FROM CONQUEST
TO STRUGGLE

FROM CONQUEST TO STRUGGLE

JESUS OF NAZARETH IN LATIN AMERICA

David Batstone

State University of New York Press

Published by
State University of New York Press, Albany

© 1991 State University of New York

All rights reserved

Printed in the United States of America

For information, address State University of New York
Press, State University Plaza, Albany, N.Y., 12246

Library of Congress Cataloging in Publication Data

Batstone, David B., 1958–
    From conquest to struggle: Jesus of Nazareth in Latin America /
David B. Batstone.
        p.   cm.
    Includes bibliographical references.
    ISBN 0-7914-0421-8. —ISBN 0-7914-0422-6 (pbk.)
    1. Jesus Christ—History of doctrines—20th century.
2. Liberation theology.   3. Theology, Doctrinal—Latin America—
History—20th century.   4. Latin America—Church history—20th
century.   I. Title.
BT198.B27   1991
232'.098—dc20   89-49227
                                                                          CIP

10   9   8   7   6   5   4   3   2   1

To Wendy

nobody, not even the rain
has such small hands

—e.e. Cummings

Contents

Foreword

From the prison cell where he was awaiting execution for his part in the plot against Hitler's life, the German Lutheran theologian Dietrich Bonhoeffer asked, "Who is Jesus Christ for us today?" The question sounds fairly conventional—just the sort of question a theologian would ask—but for Bonhoeffer, and all others who find themselves in straightened circumstances, the innocent-looking word "today" makes the question agonizingly immediate. Those who ask it know who Jesus Christ was for those who lived *yesterday*—or a millennium ago—and safe academic games can be played by measuring the claims of this Council over that one, contrasting the Christology of Antioch with that of Alexandria, weighing Luther and Calvin against each other, or comparing Kierkegaard to Gruntvig. But for Bonhoeffer, whose life was on the line, the time for academic games was past. The question was immediate and imperious.

The same is true for Christians in Latin America today. They, like Bonhoeffer, are living in tremulous times, in which violence, warfare, torture, rape and 'disappearances' are the order of the day. But for many of them, that is not quite the whole story; it is *precisely because they are Christians* that violence, warfare, torture, rape and 'disappearances' are the order of the day. To be part of the church is not to be in a safe, tame place, but to be in the thick of the struggle, marked for death because Christianity is a threat to what Paul called "the principalities and powers," the forces of evil that run rampant through the land. (I write these words only days after six Jesuit priests were martyred in San Salvador, and realize that they represent only the most visible instance of thousands of widespread deaths of which we never hear.)

As a result, many outsiders, far from the struggle and safe from its consequences, inaccurately describe liberation theology as nothing but a "political" movement, often covered with a veneer of Marxism and leading the faithful down a garden path of deception.

It is one of the virtues of Dr. Batstone's full treatment of the role of

Jesus of Nazareth in liberation theology that many such misunderstandings will be laid to rest. This does not render liberation theology antiseptic and apolitical, but recognizes that *every* theology is political, since it is
dealing with a world that is God's world but is being claimed as the private property of those who do not acknowledge the divine claim. Whatever anyone does in the world today, Jesus of Nazareth not excepted, will
impact political structures. So Latin Americans in their own situation
have to ask, "Who is Jesus Christ for us today?"

Their approach must be seen in this context: Early Christians encountered a first century Jew, a rabbi or "teacher," who shared their lot,
got hungry, discouraged, had a tremendous ability to be *simpático* with
the poor since he was one of them, and enlisted their involvement in a
very risky vision called the Realm of God. Even though the state authorities could not abide the vision, and brutally destroyed its initiator, the
friends and followers of Jesus had a series of encounters that persuaded
them that he was still alive.

As they shared their story with others, they found that they could
not adequately describe its central character solely in human terms. He
outstripped all their categories. He was — somehow — God in their
midst. They employed many titles trying to share this unique conviction:
Messiah or Christ (meaning, in Hebrew and Greek, "God's Annointed
One"), Son of God, Son of Man, Logos, Savior, "very God of very God."
By the fourth century their explorations coalesced in a widely shared
confession that he was not only "true humanity" but "true God" as well
— as much of God as could be contained within a fully human life.

Such a position is frequently described as a "Christology from below," starting with a very human Jesus and finally discovering that he is
the risen Christ. The mistake of many later Christians has been to *begin*
where the early Christians *finished,* namely with Jesus as "God." And it is
difficult, if not impossible, to move from that starting point (this time a
"Christology from above") to an affirmation of the full humanity of Jesus of Nazareth, Jeshua bar Josef, "tempted at all points like as we are."

A "Christology from below," then, allows Christians to affirm that
in One whom they already know as a fully human being, God has not
only approached, but has shared their life to the full, and this tells them
something of who he is 'for today.' They are hungry? So was he. They are
poor? So was he. They are tortured? So was he. They are killed? So was
he. They are empowered to live lives of love? So was he. Wherever they
go, whatever they do, God has already been there in this Jesus.[1]

---

1. The above five paragraphs have been adapted from my *Gustavo Gutiérrez: An Introduction to Liberation Theology,* Orbis Books, Maryknoll, New York, 1990.

The theologians whose work Dr. Batstone reviews in the pages below have adopted a Christology from below as their way of spelling out in their own lives 'who Jesus Christ is for them today.' In his clear exposition of many varieties of answers to this key question, the author is both humble enough to acknowledge that it is hard for a "gringo" to interpret the faith of Latin American culture, and courageous enough to offer his own pointed critiques when called for, as a basis for further discussion.

He goes on to make a point of crucial significance: we cannot truly understand how Latin American Christians deal with the person of Jesus of Nazareth apart from what are called the "base communities," those extraordinary groups that have grown up all over the continent— one hundred thousand of them at least—in which very 'ordinary' and unlettered people struggle together over the meaning of the Bible for their lives, and thus, preeminently, the meaning of Jesus Christ for their lives. Whatever liberation theology is, in other words, it is not a theology of the academy, formulated in library stacks and advanced seminars, but a theology that springs out of the view from below, the view from the underside of history. In this way of *doing* theology, people place a Biblical passage and their immediate situation side-by-side and work with the Jesus story until fresh connections emerge. The task, as they see it, is not merely to discover what the Holy Spirit might have said long ago (in the Bible), but to discover what the Holy Spirit is saying today (in the community as it reads the Bible).

If the results are "radical," as critics often assert, that is not because a covert politicization is taking place, but because the very message of the Bible and its embodiment in Jesus of Nazareth is radical, in the sense of getting to the *radix* (the "root") of things.

For his help in steering us through what might otherwise seem a labyrinth for newcomers, enabling us to see an overarching pattern in the diverse positions he discusses, and putting us in touch with the radix, Dr. Batstone places us all in his debt.

Robert McAfee Brown

Professor Emeritus of Theology and Ethics
Pacific School of Religion
Berkeley, California

Acknowledgments

Elisha, the primary character in Elie Wiesel's novel *Dawn*, is faced with a most monumental decision: whether or not to transform himself from a victim into an executioner. As Elisha agonizes over his dilemma, he is startled to discover that the room in which he is situated suddenly becomes filled with a host of characters, long since dead . . . yet alive. He is not alone.

> I was the center of a multitude of circles. I wanted to close my eyes and stop up my ears, but my father was there, and my mother, and the master, and the beggar, and the boy. With all those who had formed me around me I had no right to stop up my ears and close my eyes.

Here Wiesel articulates the feelings I have sensed throughout the writing of this book. All those who have helped to "form me" have been present as I struggled to bring these thoughts and ideas to creation. For that reason I feel it somewhat misleading to take full credit for this work, putting my name alone under the title. Without holding them responsible for my results, I wish to express to them due appreciation.

Thanks goes first to John Hirt, who lit a fire under my feet and sent me scurrying off the path I—then a student at Westmont College—was walking; his prophetic message and friendship moved me to search for uncharted roads. Once that journey had begun, Athol Gill suggested new ways to read the gospels as signposts "on the way." Perhaps most importantly, he sought to live out these convictions in exemplary fashion. The year I lived with Athol and the other community members of the House of the Gentle Bunyip in Melbourne, Australia, left a deep impression on my life, providing me with a lasting vision of discipleship and faith.

My personal journey continued to Switzerland, where during my studies at Rüschlikon Thorwald Lorenzen became, in a relatively short period of time, a true theological mentor. Thorwald's passion for life—

which is manifest in his concern for human rights abroad and for human relationships 'at home' — quite profoundly shapes the contours of his theological reflections. Traces of his course and seminar on Christology undeniably filter their way into these pages.

These experiences and teachings led me to Oakland, where for the last eight years I have participated in a fragile experiment in intentional community with remarkable companions: Cathy and Steve (co-travelers from the beginning), Brad, Brett, Santiago, Cynthia, Maurice, Rusty, Don (thank God I was given such a brother), Todd, Susan, Katy, Kevin, John, Pam, Steve B., Jim, Carl, Mindy, Mark, Harold, Laurie, and René. On the other side of the Atlantic, I have been deeply influenced as well by the creative music and close friendships of Tom and Warbeck (yes, your music too!), Rick and Lorraine, and Ali and Bono. You have all helped write this work in more ways than you can know.

Bill Herzog's contribution is duly noted in these pages, but his input reaches even further back to several classes he taught on the parables of Jesus and Christology. I only hope that Bill publishes some of his own material before his students do it for him bit by bit in their own works. Many thanks as well to Jorge Lara Braud, Margarita Melville, and Ben Reist for their frank advice and constant encouragement.

Words of gratitude are difficult to limit here. Of course, Linda, Mom and Dad are among those who cannot be left out. But so many more people should rightfully be mentioned since they are part of that 'Wiesel-ian' crowd that accompanies me no matter where I go. Yet three will have to suffice. Carlos Sanchez and Miguel Tomás Castro — *hermanos, compañeros, profetas* — of the Baptist Association of El Salvador, must be especially thanked for their testimony and light. If only my ministry to my own people becomes half as compassionate as theirs, I shall be most grateful. And finally, Wendy Brown, *compañera por la vida*, has waited for this day of publication as anxiously as have I. For all of her efforts to help us both survive, and even nourish our love, I thank her.

Introduction: Mapping Out a Horizon of Interest

Albert Schweitzer's renowned investigation into the life of the historical Jesus[1] sounds a rather ominous note for the modern study of Christology:

> The Jesus of Nazareth who came forward publicly as the Messiah, who preached the ethic of the Kingdom of God, who founded the Kingdom of Heaven upon earth and died to consecrate his work, never had any existence. He is a figure designed by rationalism, endowed with life by liberalism, and clothed by modern theology in a historical garb.[2]

The crux of Schweitzer's study convincingly demonstrates that the 'liberal' theologians of nineteenth century Europe had effectively created a Jesus in their own image. Yet, in so doing they had failed to recognize their unconscious (perhaps partly conscious?) desire to ascribe familiar thoughts and ideas to a historical figure who was surely a stranger to their own European milieu.

The "quest"[3] for the historical life of Jesus began in Europe during the eighteenth century as an outgrowth of the era's evolving understanding of the relationship between human existence and the passage of history.[4] The classical problem of divine and human natures, which largely arose in the fifth century and persisted to govern Christological thought until the time of the Enlightenment, ceased to be the crucial topic of debate. The location of revelation within history replaced it as the theme of utmost concern. As a direct result, theologians were challenged by a new question which was uniquely posed by the dawning age: What is the religious ideal and how is it related to the historic individual, Jesus of Nazareth?

Of course, the creation of a new historical method alone did not precipitate such an intense marshalling of energies within the religious

1

world of Europe. The debate which raged over the identity and significance of Jesus of Nazareth was, in many respects, part of a larger battle
to establish the ultimate source of religious (and thus social) authority,
and moreover to determine by what criteria such judgments were to be
made. As more than one historian has recognized, "historical investigation . . . turned to the Jesus of history as an ally in the struggle against the
tyranny of doctrine."[5] Biblical researchers became increasingly convinced that the actual historical figure of Jesus had become obfuscated
and distorted after passing through the dogmatic affirmations and
creeds elaborated by the Christian church in the centuries since his
death. They undertook the task to 'clear away the rubble' in order to liberate a rational Jesus who could be followed without the mediation of an
ecclesiastical authority.[6]

    This interest in grounding Christian faith in the historical figure of
Jesus has dominated Christological studies in the countries of the North
Atlantic to the present day. Historical surveys charting the course of its
development have been elaborated extensively elsewhere and need not
be repeated here.[7] It is important to underline, however, that scholars
have had little success in reaching a consensus regarding the essential
character of the life and message of Jesus. In fact, as was indicated above
by reference to Schweitzer's study, the images of Jesus at which scholars
have arrived appear to be as varied as the commitments which they have
brought to that interpretive task.[8] In both the 'old' and 'new' quest, each
succeeding generation of scholars was able to critically discern the ideological biases which infused the Christologies of their predecessors, only
to inadvertently repeat the same process with their own professedly "objective" approach. In recognition of this phenomenon, Alister McGrath
concluded thus his investigation of the modern Christological experiment in Germany:

> modern Christology is obliged to proceed upon the assumption that
> the gospels contain a mixture of history and theology which . . . is im-
> possible to untangle. Among the casualties of this contemporary un-
> derstanding of the nature of the gospels . . . [is] the view that it was pos-
> sible to reconstruct a non-theological, presuppositionless account of
> the history of Jesus.[9]

    The admission of the relativity of that task, however, certainly does
not negate the relevance of the historical Jesus for the creation of modern Christologies. Although the notion of partiality is commonly anath-
ema to the apologists of scholarly science, a critical theory of knowledge
suggests otherwise: there is no knowledge which is disinterested. As ev-

idence of that fact, each attempt to recover the life of Jesus during the last two centuries inevitably emphasized certain aspects of his story over others, highlighting those events which best conveyed the meaning of the gospel to its present age. No interpreter can avoid the necessity of making such choices; the only true deception occurs when one denies that such choices have been made.[10]

Only when the myth of hermeneutical—i.e., the science and actual process of interpretation—objectivity has been properly dispelled may the evaluation of diverse and even conflicting images of Jesus proceed on the basis of a more frank and fruitful dialogue. For instance, it cannot be overlooked that the Anglo-European interpreters of the last two centuries consistently limited the significance of Jesus' life to the concerns of the individual to the exclusion of the social and communal. The apocalyptic message of Jesus, full of cosmological reference which related it to every aspect of human reality, was commonly stripped of its rich historical significance and confined to the individual's locus of concern for personal morality and meaning.[11] In that respect, Jesus was not permitted to be a figure of his own time whose enduring significance might be understood in light of the specific activities, commitments, and options he made within a limited historical existence. He was more often than not taken out of those historical structures so that he could speak a 'universal' truth to a modern society.

It is with an eye trained to this history that, laden with a series of crucial questions, one approaches the Christologies under development in the theology of liberation of Latin America.[12] It must be asked whether the Jesus of Latin America is not perhaps a figure designed by Marxist analysis, endowed with life by revolutionary enthusiasm, and clothed by modern theology in political garb. In other words, is this Jesus nothing more than a vacuous symbol filled with the hopes and aspirations of liberation theologians bent on radical social transformation? Does a theology of liberation of the oppressed actually flow from the life and teachings of the Jesus we find in the gospels, or is he merely the bow which is put on top of a package already wrapped? Moving one step further, what would it truly mean for liberationists to write Christologies which pose a Jesus who is not alien to the contemporary historical and socio-cultural situation in Latin America and, therefore, speaks directly to the concerns of its people? Would this effort be a perversion or a fulfillment of the perennial task of explicating the significance of Jesus for the present day?

As even these limited queries manifest, the rise of liberation theology in Latin America has elicited a renewed interest in the debate surrounding the historical Jesus. It is a theological movement which has staked its foundation in a 'Christology from below'; that is, rooted in a Jesus who was fully incarnated in the historical structures and realities of this world and therein revealed the character of God and God's will. So central is this affirmation to the work of liberation theology that it claims to have "rehabilitated the figure of the historical Jesus within theology" by overcoming a highly abstract conception of Christ and basing Christian existence itself on the historical following of Jesus.[13]

That commitment should not suggest, however, that liberation theology has thereby invoked a staid historicism by which to orient its present understanding of Jesus Christ. To the contrary, it places on an equal plane with the past revelation of God's activity the historical, dynamic presence of the spirit of Christ in the present moment of human history. Revelation is viewed as an open process which constantly challenges Christian faith to encounter Christ anew in changing historical conditions and diverse cultural milieus. Hence, liberation theologians do not carry out a study of the life and practice of the historical Jesus simply in order to delineate how the Latin American faith community might imitate his actual steps (as if that were possible). Their results are presented to the Christian community as an invitation to participate in the search for those paths upon which it might find the risen and living Jesus walking today. In the words of Raúl Vidales, "a Christology based in the theological perspective of liberation has its point of departure in a double frontal pole—the word and the praxis of liberation, both converging dialectically in the concrete historical process."[14]

The first chapter of this book serves to confirm the suspicion that every Christology reflects a certain horizon of interest, but it is uncovered this time from within the historical context of the Latin American continent itself. Starting with those popular images of Jesus which reflect the centuries of oppression under which the people of Latin America have suffered, and moving to those Christologies of liberation which have been developed primarily during the last two decades, the chapter demonstrates how the historical experiences of a people inform their understanding of faith. It indicates once again that the social location and ideological/practical commitments of the interpreter are not to be considered elements extraneous to the hermeneutical process.

Having laid this groundwork, the focus of my study shifts to a critical analysis of the methods of interpretation which Latin American liberation theologians utilize when they approach the historical Jesus and attempt to appropriate the significance of his life, death and resurrection to the development of their own Christologies, i.e., in the creation of new gospels for their contemporary situation. Of course, it would be impossible to consider here all of the Christologies which have been written in Latin America during the last two decades, and cumbersome to attempt to treat the myriad of themes which are posed by their diverse efforts. Therefore, it has been necessary to confine myself to the works of a few key Latin American theologians as they deal with what are to be considered central themes. The elaboration of this scheme facilitates a comparative analysis of their distinct approaches and yet points to more general conclusions concerning the movement as a whole.

It is greatly regretted that I have not been able to feature within that consideration the voices of more Latin American women. Although their testimonies are unmistakably present herein, both on an academic and popular level, I am still well aware of the unbalance of gender. To that extent, I feel quite trapped by the ideology of machismo which effectively dominates the Latin American culture (not to mention my own in perhaps more subtle ways!). It is certain that liberation theology is very much on the forefront of the dialogue taking place between women and men; nevertheless, the scarcity of women liberation theologians in Latin America is glaringly apparent. In this context, the words of Elsa Tamez, a respected Biblical theologian from Costa Rica, serve as a profound caveat to everyone who struggles for the liberation of society as a whole: " ... If there is no qualitatively and quantitatively significant presence of women, if the importance of women and their achievements for the liberation process [are] not appreciated, and if the fulfillment of women is not fostered, the route to the liberation of society will be longer, less complete, and more conflictive."[15]

Throughout this study, special emphasis is placed on the life of Jesus of Nazareth as a historical figure who lived and died for those particular options which he deemed consonant with the will of a near and present God. In chapter Two, the treatment which various liberation theologians have given to Jesus' earthly practice and message will be examined in light of the historical and social structures which shaped his world. In the chapter which follows, the focus shifts to their understanding of Jesus' cross and resurrection as the central events leading to the birth of the Christian faith.

In chapters Two and Three, however, my efforts are not devoted simply to the comparison of particular exegetical results, i.e., analytical interpretations of given passages of Scripture, but primarily to the presuppositions and methods which produce those results. Hugo Assmann is right when he states that there is "no possibility of resolving the conflict in Christologies by means of a simple recourse to 'better' exegesis in order to arrive at an objective purification of Christological doctrine."[16] Nonetheless, exegetical decisions are made on the basis of particular hermeneutical assumptions and those decisions, to a lesser or greater degree, determine the image of Jesus which will become operative for one's Christology. Therefore, method and exegesis are not treated in this study as distinct entities, but as integral elements within any system of interpretation.

It is virtually universally accepted in liberation theology — as a result of the lessons learned from the two European quests, if nothing else — that the gospels as the primary source of that which we know about Jesus' life are not biographies of that life per se, but are testimonies which were already interpreting the meaning which Jesus signified for specific communities. That discovery indicates to liberation theologians that the Christological task is not exhausted with a historical investigation of the life of Jesus, but must continue to search for those means by which this figure is enabled to be proclaimed as good news today. In every new context the person and message of Jesus must be mediated historically so that it might address the concerns of the contemporary situation. José Míguez Bonino goes so far as to say that there is not even any "meaning in an idealistic search for a theological image of Christ [which is] divorced from present historical realities."[17] In other words, each theologian must choose a hermeneutical bridge which allows one to speak meaningfully about the Jesus who offers salvation today to a world very far removed from the realities of first century Palestine. It is my conviction that fidelity to the memory of Jesus in fact requires a 're-presentation' of his significance for concrete salvation in every new historical situation.

Chapter Four develops these themes as it explores the major methodological issues which arise as liberation theologians seek to relate the Jesus of history to the Christ of faith (whom they consider no less 'historical' for present discipleship). In line with the hermeneutical approach proposed by Juan Carlos Scannone, I present this challenge as a twofold task:

> On the one hand, it must try to discern, interpret, and criticize the present-day situation in salvific terms. It must explore the possibilities and ambiguities of the present, the historico-cultural project that is emerging from our [the Latin American] people, and the historical roots that sustain the whole process. On the other hand, it must reread and reinterpret the riches of our faith, using the praxis and culture of the Latin American people as its hermeneutic locale.[18]

Operating within this framework, the chapter reaffirms that the Christologies in formation within liberation theology are legitimate readings of the images of Jesus presented by the earliest faith communities, even though they are certainly informed by the meaning-world and historical experiences of present-day Latin America.

The concluding chapter of this study is offered as an epilogue to all of that material which has preceded it. It unveils how the witness of the Christian base communities of Latin America serves as a challenge to liberation theologians, prodding them to free their discipline from the world of ideas in order to rewrite theology from the perspective of those engaged in a concrete commitment to bring about the transformation of history. Although it primarily treats issues which pertain directly to the pastoral setting of the *iglesia popular* [popular church] of Latin America, chapter Five builds a case for the conviction that the praxis and reflection of these Christian communities are central to the creation of Christological images. As Gustavo Gutiérrez affirms, liberation theology is essentially a "theological reasoning that is verified—made to be true—in a real, fertile involvement with the liberation process."[19]

In advance, I would like to stress that it is with considerable reticence that I, as an author born and raised in the United States, embark on this task. It is true that many of the interests and biases reflected herein are based on my own experiences in Central America over the course of the last six years. During this time, I have served as director of a humanitarian aid and development agency which collaborates with national churches and popular organizations in the search for the self-determination and eventual liberation of their people. Nonetheless, I am fully aware that I am a product of my own culture and may never claim to share the experience and insight of the Latin American people, nor completely understand the full depth of their struggle.

Cognizant of these limitations, I have sought to avoid the temptation to write those Christologies which I might deem appropriate for their particular situation. I do, however, have the boldness to critically appraise writings produced by Latin American authors for whom I have the greatest respect and admiration. Despite the frank tenor of those criticisms at times, let it be said from the outset that it comes from an unflinching solidarity and sympathy for those goals and commitments for which the liberation movement stands.

In that regard, I cannot help but take to heart the strong words of warning issued by Enrique Dussel:

> The presence of European theologians in Latin America who neither know Latin America's situation nor understand its history and temperament, and who yet have the audacity, the presumption, to wish to propagate 'Christian teaching' here today, can only be most corrupting and detrimental. We have simply to tell them that they are committing

a basic methodological error. These theologians speak words and pro-
pound dilemmas that belong to Europe [read also the United States],
not to Latin America.[20]

If I have fallen into that error of imposing issues which are foreign
to Latin American soil, it is most deeply regretted. I would then consider
to have failed in those efforts which I have made with the sincere intention of furthering and strengthening that liberation process.

Notes

1. When the name "Jesus" is used in this book, it refers to the figure who
was born, lived and died within human history nearly 2000 years ago. At times,
this figure will also be referred to as 'the historical Jesus' or 'Jesus of Nazareth.'
The title "Christ" or "Jesus Christ," on the other hand, will be treated as a theological affirmation applied to Jesus as a postpaschal reflection of his significance
for faith and history. As will become clearly evident, I do not seek to thereby imply that the Jesus who we find in the gospels comes to us uninterpreted by the
first evangelists. Surely, they have already presented the life of Jesus to us in the
light of the resurrection.

At times, certain theologians, both Anglo-European and Latin American,
will not differentiate between "Jesus" and "Christ," even to the extent of using
the two titles interchangeably. Obviously, such usage in itself already reflects a
specific Christological and historical understanding, as does the distinction
made here in my study.

2. Albert Schweitzer, *The Quest of the Historical Jesus,* trans. W. Montgomery
(New York: Macmillan, 1956), 398. The original German edition, *Von Reimarus
zu Wrede,* appeared in 1906 and the first English translation was published
in 1910.

3. The European search for the life of Jesus is commonly known as the
"quest for the historical Jesus," a phrase taken from the title of the English translation of Schweitzer's study.

4. In the words of Alistar McGrath, with the Enlightenment came "the replacement of a predominantly metaphysical understanding of reality by an essentially historical understanding ... [which] necessitated a transformation of
the traditional approaches to Christology ... ," *The Making of Modern German
Christology: From the Enlightenment To Pannenberg* (Oxford: Basil Blackwell,
1986), 2.

The development of a historical-critical method gave Biblical researchers
confidence that they could indeed return to the earliest sources of Christianity
and reconstruct, in a completely objective manner, the life of him whom they
considered to be its founder. Their investigation was carried out with the as-

sumption that the gospels were written as descriptive, positivistic historiographies—a style which the researchers had committed themselves to write.

5. Schweitzer, *Quest*, 4.

6. In one of the first attempts to reconstruct a historical account of the life of Jesus, Herrman Samuel Reimarus—in a series of *Fragments* which were published posthumously by Lessing from 1774–1778—made quite clear his intentions to demonstrate the implausibility of the dogmatic Christ. He presented Jesus as a prophet who, since he was not aided by the divine intervention which he had faithfully awaited, failed in his attempt to bring about the Kingdom of God. The apostles, left to their own wiles, deceptively arranged an event in which it appeared that Jesus had risen from the dead.

These results proved to Reimarus that the creation of the church rests on a fraud, and since its clericalism is based upon the ascension of authority from these apostles, it serves as yet a further deception. In other words, the supernaturalism by which the church had surrounded the figure of Jesus was simply a smokescreen to hide the fact of his utter failure and bind the rational worship of God to the superstitions of a revealed religion.

7. In addition to Schweitzer's *Quest*, among the best of those books which seek to analyze the development of the modern Christological project in the North Atlantic are Alister McGrath, *The Making of Modern German Christology;* N. Smart, et al., eds., *Nineteenth Century Religious Thought in the West*, 2 vols. (Cambridge: Cambridge University Press, 1985); Hans Frei, *The Eclipse of Biblical Narrative: A Study in Eighteenth and Nineteenth Century Hermeneutics* (New Haven: Yale University Press, 1974); Jeffrey Stout, *The Flight From Authority: Religion, Morality and the Quest for Autonomy* (Notre Dame: University of Notre Dame Press, 1981); James M. Robinson, *A New Quest of the Historical Jesus* (Chatham: W & J MacKay Co., Ltd., 1959); Carl Braaten and R. N. Harrisville, eds., *The Historical Jesus and the Kerygmatic Christ: Essays on the New Quest of the Historical Jesus* (Nashville: Southern Press, 1964); and Norman Perrin, *Rediscovering the Teachings of Jesus* (New York: Harper & Row, 1967).

8. Schweitzer marveled that "it was not only each epoch that found its reflection in Jesus; each individual created Him in accordance with his own character. There is no historical task which so reveals a man's true character as the writing of the life of Jesus," *Quest*, 4.

9. McGrath, *German Christology*, 214.

10. This realization signals the intractibility of the Christological problem whether it is approached from Europe, the United States, or Latin America. It therefore provides us with our first clue that if liberation theology is to be condemned based on the supposed manipulation of a self-evident and self-disclosing image of Jesus, then the whole of the modern Christological project must be condemned along with it, for the biases and ideologies of North Atlantic theologians are found to be patently obvious in their own quests.

This background also gives historical support for the method by which the remainder of this book proceeds. It explains why my investigation does not seek to measure the Christologies under development in Latin America in relation to an alleged 'original Jesus,' but aims to evaluate the particular hermeneutical keys and epistemological commitments which orient those investigations and which lead to the stress of certain aspects of Jesus' life over others.

11. An early work by Franz Volkmar Reinhard, published in 1781, was in many ways representative of a whole genre of the 'lives of Jesus.' In his essay entitled "The Plan which the Founder of the Christian Religion Adopted for the Benefit of Mankind," Reinhard assumes that although Jesus regularly employed the apocalyptic conceptuality and terminology familiar to his Jewish world, he actually only used them as tools to communicate another, more hidden message. On that basis, he proposes that Jesus redefined the terms "kingdom of God" and "kingdom of heaven," which historically had connoted social and political expectations, to symbolize a "universal, ethical reorganization" of humanity. Jesus, then, had no thought of building an earthly kingdom; for Reinhard, 'political' and 'purely ethical' were distinct and exclusive concepts, the one incorporated into the social order and the other limited to personal piety. In fact, he suggests that Jesus would have welcomed a separation of the state and religion so as to eliminate the unwarranted forages which each realm makes into the other. This background suggests that Reinhard was possibly more influenced by the secularizing ideology of the French Revolution than that of the apocalyptic Jesus of first century Palestine.

It was not only the rationalists, however, who considered apocalyptic imagery too primitive for the enlightened Jesus. The Hegelians, as well, moralized away his use of apocalyptic imagery. Cf. Bruno Baur: "It is impossible that such [apocalyptic] sayings can . . . be taken in the mouth of Jesus as other than figurative or even regarded solely as authentic expressions of Jesus," quoted in Peter Hodgson, *The Formation of Historical Theology: A Study of Ferdinand Christian Baur* (New York: Charles Scribner's Sons, 1966), 230. Consequently, the correct interpretation for Baur: " . . . the essential task of his messianic designation [is] the ethical reform of the intentional virtue of the people . . . ," ibid., 231.

12. The term "liberation theology" will be widely used in this study to describe that theological movement in Latin America which reflects two primary characteristics: (1) it understands its theological context to be shaped within a particular historical reality, the oppressive conditions of the "dependent world" ['underdeveloped world' or 'Third world' are misnomers which represent a distorted picture of reality; see Peter Berger, *Pyramids of Sacrifice: Political Ethics and Social Change* (New York: Basic Books, 1974), especially 50–1)], and (2) it understands its theological motivation to arise from a particular historical commitment to bring about the economic, social, political and spiritual liberation of its people from those conditions.

At the same time, it is imperative to acknowledge that liberation theology is not a monolithic phenomenon which may be covered with one stroke of the brush. It would be more accurate to speak of the continual and spontaneous creation of theologies of liberation, thereby recognizing the breadth and diversity of the movement. In that respect, the use of the term "liberation theology" ought not be limited to Latin America alone. In fact, a theology of liberation arose within the Black community in the United States almost simultaneously to its growth in Latin America. Black theology has developed its own independent set of theological paradigms which correspond to the history of black slavery and oppression. The same could be said for the feminist movement which has dynamically refashioned theological construction out of a commitment to the liberation of women from the patriarchal structures of nearly every contemporary society. Moreover, distinctive theologies of liberation are being nurtured in other areas of the dependent world, most notably in Asia and Africa.

13. Jon Sobrino, *Christology at the Crossroads: A Latin American Approach*, trans. John Drury (Maryknoll: Orbis Books, 1978), 79.

14. Raúl Vidales, "How Should We Speak of Christ Today?" in *Faces of Jesus: Latin American Christologies*, ed. José Míguez Bonino, trans. Robert R. Barr (Maryknoll: Orbis Books, 1984), 143.

15. Elsa Tamez, *Against Machismo* (Oak Park, IL: Meyer-Stone Books, 1987), vii.
The relative scarcity of women theologians is quite tragic for the formation of our communal theology, and that loss extends beyond the contribution they could make to feminist liberation. I concur with Frei Betto who remarked that women, at least on a quite general level, "have a greater ability to link, in their theological work, the heart and head, feeling and thinking, intuition and rationality," ibid., 95. Is it no coincidence that our male-dominated discipline has been so lacking in these very attributes over the course of the last twenty centuries?

16. Hugo Assmann, "The Actuation of the Power of Christ in History: Notes on the Discernment of Christological Contradictions," in *Faces of Jesus*, 126.

17. José Míguez Bonino, "Who Is Jesus Christ in Latin America Today," in *Faces of Jesus*, 3.

18. Juan Carlos Scannone, "Theology, Popular Culture, and Discernment," in *Frontiers of Theology in Latin America*, ed. Rosino Gibellini, trans. John Drury (Maryknoll: Orbis Books, 1979), 236–7.

19. Gustavo Gutiérrez, *The Power of the Poor in History*, trans. Robert R. Barr (Maryknoll: Orbis Books, 1983), 201.

20. Enrique Dussel, "Histoire de la foi chrétienne et changement social in América Latina," in *Les luttes de liberation bousculent la theologie*, eds. Dussel et al., p. 95, quoted in Claus Bussmann, *Who Do You Say?*, 16.

CHAPTER ONE

The Latin American Christ:
From Conquest to Struggle

Methinks the Christ, as he sojourned westward, went to prison in Spain, while another who took his name embarked with the Spanish crusaders for the New World, a Christ who was not born in Bethlehem, but in North Africa. This Christ became naturalized in the Iberian colonies of America, while Mary's Son and Lord has been little else than a stranger and sojourner in these lands from Columbus' day to this.

—John Mackay[1]

Every discussion of Jesus Christ in Latin America must take into account an inescapable contradiction. On the one hand, the history of Christian theology in Latin America is inextricably bound to its development and formation in the countries of the North Atlantic. The birth of Christianity in Latin America was itself essentially a product of the Spanish conquest of the continent which began in the sixteenth century and which was consolidated by means of the subsequent colonization of the culture by the church and the crown—"the great two-headed Spain of the faith and the *conquista*."[2] Moreover, despite the achievement of relative political independence from Spain in the nineteenth century, Latin American countries soon became economically dependent on the 'Christian nations' of Britain and later the United States. As the continent's resources increasingly became an integral part of the Northern economies, the somewhat sporadic state of colonialism shifted to the more regular, systematic control of neocolonialism.[3] Though the church did lose a significant degree of socio-political power in the transition, it nonetheless generally acquiesced to the capitalistic ideology of accumulation or, alternatively, insisted that religion had no relevance within the material realm of economics and politics.

13

On the other hand, the Latin American approach to the theological task is quite distinct from that of the North Atlantic, primarily due to the nature of the subjects from whom challenges are posed. Gustavo Gutiérrez characterizes this difference quite profoundly:

> A goodly part of contemporary [North Atlantic] theology seems to take its start from the challenge posed by the *nonbeliever*. The nonbeliever calls into question our *religious world*, demanding its thoroughgoing purification and revitalization.... In a continent like Latin America, however, the main challenge does not come from the nonbeliever, but from the *nonhuman*—i.e., the human being who is not recognized as such by the prevailing social order.... These nonhumans do not call into question our religious world so much as they call into question our *economic, social, political, and cultural world*.[4]

The individual's search for personal meaning and self-realization, therefore, does not motivate the theological endeavor in Latin America in the same manner. The center shifts to those whose right to be subjects of their own history has been taken away from them—the voiceless, a people of the underside.

Of course, the existence and, more tragically still, the prevalence of the "nonhuman" in Latin America did not come into being by mere accident, nor was it simply a product of the cruel fate of nature.[5] That process of dehumanization was systematically carried out by foreign nations driven by unrelenting avarice and sanctified dreams of imperial expansion. What some have identified as the forward progress of history towards greater civilization and material comfort is thereby unmasked to be a limited, 'first world' ideology. "The progress is history's suffering," U.S. theologian Rebecca Chopp laments, "we are its origin, its destiny, its cause."[6]

The Spanish Legacy

The exploitation of the Latin American people began with the arrival of the first Spaniards on its shores. Although *Cristobal* [translated literally, "Christ-bearer"] Columbus was clearly convinced that he was carrying out his mission of evangelization with the blessing of God, the extension of Spanish power and wealth were never far from his mind.[7] Unfortunately, it was the might of the sword which was wielded to carry out both objectives.

The magnitude of the genocide committed by the Spanish conquistadors against the indigenous people of Latin America is staggering.

Historians estimate that when the first 'explorers' reached the Pacific hemisphere the combined population of the Aztecs, Mayas and Incas—the three major races of pre-Columban Latin America—numbered somewhere between 70 and 90 million people. Only a century and a half later that number had been reduced to approximately 3.5 million; the majority of the native inhabitants had been massacred, while some were taken back to Europe as slaves.[8]

Of course, the conquest of the Latin American continent and the Carribean did not take place without the active resistance of the indigenous tribes who struggled against the foreign domination of their land and culture. Countless millions lost their lives rather than acquiesce to the designs of Spanish rule. The story is told of Hatuey, the Indian chief of the Guahaba region—now known as Haiti—who fled with his people in canoes so that they would not be taken as slaves to work in mines and to cultivate fields which had once been their inheritance. Hiding in the caves and mountains of eastern Cuba, Hatuey pointed to a basket of gold and lamented: "This is the god of the Christians. For him they pursue us. For him our fathers and brothers have died." Shortly thereafter, Hatuey was captured and tied to the stake. Before setting him on fire, the Spanish priest offered Hatuey eternal salvation in heaven if only he would agree to be baptized. When Hatuey is told that all good Christians are in that heaven, he chooses hell and the fires proceed to burn the body of a man with a 'lost soul.'[9]

Bartolomé de Las Casas had been the owner of one of the sizable plantations upon which the Indians had been forced to work the fields as unpaid serfs. At the age of forty, however, he underwent a conversion experience which opened his eyes to the inhumane treatment which had been carried out against the land's indigenous population. He subsequently worked quite actively within and outside of the church in an attempt to stop the unrelenting conquest of their lands and their human dignity. Only ten years after the conquest of Peru by Francisco Pizarro's crusade, Las Casas—then a bishop in the church—returned to Spain and had this to say to King Charles I of the brutal repression exacted by the conquistadors:

> Daily in the land of New Castile, atrocities are committed at which Christian humanity shudders to look upon. . . . Drunk with power, and utterly devoid of any sense of responsibility, the new lords of this plantation state only indulge their unbridled caprices. . . . I must say, this would become the Crescent far better than the spotless Cross.[10]

Sadly, Las Casas was one of only a few lonely voices of protest sounding within the halls of the Latin American church. For in reality, its ecclesiastical and doctrinal authority were issued from Spain and Rome by a Catholic church brandishing its power in a manner parallel to that of the imperial throne. For all intents and purposes the colonized society could be characterized as a theocracy; it was 'blessed' with a unified political and religious structure, ruled by Catholic teaching, and headed by a royalty imbued with sacred election.[11] Evidence of this intimate marriage between the church and the political structure is demonstrated by virtue of the fact that the Pope regularly granted to the Spanish kings the privilege of nominating bishops to ecclesiastical sees in Latin America! For centuries priests and bishops continued to travel over from the Old World to take on positions of leadership and teaching within the church.[12] Astonishingly, the crown also had the right to seize a portion of the tithes gathered by the Latin American church as a reimbursement for the heavy costs of 'winning' new converts by the sword.[13]

One of the primary functions of the national church, in return, was to baptize and justify the newly established social order as representative of the reign of Christ over creation. In essence, this 'natural order' of creation was a near copy of the feudal land system — marked by a minority of owners with extensive land holdings who had at their disposal a considerable number of serfs — which had been firmly established within Spain. The communal land system of the native, 'pagan' culture was condemned and largely destroyed, securing a class stratification which has continued to characterize Latin American society to the present day. Without a doubt, there were notable exceptions of resistance to these structures of conquest; for example, the work of the Jesuits to fashion Indian farming communities under the protection and seal of the church. Even these efforts, however, were quite regularly undermined by the collusion of the religious and political hierarchy which operated with impunity.

The popular Christology which took root — or perhaps better put, was imposed — in Latin America reflected a synthesis of this historical experience of domination together with the traditional Catholic understanding of dogma and revelation. Georges Casalis has demonstrated in his typology of Latin American Christologies that this amalgamation resulted in the formation of two primary categories of Christ figures.[14] Though his typology does appropriately uncover the ideological motives behind the dominant Christologies of the traditional Latin American church, it does not tell the whole story of popular religiosity. As will be treated at more length in chapter Five, the poor have sustained subversive images of Jesus Christ within its culture which have served as a constant protest against the oppression under which they have been forced to suffer. Their existence underscores the fact that the social consciousness and religious sentiments of a dominated people is never completely co-opted by a ruling class; though perhaps alienated from its own culture, the popular consciousness is never fully bereft of elements of resistance as well.

The first image in Casalis' typology reflects the experience of Latin America's victims: a "suffering Christ" who has been thoroughly defeated and humiliated. It relies on a portrayal of Jesus of Nazareth as one who remained passive in the midst of his suffering as an outright acceptance of his God-given destiny. The religious and political authorities of Latin America promoted the image of the suffering Jesus as one in whom the poor could understand the virtues of their condition and even provide it with transcendent meaning.[15] More importantly, it reinforced the omnipresent message that their social world had been created in such a way as to preclude the possibility of meaningful change.

Given this background, it should be considered as no coincidence that the Latin American cult of popular piety has traditionally centered around the celebrations of Holy Thursday and Good Friday, while Easter is passed with significantly less fanfare. In many ways it marks the identification of the poor with a powerless Jesus:

> What do these great [Holy Week] processions of millions of women, men, and children — largely miners and country folk — reveal to us? And why miners and country folk? Is it perchance that, behind all this, there lurks the conscious or unconscious acceptance of one's situation of impotence and powerlessness, of being subjugated and oppressed, of inhumanity?[16]

The other strand in Casalis' typology can be traced to the royal-theocratic image of Christ which made the trip to the New World with the conquistadors. Jesus is depicted as a celestial monarch who reigns after his death as the leader of an imperial, military kingdom. Here, it is his resurrection which takes center stage. The resurrection, however, is not understood in relation to the new life of a crucified Jesus; rather, this figure moves from the incarnation (birth) to the ascension without pausing even for a moment's glance at the mission and death of the Savior. This Christ came to be identified with the authorities who manifested effective control—whether it be that power emanating from the throne or that practiced day in and day out by the landowners — over the lives of the native people and the poor. "Obedience to the great king of Spain and submission to the King of Heaven were demanded as one single act."[17]

Regardless of the specific categories one adopts, it seems clear that the Jesus Christ of Latin America was a figure designed to legitimate the presence of colonial rule and to justify the structures of privilege and

power which remained intact even after the arrival of national independence. The prevalence of these Christological images in every mass, catechism, and religious celebration unquestionably contributed to the internalization of the dominant ideology within the popular culture. In
that regard, Hugo Assmann indicates that the Christological efforts of
the Latin American church only served to yield "alienating Christs"
which would impede, if not forbid, the creation of any movement of
struggle against oppression:

> The Christ of oppressive Christologies really has two faces. On the one
> side are all the Christs of the power establishment, who do not need to
> fight because they already hold a position of dominance; on the other
> are all the Christs of established impotence, who cannot fight against
> the dominion to which they are subject.[18]

The Birth of a Theology of Liberation

It is from within this historical context that the rise of liberation theology in Latin America may best be appreciated.[19] In many respects, one
could say that this theological movement was born as a response to the
gradual politicization of the continent and the concomitant demand
pressed upon the church to break its complicity with an oppressive state.
A new theological reflection evolved as a resource and inspiration for
those seeking historical and political liberation from centuries of
oppression. That effort was motivated as well by a desire to move other
Latin American Christians to participate in this liberation process as a
consequence of their faith in Jesus Christ.[20]

Perhaps more appropriately, and yet certainly not in contradiction
to the aforementioned, the rise of liberation theology in Latin America
can be traced to the radical changes which were taking place in the Roman Catholic Church following the pronouncements of the Second Vatican Council (1963–1965). Convened by Pope John XXIII, the Council
placed special emphasis upon the incorporation of the laity into the worship and administrative life of the local parish. Clerics were encouraged
to lead mass in the local language of their congregations and to invoke
their participation in the interpretation of Scripture. In turn, the
Church was called to be a "sign of the times," transforming itself from a
symbol of grace outside the worldly realm into a servant which lives "the
joys and the hopes, the griefs and the anxieties of people of this age, especially those who are poor and afflicted. . . . "[21]

In the words of one liberationist, Vatican II "had the effect of a violent earthquake" within the Latin American church.[22] For quite prac-

tical reasons, its ramifications were experienced almost immediately in the region. Although the relocation of priests and sisters, both national and foreign, to the rural areas and barrios admittedly was an important factor in this development, it was perhaps ironically the scarcity of their numbers which was even more significant. In pre-Vatican II times, the paucity of clerics had meant that 'out of the way' parishes would only be visited once a month (if they were lucky) at which time mass would be celebrated and the rites for past births and deaths performed. With the formation of new pastoral models, however, catechists were regularly given leadership roles in the parish so that religious activities could be realized when the cleric could not be present. These catechists were trained to facilitate small groups in Biblical reflection and encouraged to explore ways in which the parish might confront the perceived needs of the surrounding community. The new perspectives which the poor brought to religious faith and Scriptural interpretation sowed the seeds which slowly grew into what has come to be known as a theology of liberation.

Partially as a response to the burgeoning changes already taking place on the 'base' level of the Church, the bishops of the Latin American Episcopal Conference (CELAM) held a major meeting in Medellín, Colombia in 1968 in order to consider the implications of Vatican II for Latin America. At the Medellín Conference the bishops addressed the tragic social, economic, and political situation within which the majority of their population lived. For perhaps the first time they asserted that these historical conditions should be a central concern for the ministry and theology of the Church and resolved themselves "to be certain that our preaching, liturgy, and catechesis take into account the social and community dimension of Christianity. ... "[23] In short, the Conference proposed theological and pastoral guidelines which would move the Latin American Church to accompany its poor and enable them to become "subjects of their own development."[24] It legitimated the attempts at renewal which had already taken place within the Church and provided a further impulse for the creation of fresh theological reflections based in Latin America's own social reality.

In many respects the preparatory meetings and preliminary papers which set the stage for the Medellín Conference were quite important in themselves for the genesis of liberation theology. The delegation of 130 bishops who were to attend the conference were divided along theological and social lines. Among that number, a significant group propounded a developmental solution to the problems afflicting their continent which promised to progressively lift their people out of the depths of poverty. Others advocated a total liberation from the structures which maintained this situation of dependence. These underlying currents, then, were quite evident in the various position papers which sought to influence the final shape of both the agenda and the final documents of the Conference itself. In this respect, the gathering of bishops provided the occasion for a critical mass of theological reflection upon the themes which were most troubling to the awakened clergy and laity of the church.

The emergence of liberation theology as an academic discipline is most often dated with the publication in 1971 of Gustavo Gutiérrez' seminal work *A Theology of Liberation*.[25] It cannot be overemphasized, however, that grassroots theological reflection had already been established within ecclesial base communities well before that time and had promoted the production of informally written materials throughout the continent. As Gutiérrez himself admitted in the introduction of his book, "many in Latin America have started along the path to liberation ... ; whatever the validity of these pages, it is due to their experiences and reflections."[26]

From the start, Gutiérrez and the other early liberation theologians expressed their conviction that the world and its history raise specific questions and challenges which should be the starting point for any theological endeavor. On that basis, they roundly critiqued a North Atlantic theology which "seems to have avoided for a long time reflecting on the conflictual character of human history, the confrontation among [human beings], social classes, and countries."[27] They called for a re-evaluation of the church's approach to revelation, one which would move away from the speculation of that which happens in the supernatural or ideal realm toward a fundamental concern for its relation to the world of humanity. Within their redefinition of theology was contained the means by which they proposed to carry out this task: "theology as a critical reflection on Christian praxis in the light of the Word."[28]

Liberation theology, then, was created as a challenge to those theological systems which have traditionally framed God's salvific work exclusively, or even primarily, within the spiritual and personal ('transcendent') orders of otherworldly reality. As Juan Luis Segundo explains, it has sought to

> maintain that there are not two separate orders — one being a supernatural order outside history and the other being a natural order inside history; that instead one and the same grace raises human beings to a supernatural level and provides them with the means they need to achieve their true destiny within one and the same historical process.[29]

For that reason liberationists proclaim a God who reveals Self in the unfolding of historical events themselves. They suspect that as long as the central doctrines of the Christian faith—of God, Christ, salvation and sin, only to mention a few — are not based in a critical reflection grounded in history, those doctrines will surely be utilized by those who hold positions of power to maintain their hegemony.

Although qualifiers such as "new" and "radical" certainly describe the impact which liberation theology has brought to bear on the Latin American Church, it should not be assumed that the movement considers itself as anything but the proper expression of 'authentic' Christianity. It believes that the full significance of the Scriptural testimony of God's acts of salvation and liberation, leading from the exodus of God's people from Egypt to the good news preached and lived by Jesus Christ, has been continually compromised and tempered by an established church more interested in stability than vitality. Liberationists contend that the various forms of 'escapist' religion which ignore the crises of the human drama—and yet nevertheless predominate in contemporary society—are false distortions of a living faith which realizes itself in concrete activity in the world. Thus, they conceive of their task as a reclamation and fulfillment of Biblical revelation and Christian praxis.

It would be a mistake, however, to assume that Latin American bishops and theologians spoke with one unified voice after the Medellín Conference. Efforts toward a clear theological option in favor of the marginalized of Latin America was not an easy, and by no means, universal, choice. As evidence of that fact, the development of Christologies which consciously took these historical realities into account elicited a reactionary response from those sectors of the church who saw their own 'orthodox' Christologies, replete with titles and substantive nouns extracted from an alien conceptual world, under challenge.[30] They justifiably perceived this new theological movement as a threat to their own interests, be they ecclesiastical, economic or social. In short time, the Latin American Church became engaged in a serious Christological debate over the existence of a myriad of conflicting images of Christ which struggled for prominence. Assmann was quite correct when he suggested that this discussion was really only the beginning of a much larger battle, for the issues underlying the conflict had deep roots: "there is no immediate prospect of a solution [to the debate on conflicting Christologies] ... because there is no immediate prospect of a solution for the serious social contradictions which exist in a 'Christian' Latin America."[31]

As a result, it has become quite clear to Latin American theologians — though perhaps still not admitted among those who claim that only the liberationists have made a political stance[32]—that one's social location and ideological commitments will determine, to a great extent, the image of Jesus at which one arrives. For every interpreter will unavoidably ground hermeneutics in that particular ideology[33] to which one is committed. Echoing the conclusions reached by Schweitzer in his study of the European quest, Míguez Bonino reaffirms that "in the course of history, the face of Jesus has frequently taken on the features of the person — ideal or historical — who best represented what at that moment [people] most closely linked with the Christian religion or with the fullness of humanity." Taking that history into account, Míguez Bonino does not find it surprising that in Latin America today there are only reactionary, reformist and revolutionary readings of the germinal events of the Christian faith, for there are only reactionary, reformist and revolutionary engagements within the present historical process.[34]

Given the intractibility of that problem, liberationists contend that the challenge for all theologians, be they from Latin America or anywhere else in the world, is to move beyond a simple process of justification and determinism within one's own Christological reflection. However, contrary to common (post-Enlightenment) wisdom, such a safeguard is not thought to be gained simply in the elaboration of a completely 'objective' scientific method that will produce results which are supposedly neutral and free of bias. In reality, that would only serve to mask an interpreter's true underlying commitments. What is most essential is that, as a theologian, one comes to terms with the ideology manifest within one's own interpretations in order to open oneself and others to honest criticism.[35]

Liberationists believe that this can best be done by immersing oneself in an active praxis which is based on the "spirit of Jesus" — i.e., the ethical demands of one's Christology — followed by a critical analysis of one's experiences, and culminating with a re-evaluation of the Scriptural sources which have contributed to the formation of one's Christology; from there, the circle then turns again in search of new discoveries and understandings. Such a methodological circle is necessary "since there is no direct route from divine revelation to theology: the mediation of some praxis is inevitable."[36] Ample consideration of these hermeneutical commitments will be provided in the ensuing pages.

Does Liberation Theology Say Anything New?

Not everyone was convinced that Gutiérrez' book as well as other works written by Latin American liberation theologians in the early 1970s delivered the radical break from North Atlantic theology which they had promised.[37] In an "open letter" addressed to Míguez Bonino, German political theologian Jürgen Moltmann, while finding much to praise in the nascent movement, nonetheless questioned whether it really offered anything distinct from that which had already been mapped out in the progression of post-Enlightenment thought in Europe:

> Gutiérrez presents the process of liberation in Latin America as the continuation and culmination of the European history of freedom. . . . This is all worked through independently and offers many new insights —but precisely only in the framework of Europe's history, scarcely in the history of Latin America. Gutiérrez has written an invaluable contribution to European theology. But where is Latin America in it all?[38]

Although Moltmann's critique was not well received in Latin America, his analysis was, on some levels, difficult to refute. For it cannot be denied that the major theological categories of liberation theology are largely worked out within the philosophical and conceptual framework of post-Enlightenment thought. It also seems indisputable that the liberation movement, especially in its initial phases, relied on the Biblical research of that heritage for its cogent support. Even liberation theologians will readily admit that they highly value those emancipatory factors which have been operative within the European heritage.[39]

Nevertheless, it is difficult to understand how Moltmann could have failed to see the essential character of Latin America "in it all." Gutiérrez, Míguez Bonino, and other liberation writers incorporated into their theological works an in-depth analysis of the social, political, and economic dependency of their own continent and built a strong case that the yearnings for liberation which those conditions produced should be the basis upon which to construct a theology.[40] In so doing, they had inverted that method typically employed by theological reflection in Europe and North America. In simple terms, rather than approaching their pastoral setting with a fixed body of doctrines which merely lacked implementation, they consciously placed a priority on that pastoral setting—viz., a presence with the exploited and marginalized sectors of the society—as a lens from which to view Scripture and the tradition of the church. In this vein, Leonardo Boff included in his first major work on liberation theology the following caveat:

> The predominantly foreign literature that we cite ought not to delude anyone. It is with preoccupations that are ours alone, taken from our Latin American context, that we will reread not only the old texts of the New Testament but also the most recent commentaries written in Europe.[41]

In many respects, then, the distinctive character of liberation theology is to be found in the method which guides its orientation and not always, or even necessarily, in the theological categories and references

of its elaboration.[42] This recognition indicates three important considerations which are absent (or implicitly discounted) from Moltmann's
critique. Firstly, the pastoral setting within which liberation theology is
fashioned causes it to stress specific options of faith that are largely ignored in the theological systems which originate from locales shaped by
vastly different historical conditions. Theology as a second act seeks to
articulate that which has been learned about God and God's truth based
upon a critical reflection of a practical engagement. Perhaps an actual
narrative from Latin America might best exemplify this priority of the
pastoral setting.

Bishop Urioste has seen more suffering than one would care to see
in a lifetime. He was a close advisor to assassinated Archbishop Oscar
Arnulfo Romero and has personally ministered to his country in a time
when corpses daily littered El Salvador's streets and fields. He once
shared with me how a woman from his diocese helped him come to
terms with these modern day crosses.

The woman visited him after she had found her nephew and his
wife dead alongside one of the roads which lead out of the capital of San
Salvador. The National Guard had arrived at their home late one night,
charging that the two young people were part of the guerilla movement.
Perhaps they were involved in a labor union or had been overheard criticizing the government; it does not take much to be considered subversive in most Latin American countries. They were forcibly removed
from their home and nothing was heard about them until two days later,
when their mutilated bodies were found at the edge of town. The head
of her nephew had been decapitated, a common style of execution used
to intimidate.

As Bishop Urioste retold the story, the sadness visiting his face betrayed the tragedy which had accompanied its first hearing. "What can
one say to a woman who has just undergone such suffering? I was
speechless, because I could not bring myself to tell her that everything
would be O.K. I knew I would say that only to comfort myself, not her."
So he sat next to the woman without saying a word, sharing with her the
agony of the silence of the cross.

After a few minutes, the woman lifted her head and said to the
grieving priest, "Don't be sad, Padre. I want to read you something that
has helped to comfort me." And as she spoke these words, she began to
turn the tattered pages of her Bible, finally arriving at the passage
marked with the stain of tears:

> My God, my God, why have you forsaken me? 'How far from saving
> me,' the words I groan. I call all day, my God, but you never answer; all
> night long I call and cannot rest.

> Yet, Holy One, you make your home in the praises of Israel, in you our ancestors put their trust and you rescued them; they called to you for help and they were saved. They never trusted in vain. For God has not despised or disdained the poor one in poverty; God has not hidden God's face from the poor one, but has answered when the poor have called (Psalm 22).

Having recounted the faith of this woman, Bishop Urioste proceeded to explain to me the theological lesson she had taught him. At least since the Biblical story of Job, and no doubt before, it has been assumed that fortune and success are a sign of a righteous life, while poverty and suffering are instruments of God's punishment. If that be the case, then Calvary presents at least two major question marks. Firstly, how could Jesus' mission have failed? And secondly, how could God have been present in such an ignominious death? There are no absolute answers to either of these problems. However, it seems that at the edge of existence the presence of God mysteriously appears and promises a resurrected day for those who have every reason to abandon hope. When all events point to the conclusion that God has cursed those in suffering, the suffering ones find God is walking with them. So the woman from El Salvador did not interpret either her poverty or the death of her family members as a punishment from God, but experienced the presence of God as a hope in her despair.

Strangely enough, the abandonment of God is more a problem for us in the developed world who know very little about death and pain as daily encounters in life, and understand the process of accumulation much better than that of loss. Who has not felt an alienation from God when misfortune has come to one's door? Who is not inclined to doubt the very existence of God when reflecting on the evil which operates in the world?

One cannot ignore the deep mark which our socio-economic system inculcates on our collective psyche. Ownership is the dominant mode by which the members of our culture develop a sense of identity and by which we determine our social relations. The seemingly unlimited ability to possess capital and material objects gives us a sense of security and control in relation to the dynamics which interact to create our social system. In some sense, then, the inability to 'own' or have some level of control over the activities of God produces in us a religious alienation. When the unfortunate events of history occur and leave a trail of suffering in their wake, we suppose they testify to an absence of God; a present and existing God would surely be responsive to our personal needs and pursuits. In this context, Jon Sobrino once remarked to me, "The developed world so believes that it has the right of private ownership for everything that it enters into a crisis once it discovers that it cannot own God."[43]

The story of the bereaved Salvadoran woman — or should it be called the story of the bereaved bishop? — indicates the vital role which the Latin American experience plays in the formation of its theological reflection. The continent's history of suffering has engendered in its people a strong social consciousness which informs the interpretive priorities of its theological method. For suffering, despite its quality as an unjustifiable negative experience, may nonetheless serve as an "interruption of structures that attempt to control rather than inform history; an interruption of theories that deny the dangerous memories and transformative narratives of cultural traditions."[44]

In that context, Tamez explains how a popular consciousness shaped by centuries of suffering demands the stress of essential aspects of human reality over more peripheral concerns, thereby structuring the grid through which the past testimonies of faith will be read:

> The story told in the various Biblical accounts is one of oppression and struggle, as is the history of our Latin American people. In fact, our present story can be seen as a continuation of what we are told in Biblical revelation. . . . Oppression and liberation are the very substance of the entire historical context within which divine revelation unfolds, and only by reference to this central fact can we understand the meaning of faith, grace, love, peace, sin and salvation.[45]

In sum, liberation theology seeks to interpret the traditions and symbols of Christian witness in light of the concerns and categories which fashion their own Latin American experience of human reality.

Critics of liberation theology also often overlook a second key element which distinguishes the movement from the major currents of European and North American theology. Unlike so many scholars of the North Atlantic, it is unable to ignore the inescapable presence of ideology within any given theology; the polarized realities of Latin America make those ideological commitments quite overt.[46] Although it is true that liberationists rely extensively on a Marxist social analysis largely developed in Europe, it is the integration of that analysis into their own theological method which is unique. In that respect, their collective historical experience provides them with a host of suspicions that challenge what we might consider even the most innocuous of theological systems.

Once again it is a peasant woman from El Salvador who helps to illustrate this point. I met Ana in a refugee camp after she had fled from her home in the countryside. She was a widow whose husband had been killed by the military because of his work as a community organizer within their local Catholic parish. She had come to the camp for the sake of her children, hoping that at least she could give them the gift of life; she had nothing else to offer them. They now shared their living space with over two hundred people in large dormitories constructed out of corrugated iron. A daily diet of tortillas and beans for the adults, with limited vegetables and fruits for the children, sustained them "until it's all over."

Ana admitted that she does not know what it would mean to be "over," for the peasants of El Salvador have always seemed to struggle against a poverty which kills — a different kind of violence, to be sure, but one just as deadly. But her faith in God tells her that this hell must end. With a powerful moral force, she informed me:

> I, as a mother, feel the weight of this war. In our country the law of God is being violated. We are not living by the law of God, but by the law of evil human beings. A small amount of people are living the way that everyone should.

> There needs to be a change so that we all can live the way that God desires. Although we are treated like animals and receive no respect from those who have power in our country, we know that we are human beings because God loves us. Isn't that what it means to be made in God's image?

During the same time I was coming to know Ana and other refugees in the camp, U.S. theologian Michael Novak was invited to El Salvador to address the National Association of Free Enterprise — a powerful Salvadoran organization which represents the interests of the wealthy oligarchy. Novak entitled his lecture "A Theology of Creation." He proposed that in creation God had given to each individual the gifts and talents which are necessary for productive work. Foremost among these gifts was that of the intellect, which possessed the creative potential of multiplying capital out of the productive force possessed by each individual. It would be a sin, he explained, to limit the freedom of individuals to use capital and the modes of production, for God had made us in the divine image to be creators upon the earth. The fruits of bountiful profits, therefore, were to be fully enjoyed because they are the sign of the divine blessing given to a "faithful steward."

Novak presents a theology of creation which is by no means foreign for most of us who live in the United States. We have been taught from birth that God has especially blessed our country because we have responsibly used the talents which have been given to us. And on an individual level, it is common wisdom that anyone can succeed as long as one works hard enough.

But Ana's experience provides her with certain basic suspicions regarding the ideological content of any theology which legitimates private gain at the expense of the community and she does not need the help of a Marxist social analysis to uncover it! She would have every reason in the world to believe that the peasants of El Salvador are not deserving of the dignity which has been granted to all human beings by divine creation. The teachings of the church have traditionally communicated to them that they should accept their preordained state as a source of productive labor — how often the dictum "slaves obey your masters" was used from the pulpit! The unmistakable message was that the social order had been divinely established and it was a sin to try to change it.

Nonetheless, Ana implicitly perceives the logical implications of such a theology: God has only blessed a small minority of the population with the gifts necessary to be successfully creative, while the vast majority of the people have either been created without these gifts or have failed to use them properly. Ana reads the Bible in a quite different way. She finds in the book of Genesis and throughout Scripture a God who created human beings in order to care for the creation and each other. It was in the Fall, and not in Creation, when that harmony was destroyed and human beings sought to usurp the role of God for the power to dominate and control. In her theology, then, the pursuit of individual happiness is subservient to the care of the human family, for selfishness is a violation against God and all of God's creatures. In short, for Ana the value of the human person can never be determined in relation to one's economic value, for God has given every person a dignity and value which cannot be eradicated by any earthly power.

Although Ana has not had access to the sophisticated tools of social science, her personal experiences have nonetheless enabled her to unmask the human attitudes which are bound up with the social structures. In turn, the suspicions generated from that insight are used to critically evaluate the underpinnings of theologies which have been presented to her as an explanation of her world.

In much the same way, liberation theologians incorporate social analysis as a primary step in the reflective process. They do not pretend to claim that their method will thereby provide 'correct' explanations, much less solutions, to the human dilemma. Rather, they believe that "an adequate analysis, drawing upon all of the resources of [their] personal and communal experience in light of a proper use of the social sciences, will allow the right questions to emerge."[47] The responsibility of theology, they conclude, is to respond to those questions with integrity.

Thirdly, Moltmann's critique fails to take into account the true subjects of liberation theology; it is not simply a theological theory, but can more accurately be characterized as an ecclesial-political movement.[48]

Liberation theologians stress that they have not attempted to write the definitive theology for Latin America, but view their reflections as part of a process which is moving in a forward trajectory—a beginning step, not the final product. They are seeking to equip their people with the tools which will make possible the creation of more indigenous theologies arising out of their own historical experience and struggle for concrete liberation.

However, as the Salvadoran women of the preceding stories manifest, this process is dialogical. It is the movement of the base which provides the motivation and direction for those theologians who have made a commitment to the popular struggle.

Beatriz Melano Couch thus explains that the theological method which guides liberation theology is "a hermeneutics of suspicion and a hermeneutics of hope born of engagement."[49] The collective suspicions of the community regarding the present construction of reality will lead to a hope that a more liberative knowledge and vision for seeing the world can be imagined. That hope, in turn, arises from an active engagement on behalf of real change for those who are victims of personal and structural exploitation. This method, then, seeks to fashion "a theology which does not stop with reflecting on the world, but rather tries to be part of the process through which the world is transformed."[50]

Summary

"The debate on the theology of liberation begins to be a fruitful one when it broadens into a debate of the history of Latin America, which is also part of the history of the church and its theology."[51] For it is in Latin America's story of conquest and oppression that we find images of Jesus which served to reinforce the social, political, and ecclesial structures imposed and maintained by the conquistadors, while masking Jesus' liberative message of historical liberation. The cross and resurrection were commonly dichotomized to present either a suffering Jesus who was impotent before the powers which controlled his fatal destiny or a celestial Jesus who had triumphantly risen to assume the reign of an imperial kingdom. Thus, be it conscious or not, the primary function of Christology in Latin America was to baptize and sacralize the conquest of the continent and make a virtue out of the consequent suffering of its people.

Liberation theology arose in Latin America as an effort to reconcile theology and the practice of the church to the reality of these sinful conditions of human alienation. The existence of millions of nonpersons within its continent challenged its theologians to put their discipline at the service of a project which struggles to open the historical process for those who have been excluded from it. For that reason, liberation theology has been especially critical of those speculative theologies which debate over possible ideas which might explain the 'essential nature' of God while ignoring the very signs of God's liberative presence as they are unveiled within human history. In contrast, it poses theological reflection as a second step which responds to an active engagement for the liberation of the world.

In like manner, its Christology aims to uncover the significance of Jesus Christ for the lives of human beings and communities who are engaged in the creative process of liberation within the present historical structures. Liberationists thereby seek to rediscover the Jesus who was crucified because of his active praxis on behalf of the marginalized and excluded and was resurrected to work with his disciples to transform their present reality into a 'new creation.'

Notes

1. John Mackay, *The Other Spanish Christ: A Study in the Spiritual History of Spain and South America* (New York: Macmillan Co., 1932), 41. Mackay's book is obviously dated, but contains an endless supply of perceptive insights into the legacy of Spanish spirituality.

2. Saul Trinidad, "Christology, *Conquista*, Colonization," in *Faces of Jesus*, 54.

3. Rebecca Chopp, *The Praxis of Suffering: An Interpretation of Liberation and Political Theologies* (Maryknoll: Orbis Books, 1986), 11. Chopp suggests that Protestantism functioned as an ideological justification of neocolonialism in this period of Latin American history in the same way that Catholicism had served in the colonial era. Míguez Bonino draws much the same conclusion in *Revolutionary Society*.

4. Gutiérrez, "Praxis de liberación, teología, y anuncio," in *Liberación: Diálogos en el CELAM* (Bogotá: CELAM, 1974), 69.

5. Eduardo Galeano challenges any such pretension when writing about Latin America's plight: "There are those who believe that destiny rests on the knees of the gods; but the truth is that it confronts the conscience of man [*sic*] with a burning challenge," *Open Veins of Latin America: Five Centuries of the Pillage of a Continent* (New York: Monthly Review Press, 1973), 283.

6. Chopp, *Praxis of Suffering*, 20.

7. Christopher Columbus, who was a very religious man, wrote of his mission to carry Christ to the New World as a fulfillment of the Old Testament

prophecies: "The truth is that all things will pass away, but God's word will not pass away, for all that God has spoken is to be fulfilled. [As the Bible says,] 'Surely have the coastal dwellers hoped in me, and the ships of Tarsus from the very first; to bear their sons from afar, and their silver and gold along with them, to the name of their God, the Holy One of Israel, who has given them glory' (Isaiah 60:9). . . . How clear it is that he meant these lands! . . . and that it was from Spain that his holy name would spread far and wide among the gentiles. . . . And after saying this by the mouth of Isaiah, he made me his messenger, and showed me where to go," quoted in Saul Trinidad, "Christology, *Conquista*, and Colonization," 56.

Trinidad has added his own commentary to Columbus' manifesto: "Columbus' praxis, [i.e.] his 'pastoral' behavior, is the very negation of the incarnation, indeed of the faith itself—for faith should have asked, 'What does it mean to believe in Christ as I stand here before the American Indian?,' " ibid.

8. Galeano, *Open Veins*, 50.

9. This story follows the recounting given by Eduardo Galeano in *Memory of Fire: Genesis*, Vol 1., trans. Cedric Belfrage (New York: Pantheon Books, 1985), 57.

Surely John MacKay was right when he poetically contested: "The royal coffers of Spain brimmed over with gold, and that became her ruin. She had emerged from her 'cavern' to conquer and catholicize the New World. She conquered it, and in its catholicization de-Christianized herself, and returned not to a cavern but to a grave," *Spanish Christ*, 41.

10. Bartolomé de las Casas, quoted in Bussmann, *Who Do You Say?*, 7.

11. In the words of Míguez Bonino: "The ancient dream of a 'Catholic kingdom,' a unified political and religious structure ruled by Catholic teaching down to its last details—the dream that could never be realized in Europe—was transported to Latin America. 'Christianization' meant the inauguration of this dream in this land—the dream of creating Christianity 'from top to bottom,' " *Polémica, Diálogo y Misión: Catolicismo Romano y Protestantismo en América Latina* (Uruguay: Centro de Estudios Cristianos, 1966), 23.

12. Gutiérrez provides this biting critical overview of the history of the Latin American church: "The Church in Latin America was born alienated. It has not, from the start and despite some valiant efforts to the contrary, been the master of its own destiny. Decisions were taken outside of the subcontinent. After the wars of independence of the last century, a sort of ecclesiastical "colonial treaty" was established. Latin America was to supply the 'raw materials': the faithful, the Marian cult, and popular devotions; Rome and the Churches of the Northern hemisphere were to supply the 'manufactured goods': studies of Latin American affairs, pastoral directives, clerical education, the right to name bishops—and even supply them—money for works and missions. In other words, the generally dependent situation of Latin America is just as real in Church affairs," "Contestation in Latin America," in Teodoro Jiménez Urresti, ed., *Contestation in the Church*, Concilium 68 (New York: Herder/Seabury, 1971), 45.

13. Chopp, *The Praxis of Suffering,* 9.

14. Georges Casalis, "Jesus—Neither Abject Lord nor Heavenly Monarch," in *Faces of Jesus,* 72–76. For a more extensive study of the diverse images of Jesus in Latin America, see *Cristianismo y Sociedad* 13, no. 43–44 (1975); both issues are focussed entirely upon this subject.

15. Ibid., 73.

16. Trinidad, "Christology, *Conquista,* Colonization," 59.

17. José Míguez Bonino, *Doing Theology in a Revolutionary Situation* (Philadelphia: Fortress Press, 1975), 5.

18. Hugo Assmann, "The Power of Christ in History: Conflicting Christologies and Discernment," in *Frontiers,* 149.

19. My analysis has thus far concentrated on the Catholic antecedents of the development of Christology in Latin America. One cannot ignore that a liberation movement has also taken root within the Protestant churches, albeit to a lesser extent within an already minority tradition. Míguez Bonino helps to explain the convergences and divergences of the Protestant movement to that of its Catholic counterpart: "The points of resemblance would include a gradually growing and deepening awareness that leads one from one step to the next: from a rather vague and charitable concern with social issues to works of social service, then to an awareness of structural conditioning factors, and then to a realization of the priority of the political realm and the inevitable association of theological reflection with socio-political analyses and options. The points of difference would include: membership in a minority religious community with a tradition of avoiding explicit politics while maintaining de facto ties with the system of liberal capitalism and the 'neocolonial' setup, and a theological tradition going back to the Reformation," "Historical Praxis and Christian Identity," in *Frontiers,* 261.

20. Jon Sobrino, *Jesús en América Latina: Su Significado Para La Fe y la Cristología.* (San Salvador: UCA Editores, 1982), 22. Cf. also Leonardo Boff: " ... It is the overall context of dependence and oppression at every level of life that prompts Christology in Latin America to ponder and love Jesus Christ as Liberator. The theme was not willed into being by a few theologians. ... It arose as a concrete demand of faith for Christians who felt summoned to wipe out the humiliating conditions imposed on their fellow [*sic*] human beings. In Jesus Christ, they found motives and stimuli for the cause of liberation," *Jesus Christ Liberator: A Critical Christology For Our Time,* trans. Patrick Hughes, Maryknoll: Orbis Books, 1978), 267.

21. *"Gaudium et spes,"* no. 1, in Walter M. Abbot, ed., *The Documents of Vatican II* (New York: Guild Press, 1966), 199.

22. José Comblin, "The Church in Latin America after Vatican II," *LADOC* 7 (Jan.–Feb. 1977): 1.

Atilio René Depertuis confirms this notion: "Motivated by the situation of poverty and dependence of the continent and inspired by the fresh air that was blowing through the opened windows of Vatican II, a new kind of theological reflection was fostered among Roman Catholics, focusing on the need for liberation . . . ," *Liberation Theology: A Study in Its Soteriology* (Burrian Springs, MI: Andrews University Press, 1982), 82.

23. From the Medellín document "Peace," no. 24, published in *The Church in the Present-Day Transformation of Latin America in Light of the Council*, Vol. 1 *Position Papers;* Vol. 2, *Conclusions* (Washington, D.C., U.S. Catholic Conference, 1970). Hereafter, references to Medellín documents will be by name of volume and paragraph number.

24. In Spanish, *"autores de su propio progreso."* This phrase is used in the following places of the Medellín *Conclusions:* "Elites," no. 9; "Peace," no. 16; "Education," no. 3; "Pastoral Accompaniment," no. 10–12.

25. Gustavo Gutiérrez, *Teología de la Liberación: Perspectivas* (Lima: CEP, 1971). Published in English as *A Theology of Liberation: History, Politics, and Salvation,* trans. Sister Caridad Inda and John Eagleson (Maryknoll: Orbis Books, 1973).

26. Gutiérrez, *Theology of Liberation,* ix. Gutiérrez himself points to 1968 as the birthdate of Latin American liberation theology in *The National Catholic Reporter* (Dec. 11, 1982): 11.

27. Ibid., 35.

28. Ibid., 13.

29. Juan Luis Segundo, *The Liberation of Theology,* trans. John Drury (Maryknoll: Orbis Books, 1976), 3.

30. Raúl Vidales explains that it was not only the "reactionaries" who, after Medellín, resisted the creation of Christologies which were grounded in the historical realities of Latin America: "Confronted with this vital demand, the image of Christ was still presented, however latently, by a particular theology which, although it recognized Christ as sensitive to the socio-economic problems of the people, did not locate him in active relation to the complexity of an imperialist system of domination within which one develops one's practice," "La Práctica Histórica de Jesús—Notas Provisorias," *Christus* (Mexico) 40, no. 481 (1974): 43.
That next step for which Vidales calls would lead Christology to a much more overt political stance vis-à-vis the oppressive powers of Jesus' day, but more importantly, those of contemporary Latin America as well. It was this shift which many church leaders and theologians were not willing to make.

31. Assmann, "Power of Christ," 138. He adds, "The conflict of differing Christologies cannot be analyzed or resolved outside the dialectics of socio-political conflicts," ibid.

32. In response to such a position, Assmann contends that everyone brings a specific ideological commitment to Christology: "Some Christologies claim to be apolitical. They offer us a Christ who 'has' power but does not exercise it, and who never takes sides. They are simply ways of concealing the fact that an option for one side has already been made. The newer political Christologies are ways of stripping the mask off these allegedly apolitical Christs and revealing their true countenance," ibid., 149.

33. Due to the immediate negative response often provoked by the word "ideology" in North America, I find it necessary to define the term as it will be used in this study. Adopting an explanation offered by Juan Luis Segundo, ideology will be considered as "a system of goals and means that serve as the necessary backdrop for any human option or line of action," *Liberation of Theology*, 104–105. Ideology, therefore, should not necessarily be condemned as intrinsically evil, but considered the fundamental manner in which humans perceive and act—for good and for evil—upon their reality.

At the same time, ideology must not be equated with (or replace) faith. Faith evokes a diversity of ideologies, depending upon the particular social and historical context within which one is living. To quote Segundo once again: "Faith . . . is the total process to which [the human being] submits, a process of learning in and through ideologies how to create the ideologies needed to handle new and unforeseen situations in history," ibid., 110, 120. For a more elaborate discussion of these themes, see chapter Four of Segundo's *Liberation of Theology* or the quite extensive overview in *Faith and Ideologies*, vol. 1, *Jesus of Nazareth: Yesterday and Today*, trans. John Drury (Maryknoll: Orbis Books, 1984).

34. Míguez Bonino, *Revolutionary Situation*, 2. Míguez Bonino maintains that despite these conflicting results, Christology should not seek to "rise above history" in order to resolve these tensions, for "theology cannot claim to have some purely kerygmatic truth . . . which is unengaged or uncompromised in concrete historical praxis," ibid., 99.

35. A method which Ricoeur called the "hermeneutics of suspicion." Cf. Segundo, *Liberation of Theology*, 8.

36. Míguez Bonino, "Historical Praxis and Christian Identity," *Frontiers*, 262. Cf. Jon Sobrino, *Christology at the Crossroads*, xxv.

37. A limited list of those of some note include Hugo Assmann, *Teología desde la Praxis de la Liberación: Ensayo Teológico desde la América Dependiente* (Salamanca: Sígueme, 1973); sections of this book later published in English as *Theology of a Nomad Church*, trans. Paul Burns (Maryknoll: Orbis Books, 1975); Míguez Bonino, *Revolutionary Situation;* Rubem Alves, *A Theology of Human Hope* (Washington, D.C.: Corpus Books, 1969); Enrique Dussel, *América Latina: Dependencia y Liberación.* (Buenos Aires: Fernando Garcia Cambeiro, 1973); José Porfirio Miranda, *El Ser y el Mesías [Being and the Messiah]* (Salamanca: Sígueme, 1973); Juan Luis Segundo, *De la Sociedad a la Teología* (Buenos Aires: Ediciones Carlos Lohlé, 1970).

38. Jürgen Moltmann, "On Latin American Theology: An Open Letter to José Míguez Bonino," *Christianity and Crisis* 36 (1976): 59.

39. In fact, Sobrino maintains that liberation theologians wish not only to recognize that tradition which leads us through Kant, but to equally embrace the contributions made by Marx and his followers: "In the face of the liberating movement of the Enlightenment, [Latin American theology] spontaneously orientates itself toward the challenge presupposed by the Second Enlightenment: the liberating function of knowledge does not reside in its capacity to explain an existing reality, nor again to lend meaning to a faith threatened by this reality, but in its capacity to transform a reality . . . ," "El Conocimiento Teológico en la Teología Europea y Latinoamericana," *Estudios Centroamericanos* 30 (1973): 431.
In reference to this desire by liberation theologians to incorporate both challenges of the Enlightenment, Chopp somewhat ironically remarks, "This claim leads one to wonder if liberation theology is not really the *true* inheritor of the Enlightenment tradition of modern theology," *The Praxis of Suffering*, 150.

40. For example, cf. Part Three of Gutiérrez' *Theology of Liberation*, 79 – 142. Entitled "The Option before the Latin American Church," he treats, according to subsections, the following themes: "A New Awareness of Latin American Reality," "The Decade of Developmentalism," "The Theory of Dependence," "The Liberation Movement," "The Commitment of Christians [in the process of liberation]," "Towards a Transformation of the Latin American Reality," and "A New Presence of the Church in Latin America."
Míguez Bonino likewise devotes nearly half of his book *Revolutionary Situation* (1–83) to these topics. The four chapters in his analysis are entitled: chapter One, "Beyond Colonial and Neocolonial Christianity"; chapter Two, "Understanding our World"; chapter Three, "The Awakening of the Christian Conscience"; chapter Four, "The Theology of Liberation."

41. Boff, *Liberator*, 43.

42. Enrique Dussel, "Sobre la Historia de la Teología en América Latina," in *Liberación y Cautiverio: Debates en Torno al Método de la Teología en América Latina*, ed. Enrique Ruiz Maldonado (Mexico City: Venecia, 1976), 55–70.

43. Large sections of this narrative have been previously published in David Batstone, "Don't Be Sad Padre," *On Being* (Australia) 16, no. 8 (Sept. 1989): 12–3.

44. Chopp, *The Praxis of Suffering*, 127.

45. Elsa Tamez, *Bible of the Oppressed* (Maryknoll: Orbis Books, 1982), 1. Tamez observes, on the other hand, that there is almost a complete absence of reflection on oppression in the Biblical theology produced in the countries of the North Atlantic. "But the absence is not surprising, since it is possible to tackle this theme only within an existential situation of oppression," ibid., 4.

46. Responding to Moltmann's critique that the only distinctive thing about Latin American theology can be traced to Marx and Engels, Segundo exclaims:

"Who would believe such a remark after reading what so many important German theologians have to say about ideology! One would think they are doing theology in the Amazon jungle!" *The Historical Jesus of the Synoptics*, vol. 2, *Jesus of Nazareth Yesterday and Today* (Maryknoll: Orbis Books, 1985), 193, n. 6.

47. Michael Cook, "Jesus from the Other Side of History: Christology in Latin America," *Theological Studies* 44 (June 1983): 265.

48. Dussel, "Sobre la historia," 57.

49. Beatriz Melano Couch, "Statement," *Theology in the Americas*, 306.

50. Gutiérrez, *Theology of Liberation*, 15.

51. Pablo Richard, "Teología de la Liberación en la Situación de América Latina," *Servir* 13 (1977): 33–4. Richard adds: "We must give an account of our theology of liberation, not by attempting to answer abstract questions, but by transforming our whole Latin American history, at least from the time of Christopher Columbus until today," ibid.

CHAPTER TWO

The Mission of the Historical Jesus

> *This proclamation of the kingdom, this struggle for justice,
> leads Jesus to death. His life and his death give us to know that
> the only possible justice is definitive justice . . . , starting right
> now, in our conflict-filled history, a kingdom in which God's
> love will be present and exploitation abolished.*
> —*Gustavo Gutiérrez*[1]

Padre J. Guadalupe Carney was a U.S. born Catholic priest who
worked for nearly twenty years with the poor communities of Honduras:
the banana workers in the country's valleys, the landless campesinos on
its hillsides, and the indigenous tribes high in its mountains. He credited
these humble people for his conversion from a spirituality rooted in a
self-centered faith to one nurtured by a service to others. In 1983, he
'disappeared'—a Latin American euphemism for murder with a clandestine burial, usually at the hands of military security forces—in the
jungles of Honduras, the consequence of his prophetic ministry against
the economic exploitation and military repression of the Honduran
poor.

Ten years before his murder, Carney wrote and circulated a paper
entitled "Does There Have To Be Rich and Poor: The Class Struggle?"
While perusing below an abbreviated excerpt from that document, the
reader is encouraged to reflect upon a question which would surely be
posed by the majority of U.S. churches (most likely, even the most progressive) and their theologians: Has Padre Carney rendered here a
meaningful account of the gospel within present-day Honduras, or has
he simply manipulated religious terminology to politicize God and make
the gospel captive to a limited ideology?

> What does God think of the class struggle, of having rich and poor
> classes, of some families eating better than others? Do you think God
> wants his children to live like that? Is that the way God made the world

> to be? Because some persons are more capable of earning money than others, does God therefore want them to have more than others? . . . We shouldn't call ourselves Christian until we are disposed to share everything we have with our brothers and sisters, our neighbors. It seems to me that the saying of Marx that 'each one should give according to his capacity, and each one should receive according to his need' (which was the same as the system of the first Christians described in Acts 2:42– 47) is another way of saying with Jesus, 'Love your neighbor as yourself.'[2]

The question presented immediately preceding this passage—pure gospel or political ideology? — was deliberately meant to prejudice the reader's interpretation and highlight the subconscious grid which determines our own world of meaning. For once it has been established that these two concepts are mutually exclusive, the issue has, for all intents and purposes, been decided.

For many, the spurious mix of Marxist social analysis and revolutionary commitment with the Christian gospel would be reason enough to reject Padre Carney's assertions out of hand. Perhaps for others, the political implications of his message would not be quite so disturbing as the apparent relativization and compromise of Christ's universal proclamation of salvation and grace to a specific situation; at root, it is the fear that such an interpretation would confine Christ's import to other contexts, both past and present. Regardless, both viewpoints manifest a concern that the distinctly religious message of Jesus transcend provisional historical ideologies and socio-political strategies so that it might bring a word of reconciliation between God and humanity.

It is from this vantage point that German theologian Walter Kasper delineates the limits for any Christology which seeks to address the concrete problems which afflict the world:

> Christology can approach and tackle the legitimate concern of the modern era and resolve its problem. . . . [But] liberating reconciliation, as it occurs in and through Jesus Christ, is primarily a divine gift and only secondarily a human task. Here precisely is the border line between Christian theology and ideologies or utopia. . . . [3]

Incidentally, it is this very preoccupation which also undergirds the Vatican's generally critical evaluation of liberation theology: "Faith and ideology are in contradiction."

Without a doubt, Carney takes a number of steps in his document which metaphorically "tear the veil" dividing the sacred from the profane, such as: (1) adopting a modern social analysis (Marxist) of the condition of sin inherent in the legally structured social and economic marginalization of a people; (2) identifying the presence of God's character and will within a conflictual historical situation, and therein choosing for one side (the poor) against the other (oppressor); and (3) seeking a liberation (redemption) of the society through the mediation of a historical praxis (discipleship) instigated by human beings. In sum, Carney sought to explicate the significance of Christ's presence within that ideology which, in his opinion, best articulated the causes lying behind the alienation of Honduran society and presented a vision (utopia) of a new society which would make effective Jesus' maxim, "Love your neighbor as yourself."[4]

Assuming for the moment that Carney had in fact misconstrued the gospel of Jesus Christ, several approaches present themselves as alternatives which he might have more appropriately utilized. He could have presented Jesus' proclamation as a universal ideal of truth (elements of this approach are admittedly already present) which, though it might be ahistorical in character, nevertheless inspires human values independent of all partisan ideologies. Or, from a different perspective which views the entire focus of Jesus' ministry as essentially interpersonal, perhaps Carney was mistaken in directing the gospel to what is fundamentally a socio-economic problem. Since Jesus never addressed the larger social and political concerns of his day, but oriented his message and activities toward the conversion and well-being of individuals, any relevance of his message to the conditions which preoccupied Carney may only be applied indirectly: from the individual out to the society. Or, finally, he could have presented the historical life of Jesus as a model—of faith (e.g., complete trust), action (e.g., nonviolence), or obedience (e.g., unquestioning acceptance of one's destiny)—which ought to be imitated as a specifically Christian contribution to the Honduran situation.

Essentially, all of these methodological alternatives emanate from a basic presupposition that the life and ministry of Jesus must convey a religious truth which is expressed in timeless forms and which moves unfettered across generations and cultures. Representing such a perspective, Hans Küng suggests that Jesus of Nazareth is an enigma who equally transcends every articulation of his meaning for human existence:

> Jesus apparently cannot be fitted in anywhere: neither with the rulers nor with the rebels, neither with the moralizers nor with the silent ascetics. He turns out to be provocative, both to the right and to the left. Backed by no party, challenging on all sides: 'The man who fits no formula.'[5]

Albeit in a distinct way, this is the conclusion reached as well by those scholars who participated in the renowned quest for the historical Jesus in nineteenth century Europe. They sought to elevate the personality of Jesus as a universal key which would permit the easy flow of religious meaning from the first century to their own era. For those scholars, Jesus was essentially a religious genius who, through the progressive realization of his true being, achieved the unity of a divine-human consciousness which was held to be the ultimate possibility for all human beings.[6] They went to great lengths to remove Jesus from the historical conditions of his own day, placing special emphasis on those gospel passages dealing with his personal relationship to the "Father" and his powerful personal influence upon those who came into contact with him. In brief, they patently depicted Jesus as the ultimate, transcendent individual who, unaffected by the winds of history, incarnated the model by which to enter into communion with God.[7]

In the remainder of this chapter, I shall evaluate the treatment which a few representative Latin American liberation theologians accord to the historical mission of Jesus. Interestingly enough, these theologians are confronted with nearly the same hermeneutical options which were forced upon our interpretation of Padre Carney's 'Honduran gospel.' They must first make a fundamental decision regarding the character of truth—be it religious or other—and its mode of communication within human history. For if it is presupposed at the start that Jesus proclaimed truth solely in the form of a universal religious ideal, then the historicity of that message will be treated merely as the "husk from which the kernel" (Harnack) may be extracted. The same identical message could then be proclaimed in our own setting with a confidence that it would carry the same power and inspiration it held for those whom Jesus addressed in the first century.

To the contrary, if it is assumed that Jesus, due to the necessarily limited character of every human being's real-life history, sought to comprehend and enunciate an understanding of God's will and character within the structures which shaped his view of reality, then one's interpretation will reveal a very different notion of truth and its communication in history. Jesus' message of the coming of God's grace and salvation would then take on concrete features which would place it squarely in the midst of a conflictual world subject to social chaos and political drama. Posed within that framework, it is the response which he makes to his own concrete situation which could very well point toward those aspects of his life and message which are of enduring value.

Perhaps what is at stake here, therefore, is not so much an absolute image of Jesus—a dubious goal at best—as the illumination of a vision of life, that is, a way of seeing reality. In that regard, it would be of primary interest to determine how Jesus understood God's truth within the limits and demands of his own history, and in what ways he chose to express that faith in words and deeds during his own life. Segundo believes that by treating the issue in this way we will be at the same time "elucidating the relationship between faith and ideologies as it is to be found in the central event of Christianity."[8] If that is the case, then a better understanding of Jesus' own vision of faithful living may also provide new insights for pressing questions which challenge the modern world, such as the one asked by Padre Carney: "What does Jesus think of the class struggle, of having rich and poor classes . . . ?"

In Search of a Method

According to the records of the early historian Flavius Josephus, the overriding interest of the Jewish people living in Palestine during the first century was to be liberated from all kinds of domination by others, so that God alone might be served.[9] Since their return from the Babylonian exile (586 – 538 B.C.), the Jewish people had suffered continual domination at the hands of one foreign power after another. Control of their land had passed hands from the Persians to Alexander the Great, followed by the Egyptian Ptolemies until one hundred years later the Syrian Seleucids, and finally, after a short respite of relative independence with Maccabean rule, Palestine became a colony of imperial Rome.

Remarkably, despite centuries of foreign domination, the Jewish people never ceased to yearn for the establishment of a theocratic state which would regain the legendary sovereignty enjoyed during the Davidic reign. Perhaps nowhere were these aspirations for liberation more profoundly expressed than in the apocalyptic hopes which infused the Jewish religious spirit during the latter stages of this epoch. The conceptual world of apocalyptic envisioned the restoration of Yahweh's people into a holy community in which justice and cultic purity would reside in a glorified Zion.

Yet, although apocalyptic came to be an integral element within the Jewish conceptual world, it was never accepted in first century Palestine with unanimity. Its symbolic value and creative extension, along with everything else in the society, were determined in relation to the strong influences wielded by nation and cult. Those visionary hopes for a new reality which encouraged the rise of apocalyptic eschatology tended to be strongest among those Jews who were especially marginalized by the presence of occupational forces. A more pragmatic approach, on the other hand, was typically adopted by those Jewish leaders exercising relative control over the political and religious institutions of the country. The utilization of apocalyptic, therefore, was itself largely subject to a community's location within the power structures of the society.[10]

The mainstream of North Atlantic scholarship over the last century has recognized the prevalence of the apocalyptic meaning-world in the society within which Jesus lived; likewise, its historical investigation of the gospels has tended to locate the center and framework of Jesus' preaching and mission in the approaching reign of God.[11] Nevertheless, at the same time, the vast majority of that scholarship has elected to either eliminate or reinterpret those apocalyptic notions so frequently used by Jesus in order that they might make his message more intelligible and relevant for the present day.

For example, Rudolf Bultmann dismissed apocalyptic language as a meaningful way to speak of Jesus' salvific significance for the world because it was absolutely alien to the contemporary conception of humanity. He contended that the eschatology of Jesus' proclamation was based on a cosmology of a pre-scientific age which, when interpreted literally, masks the true nature of his message.[12] And if that were not reason enough, as far as he was concerned, the failure of the final Parousia to arrive was sufficient cause to discard the apocalyptic meaning-world of Jesus anyway.[13]

As a foundation for his own method of interpretation, Bultmann believed that the events surrounding the life of Jesus communicated a message of salvation through the medium of the "word," a truth about human existence which challenges humanity today as powerfully as it did in the first century. In order to discover that word, Bultmann maintained that Biblical theologians would need to investigate the historical message of Jesus. However, his conception of that task did not involve a reconstruction of Jesus' specific activities or concrete strategies.[14] The grid he utilized to recover that message was an interpretation of Jesus' own existential self-understanding within the conceptual world of the first century. Hence, without sensing any inherent contradiction, he sought to evaluate the ideas of Jesus without reference to the deeds and events which placed that self-understanding in a particular social, historical and political context.

It should be no surprise, then, that Bultmann's Jesus has little to say about the actual social relations of this world; ultimate value is transposed onto the existential decision of the individual in relation to a transcendent God. In truth, a system of ethics based on social realities has no place in a world successfully demythologized of the historical concerns of Jesus. As Bultmann himself explained,

> The real significance of 'the Kingdom of God' for the message of Jesus does not in any sense depend upon the dramatic events attending its coming, nor on any circumstances which the imagination can conceive. It interests him not at all as a describable state of existence, but rather as the transcendent event.[15]

What Bultmann essentially left unsaid has been repeatedly confirmed by other theologians who share his perspective: Jesus as the Savior of the world transcended the meanings those apocalyptic images elicited within the conflictual religious and social struggles of nation and cult.[16] In its place, a referential ideal of one type or another has been perennially sought which would explain 'what Jesus really meant' when he made statements of an apocalyptic bent. It seems readily apparent that "their loss of confidence in apocalyptic as a vision of world-transformation led them away from social understandings of world toward more personal and interior definitions."[17]

In light of this background, it is somewhat surprising to discover in the early works of several pioneer liberation theologians that Jesus' message of the reign of God was often placed outside the social forces at play in his apocalyptic world. For instance, Leonardo Boff asserted in *Jesus Christ Liberator*—which was perhaps the first attempt to write a systematic Christology from a Latin American perspective — that "the great drama of the life of Christ [Jesus] was to try to take the ideological content out of the words 'kingdom of God' and make the people and his disciples comprehend that he signified something much more profound. ... "[18] Boff supposed that this more "profound" message was the proclamation of a universal liberation which transcended the regional interests which preoccupied the majority of first century Jews: "It is not liberation from the Roman subjugation, nor a shout of rebellion by the poor against Jewish landowners. ... The kingdom of God cannot be reduced to a single dimension of the world. It is the globality of the world that must be transformed in the direction of God."[19]

Boff's position in *Liberator* is perhaps best represented in his exegetical treatment of the temptation narratives (Matt. 4:1 – 11; Lk. 4:1 – 13). He claims that the essence of the three temptations placed before Jesus is the demonic challenge to reduce the universal character of the reign of God to a particular ideology of mere "intrahuman dimensions."

Specifically, Satan offered Jesus a concretization of the reign of God in three spheres: (1) political domination; (2) religious power; and (3) the reign of the social and political miraculous. Boff's Jesus, however, realized that any attempt to "regionalize" God's reign within any of these limited realms of history would be a perversion of God's actual will for the world. "Liberation is real liberation," Boff argued, "only when it is universal, all-comprehensive — when it is a translation of the absolute meaning that is the object of every human being's quest."[20]

Boff did emphasize, however, that Jesus' message challenged the guardians of the social and religious order because it relativized the boxes within which they sought to enclose and control both morality and theology.[21] Moreover, he demonstrated that Jesus' solidarity with the poor and oppressed, as well as the miracles done on their behalf, shattered their elevation of law above human beings. In that regard, Jesus' universal message overcame the absolutizations by which those powers had effectively enslaved the majority of the Jewish people. Nevertheless, Boff was quite convinced that "in all his attitudes, whether in moral disputes with the Pharisees or in his temptation to distribute power among his disciples ... , Jesus always refuses to dictate particularizing norms. He always refuses to formulate solutions or foster hopes that would regionalize the reign of God."[22]

In Boff's first Christology, then, Jesus is primarily concerned with the totality of human history and the conversion of persons within it—a tremendously significant Christological affirmation in its own right! Boff thereby sought to ensure that the proclamation and activities of the historical Jesus would not be exhausted in the limit-realities of his own time, but would have relevance for the present world of Latin America as well.

In *A Theology of Liberation*, Gutiérrez was likewise reticent to locate the message of Jesus within the narrow apocalyptic expectations of the Jewish people. In fact, he assumed that Jesus would have gone to great lengths to avoid the current of religio-political messianism which was so prevalent in the Jewish world. Although "messianism can be efficacious in the short run," Gutiérrez surmised, "the ambiguities and confusions which it entails frustrate the ends it attempts to accomplish."[23] Therefore, Gutiérrez carefully avoided tying Jesus' historical project to any concrete option of the first century which might have compromised his underlying aim of total liberation: "the deep human impact and the social transformation that the Gospel entails is permanent and essential because it transcends the narrow limits of specific historical situations and goes to the very root of human existence...."[24]

Possibly for this reason more than any other, Gutiérrez in this first work paid little attention to the specific historical context of Jesus' message in favor of a Christology which highlights the universal proclamation of a new humanity and a qualitatively more humane society.[25] He was careful to explain, however, that this universality goes to the very heart of political behavior precisely because of its radical salvific character: "the liberation which Jesus offers ... transcends national boundaries, attacks the foundation of injustice and exploitation, and eliminates religio-political confusions, without therefore being limited to a purely 'spiritual plane' "[26] Therefore, the liberation of the Jewish people was certainly of interest to Jesus, Gutiérrez concludes, but only on a much deeper level of reality with more "far reaching consequences."[27]

Without a doubt, both Boff and Gutiérrez rooted their gospel of universal redemption in historical categories of reality which define the efficacy of Jesus Christ for humanity in concrete terms of liberation. At the same time, however, they tended to minimize the particularity of Jesus' historical ministry within a specific time and space in order to highlight its universal consequences for all levels of human reality. To that extent they both implicitly set up a false hermeneutical alternative in their consideration of the historical Jesus: ultimate, transcendent meaning or limited, historical experience.[28]

To insist that the reign of God which Jesus announced is not "a liberation from any specific, historical evil" (Boff) leaves an unresolved tension between the transcendent (ideal) character of truth as ostensibly presented by Jesus and its historical actualization within present reality. Put in practical terms, while the contemporary Christian community in Latin America is challenged to make specific historical options in favor of the struggle of the poor, it is suggested that Jesus avoided making such choices between ideologies so that he would not compromise the universality of his message. It would seem more consistent with a Christology which stakes its grounding in history to take as its starting point the particular: the reason Jesus' life has universal import for the liberation of humanity and the total scope of reality is because of the fact that he embodied his message and cause in a specific ideology (-ies) which gave it meaning. "In short, his divine revelation has an impact on us because of the ideology that incarnates it, that puts limited, three-dimensional human flesh on it."[29] As will be discussed at greater length in the next chapter, in their later works, both Boff and Gutiérrez fully incorporate this perspective into their Christologies and therefore present a significantly more integrated image of Jesus of Nazareth.

In 1975, liberationists from throughout Latin America gathered together in Mexico City to celebrate a congress focussing on the methodology which was under formation in their theologies.[30] One of the key conclusions reached during the course of their sessions was fundamental: if liberation theology was to remain consistent to the principles which served as the foundation for its theological method, then that method itself must remain vulnerable to change and growth. For if theology was indeed to be a reflection on praxis, the experience of that praxis would surely lead to continually new and different conclusions regarding the structure of reality and the framework required to understand it.

Segundo presented a paper at the Mexico congress which demonstrated that this process was already under way in the short span of time since liberation theology had come to life. He distinguished two stages through which the movement had passed: (1) the rise of a specifically Latin American theology dating roughly from the Medellín conference of bishops which, though it played a pioneering role in widening the social and political concerns of their theological systems, was altogether too reliant on limited exegetical results (especially an exaggerated emphasis on the Exodus event and unsubstantiated theological maxims); and (2) the "continuation today" which he defined as a transition in method since that early wave of writings which could be linked to the growing experiences of the movement as a whole.[31]

The evolving development of a liberation methodology identified by Segundo brought with it a commitment to elaborate Christologies which treated the full scope of Jesus' life instead of relying on a few key passages which might reinforce more general systematic points. For example, the parable of the sheep and goats in Matthew 25 and the announcement of good news to the poor in Luke 4:16ff. were two of the primary New Testament texts commonly highlighted in early works on liberation theology. The initial failure to carry out a more extensive Christological project had elicited criticisms from many quarters charging that liberation theology suffered from a "Christological vacuum" or that it had "prescinded from Christ."[32] The spate of Christological works which were published in Latin America in the ensuing years, however, effectively served not only to silence those critics but in the process also evoked a renewed interest in the figure of the historical Jesus as a determinative element in theological construction.

The Christology proposed by Ignacio Ellacuría—martyred (1989) for his uncompromising stance for peace in El Salvador — in his book *Teología Política*[33] was an important step in that development. Ellacuría attempted to locate Jesus' mission within the socio-political world of the first century and therein come to terms with its implications for the mission of the modern church. He presented an understanding of the historical options to which Jesus committed himself which was fully cognizant of the power relations and conflicts which polarized his Jewish world. Ellacuría admitted that the gospels nowhere report that Jesus laid out a strategy for the overthrow of the Roman occupation of Palestine nor a popular insurrection against their surrogate Jewish rulers. At the same time, he emphasized that they made no attempt to hide the fact that the teachings and activities of Jesus were thoroughly immersed in the popular current of messianic apocalypticism. Ellacuría was convinced that this contextualization in itself was significant:

> Despite the ambiguities surrounding his life, Jesus chose that lifestyle [of eschatological messianism] and no other. It is a theological datum of the greatest importance. Salvation history has an intimate relationship with salvation in history.... One may be able to go through this dimension and eventually beyond it, but one cannot bypass it if salvation is to be effective and real.[34]

Ellacuría further demonstrated the essentially political character of Jesus' messianic ministry as it conflicted with the interests of the religious leaders and the priestly class who maintained positions of social power due to their control of the religious cult. He presented the "prophetic-messianic actions" of Jesus as a destabilization of their balance of power, not the least of which included "cleansing" of the temple marketplace, one of their primary sources of economic power.[35]

However, Ellacuría surmised that during the course of his public ministry Jesus gradually shifted the focus of his messianic work. Based on his reading of the gospel texts, he concluded that Jesus eventually began to perceive the vital difference separating a "true messianism" from a "false" one: "He gradually came to realize that the kingdom must be universal. In his preaching he favored the concept of the poor and poverty over the concept of Jew and Jewishness. In other words, he gave preference to a humanistic, social concept over a religio-political concept."[36] On that basis, Ellacuría concluded that Jesus left behind the more limited concerns of his own social and political situation so that he could proclaim a universal message of the reign of God. He believed that this later commitment was, in reality, more socially inclusive because its concerns extended beyond the boundaries of the Jewish faith. Put succinctly, Ellacuría's "Jesus worked to transform a politicized religion into a politicized faith."[37]

The publication of *Teología Política* certainly pointed the Latin American study of the historical Jesus in new directions. However, by no means did it provide liberation theologians with any definitive images of Jesus. If anything, Ellacuría's results simply signaled some of the central issues which would continue to occupy their efforts to uncover Jesus' significance for their own Christologies. In the first place, it indicated that the modern interpreter faces a crucial hermeneutical choice regarding the essential character of Jesus' proclamation and activities: in Ellacuría's terms, was it a "humanistic" message designed for universal import or a "religio-political" message oriented to his own particular social situation? Although these categories are certainly not mutually exclusive (and are treated as such here only for analytical purposes), the emphasis of one category over the other will inevitably shape the image of Jesus at which an interpreter arrives.

Secondly, yet closely related to the first consideration, Ellacuría found it necessary to define the nature of Jesus' relationship to the messianic expectations and apocalyptic meaning-world which are so prevalent in the gospel presentations of his message and activities. The interpreter's judgment whether Jesus immersed himself in that apocalyptic world, came to wholly reject it, or devoted himself entirely to a reinterpretation of it — given the historical context within which Jesus lived — will have determinative consequences for the interpreter's Christology.

If these central issues appear to echo the concerns which drove the quests for the historical Jesus of an earlier era in Europe, it should be viewed as no coincidence. In reality, it demonstrates that these dilemmas are endemic to the formulation of Christology within the modern world. The demand to relate the Jesus of history to the Christ of faith falls upon every Christian community and every generation of believers, regardless of the cultural and social structures which nurture them. Although the structure of that task might not change, the paradigms by which it is understood and treated will undoubtedly vary in each new situation. It is of considerable interest, therefore, to understand how those issues are resolved (or left unresolved) from a Latin American perspective so that we might better understand the hermeneutical decisions which are implicit in our own approaches to Jesus.

J. Severino Croatto: Jesus, The Enactor of Universal Humanization

One of the more evident signs that liberation theology is a reflection in process is given in the diversity of its Christologies. For that reason alone it is not possible to choose one Latin American author whose approach to the historical Jesus could be considered typical of the liberation movement as a whole. In fact, the solutions which different Latin American authors have provided to the central issues raised by Ellacuría's reconstruction actually illustrate the viability of the options.[38]

J. Severino Croatto, a respected Biblical theologian from Argentina, is in many ways representative of those interpreters who find little basis for understanding Jesus' historical project in religio-political terms. He points to the absence in the gospels of any political strategy or program which Jesus might have used to bring about the liberation of the poor from the yoke of Roman oppression.[39] Based on his conviction that the gospels are in many respects socio-politically "ambiguous" — that is, they leave unsaid the urgent demands for Christian discipleship in the political, socio-economic, and cultural dimensions of life — Croatto contends that the modern interpreter must "decontextualize" the gospels in order to express their hidden or, perhaps more accurately put, potential depth of meaning.[40] In practical terms, Croatto dislodges from the narrative accounts of Jesus' words and deeds a core message of universal liberation which is "oriented to the recovery of humankind and its natural values." And it is from this axis that the word of revelation interacts with the reality of the contemporary community of faith.[41]

By no means does Croatto suggest that Jesus was unconcerned for the welfare of the oppressed majority who lived in Palestine during his own day; to the contrary, he stresses that Jesus was unquestionably interested in their "ultimate" liberation. But he claims that if Jesus had involved himself in the particular conflicts of his social context, he would have obscured his real message in a tangled web of limited, parochial concerns. In Croatto's opinion, it was for this very reason that Jesus distanced himself from the hopes of liberation espoused by the Zealots; it was "the anthropological [humanistic] and not the nationalist thrust of the praxis of Jesus [that] universalizes it."[42]

Croatto assumes that Jesus recognized the limitations of determining his activities in relation to a political commitment. He argues that only a socio-critical analysis of reality — which in itself is unique to the modern world — would have enabled Jesus to discern those elements of humanization which may, from a theological perspective, justly demand a revolutionary political project. In his analysis of first century Palestine, however, the only forces which actually motivated revolutionary movements revolved around one of two elements: the cult of law and the ideology of election.[43] Since Jesus did not want to confuse his distinct message of liberation for all of humanity with these restrictive ideologies, Croatto believes Jesus essentially rejected political imagery (read apocalyptic messianism) as an appropriate mode of communication about the reign of God.

Nonetheless, Croatto does affirm that Jesus' ministry had broad social implications. He underlines that Jesus proclaimed to the poor and oppressed that they were to be the privileged recipients of God's reign, and denounced those obstructions upheld by the cult and Torah which blocked their potential humanization. Jesus was especially condemnatory of the scribes and Pharisees for withholding from the marginalized the possibility of redemption due to their ignorance of the Law and/or their inability to follow it. He deliberately confronted that legalism in many of his activities — e.g., healing on the Sabbath — so as to lay bare the false consciousness of values which places Law over the welfare of human beings.[44]

Due to this threat which Jesus posed to their social world, the Jewish leaders plotted his arrest and execution. But in order to achieve that goal, Croatto contends that they needed to manipulate Pilate into sentencing to death someone whom they knew was innocent of any political crime. He suggests that it was not an easy deception to arrange, for "[Pilate] grasps Jesus' *transcendent mission* better than did the Jews and would not have on his own accord seen him as a danger to Roman hegemony."[45]

The "transcendent" character of Jesus' mission which the Jewish leaders did not understand, Croatto explains, was its dynamic function as the constitutive "event" and "word" of liberation.[46] Although Croatto recognizes that messianic apocalypticism was the "dominant atmosphere" in Jesus' world and the primary language utilized to express socio-political liberation, he asserts that Jesus made a deliberate attempt to express his message in such a way which would avoid its "dualism."[47] Hence, the perspective from which he believes Jesus spoke entails a quite different understanding of eschatology: a universal reality expressing "two moments of the same history." In other words, Jesus preached a gospel of the "eschatological" self-manifestation of God who comes from beyond history to challenge human beings to break free from the bondages of sin within history so that they might participate in the creation of a new reality.[48]

Croatto claims that this message is most clearly laid out in the "sermon on the mount." Based on a dubious exegetical leap, he contends that although Matthew and Luke placed the sermon toward the beginning of their accounts of Jesus' ministry, it surely took place at the end of his public life.[49] The beatitudes, then, are underlined as the synthesis of Jesus' proclamation and the cumulative reflection of his own personal experiences. They are also, not coincidentally, the most complete expression of Croatto's image of Jesus: the liberator-teacher from Nazareth who conscientizes the poor and oppressed of their right to access of God's reign of salvation by means of a de-apocalypticized proclamation of universal humanization.

Segundo Galilea: Following (the Absolute Values of) Jesus

Croatto's approach to the public ministry of Jesus is shared by several other key Latin American theologians, but perhaps no one has drawn out its practical consequences more clearly than Segundo Galilea, a Chilean priest who has written most extensively in the area of pastoral theology. In his primary work on Christology *Following Jesus,* Galilea indicates the centrality of the life of Jesus for our own personal and collective discipleship: "Any real following of Christ springs from a knowledge of his humanity, his personality traits, his way of acting, [all of] which by themselves make up the demands of our Christian life."[50] He emphasizes, however, that this knowledge of Jesus will not come solely from Biblical exegesis or historical theology, but will be mediated most particularly by a present encounter with Jesus in faith and in love.

Although Galilea admits that many of Jesus' own disciples understood him to be a political Messiah, he claims that they had completely misinterpreted the primary purpose of his public ministry: to demand the immediate conversion of human beings and societies. In line with that proposition, Galilea argues that Jesus did not seek temporal or political ends:

> Jesus was fundamentally a religious leader who announced the kingdom of God as a religious, pastoral message. Not by his stance before the established authorities, or in the content of his preaching ... or in the orientation he gave his disciples did there appear anything comparable to a political messiah. ... [51]

According to Galilea, the core of Jesus' ministry was the truth which he taught about human beings, a word and witness which restored to them their capacity to live according to those universal values which were represented by the reign of God. In that regard, Jesus' message was thought to have conveyed a quite radical social message. For although Jesus' proclamation was not socio-political per se, Galilea stresses, it did provide the standard by which all persons and structures that were not aligned to the ideals of that reign were to be judged. Jesus thereby imparted an absolute truth which was able to transcend (and necessarily so) the limit-realities of his own situation. His message was a truth about humanity that will always be valid for the evangelization of people, societies, and cultures. In fact, it unmasked the "idolatry" which Galilea believes was intrinsic to the messianic expectations of the Jewish people; idolatrous since it sought the realization of a liberation which was in reality less than complete. Hence, Galilea concludes that "while instituting no socio-political programs, Jesus laid down once and for all the rules for any system or program which seeks to style itself human."[52]

Based on this understanding of the essential character of Jesus' historical mission, Galilea draws some important implications for the contemporary Christian community. Not only does he suppose that Jesus supplies the absolute ideals by which the community should fulfill its own mission in the world today, but also the model by which to achieve them. It is in following Jesus, Galilea contends, that faith finds its true expression, regardless of the fact that "in times like these when ideologies give a privileged place to the economic sphere and make the problem of production and the distribution of wealth the cornerstone of their historical success, the work of Jesus appears anachronistic and condemned to being admired but not imitated."[53]

For that reason, Galilea maintains that the community "finds its true liberating significance in the path of Christ who liberates completely . . . , although through non-political mediations."[54] It discovers in him a "true pastoral equilibrium of prophecy and politics" which is able to transcend all human ideologies so that the Christian community may serve as the critical conscience which brings society nearer the reign of God.[55]

Despite the obvious 'absolute' bent to their images of Jesus, it would be a grave mistake to conclude that Croatto, Galilea, and the other Latin American theologians whom they represent have written ahistorical Christologies. To the contrary, they all seek to delineate the historical implications of Jesus' proclamation for the ultimate redemption of the psychological, social, and economic realities of human existence. But in order to accomplish that goal, they believe that Jesus deemed it necessary to elucidate a religious teaching that went beyond the symptoms of human alienation in order to challenge its very roots. In Galilea's estimation, it was this message which truly subverted the historical structures of sin which were well established in the first century: "[Jewish theocracy and Roman totalitarianism] are struck down at their very foundation, not through a political strategy, but through the proclamation of the truth about God and humanity."[56]

In light of a human history which is rife with examples of oppressive powers which have held themselves up as the final solution to the world's condition — yet often at the expense of human existence itself — that message is unmistakably 'good news.' It is debatable, however, if it is necessary to remove Jesus from the exigencies of the social world of his own time in order to maintain the force of that message today. Moreover, it may very well be that a dynamic paradigm of historical existence is forfeited in the process.

Jon Sobrino: The Two-Stage Ministry of Jesus

In an effort to integrate those gospel passages which suggest that elements of both a religio-political and a universal humanistic message

were present within Jesus' historical mission, Jon Sobrino offers a reconstruction of Jesus' life which presents both in chronological sequence.
His effort is made possible by recourse to a distinct understanding of the
relationship which exists between history and Biblical hermeneutics.

Within his investigative method, Sobrino employs historical categories such as conflict, crisis, ignorance, and temptation in order to illuminate the actual elements which shaped Jesus' public ministry. He crit-
icizes those efforts of past quests for the historical Jesus which, while
highlighting his "higher consciousness" or "transcendent personality,"
effectively removed Jesus from his own historical context. Those attempts failed, contends Sobrino, because they were blinded by an allegiance to the Hellenic principle of eternal perfection, viz., since Jesus was
the perfect human being, he was untouched by such imperfections as ignorance and conflict.[57] The Scriptures, to the contrary, describe the relationship between humanity and God in terms of historical process; the
human being and the community grow in faith as they pass through the
challenges which life/God bring them.

Thus, it is from within the framework of historical process that Sobrino approaches Jesus' struggle with the powers of sin. Given the limitations of language and understanding, Sobrino recognizes that to
speak in such concrete terms entails a risk of falling into complex ambiguities. Nevertheless, he sees a worse danger in a reliance on abstract terminology in which the concrete elements of the life of Jesus inevitably
become diluted.[58]

Further clarifying the presuppositions of his method, Sobrino de-
cides to consider the life and death of Jesus from a determined starting
point: the reign of God. In giving a rationale for this choice, Sobrino
claims that the reign of God was the image which dominated Jesus'
preaching and gave meaning to the bulk of his activity. Nevertheless, he
thinks it would be unproductive to seek to contextualize Jesus' activities
within the first century Jewish notions of God's reign and the expectations which surrounded its coming. He proposes a reverse method: "the
concrete contents of the kingdom should rise from his [Jesus'] ministry
and activity considered as a complete whole."[59] Paradoxically, then,
though the reign of God is determinative for the shape of Jesus' mission,
the person and ministry of Jesus define the actual content of its
meaning.[60]

On that basis, Sobrino traces the development of Jesus' proclamation of the reign of God as a reflection of his maturing faith and self-
understanding within a determined historical process. He reconstructs
this history with considerable reliance on the Marcan narrative, wherein
he perceives two structurally distinct periods of maturity which are separated by a central watershed experience, the "Galilean crisis."

In the first stage of Jesus' public ministry, there was very little in his message which had not already essentially been expressed in the apocalyptic world of Jewish teaching and in the preaching of John the Baptist. Thus, in many respects Jesus' early message was a radicalization of what was already present within that tradition. He did not proclaim himself nor demand that others follow him. He simply called his hearers to accept the reign of God, the coming of which was near, and undergo a conversion to it.[61] Moreover, the 'early' Jesus maintained a dialectical vision of God's reign in history: a hope for a future kingdom which, even in the midst of a conflictive struggle with evil in the present situation, is glimpsed within historical acts of love and justice.[62] In other words, he balanced a tension between waiting for the reign of God to come as a gift and participating in its present construction as a responsibility.

Although Jesus did not specifically provide a concrete plan for the implementation of God's reign, Sobrino continues, he did present it as the ultimate reality of God's justice which comes in judgment of all present structures and authorities. Invoking God's justice in very concrete terms, Jesus announced that the privileged recipients of God's coming reign were to be the poor and outcast, whom Sobrino defines as those who suffered from real economic oppression or those who were alienated from the structures of power because of their physical or moral condition. Jesus' practice of miracles for their benefit further served as signs of the imminent arrival of God's reign; yet, they were also more than signs, since they effected the objective transformation of oppressive structures of sin within first century Palestine.

It was Jesus' clear preference for the poor, both in his historical activity and in his hope for their future liberation, that threatened the security of the Jewish authorities. Although those leaders partially shared his eschatological hope for the future arrival of God's reign, what made him heretical in their eyes was whom Jesus claimed to be the beneficiaries of that future and the implications of that belief for the socioeconomic and political structures. In summary, Sobrino's recovery of the apocalyptic Jesus within this first stage enables him to express the radical social import of his mission, especially since he demonstrates that Jesus identified the proclamation of the reign of God with the actual realization of God's reign in practice.[63]

Sobrino proposes that increasing tensions with the Jewish rulers as well as the seemingly irrepressible persistence of oppressive social conditions led the masses who had followed Jesus in this first stage of his public ministry to abandon him. That setback was coupled with another major crisis. Jesus had expected the reign of God to arrive before his disciples had come back from their mission journeys, yet they had already returned without any tangible sign that God's final reign had indeed begun. This "failure" threw Jesus into deep despair, tempting him to withdraw from public life and form a secluded sect. It is this crucial point in Jesus' life that Sobrino refers to as the "Galilean crisis." He understands it as a rupture in Jesus' public ministry that "affected not only his outer attitude but also the very depths of his person and conception of God and the kingdom."[64]

Sobrino believes that rather than succumb to fatalism Jesus underwent a radical shift in his self-understanding and mission. He began to realize in this second stage that the imminent arrival of God's reign was no longer essential; consequently, he gave up his apocalyptic notions and developed a new vision of God's activity in the world. The eschatological miracles so dynamically practiced in the first phase of his ministry largely ceased. He also drastically reduced another central feature of his earlier ministry: the prophetic denunciation of those sins which opposed the structures of justice promised by the reign of God. Jesus perceived that what was now needed was the "power of love in suffering" which would require him to take the burden of sin upon himself.[65] In basic terms, Jesus accepted his fate. He called on his disciples to "take up the cross" which he knew that he would have to bear. In this reformulated proclamation of Jesus, a decision for his own person became one with a decision for the reign of God.

The hermeneutical key Sobrino employs to bring continuity to this shift within Jesus' mission is his interpretation of the historical development of Jesus' faith. He claims to discover the "real historicity of Jesus" in the progressive evolution of both Jesus' relationship to God and the choices which he made based on that trust.[66] Acknowledging the difficulties of comprehending what Jesus actually thought of himself and of God, Sobrino nevertheless maintains that the character of Jesus' faith may be determined in relation to the concrete attitudes and actions he displayed in response to specific situations and conflicts.[67]

Although Sobrino's approach unquestionably contributes to a historical method of interpretation, his utilization of that hermeneutic leads him at times into some of the same traps sprung by earlier quests for the life of Jesus. For on the one hand, Sobrino may justifiably claim that conflict, temptation, et al., are categories required to elucidate the process of human transformation and conversion within history. He may also legitimately assume that the gospels narrate such transformation within the lives of both Jesus and his followers. It is even valid and necessary to suppose that Jesus not only fashioned his reality, but was shaped by it. Sobrino is not justified, however, in reconstructing a chronological history of Jesus or his faith. As much as he wishes to uncover a historical process of change and development within the subjective mind of Jesus, the gospels do not provide the resources required to achieve such a task.[68]

Therefore, when Sobrino asserts that "the 'historical Jesus' is nothing but the 'history of Jesus,' "[69] he — as well as Ellacuría in the aforementioned seminal work — ignores the fatal blow which William Wrede dealt to liberal European scholars a century earlier on this same issue. Relying particularly on the structure of the gospel of Mark, the liberal school had sought to reconstruct the chronological history of Jesus' progressive development into the Christian messiah. It made frequent recourse to the principles of "natural psychology" in order to explain the apparent changes in the strategic activity of Jesus' ministry and within his own self-understanding. During the first stage of its chronology, Jesus was thought to have fully accepted the popular Jewish ideas surrounding the coming of the messianic age which would result in the creation of an earthly kingdom. The practical consequences of the preaching of these orthodox (Jewish) ideas, however, led Jesus to see their transitory quality, thereby compelling him to formulate his own unique Christian message of an "inward kingdom of repentance."[70]

Wrede, following in the skeptical tradition established by Bruno Baur, seriously doubted the historical authenticity of the gospel narratives. Though accepting the priority of Mark as a source for the other synoptics, he rejected the notion that it is a chronological retelling of the history of Jesus. The gospel material, Wrede so convincingly demonstrated, had been arranged dogmatically, each writer (including Mark) ordering the events in such a way that best reflected the meaning of Jesus for their particular community. It is this dogmatic element, and not a historical interest, which binds together and directs their presentation.[71] Wrede therefore concluded that they could not be interpreted as eye witness reports of the progression of Jesus' ministry. The essential results of Wrede's research have stood the test of time.

In the treatment which Sobrino gives to the story of Jesus' temptation, he inadvertently exposes the vulnerability of his own attempt to reconstruct a chronology of Jesus' faith. He argues that the "critical crises of self-identity" reflected in the temptation account, as well as the choice Jesus is forced to make therein between a "false and true messianism," date the passage in such a way that suggests that it has been wrongly placed by the gospel writers at the beginning of his public ministry. He thereby proposes that the story should be considered an "interpolation" of the gospel writers which actually belongs later in the chronology.[72] But that decision in itself reveals a contradiction in Sobrino's method: the criterion by which he discerns the proper order of events in the gospel is the very notion of Jesus' faith that his reconstruction is said to chronicle.

Behind Sobrino's two-stage reconstruction appears to lie a more subtle motive: an attempt to detour Jesus' "failed" apocalyptic expectations. Sobrino quite openly argues that the Christian community must somehow adjust to the "fact" that Jesus had wrongly foreseen (ignorance) the immediate end of the world, for that misjudgment presents every Christology with a daunting contradiction. Put simply, if Jesus had unwaveringly sought the arrival of God's reign throughout his ministry and that reign did not come either in his lifetime or in the two thousand years since his death, then his life and message may only serve as another example of a failed messianism. Confronted with that option, Sobrino chooses instead to portray Jesus as the obedient Son who realized that failure head-on and, despite the absence of familiar ground upon which to stand firm, maintained his trust in God. In Sobrino's framework, then, Jesus accordingly transformed the character of his ministry to center on the transcendent significance of his own destiny and his personal relationship to the "Father."[73]

Hence, the apocalyptic failure becomes for Sobrino a primary referent from which the development and character of Jesus' mission can be interpreted. Although Sobrino clearly does not wish to 'individualize' Jesus' understanding of the arrival of God's reign into history, he nonetheless rejects apocalyptic language and its socio-political critique as a meaningful way to speak of the reign of God. In Sobrino's first stage, Jesus was a Galilean prophet who utilized apocalyptic as a transformative vision which served to disrupt the social world of his hearers and to threaten the control of the Jewish rulers. In his second stage, "fidelity to the Father now stands in the presence, not of the Father's imminent coming, but of Jesus' imminent death."[74] Though Sobrino denies that Jesus thereby chose to address individual concerns rather than structural change — what he justifiably considers a false alternative[75] — the reader cannot help but sense a shift towards a more personal gospel. The 'history' of Sobrino's Jesus seems to convey what is surely an unintended message: love may become historical in personal acts of faith but is largely ineffective in relation to the structures of the world.

Perhaps an example here may help to illustrate this point. When considering the relationship which existed between Jesus and the Zealots, Sobrino marks a clear distinction in their approaches both in terms of their understanding of power and in their strategy of societal transformation:

> ... The Zealots favored armed insurrection. According to Jesus, how-
> ever, God's coming was an act of grace. . . . The basic temptation facing
> him and others was the temptation to establish God's kingdom through
> the use of political power. The only true power in Jesus' eyes was the
> power embodied in truth and love. That is why he . . . call[ed] for par-
> don and love of enemy rather than vengeance. . . . Over against the no-
> tion of God as power, Jesus sets the notion of God as love. . . . [76]

In this presentation of Jesus' attitude towards power, at least two
ideologies are implicit. In the first place, Sobrino assumes that the use of
political power chosen by the Zealots is inherently opposed to a different
category of power utilized by Jesus, viz., one that is "embodied in truth
and love." That notion is reinforced by the subsequent theological affirmation that Jesus does not reveal a God who wields power, but one who
loves. It should be mentioned that Sobrino does offer qualifications to
that conclusion at other points in his writings, e.g., the "universal love"
of Jesus, though not political in itself, often becomes such in concrete situations because it always finds itself opposed by the "oppressive weight
of power."[77] Nevertheless, an ideology elevating the ideal of truth and
love over coercive, political power prevails.

In the second place, although Sobrino believes that Jesus concurred
"with the Zealots on the idea that there must be come historical and
socio-political mediation of the kingdom of God," Jesus is thought to
have envisioned a very different society which is comprised of a reconciled human community.[78] Conversely, the Zealots by virtue of their option for armed insurrection and animosity for the enemy, thereby prove
their false conception of a new society. Once again, Sobrino provides a
disclaimer, noting that he does not thereby seek to imply that the history
of Jesus is a confirmation of pacifism. As far as he is concerned, the real
issue is the human 'will to power' which makes the search for justice an
affirmation of one's ego. In short, "the human heart must be pure."[79]

However complete the attitude of Sobrino's Jesus towards power
might seem within an ideal world, or for that matter within one as far
removed from ours as first century Palestine, the imitation of that attitude within the contemporary scene is laden with problems. That is most
especially the case in the polarized social and political situation which
characterizes Latin America today. It is self-evident that the resolution
of the Latin American crisis lies in a political option of some form which
can challenge and reverse the vast inequities of wealth and structural
violence which dominate the society. Keeping that context in mind, it is
not clear how Jesus as a fully human person within the conflictual situation of his own time was able to find options which embodied truth and

love but at the same time were not coercive, which were stridently against the injustice of the authorities but were predicated on reconciliation and a pure heart.

Our own experience of historical realities suggests that notions such as power, love, truth, and reconciliation are not self-contained categories. A life lived free of concrete strategies, commitments and ideologies is alien to the only kind of reality that we know, i.e., human history. Power, for instance, will be a fundamental factor in every historical situation. The choice forced upon each community and individual is not whether to use power *or* love *or* truth, but whether power will be used in a loving or unloving way, in a truthful or untruthful way. And in each new concrete situation those effective (or 'power-ful') strategies may well be redefined.

Turning to a more contemporary example from the dependent world, it can be demonstrated how an idealized attitude of love over power/coercion/revolution often lends itself to specific ideologies which may very well be antithetical to Jesus' historical life and message. It was reported in the Philippines — a country which has suffered a history of oppression and foreign domination similar to that of Latin America — that the army has decided to imitate the popular education which the insurgency has so successfully carried out among the poor majority. The soldiers are relocating their base camps to marginal barrios which have traditionally been treated only with suspicion by the government and military. Their strategy calls for "political organizing, civic action programs, and cultivation of informants and village defense networks to win popular grassroots support." But as important as the organizing initiatives might be, high priority is being placed on political education. As the army chief of staff describes it, "Christian values are stressed in the community teach-ins, while the rebel brand of liberation theology — so popular in depressed communities — is decried as Marxist propaganda. While they teach revolution, we teach love."[80] As the toll of human rights committed by the military in the Philippines continues at a tragic rate, one is left to wonder what exactly is the content of the army's notion of Christian love.

In order to define such abstract notions as love, power, and truth in our reality, then, requires a historical context which provides them with content and shape. If that is to be accepted, then it would seem imperative for a liberation Christology to uncover the specific historical options which Jesus made within his particular context. It is clear that Jesus at least distanced himself from the option chosen by the Zealot faction; that said, however, does not in any sense imply that Jesus rejected social or coercive power. It is important, therefore, to investigate what types of power Jesus did use and the possible reasons for those choices. In that respect, a full incarnation of Jesus in the first century enables an understanding of the values and ends for which he struggled and died, thereby encouraging us to look, in dialogue with his living Spirit, for those means which may bring about salvation and liberation in our present contexts. Most certainly, Sobrino does not ignore that task; yet, his concern to maintain the universality of Jesus' earthly existence often does lead him to create somewhat of a dichotomy between history and religious truth, as well as between personal sanctification ("pure heart") and socio-communal redemption.[81]

Interestingly enough, Sobrino draws a clear distinction between the ethical framework of Jesus and that suggested for the modern believer. The failure of the Parousia to come, Sobrino argues, causes the modern believer to approach the world from a fundamentally different vantage point: "The difference is in the search for a hermeneutic that ... interprets discipleship within a history that apparently is not near its end, and that therefore demands a series of religious, social, economic, and political analyses which will organize history on a path towards the reign of God."[82] Hence, the primary significance of the ministry of Jesus for Sobrino is not so much the scope of his ethical choices as it is his revelation of how the disciple of any age may respond to the absolute mystery of God in trust and obedience to the mission of God's reign.[83] In that sense, he hails the historical Jesus as the "principle that enables us to draw closer to the totality of Christ both in terms of knowledge and in terms of real-life praxis."[84]

Juan Luis Segundo: The Apocalyptic Jesus

Undoubtedly, the decision made by many liberation theologians to present Jesus' message as a predominantly humanistic word of universal liberation is partly due to the nature of the gospel texts themselves. On the surface at least, they do not easily lend themselves to a reading which permits a socio-political "hermeneutics of freedom" and, as a result, seemingly depict a Jesus who devoted his energies primarily to the conversion and well-being of individuals. Juan Luis Segundo confirms that it was often for that very reason liberation theologians, especially in the early stages of the movement, tended to turn to other sections of Scripture to find more direct evidence of God's concern for the socio-political dimensions of human reality:

> ... The Gospels seem to center Jesus' main interests on another plane entirely, on an apolitical plane. The young Christian is often advised in

> advance that he must 'translate' the language of Jesus into political di-
> mensions ... [but] such 'translation' is not an easy process. ... That is
> not one of the least reasons why liberation theology prefers the Old Tes-
> tament and, in particular, the Exodus account.[85]

It is also surely not one of the least reasons why liberation theology, especially in its early formation, tended to "prescind from Christology."

Segundo announces, however, that any such avoidance of the gospels is a serious mistake, for the gospel presentation of the historical Jesus can be a tremendous resource for theological reflection within the
present context of Latin America. Even though he does not deny that Jesus' teaching was "overwhelmingly interpersonal," he contends that the
gospel texts (especially the synoptics) are best interpreted and understood by means of a socio-political key.[86]

The reason that other theologians have often failed to see this, postulates Segundo, has been their acritical projection of modern categories
of socio-political analysis to a completely distinct world of the first century. Since the gospels do not permit a link between Jesus and the overtly
political Zealot movement, interpreters frequently conclude that Jesus'
message was not political. But that decision is based on our modern ideology of the autonomy of secular politics which was not shared by Jesus
and his contemporaries:

> The fact is that the concrete, systematic oppression that Jesus con-
> fronted in his day did not appear to him as 'political' in our sense of the
> term; it showed up to him as 'religious' oppression. More than the of-
> ficials of the Roman Empire, it was the religious authority of the Scribes
> and Sadducees and Pharisees that determined the socio-political struc-
> ture of Israel. In real life this authority was political, and Jesus really
> did tear it apart.[87]

Thus, Segundo proposes that Jesus' principal conflict was with the
religio-political authority represented by the Jewish leaders. The Romans, as a general rule, allowed these surrogate authorities to run the
daily affairs of their own people as long as they maintained the social order and expedited the collection of taxes.[88] Therefore, those who controlled the medium of salvation in the Jewish society were also in a position to determine the socio-political structures; as a result, religious
purity and impurity served a vital ideological function.[89] The social and
economic realities of the Jewish society were determined by a matrix of
poor and "sinner" in one class and wealthy and "righteous" in another,
with room for few in between. It is in this historical context that the gospels narrate Jesus' struggle with the Sadducees and Herodians as those

occupying positions of authority and with the Pharisees as the theological guardians of that social order.

Segundo believes that Jesus especially scandalized the Jewish authorities with his proclamation of the imminent arrival of the reign of God. He contends that Biblical theologians have often been "so irrevocably dominated by a false conception of the divinity of Jesus and its consequent idealism" that they have been unable "to see how the efficacy and relevance of Jesus' project within the world of Israel depended on having activated an expectation which, from outside that world, could be considered simplistic and limited: that hope based in Jewish nationalism for the reign of God over Israel."[90]

It is all too often overlooked how ideologically explosive the term "reign of God" was within Jesus' own social milieu. Segundo points out that it did not have the same metaphorical and hence purely religious import in first century Palestine which makes that term so safe within our own theological meaning-world. The apocalyptic notion of the reign of God was admittedly a nationalistic, culturally-bound vision of human hope. Segundo contends that it was nonetheless Jesus' discernment that among the limited possibilities posed by his environment it best expressed the character of God's engagement in the historical process. Therefore, though Jesus was surely aware of the contentious linguistic baggage which accompanied the use of apocalyptic notions, he consciously chose to express his message in that language and no other. The reason for that, Segundo maintains, is that Jesus "realized that he could never demand faith from people if he addressed them in neutral, antiseptic terms."[91]

So, rather than seek to avoid the messianic expectations of the Jewish people, Jesus embodied his teaching within the very conceptual world which fanned those hopes. To dispel any doubt concerning the messianic character of Jesus' mission, Segundo adds that the best proof of the degree to which Jesus adopted and employed it may be seen in the response of his own disciples: "The fact [is] that the close circle of people around him, who benefited from his clearest explanations, thought right up to the end that in Jesus they would see literally the full restoration of the monarchy and the independence of Israel."[92]

In the parables, a style of teaching utilized uniquely by Jesus, Segundo discovers that apocalyptic message most clearly highlighted.[93] The apocalyptic imagery operated to subvert the world within which it was expressed, making what might otherwise be interpreted as a strictly humanistic message take on a decidedly political tone. For instance, those parables which announced unrestricted entrance into God's reign for all people without any moral precondition — e.g., the parable of the wedding banquet — challenged the religious ideology of the Pharisees who thereby justified the social division of Palestine. Other parables such as that of the laborers in the vineyard, which narrate a reverse of the prevailing social scripts and socio-religious values, would have shocked a quite different set of hearers, the landless peasants, as well:

> The scandal derives from the fact that the privileges resulting from the division of labor are always attributed to virtuousness. It is assumed that they are grounded in the will of God. Oppression thus becomes sacred, even penetrating the mind of the oppressed. But the God of Jesus does not think that way, refuses to play that role.[94]

On that basis, Segundo argues that Jesus judged a world in which peasant farmers plant and harvest the crops while the urban landowners 'virtuously' claim the profits.[95] The parable signals that the end of this world has already begun!

The content of the parables alone make it impossible for the Biblical interpreter to hold that Jesus passed by the grave social problems of his time. Placed into juxtaposition with his activities on behalf of the poor and dispossessed, the parables reflect Jesus' concrete hopes for their actual messianic liberation. In that regard, it is not enough to simply say that Jesus identified with the poor. His historical mission went beyond that:

> To be able to comprehend the originality of his concrete historical action, we have to situate ourselves within the perspective of the exercise of his messianism and of the construction of the Kingdom; in this context are to be placed the parables. . . . The dynamism of his action becomes revolutionary to the extent that his messianism . . . calls men and women to responsibly 'become aware of their condition' [*toma de conciencia*] in order to take efficacious historical actions which transform those conditions.[96]

Jesus taught these parables, then, not only to impart didactic material, but also to unmask the religious ideologies which supported the mechanisms of marginalization and exploitation in the Israelite society. By means of that process, Jesus sought to break the consciousness of domination which reinforced the poor's fatalistic conception of their own alienated condition. It was an attempt "to dismantle the ideological mechanism wherewith the poor themselves turn the popular religion they practice into an instrument of oppression that benefits those with power in Israel."[97]

Segundo suggests that Jesus was not so convinced regarding the use of miracles to serve as a means of conscientization. Jesus obviously did employ unique powers to help the sick, disabled, and poor; acts which concomitantly served as "a momentary eschatology when the powers of the new age touch human life and transform it."[98] At the same time, however, Jesus discovered that miracles could serve to block consciousness of the character of the messianic kingdom about which he proclaimed and unwittingly discourage the active participation of common people to help bring it about. Despite the credibility these concrete signs might have given his message initially, they later attracted people only looking for handouts instead of those seeking true liberation. Segundo surmises that it is out of this dilemma that the "messianic secret" arose: Jesus saw the wisdom of maintaining a low profile so that he would have the opportunity to spend more time carrying out authentic "consciousness-raising."[99]

In review, Segundo urges a reconsideration of the apocalyptic teachings and actions of Jesus which locate him squarely within the social and historical world within which he was immersed.[100] Jesus' proclamation of the imminent arrival of God's reign may then be seen in its concrete function of reversing the prevailing value judgments in Israelite society. Since it was his unswerving commitment to the proclamation and enactment of that reality which brought Jesus to his death, an understanding of his relationship to that determined worldview is by no means inconsequential. For it is those goals and means Jesus lived subjectively as absolute values within the structures of his own situation. Expressed in other words, "the fact that God reigns can only mean that God's values have been fleshed out in reality. And Jesus pointed up what those values were in a most conflictive and radical way."[101]

For that reason, Segundo does not want to forfeit the historical character of Jesus' project in the interests of extending his universality. He believes that it is wrong to assume that the universal import of Jesus' life may be uncovered once his concrete ideologies and historical options have been capably shed, as if the absolute character of Jesus' revelation is forfeited by virtue of the fact that it is historically conditioned. For it is only through historical mediation itself that revelation reaches us at all.

Of course, the very nature of history inherently places limitations upon any particular project, and since Jesus was a figure of history, his life and mission are subject to those realities. At first glance, then, the historical character of Jesus' life might seem to diminish the universality of his message about total liberation, applicable to all human beings and all phases of human existence. Segundo contends that, to the contrary, it is that particularity itself which gives the life of Jesus universal import. Liberation, like salvation, only has a credible meaning when it takes on (incarnates) some concrete form. It is "the obligation of summoning human beings to a universal liberation while bearing real witness to some concrete liberation ... [that] explains the curious dialectic in Jesus' life."[102]

In order to explain this dialectic within a modern worldview, Segundo adopts the evolutionary categories developed by French scientist/theologian Teilhard de Chardin.[103] Segundo believes that an evolutionary worldview moves human understanding beyond the static parameters which typically limit our perception of linear history. An evolutionary system offers an interpretation of historical events which elucidates both their contribution to their own historical process as well as their contribution towards the future culmination (Omega point) of the total historical process itself.

It would be an error, in Segundo's opinion, to conceive of this process as an unrelenting march of nature and history towards a predetermined end. In actuality, it moves in a circuitous path which is brought about by the seemingly antithetical forces of "entropy" and "neguentropy," both of which contribute to the shape of history's future. Entropy is the degeneration of energy (symbolized by death) and neguentropy is the living force which stimulates growth toward completeness. The accentuations, accumulations, and repetitions of entropy and neguentropy in the evolutionary process periodically lead to the crossing of new thresholds which transcend, at least in the world of comprehension, the cumulative effect of tiny changes which have taken place in successive occurrence. These small changes seem to join together in some unforeseen journey toward new visions which we call "revelation."

Segundo proposes that Jesus placed his life in the service of the path of neguentropy, for he sought to integrate into the historical process those who had been marginalized and excluded so that they might become its living subjects. Yet, at the same time, Jesus was also forced to adapt himself to the forces of entropy, thereby accepting the need to adopt specific ideologies which perhaps, on the surface, seem contrary to the universal life force of neguentropy. Although Jesus fully recognized the ideal possibilities of human relationships and structures, he had to realistically incorporate time and entropy within his daily reality.

However, Segundo stresses that Jesus' "liberty never accepted — in bad faith — complicity with an entropy greater than that which was demanded by the efficacy of his historical project."[104] For example, Jesus made enemies, in itself the antithesis of integration; he showed partiality to the poor and opposed those who oppressed them. It was this type of willingness to so adjust to historical realities that Segundo terms "flexibility," a quality which is essential for the effective growth of the evolutionary process, since concessions to entropy are at times required for its positive development.[105]

Of course, once Jesus' life is placed in such an authentic historical context, his activity becomes more ambiguous and partisan; for some, perhaps, less distinguishable from the powers of sin. Yet, for Segundo, this is no more a scandal than the fact that Jesus and the reign of God made themselves subject to the law of death and thereby 'crashed against the rocks' of their adversaries. In fact, it appears that Jesus was so aware of the power of death which opposed his project that he chose to "submerge in it his aims. Thus, that grain of humanization which characterizes the reign of God needed to die in order to liberate . . . all of its possibilities. And with it needed to die Jesus."[106]

Somehow amidst the mystery of death and degeneration an advance was made in the process of liberation toward its ultimate point. All of that, however, is only truly apparent to the eyes of faith. As Segundo notes, "Jesus' victory over Sin is as invisible as his victory over death. And only when, with the resurrection, the ultimate is presented to faith, will it also include this transcendent data of the victory . . . "[107] Jesus' resurrection, then, is the event that enables a conversion for the one who has faith, creating a new vision of that which may potentially take place within time and entropy.[108]

Segundo is hopeful that a recasting of our conceptual framework may allow us to see the particular and universal in Jesus' life as a dialectical unity. If that were to be accepted, he believes that the Christian community would be freed from the obligation to dogmatically follow one line (idealistically) of action. It might possibly then discover creative "flexibility" in the elaboration of a liberative praxis within its own context. He is convinced that as long as the faith community ignores the demands of efficacy and entropy within the historical process, it will skew the central paradigm of the crucified and resurrected Jesus.[109] In that respect, Segundo offers a liberation method which fully responds to Moltmann's call for historical thinking in our Christology:

> To look for what corresponds to God in the world, to the last things in the things before the last, to the great hope in the lesser hopes. . . . Must we not go beyond that and from the start, understand God in the world, the beyond in the this-worldly, the universal in the concrete, and eschatology in the historical, in order to arrive at a political hermeneutics of the crucified Christ and a theology of real liberation?[110]

Reign of God, Utopia, and Historical Engagement

Each of the Christologies which have been discussed in this chapter have attempted in one way or another to demonstrate the vital bond linking the mission of the historical Jesus to the central proclamation of Latin America's popular church: God's promise to transform the personal and communal realities of human existence. In order to responsibly carry out that task, it was shown that each theologian chooses to highlight those gospel passages which, in their opinion, most truthfully speak of the presence of Jesus Christ within their context. In other words, each theologian seeks to faithfully relate the Christ of faith to the Jesus of history. The fact that they arrive at different images of Jesus, therefore, does not necessarily indicate that some have misconstrued the gospel witness while others have read it correctly.

In reality, Jesus' mission was broader than what was allowed by either of the categories by which my evaluation was structured. The gospels unquestionably reflect Jesus' concern for the conversion and welfare of the human person; moreover, his activities and teachings communicated truths about the human condition which extend (even universally) beyond the situation to which they were originally addressed. For that matter, the words and deeds which Jesus directed to the socio-political conditions of his time also obviously convey a more widely humanistic message of hope and liberation. For it was not the existence of structures themselves which preoccupied Jesus, but the effect those structures had on the lives of human beings.

The previous discussion did show, however, that all too many liberation theologians choose to reject the image of the apocalyptic Jesus as a meaningful way to speak of his significance for the present world. They commonly turn to other images which appear more likely to correspond to Jesus' concern for the total liberation of human reality. In many respects it is a curious hermeneutical decision, for nearly all liberation theologians utilize the apocalyptic notions of 'reign of God' and 'utopia' as central features to express their own understanding of the relationship which exists between God and their Latin American history.

For instance, in his book *Doing Theology in a Revolutionary Situation*, José Míguez Bonino devotes an entire chapter to the theme of eschatology, which he entitles "Kingdom of God, Utopia, and Historical Engagement."[111] Therein he presents a challenging consideration of the reign of God as a future vision of the world which mobilizes the church to historical actions of love and justice in the present. However, Míguez Bonino claims to discover support for that vision much more readily in the Old Testament than in the New Testament. Surprisingly, he claims that the

New Testament provides "scanty elements" which relate the reign of God to history in such a way that would demand "a serious concrete engagement."[112] That evidence which he does find in the New Testament revolves around the Pauline notions of 'body' and 'resurrection'; without explanation, no reference is made to the mission of the historical Jesus.

If Sobrino's study is any indication, perhaps the reason for this oversight by many liberation theologians can be traced to their assumption that Jesus' apocalyptic expectations themselves were proven by subsequent history to be in error. Of course, Jesus' ostensible miscalculation of the imminent arrival of the kingdom is not a new datum for Christological investigation. Schweitzer had thereby demonstrated "the futile implications of making eschatology the center of an investigation of Jesus' ministry . . . [which] in effect cut off discussion of the reign of God as a socially transforming reality that could influence the course of events in the world. . . . "[113] In the next generation of scholarship that assumption was confirmed by Bultmann who effectively argued for the implausibility of using apocalyptic imagery as a tool to interpret the significance of Jesus for the post-Enlightenment world: " . . . mythical eschatology is untenable for the simple reason that the Parousia of Christ did not come to an end, and as every schoolboy knows, it will continue to run its course."[114] On that basis, the tradition leading from Schweitzer through Bultmann to the new quest largely dismissed the contemporary relevance of Jesus' apocalyptic message on the grounds that the kingdom of God had not arrived as a natural phenomenon to end human history.[115]

William Herzog, a Biblical theologian from the United States, has signaled a way out of this self-enclosed critique. He proposes that apocalyptic will always be rejected as long as it is assumed that its primary referent is directed to the natural world. In response to Bultmann's dictum, he proposes that the actual sense of apocalyptic imagery is most aptly captured in terms of a social world "which may live and die while the [physical] world continues its natural movements and cosmic rhythms."[116] Herzog claims that it is not even necessary to suppose that these distinctions were present in the mentality of first century Jews, for language about the natural world could not (and cannot) be so easily isolated from a group's perceptions of its social world; for the human community the two are intricately intertwined.

He defines "world," then, as a social and cultural category which identifies the structure of historical conditions existent within a determined reality and which is supported by the various ideologies which give it legitimacy. "Taken together, a society's traditions, institutions, and practical arrangement form a symbolic universe."[117] Possibly no more vital source for these sanctioning ideologies can be found anywhere else than in religion. Herzog underlines that the role of religion is so crucial because "with its blessing and legitimating force, any social construction of reality, including its prejudices, distribution of wealth, class or rank stratification, policies and exploitation, becomes the Divine construction of reality."[118]

That process was clearly manifest in the control of nation and cult demonstrated by the Jewish leaders of first century Palestine. In fact, it most likely inspired Jesus' bitter denunciations of the Pharisees over the true character of Hebrew law. The central issue for Jesus was not the ultimacy of law as such, but the predominance of a social world which used law as one of its pillars. For good or bad, law serves to place a religio-ethical sanction on any particular construction of reality. Framing the law in that context explains "why world is usually accepted not merely as 'what is' but more insidiously as 'what must be,' or 'what ought to be,' or 'what has been ordained to be.' "[119]

Herzog demonstrates that Jesus utilized apocalyptic to subvert world, i.e., he adopted its imagery and language as an incisive judgment on the existing historical structures and as an alternative foundation upon which to construct a new reality. Jesus' teaching and his praxis of the reign of God "offer[ed] glimpses of another world where the power relations and social givens of this world are suspended and examined, perhaps even subverted and shattered."[120] Jesus' mission, then, was not only directed toward the vision of a future world but was also committed to the actual transformation of history itself.

What makes Herzog's presentation of the apocalyptic Jesus so suggestive for Latin American liberation theology is the fact that many liberationists have come to understand the reign of God in a quite similar fashion within their own eschatologies, yet independently of the historical Jesus. They, too, have recognized the utopic function of the reign of God as a challenge to the existing order of social reality and as a stimulation for the imagination of new possibilities within their own historical situation. For that reason, their own understandings of the relationship between the reign of God, utopia, and historical engagement hint at some potentially provocative ways to comprehend Jesus' historical mission as well.

"Utopia," writes Gutiérrez, "is characterized by its *relationship to present historical reality*."[121] If it is not linked to a concrete commitment to bring about transformation in the reality within which it operates, it loses its authentic character and becomes a false illusion. Gutiérrez draws a simple model to illustrate the role which utopia plays within the liberation process. He first distinguishes between two levels of meaning:

(1) scientific-rationality which creates "real and effective political action" and (2) faith, which is conceived as the freedom from the power of sin and the path to communion with God and all humanity. In Gutiérrez' model, these two levels of meaning cannot relate in a direct, immediate manner without causing the distortion of one or the other. Theological enterprises which have in fact done that very thing in the past have typically sought faith norms to guide the implementation of appropriate human action, thereby usurping that orientation which rightfully ought to arise from a scientific analysis of a given historical situation.[122] Rationality and faith maintain their distinctive character, therefore, only when they are mediated by a third level of meaning, utopia, through which human beings project that vision which, though it is not yet a reality, is in the process of becoming one; indeed, it is alive in the social consciousness of a people.

When it presents this new vision of world, utopia prods the rational/scientific realm to seek new paradigms and specific strategies which move the world beyond the present construction of reality. Faith, inspired as well by the vision of utopia, affirms that its historical concretion is actually possible and that its realization will bring humanity into closer communion with God and one another, i.e., towards reconciliation. Based on this conceptualization of liberation, Gutiérrez concludes that "faith and political action will not enter into a correct and fruitful relationship except through the effort to create a new type of person in a different society, that is, except through utopia. . . . "[123]

Though he could not properly be called a theologian, Paulo Freire has nonetheless also greatly contributed to the Latin American conception of the historical mediation linking utopia to ultimate reality. Freire proposes that in order to serve its proper function, utopia must not only denounce and unmask those ideological mechanisms which support the existing order, but also must announce a vision of the world as it could (and should) be.[124] In Freire's system, however, both denunciation and announcement do not simply have their reference within a body of absolute ideals which are self-evident and applicable to every historical situation. To the contrary, they are to be discovered in the midst of a historical praxis which seeks the transformation and liberation of a particular situation: "In order for the oppressed to be able to wage the struggle for their liberation, they must perceive the reality of oppression not as a closed world from which there is no exit, but as a limiting situation they can transform."[125]

Freire explains that human beings live within a "thematic universe" which is constituted by a complex of interacting themes—"the ideas, values, concepts, and hopes, as well as the obstacles which impede . . . full humanization."[126] Within every given historical reality, these themes are interwoven by the dominant classes in such a way as to present a closed system which conveys the air of permanency. In order for the popular sectors to overcome an oppressive situation, particular acts are required which may strip that world of its legitimacy. These acts demonstrate that their situation is not "the impassable boundaries where possibilities end, but the real boundaries where all possibilities begin."[127]

As regards utopia, then, it both demystifies the themes which justify and support an established thematic universe and offers clues on how to refashion that world with new themes which 're-present' the arrival of a more humane world. In Gutiérrez' estimation, "this is what we [Latin American theologians] mean when we talk about a utopia which is the driving force of history and subversive of the existing order."[128]

Recognizing the risk of oversimplification, one may say that the difference between the claims "the reign of God is an ideal" and the "reign of God is a utopia" lies in the respective links they forge with historical activity. When the reign of God functions as an ideal, it always stands above history as an absolute critique against all human constructions of reality; or, in the terms proposed by Freire, it is an eternal thematic universe which equally judges all situations. Once that framework has been established, it is useless to speak of historical mediations which might lead to human participation in the building of God's reign, for every translation of the absolute to the concrete, or from the universal to the particular, is already less than 'ideal.'

When the reign of God functions as utopia, on the other hand, we are speaking of 'myth,' which means a force that moves men and women within history.[129] It invites and inspires human beings to make concrete, historical options which break with oppressive situations in order to create the conditions within which new themes may be generated. In essence, it suggests a causal relationship between activity in history and the dawning of that utopia; the utopian truth of the reign of God becomes a 'topia' (place).

Liberation theologians have directed their strongest criticisms toward European political theologians on this very point. Political theologians have commonly defined God's reign in history as "real presences of his coming universal presence" and recognize that "no theology of liberation, unless it wills to remain within idealism, can do without the materializations of God's presence."[130] Yet, as Míguez Bonino points out, when it comes to articulating a translation of that vision within actual historical structures, their eschatology often takes an unexpected turn: "Why is it, therefore, that at the crucial point ... most European theology draws back from these 'materializations' and finds refuge in a 'critical function' which is able to remain above right and left, ideologically neutral, independent of a structural analysis of reality?" Míguez Bonino then answers his own question: they fear that speaking of God's reign in the same breath as such ideologically-laden realities as economic structures and social organizations will inevitably result in the sacralization of transient, human constructions.[131]

Liberationists raise the possibility that these eschatological reservations actually impede concrete mediations of the reign of God within human history. Although the reign of God is certainly not presented by European political theologians as a denial of this history, it nonetheless at times serves as an extensive relativization of historical realities. Consequently, the reign of God remains in the realm of image-reality where it is untainted by the ambiguities of historical conditions.

In response, Latin American theologians suggest that the reign of God as utopia has the capability of generating 'functional ideologies' which may guide liberative practice toward the effective realization of that hope. Though the reign of God is surely not thereby given in its totality as the final consummation of the present historical process, it nevertheless dynamically operates by means of historical mediations which are realized in every level of that reality: political, economic, social and religious. Utopia so conceived does not merely stand outside history as its judge, but accompanies the struggle for a more just society at all times. "The foretastes of utopia are experienced in everyday life," underlines Tamez, "and it is in everyday life that we begin to build this utopia. There is no place else."[132]

Yet, as has already been suggested, very few liberation theologians have effectively incorporated into the hermeneutical methods which govern their investigations of the historical Jesus these profound insights on the reign of God as a utopian vision which compels historical engagement. Despite the fact that the apocalyptic world of the first century provided the context within which the reign of God was understood as a utopian vision for historical hopes, that world has been commonly rejected by liberationists as a meaningful key to interpret Jesus' discourse. Contrary to the thinking which has marked their own eschatological reflections, they have all too often lifted Jesus' message of the reign of God out of the social world which determined his own mission so that its universal character would not be compromised by more transient interests and ideologies.[133] What makes that hermeneutical decision so tragic is the fact that they are most likely overlooking a paradigm, already familiar to them at other levels of their theological reflection, which could both broaden their understanding of the life of the historical Jesus and enrich the creation of their own Christologies today.

Of course, it cannot be ignored that the apocalyptic world of Jesus is unmistakably alien to the world of modern day Latin America, and for that reason alone does not possess the dynamic power necessary to generate themes which may spark present historical engagement. For utopia, like ideology, is not a fixed notion which manifests itself identically in every new historical context. Utopia is a vehicle of the creative imagination which arises from the cultural and social fabric of a people who struggle for the transformation of their world. Therefore, it is perhaps not the specific form of Jesus' utopian vision which is consequent for present reality, nor the specific ideologies he used to make that vision real, but the hermeneutics which relate the values and goals implicit within that vision to the concrete historical process.

As has already been demonstrated, Segundo is one of a few liberationists who has already recognized this fertile ground for understanding the historical mission of Jesus. Based on his investigation of the synoptic gospels, Segundo warns that an idealization of the message of Jesus of Nazareth will inevitably be matched by an idealization of the present proclamation of the church, and vice versa:

> ... whatever concrete version which intends to continue, in the mark of Jesus, the project of God's reign will have to renounce any idealistic purism which, in the name of utopias which cannot be realized (and which will never be realized) believes that the closer it gets to Jesus the freer it will be of ideologies ... For the faith of Jesus ... was also incarnated in a limited and imperfect ideology. ... [134]

Undaunted by its obvious particularity, Segundo establishes the conceptual world of apocalyptic messianism as that limited ideology which Jesus utilized to communicate God's will for the liberation of human beings from those conditions which oppress them.

Segundo contends that Jesus spoke of the coming reign of God as a denouncement of the existing order of social reality and as an announcement of a dynamic reality which is moving in history to bring that utopia "near." In other words, Jesus' proclamation and actions not only effected a critical judgment of the present world—a perspective likely shared by the Essenes and other separatist sects—but also "set in motion mechanisms that ... [were] *constitutive* of the actual reign of God."[135] Hence, it was not first a religious ideality which measured the achievements of history in order to goad humanity on to unreached (unreachable?) heights, but " ... it is *from within* historical causality that human beings collaborate with the kingdom. ... "[136] In that respect, the themes which Jesus used to point to the establishment of God's reign were such as to galvanize the imagination of the poor and trigger a bitter conflict with the religio-political authorities of Israel.

As Segundo's results suggest, a reconsideration of the apocalyptic world of Jesus from the eschatological perspective of liberation theology may provide some fresh ways of understanding Jesus' reflection and action upon the world. It may signal what Jesus intended for the reign of God to bring on earth and why he chose that particular ideologically explosive language to express God's salvific plan for humanity. It also may uncover those themes which enabled Jesus to demystify the oppressive society within which he lived and demonstrate his enduring faith in the possibility of world-transformation. Perhaps further still, it may serve to illuminate the strategies and paradigms Jesus adopted to make that message good news for his contemporaries. In turn, the apocalyptic proclamation of the historical Jesus may 're-present' the world to Latin Americans in such a way that will reveal the real boundaries where all possibilities begin. For as Herzog intimates, "to enter into this vision is to experience apocalypse then so that we might know where to look for apocalypse now."[137]

Summary

This chapter began with a question regarding the nature of religious truth and its proper communication in present-day Honduras: was Padre Carney's gospel a legitimate rendering of the proclamation of Jesus Christ, faithful to that testimony offered by the New Testament evangelists to their own communities? It was indicated at that juncture that at least two essential characteristics of Carney's gospel would make it suspect in many contemporary theological circles: (1) the fact that it addressed a political problem which was essentially socio-economic in nature, though therefore undeniably a vital human concern and (2) the fact that it allied itself to a particular ideology which it deemed most consonant at that point in history with the utopian vision of God's reign.

That debate was presented as a window through which a hermeneutical challenge of a different order could be viewed. It was proposed that Biblical theologians, be they from the countries of the North Atlantic or Latin America, must struggle with many of the same dilemmas when they seek to interpret the life of the historical Jesus within his own time. In fact, when the writings of several representative Latin American theologians were evaluated in relation to their understanding of the general orientation of Jesus' public ministry, it was discovered that they often stumbled and divided on these very issues concerning the communication of religious truth.

It was indicated that several liberation theologians place the mission of Jesus within a decidedly religious framework which transcended, or at best indirectly undermined, the social world and political drama which existed in first century Palestine. It was also found that many of them take special care to free Jesus from particular ideologies which might compromise his universal message of the total liberation of humanity and of all creation. Within that framework, the apocalyptic world of Jesus is frequently rejected as a meaningful way to express the essential orientation of his historical mission. Consequently, those gospel passages which are chosen for their Christologies tend to highlight the essentially humanistic message which Jesus imparted to alienated human beings both as a call for conversion to a new way of being and as a word of hope for the ultimate salvation of the world. This image of the historical Jesus as the liberator of the human condition, firmly grounded in the gospel texts, elicits profound implications for the spiritual, social, political and economic realities of present-day Latin America.

At the same time, it was proposed in this chapter that the force of that liberative gospel is not compromised, but in fact strengthened, when the mission of Jesus is immersed in the socio-historical context within which it took form. While not allowing for a biography of the history of Jesus, the gospel texts do permit a sketch of various key activities and teachings which suggest his allegiance to a determined historical utopia (reign of God) and his option for particular ideologies which might bring that utopia near. Although commonly overlooked by liberation theologians in relation to the historical Jesus, this apocalyptic hermeneutic has produced within their own theologies some rather provocative ramifications for the imagination of new worlds. Therefore, those liberationists who have applied these insights to their investigations have illuminated a lightly-trodden path which promises to assist in the recovery of the social and political elements of the good news proclaimed and lived by Jesus of Nazareth.

Notes

1. Gutiérrez, *Power of the Poor*, 14.

2. Padre J. Guadalupe Carney, *To Be A Revolutionary: An Autobiography* (San Francisco: Harper & Row, 1985), 307–9.

3. Walter Kasper, *Jesus The Christ*, trans. V. Green (New York: Paulist Press, 1976), 16 – 7. In respect to the "solutions" which Christianity might offer to a wounded world, Kasper adds: "Thinking about Christology discloses the help which is needed at the moment and which theologians (who are certainly not the whole Church) can give modern society and the Church in their search for an identity," ibid., 17.

But it must be asked, what ideology is it that will be given by theologians who are determining the "help needed at the moment?" And what solutions are they to devise which maintain the "border line" between Christian theology and ideologies or utopias? Historically, Kasper's hermeneutical method has been the recipe for apolitical church dictums which, intentionally or not, support the ideology of the status quo.

4. Padre Carney's document embodies, on many levels, the definition which Segundo Galilea has given to liberation theology: "Liberation theology is rooted in three assumptions that form the Christian's view of the present juncture in Latin American history: (1) The present situation is one in which the vast majority of Latin Americans live in a state of underdevelopment and unjust dependence; (2) viewed in Christian terms, this is a 'sinful situation'; (3) hence it is the duty of Christians in conscience, and of the church in its pastoral activity, to commit themselves to efforts to overcome this situation," "Liberation Theology and New Tasks Facing Christians," in *Frontiers*, 167.

5. Hans Küng, *On Being A Christian*, trans. E. Quinn (Garden City, NY: Doubleday, 1976), 212.

6. Despite their best efforts to arrive at an objective knowledge of Jesus, the 'liberal' researchers fashioned him into an image which was consonant with the religious ideals of their own time. The strong criticism which George Tyrrell directed specifically towards the Christology of Adolph Harnack surely has some validity when it is considered against the wider backdrop of the liberal project: "The Christ that Harnack sees, looking back through nineteen centuries of Catholic darkness, is only the reflection of a Liberal Protestant face, seen at the bottom of a deep well," *Christianity at the Crossroads* (London: George Allen & Unwin, Ltd., 1963; London: Longmans, Green & Co., 1909), 49.

7. B. H. Streeter was not the only Biblical interpreter who thereby understood that Jesus' own historical context faded into insignificance when faced with the power of his personality: "Above all in the mind of our Lord do we trace the individuality and independence that belongs to an all-commanding genius. He is no mere re-echoer of the ideas of his time, eschatological or otherwise, "Prof. Burkitt and the Parables of the Kingdom," *The Interpreter* (1910): 246.

Schweitzer, undoubtedly in an unconscious way, affirmed the very personality theory of religion which he had set out to destroy. Although he did indeed place Jesus within the context of the Jewish apocalyptic world, that message was capable of transcending the very social and historical conditions which had given it form. For while every other Jewish apocalyptic movement of the first century was subject to the social chaos and political drama transpiring in the first century, the movement of Jesus alone was held to be above and beyond it. In Schweitzer's own words: "The Baptist and Jesus are not, therefore, borne upon the current of a general eschatological movement. The period offers no events calculated to give an impulse to eschatological enthusiasm. They themselves set the times in motion by acting, by creating eschatological facts. . . . It was the only time when that ever happened in Jewish eschatology," *Quest,* 370. In this sense, Schweitzer was at one with the liberal school in its conviction that the unique personalities of John the Baptist and Jesus were solely responsible for their message.

The conclusion of Schweitzer's investigation hints that Jesus is as foreign to our own time as he was to his own, for both then and now he moves outside the bounds of history and beyond the contradictions of social realities. Schweitzer considerd that the grave error of historical investigation in the nineteenth century had been the attempt to search for a figure who was wholly human like ourselves. For while we search for him in history, "He comes to us as One unknown, without a name, as of old, by the lake-side. He came to those who knew Him not. He speaks to us the same word: 'Follow thou me' . . . ! And to those who obey Him . . . they shall learn in their own experience Who He is," ibid., 403.

In the religion of Schweitzer, therefore, Jesus meets us in the present as a mystical, mysterious figure, calling us to faithfully follow and respond to our moral duty. In many respects, his Christological results represented the final perfection of the Kantian ideal.

8. Segundo, *Liberation of Theology,* 110.

9. See *The Work of Josephus* (17,11,2), trans. William Whitson (Peabody, MA: Hendrickson Publishers, 1978), 471–3.

10. Paul D. Hanson, *The Dawn of Apocalyptic: The Historical and Sociological Roots of Jewish Apocalyptic Eschatology,* revised ed. (Philadelphia: Fortress Press, 1979), 21. Hanson makes a clear distinction between prophetic eschatology and apocalyptic eschatology. Nonetheless, the continuity which binds the two together is found in a hope in God's liberating activity on their behalf: " . . . The visionary element which lies at the heart of apocalyptic extends throughout Israel's religious history; that is, the element of the prophet's vision of the saving cosmic activities of [Yahweh] . . . ," ibid., 16.

11. Kasper, *Jesus the Christ,* 72. Cf. Norman Perrin: " . . . Weiss and Schweitzer were right in claiming that Kingdom of God was an apocalyptic conception in the message of Jesus. In general this came to be accepted . . . ;" and further on he adds, " . . . in 1927 a conference of English and German theologians agreed that Kingdom of God was an apocalyptic concept in the message of Jesus, and from that moment forward this was accepted as a basic tenet . . . ," *Jesus and the Language of the Kingdom* (Philadelphia: Fortress Press, 1975), 35.

12. Bultmann believed that a "demythologization" of the conceptual world of the first century would yield the universal significance of Jesus' message. In other words, once the mythical elements of apocalyptic eschatology were interpreted by means of a modern existential philosophy, rather than an ancient cos-

mology, the proclamation of Jesus and the early community would challenge people today as it did at the time of its first expression. Bultmann found Heidegger's existential analysis of the ontological structure of being to be the most useful key for expressing the modern understanding of human existence.

13. Bultmann declared that "even if we believe that the world as we know it will come to an end in our time, we expect the end to take the form of a natural catastrophe, not of a mythical event such as the New Testament expects," "New Testament and Mythology," in *Kerygma and Myth*, ed. H. W. Bartsch, trans. Reginald H. Fuller (New York: Harper & Row, 1961), 13.

14. Undoubtedly, he was directing these limitations against those who were attempting to arrive at a psychological portrait of Jesus and his personality. However, in the attempt to shut the door completely on such ill-fated research, he locked out the "word become flesh" in the process.

15. Bultmann, *Jesus*, 41. The implications of Bultmann's Christology for his social ethics are reflected in another passage: "No program for world-reform is derived from the will of God. ... That property can be used ... as a means of production ... is completely outside the thought of Jesus. For everyone has to decide for himself whether his property is of this character ...," ibid., 105.

16. Surely, this is the result if not the intent of Küng's depiction of Jesus: "[Jesus] belongs neither to the right nor left, nor does he simply mediate between them. He really rises above them: above all alternatives, all of which he plucks from the roots," *On Being A Christian*, 262.

17. Herzog, "Apocalypse Then and Now: Apocalyptic and the Historical Jesus Reconsidered," *Pacific Theological Review* 18, no. 1 (Fall 1984): 22. Herzog claims that "nearly every form of moral religion or philosophical theology that displaced apocalyptic reflected the Enlightenment fondness for the individual," and he adds, "... it mattered little whether they chose as their vehicle psychology, existentialist philosophy or revivalist religion," ibid., 18.

Raúl Vidales rightly perceives the danger inherent to any Christological hermeneutic which shuns the historical conditions which shaped Jesus' concrete ministry. He claims that concrete acts of liberation in history are not motivated by the force of a universal ideal which is developed independent of that history itself. To the contrary, he argues: "An ahistorical reading of the gospel places it without recourse into a universal and abstract plane which confer it a neutral character, in a supposed 'message for all' beyond the conflicts and antagonistic divisions of a society divided in classes. An ahistorical reading favors a message equally announced to 'exploiters' and 'exploited' ... , "La Práctica Histórica de Jesús," 44.

18. Boff, *Jesús Cristo Libertador: Ensaio de Cristología Crítica para o nosso Tempo* (Petrópolis, Brazil: Editora Vozes Ltda., 1971); *Jesús Christ Liberator*, 60.

19. Ibid., 239. Or once again at another juncture, Boff wrote: "The kingdom of God that Christ announces is not a liberation from this or that evil, from

the political oppression of the Romans, from the economic difficulties of the people, or from sin alone. The kingdom of God cannot be narrowed down to any particular aspect. It embraces all … " ibid., 55.

20. Ibid., 14–5. There are aspects of Boff's interpretation of the Temptation of Jesus which are quite profound: e.g., his explanation of the nature of power and, within that understanding, Jesus' commitment to "conversion" rather than domination. What is being critiqued here is the supposed contradiction between universal truth and "regionalized" concretion.

21. Ibid., 23.

22. Ibid., 15.

23. Gutiérrez, *Theology of Liberation*, 228.

24. Ibid., 231.

25. Gutiérrez gives seven pages to Jesus' historical context, with the majority of that effort devoted to his relationship to the Zealot movement, *Theology of Liberation*, 225–232. He stresses that Jesus confronted groups in power and died at the hands of the political authorities.

26. Ibid., 228.

27. Ibid., 231.

28. They clearly do not accept this hermeneutical polarity in other themes treated in their writings. For instance, when discussing the efficacy of ethics, Gutiérrez asserts that the "universality of Christian love is only an abstraction unless it becomes concrete history, process, conflict; it is arrived at only through particularity," ibid., 275.

29. Segundo, *The Humanist Christology of Paul*, vol. 2, *Jesus of Nazareth Yesterday and Today* (Maryknoll: Orbis Books, 1986), 163. In this regard, Segundo maintains that the universal significance of the historical Jesus may only be spoken of as "virtual" and not realized, 21.

30. The papers from the congress were published in a volume entitled *Liberación y Cautiverio: Debates en Torno al Método de la Teología en América Latina*.

31. Segundo, "Condicionamientos Actuales de la Reflexión Teologíca en Latino-américa," in *Liberación y Cautiverio*.

32. Criticisms which Hugo Assmann admits were probably justified, "Power of Christ," 125.

33. Ignacio Ellacuría, *Teología Política* (San Salvador: Ediciones del Secretariado Social Interdiocesano, 1973); published in English as *Freedom Made Flesh: The Mission of Christ and His Church*, trans. John Drury (Maryknoll: Orbis Books, 1976).

34. Ellacuría, *Freedom Made Flesh*, 49.

35. Ibid., 32. Despite the fact that he draws some questionable conclusions in regard to the links between Jesus and the Zealots, Ellacuría's section on "the political character of Jesus' mission" (23–86) is quite suggestive of fresh ways to understand the historical ministry of Jesus.

36. Ibid., 63.

37. Ibid., 68.

38. In order to avoid any possibility of misconception from the start, may it be said that I am addressing the differences in their hermeneutical approaches to the historical Jesus. I do not wish to imply that some Latin American theologians are committed to the liberation of the poor and the actualization of salvation in history, while others are not; clearly that motivation moves them all.

39. J. Severino Croatto, *Exodus: A Hermeneutics of Freedom*, trans. Salvator Attanasio (Maryknoll: Orbis Books, 1984), 62.

40. Croatto, "The Political Dimension of Christ the Liberator," in *Faces of Jesus*, 103, 121.

41. Ibid., 113.

42. Ibid., *Exodus*, 64.

43. Ibid., 63.

44. Ibid., 50.

45. Ibid., 61, italics mine.

46. Ibid., 49.

47. Croatto defines apocalypticism as a vision which "separates and distinguishes two worlds, and considers the second, the world of definitive salvation, to be the only one that is the exclusive work of God," "The Political Dimension of Christ," 111.

48. Ibid.

49. Ibid., 110. To support this view, he notes the allusions which Jesus made to the persecutions he had suffered at the hands of his opponents during the course of his ministry and the "maturity" which the sermon presupposed on the part of his listeners.

50. Segundo Galilea, *Following Jesus* (Maryknoll: Orbis Books, 1981), 13.

51. Ibid., 103. The primary aim of *Following Jesus* is to bring together two traditions which approach the Latin American reality in quite distinct ways: the religious contemplative and the committed militants. Galilea believes that elements of both of these lifestyles are necessary for a wholistic Christian existence in a situation of struggle. The crux of his argument is to be found in chapter

Five, entitled "Contemplation and Commitment." He believes that Jesus was able to keep these two worlds in tension: "his contemplation leads to a commitment which is not directly temporal but rather pastoral-prophetic. It had socio-political consequences more proper to the ministry of evangelization than to temporal-political action," ibid., 65.

52. Segundo Galilea and Raúl Vidales, *Cristología y Pastoral Popular* (Bogotá: Paulinas, 1974), 41.

53. Galilea, *Following Jesus*, 36. It sounds strange coming from a Latin American that ideology is blamed for elevating the economic sphere and the distribution of wealth to a "privileged place," since the vast majority of his continent suffers daily from the real consequences of greed and economic dependency. Surely Karl Marx or his followers did not set out to elevate the economic sphere, but rather developed a theory in response to the conditions already established by determined social structures. It would seem more true to the historical experience of Latin America, then, if Galilea had said that any faith which seeks to follow Jesus and does not respond to that central reality of economic exploitation is itself "anachronistic." To be fair to Galilea, numerous sections in his writings do indeed suggest that very notion.

54. Ibid., 105.

55. Ibid., 43.

56. Ibid., 107.

57. Sobrino, *Christology at the Crossroads*, 101–2.

58. Sobrino, *Jesús en América Latina*, 55.

59. Edward Schillebeeckx, *Jesus: An Experiment in Christology* (New York: Harper & Row, 1979), 143, quoted in Sobrino, *Jesús en América Latina*, 165.

60. In Sobrino's estimation, both Jesus and the reign of God can only be known in mutual discovery: "In historical terms we can only come to know the historical Jesus in and through the notion of God's kingdom. By the same token we can only come to understand what is meant by the kingdom of God in and through Jesus," *Christology at the Crossroads*, 41.

61. Ibid., 41, 60.

62. Ibid., 110.

63. Ibid., 4.

64. Sobrino, *Jesús en América Latina*, 354.

65. Sobrino, *Christology at the Crossroads*, 94–5.

66. Sobrino, *Jesús en América Latina*, 139.

67. In this respect, Sobrino's efforts are reminiscent of the exegetical work of German Biblical theologian Ernst Fuchs. Recognizing that the liberal 'lives-

of-Jesus' had sought to recover a pure religion of Jesus which had been cor-
rupted by centuries of ecclesiastical dogma, Fuchs maintained that their efforts
were essentially pointed in the right direction but aimed at the wrong target. As
far as he was concerned, the object of historical research should not be the religion of Jesus per se, but his personal acts of faith.

Although Fuchs was not interested in reconstructing a chronology of Jesus'
faith in the style of Hase and Holtzmann, he believed that the essential character
of Jesus' life could nevertheless be determined by reference to specific, concrete
situations which are recounted in the gospels. For example, when Jesus was
jarred by the fate of John the Baptist, he was confronted with a "historic" decision of faith: "Jesus himself did of necessity face a problem similar to the one his
disciples faced after his death. Jesus lived through the experience of the violent
death of John the Baptist. But if at the time of his own baptism Jesus without
doubt recognized the gravity of eschatological judgment implied in the Baptist's
message, then after the Baptist's death he would have to decide what this death
meant for him," *Studies of the Historical Jesus* (London: SCM Press, 1964), 23.

Fuchs believed that it was in the context of this crisis that Jesus made an "authentic" decision for God and placed his trust in God's will for the destiny of his
life. In theological language, the continuity of the kerygma lies in the witness of
faith becoming the ground of faith.

68. Sobrino even admits that such an undertaking must be done "systematically" and not "historically" due to the lack of hard evidence available to make
such determinations; see *Christology at the Crossroads*, 73. Such an approach
would be fine if Sobrino then limited himself to making systematic points rather
than drawing historical conclusions about the history of Jesus of Nazareth. Yet,
he has based his reconstruction of the life of Jesus on the historical development
of Jesus' faith. Moreover, he devotes an entire chapter to the prayers of Jesus as
a source for understanding the history of that faith (chapter 5: "The Prayer of
Jesus," ibid., 146–178).

69. Ibid., 85.

70. A phrase widely used by Heinrich Holtzmann and other liberal scholars. See Schweitzer, *Quest*, 205.

Hase (1829) was perhaps the first to speak of a process of development in
Jesus' self-understanding of his messianic activity. Yet, he claimed that not all of
the disciples understood the shift that took place in Jesus, for the writers of the
synoptic gospels largely remained wedded to their apocalyptic worldview and
did not differentiate Jesus' sayings in the first and second stages of development.
Only John, Hase argued, was able to remove the blinders from his eyes, for the
nonapocalyptic fourth gospel alone was able to present with clarity the ideas of
Jesus himself during the second stage of his ministry. For this reason, Hase and
later Schleiermacher attributed historical priority to John's gospel because they
believed that only there was the true consciousness of Jesus reflected. Holtzmann
would later popularize these findings, but with a priority given to the Marcan
gospel.

71. In a frontal attack on the results of the liberal research, Wrede charged: "Mark knows nothing of any development in Jesus, . . . he knows nothing of any conflict in the mind of Jesus between a spiritual and popular, political Messianic idea; . . . he knows nothing of the idea that the question about the Messiah's being the Son of David had something to do with this alternative between political and non-political; . . . he does not know that the first period was a period of success and the second a period of failure . . . ," quoted in Schweitzer, *Quest*, 332.

72. Sobrino, *Christology at the Crossroads*, 96–9.

73. Ibid., 94–102.

74. Ibid., 94.

75. He contends that the two are dialectically interrelated. A person must be truly converted to the gospel and be willing to renounce one's own 'will to power' in order to be truly capable of doing the work of justice required by God's reign. See ibid., 121.

76. Ibid., 214–5.

77. Ibid., 214.

78. Ibid.

79. Ibid., 122.

80. Gwen Robinson, "Philippine Army Trying to Win Hearts and Minds," *San Francisco Chronicle* (24 October 1988).

81. Comments which Sobrino makes in the preface to the English edition of *Christianity at the Crossroads* demonstrate that he is well aware of these dangers: "Considering Christ as Love . . . Christians maintain an apparent neutrality vis-à-vis the flagrant inequities in society. Such neutrality is wholly contrary to the partiality that Jesus displayed in favor of the oppressed. By the same token, Christ as Power has justified the sacralization of power in the political and economic realms. . . . So we have the abstract Christ, the impartial Christ, and the power-wielding Christ. These are symbols those in power need. These are the symbols that they have used, wittingly or unwittingly, to maintain the Latin American continent in its present state," xvi.

82. Sobrino, "El Jesús Histórico, Crisis y Desafío para la Fe," *Christus* (Mexico) 40, no. 481 (1974): 17. In Boff's first book, almost the identical theme and its consequences are outlined in regard to the failure of the arrival of the Parousia. He too maintains that history did not unfold according to what a literal interpretation would render of Jesus' apocalyptic expectations: "We must take due account of the differences between Jesus' situation and our own. In his day there was an apocalyptic atmosphere and people were looking for the immediate breakthrough of the kingdom. In our eyes the Parousia has been held up and

history still has a future. Hence there must be differences in the way we organize love and justice in society," *Liberator*, 292.

83. Sobrino, *Christology at the Crossroads*, 106.

84. Ibid., 9.

85. Segundo, *Liberation of Theology*, 111.

86. Segundo, *The Historical Jesus*, 83. One reason Segundo offers for why Jesus' message might seem more "interpersonal" and less "political" to the modern mind is the fact that Jesus lived in a much "less organized society," ibid. I cannot say that I find that argument convincing; was the Old Testament world any more complex so that its message would be more overtly political?

87. Segundo, *Liberation of Theology*, 95, n. 5. Segundo agrees with Gutiérrez' assertion that the realm of politics is the most prevalent and pervasive factor within modern society. Yet, he believes that it is a mistake to suppose that Jesus shared this perspective: "The discovery of the pervasive influence of politics is our contemporary discovery, not his," ibid.

88. Tamez essentially concurs with Segundo's historical judgment that some Jews did not suffer from the Roman domination, but actually profited from it. Within this class which possessed economic and political power in Palestine and profited from the high inflation of the empire she includes the council of elders (typically men from the noble families), the chief priests, the large landowners, the rich merchants, "and others who exercised some political and ideological control (the scribes, Pharisees, Sadducees)," *Bible of the Oppressed*, 66.
Ellacuría uncovered important evidence which supports the notion of this collusion between Jewish religious leaders and Roman rulers: from the years 15 –26 A.D., Roman ruler Valerius Gratus appointed four different high priests to positions of leadership. The last of these, Caiphas, most likely played a major role in the condemnation and execution of Jesus, *Freedom Made Flesh*, 42. Given the colonial experience of the Latin American church during which time the Spanish king appointed bishops to his liking, it is difficult to imagine how these power dynamics are overlooked by some liberation theologians.

89. Segundo, *The Historical Jesus*, 71–85.

90. Segundo, *Historía y Actualidad: Las Cristologías en la Espiritualidad*, vol. II/2, *El Hombre de Hoy ante Jesús de Nazaret* (Madrid: Ediciones Cristiandad, 1982), 927.

91. Segundo, *Liberation of Theology*, 129. Segundo adds: " . . . he could not demand faith from people independently of the ideologies conveyed by faith — which is what we so often have tried to do," ibid.

92. Segundo, *The Historical Jesus*, 55. Segundo contends that there is good reason to believe that this aspect of the gospels could not be the result of later redaction: "Everything that the Synoptics tell us about the misunderstandings of

the apostles, the leaders of the Christian churches by the time the evangelists were composing their works, bears the clear mark of being prepaschal," ibid. Cf. Ellacuría, *Freedom Made Flesh*, 49–51.

93. Segundo, *The Historical Jesus*, 120–149. "Thus they [the parables] are attacks on the oppressive religious ideology of the Israelite majority and, for that reason, a revelation and defense of the God who has chosen sinners and the poor as the preferred recipients of the kingdom," ibid., 120.

94. Ibid., 127.

95. Vidales describes the socio-economic oppression suffered by these landless peasants: "The concentration of goods and wealth in the city benefited only the upper classes, while making life increasingly difficult for those becoming landless and impoverished. The low salaries of the skilled laborers and even more those of the manual workers added to the possibility of contracting slaves, making the struggle for a salary ever more distressing," "La Práctica Histórica de Jesús," 51.

96. Ibid.

97. Segundo, *The Historical Jesus*, 132. See also *Las Cristologías en la Espiritualidad*, 887.

98. A phrase written by William Herzog with which Segundo would surely resonate, "The Quest for the Historical Jesus and the Discovery of the Apocalyptic Jesus," *Pacific Theological Review* 19, no. 2 (Spring 1985): 35.

99. Segundo, *The Historical Jesus*, 145. In *Liberation of Theology*, Segundo makes this same point: "He [Jesus] first points up the concrete liberations he is effecting, only to try to draw people's attention away from them later in order to emphasize a broader and more profound message. That, in my opinion, is the proper explanation for the 'messianic secret.' The explanation of liberal exegesis is incorrect," 124, n. 11.

Ellacuría writes in a similar vein: "Whatever the critical interpretation of the miracles may be, it is clear that the primitive community saw Jesus' satisfaction of [humanity's] concrete needs as a sign of the presence of the kingdom. So true was this that it sometimes led the crowd into erroneous interpretations of Jesus' prophetic character," *Freedom Made Flesh*, 40.

See also Sobrino, *Christology at the Crossroads*, 48–9.

100. Biblical theologians are all too often so blindly committed to an ideal image of Jesus that the value systems and intentions of his own life are cast aside. In that regard, Segundo observes: "We are so accustomed to [seeing] in Jesus the 'perfect human' who, in our opinion, ought to have represented God upon the earth—and with the corresponding universal values—that we are no longer able to perceive, not even in our reading of the gospels, how profoundly and exclusively Jewish Jesus truly was. While making him a citizen of the world, we convert him into an actor on stage."

Segundo makes this statement while discussing the encounter of Jesus with the Syro-Phoenecian woman. He laments the fact that once Jesus is made a 'citizen of the world,' then everything has its significance in reference to other life situations, but never to his own. He satirically suggests, "If he did insult the Syro-Phoenecian woman, then he did it for the learning of future generations." See *Las Cristologías de la Espiritualidad*, 928.

101. Segundo, *The Historical Jesus*, 150.

102. Segundo, *Liberation of Theology*, 124, n. 11.

103. Segundo, who utilizes Tielhard's categories throughout his writings, in turn revises and filters them through a grid borrowed from Gregory Bateson's evolutionary philosophical system. It must be mentioned, however, that Segundo finds it necessary at times to distance himself from aspects of Tielhard's system. See *Las Cristologías en la Espiritualidad*, 936 – 942. In this volume, Segundo relies almost exclusively on one of Bateson's primary works, *Steps to an Ecology of the Mind* (New York: Ballantine Books, 1972).

104. Segundo, *Las Cristologías en la Espiritualidad*, 933.

105. Ibid., 913–933.

106. Ibid., 926.

107. Ibid., 933.

108. Ibid., 954.

109. Ibid., 934.

110. Moltmann, *Crucified God: The Cross of Christ as the Foundation and Criticism of Christian Theology*, trans. R. A. Wilson and John Bowden (London: SCM Press, 1974), 321.

111. Míguez Bonino, *Revolutionary Situation*, 132– 153.

112. Ibid., 140.

113. Herzog, "Quest," 31.

114. Bultmann, "New Testament and Mythology," 5.

115. Though Käsemann, Bornkamm and other 'new questers' unquestionably established significant advances in the study of the historical Jesus, in this particular area they did not move beyond Bultmann's "demythologization" of the apocalyptic Jesus. When they spoke of the acts of Jesus as "eschatological," it was not placed in the context of the contemporary Jewish eschatological expectations, but interpreted as acts which make the reality of the end ("eschaton") present for the hearer and beckons one to a decision regarding one's existence. Their dismissal of the apocalyptic world of Jesus led them to dismiss any understanding of Jesus' message outside of interior dimensions.

The image of Jesus which Bornkamm provided in his major work is perhaps emblematic of the Christological images produced by the new quest. Bornkamm sought to demonstrate that the historical Jesus confronted human beings of his own time with the word of God just as the kerygma does us today: "the word of Jesus long ago has become today's word," *Jesus of Nazareth*, trans. Irene and Fraser McLuskey with James M. Robinson (New York: Harper & Row, 1960), 18.

Bornkamm's Jesus offers God's grace to everyone, even those who were condemned by the Jewish legal system, which includes the poor and reprobate. But this grace extends solely to their existential condition, for the message of Jesus is absent of any hope for the transformation of societal conditions or political structures. For the poor as well as the guardians of the law and tradition (thus those with social and economic power), Jesus has the same message: "In the encounter with Jesus, time is left to no one: the past whence he comes is no longer confirmed, and the future he dreams of no longer assured. But this is precisely why every individual is granted his own new present," ibid., 62–3.

Therefore, though Bornkamm's Jesus speaks of the present dawn of God's reign in terms which show that the present reveals the future as salvation and judgment, that word is thought to have little relevance for the unredeemed structures of social reality: "Jesus' attitude and message can in no way be interpreted as a 'reversal of all values,' or a systematic revolution in the realm of moral and social standards," ibid., 80.

116. Herzog, "Quest," 32.

117. Ibid. In slightly more technical language, "world is a social construction of reality involving two basic processes: (1) the objectification of society through its institutions, roles and traditions; and (2) the legitimation of society by giving normative dignity to its practical imperatives," ibid.

Much of Herzog's understanding of the social system is drawn from the theories of Peter Berger and Thomas Luckmann in *The Social Construction of Reality* (Garden City, NY: Doubleday, 1966). Another important Berger text relevant to this theme is entitled *The Sacred Canopy* (Garden City, NY: Doubleday, 1967); see also James T. Borhek and Richard F. Curtis, *The Sociology of Belief* (New York: Kreiger, 1983; 1975).

118. Ibid., 33.

119. Ibid. Herzog cites a quote from Peter Berger which further illuminates the nature of 'law': "The fundamental 'recipe' of religious legitimation is the transformation of human products into supra- or non-human facticities. The humanly made world is explained in terms that deny its human production. The human *nomos* becomes a divine cosmos, or at any rate, a reality that derives its meanings from beyond the human sphere," *The Sacred Canopy*, 89, quoted in Herzog, "Quest," 33.

120. Herzog, "Quest," 35. In many respects, Herzog offers a reinterpretation of Marx's notion of 'superstructure'; that is, the manner in which religion,

philosophy, and nearly every other epistemological category is organized to reinforce or challenge a determined socio-economic reality. The difference, however, is that Marx, undoubtedly partly in response to a politically reactionary nineteenth century church, claimed that religion was the only one of these categories which was intrinsically unable to subvert an established superstructure. Marx conceived of revolutionary economics, revolutionary sociology, and even revolutionary philosophy, but religion alone was destined to always serve as an ideology of legitimation; thus its label as 'the opiate of the masses.' Herzog, to the contrary, suggests that religion can either sanction or subvert "world," and may play a vital role in either fundamental option. In a similar way, most Latin American liberation theologians have made this selective appropriation of Marxist thought.

121. Gutiérrez, *Theology of Liberation*, 233. Liberation theologians have been quite influenced by the writings of Ernst Bloch; see *Das Prinzip Hoffnung*, 2nd ed. (Frankfurt: Suhrkamp, 1969).

122. Gutiérrez, *Theology of Liberation*, 236.

123. Ibid.

124. Paulo Freire, "Education and Cultural Action: An Introduction," *Conscientization for Liberation*, ed. Louis M. Colonnese (Washington, D.C.: United States Catholic Conference—Latin American Division), 119.

125. Paulo Freire, *Pedagogy of the Oppressed*, trans. Myra Bergman Ramos (New York: Continuum, 1970), 34.

126. Ibid., 91–2. Freire explains that these themes have been called "generative themes" because "however they are comprehended and whatever action they may evoke they contain the possibility of unfolding into again as many themes, which in their turn call for new tasks to be fulfilled," ibid., 92, n. 19.

127. Alvaro Vieira Pinto, *Consciência e Realidade Nacional*, vol. 2 (Rio de Janeiro, 1960), 284, quoted in Freire, *Pedagogy*, 89, n. 15.

128. Gutiérrez, *Theology of Liberation*, 234.

129. Raul Vidales & Tokihiro Kudó, *Práctica Religiosa y Proyecto Histórico II: Estudio sobre la Religiosidad Popular en Dos Barrios de Lima* (Lima: Centro de Estudios y Promoción del Desarollo, 1982), 42.

130. Moltmann, *The Crucified God*, 314.

131. Míguez Bonino, *Revolutionary Situation*, 149. Hugo Assmann's criticism is much harsher: "It was at this precise point, in my view, that European 'political theology' began to get cold feet. Frightened by its own boldness, it began to go off into vague generalities that did not correspond with the scientific idiom and terminology that was available, however fragmentary and imperfect, to describe the conflict-ridden play of power in history. To put it plain and simply,

European theologians did not dare to go further in their analysis of the historical mediations of power at play," "Power of Christ," 146.

132. Tamez, *Against Machismo*, 135. Tamez, in turn, cites the work of Vidales in relation to this point.

Cf. Sobrino: "The utopian hope takes on flesh and blood amid the groaning and suffering of human beings." Sobrino, *Christology at the Crossroads*, 240.

133. In his first Christology, Boff wrote in this vein: "The potential perversion lies in regionalizing the kingdom of God in one way or another. One may localize it in terms of political power, or in terms of religious and sacerdotal power, or even in terms of prophetic and charismatic power. This was Jesus' temptation and it accompanied him throughout his life," *Liberator*, 281.

134. Segundo, *Las Cristologías de la Espiritualidad*, 933–4.

135. Segundo, *The Historical Jesus*, 158.

136. Ibid., 159.

137. Herzog, "Apocalypse Then and Now," 25.

The convergence of those themes which were prevalent within Jesus' world and the utopian themes which are operative within present-day Latin America seem to suggest that in times of severe social and political oppression, utopian elements will spin to the center of a revolutionary meaning-world. If that is the case, then apocalyptic may serve liberation theologians as a hermeneutical key pregnant with undiscovered truths for a recovery of the life of Jesus.

CHAPTER THREE

The Death and Resurrection of Jesus of Nazareth

Only when taken in conjunction with his life and death does Jesus' resurrection have a realistic meaning. Otherwise it becomes either pagan mythology, or a modern ideology of a future reconciliation without the conversion of historical evils.
— *Leonardo Boff*[1]

The recent history of the church in Latin America sets the images of cross and resurrection in sharp relief. As Sobrino articulates, "a people who have suffered so much, who have been disfigured, tortured and assassinated, do not need demythologization or a sophisticated hermeneutic in order to find in that Son a dear brother."[2] Of course, the fate of the Latin American church is itself directly related to the historical options which it has made in response to the gospel.

The Medellín Conference called upon the church to defend the rights of the oppressed, to promote grassroots organizations and, in general terms, to make "a preferential option for the poor." The pastoral consequences of this momentous conference were many, but perhaps none as significant as the explosion in the growth of *comunidades eclesiales de base* [base ecclesial communities] throughout the continent, most particularly in marginalized rural areas and in the city barrios.

Within the base communities, campesinos and factory workers began participating in and taking responsibility for the daily leadership and teaching of the community members. The "delegates of the word" —as the lay leaders are commonly called—regularly led the community in discussions upon biblical passages, paying particular attention to those meanings it might have for the concrete demands of the community's present situation. The dialogical style of these meetings encouraged the poor to evaluate their reality in such a way that empowered them to transform it. Not surprisingly, within a relatively short period of time the base communities began to present a profound social challenge to the politically oppressive regimes of Latin America.

The impact of the base communities was deeply felt in the country of El Salvador. Most notably in the archdiocese of San Salvador—due to the unflinching encouragement and support of first Archbishop Luis Chávez y González and later Oscar Romero—the proliferation of new communities and lay leaders was quite impressive. The eventual maturation of these communities led to their involvement in initiatives which sought to win new economic and social freedoms, such as the creation of agricultural cooperatives, the organization of unions within sugar refineries and coffee plantations, and campaigns for accessible bank credit and the lowering of prices on agricultural inputs. The response of the government was predictable and swift: brutal military repression. Thousands of community members were assassinated and disappeared, delegates of the word were targeted as 'subversives,' and numerous priests who were perceived as leaders supporting the movement were killed.

In one of many tragic incidents, Father Octavio Ortiz, a Salvadoran priest who was working with the base communities in the barrios of San Salvador, was murdered as he led a weekend retreat for catechumens. Army tanks, followed by military troops, broke through the gates of the Catholic retreat center and machine-gunned the gathering, killing Father Ortiz and four youth workers in the church. The official military report claimed that Ortiz had been leading "guerilla warfare training," citing the fabricated discovery of a cache of weapons on the premises.[3]

The murder of Padre Ortiz and that of other priests, most notably Padre Rutilio Grande, deepened not only the prophetic ministry of the base communities themselves, but also that of their archbishop, Oscar Arnulfo Romero:

> Fr. Grande's death and the death of other priests after his impelled me to take an energetic attitude before the government. . . . I support all of the priests in the communities. We have managed to combine well the pastoral mission of the Church, preference for the poor, to be clearly on the side of the oppressed, and from there to clamor for the liberation of the people.[4]

As repression increasingly silenced the protests of human rights and church workers, Romero became the voice of those who had no voice. He encouraged mothers who had lost a loved one by abduction or murder to form a committee of 'mothers of the disappeared.' He regularly visited poor communities and held dialogues with them about their situation and struggles. He weekly gave sermons during the Sunday morning mass in the cathedral—also broadcast via radio throughout the country—in which he would relate the lectionary reading to the present life of the country. At the end of the sermon, he usually read off a litany of specific human rights abuses which had been carried out that previous week — often the only outlet for such subversive information! As one historian describes his ministry, Romero was an archbishop of the people:

> During Oscar Romero's three years and one month as archbishop, the role of the church in the political life of the country expanded with each succeeding crisis. At the same time, under increasing difficulties brought about by waves of persecution against the priests, religious, and CEB [ecclesial base communities] members . . . , the focus increasingly was on the diminutive archbishop of San Salvador, both within and outside the country.[5]

Of course, as popular as he was with the poor, Romero became a considerable threat to the wealthy oligarchy and to the military institution. Not only was he feared for his words, but also for the symbol of hope he represented to those Salvadorans who struggled for the transformation of their society. Finally, he 'went too far' when, during a Sunday morning homily on national radio, he ordered soldiers to disobey their commanding officers whenever they were told to murder civilians ("your brothers and sisters"). The next week Archbishop Romero was assassinated by a security force death squad as he said mass at a hospital chapel in San Salvador.

In a series of meetings held in 1985 — five years after his death — a gathering of delegates of the word, priests, and religious workers from the base communities of San Salvador shared with visiting internationals reflections on their recent history.[6] They revealed that over 600 of their members had been martyred within the previous eight years and many more had been forced to leave the country or flee to the mountains in order to join the armed resistance. Each family had their own story of suffering to tell as they spoke of relatives and friends who had died *"para el pueblo"* [for the people]. They spoke with grief about the loss of Father Octavio, of numerous other priests, and of hundreds of delegates of the word. And yet, amidst the memories was the ongoing struggle which continued to bring repression to those Salvadorans present.

What was perhaps most remarkable, however, was the Salvadorans' hope and courage that a change would eventually come, an attitude which was evident in nearly everything they said. When asked how this could be so, given the tragic events which had afflicted their communities, a Salvadoran nun seemingly spoke for the group when she responded:

> It is true that we have seen many people crucified in El Salvador. . . . Nevertheless, we do not lose hope. Near the end of his life, Archbishop Romero was receiving many death threats because of his work on behalf of the poor. At that time, he said to us, 'If they kill me, I will rise again in the Salvadoran pueblo.'[7] And, you know what, it has happened. Archbishop Romero is not dead. We feel him amongst us here. . . . After passing through the experience of the assassination of Romero, we now understand what the resurrection of Jesus means for our lives and for the lives of all of those who have been killed.[8]

This modern parable from El Salvador paints a backdrop for our study of the death and resurrection of Jesus within liberation theology. It is obvious that the base communities of San Salvador were able to link their own historical situation to the drama of the passion and resurrection which is played out in the gospels. In order to do that, however, they necessarily made some fundamental assumptions regarding the enduring significance of the Jesus event for the ongoing interpretation of human history. Moreover, based on their own experiences of Golgotha, the Salvadoran communities came to interpret the cross and resurrection as a unity — it was with the resurrection of Jesus (Romero?!) that the full meaning of his life and death were unveiled. These reflections lie in sharp contrast to the past Latin American Christologies which justified the conquest and centuries of oppression. It was suggested in chapter One that a separation of Jesus' death from his resurrection had led to the creation of alienating images of Jesus, represented by either a suffering Jesus or a celestial Messiah.

With that in mind, it is of particular interest to see how several key liberation theologians approach the death and resurrection of Jesus as a salvific event which took place in a particular time and place, while at the same time appreciating its significance within a supra-historical level of reality which provides every event with its ultimate meaning. At issue is how the salvific significance of the cross and resurrection was historically mediated, and by what channel that meaning is transposed to present reality. The relationships drawn between the life, death and resurrection of Jesus of Nazareth shall be treated therein as a key category of evaluation. It will be assumed that every interpreter must decide whether or not these central elements of the Jesus event are to form an organic unity, and if not, which of those elements will serve as a primary reference for the rest.

Gustavo Gutiérrez: The Universal Redemption of Jesus Christ

Despite the unmistakable maturation and adjustment in Gutiérrez' thought, which can be traced from *A Theology of Liberation* to *The Power of the Poor in History* and beyond, "there can be little doubt that [he] has had one overriding purpose—to study, explain, and strengthen the 'potentiality' of the poor. . . . " Gutiérrez has consistently placed other themes at the service of this guiding interest, thereby seeking to place that potentiality into written form.[9] Perhaps for this reason more than any other, Gutiérrez has never quite clearly elaborated a systematic Christology.

Gutiérrez does, however, place Jesus Christ at the very center of his understanding of history. He explains that there exists in the eyes of faith only one history, neither wholly sacred nor profane, but "Christofinalized." As the Redeemer of the world, Christ is the point from which all events—past, present, and future—are to be measured. For the faith community, then, "there is only one human destiny, irreversibly assumed by Christ, the Lord of history. His redemptive work embraces all the dimensions of historical experience and brings them to their fullness."[10] In short, Gutiérrez professes that Jesus Christ is "the great hermeneutical principle of the faith, and . . . the basis and foundation of all theological reasoning. . . . "[11]

In light of these expansive Christological affirmations, one would expect Gutiérrez to demonstrate how the concrete history of Jesus of Nazareth might serve as an interpretive key for the content of Christian faith. For if Jesus was indeed, as Gutiérrez claims, "the irruption into history of the one by whom everything was made and [by whom] everything was saved,"[12] it would seem important to understand how the life of this particular Jewish prophet of the first century revealed the will and plan of God for human destiny. Such expectations, however, are largely disappointed; except on rare occasions, the primary focus of Gutiérrez' Christological work is directed to the living presence and activity of Jesus Christ within the world today.

The redemptive work of the "historic Christ" is proclaimed in *Theology of Liberation* as the center point of salvation history. Relying primarily upon a Christology drawn from the Pauline epistles, Gutiérrez explains that the cross and resurrection free the world from all sin and alienation:

> The redemptive action of Christ, the foundation of all that exists, is also conceived as a re-creation and presented in the context of creation (cf. Col. 1:15–20; I Cor. 8:6; Heb. 1:2; Eph. 1:1–22). . . . But the work of Christ is presented simultaneously as a liberation from sin and from all

its consequences. . . . Creation and salvation therefore have, in the first
place, a Christological sense: all things have been created in Christ, all
things have been saved in him (cf. Col. 1:15–20).[13]

If Christ does bring about a "new creation," Gutiérrez continues, then
all the earmarks of the "old" world are already overcome, even if "not yet
completely." It is a promise that "is gradually revealed in all its universality and concrete expression," thereby guiding human beings to "incip-
ient realizations towards its fullness."[14]

Yet, Gutiérrez does not elaborate why the life, death and resurrection of this particular human being, Jesus of Nazareth, led to such far-
reaching consequences for the world. The same could not be said for the
historical treatment he gives to another "paradigmatic event of liberation," the exodus. He carefully demonstrates the relationship between a
"historical act" of liberation in the exodus to a more comprehensive revelation of salvation history for the Jewish people. Moreover, the release
of the Jewish slaves from conditions of oppression is taken as a universal
sign of God's concern for the poor, a sign which Gutiérrez then employs
as a hermeneutical paradigm to interpret God's activity in the remainder
of the biblical witness.[15] Though the resurrected Christ is then presented within that rubric as the fulfillment of this same liberating process revealed by God in the exodus, Gutiérrez does not attempt to explicate how that came to be through Jesus of Nazareth.[16]

The most salient aspect of the historical Jesus in *Theology of Liberation* is perhaps the very fact of the incarnation itself, i.e., as the word of
God, he actually "pitches his tent" within human history. Gutiérrez then
moves directly from the incarnation to the cross and resurrection, all of
which he believes are events that fully express the Christian proclamation of God's act in Jesus Christ: "By his death and resurrection he re-
deems [humanity] from sin and all its consequences, as has been well
said in a text [Medellín] that we quote again: 'it is the same God, who in
the fullness of time, sends his Son in the flesh, so that he might come to
liberate all [humanity]. . . . ' "[17]

The absence of any other explanation leads one to believe that Gutiérrez' Christology implicitly relies on a classical interpretation of that
redemption effected on the cross. Represented by a host of satisfaction
theories, the classical interpretation seeks a metaphysical solution to the
problem of sin which enslaves the world and all humanity. Associated
most commonly with Saint Anselm, such interpretations posit an offended God—or, in another scenario, a God who must unwillingly share
dominion of a world partially ensnared by Satan—whose dignity must
be restored by the death of a worthy representative of a fallen humanity.
The Son of God was posed as the sole 'substitute' who could span the

infinite distance between God and humanity created by that offense. For that reason, the Son was incarnated in human flesh so that he could die for the sins of the world and satisfy the inner logic of divine reality.

Satisfaction theories, however, do not take into account the historical drama of the cross, for their interpretation unfolds within a predetermined, ideal world. On that note, Sobrino argues that "Anselmic" theories of the cross and various others fashioned after it,

> ignore the intrinsic relationship that exists between Jesus' proclamation of liberation, his denunciation of oppression, and his historical death on the cross. . . . It never views the matter in terms of the power of the real sin in history, which brings death to the Son — not in idealistic terms but in real terms.

The danger of viewing the death of Jesus in isolation from the rest of his life, Sobrino adds, is that one then seeks to arrive at knowledge of the cross on the basis of a preconceived idea of God, when in actual fact a reverse hermeneutic is indicated by Biblical revelation, viz., the interpreter ought to understand God on the basis of the life which led Jesus to a cross.[18]

Gutiérrez does admit towards the end of his book that, at least up to the time of its publication in 1971, an adequate study of the concrete ministry of Jesus was yet to be done by liberation theologians, and suggests a clue why that was possibly so:

> To approach the man Jesus of Nazareth, in whom God was made flesh..., what it is that gives his word an immediate, concrete context, is a task which more and more needs to be undertaken. One aspect of this work will be to examine the alleged apolitical attitude of Jesus, which would not coincide with what we mentioned earlier regarding the Biblical message and Jesus' own teaching.[19]

Thus, Gutiérrez here intimates that the reason the exodus tradition tended to be the paradigmatic, historical model for salvation in his liberation theology was because, at face value at least, it more readily translated into a political theology of liberation.[20]

Scattered passages in several of Gutiérrez' later works, however, reflect a deepening of his understanding of the life which led Jesus to a cross and its consequent meaning for human redemption. In *Power of the Poor*, for example, he affirms that

> having faith means believing that a certain human being of our own history, a Jew named Jesus, who was born of Mary, who proclaimed . . . the gospel to the poor, and liberation to those in captivity, who boldly

> confronted the great ones of his people and the representatives of the
> occupying power, who was executed as a subversive, is the Christ, the
> Messiah, the Annointed One, the Son.[21]

Presented almost in creedal form, this statement is a beautiful integration of two titles, Jesus and the Christ, which are held together by an act
of faith. It is the profession of a single identity which binds the Jesus of
Nazareth who was crucified in first century Jerusalem to the risen Christ
who is present in the world today: "Jesus has already come into the
world. . . . He is historical fact. But far from closing history, this fact
opens it to unsuspected thoroughfares."[22]

It would seem that this inextricable unity between Jesus' life, cross,
and resurrection is fundamental for a theology committed to historical
liberation. For as important as it is for Gutiérrez to proclaim that Jesus'
resurrection "uproots him, rips him up out of a particular date and
space, [and] forces upon us an understanding of the universality of the
status of the children of God,"[23] that redeemed existence nonetheless requires a historical context through which it may be defined and realized.
Although theologians committed to social and political liberation have
no difficulty in elaborating the consequences of Christ's universal redemption to oppressive situations, such a Christology could be elaborated with equal ease to legitimate a personalized, interior reconciliation
which transforms only the hearts of individuals. Worse yet, 'glorified'
Christs which are divorced from the crucified existence of Jesus have
been used throughout 'Christian' history to justify untold atrocities; the
celestial Christs of the Spanish conquest of Latin America are merely examples of a longer, tragic legacy.

In that respect, the historical mission of Jesus who proclaimed
God's reign of justice and liberation to be established in favor of the
poor, the oppressed, and the marginalized of this world is a paradigmatic event which ever impedes Christology from being fully co-opted
to legitimate structures, systems, and actions which are anti-human.[24]
For as Gutiérrez explains in *Power of the Poor,*

> . . . it was precisely the coherence of Christ's word with his practice that
> led him to his death. A Christological approach [so conceived] makes it
> possible to subsume the experiences of . . . the faith that the poor have
> realized throughout history, and incorporate these experiences and re-
> flections into a valid and authentic theology.[25]

It is the resurrection of this crucified Jesus which gives the poor and dispossessed a living hope for a liberation from the sinful realities which

victimize them. It reveals that love cannot be suppressed and killed, for it always springs back into new life.

Of course, as Gutiérrez recognizes, these determinations do not depend on historical research alone; their true realization is reliant upon an active praxis which seeks to make concrete the confession that "Jesus is the Christ." In *We Drink From Our Own Wells*, he suggests that it is in acting out this commitment that our "encounter with the Lord" takes place: "It is in our historical following—in our walking the path of Jesus —that the final judgment on our faith in Christ will be made. The following of Jesus is the solid ground on which can be built a reflection on Jesus as the Christ, a Christology; otherwise, it will be built on sand."[26]

The unity of the cross and resurrection, therefore, welds together two equally important Christological claims: (1) God's love and being were incarnated in the person of Jesus of Nazareth; (2) the Spirit of this same Jesus moves in present history to bring about personal and communal transformation. A Christology so conceived neither "petrifies" faith in a past event, nor allows it to escape into "the blue sky of the abstract,"[27] and thereby fully expresses the "paschal core of Christian existence and all of human life."[28]

Leonardo Boff: Jesus of Nazareth as the Concrete Mediation of Liberation

The other Latin American theologians whose works are evaluated in this chapter have devoted considerably more attention to Christology than Gutiérrez; correspondingly, their works will be placed under closer scrutiny. For that reason, the evolutionary development in Leonardo Boff's understanding of the cross and resurrection of Jesus—a progression already detected in Gutiérrez' writings — will be charted. That choice of presentation is more than just a matter of style, for in order to gain a proper perspective on Boff's Christological thought, his later writings should be considered separately from his first study, *Jesus Christ Liberator*.

It must be mentioned, however, that the obvious disparities that mark Boff's early Christological formulations from his later efforts cannot solely be attributed to a maturation in his theological thought. The Preface to *Liberator* places that book within a determined historical context: the country of Brazil during a period of history (early 1970s) when it was suffering under an intensely repressive military government. At that time, the mere mention of the word "liberation" in the media brought tremendous repercussions to those responsible for its publication. Boff enigmatically relates the effect which these conditions had on his own work: "The book did not say all that its author wanted to say; it only said what could be said."[29]

For a combination of reasons, then, though it did in some regards point towards a new direction for a Latin American Christology, *Liberator* was perhaps more representative of the Christologies of existential human understanding which had been written within North Atlantic scholarship.[30] That appears to be so despite Boff's stated working premise that every Christology ought to be shaped by the particular socio-historical context out of which it arises: "a Christology thought out and vitally tested in Latin America must have characteristics of its own."[31] The forthcoming material, however, did not support his claim.

Perhaps nowhere does that become more evident than in a chapter he entitled "Where Can We Find the Resurrected Christ Today?" Surprisingly, he did not even make scant reference therein to his Latin American context, but spoke of Christ predominantly in transcendent, universal terms: the cosmic Christ, the archetype, God with us, the Christ of the future ("Omega point"), the universal liberator of humanity, the conciliator of opposites (mediator), and Christ in the church as a sacrament of the presence of the Lord.[32] All of these titles are "true and applicable to a variety of concrete situations," notes Michael Cook, "but what is distinctively Latin American in all this?"[33] Although Boff did make some veiled references to the Christ who is present with those who struggle in history to carry his cause forward, an explication of the meaning of a resurrected Christ in a 'crucified' Latin America was glaringly absent.

Boff's early Christology was essentially "an attempt to build a new understanding of the mystery of the incarnation from an analysis of what we can glimpse of the mystery of the human."[34] He highlighted the resurrection as the confirmation of the truthfulness of Jesus' earthly existence; fundamentally, he sees it as an affirmation of the incarnation itself. Despite humanity's refusal to recognize and accept the "cosmic realization of the kingdom" which Jesus proclaimed, God was nonetheless able to realize that kingdom in the life of God's son. In that regard, Jesus of Nazareth was the embodiment of God's truth within history, and from that point onward he explains humanity's future destiny; his "present existence is our future."[35] This Jesus, who thus fulfilled within the structures of the world the potentialities of his human nature, was then transfigured by means of the resurrection into the realm of universal existence.[36]

Continuing in this vein, Boff presented the death of Jesus as a sign of the complete realization of his own authentic existence. Jesus is the perfect example of faith, the one who was obedient to the will of God even to the cross. Moreover, he was a being for others who fully identified with human suffering and death. Boff professed that it is the originality of this life which brings us salvation:

> Has the death of Christ, considered in itself, have theological relevance for us today? Yes it has . . . , [for] the universal meaning of the life and death of Christ . . . is that he sustained the funadmental conflict of human existence to the end: he wanted to realize the absolute meaning of this world before God, in spite of hate, incomprehension, betrayal, and condemnation to death.[37]

It is his faithfulness to that task which also makes Jesus the "absolute reference point" for human existence and self-understanding.[38]

In *Liberator*, Boff did not to any significant degree incorporate into his Christology the historical conflicts which brought Jesus to die on a cross. He did explore Jesus' contentious relationship to the scribes and Pharisees and recounted the manner by which they had him condemned to die as a religious heretic.[39] However, consistent to his paradigm of the universality of Jesus' existence, even here Boff stressed Jesus' role as mediator and his cross as the symbol of the reconciliation of all antitheses. Jesus did not simply suffer his death, he also embraced it as a sign of love and forgiveness, thereby overcoming the alienations and divisions which separate human beings from one another (including him from the scribes and Pharisees) and from God.[40] It is from that perspective, then, that Boff confessed, "By the cross, Christ created the new humanity, a *milieu divin*, a reconciled world within the divided world. . . . " In actual fact, however, it was essentially in the resurrection—an act of God which transforms "a sign of hatred" into the general reconciliation for all humanity—that Boff discovers the meaning of the life and death of Jesus for the world.

Once again, it is difficult to comprehend how Boff arrived at this image of Jesus starting from his own Latin American situation, a reality torn apart along social, economic, and political lines. In the region at large, it would not be an exaggeration to say that a person who offers even the least form of resistance against these oppressive conditions regularly risks torture and execution. For that reason alone, most Latin Americans can readily identify with Jesus' intense struggles with the societal authorities of his day, a conflict which eventually brought him to a swift trial and a brutal crucifixion.[41]

In the shadow of these historical crosses, past and present, many of Boff's statements—e.g., Jesus "knew how to put an *and* where we put an *or*" and "[Jesus] succeeded in reconciling opposites and being the mediator of human beings and all things"[42]—were somewhat ambiguous in relation to historical reality. It would seem more true to the experiences of Latin America, not to mention the experiences of Jesus narrated in the gospels, to understand the cross as a symbol of the struggle between historical antitheses: love and hate, inclusion and exclusion, justice and injustice. From that vantage point, Jesus of Nazareth was murdered because he made historical options in favor of one reality over another. Although interpreting the cross thus might very well compromise Boff's image of Jesus as the "archetype of the most perfect individuation"—in Jungian language, the integration of all the conflicts and existential dramas that polarize one's essential being[43]—it frames the passion of Jesus in such a way that is realistic to the historical dynamics forced upon Latin Americans.

With the publication of *Liberator* into English in 1978, Boff added an epilogue which significantly modified the landscape of his Christological hermeneutic in consideration of these Latin American concerns. He announced that a change in the political atmosphere within his country had permitted him to now "introduce a more open and straightforward type of socio-analytic thought"[44] and, as a result, to more consistently base his Christological reflection in terms of themes which encompass the possibility of structural change in socio-historical situations marked by domination and oppression.[45] In order to carry out that task, he acknowledged that his method of interpretation would need to incorporate two fundamental elements: "(1) the relevance of socio-political liberation for Christology; (2) the social setting that is the point of departure for this Christological reflection."[46] He explained that both of these factors would, in turn, be informed by a concrete praxis which works toward the actual liberation of the oppressed.

Anticipating criticism that such a hermeneutical method would be socio-politically "biased," he argued that since historical reality itself forces choices between conflicting commitments, to assume a neutral starting point for Christological reflection would be an illusion. Although most theologians claim to craft their Christologies in apolitical fashion, his experience suggested otherwise: "if a different kind of Christology with its own commitments appears on the scene and confronts the older 'apolitical' Christology, the latter will soon forget its 'apolitical' nature and reveal itself as a religious reinforcement of the existing status quo."[47] He felt quite justified, then, in pursuing that image of Jesus which appears when examined in the light of a liberation interest, as well as evaluating the interpretations of Jesus' message and salvific praxis within a matrix determined by the present Latin American situation. He wished only that other interpreters would be as transparent regarding their own horizon of interest.

This pronounced shift in Boff's post *Liberator* method is manifest in the subsequent precedence of praxis over theory and the concomitant Christological precedence of the historical Jesus over the Christ of faith.[48] Within his reconsideration of Christology, it is now the life and death of Jesus which give meaning to the resurrection, while the resurrection operates to universalize the experience of his crucified existence. Boff suspects that if the historical causality which lies behind the cross is divorced from the resurrection event—a tendency of his earlier Christology—then the latter is always in danger of mystification and idealization. When that happens, the resurrection essentially becomes a "symbol of a world totally reconciled to God for all future time without having to pass by way of conversion from the causative mechanisms of the wickedness of the present."[49]

In order to avoid any such abstraction, Boff proposes that the total liberation which the resurrection represents may only be defined in relation to Jesus' struggle to establish God's reign in human history:

> The *timeless* meaning of the death of Christ ... should be extracted from this *historical* context of that death, rather than from a theological one. Only thus will that meaning cease to be ahistorical, and at bottom empty and vacuous. And only thus will it acquire genuinely valid dimensions for contemporary faith as well.[50]

He proposes that the historical "trajectory" of Jesus' life and death provides Christology with a meaningful alternative to classical theories of redemption which hinge on the demands of metaphysical necessity. As was elaborated in the previous section, classical models typically project the concrete character of the life and death of Jesus into another world of meaning within which his significance for human existence is defined. Boff argues that these "images and representations ... are then petrified and put forth as valid for all places and ages. That is how we end up with all sorts of abstract and hollow talk about redemption, death, the behavior of the historical Jesus, and the intraworldly value of the resurrection."[51]

He does accept that some of these religious notions, most particularly "sacrifice" and "ransom," may actually "reveal the transcendent truth of the truly historical character of Jesus' destiny."[52] Nevertheless, he warns that they may easily become distorted when placed within a predominantly metaphysical world of thought which seeks an explanation of Jesus' death in the 'mind' of a God concerned with repairing divine honor or, in more modern conceptions, divine Self-unity.[53] The problem with such "ethico-juridical" theories of redemption, he explains, is that they leave "no room for asking how liberation from social sin, redemption from structural injustices, or a struggle against hunger and human misery are to be identified in any way with Jesus Christ's redemption."[54]

Accordingly, he contends that the redemptive work of Jesus ought to be interpreted within a historical framework which addresses the personal and communal realities which actually concern human beings. His own application of that method yields the following elements (in excerpted form) for a contemporary Latin American gospel[55] of death and resurrection:

> To suffer and die for the sake of the crucified means to put up with the fact that the system defames the values of those who fight against it.... [Yet] to die that way is to live.... The message of the passion is always to go hand in hand with the message of the resurrection. Those who died as insurrectionists against the system of this age and refused to be 'conformed to this world' (Rom. 12:2) are now the 'resurrected.' Insurrection for the cause of God and others is resurrection.... The resurrection [then] seeks to point up the true meaning and guaranteed future of the seemingly fruitless struggles for justice and love in the process of history. In the end, they will triumph. In the end, sheer goodness will reign.[56]

Obviously, Boff is not concerned here simply with the facts surrounding the historical Jesus. Although his method does seek to demonstrate that Jesus' mission realized concrete acts of liberation within the world in which he lived, it also attempts to show that his life represents a dimension which affects our present history as well. In effect, he has issued an invitation to those who are struggling for justice and love in the world to accept the good news that Jesus has revealed God's solidarity with them even when they suffer: "To preach the cross today is to proclaim the way of Jesus ... Living that way is already resurrection.... "[57]

Of course, given its clear commitment to historical liberation one would not expect a unanimity of support for Boff's image (post *Liberator*) of Jesus Christ. German theologian Claus Bussmann is surely not alone when he questions whether Boff's interpretation of the Christ event is a legitimate rendering of the resurrection proclamation of the early Christian community. Bussmann's primary concern is that "Boff says basically nothing in connection with Jesus' resurrection other than what he has already said about the activity of Jesus in the world.... "[58] That assumption, Bussmann contends, is quite tenuous, for he believes that Jesus' proclamation of the reign of God cannot be so clearly identified with the post-resurrection reflections of the early Christian community. In particular, he charges that Boff's approach is strongly reminiscent of Willi Marxsen's well-worn dictum "the Jesus affair is not over," only reworked by means of a liberation key.[59]

Since Bussmann's critique raises some rather central issues regarding the relationship between the historical Jesus and the Christ of faith, it should not be taken lightly. For it cannot be ignored that Boff does present the life, death, and resurrection of Jesus of Nazareth as a unity which is not dissolved by a discontinuity in time. By means of his resurrection, the proclaimer is enabled "to continue his activity among men and women and arouses them to the struggle for liberation."[60]

Yet, at the same time Boff does not think that its significance is therein exhausted. In his estimation, if the resurrection was merely an event that signaled that "God's cause goes forward" (Marxsen), then that liberation announced by Jesus would only be partial and truncated. Confined to the historical life and death of Jesus alone, the process of redemption would lack the universality and totality which mark true liberation. It would still be entrapped within an "indefinite circularity of oppression-and-liberation," a closed system which would preclude the possibility of change and transformation in an open future.[61]

Perhaps if Boff understood Jesus' cause solely in existential terms, i.e., the communication of a message concerning personal existence, then the projection of that message from the cross forward to the post-resurrection community could be posed as a movement of complete continuity. But that is not the case; to the contrary, Boff presents Jesus' cause as a concrete struggle for the creation of a new historical reality. In that sense, it was a cause that failed, for the new reality did not take place and its proclaimer ended up on the cross. To all appearances, death and oppression continued their unrelenting reign as the bearers of ultimate reality over the persons, relationships and structures of this world.[62] According to the gospel of Mark, Jesus was abandoned even by God, the One in whom he had placed total faith and confidence.[63] Completely disillusioned, his disciples fled to the safety of Galilee, deceived by yet another false utopia built on broken promises and empty dreams; thus, "not only did it frustrate the disciples' hopes, it also destroyed their faith."[64]

In Boff's interpretation of the gospels, it was only their experience of the resurrection which enabled the disciples to reinterpret the life of Jesus and move beyond the ultimate tragedy of the cross. It was not merely a theological decision or a subjective realization which occasioned their complete reversal. Nor was it simply a recapturing of the ideas and hopes of a resurrection of the dead spawned by the apocalyptic horizon. In truth, it was only the apparitions of the crucified, dead, and buried Jesus before the disciples which enabled them to recuperate their faith and reunite as a community once again. They were "surprised and dominated by an impact that was beyond their possibilities of imagination. Without this, they would never have preached the crucified as Lord."[65]

For most liberation theologians, it is crucial to affirm at this point that the resurrection concerns the figure of Jesus, and not merely the faith of his disciples. As Boff repeatedly stresses, "according to the New Testament something happened to Jesus and that something provoked faith in the apostles, and not vice versa."[66] He is not speaking here, of course, simply in biological terms; that is, material proof that a cadaver had in actual fact been resuscitated by means of the resurrection. For although the disciples recognized the crucified Jesus as the one who had been risen, they also understood that he "was not reanimated for the kind of life he had already had."[67] It is the complete transformation of Jesus' person, both body and soul, into a new realm of being.[68] The reason that this affirmation is so important for liberationists is because once it has been determined that something did indeed happen to Jesus, then we are able to create hope that something concrete can happen in our history as well.

The resurrection, then, not only justifies the person of Jesus of Nazareth before the world, it goes beyond that to manifest the reign of God in its fullness and reveal the possibilities of transformation for all reality. It represents a liberation from those conditions against which Jesus struggled — illness, disease, personal alienation, guilt, poverty, oppression — and announces a victory over the sinful structures which brought him, as well as all other human beings who have committed themselves to love and justice, to violence and death. In that regard, it shows "that the oppressed and liquidated have a life reserved for them, the life that has now been manifested in Jesus Christ. They may take courage, then, and live the freedom of . . . [those] who are not subject to the inhibiting powers of death."[69] The end of history in all its totality and universality is presented within history as an anticipation of its future reign.[70]

In light of the foregoing, it does not seem that Bussmann's critique has adequate foundation. The resurrection signifies for Boff an entirely new dimension of the message and figure of Jesus. The Jesus affair does not simply carry on unchanged after its destruction by the historical powers which opposed it. To that end, Boff emphasizes that the faith community is not called to live merely on nostalgia: "Jesus of Nazareth, dead and buried, does not merely live on by means of his remembrance and his message of liberation for the oppressed conscience. He himself is present and lives a way of life that has already surpassed the limitations of our world of death and realized every dimension of all its possibilities."[71]

In conclusion, it is the act of God in resurrection that announces this suffering and crucified servant as the true messiah and liberator. The cause of the historical Jesus is raised up into a new life for the faith community, one which opens up the historical process to the possibilities for a resurrected reality. Echoing a conviction held by many liberation theologians, Boff believes that the unity of the Christ event—life, death, and resurrection—unveils a paschal dialectic lying at the very heart of human life which must be discovered in every situation anew by means of discipleship.

The faith community is called to confront those situations where death and alienation still reign and seek to concretize God's utopia on personal and communal levels. Contrary to common theological wisdom, however, abstract reflection (theory) alone does not provide us with that access.[72] It is only gained by means of a critical analysis and reflection upon historical praxis which aims to actualize the universal redemption revealed in the resurrection. In other words, a truly liberative Christology seeks to detect and establish those concrete mediations that do flesh out the redemptive work of Jesus Christ in history.[73]

Jon Sobrino: The Trial of God and Humanity in History

Jon Sobrino, a Jesuit priest who is a native of Spain, has lived and worked in El Salvador during the last two decades, one of the most tragic periods of that country's history. The 1989 massacre of six of his Jesuit brothers—a fate Sobrino escaped merely by a quirk of schedule—was a very personal encounter with the dark forces of death. In a candid interview, Sobrino provided an open and frank appraisal how this daily reality affects the shape and content of his theological reflections:

> Liberation theology is not merely an academic discipline, but is done from the perspective of the poor. If theology is not for the poor, who is it for? For who else would theology be in this continent? Here, poverty means death; both slow death, due to the unjust structures, and immediate death, as is reflected in the 70,000 Salvadorans assassinated in this country and the 100,000 civilians killed in Guatemala during the last decade — all because they said they didn't want to be poor. God does not will death. Theologians here are deeply affected by this reality.[74]

It is from within this historical context that Sobrino's Christology attempts to rescue the historical Jesus from those abstractions which have allowed his image to serve in Latin America and in other parts of the world as a legitimization for social and economic exploitation. He argues that the oppressive powers which currently prevail in most of Latin America "want to see absolute religious symbols that command respect in and of themselves, even though they may be tangential or even contrary to history." In response, Sobrino deems it vital that the interpreter not allow Jesus' life and message to be 'limited' to the proclamation of universal reconciliation, while masking the historical manifestations of those sins against which Jesus struggled and which eventually brought him to his death.[75] It is these commitments that clearly inform the hermeneutical suspicions which Sobrino brings to the task of understanding Jesus Christ.

Sobrino describes his first major systematic effort at Christological formulation as "a Christology at the crossroads" because "behind it lies a long tradition, part of which it proposes to reject. Before it lies a new and authentically Latin American Christology which does not yet exist, which yet remains to be formulated, and toward which this book moves."[76] The method that he suggests will yield this distinctive Latin American Christology is one rooted in the Trinitarian reality of God, a starting point which radically transforms the precondition of Christology. It is a method which is mediated by a concrete praxis in the Spirit, yet realized in accordance with the life and destiny of the historical Jesus.[77]

Sobrino points to the cross of Jesus as one particular area of interpretation upon which the historical experience and praxis of Latin American communities have shed new light. He adds that in many respects this historical consciousness is a relatively recent phenomenon. The popular piety which had sprung from the 'spirituality of the conquest' had to a great extent appropriated Jesus' passion as the model by which to justify the destiny of the Latin American poor and encourage their passive acceptance of suffering within God's will. However, the changing faith of the Latin American Church has imagined new ways of seeing the cross:

> While the resurrection remains the paradigm of liberation, the cross is no longer seen simply as a symbol of suffering or as the negative dialectical moment which immediately and directly gives rise to the positive movement of liberation. ... From their concrete experience in the effort to achieve liberation, people are now beginning to realize that they cannot prescind from the cross of Jesus if their experience is to be truly Christian.[78]

Consequently, these reflections have led the popular church away from interpretations of the cross which depend on mythical scenarios (satisfaction theories) to explain the redemption of humanity. In their stead, it has sought interpretations which recover the life and message which brought Jesus of Nazareth to his historical cross. It has attempted to integrate into its interpretation of the cross the dynamics of conflicting interests and powers which marked Jesus' passion, exploring the reasons why, in the first place, the authorities sought his death and why, in the second place, Jesus nonetheless remained committed to continue "walking down the road to Jerusalem."

Although he operates within the framework set by these historical priorities, Sobrino believes that the distinctive features of Jesus' cross can nevertheless best be elucidated in terms of both its theological (effect on God) and soteriological (effect on humanity) significance. He maintains that this approach may help to overcome the two main obstacles which frequently prevent a comprehension of the cross of Jesus in all its profundity: "One is the danger of isolating the cross from the concrete history of Jesus; the other is the danger of isolating it from God."[79]

Adopting an interpretive scheme largely developed elsewhere by Moltmann,[80] Sobrino attests that the cross of Jesus of Nazareth suspends a question mark over the true character of God's being: "Is God the God of religion, in whose name one can subdue human beings? Or is God the God whom Jesus proclaims in the good news about human liberation?"[81] At stake, essentially, is the actual manner by which access to this God may be found.

Sobrino points out that the Jewish authorities saw the issue from that perspective as well, as is indicated by the fact that they had Jesus condemned to die on the charge of blasphemy. The conception of God which Jesus promoted was one that challenged their system of obligations and privileged locales (temple and cultic worship) through which one would need pass in order to gain favor from God. For Jesus, on the other hand, the only privileged access to God could be gained through the medium of human beings themselves, most particularly through those who are totally dependent on God for their sustenance, viz., the poor and marginalized. Jesus' actions and teachings on their behalf revealed a God of grace before whom one cannot justify oneself, but before whom one may only find hope.[82]

Sobrino believes that the debate regarding the authentic understanding of God's character is also manifest in Jesus' clash with the Roman Empire. Jesus desacralized the divine claims which undergirded its doctrine of *Pax romana* and relativized its notions of a deity who operated solely on the basis of dominant power. In the name of his God, Jesus condemned the oppression and social marginalization which resulted from that system and in the process stirred up hopes for a new day when the value of all human beings would be respected. For that reason, Jesus was executed as a political agitator, evidenced in part by the manner of his execution (crucifixion) and the inscription placed above his head on the cross (King of the Jews).

On that basis, Sobrino underlines that the cross was not the result of a Roman or Jewish misunderstanding, but the consequence of a life in which incarnated love posed a threat to a religious and social stability which had been built on oppression.

> Framed in this context of a basic theological conflict, Jesus' trajectory to the cross is no accident. He himself provokes it by presenting the basic option between two deities. His course is also a trial of the deity, with Jesus appearing as a witness on one side and those in power as witnesses on the other side.... [83]

At root, the representatives of both the political and religious establishment kill Jesus based on their conception of God.

By itself, however, the death of Jesus on the cross does not answer the question of God's essential being nor reveal the true interpretation of God's power. In fact, what intensifies the dispute even further and actually lends credence to the theological claims of the authorities is the appearance that Jesus died in complete discontinuity with his own cause. "In order to appreciate the uniqueness of Jesus' death," Sobrino suggests, "one need only hear Jesus' proclamation of the imminence of the kingdom, and then hear his cry on the cross as his Father abandons him."[84] After the cross it can only be concluded that either the authorities had been right all along and it was Jesus of Nazareth who had misplaced his trust in a false conception of God or there must be a radical alteration in the understanding of God held by the Jewish and Roman authorities, for that God would operate on the basis of weakness, not domination.[85]

In bringing this Jesus back to new life, God alone delivers an answer to the questions posed by the cross, for God's act at Easter is a confirmation of the historical path which led Jesus to his death. Moreover, it is a sign that the One in whom Jesus had placed his trust, a God who reveals the divine presence through mediations of weakness and love, is indeed the only true God. Paradoxically, however, the uncertainty of the cross is also subject to that answer which is given by those human beings who stand before it. For although Jesus' resurrection is an eschatological happening — when the final reality of history makes its appearance in the midst of history — it is not immediately comprehensible as such. The reality of resurrection, and thus also the decision concerning the revelation of God in the life of Jesus of Nazareth, may only be appropriated as an act of faith. "This means that the meaning of the resurrection cannot be grasped unless one engages in active service for the transformation of the unredeemed world."[86]

In light of all that has been written thus far, it is clear that Sobrino's treatment of the life and death of the historical Jesus is at one and the same time a 'theo-logical' issue. It does not follow, however, that Sobrino is thereby proposing an ahistorical explanation for the meaning of the cross, the primary significance of which could be transposed to a removed realm of divine reality. For to the contrary, Sobrino believes that God was present in the person of Jesus of Nazareth and fully immersed God-self in and subjected God-self to the mechanisms, ambiguities, and contradictions of human history. In that respect, the incarnation was the complete identification of God's being with the historical path that led Jesus to carry out acts of love and forgiveness, to proclaim the good news of a reign of justice, to conflict with the social authorities, and ultimately to his death upon the cross.[87] Therefore, a decision about God also implies a decision about history and its proper interpretation.

> The cross poses the problem of God . . . in terms of theodicy (the justification of God). On the cross, theodicy is historicized. The Son is not crucified by some natural evil. . . . He is crucified by a historicized evil, i.e., the free will of human beings. What justification is there for a God who allows the sinfulness of the world to kill his Son (and hence other human beings as well)?[88]

In essence, Sobrino is attempting to turn classical Christological hermeneutics upside down. The first element in the divine-human equation is to be determined and defined by the second, the historical drama which transpired in the life of the human Jesus. Preconceived notions of divinity may no longer seek their incarnation in the life of Jesus, but are themselves subject to the character of God which he revealed. As a result, both elements, divine and human, are explicated in terms which make sense only in relation to history itself. In respect to the present theme, then, Sobrino asserts that "the cross is not the result of some divine decision independent of history; it is the outcome of the basic option for incarnation in a given situation."[89]

On that basis, Sobrino concludes that Jesus of Nazareth revealed the unexpected character of a "crucified God." The God who identified Self wholly with the plight of a broken humanity in all its suffering and struggles also became unavoidably vulnerable to those sinful realities and structures which produce such horrendous human conditions. God maintained this solidarity with humanity to such a profound level that God crucified God's Son (which is also dialectically God-self) in order to experience within the very being of God the most negative side of history. In that sense, God's action is demanded by the existence of that theodicy — put simply, the power and reign of evil — in history which discredits the existence of a loving and near God. As Sobrino explains,

> There is only one possible response on God's part. God himself must be part of the whole process of protest.... [Hence,] on the cross we find a process within God himself.... God 'bifurcates' himself on the cross, so that transcendence (the Father) is in conflict with history (the Son). In God's abandonment of the Son, however, we find not only God's criticism of the world but also his ultimate solidarity with it.[90]

Sobrino does not believe that it is sufficient for theology to posit a good deity who has ultimate power over an evil force which, though in some sense already defeated, nonetheless wreaks havoc in history. A God so conceived remains essentially apathetic to the injustice, oppression, suffering, and death which dominate the societies of Latin America and the rest of the dependent world. For that reason, Sobrino holds that it is only when theology accepts a God who has experienced these negatives from within history ("suffered in his own flesh") that it will be able to see God mediated in Jesus' cross and in the crosses of all of those who suffer in history.[91]

In this explication of the redemptive work of the cross of Jesus, it is obvious that Sobrino's primary concern is to express how the suffering and death of Jesus, as well as that of the Indians, campesinos and urban poor of Latin America, may be seen as a mediation of God. Echoing the conviction of Bonhoeffer that "only a God who suffers can save us," he conceives of God as One who is profoundly moved and affected by the events of history. In that respect, his effort is an important contribution to a theological method which seeks to discover in what sense suffering and death may be a mode of being for God.[92]

Saying that should not necessarily indicate a theory of redemption which would substitute Anselm's conceptual world with a Hegelian philosophy of Spirit. In this latter scenario, the existence of sin in the world would be an offense to the completion of God's being. The alienation of God from God's creation could not have been reconciled, so the theory would go, by the suffering and death of countless numbers of innocent people throughout history, for evil would still have an existence independent and outside of the divine reality. It could only be the death of God in the person of God's Son which would permit the assimilation of evil within the divine reality and once again reconcile God to the world. In Hegel's explanation, sin and death thereby become part of God's complete character: "The death of Christ is the death of this death itself, the negation of negation. . . . The reconciliation believed in as being in Christ has no meaning if God is not known as the Trinity, if it is not recognized that He *is* but is at the same time the Other. . . . [93]

A Hegelian interpretation of the cross, however, leaves an inescapable dilemma. If God is indeed required to make evil a part of God's identity and being in order to overcome it, what actually has been gained on the cross? It would appear less a defeat of evil than it would its sacramentalization within human history. For once evil has been subsumed within God's character, it becomes an eternal presence against which love and hope must struggle world without end! As Leonardo Boff suggests:

> . . . We may not force God and the cross into a bond that would be intrinsic to the divine identity. If we could, we would be lost. If suffering is an expression of God's very essence, if God hates, if God crucifies, then there is no salvation for us. . . . How would we speak of redemption that comes from God, were God also in need of redemption?[94]

The cross is clearly a symbol of antitheses: a historicized theodicy which brings a historicized love to its end. But to join these two realities into a single synthesis would rob the event of its liberative import and hope. The oppressed should be seen as the mediation of God not because the cause of their oppression is now part of God's character, but rather because God's character has identified with their character, or being, in the life, message, and death of Jesus. In that sense, God does indeed become vulnerable to the tragedy of history and suffers the effects of a world which rejects the divine offer for a transformed reality.

To say that God is not in need of redemption is not the same as saying that God is a perfect (immutable) Being who is unaffected by historical reality. Quite to the contrary, most liberationists would want to affirm with the Apostle Paul that God will only be "all in all" once the redemption of humanity and all of creation has taken place. As strange as it may sound to those of us inculcated with classical categories of theological thought, God's 'completion' is integrally related to our redemption. In that sense, the destiny of God's future is connected with the unfolding of human history itself.[95]

Therefore, to use the terminology which is utilized by Sobrino, it is not so much God who is on "trial" in the life of Jesus as are the distinct visions of history which seek divine justification for their fundamental

value and structure. And in that trial it is the human community which
has been called to be the jury; however, in this court the members of the
jury are not required so much to make a speculative judgment as they
are a decision fleshed out in concrete praxis ("Which side are you on?").
Such a 'theo-logy' of Jesus' cross still serves to place God in solidarity
with those who suffer. However, in this case God does not undertake the
cross to eternalize it and deprive us of all hope, but assumes it because
God means to put an end to all the crosses of history.[96] At various points
in his study, Sobrino demonstrates that this is his actual theological understanding of the cross:

> Latin American theology turns theodicy into anthropodicy, into the
> question of justifying human beings rather than God. . . . The possibil-
> ity of justifying God is not to be found in speculating about some pos-
> sible logical explanation that will reconcile God with suffering history.
> It is to be found in a new realization of Jesus' cross, so that we may see
> whether that will really give rise to a new resurrection.[97]

In an article which Sobrino wrote six years after the original publication of his first Christology, his theological focus on the cross and resurrection recedes noticeably to the background in favor of a soteriological emphasis; that is, its unique significance for human salvation.[98] It is
the figure of Jesus as a "being-for-others"[99] which now takes center
stage. As a foundation for that approach, Sobrino demonstrates how Jesus of Nazareth was fully engaged in a struggle to announce and enact
his message of salvation for the forsaken, most particularly represented
by the poor and oppressed, to whom he pointed as concrete signs of liberation. It was after the resurrection that Jesus' existence as a being-for-
others became universalized, resulting in the "eschatologization" of the
salvific value of his life and death. Throughout, Sobrino does not consider the particularity of the historical Jesus and the universality of
Christ to be in contradiction or discontinuity. In fact, it is the very particularity of Jesus' destiny that permits an understanding of the meaning
of salvation itself and defines the process by which Christ became the
Savior of the world.

Sobrino delineates five primary elements which express the salvific
work of the cross and the resurrection of Jesus. In so doing, he aims to
recover the significance which the cross and resurrection would have
had for the first Christian communities, and which subsequently served
as the basis for those soteriological models which we find in the New Testament. They are, in shortened form: (1) Jesus gave of himself; historically he lived his life in favor of the poor and eschatologically he deliv-

ered himself unto death; (2) Jesus received the objective consequences of the historical sins of others and eschatologically he bore the sins of the world; (3) Jesus historically obeyed the salvific will of God even to a tragic end, while accepting that cross made him the eschatological Savior; (4) Jesus' historical commitment and death made God's offer of salvation real and credible, eschatologically that message was confirmed in his resurrection; (5) Jesus forgave sins, but in doing so he also introduced men and women to the very life of God.[100]

When Sobrino claims that Jesus and his activities have been "eschatologized" in the resurrection, he conveys that the resurrection event which universalized the message of Jesus was simultaneously the identification of Jesus' person as the identity behind that message, i.e., "the proclaimer became the proclaimed." After the resurrection it was Jesus himself who began to be preached in the announcement of the good news of salvation. Hence, though the resurrection does project history forward toward its ultimate and transcendent end (eschatology), its absolute point of reference remains the historical destiny of Jesus.

In these five theses, Sobrino consistently maintains a dialectical tension between particularity and universality, history and eschatology, cross and resurrection, Jesus and Christ. The proclamation of Jesus Christ is thereby presented as both a dialectic and a unity, for only thus does Sobrino believe that the full mystery of redemption may be comprehended. He warns that when the resurrected Christ is presented simply in divine predicates, that figure may conveniently serve as a theological alibi for not considering the permanent value of the historical Jesus. On the other side, should that Christology fall into a 'Jesus-ology,' it leaves him hanging on a cross.[101]

Because Sobrino understands Jesus' resurrection as an eschatological happening, its interpretation yields not so much a fixed series of doctrines and creeds as it does the basis for a new vision of life. In that regard, he intimates that the truth of the resurrection may not be authentically understood in a theoretical manner, but may only be mediated by means of experiential knowledge. In the process of the faith community's own praxis within the struggles of history, it may anticipate the future promise revealed in the resurrection and experience it in the transformation of every unredeemed reality, even in the midst of an evil and unjust world. And with each concretion, a new horizon of understanding is opened which widens one's vision of history and strengthens one's hope. For "the resurrection sets in motion a life of service designed to implement in reality the eschatological ideals of justice, peace and human solidarity. It is the earnest attempt to make those ideals *real* that enables us to comprehend what happened in Jesus' resurrection."[102]

Sobrino calls this praxis "the historical following of Jesus," which he proposed as the paradigm for universal Christian existence and, correspondingly, the starting point for Christological reflection. "In the resurrection of Christ the definitive promise of the goal towards which we walk appears; but in the historical Jesus appears the manner to walk that path."[103]

Juan Luis Segundo: "Multiplying" the Jesus Event

Juan Luis Segundo claims that academic Christology has all too often built its work on a faulty foundation. In the first place, it frequently operates under the assumption that a method of interpretation freely secured from subjectivity and ideology will permit the discovery of a singularly true image of Jesus Christ. Its Christology, then, becomes a discourse limited to one Christ, one Messiah, one Savior, all of which are interpreted by means of a specific category deemed consonant with the historical Jesus. The fundamental error of such efforts, he contends, is the attempt to arrive at one absolute image of Christ based on a unidimensional understanding of the function and mission of Jesus of Nazareth.

Moreover, Segundo contends that academic Christology often wrongly assumes that interest in Jesus is aroused when people are able to recognize him as a divine figure of the stature of God. On that basis, the central interest of its Christology is typically devoted to the formulation of absolute categories which facilitate an understanding of the person of Jesus as a union of two natures, human and divine. Segundo, however, begs to differ:

> If people came face to face with a specific, limited human being, ambiguous as everything involved in history is, and came to see him as God or a divine revelation, it was because that human being was of interest, was humanly significant. And if people arrive at the same final vision of him today, it will only be because the latter is verified again: that is, because he is of interest and humanly significant to them.[104]

Based on that judgment, Segundo asserts that even if it were possible to bring together into a single, coherent synthesis all of that which has been written about Jesus in the Scripture and the tradition of the church, the result would be of limited use. It still would not address the most fundamental concern of Christian faith: what significance does this Jesus have within our world of meaning? For that reason, Segundo quite intentionally denominates his efforts as an "anti-Christology," which he defines as a reflection which starts off from the historical data about Jesus and multiplies the readings of his message in relation to the human problems of later times and of the present day.[105] In real terms, then, he is 'anti' every attempt to make Christology a monistic reflection.

In light of that background, it is not surprising that Segundo finds Bultmann's hermeneutical method as the most promising for integrating our experience of Christ in the present reality with "the summons issued to us by the Absolute in Jesus."[106] He believes that the gulf which separates our world from that world within which Jesus lived requires that two crucial aspects of Bultmann's method be carried out: (1) a reinterpretation of the gospel accounts and words of Jesus which sheds his mythical conceptual world; (2) the development of modern categories of understanding that best incorporate those contemporary meaning-worlds which orient our daily comprehension and behavior.[107]

Segundo maintains that though the writers of the New Testament were in a historical sense chronologically closer to the life of Jesus, they surely found themselves confronted with the same challenge of expressing the enduring significance of Jesus of Nazareth within their contemporary circumstances. For they too

> start out from the concrete, historical interest he aroused in his own time and place and move on to the human problems of later times. . . . Those problems are bound up with meaning-worlds that are radically akin to his (by virtue of the values sought . . .) and that are open, by existential logic, to *the transcendent data brought by Jesus within his own historical coordinates.*[108]

In sum, Segundo presupposes that Christologies have the dual responsibility of being valid for their own context and faithful to the history of Jesus at the same time.[109] Of course, that statement sounds less complicated upon a first hearing than it is in reality. In view of the complexity of that hermeneutical problem, it would seem important to uncover what Segundo means when he makes reference to the "transcendent data brought by Jesus within his own historical coordinates," and understand how that data promises to guide a creative multiplication for the writing of contemporary gospels.[110] It is perhaps in Segundo's treatment of the cross and resurrection of Jesus that these issues are most clearly outlined.

In his multi-volume work on Christology, Segundo conspicuously omits from his treatment of the "historical Jesus of the synoptics" any discussion of the cross as a salvific event. It is not until he arrives at the second part of his study on Jesus, an analysis of the interpretive key Paul utilized to express his significance, that the cross is presented as such; that is, as Paul's interpretation of the meaning of the cross for the audience which he was addressing. This arrangement of materials is itself illustrative of Segundo's conviction that any expression of the salvific import of the cross of Jesus will be articulated, and therefore understood, within the meaning-world of the interpreter alone.[111]

Segundo argues that the New Testament interpretations of Jesus' salvific work—Jesus as sacrifice, as ransom, as the new Adam—must not be allowed to predicate the meaning that it may have in our own cultural and historical context. All of these images of Christ were carefully crafted in response to issues which were specifically relevant to their own era. That does not deny that these representations may still serve to evoke new ways of looking at the relevance of Jesus for our own reality. It does indicate to Segundo, however, that the task of the modern interpreter is to "deconstruct or dismantle that language which is no longer ours" in order to discover within traditional Christologies of the church those keys which will assist in the explication of Christ's salvific work within our own language and our own meaning-world.[112]

Segundo fears that adopting absolute categories to interpret the significance of Jesus may serve to strip both Jesus and his cross of their bite and scandal.[113] He points out that universal theories of redemption all too often assume

> that the incarnation could have taken place, without major inconvenience, a thousand years before or after its historical date. In one case or another, Jesus would have died in order to redeem us from our sins, and his sacrifice, carried out under other authorities . . . , would have been valid for our pardon.[114]

In contradiction to such a scheme, he proposes that it is the historical particularity of Jesus' cross which signals its enduring significance.

As was indicated above, Segundo believes that the Christologies which are found in the gospels reflect the interests and ideologies of their creators; it was the concerns of their own socio-historical context which shaped their distinctive content and construction. In order to recover the events which gave rise to those images of Jesus Christ, then, it is necessary to select that interpretive key which best deciphers the various "codes" in which those events have been expressed.[115]

In respect to the synoptic gospels, Segundo's investigations lead him to the conclusion that they are best interpreted by means of a political key.[116] Although he realizes it would be "sheer reductionism" to think that solely one hermeneutical key could explain every aspect of Jesus' life as found in the synoptic gospels—e.g., he admits that a political key does not adequately explain numerous elements of Jesus' strictly moral and religious teaching—he nevertheless proposes that it best expresses the intent of the synoptic Jesus.[117]

In the previous chapter, Segundo's understanding of the religio-political character of Jesus' historical mission was sketched in broad outline. At that point it was indicated that Segundo highlights the Jewish leaders as Jesus' primary adversaries; his project posed a threat to the social and political power which they enjoyed in Palestine during the early part of the first century. At the same time, it was also noted that Segundo does not see Jesus' religio-political message in conflict with a more universal, humanistic gospel:

> Jesus never for a moment gives up his central intention of revealing God and the import of that revelation for human existence as a whole. But in so doing, he clearly makes use of political ideology. . . . Jesus makes himself heard and understood by involving himself, in God's name, in the socio-political tensions of contemporary Israel. . . . It is thus that he acquires disciples and adversaries.[118]

The life and teaching of Jesus eventually became such a threat to those who opposed his project that they had him killed. He is sentenced to die in a manner consistent with the path he had chosen to live: as a political subversive.[119] Jesus' death on the cross and his apparent abandonment by God signaled to the community of his disciples the end and, worse yet, the failure of his message and cause. Accordingly, Segundo describes Jesus' cross as an event which seemed to be the most radical lie that history could give to a small community deprived of its leader.[120]

In the resurrection, however, God transformed the cross into a "transcendent datum" which is not a closed door, but an open one through which life, justice, and love flow within history.[121] It is to these experiences of having 'seen'—whatever that word entails—the risen Jesus that all of the gospel testimonies (with the possible exception of Mark) point as the foundation of the ongoing existence of their faith communities. In that regard, Segundo emphasizes that the resurrection became the benchmark for all their reflections about Jesus of Nazareth: "The creative Christologies . . . [of the gospels] would not have had the ability to take off from the historical Jesus if they had not been convinced that the statement, 'Jesus rose from the dead,' was *just as true* as the statement, 'Jesus died on the cross. . . . ' "[122]

What Segundo finds most startling about the resurrection accounts of all four gospels is that the literary genre utilized therein does not change from that used to narrate Jesus' prepaschal life. "It as if we were on the same plane of realities, as if anyone who chanced upon these scenes could have witnessed and verifed the same thing."[123] Nonetheless, Segundo believes that a closer analysis, which he unfolds in four stages, reveals a profound difference between the prepaschal and paschal narratives.

To begin with, it is of considerable note that in regard to the content of the paschal events, the gospels agree on very little beyond the discovery of the empty tomb. "From there on, they disagree on everything: where, when, and to whom the risen one appears; what he says to them; what they believe they know about him; and when he withdraws once and for all from their presence."[124] This diversity especially stands out in light of the general unanimity, particularly within the synoptics, in the narration of prepaschal events.

Second, Segundo claims to detect in the postpaschal accounts a shift in the content of Jesus' teaching as well. It seems as though the disciples gain a new level of comprehension relative to the teaching which Jesus had delivered to them during his earthly ministry (cf. disciples on the Emmaus road) which thereby enables them to envision its future and universal implications. "The experience [lying] behind them is an understanding of Jesus and the following of Jesus which takes place on the psychological and historical level, but which finds its logical origin in the reality of the risen one."[125] In some cases, this even meant a radical change in the nature of that ministry which Jesus had unleashed during his own historical mission. One means Segundo uses to demonstrate this point is by reference to a logion put into the mouth of the risen Jesus by both Matthew and Luke: "Go therefore and make disciples of all nations, baptizing them in the name of the Father, the Son, and of the Holy Spirit" (Matt. 28:19; Lk. 24:47). Here, a mission which had previously been restricted primarily to the Jewish people (Mt. 10:5; 15:24) is universalized after Easter to encompass Jew and non-Jew alike.[126]

Third, the gospels consistently narrate the difficulty which those people who knew Jesus in his prepaschal life have in recognizing him in his resurrected state. Be it in the gospel of John, when Mary Magdalene confuses him with the gardener and Thomas will not believe until he sees the marks of crucifixion, or in Matthew where the disciples meet the risen Jesus "but some doubted" (Mt. 28:17), or in Luke where "their eyes were kept from recognizing him" (Lk. 24:16); throughout Jesus has changed and is only recognized by "some characteristic of him that remains or reappears despite the transformation he has undergone."[127]

Finally, the resurrection, unlike the cross, is never presented as an event which could have been observed by simply anyone, believer and non-believer alike. In fact, collectively the four gospels do not put forth even one impartial witness, or for that matter anyone who had not been a follower of Jesus before the paschal events.

> The resurrected Jesus appears only to those who have believed in his original exhortation and stuck with the values he represented, however weak may have been their understanding of his major ideas and however vacillating may have been their faith when confronted with the scandal of the cross. I repeat: the risen Christ appears *only to them.*"[128]

Hence, it appears that the resurrection became a verification only to those who had already been engaged with Jesus in the realization of a new value structure within human reality, i.e., the reign of God. For these disciples, the resurrection was a confirmation that the historical project of Jesus was indeed the aim of God's ongoing activity in history as well. But to those who had rejected Jesus' vision of God's reign, no universal, verifiable revelation was given; to them Jesus was still the Galilean subversive whose life and message were cut abruptly short on the cross.

These four observations of the resurrection accounts point Segundo to the conclusion that after the resurrection Jesus' disciples attained a new level of comprehension about the person of Jesus and the values for which he lived and died. Although this complex of values, experiences, and beliefs were not such that could be verified by means which the modern world considers scientific or historical, it was obviously nevertheless for them 'objective truth.' It was objective for them in the sense that it became the basis upon which they perceived their own historical reality and upon which they staked their own lives. It is this body of truth-knowledge that Segundo refers to as "transcendent data." "They are data because they do not deal with what ought to be (values) but rather with what is: with reality and its more remote possibilities or probabilities."[129]

In the same manner that Segundo does not elaborate a normative theory of redemption which might explain once and for all the final meaning of Jesus' cross, neither does he formulate a doctrine of resurrection. He is obviously more interested in developing what may appropriately be termed a "resurrection hermeneutics," i.e., the process by which the resurrection may be verified within present historical situations. From that perspective as well, Segundo proclaims the unity of the resurrection and the cross for the modern believer:

> With the resurrection of Jesus we come to a borderline. We cross a
> threshold into the ultimate. But that ultimate is not an abstract cate-
> gory. It is the concrete datum employing the response of total reality to
> the question of the ultimate fate of the values ... that Jesus kept in his
> limited, ideological human existence faced with death.... [130]

But the cross and resurrection only become a unity for those who,
like the disciples, opt for those values exemplified by Jesus and "wager
their life" (faith) that they represent the ultimate reality. Though that
wager is certainly real once it is made concrete in one's own historical situation, its ultimate validation will not arrive until the end of history.
However, in what could only be described as a paradox, the resurrection
operates eschatologically to unveil the future, allowing us to see the victory of life and the cause of humanization as already present.[131]

Summary

The cross and resurrection of Jesus are heralded by Latin American liberation theologians as the central events of Christian faith. In true
Biblical fashion, they proclaim that Jesus died to deliver us from sin and
that he was raised to new life in order to bring salvation to the world. It
is in his resurrection that they discover the complete end and goal of history, and in his person that they understand the manifestation of the
reign of God in all its fullness. In short, Jesus Christ is proclaimed the
historical, universal and cosmic liberator.

Though liberationists believe that the redemption effected by Jesus
Christ has these transcendent and universal dimensions, they emphasize
that these truths must nonetheless be mediated and rendered visible in
concrete acts of salvation. So Jesus himself "translated this universal liberation into practice by implementing a concrete approach to liberation
within his particular situation."[132] He died to deliver human beings from
the sin which lay at the root of an unjust, exploitative world. Thus, the
cross was not "the result of some divine decision independent of history;
it [was] the outcome of the basic option for incarnation in a given situation."[133] He was sentenced to die because of the threat posed by that specific ideology — evident in his words and deeds — which he had chosen
to express the salvific will of God. He entered into the social, political
and religious life of his time in order to reveal a truth about God concerning all of those realities which affect human existence. To preach
the cross of Jesus today, then, means to place it within the conflict, crisis,
suffering, and confrontation which occasioned its historical occurrence.

The resurrection confirms the life of this crucified Jesus. It affirms that the God in whom Jesus placed his trust is not a God of the dead, but of the living. It is this God who breaks the vicious cycle of oppression and exploitation, thereby revealing a hope against injustice and death and the possibility, indeed the promise, of the transformation of an unredeemed world. To have faith in this risen Jesus demands a commitment to 'take up one's cross' in solidarity with the crucified of this world and verify within one's own praxis the reality of his resurrection within present history.

It was clearly this gospel which Oscar Romero proclaimed and enacted within his own life. He believed that the cross and resurrection of Jesus addressed the very paschal core of human existence. Romero proclaimed that the "radical truths of the faith become really truths ... when the church involves itself in the life and death of its people. So the church, like every person, is faced with the most basic option for its faith, being for life or death."[134] Like so many other martyrs in Latin America today, Romero found that to choose for life meant to suffer and die for the sake of others. But in light of the resurrection of Jesus, Romero's life was one more sign that to die that way is to live.

Notes

1. Leonardo Boff, *Passion of Christ*, 68.

2. Sobrino, *Jesús en América Latina*, 188.

3. The details of this incident were related to me by Octavio Ortiz' father, San Antonio Abad (San Salvador), 28 August 1988.

4. Oscar Romero, interview by Tommy Sue Montgomery, 14 December 1979, *Revolution in El Salvador: Origins and Evolution* (Boulder, CO: Westview Press, 1982), 111.

5. Ibid.

6. The meetings were organized as part of a delegation sponsored and led by Central American Mission Partners (CAMP). I was present at all of the meetings, including a large gathering commemorating the fifth anniversary of Romero's assassination, San Salvador, 17–24 March 1985.

7. *"Si me matan, resucitaré en el pueblo salvadoreño."*

8. Salvadoran church workers, interview by author, San Salvador, 22 March 1985.

9. Curt Cadorette, *From the Heart of the People: The Theology of Gustavo Gutiérrez* (Oak Park, IL: Meyer-Stone Books, 1988), 115.

10. Gutiérrez, *Theology of Liberation,* 153.

11. Gutiérrez, *Power of the Poor,* 61.

12. Ibid.

13. Gutiérrez, *Theology of Liberation,* 158.

14. Ibid., 161.

15. Ibid., 153.

16. The first discussion of the historical Jesus in *Theology of Liberation* does not come until page 225, well after he has laid the foundation of his Christological framework. In a subsection entitled "Jesus and the Political World," Gutiérrez discusses the life of the historical Jesus in relationship to social ethics, 225–232.

17. Gutiérrez, *Theology of Liberation,* 176; cf. *Poor in History,* 63. In his consideration of the debate which took place between Bultmann and Bonhoeffer over the interpretation of the Word of God in history, Gutiérrez sides with the latter when he "defines 'thinking theologically' as thinking from a point of departure in the 'incarnation, crucifixion, and resurrection of Jesus Christ,' " *Poor in History,* 227.

18. Sobrino, *Christology at the Crossroads,* 193.

19. Gutiérrez, *Theology of Liberation,* 226.

20. Cf. Segundo's statement on this subject which was quoted in chapter Two.

As a sidelight, it is interesting to note that Gutiérrez was not alone with his early emphasis on the exodus. In his 1982 overview of salvation history from a Latin American liberation perspective, Dupartuis devoted almost his entire study to a consideration of the Old Testament. In his extremely brief section on the New Testament, he provides the reader with a clue to the underlying reason: "When the New Testament tells of the saving work of God in Christ, the major portion of the vocabulary it uses is drawn from the Exodus event. Such New Testament words as 'redeem,' 'redemption,' 'deliver' . . . have an Exodus ring to them. The liberation that Jesus brings, however, in light of the Gospels, is not political," *Soteriology,* 275.

21. Gutiérrez, *Power of the Poor,* 13.

22. Ibid. Gutiérrez writes in a later text, "To profess 'this Jesus,' to acknowledge 'Jesus the Christ,' is to express a conviction. It is not simply putting a name and a title together; it is an authentic confession of faith. It is the assertion of an identity: the Jesus of history, the son of Mary, the carpenter of Nazareth, the preacher of Galilee, the crucified, *is* the Only Begotten of God, the Christ, the Son of God," *We Drink From Our Own Wells: The Spiritual Journey of a People,*" trans. Matthew O'Connell (Maryknoll: Orbis Books, 1984), 46. He further adds, "The

affirmation that Jesus of Nazareth is the Messiah, the Christ, is the nucleus of Christological faith," ibid.

23. Gutiérrez, *Power of the Poor*, 15.

24. Gutiérrez formulates the meaning of the cross in relation to what it tells us about the nature of God. Borrowing a theme developed by Bonhoeffer, he discusses the significance of a God who suffers, and thereby enters into identification with the suffering of the world: "God is a God who saves us not only through his domination but through his suffering. Here we have Bonhoeffer's famous thesis of God's *weakness*. ... It is of this God, and only of this God, that the Bible tells us. And it is thus that the cross acquires its tremendous revelatory potential with respect to God's weakness as an expression of his love for a world come of age," ibid., 230.

25. Ibid., 104–5. Two other statements of note in *Power of the Poor* reinforce that point: "Of course, his practice took him to a violent death. He dies in solidarity with the violent death of the oppressed in the world. ... He died before his time, by execution. Nor were his days thereby ended, for his resurrection is an affirmation of life, confirming him as the Christ, the messiah, and setting the seal of God's approval on his message of justice and life, the message that defied a homicidal society," ibid., 96.

Moreover, he writes: "The universality of the new covenant passes by way of Christ's death and is sealed by his resurrection. Jesus' death is the consequence of his struggle for justice, his proclamation of the kingdom, and his identification with the poor, ibid., 15.

26. Gutiérrez, *We Drink From Our Own Wells*, 50–1. In one of his more profound statements on discipleship, Gutiérrez adds, "To the question, 'Who do you say that I am?' we cannot give a merely theoretical or theological answer. What answers it, in the final analysis, is our life, our personal history, our manner of living the gospel," ibid.

27. Gutiérrez, *Poor in History*, 143.

28. Gutiérrez, *Theology of Liberation*, 35. Gutiérrez describes how he understands Jesus Christ as the hermeneutical principle of Christian life: "This then is the fundamental hermeneutical circle: from humanity to God and from God to humanity, from history to faith and from faith to history, from the human word to the word of the Lord and from the word of the Lord to the human word, from the love of one's brothers and sisters to the love of the Father and from the love of the Father to one's brothers and sisters, from human justice to God's holiness and from God's holiness to human justice," *Power of the Poor*, 61.

29. Boff, *Liberator*, Preface (not part of the original text; written in 1978 with the publication of the book in English), xii.

30. Segundo confirms this notion with his appraisal of Boff's work: "I think that Leonardo Boff's *Liberator* suffers from the fact that it was his first

work completed after his theological studies in Europe," *The Historical Jesus,* 190, n. 2.

31. Boff, *Liberator,* 43.

32. Ibid., 206–225.

33. Cook, "Christology in Latin America," 269.

34. Boff's own description of the motivation behind his *Liberator* in "Images of Jesus in Brazilian Liberal Christianity," in *Faces,* 26. In *Liberator* it is the incarnation itself which shapes Boff's understanding of redemption. For example, Boff asserts that "by means of the Incarnation we come to know who in fact we are and what we are destined for," ibid., 205. Cf. also the discussion on p. 122.

35. Ibid., 236.

36. "Jesus lived the human archetype just as God wanted, when he made him to his own image and likeness . . . ," ibid., 118.

37. Ibid., 118–9.

38. Ibid., 229.

39. The Pharisees, for example, are angered by Jesus' "universal message" which relativizes their interpretation of law and the foundation of their religious system. However, Boff does not explore the socio-historical factors underlying these threats. For instance, he supposes that Jesus was condemned as a blasphemer by the Jews although, in Boff's words, "they knew his mission was not political." Moreover, Boff suggests that during the trial before Pilate (whom he believes saw no inherent danger to Jesus' ministry), the Jewish leaders were able to use deceptive tactics to transform religious accusations into those of a political character. See *Liberator,* 104–118.

40. Ibid., 237–8. Boff consistently portrays Jesus as an ideal Christ figure who is free from the ambiguity/impurity of taking an oppositional stand; consider the contradictory statement made earlier in this passage: "Christ is not *against* anything. He is in favor of love, spontaneity, and liberty. It is in the name of this positiveness that at times he has to be against something," ibid., 68.

41. Tamez articulates this concern in practical terms: "When we Christians speak of oppression in Latin America, we cannot afford to do it in abstract, universal, nonanalytic terms. We are speaking, after all, of an experience that is very concrete: of political and economic tyranny, of despoilation, torture, assassination, imprisonment, disappearance. . . . The same could be said of the Biblical experience of oppression," *Bible of the Oppressed,* 3.

42. Boff, *Liberator,* 245.

43. Ibid., 240–2.

44. Ibid., Preface, xii.

45. Ibid., Epilogue, 264–5.

46. Of course, Boff recognizes that this exegetical task is not done in a vacuum: "When we inquire about Christ's liberation and its meaningfulness in terms of the liberating process of Latin America, we are already pointing the response in a certain direction and setting up a viewpoint through which we will scan the words, life, and historical journey of Jesus Christ," "Christ's Liberation via Oppression," 101.

47. Boff, *Liberator*, Epilogue, 266.

48. Leonardo Boff, *Jesucristo y Nuestro Futuro de Liberación* (Bogotá: Inter-American Press Service, 1978), 23.

49. Boff, *Passion of Christ*, 3.

50. Ibid., 22.

51. Boff, "Christ's Liberation via Oppression, p. 102.

52. Ibid., 116.

53. Boff takes issue with Moltmann's theology of the cross here. He charges that when Moltmann identifies suffering with the realization of the divine Self, he risks reducing the cause of Jesus' death to the struggle going on within God, thereby finding the cause of the cross within the nature of God's own Self, *Passion of Christ*, 111–6. See my discussion of Jon Sobrino's theology of the cross later in this chapter.

54. *Passion of Christ*, 89.

55. I agree completely with Juan Luis Segundo who, when quoting this selection from Boff's writings, names it exactly this: "a gospel for Latin America." For those who wish that he would treat the term "gospel" more metaphorically, he comments, "I grant that Boff's version is partial because it refers to only the passion and resurrection, but it is no more partial than, say, the Letter to the Hebrews. So what exactly is the problem in giving it the same status as the four canonical Gospels or what Paul called his gospel?," *The Historical Jesus*, 6.

56. *Passion of Christ*, 130–133. I prefer the translation given here, which is taken from the translation of Segundo's work, *The Historical Jesus*, 3–6.

57. Ibid.

58. Bussmann, *Who Do You Say*, 126. It must be mentioned that Bussmann is extremely sympathetic to the cause of liberation theology, and his book more than anything is structured so as to permit Latin American theologians to present their own case. Nevertheless, at some points I disagree with his editorial comments.

59. In essence, Marxsen suggested that the resurrection should not truly be considered a historical act, but rather a product of the disciples' interpretation

of the 'appearances' of Jesus. In other words, 'resurrection' is more a matter of speaking than a real event in history. Along with Bultmann, however, Marxsen did not seek to thereby imply that nothing happened after the death of Jesus. What he did intend to convey is that what did happen is only accessible to faith (*geschichtlich*) and inaccessible to the historian (*historisch*) as such.

60. *Liberator*, Epilogue, 291. Boff adds, "The meaning of the resurrection as total liberation only becomes clear when it is set in a context of Jesus' struggle for the establishment of the kingdom in this world," ibid.

61. Boff, *Passion of Christ*, 66. Boff does not believe that one can understand "the *full* import of the historical Jesus derived from mere analysis of history itself. It must be read and interpreted on the basis of the complete revelation of his course that is to be found in the resurrection," *Liberator*, Epilogue, 280.

62. In Boff's estimation then, "the cross demonstrates the conflict-ridden nature of every process of liberation undertaken when the structure of injustice has gained the upperhand," *Liberator*, Epilogue, 290.

63. Boff considers the declaration of Jesus in Mark, "My God, my God, why hast thou forsaken me," to be perhaps the only historically authentic words uttered by Jesus on the cross in the gospel accounts. See ibid., 111.

64. Boff, *Jesucristo y la Liberación del Hombre* (Madrid: Ediciones Cristiandad, 1981), 465.

65. Ibid. Boff emphasizes that it is this interpretation of the resurrection which clearly counters the assertions of Marxsen: "The personal encounter [with Jesus] is much richer than simple seeing; it is a communion of persons, a being in a mutual presence . . . ," ibid.

66. Ibid., 466. In response to Bultmann, Boff believes that this recognition is quite fundamental for faith in the present day: " . . . In light of I Cor. 15:38, the oldest testimony written of the resurrection . . . we must ask Bultmann if the relation of the resurrection to history is as irrelevant as he thinks. The resurrection is not a myth which one could say that nothing happened . . . ," ibid., 462.

67. Boff, *Passion of Christ*, 66.

68. Boff distinguishes between the Hebrew and Greek conception of body, noting that the Hebrew conception is tied to essential identity and not cellular physiology. Hence, "the body of resurrection will possess the same personal identity, but not material as that which we had in temporal space. We cannot confuse corporal identity with material identity," *Liberación del Hombre*, 530. See larger discussion on 497–533.

69. Boff, *Passion of Christ*, 67. In "Christ's Liberation via Oppression," Boff quotes a profound statement written by James Cone in support of his interpretation: "His resurrection is the disclosure that God is not defeated by oppression

but transforms it into the possibility of freedom. For men and women who live in an oppressive society, this means that they do not have to behave as if *death* is the ultimate. God in Christ has set us free from death . . . ," 123.

70. In his reflections on the resurrection, Boff actually appears closer to Pannenberg and Moltmann than he does to Marxsen! See Wolfhart Pannenberg, *Jesus—God and Man*. Pannenberg presents Jesus Christ, as a result of his resurrection, as the pre-determined ("proleptic") end of history. Moltmann reinterprets this approach within the context of a more specific concern for justice within history; cf. *Crucified God*.

71. Boff, *Liberator*, 207.

72. Ibid., Epilogue, 279.

73. Boff, "Christ's Liberation via Oppression," 102.

74. Jon Sobrino, interview by author, San Salvador, 16 January 1988. In *Jesús en América Latina*, Sobrino quotes Assmann in order to dramatize this very point: "If the historical situation of dependency and domination of two-thirds of humanity, with its 30 million annual deaths from hunger and malnutrition, does not become the starting point for whatever Christian theology today, that theology will not be able to historically situate and concretize its fundamental themes," 78.

75. Sobrino, *Christology at the Crossroads*, xvi–xix.

76. Ibid., xv. In actual fact, he described his book as such in the Preface which he added to its English publication in 1978. Subsequently, the English title was taken from that statement. The original title in Spanish, as noted previously, is *Cristología desde América Latina*. The majority of the material in this section will be drawn from that book and from *Jesús en Latin América*, a shorter book written in 1982 in order to respond to the questions and criticisms raised by the earlier text.

77. Ibid., xxiv. It must be pointed out that Sobrino's usage of the term "historical" can at times be misleading. He does not limit its meaning to that which may be discovered by means of historical investigation. Often he uses the term interchangeably with the term "kerygmatic." Thus, the kerygmatic presentation of Jesus in the gospels is commonly accepted as historical (although at the same time he does clearly recognize their nature as theological documents). For instance, in a discussion of the definition of doxological and kerygmatic statements, Sobrino remarks, "I call the latter 'historical statements' for the sake of more readily understandable nomenclature," ibid., 344, n. 6. In other words, faith reflections concerning events which have transpired in history would be considered historical by Sobrino as much as the event itself.

Although I would agree that our knowledge of every event comes to us already interpreted, and that a purely objective account does not exist, it nevertheless appears to me necessary to maintain more rigor in the descriptive categories theology employs; otherwise, the consequent ambiguity obfuscates our own analysis of historical categories within the present reality.

78. Ibid., 180.

79. Ibid., 181.

80. Moltmann, *The Crucified God.* The order of Sobrino's presentation in *Christology at the Crossroads* is obviously dependent upon Moltmann's study, a fact which can be detected simply by reading the chapter titles of Moltmann's book: chapter One: "The Identity and Relevance of Faith"; chapter Two: "The Resistance of the Cross against Its Interpretations"; chapter Three: "Questions about Jesus"; chapter Four: "The Historical Trial of Jesus"; chapter Five: "The Eschatological Trial of Jesus"; chapter Six: "The Crucified God"; chapter Seven: "Ways towards the Psychological Liberation of Man"; chapter Eight: "Ways towards the Political Liberation of Man."

81. *Christology at the Crossroads,* 204.

82. Ibid., 204 – 9. It is remarkable to see the extent to which Sobrino, the Jesuit, has accepted here the theological framework of the Protestant theologians of the new quest (not to mention Karl Barth!). Cf. Käsemann: "Jesus came ... to say how things stand with the kingdom that has dawned, namely that God has drawn near man in grace and requirement. He brought and lived the freedom of the children of God, who remain children and free only so long as they find in the Father their Lord."

83. Sobrino, *Christology at the Crossroads,* 203 – 4. Sobrino disputes Bultmann's conviction that Jesus was crucified by the Roman's as a result of a "misunderstanding," i.e., of Jesus' purely religious ministry as somehow political. He challenges Bultmann's view on both a historical and a theological level; see ibid., 211 – 5.

84. Jon Sobrino, "Tésis sobre una Cristología Histórica," *Estudios Centroamericanos* 30 (1975): 469. See also the discussion in *Christology at the Crossroads,* 217 – 9, at which point Moltmann is quoted: "Jesus preached God's approaching nearness in grace as no one ever had before in Israel. ... Someone who had lived and acted in this way, who was wholly conscious of the nearness of God, could not experience death on the cross as confirmation or as mere misfortune. He could only experience it as hellish abandonment by the very God whose loving nearness he had proclaimed," 218.

85. Sobrino, *Christology at the Crossroads,* 219. Of course, behind all of these affirmations is the foundation laid by Barth's conception of God. Sobrino and Moltmann both pose the cross as a critique of all theological understandings which presuppose an understanding of God's character outside of God's revelation in Jesus Christ. For instance, Sobrino quotes Barth to support one of the primary themes of his book: "Whenever Christian faith focuses one-sidedly on

the Christ of faith, and wittingly or unwittingly forgets the historical Jesus, and to the extent it does that, it loses its specific structure as Christian faith and tends to turn into religion," ibid., 275.

86. Ibid., 380.

87. Ibid., 202. Sobrino rhetorically asks, "Is God revealed only at key highpoints in Jesus' life such as his baptism, his transfiguration, his crucifixion, and his resurrection? Or does the revelation of God take place all along in the revelation of the Son . . . ?" Sobrino affirms the latter option, ibid.

88. Ibid., 371.

89. Ibid., 214. Sobrino presents an extensive case for these premises in chapter 10, entitled "The Christological Dogmas," 311 – 345. Cf. also his treatment of Jesus' particularity as the starting point for affirmations about God and humanity in *Jesús en América Latina*, 43 – 7.

Segundo has also written at some length supporting this notion. For example, he writes, "Whoever has not had the experience (earthly) of love (*agape*) cannot form a correct concept of God and employ it in a sentence such as *God is love* or *Jesus is God*. The semantic path is the inverse: out of the experience comes the content that is necessary to give to the term *God*. If, then, the affirmation that Jesus is God is equal to saying that Jesus, with the values that are represented, in an iconic way, in his life, constitutes the absolute for me, then language will gain something in meaning and clarity," *Las Cristologías de la Espiritualidad*, 647.

Once again, at another point in this same work, Segundo adds, "In the affirmation 'Jesus is God' the information did not pass from an already known proclamation to a historical figure of Jesus, ambiguous and indecisive. On the contrary, the concept of divinity . . . had to be filled with the attributes that arose from the concrete history of Jesus. This means that every 'cosmic' interpretation of Jesus must begin with that which we know of his history, and not with that which we supposedly know about who is, or can be, God," ibid., 892.

90. Sobrino, *Christology at the Crossroads*, 225.

91. Ibid., 195–8.

92. Ibid., 196–7.

93. G. W. F. Hegel, *Philosophy of Religion*, vol. 3 (London: Routledge and Kegan Paul, 1968), 98– 100.

94. Boff, *Passion of Christ*, 114–5.

95. David Batstone, "The Transformation of the Messianic Idea in Judaism and Christianity in Light of the Holocaust: Reflections on the Writings of Elie Wiesel," *Journal of Ecumenical Studies* 23, no. 4 (Fall 1986), 593. In this article, I explore these themes of the mutuality of divine and human redemption in relation to the writings of Elie Wiesel.

Wiesel recounts a legend which in many ways captures the mystery of this understanding of redemption: "Legend tells us that one day man spoke to God in this wise: 'Let us change about. You be man, and I will be God. For only one second.'

God smiled gently and asked him, 'Aren't you afraid?'

'No. And you?'

'Yes, I am,' God said.

Nevertheless, he granted man's desire. He became a man, and the man took his place and immediately availed himself of his omnipotence: he refused to revert to his previous state. So neither God nor man was ever again what he seemed to be. Years passed, centuries, perhaps eternities. And suddenly the drama quickened. The past for one, and the present for the other, were too heavy to be borne. As the liberation of the one was bound to the liberation of the other, they renewed the ancient dialogue whose echoes come to us in the night, charged with hatred, with remorse, and most of all, with infinite yearning," *Town Beyond the Wall* (New York: Avon Books, 1964), 190.

96. Boff, *Passion of Christ*, 114.

97. Sobrino, *Christology at the Crossroads*, 224.

98. Sobrino, "Temas Fundamentales para la Cristología," in *Jesús en América Latina*. This book is a collection of essays, some of which were published previously. "Temas Fundamentales" and one other essay were published therein for the first time (1982).

99. In Spanish, *'pro-existencia'* (literally, pro-being or pro-existence) or again later, *'pro-existencia parcial en favor de otros'* (pro-being on behalf of others). Although Sobrino does not acknowledge it, Jesus as a 'being-for-others' was first fully developed by Bonhoeffer in his short Christology. Sobrino is here extrapolating from some terms used by Karl Rahner, that Jesus is not *'supra-existencia'* nor *'contra-existencia,'* but *'pro-existencia.'* ibid., 44.

Bonhoeffer has had a tremendous, though not always recognized, influence on Latin American liberation theologians. Based on my relationships with the churches of Central America, I have discovered that many communities, especially Protestant, began their theological journey toward liberation theology inspired by their reading and discussion of *The Cost of Discipleship*, trans. R. H. Fuller (London: SCM Press, 1959).

100. Ibid., 45–7.

101. Sobrino, "El Jesús Histórico, Crisis, y Desafío," 17.

102. Sobrino, *Christology at the Crossroads*, 225.

Cf. Moltmann: "Those who hope in Christ can no longer put up with reality as it is but, beginning to suffer under it, move to contradict it. Peace with God means conflict with the world, because the goad of the promised future stabs into the flesh of every unfulfilled present," *Theology of Hope*, trans. James Leitch (London: SCM Press, 1967), 313.

103. Sobrino, "El Jesús Histórico, Crisis, y Desafío," 17. In his earlier work, Sobrino hailed the historical Jesus as the "hermeneutic principle that enables us to draw closer to the totality of Christ both in terms of knowledge and in terms of real-life praxis," *Christology at the Crossroads,* 9.

104. Segundo, *The Historical Jesus,* 17.

105. Ibid., 16–8, 39.

106. Ibid., 35. In actual fact, Segundo cites both Bultmann and Rahner as those theologians most helpful in pointing towards an "anthropological faith," i.e., in terms of what Jesus has to say about human existence. Essentially, however, the hermeneutical method is associated with Bultmann's work. Segundo turns to Rahner for a better explication of the preunderstanding both Rahner and Bultmann find in Heidegger's work. See the discussion on 32–8.

It would be important to note here as well that Segundo distinguishes between the phrases "Jesus is absolute" and "the Absolute in Jesus." The foundation for this distinction can be found in his understanding of faith and ideology. The Absolute who encounters us in the message of Jesus challenges us to conversion, to the change of values and activities which rule our lives. It is a call to complete faith in the God who acted in Jesus to bring salvation. However, faith as a surrender of one's trust to God may not be equated with a specific ideology, for ideology will necessarily change depending upon both the context and commitments of the believer. Despite its foundation in relative values, ideologies are nonetheless lived subjectively as absolute values within a particular context; yet, faith may require at some point a change of ideologies as one's context changes. "So even though Christian faith could be said to have absolute value, it lacks any precise instrument for measuring the historical life of Christians by pre-established standards," ibid., 107.

107. Ibid., 32–8. At certain points, however, Segundo diverges from Bultmann, more in the area of content rather than in method. For instance, in regard to the second element, that of uncovering a preunderstanding within which Jesus' significance may be meaningfully presented to today's world, Segundo suggests an alternative meaning-world than that employed by Bultmann. Transcendental anthropology—the preunderstanding used extensively by Bultmann (cf. Heidegger)—claims to be immersed in concrete, historical categories. Segundo charges that in actuality it is based in "abstract, existential categories" which prescind from the very history within which that existence is said to be shaped. For that reason alone, he does not consider it to be the most appropriate theory from which to form a preunderstanding which encompasses the experiences of the Latin American people. He recognizes that every preunderstanding is inherently shaped by the ideological world of its creator; consequently, not only Bultmann but every interpreter must always be subject to the self-criticism provoked by one's own praxis and that of one's community.

In the first chapter of *Liberation of Theology,* Segundo also deals with Bultmann's hermeneutical circle. At that point, he elaborates on Bultmann's failure to include the consideration of ideology within the steps of his hermeneutical process.

108. Ibid., 39, italics mine. Segundo realizes that many theologians would undoubtedly criticize him for turning Christology into anthropology. I agree with his appraisal that such criticisms are based on a false epistemological dichotomy, viz., that we have a choice of starting with divine, otherworldly, knowledge or with knowledge grounded in human understanding (which is implicitly inferior by its very nature). In my opinion it is only by starting with our own human reality that we can arrive at any understanding of God's revelation in Jesus Christ; if not, what would have been the point of incarnation?

109. Ibid., 10.

110. Ibid., 39.

111. "My aim is to arrange and verify the most historically reliable data about Jesus of Nazareth, so I shifted postpaschal data from the domain of history to that of faith's interpretation of Jesus and events." ibid., 166. He provides a more complete explanation for this Christologically motivated arrangement of material in the Introduction of *The Humanist Christology of Paul*, 1–11.

112. Segundo, *The Historical Jesus*, 194, n. 15. The term "deconstruction" of redemptive language has been adopted from Boff. Essentially, Segundo uses it in the same way as Bultmann's demythologization, but he believes it clarifies some of the difficulties which the latter term carries with it. In Boff's words, "To deconstruct means to see the building in terms of its construction plan and redo the construction process, pointing up temporal nature and possible obsolescence of the representational material, while at the same time, revealing the permanent value of its import and intent . . . ," ibid.

113. Segundo, *The Historical Jesus*, 39.

114. Segundo, *Las Cristologías de la Espiritualidad*, 833.

115. Segundo, *The Humanist Christology of Paul*, 182. Despite his fresh approach to Biblical hermeneutics, it should not be overlooked that Segundo is thoroughly steeped in the historical-critical tradition. He outlines three basic criteria for establishing the "historical trustworthiness" (not truth or falsity) of a given text. First, he assumes that the post-Easter experiences of the early Christian community reinterpret the prepaschal events. As a result, he considers those texts which make no reference to the passion, death, and resurrection of Jesus historically trustworthy. For example, on that basis he considers the messianic titles 'Son of Man' and 'suffering servant' as later redactions of the gospel writers and/or their communities. Second, though not unrelated to the first criterion, he eliminates from consideration those texts which betray an awareness of the existence of the church. Finally, he details the literary criteria. Here he is largely in concert with the results of North Atlantic historical investigations that Mark (or pre-Mark) and Q were sources utilized by at least the two other synoptic writers and possibly by John. See *The Historical Jesus*, 45–70.

116. Segundo, *The Historical Jesus,* 71–85. Segundo does find that the political key is more appropriate for the gospels of Mark and Luke than it is for Matthew.

117. Segundo admits that after the resurrection of Jesus the early Christian communities do not reaffirm Jesus' political message and seem to shift the emphasis from Jesus' prophetic denunciation of oppressive conditions and structures to a proclamation of Jesus' person as Messiah. In that regard, he writes, "Now 'salvation' in 'the name of Jesus' takes the place of the 'year of grace,' that is, the realization on earth of the values of the kingdom that will transform the plight of the poorest and most exploited members of Israelite society. . . . "
The reason he offers for this transition is that the paschal experiences were too overwhelming for the communities: "At first the cross seemed to be the most radical lie that history could give to the pretensions of a small community deprived of its leader and defender. By the same token, the experiences of the risen Jesus constituted the most powerful confirmation that reality could offer a seemingly defeated and disrupted community. . . . And whether we approve or disapprove, it was only natural that it would center the attention and preaching of the Christian community on a point other than the one that was central for Jesus himself." Thus, although the early communities might not have confirmed that key which seems to be central in the life of the synoptic Jesus, Segundo believes it is still the place from which to start our own Christologies, ibid., 182–8.
I personally find his arguments in this section quite unsatisfactory. Most promising of the motives that he suggests lies behind this "shift in emphasis" is the recognition of the changing milieu and demands placed upon a nascent community. However, to claim that the "paschal experiences had too much of an impact on the nascent church for us to expect that it would simply pick up the pre-paschal themes of Jesus" does not appear to have sufficient foundation.

118. Ibid., 94.

119. "In the end, all four Gospels attribute the violent death of Jesus to the religio-political authorities, who saw him as a threat to their own power," ibid.

120. Ibid., 185.

121. Ibid., 10.

122. Ibid., 167. Within his study of the synoptic gospels, Segundo devotes solely two brief appendixes to the resurrection accounts. At times, he treats the gospels as if they were only collected data about the historical Jesus from which we may understand the launching of other New Testament Christologies. For example, he describes his approach to the New Testament material in the following manner: "I made it clear that it was not my intention to explore the special Christology of each of the Synoptics. I have looked in them for the most historically certain data about Jesus of Nazareth. Forced to choose between Christologies, I prefer to move from the history of Jesus and an appendix on the historical experiences of his resurrection by the disciples to the Christology of Paul in his Letter to the Romans," ibid., 218, n. 3.

But would it not be important to consider the Christologies within which that "data" are presented in order to understand why that material has been arranged and presented differently by each gospel writer? Surely the gospel writers had interests and ideologies as strong as Paul, but chose a different form, viz., narrative, by which to express their own Christologies; in fact, the choice of a narrative form itself is no doubt tied up with those commitments. Segundo himself stresses that Jesus always appears to us as already interpreted and that "we have no access to him except through *those interests* in one way or another," ibid., 17.

In a later discussion, Segundo seemingly confirms this very point: "Hence the wrongheadedness of many exegetes (e.g. Pannenberg) in resorting to Paul (I Cor. 15:5–8) for their discussion of the resurrection, not only because he has the older formulation of the event, but also, and at bottom, because they think his formula is *more sober.* Exactly the opposite is the case. Paul's list makes one think of a historical sequence as verifiable as, for example, that relating to the death of Socrates. By contrast, the gospel accounts, with their odd literary genre, are much more reticent in identifying the facts narrated with any historical material," 218–9, n. 9.

123. Ibid., 167. Segundo finds most surprising that John resorts to the same literary style here as do the synoptic writers: "The author of the fourth Gospel knew how to create new literary genres combining symbolism, philosophy, and theology in order to recount the activities of the prepaschal Jesus. But he *goes back* to the literary genre of the Synoptics (or one very similar to it) where we would least expect him to: in narrating the appearances of the resurrected Jesus," ibid., 167–8.

124. Ibid., 168.

125. Ibid., 170.

126. Ibid., 169.

127. Ibid., 170.

128. Ibid., 171. In more explicit terms, Segundo adds, "Jesus' appearances confirm the existing faith of the witnesses; they are not a valid proof independent of that already existing faith," ibid., 170. A similar view has been developed extensively elsewhere in European theology, most notably by Ebeling and Rahner.

129. Ibid., 173.

130. Ibid., 175.

131. Ibid., 10. Segundo adds: "They [the evangelists] tell us that the disciples had an opportunity to peep into the ultimate and there verify, in the risen Jesus, a basic transcendent datum. The ultimate in the midst of history . . . ," ibid., 175.

The notion of eschatological verification has also been developed extensively in European political theology. For instance, Dorothy Soëlle has put forth a similar understanding of the cross and resurrection which seeks its verification in the transformation of history: " . . . [The] differentiation and communication of the kingdom of God and the world need not be made in idealistic terms; the starting point is the particular history of Jesus, which ends on earth with the cross and eschatologically with the liberation of all things," Soëlle, *Perspektiven der Theologie* (1968), 71–2, quoted in Moltmann, *Crucified God*, 330, n. 8.

132. Boff, "Christ's Liberation via Oppression, 103.

133. Sobrino, *Christology at the Crossroads*, 214.

134. Oscar Romero, quoted in Phillip Berryman, *The Religious Roots of Rebellion: Christians in Central American Revolutions* (Maryknoll: Orbis Books, 1984), 331.

CHAPTER FOUR

Christ in Latin America Today

What is a matter of life and death for our human (and Christian) existence today is our ability to create Christologies that are valid for our own context and, at the same time, faithful to Jesus of Nazareth, the historical Jesus.

—*Juan Luis Segundo*[1]

How does one even begin to respond to the most elemental (even if surreptitiously so) of all Christological questions: Who is Jesus Christ in Latin America today?

For some, the answer will seem quite obvious: he is the same figure that he was yesterday, is today, and will be tomorrow. Put simply, a faithful reading of the New Testament witness will reveal his enduring significance to the Christian community just as it has to past generations and cultures. Others, who manifest the concern to be more contextual would argue that this first approach ignores the vast gulf which separates the meaning-world of the first century from that of the present day. Hence, though they would concur that the image of Jesus which appears in the New Testament will provide the substance of a contemporary understanding, they would stipulate at the same time an additional methodological condition: the necessity of updating the language and conceptual framework within which that Biblical Christology was formed so that it might become more meaningful and relevant to a modern world. Interpreters of this second persuasion, then, view their primary challenge as one of translation — the perennial task of enabling a revealed truth, given once and for all, to speak in new situations with the same dynamism which occasioned its original presentation.

At numerous points throughout the course of this study I have sought to expose the limitations of both these Christological methods, despite their broad acceptance within the Christian church. The first inadequacy is that they fail to appreciate the ongoing activity of the Spirit of Jesus in that history which has transpired from the time of the closing of the Scriptural canon until the present day. For all intents and purposes, it is assumed that nothing new about Jesus has been learned—or given to be learned — since the ascension event. In other words, Jesus Christ, as the definitive witness of God's being and will, is revealed only twice in the course of human history: once in the first century in Palestine through the person of Jesus of Nazareth, and the other time in the future when he returns from his heavenly abode as the 'Son of Man.' The first revelation is taken as actual, and the second one as promise.

On another level, these methods fundamentally misrepresent the very character of those texts to which they appeal as an absolute source for their own Christologies. They suppose that the interpreter need only accumulate everything which may be known about Jesus as he is presented in the Scripture and then apply those findings to the present situation.[2] In that regard, they presuppose a unidimensional understanding of Jesus which may be discovered simply by starting from the first book of the gospels and running all the way through to the last book of Revelation. Those inconsistencies which might appear are quite handily subsumed within a larger whole which is held to constitute Jesus Christ's universal character as the Savior of the world.

One need not go farther than the Biblical texts themselves, however, to demonstrate that both of these premises suffer from a lack of methodological rigor. If they were to be accepted uncritically, one would likely walk away from the New Testament not so much with a prepackaged solution to the Christological quest as one would with a disturbing question that has no ready answer: Which of all the witnesses to the life of Jesus has given the true and proper interpretation?

The Dialogue Between Historical Testimony and Living Faith in Liberation Theology

Even a cursory reading of the New Testament manifests that the fourth gospel presents an image of Jesus quite distinct from that reflected in the synoptic texts. A closer investigation would reveal that, despite their initial appearance of unanimity, the three synoptic gospels paint irreconcilable portraits of Jesus as well. The gap widens further still once the Pauline writings — whichever epistles are included under that category—are taken into account, not to mention their own rupture with that image of Jesus found in James' epistle, and that from the Christology of the Letter of Hebrews, and thus the litany could continue.

This observation presents a special challenge for those who seek to interpret the New Testament:

> The *poor* were a central object of Jesus' message as it is presented in the Synoptic Gospels (in different shadings, to be sure); but that central theme disappears completely in the Christology ... of the first eight chapters of Paul's Letter to the Romans. In the interpretation of both the Synoptics and Paul, Jesus is apparently quite insensitive to the monstrous evil embodied in the almost absolute power of the Roman Empire, but in the community from which we get the Book of Revelation (or, the Apocalypse), Jesus becomes the slain Lamb who emerges victorious over the Beast, the very embodiment of that absolute power in its various transfigurations. Who interpreted Jesus correctly?[3]

And Segundo here only skims the surface of the crisis that this plurality presents to a systematic elaboration of a uniform, Biblical Christology.

For that reason, the answer one gives to the question "Who was right?" generally determines the shape of one's Christology. All too often a singular image of Jesus is chosen as the normative center around which the other Christological elements of the New Testament are thought to coalesce. For the sake of elucidation, let it be supposed that the portrayal of Jesus as the new Adam as it is developed in Paul's epistle to the Romans is the Christology *par excellence* of the New Testament. In that case, the gospel material which treats Jesus' faithful and unswerving obedience to the will of God and to the demands of God's reign, as well as those narratives which relate Jesus' refusal to succumb to the wiles of temptation, would undoubtedly come to the forefront in order to reinforce the general character of that image. Moreover, recourse could surely be made to those statements from the Letter to the Hebrews which highlight Jesus' sinlessness and purity, as well as the description of Jesus as "the innocent Lamb who was slain" in the Book of Revelation. Varying degrees of support could be drawn from material contained in other sections of the New Testament as well until a systematic Christology could be presented to the contemporary faith community as the dogmatic norm for its understanding of Jesus as the new Adam.

But the final product would be partial, as would any other systematic Christology which would purport to speak for the whole of the New Testament witness. The creation of the new Adam Christology is unique to the cultural milieu, religious identity, community life, and general meaning-world within which the Apostle Paul sought to explicate the significance of Jesus' life, death and resurrection. Paul wrote within a 'life situation' (*Sitz im Leben*) that was obviously worlds apart from that setting within which Matthew, for instance, elaborated his gospel. Thus, to selectively lift out elements of Matthew's presentation of Jesus — described succinctly, the coming into being of the Christian messiah — and arbitrarily combine them with fragments shaped within Paul's representation, would merely serve to distort the richness which each Christology has to offer in its own right. Perhaps most importantly, although its intended goal would be to make the significance of Jesus nearer and clearer to the modern faith community, the aggregate product of such an undertaking would more likely move the community further away from a comprehension of Jesus within its own life situation.

If a rather crude parallel would not offend, it would be equally ludicrous to seek to define to a group of music students the depth of the C-major key by mixing fragments from Mozart, Brahms and the Beatles, thus forming one comprehensive musical score. Would not the essence of that key be better appreciated by a presentation of complete and independent scores from each of the respective artists? Surely the distinct styles and rhythms represented by a diversity of musical scores would facilitate a more profound understanding of its object.

In the same way, liberationists believe it would do more justice to the Christologies of the New Testament if each was esteemed as a unique creation of the writer and/or community that gave it form, and each was given full play in accordance with its own hermeneutical 'key.' In the process, the modern interpreter would gain insight into the actual intentionality lying behind the development of these Christologies and recognize the multiplicity of meanings which Jesus may potentially take on within varied historical, social, and cultural contexts. It seems likely that the early Christian communities understood their Christological task in that very manner, for "when the first gospel, Mark, was written, it already presented to us an historical Jesus and Risen Lord as one single figure. In this way, Jesus became the eternal contemporary of the church in its many circumstances."[4]

The Christological method employed by Paul also clearly lends credence to this approach. Even though his major works (Thessalonians, Corinthians, Galatians and Romans) were likely written no later than thirty years after Jesus' death and well before the creation of the first synoptic gospel, Paul evidently did not regard it necessary to simply repeat the words and deeds of Jesus in order to reinterpret his significance for the existence of human beings in his Hellenic world. In fact, except on rare occasions Paul omits any historical reference to Jesus' mission or to his central message of the approaching reign of God.[5] As astonishing as it might seem, Paul's extended proclamation of "the gospel of Jesus Christ to save all who believe" (Romans 1:16) primarily utilizes only two central events of that salvation history out of which it was born: the cross and the resurrection.

Although the gospels had not yet been written, it probably can be safely assumed that the communities to which Paul wrote had access to collections of sayings and narrative accounts which recalled the life of Jesus in some form. And it must be further admitted that Paul likely pre-supposed the existence of an ongoing catechesis based on these frag-mentary sources within the communities to which he wrote. Neverthe-less, as Segundo notes,

> even granting all that, we cannot readily see how those communities could move from an understanding of 'the elementary teaching about Christ' (Hebrews 6:1) to Paul's abstract categories. Without clarifying explanations or bridges, Paul uses those abstract categories to deal with Jesus explicitly, apparently attributing no importance whatsoever to the events and teachings that the Synoptics took so much trouble to re-cord and explain.[6]

The same structure is evident in Paul's sermon on Mars Hill as re-corded in the Book of Acts. In seeking to explain the meaning of Jesus' resurrection to the Athenians (Acts 17:16–32), Paul exposed the differ-ence between their own understanding of religion and that faith which trusts in a living God "in whom we live and move and exist" (v. 28) Paul declared that those who have a relationship to this God "do not suppose that God's nature is anything like an image of gold or silver or stone, shaped by the art and skill of human beings" (v. 29). For that matter, this God of resurrection, i.e., God of life, may not be found in any fixed im-age or human-made temple, for God is a creative presence within this world which humanity shares (v. 24). Paul proclaimed that the only way to find this God is to "feel around for him, for God is actually not far from any one of us" (v. 27). Therefore, Paul concluded, the resurrection of Jesus is not the end of God's revelation, but the new beginning!

What Paul obviously did do was 're-present' the image of this res-urrected Jesus into those categories (which are truly only 'abstract' to those who were outside of his world) that allowed him to express that this figure had something of ultimate significance to say to the Hellenic cul-ture and, by implication, to human beings of every other culture. That need not imply that Paul was unfaithful to the Jesus tradition or, as is claimed by various interpreters who naïvely seek to recover an original 'Jesus-ology,' that he distorted an essentially material gospel with spiri-tualized, Hellenic thought forms. In actual fact, Paul created his own gospels which differ from those clearly identified as such in that he did not narrate the past but imaginatively interpreted it and represented it in terms of what the living Spirit of Jesus was saying in his own time. "Instead of referring to Jesus and what he said to his historical listeners," Segundo observes, "Paul infers from that what Jesus would have said to those outside Israel who have honestly tried to fathom what it means to be a human being in a universe apparently condemned to uselessness and absurdity."[7]

Liberationists contend that the existence of diverse New Testament Christologies is itself a statement concerning the Biblical understanding of revelation: divine revelation and the human interpretation of it are never a 'closed book,' but are always as open as the ongoing historical process which unfolds towards its undetermined future. Nowhere in the Scriptural witness is it suggested that God had prescribed a given point in time when God's self-communication would cease. In fact, was this not one of the very sins for which Jesus condemned the Pharisees, viz., their inability to see that God's character was not to be enclosed in Torah or Law, but rediscovered anew as that tradition encountered the present reality?

It was partly this very conviction which led the early communities to turn collections of Jesus' sayings and deeds into gospels, else they would have closed the fonts of revelation and maintained those collections as sacred texts in their original, scattered form. Even if it were supposed that their purpose was to gather that material into a comprehensive account of Jesus' history, that still would not explain the production of four gospels, all of which were retained without apparent contradiction.[8] These clues indicate that the early communities were writing narrative accounts not only about 'what happened once upon a time' but also about 'what is happening now.' The character of Jesus as a human logos, or word, of revelation required (and requires) of faith not only a record of his history but also a Christology which interprets those events contemporary to any given community of faith.[9]

By the time of the writing of the final canonical gospel at the end of the first century, the community of the Apostle John can still affirm the identity of Jesus with his risen presence. So profound is this identification that the Johannine community is able to faithfully put into the mouth of Jesus of Nazareth the confession: "The Spirit who comes, who reveals the truth about God, will lead you into all truth. It will not speak on its own authority, but will speak of what it hears and will tell you of things to come" (John 16:13).[10]

The question of truth in the New Testament, liberationists are quick to point out, nonetheless extends beyond the early communities' own experience of the presence of the Spirit in their history. The gospels, for instance, were written well after the establishment of the first Christian communities in response to the growing numbers of divergent under-standings of Jesus Christ which had sprung to life. In effect, their own Christologies served as a challenge to other competing Christologies which threatened to dissolve the historical truth of Jesus into an abstract symbol or myth. In these redeemer myths, human salvation was com-monly accomplished by a divine figure who did not need to pass through the struggles and conflicts of history, for it was in the spiritual realm that they supposed the real battle of good and evil was being fought. The narration of the life of Jesus in the canonical gospels, therefore, reflected their passionate concern to ground Christian faith in the life and death of a particular historical figure. The four evangelists and their commu-nities thereby demonstrated that this historical Savior was vitally con-cerned with a salvation which affects the persons and structures of the only kind of reality they knew, human history.

Though it has already been established that Paul did not attempt to recount the story of Jesus in a similar way, he was nevertheless keenly aware of the historical foundation and content of Christian faith as well. In one of his earliest epistles to the church in Corinth, he reminds di-vided factions in the community that the center of their faith was to be found in neither the performance of miracles nor the creation of new religious myths. "As for us," Paul writes, "we proclaim the crucified Christ, a message that is offensive to the Jews and nonsense to the Gen-tiles" (I. Cor. 1:23). After dealing in the letter with some pastoral issues which had arisen in the community during his absence, he returns to re-mind them once more of the essential character of the "gospel" he had preached and on which their "faith stands firm": "Christ died for our sins ... that he was buried and that he was raised to life three days later ... that he appeared to Peter and then to all twelve apostles. Then he appeared to more than five hundred of his followers at once. ... " (I Cor. 15:3–6). For Paul, then, the central aim of the gospel is to proclaim that this Christ who offers the possibility of salvation for all humanity is one and the same with the Jesus of history.

Hence, to claim that each generation and culture must rediscover the significance of Jesus of Nazareth for faith does not necessarily imply that Christology is simply placed at the caprice of pragmatism or must endlessly waver atop an ocean of contradictory values. The authors of the New Testament did not merely pull their Christologies 'out of the air,' thereby inventing a Jesus who could legitimate their personal or com-munal interests. Much to the contrary, the early Christian communities selected and, to a certain point, historicized those memories of Jesus which, even years after his death, still functioned in their communities as a redemptive word. Each of the testimonies, however, interpreted those memories in a manner corresponding to the concerns of their own life situation; for that reason, we are left with numerous, diverse testimonies of the historical reality of Jesus.

Acknowledging this creative process in the New Testament, Sobrino synthesizes its relevance for liberation theologians who desire to express the meaning of Jesus Christ for their communities today:

> Latin American Christology learns two important lessons from the New Testament. The first is that one cannot theologize about the figure of Jesus without 'historicizing' him . . . ; that is to say, one cannot speak theologically about Christ without returning to the historical Jesus. The second is that one cannot historicize Jesus without 'theologizing' him, that is, without speaking about him as the good news of God.[11]

For obvious reasons, present-day Latin American communities of faith cannot draw upon their own direct memories of Jesus of Nazareth; that was a singular privilege enjoyed by the first few generations of believers. Nonetheless, they can write Christologies on the basis of those memories which they receive by mediation of the New Testament witness in dialogue with those Christic images which they discover in their own praxis.

Liberation theologians believe that the interpretive work which is implied by that task should be done in full awareness of the contributions and limitations represented by the North Atlantic quests for the historical Jesus. On the one hand, a recovery of the biography of Jesus has been shown to be a dead-end street. On the other hand, in accordance with the findings of the new quest, the radical skepticism of Bultmann must be moderated.[12] Therefore, despite the fact that the gospel texts do undeniably present narrative and didactic material informed by the specific interests of the gospel evangelists and their communities, liberationists believe that an investigation of the historical Jesus may still uncover a significant corpus of his words and deeds which may be verified with a reasonable degree of certainty.

From this body of data can be determined what Segundo calls the "historical coordinates" of Jesus' life: (1) the value systems that he chose which reveal the 'heart' of the God in whom he believed; (2) the theoretical and practical strategies, or means, Jesus utilized in order to posit those values in the concrete reality of first century Palestine. "If we take those two things into account, then the life of Jesus shows up in all its meaning, [that is,] the meaning which Jesus himself gave it, but also in all its *limitedness*."[13] Though the particular ideologies and paradigms which Jesus adopted unavoidably restricted the infinite world of meanings which his message and activity might have potentially embodied, only thus could he embody values which would make human comprehension of his mission and cause possible.

For as elusive as the historical figure of Jesus might seem, the search for his essential significance is by no means inconsequential. Experience has taught liberationists that a Christology which prescinds from historical grounding in its starting point, method or analysis must be inherently suspect of abstraction for the sake of some predetermined objective. Therein lies the profundity of the warning sounded by Jose Porfirio Miranda, who writes in light of the five centuries of suffering endured by the Latin American people:

> No authority can decree that everything is permitted: for justice and exploitation are not so indistinguishable. And Christ died so that we might know that not everything is permitted. But not any Christ. The Christ who cannot be co-opted by accommodationists and opportunists is the historical Jesus.[14]

As Miranda here so emphatically contests, not every Christology in the tradition of the church is above reproach, regardless of the plurality of models which we find in the New Testament. Though recognizing the fact that the context of faith communities will always change, and given that Jesus Christ cannot be fit into any one formula, it must be underlined that the unalterable content of faith is nonetheless to be discovered in Jesus of Nazareth. Since this latter statement by itself is open to potential misinterpretation and confusion, it will be expressed in yet another way: the historical coordinates which frame Jesus' cause and led him to his death on a cross serve as the criteria for determining the truthfulness of every Christology.

The historical experience of Latin America has provided its theologians with a set of suspicions regarding Christology which are perhaps akin to those held by Thomas after the death of Jesus. When told by the other disciples that Jesus had made himself present to them and that he was once again fully alive in their history, Thomas exclaimed, "Unless I see the scars of the nails in his hands and put my finger on those scars and my hand in his side, I will not believe" (John 20:24). Metaphorically speaking, liberation theologians are equally suspect of any claim of Christ's presence if they cannot recognize in that figure of proclamation the "scars" of the crucified Jesus. For they are convinced that it is his cross which calls into question all knowledge about God: "out of love and solidarity God becomes poor and was condemned, crucified and murdered. . . . Thus we are shown that God's preferred mediation is neither the glory of history nor the transparency of historical meaning.

God's preferred mediation is the concrete, real-life suffering of the oppressed...."[15]

If it is to be accepted that revelation is an open process and that Jesus Christ continues to be active in the unfolding of history, it is essential for liberationists to clarify how that presence is to be recognized as such in coherence with the New Testament witness. They do not seek historical data about Jesus of Nazareth, however, in the hope of uncovering the absolute means by which human existence might be eternally directed. It is contradictory to the notion of incarnation itself to suppose that Jesus was anything less than fully immersed in the struggles against sin which afflicted his own world. The historical options which he made in first century Palestine correspond to the conditions of the social and religious world which shaped his reality. It would be anachronistic, then, to suppose that those same options would have equal viability and relevance within twentieth century Latin America. No contentual biblical statement, then, can be singled out as *the* criterion of Christian faith. Nor does that which is learned about Jesus from the testimony of the gospels reveal the actual steps the people of Latin America must walk in order to bring about liberation within their own context. In brief, that data which they discover about him must be historically mediated once again within their own contemporary reality.

We must again be careful to distinguish this method of Biblical interpretation from one which simply attempts to apply past revelation to the contemporary situation. Faith is not merely an accumulation of knowledge regarding the content of a sacred text. Such a method would only serve to absolutize the 'con-text' which shaped the world within which that testimony had been written. As Elisabeth Schüssler Fiorenza so ably points out, it also ignores the "false consciousness" which is readily apparent at times in the Biblical texts themselves.[16] For example, it is an affront to the Biblical testimony of liberation itself to sustain that women are mandated today to be submissive to men within our contemporary culture, or that slaves are to obediently subject themselves to the will of their oppressive masters. In both cases, it is the contemporary struggles for liberation which critique such Biblical ideologies that perpetrate oppression and thereby expose their divergence from the value coordinates which frame the very history of salvation found running throughout the rest of the Biblical witness.

For that reason, it is not only exegetical data which interests liberation theologians, but also the creative space which exists between that data and those New Testament writers who understood Jesus to be speaking in new ways within their own historical contexts. A critical reading of the texts seeks to isolate the historical data from the interpretations to which they have been subsequently subjected by the early

Christian communities. As Boff recognizes, however, each interpreter needs to be as suspicious of the interests brought to that exegetical task as of those potentially held by the original authors of the texts themselves.

> [A Biblical hermeneutic] will have to ask itself in all honesty: To what extent are the facts as narrated the projection of an antecedent theological interpretation? ... And at the same time we shall have to ask ourselves at all times: To what extent does our own interest attempt to force the text to say more than it really says? To what extent are we projecting rather than assimilating?[17]

What Boff is suggesting, then, is that liberation theologians and their communities must interact with the Jesus tradition in the same way that the evangelists and their communities did within their own context. They are similarly challenged to realize that their faith is not only a memory of the past but also a celebration of their present engagement with Christ. "On the one hand, theologians are constantly referred back to ... Jesus and his message because they must be able to explore and understand the fact of history from the standpoint of the Christ happening. On the other hand, they are immersed wholly in the process of concrete history because they are obliged to appreciate [therein] the pulse of the Word. ... "[18] The central question of biblical hermeneutics, then, should not be who of all the New Testament witnesses presented the definitive image of Jesus, but what can each of them teach us about the light which Jesus sheds on the problems of our own day.

For as important as exegetical results are for laying the groundwork for a modern Christology, immediate faith in the historical Jesus is not thereby made possible. Ultimately, faith in this figure of history is dependent on the fact that he is a living reality and meets us as such today; thus the enduring significance of Paul's words, "if Christ has not been raised from death, then we have nothing to preach and you have nothing to believe" (I Cor. 15:14). It is by virtue of his living testimony within our own situation that he takes on meaning and is believed as the Christ. That is so, Segundo explains, because historical judgments alone may never serve as the foundation of faith:

> When we declare the life and teaching of Jesus have absolute value ..., we are presuming that we can claim them with absolute certainty. But this assumption runs counter to the relativity of the countless historical judgments which serve as the logical basis for that affirmation that there actually has been an encounter with God in the midst of human history.[19]

Hence, historical knowledge cannot directly mediate an experience of Jesus. It is only when such knowledge is accompanied by a praxis immersed in our own world that we may truly encounter him.[20]

The praxis of the faith community raises central issues which serve as a focal point for both an understanding of the various Christologies of the New Testament and their challenge for human existence today. It should not be assumed, then, that the New Testament simply presents the facts and the present-day community need only carry out their appropriate application. For in reality, the meaning-world of the community — which is itself conditioned by its own culture, historical commitments and experiences — will both shape and be shaped by each successive reading of the New Testament witness.[21] It is in this sense that liberation theologians demand a method which locates truth neither wholly in the past nor solely within the world of the interpreter; it is conceived as a product of that which is revealed in their interaction.

Croatto offers a rich understanding of this dialogical relationship which exists between event and word, between proclamation and situation, and between the Biblical word on liberation and those processes of liberation which are our own.[22] He develops an interpretive method which links two poles: (1) the original historicity of a salvific event, and (2) the concrete character of the interpreter's own communal locus. Both of these poles of interpretation are encompassed by a larger field which places them in a continual interplay of mutual illumination. Since the meaning of Jesus' historical praxis is "codified" in texts which have both a linguistic structure and message, those texts by their very nature always remain open to ongoing interpretations. For that reason, new discoveries and meaning-worlds, such as those wrought by the physical and social sciences in the modern era, may shed new light on the full import of Jesus' message and praxis on behalf of the reign of God.[23]

Croatto proposes that foundational events of revelation and their "original word of interpretation" (Scripture) contain a "reservoir of meaning" which is made manifest when new questions, themselves born of historical praxis, address the text. What he has classified here as a "reservoir of meaning" may also be conceptualized as an interpretive catalyst; that is, the reactive creativity which is produced by the interaction of two meaningful events. The text is opened up from the perspective evoked by its new horizon, which serves to deepen (not simply add to) that meaning which lies "in front," and not just behind, the text. A meaningful reading of the Biblical message, then, eventuates only when a current reading of a past revelatory event supersedes its first contextual reading.[24] In that sense, "the act of interpretation is simultaneously the act of an accumulation of meaning."[25]

Thus, the surplus of meaning which a revelatory event and its word of interpretation may offer will vary according to the horizon which is brought before it. For that reason, not every revelatory event which has been witnessed to in Scripture will speak equally to every situation. This insight helps to at least partially explain why specific aspects of Jesus' mission and destiny, as well as different Scriptural interpretations of it, will be more relevant in some historical contexts than others. That admission should not be cause for alarm to those concerned that the uniqueness of Jesus Christ is thereby relativized and diminished. Behind such an anxiety generally lies a hidden assumption that a singular, fixed image of the historical Jesus which is held quite dear might be lost. But the uniqueness of Jesus is not compromised when his significance is reinterpreted for the modern faith community; to the contrary, it is only his 're-presentation' within each new context which permits a profound understanding of the confession of him as Savior.

Of course, it would be untrue to historical experience itself to suppose that those reinterpretations would ever be self-evident for any given community. Since "in the order of knowledge error is always first,"[26] that venture will always be a risk of faith which must perpetually remain open to the winds of the Spirit. When faith is seen as an ever growing and maturing process which "feels around" for the presence of God (Paul), it does not seek to secure itself in a body of content, but in a way of being. Thus, the task of explicating the current significance of Jesus is never completed once and for all. Since the historical structures within which those formulations are immersed are in a constant state of flux, an ongoing reinterpretation of the community's faith is demanded. Moreover, those formulations are always placed under the suspicion of a reflection which arises from the praxis of the contemporary faith community that is living out its commitment to bring the liberation promised by Jesus to fruition.

Given the patriarchal tradition of the Christian church not only in Latin America but also throughout the world, a final note should be emphasized before closing the current discussion. When we speak of the vital memory of the historical Jesus for contemporary Christology, it is not his maleness that is to be considered consequent for Christological reflection. His gender is not to be universalized into a symbol of either an ideal humanity or a divine logos. As feminist theologian Rosemary Radford Reuther signals, modern Christologies must instead begin with the affirmation that "the risen Christ continues to be disclosed through spirit-possessed persons who may be male or female." Hence, the importance of recognizing that the identity of Christ is not encapsulated once and for all in the historical Jesus, but is a personhood which contin-

ues to grow through the community of sisters and brothers who seek to
carry out Christic activities in their own lives.[27]

Without any contradiction to the above, it may very well be that the
message and praxis of the historical Jesus can address the question of
women/men relations in a quite radical way. Although it would surely be
anachronistic to label Jesus a closet feminist, it is clear from the Biblical
witness that he did not address women in the hierarchical fashion which
characterized his society. In his eyes, women were worthy of respect and
worthy of being heard and, though understated by the gospel writers,
even worthy of being disciples. He thereby embodied in concrete form
the reversal of values which was at the center of his proclamation of the
reign of God: "the first shall be last, and the last shall be first." In turn,
those women who were at the bottom of the status ladder in the first century manifested great courage in their response to his invitation to subvert that system as members of his community. Jesus thereby "manifests
the kenosis [self-emptying] of patriarchy," and together with "the marginalized women and men who respond to him represents the overthrow
of the present world system and the sign of a dawning new age. . . ."[28]

In summary, liberation Christology, given its predominant interest
in recognizing the activity of the living Spirit of Christ in its present historical process, deems it necessary to illuminate that path to God which
Jesus revealed in his own teaching, praxis and destiny. That work is carried out with the recognition that a separation of the resurrected Christ
from the concrete history of Jesus all too often leads to "a spiritualism
unconnected to the concrete history of the spirit which drove Jesus."[29] In
their investigation of the life of Jesus, however, liberation theologians do
not expect to find absolute answers to the questions and interests demanded by the praxis of their own faith communities. They recognize
that interpreting Jesus within the particular context within which he
lived inherently places limitations on its direct applicability. That which
they do seek to find are different images, paradigms, and keys which
may provide them with a basis from which to write Christologies which
are demanded by their own situation. As Sobrino puts it, "we learn . . . by
seeing how *Jesus* lived his history. Then, in that spirit, we learn how to
live, not *his* history, but *our own*."[30]

"New Sap Throbbing Through an Old Trunk"

The elaboration of Christologies that take as their starting point the
inhumane conditions in which the majority of Latin Americans live exposes the ideological commitments which undergird our own Christo-

logies. That challenge applies even to those Christologies which claim that they 'are not of this world.' As an illustration of that point, consider this report of a U.S. evangelistic campaign carried out in northern Nicaragua:

> The California-based Campus Crusade for Christ has brought the *Gospel of Luke* here on the silver screen as part of its Central America-wide evangelization campaign. The film's Jesus is a gentle, white miracle worker who speaks in serpentine parables in an authoritarian tone ...
>
> As a twinkling cross fades from the screen at the film's end, a local evangelist leaps on to a makeshift stage: "Step forward those of you who want eternal life! Who among you here wants to spend the rest of your days with JESUS? Who is ready to take the first step forward with Jesus, just come up to the altar, take that step!"
>
> ... They are stepping up for a package of beliefs which, as put forward by Campus Crusade, leaves no room in their earthly lives to work for social gains. Caeser must not compete with the Heavenly Father; preoccupation with this world would mean serving two masters. The task of the evangelical ... is to bring about the glorious return and Kingdom of Jesus. That is 'the only real revolution,' writes Campus Crusade's founder and director, Bill Bright.[31]

Of course, one would first want to ask Bright and other U.S. evangelicals who share his image of Christ why it is that they deem it so important that their Christology transcend the economic, social, and political realities which daily impinge upon the human community. Liberationists immediately have the suspicion that they do so in order that their own personal/class interests will not be subject to the force of moral and historical testimony.

Furthermore, if the salvation which Christ offers also promises to bring about a revolution within our lives, one cannot help but wonder what aspects of our lives are to be radically transformed by a decision in favor of that gospel. In this case, liberationists would question the relevancy and integrity of a salvation which completely ignores a history within which two-thirds of humanity are condemned to live in horrendous conditions of poverty and disease.

Finally, if we are called right now to begin spending the rest of our days with Jesus, how should we then live, i.e. by what values should we make those central decisions which determine the course of our lives? Once again, liberationists suspect that due to its divorce from history the content of that Christological faith will be determined in relation to the political and socio-economic values of the status quo.

In the case of Campus Crusade's Christology, at least, it seems that the suspicions of liberationists would be largely confirmed. For although Bright insists that his organization has never "spent a dollar for political ends," he at the same time admits that U.S. businessmen heavily support his work because, due to its language of "national salvation" and "keeping America great," they know it will keep the Bible from "being subverted."[32] And in the Latin American campaign, where "the American Way" is proclaimed in conjunction with the gospel of Jesus Christ, the practical implications of its 'otherworldliness' is even more clearly unmasked. As Campus Crusade's regional director for Central America explains, "the struggle in which we are engaged, not only in Central America but in the whole world, is an ideological one."[33]

Every Christology is under the commanding influence of a horizon of interest. Aware of that inescapable fact, liberation theologians seek to construct their Christological method in a manner which is consistent with their experience of salvation history both in the Bible and in the lives of their own faith communities. As one possible way to clarify that task, Leonardo Boff delineates the hermeneutical priority of five categories which frame a liberationist reading of the story of Jesus in Latin America today: the primacy of (1) the anthropological (human) element over the ecclesiastical, (2) the critical element over the dogmatic, (3) orthopraxis over orthodoxy, (4) the social element over the personal, and (5) the utopian element over the factual.[34]

It is the concerns and demands represented by these five categories which interact with the Scriptural texts to yield a particular and, dare it be said, 'conditioned' preunderstanding of Jesus. Of course, those interpreters who choose to read the story of Jesus with an inverse primacy of value, e.g., the personal over the social, will obviously operate under a different commanding influence and undoubtedly arrive at a quite different image of Jesus.[35] However, their choice of priorities would be no more or no less ideological than those assumed by liberation theologians. For no matter how academic or Biblical a Christology may claim to be, it is never independent from the particular, existential—in a concrete sense, in the midst of a situation — decisions which its creator(s) make. As Boff correctly argues, "The subject is immersed in history, in a socio-political context, and is moved by personal and collective interests. There is no knowing, then, no knowledge that is free of ideology, that is purely disinterested."[36]

To admit that Christology will always take place within the realm of human options and biases does not negate its possibility, but recognizes that God's revelation in Christ is ultimately concerned with human beings burdened with very particular problems. For only a historical word which interacts within the actual structures of human reality can be identified with the human 'word' who lived and died in a particular time and space in order to reveal the redemptive will of God. That word is only able to address those issues which are actually brought before it. For those who do not search for it, it will not be found.

It has been demonstrated throughout this study that a liberationist preunderstanding operates to spin certain key elements to the center of a consideration of the Jesus event as a primary datum of Christian existence. In the first place—making use of Boff's categories as a framework—it was shown in the previous chapter how liberation theologians interpret the cross and resurrection of Jesus in a manner which manifests the primacy of the human element over the ecclesiastical. The cross and resurrection are treated eminently as human events, and only as a consequence of that fact are they attributed a 'religious' value. For that reason, an explanation of their salvific significance is not sought in a metaphysical realm far removed from the drama of the history within which they took place. Much to the contrary, their essential meaning is grasped in relation to the condition of sin as a dominant presence in the structures of this world and, concurrently, to the human yearning of liberation from its very real power. The cause of Jesus' death, in turn, is discovered in relation to those historical forces against which he struggled in order to create the possibility for a new human reality. His death was not demanded by either an offended or divided God; if such language must be used, the only demands which brought Jesus to his cross were the exigencies which grew out of his historical commitment to God's reign. It is in this sense that liberation theology confesses without reservation that Jesus truly died for the sins of humanity.

Although the resurrection of Jesus does clearly signal to liberation theologians the birth of the church (*ecclesiastical element*), it only does so as a direct result of God's response to the *human* crisis created by his death. After the cross it was still not clear if the future which Jesus represented was little more than an illusion in the face of the power of sin which crushed even his historical project. Those who had followed him were forced to consider the possibility that human history was condemned to move onward in an endless cycle of oppression and death from which there was no escape. The resurrection, however, functions in liberation theology to affirm the utopian vision which Jesus proclaimed in favor of humanity and to justify the particular aims of his project.[37] The one who was risen to a new life in order to be the head of the church is confessed to be one and the same with he who gave his life for the salvation of human beings; therefore, resurrected along with him are his deepest hopes for humanity.

In chapter Three it was indicated that the primacy of the critical element over the dogmatic, as well as orthopraxis over orthodoxy, also greatly influence the manner by which liberation theologians appropriate the value of the cross and resurrection. It is clear that Sobrino, for instance, has on that basis selected the Marcan Jesus as the Biblical image which he considers most relevant for a liberation Christology. The gospel of Mark was, in several respects, written with many of the same interests which motivate the Christological work of Sobrino. Composed well after the epistles of Paul and the initial formation of a *dogmatic* tradition in the nascent church, Mark wrote a "passion narrative with an extended introduction" in order to identify the resurrected Christ with the figure of Jesus of Nazareth. Seeking to prevent the dissolution of Jesus into a Christological abstraction — a threat posed by gnosticism and the burgeoning prevalence of Hellenistic redeemer myths — Mark 'remembers' the inherent scandal of Jesus' life and death as a *critical* element for every Christological formulation.

Sobrino adopts that very structural framework which defines the life of Jesus as a movement "on the way" to Jerusalem. In view of the many modern crosses which are scattered across the hills of El Salvador, Chile, Peru and the rest of Latin America, he seeks to challenge those Christologies which "ignore or even contradict fundamental principles and values that were preached and acted upon by Jesus of Nazareth."[38] He shows the cross of Jesus to be more than a paradigm of suffering to which all human beings are subject by virtue of their essential nature. Quite simply, he presents the cross as a critique of all theological knowledge which locates God outside the realm of the sorrow and pain which tragically mark history. We discover the ultimate act of solidarity in the life and death of Jesus, who reveals God as a Being of love in a real and credible way and not in some idealized form.[39]

Beyond these considerations, Sobrino is also obviously aware that Mark is the only gospel which does not include any evidence which might provide empirical proof that Jesus had truly been resurrected from the dead.[40] Its verification, and therefore its answer to the questions which the cross raises about God and history, are left open for the reader to decide based on his or her own faith response to the testimony about Jesus. Sobrino has insightfully developed these Marcan themes in his own Christology in such a way that manifests the priority of *orthopraxis* over *orthodoxy:* "The identity of Jesus is revealed ... in the abandonment and death of Jesus on the cross, and we will only discover that identity, and so our own, insofar as we take up the cross and follow Jesus. ... Commitment (praxis as the following of Jesus) remains the first and last act."[41]

Unlike the cross, the resurrection was not an event which could have been observed simply by anyone who was alive in the first century. The question of its verification appears to lie in the realm of faith alone. For that reason, liberationists are more interested in recovering the criteria which enabled the disciples to recognize Jesus and verify his identity and presence in their midst than they are in establishing a dogma by which to measure an orthodox Christology. For "like knowing God, knowing the resurrection is not something that is given once and for all. We must keep creating our horizon of understanding, and we must keep alive our hope and praxis."[42]

It was the purpose of chapter Two to illuminate the themes and images of the historical Jesus which come into sharp focus when the last two aspects of Boff's order of hermeneutical priorities—the primacy of the social element over the personal and the utopian element over the factual—shape the interpreters' horizon of interest. The investigations which liberationists have made to recover key aspects of Jesus' public ministry indicate that he was vitally concerned about the alienation and suffering of the world's victims. He cured those who were afflicted with various disabilities and illnesses, forgave the sins of those who 'opened their eyes' to his word of judgment and promise, and to those disciples who would follow him he taught new ways of relating to God and to one's neighbor. In essence, he shifted the center of rabbinical teaching from the law to human beings.

Jesus came to the realization that the law had been manipulated by the religious leaders not only to preclude the possibility of individual acts of redemption—e.g., the healing of the man with a paralyzed hand on the Sabbath (Mark 3:1–6)—but also to exclude entire social groups from participation in the social media of salvation. In contrast, Jesus proclaimed a message of good news to the poor and socially marginalized that the reign of God was at hand, and that they were to be its privileged participants. He embodied this announcement in his own flesh, seeking out the poor, the sick, the lowly, and the reprobate, turning them into his disciples and companions.

Without denying that the message of Jesus was eminently religious, liberationists emphasize that Jesus' historical mission went to the very root of socio-political oppression. The Jewish leaders, by virtue of their special arrangement with the Roman Empire, served not only as religious authorities but also largely directed the social and political affairs of the people. Within that historical context, events such as the disciples plucking ears of corn on the Sabbath (Matt. 12:1–8) take on an entirely new dimension than that interpretation afforded by a strictly personal interest in the correct rendering of law. Jesus lifted the real need of human hunger over the demands of tradition, and thus the value of the human being over the structures of a social system which sacralizes oppression.

In like manner, through his parabolic teachings and deeds, Jesus 're-presented' the world to his followers in such a way that manifested the contradictions of a particular construction of reality supported and legitimated by the established powers of religion. In this new 'world,' the reign of God is compared to a wedding banquet in which everyone is invited regardless of one's social or religious status. The grace of God, therefore, is shown to be a reality which excludes only those who will not accept its invitation (Matt. 22:1 – 10; Lk. 14:15 – 24).

As surely as that message was understood by those who were marginalized from the social world of Palestine, it was all too clear to the religio-political leaders as well. Therefore, to suppose that the Jewish and Roman authorities were simply mistaken or confused when they brought Jesus to trial and execution underestimates their capability of recognizing a real threat to their own source of power. They have Jesus put to death for his role as a religious, social, and political subversive, believing that his message of liberation would die on the cross with him.

It was also underlined in chapter Two that Jesus made use of apocalyptic imagery, of which the reign of God was a central and integral component, to stimulate the imagination of his listeners and bring about the creation of a new consciousness of 'world.' To that end, he announced that the arrival of God's reign into history would transform all human relationships, both interpersonal and structural. In his notion of the reign of God the social scripts of a poor beggar are reversed with those of a callous rich man (Lk. 16:19–31), the despised publican switches roles with the 'righteous' Pharisee (Lk. 18:10–13), the laborers in the vineyard regain the land controlled by a greedy, absentee landowner (Matt. 20:1 – 16; Mk. 12:1 – 12), a desperate and persistent widow receives mercy from, of all people, a judge (Lk. 18:2–6), a peasant farmer is able to find the land and seed he needs to receive a sustainable harvest (Mk. 4:1–9), and those who act on behalf of the poor and needy are warmly received while those who ignore their plight are cast out, despite their claims of faithful religiosity (Mt. 25:31 – 46). Perhaps these 're-presentations' of historical reality could not be perceived as *factual;* nonetheless, their potentiality presses in on the present reality and destabilizes the established order which claims its own divine sacralization. In the announcement of the *utopian* reign of God, then, Jesus postulates the unceasing search for a new kind of human being in a qualitatively different society.[43]

The recovery of these historical and utopian elements of Jesus' mission stands as a critique of those past quests for the historical Jesus which consistently portrayed him as a religious figure solely concerned with the conversion of individual hearts. Tamez articulates the conviction of most liberation theologians when she says that something has gone "awry" in the traditional interpretation of the Biblical witness: "Struggle, life, and liberation have been replaced by passivity, resignation and submission. In other words, the gospel has been reduced to a set of individualistic terms relating only to the 'spiritual order.' "[44] A thorough reading of the gospels, on the other hand, seems to indicate that Jesus was wholly aware that human transformation was also intricately tied to the conversion of those structures which conditioned the possibility of change itself. "Thus Jesus does not simply affirm the possibilities of God and then go on to affirm human possibilities. Instead his aim is to act in such a way that human possibilities might be realized concretely in oppressive situations."[45]

It is the commitment to carry out that task which has also motivated liberation theologians to search for the presence of Jesus Christ in Latin America today. In the same manner as the early Christian communities, they have sought to witness to the good news of salvation which God has revealed in the person of Jesus. It is a confession both of that which God has done in the past and a testimony to the presence of the resurrected Jesus within their own history. It is this ongoing work which is transpiring in the lives of Christian communities throughout Latin America as they confront the problems of the actual world, trying to introduce into its solutions elements of its living faith in Jesus of Nazareth. They are seeking to imaginatively express in their own terminology and conceptuality what Jesus would have said if he were in their situation as an expression of the manifold significance of his life and message for humanity.

> Yes, the new consciousness has arrived; like a thief in the night . . . here it is in pregnant silence in the prophetic darkness.
>
> We feel it beating in the old body of the race, as if the dried-up spring should suddenly burst with water. The dead heart, the secret entrails, reinitiate the dynamism of a pendulum. . . .
>
> Come now, for the new consciousness has arrived. New sap is throbbing through the old trunk.[46]

Notes

1. Segundo, *The Humanist Christology of Paul*, 10.

2. "The first misunderstanding . . . [of the Christological task] is to suppose that of the two elements that demand historical fidelity — in this case to Jesus of

Nazareth — one is already possessed and, therefore, all the attention and creativity ought to fall on the second element. Said in other words: we possess in
substance all that we need to know relative to Jesus of Nazareth. The problem
is ... making it speak in our modern language or in making it speak about our
things ... ," Segundo, *Las Cristologías de la Espiritualidad*, 788.

3. Segundo, *The Historical Jesus*, 19.

4. Herzog, "Quest," 39.

5. One of those few occasions may be found in I Cor. 11:23-4, the words
attributed to Jesus as those that he had said over the bread and wine at the Last
Supper.

6. Segundo, *The Humanist Christology of Paul*, 2.

7. Segundo, *The Historical Jesus*, 21.

8. "Each person and each generation must experiment, discover, and edit
its own gospel about Jesus.... [So] the first Christian community had not one but
four gospels, in this way accommodating his message to determined and concrete cultures and situations ... ," José Ramón Guerrero, *El Otro Jesús* (Salamanca: Ediciones Sígueme, 1976), 15.

9. Ellacuría, *Freedom Made Flesh*, 24.

10. A further exemplification of this Biblical hermeneutic can be seen in the
Letter of Revelation, an apocalyptic message written to the seven churches of the
southern province of Asia. The apostle writes with the confidence that it was
"Christ [who], made these things known to his servant" and that the record
of events is a "message from God and the truth revealed by Jesus Christ" (Rev.
1:1–2).

11. Sobrino, *Jesús en América Latina*, 92. In turn, Sobrino maintains that it
is Latin America's own setting which has conditioned those memories of Jesus
which constitute their gospel of liberation: " ... Fidelity towards the Latin American situation ... and its demands yields an adherence to the historical Jesus,
while a comprehension of the historical Jesus has lead to a more profound understanding of the Latin American situation and its problems. In reality, this is
a single moment with two distinct and complementary moments that brings
about the 'historicization' (according to the historical Jesus) and the 'latinameri-
canization' of faith in Christ," ibid., 88.

12. Bultmann held that the gospels should not be treated as documents de-
tailing who Jesus was as historical fact, but that they should be interpreted as
fragmentary sources which are full of myth and legend. He did not think that
this fact represented any threat to Christian faith for, as he constantly emphasized, the theological claim that "God has acted in Jesus Christ" does not depend
upon the results of historical research but may only be confirmed as a response
of personal faith. Of primary importance for Bultmann is "that" Jesus was a per-

son who lived in history and not the specific content of that history. See Bultmann, *Faith and Understanding*, trans. J. C. Greig (New York: Charles Scribner's Sons, 1932), 206–215.

Ernst Käsemann and other prominent figures of the new quest claimed that it was not enough to simply posit the "thatness" of Jesus. They feared that without a material continuity to the historical Jesus, the proclamation and faith content of the church might fall into a modern form of docetism. They emphasized that their goal was not to arrive at the actual events and sayings of Jesus in order to objectify faith, but to demonstrate that the proclamation of God's offer of salvation (the kerygma) has its source in Jesus of Nazareth and not solely with the early Christian community. As Käsemann explained, "Fuchs, G. Bornkamm and I see ourselves compelled to restrict the assertion that Easter founded the Christian kerygma; we must enquire as to the meaning of the historical Jesus for faith," quoted in Robinson, *New Quest*, 84.

13. Segundo, *The Humanist Christology of Paul*, 162. In a later volume, he adds: "It is a deception when, for the sake of supposed superiority, every realization is considered failed and its means condemned as partial, unless a 'faithful' copy of the faith of Jesus is found. The faith of Jesus ... was also incarnated in a limited and imperfect ideology, as were the very criteria which were taught by him. That is the price and significance of incarnation," *Las Cristologías de la Espiritualidad*, 933–4.

14. Jose Porfirio Miranda, *Being and the Messiah: The Message of St. John*, trans. John Eagleson (Maryknoll: Orbis Books, 1977), ix.

15. Boff, *Passion of Christ*, 132.

16. Elisabeth Schüssler Fiorenza, "Toward a Feminist Biblical Hermeneutics: Biblical Interpretation and Liberation Theology," in Brian Mahan and L. Dale Richesin, eds., *The Challenge of Liberation Theology: A First World Response* (Maryknoll: Orbis Books, 1981), 101. Fiorenza believes that this fact also challenges the hermeneutic-contextual method which I have espoused in this chapter since it does not allow for a critical theological evaluation of Biblical theologies as false consciousness. Though I find her argument quite compelling, I disagree with her that historical content and hermeneutic learning cannot be separated. Even in the midst of that dialectic I believe it is possible to carry out an ideological critique of the past embodiments of historical truth. Moreover, I do not believe that her alternative—a common existential ground which links the interpreter to the author of the text—is sufficiently 'historical' for a theology of liberation. It makes it too easy for us to stay with our own oppressive models which have as their justification our own unchallenged existential validation.

At the same time, I recognize that feminist theologians have proposed a daunting suspicion that the Bible and Christian theology are inherently sexist and thereby destructive of women's consciousness. I believe this challenge should be the starting point for ongoing dialogue between Latin American theologians and feminist thinkers. For as Fiorenza so powerfully states, "Only when we crit-

ically comprehend how the Bible functions in the oppression of women can we
prevent its misuse for further oppression," ibid., 105.

17. Ibid., 8. Boff clarifies what this means for the modern Christological interpreter who wants to understand the passion of Jesus: "Let us, then, seek only
to do this: place ourselves in the situation in which the evangelists found themselves. Like them, let us, too, proceed to a theological interpretation of the Lord's
passion. Our attitude of faith is the same. Only the *Sitz im Leben* ... will be different," ibid.

18. Raúl Vidales, "Methodological Issues in Liberation Theology," in *Frontiers*, 41.

19. Segundo, *Liberation of Theology*, 170.

20. See Míguez Bonino, "Who is Jesus Christ in Latin America Today?"
5-6; also Sobrino, *Christology at the Crossroads*, xxiii–xv; *Jesús en América Latina*,
88–92.

21. So explains Vidales that the modern faith community must "reread the
Bible from the context of the other 'Bible' known as human history. It is one dialectical activity, not two separate, parallel tasks" "Methodological Issues," 40–1.

22. Croatto, *Exodus*, 3.

23. Ibid., 121.

24. Ibid., 3. Writing from this perspective as well, Segundo explains regarding Jesus: "The *actual* meaning of someone who lived and acted in the past,
has, or at least ought to have, two ... objective components: those which proceed
from the historical data that we possess about the person in question, and those
which constitute the real problematic that an individual, a group, a society, or
humanity in general are [presently] facing (consciously or unconsciously)," *Las
Cristologías de la Espiritualidad*, 787.

25. Croatto, *Exodus*, 2. It is this same conviction which leads Sobrino to
write, "To say that Christ ceases to unleash a Christian reality and a Christian
history is formally to deny that he is Christ. And if he does continually unleash a
new and novel Christian history, then it is absolutely necessary to integrate that
new history into our reflection about Christ," *Christology at the Crossroads*, xxi.

26. C. Boff, *Theology and Praxis*, xxii. Bultmann's comments on the reinterpretation of Christology in terms of an appropriate preunderstanding relevant
to the present historical context merit attention here: "We must realize that there
will never be a right philosophy which could give answers to all the questions and
clear up all the riddles of human existence. Our question is simply which philosophy today offers the most adequate perspective and conceptions for understanding human existence," "New Testament and Mythology," 55.

27. Rosemary Radford Reuther, *Sexism and God-Talk: Toward a Feminist Theology* (Boston: Beacon Press, 1983), 134–8.

28. Ibid., 137 – 8. Fiorenza, on the other hand, provocatively questions whether Jesus can in any way serve as a historical norm for contemporary faith: "... A feminist theologian must question whether the historical man Jesus of Nazareth can be a role model for contemporary women, since feminist psychological liberation means exactly the struggle of women to free themselves from all male internalized norms and models," "Feminist Biblical Hermeneutics," 107.

29. Sobrino, *Christology at the Crossroads*, xvi.

30. Ibid., 139.

31. Deborah Hunington, "The Prophet Motive," *NACLA Report on the Americas*, vol. XVIII, no. 1 (Jan/Feb 1984): 2.

32. Remarks made by Bill Bright to *The Washington Post* (November 18, 1977), quoted in Deborah Huntington, "God's Saving Plan," *NACLA Report on the Americas*, vol. XVIII, no. 1 (Jan/Feb 1984): 24.

33. Ibid., 31.

34. Boff, *Liberator*, 44 – 7.

35. On that basis, Sobrino argues that European Christology as well has specific interests which guides its Christological work. As examples, he points to the images of Jesus as "the bearer of absolute salvation" (Rahner) and as "the Omega point of evolution" (Teilhard de Chardin): "Both theologians certainly underline the salvific aspect of Christ; but given their cultural situation, their speculative Christology has to concentrate on showing how Christ can be the Savior. In Latin America the emphasis is the inverse. Certainly Christ is the Liberator for Christology; but the task is showing him [concretely] as liberator," *Christology at the Crossroads*, 91.

36. Boff, *Passion of Christ*, 1.

37. "The God who seemed to abandon him on Good Friday now appeared as his legitimator," Boff, *The Passion of Christ*, 4.

38. Sobrino, *Christology at the Crossroads*, xv.

39. Ibid., 370 – 3.

40. I consider the Gospel of Mark to have ended with the visit of the three women to the garden (16:1 – 8). The other ending(s) are likely later additions.

41. Cook supplies this analysis of Sobrino's Christology in light of the gospel of Mark in "Christology in Latin America," 274.

Parenthetically, the fact that Sobrino's image of Jesus is readily identifiable with that of Mark's gospel and not with that, for instance, of John's gospel, does not on that basis alone make his Christology any less legitimate. In fact, there are good reasons to believe that the realities of the present Latin American situation evoke this image of the crucified Jesus more than it would any other Christology of the New Testament. Certainly, the image of a Jesus who calls his disciples 'to take up his cross' and follow him on the way has powerful relevance for the people of Latin America. That judgment, however, should not imply that the Marcan Christology is the only true understanding of Jesus of Nazareth in Latin America today, or that other Latin American communities and their theologians may not find other images of Jesus in the New Testament which more ably speak to their situation.

As proof of that point, Segundo relates how a group of Latin American Christians in Uruguay met regularly with him with the goal of uncovering those Christological images that have relevance in their own context. The group discovered that the "anthropological key" which Paul used to interpret Jesus spoke perhaps most powerfully to their situation. See *The Humanist Christology of Paul*, 173–180.

To give one more example, Miranda has written a Christology for Latin America grounded in the image of Jesus found in the Gospel of John. See *Being and the Messiah: The Message of John*.

42. Sobrino, *Christology at the Crossroads*, 257.

43. Gutiérrez, *Theology of Liberation*, 231.

44. Tamez, *Bible of the Oppressed*, 58.

45. Sobrino, *Christology at the Crossroads*, 47.

46. Luis Valcarcel, *Storm in the Andes*, quoted in Pastoral Team of Bambamarca, *Vamos Caminando: A Peruvian Catechism*, trans. John Medcalf (London: SCM Press, 1985), 365.

CHAPTER FIVE

Ecclesial Base Communities: The Indigenization of Christology

> *To make real, to translate, to convert into a diaphanous and*
> *true current a language that seems distant; to communicate*
> *the foundation of our spirit in a foreign language—that is the*
> *hard and arduous task before us.*
>
> —*José María Arguedas*[1]

Segundo acknowledges at the conclusion of his *Liberation of Theology* that neither his work nor that of other theologians which are being produced in Latin America today represent a final draft. If anything, their reflections indicate one stage in the growth of a living organism which is progressively developing its own methodology and content both in continuity to, and in distinction from, the historical tradition of the Christian church. Admitting that no one may predict where the pathways opened up by this commitment will lead, he does suggest from where he expects the orientation for that journey to come: "they will take their cue from flesh and blood human beings who are struggling with their heart and mind to fashion the kingdom of God out of human materials of our great but oppressed continent."[2]

In Latin America today, the Spirit is bringing to birth committed communities which are choosing "the path of building a world in which persons are more important than things and in which all can live with dignity."[3] These base ecclesial communities have stimulated within their ranks a creative imagination which expresses in reflection and action the theological and human significance of the "irruption of the poor" on the present world scene. It would be a mistake, however, to categorize their commitment as an eminently religious engagement from those observing the process of social transformation from the outside. For the base communities are not simply religious organizations which operate in an

independent fashion parallel to the popular movements for liberation in
Latin America. They are comprised of people involved in that movement itself who, as well, seek to live their faith and break bread together
in community.[4]

The following selection, which is a transcript recording a communal discussion of the gospel story of Jesus' birth in Bethlehem, indicates why these base communities have already served as a dynamic impetus for the creation of new images of Jesus Christ in Latin America.
The participants in this particular community are residents of a fishing
and peasant village on an island of the Solentiname archipelago in Lake
Nicaragua during the mid-1970s:

> Elvis: The importance of the birth of Christ is that it was the birth of
> the Revolution, right? There are many people who are afraid of the
> word as they were afraid of Christ because he was coming to change the
> world. From then on the Revolution has been growing. It keeps grow-
> ing little by little . . . and nobody can stop it.
>
> Ernesto: And it has to grow here also, doesn't it?
>
> Pancho: We have to get rid of selfishness and do what Christ said, and
> go on with the Revolution, as you socialists say. I'm not a socialist. I'm
> not a revolutionary. I like to hear the talk and grasp what I can but
> really I'm nothing. Although I would like to see a change in Nicaragua.
>
> Manuel: But if there's going to be a change you have to cooperate with
> it. . . .
>
> Pancho: But how do you do it!? I'd like somebody to tell me. . . . But you
> can't! When we rise up they kill us.
>
> Alejandro: But look, they killed him too.
>
> Pancho: Correct, but he was Christ and we're never going to compare
> ourselves with him.
>
> Manuel: But I heard there have been other men, like Che, who also
> have died for freedom.
>
> Pancho: Right. You can die, and tomorrow we'll all be dancing and we'll
> never think that you died for us.
>
> William: Then you think that those deaths are useless?
>
> Pancho: They're useless. Or they're almost useless!
>
> Young Miriam: I say that when there's someone who will free our
> country there will be another Christ.
>
> Fernando (to Pancho): When you say, 'What can I do? Nothing!,' I
> agree with you. But when you ask another, 'What can we do?,' I would

say everything. And that day when you ask each other, 'What do we do?,' you'll already know what you are going to do. And the people all united are the same Jesus that you see in this manger scene, against whom Herod couldn't do a thing.[5]

This passage exemplifies the dialogical pedagogy which is actively shaping the Christian community in Latin America and, as a result, its theological method. Through such discussion, campesinos and workers are enabled to critically reappropriate their cultural and religious heritage and thereby reinterpret their lives based on a new understanding of the gospel. It is out of this process that the rereading of the Bible and the rewriting of theological reflection unfold as a vital expression of the struggle of marginalized people.

Míguez Bonino declares that due to this "ecclesiogenesis" in the Latin American church, theology can no longer "be artificially constructed in a theological laboratory or in a devotional hothouse."[6] On that basis, he makes an impassioned call for the formulation of a Christology (and spirituality) which arises out of Latin America's own "revolutionary situation." Although trained theologians will surely be able to assist in its articulation, make explicit its reference to the historical tradition of the church, and ask the critical questions which may be necessary for its correction, the Christological framework itself will only grow from those communities which have taken a decidedly immediate and concrete commitment to the liberation of humanity. For "in the last analysis," concludes Míguez Bonino, "it is active commitment itself, the historical praxis of the oppressed, which permits them to recover the Christ who transforms history, the liberator Christ who has been snatched from them."[7]

For if it is to be believed that God reveals God-self in history and is working therein to reconcile the world, then both history and God's activity must be re-interpreted from the perspective of the poor. In that case, history ceases to be a hypothetical element in the equation of predetermined theological constructs; instead, it is the actual foundation out of which theological and Christological reflection grows. Gutiérrez, speaking out of his Peruvian context, points out that this basic realization in the two-thirds world has required a reversal of the traditional relationship established between history and Christian theology:

Christianity as it has been historically lived has been, and is, closely tied to a culture: Western; to a race: the white race; to a class: the dominant class. Its history has also been written by a white, Western, and bourgeois hand. We must regain the memory of the 'beaten Christs of the Indies' as Bartolomé de Las Casas called the Indians of the American continent.[8]

When the presence of the poor is moved to the center stage of history, Christology's horizon of interest by necessity radically shifts as well.

Before it is assumed that what is being spoken of here is merely the opening of theological relevance to the realm of politics and social transformation, a clarification must be offered. It is not that traditional theology has completely ignored political questions and social issues; it has touched upon them, albeit to a limited extent, and most typically in the area of ethics. The obstacle, as Clodovis Boff points out, is that "this theology operates within the space offered it by its philosophical mediation. The problematic in and by which it confronts social and political questions is marked by an idealism incapable of perceiving ... [the realities of the actual situation]."[9] Its limits of truth, therefore, are determined antecedent to any historical event, regardless of what might be revealed about God in the unfolding of the historical process within which that event transpires. Hence, traditional theological constructions are all too often fenced in by their own ideological definitions of how social forces are interwoven to create a 'legitimate' construction of reality, thereby excluding the possibility of new ways of envisioning the world. Thus, "we are not faced here with new fields of application of old theological notions, but with the provocation and necessity to live and think the faith in different socio-cultural categories. ... "[10]

So it is from the communities of the oppressed that new Christological images, replete with the historical ideologies and utopic visions which mark the contemporary Latin American situation, continue to arise. That fact might surprise many people who wonder how communities of largely illiterate peasants would have the capacity to fashion the church's Christology. For those of us who have worked in their midst, however, all such doubts are quickly dispelled. Though campesinos may not write Christologies, they surely live them.

The "Irruption of the Poor"

The Latin American *pueblo* — literally people, but in a much more collective/communal sense than that word conveys to us in English — has long suffered under an exploitation which has been justified and supported by an orthodox theology. With few exceptions, the church which came to the continent with the early Spanish conquistadors overtly sided with the wealthy and powerful elite who controlled their lives. Claiming that the social order was ordained by God, the church more often than not taught the faithful to accept their lot in life, work diligently for the landowners, and wait patiently for their reward in the heavenly city. Beyond the domestic domination represented by this alliance of the church and oligarchy, whenever change could be glimpsed on the horizon the people endured invasions by one foreign power after another claiming a divine 'manifest destiny' to maintain the continent under their imperial submission.

Gutiérrez relates that this tragic history has left the church in Latin America with a mixed legacy: it is both a Christian *pueblo* and yet an exploited *pueblo*.

> We cannot forget that the dominant classes who oppress this people use Christianity to justify their privileges, but neither can we forget that the suffering of an oppressed people is revealed in popular expressions of faith. In them we find resistance and a protest against domination, as well as a vigorous witness of hope in the God of the Bible.[11]

In light of the complexity of popular religious consciousness, no Christology which seeks its indigenization in the cultural and religious roots of the Latin American poor can seek immediate signs of revelation which are overtly written on the faces of oppressed people. Such a method would only lend itself to the idealization and romanticization of the reality of oppression itself. The possibility of indigenous Christologies first requires that a prior mediation takes place which empowers the poor to be the creators of their own reality, a process which is known throughout Latin America as conscientization. Galilea has defined conscientization as a "means [of] moving from an uncritical, conformist outlook based on feelings of cultural inferiority to a creative outlook that is aware of its own identity and critical of all forms of cultural, ideological, and political alienation, however subtle they may be."[12] This awareness permits the poor to move beyond a dense, enveloping vision of a world from which there is no escape in order to acquire the ability to intervene in their reality as it is unveiled.[13] It is this critical appropriation of a peoples' communal experience, belief, spirituality and culture which provides them with the tools to recreate history out of their own collective memories.

Conscientization is so essential for oppressed peoples because, in Freirian terminology, their "very structure of thought has been conditioned by the contradictions of the concrete, existential situation by which they were shaped;" in other words, they suffer from a 'dominated consciousness' which has internalized the ideology of the oppressor.[14] The ongoing exploitation suffered by the poor together with the persistence of the dominant ideology create a closed world which devalues their own cultural and religious heritage, thereby cutting off the potentiality of their creative imagination. For this reason, it is only once the poor have effected a profound recognition of themselves that they are capable of refashioning their Christian faith and removing the mask of passive religiosity.

> To the extent that the popular classes that identify themselves as Christian ... enter, assume, and live out their religious practices ... in dialectical relation to the process of liberation (conscientization, politicization, organization and mobilization, progressive and effective participation in processes of social decision making, etc.), they recover religion's potential for protest (utopia), which assumes an active role and effectively contributes to the process of revolutionary social transformation.[15]

Yet, how is it possible for oppressed peoples to move beyond the dominated consciousness which feeds their own oppression so that they may critically reflect upon their world? The oppressed suffer within themselves a battle of identity: between their own true selves which yearn for freedom and those selves which have learned to adapt to, and thereby survive, the structures of domination. It is readily apparent that as long as they remain unaware of the root causes of their condition and are unable to recognize themselves as unwitting victims of exploitation, they will remain fatalistically identified with their dominated selves. As a result, they will likely react in a passive and alienated way when confronted with the possibility, and even the necessity, to struggle for their own freedom and self-affirmation.[16]

Although the process of conscientization may be explained in theoretical terms, its full significance is best communicated in narrative form. Especially for North Americans who have never had occasion to live and work in Latin America—or, for that matter, other parts of the dependent world—the notion of conscientization may appear as nothing more than erudite rhetoric designed to promote hidden theological and political ends.[17] It would be misconstrued, however, if it were not characterized as a fundamentally popular phenomenon which is changing the face of the Latin American church.

The ensuing testimony of a poor campesino, Lito, who lives in the northern region of El Salvador, reflects the conversion experience of literally millions of 'non-persons' in Latin America within the last two decades.

What do I remember of the sermons? In those times all was in Latin . . . with backs to the people. In order to speak to us directly the priest went up to this thing they call a pulpit. He began to speak to us with 'in-nominepatri-tefili-tespiritu-santi-deus.' And 'amen' said the people. Who knows what he wanted to say with all that.

And after that he began to speak, and he always said the same things. That we ought to respect our authorities, because Saint Paul in one of his letters said that all authority comes from God. For that reason we should never place ourselves against the authorities, he said, for that is to place oneself against God. And all of that we took in completely. With eyes closed. And that message was carried out to the Christians in meeting after meeting: that nobody was to raise up against the authorities. See how things were in those days . . . !

There was another matter in which we were oriented constantly—that of conformity. Many grandmothers, elderly, young boys and girls, came to the priest with their problems to see what ideas he might give them: 'Father, they have burned my house down,' or 'Father, I don't have work,' or 'Father, my wife is sick and I don't have any money'; then he would hear their confession and give advice. And when he came to the pulpit, he always repeated, 'Blessed are the poor, for theirs is the kingdom of heaven, blessed are those who suffer, for they shall be comforted.'

And then he would say, 'Truly, it is important to be poor, its a real privilege to be poor, no?' And we all believed him.

And the priest also would say, ' . . . When you suffer with patience, brothers and sisters, God won't let anything pass by God's eye, for God is noting all those who suffer; but when you arrive to God's house when you die, God is going to send a chorus of angels to carry you, accompanied by the Holy Virgin, and they are going to lift you up and put you on a throne already prepared for you.'

Geez, we at that mass had already seen this film. And who knows how many of our people at this moment are flying through the air. . . .

But then he would say, 'Furthermore, beloved sons and daughters, never desire what others have because that is bad. Those who covet cannot be saved. It is necessary to conform to what God gives. Because God already knows what God wants to give you and what God doesn't want to give you. If God has not given us anything, only God knows why. . . .'

. . . With that same priest we had many meetings. One day he told us, 'Look, I am going to give you a Bible and I want you to read it every night, but I am going to leave markers where I want you to read, be-

cause this book is so large and I don't want you to get lost.' And we believed that was the truth, and that since it was such a large book, for that
reason he had marked the pages where we should read. And for that
reason we always read about the same topics of patience and authorities. The catechists always met together every night. The priest didn't
attend, because he only came once a week, on Saturday.

At that time, they changed priests every five years. . . . Soon came the
time for the departure of our priest. And we began to hear news that in
our country were 'communist priests.' And when we came to hear the
news that our priest was going to leave, the army commander came to
give us the news about the new priest who was going to arrive. Who
knows how the commander knew that the priest who was going to arrive was a young priest, which parish he had been in before, and that
above all he was supposed to be a communist. That commander, I remember, never used to miss a mass. . . .

. . . Before long the new priest who had been announced as a communist came to our village. A young father. The people were waiting for
him in order to see if he had a different face. In that time, we thought
that the face of a communist had to be different. I remember that those
of us who were young at the time, always the most curious, went to the
window of the church to look inside where the priest would cross the
sacristy and the altar. We wanted to see him from afar. And we were
there, curiously looking, when all of a sudden the priest was in the
midst of us. 'Hi, boys, how are you doing?' He was dressed in a black
shirt. I still remember clearly today that first meeting. A big smile,
humble, simple. Somewhere around 22 years old. 'We're doing fine,
Father.' And we waited; we wondered to ourselves how this man would
speak. And then he spoke in our common slang. . . .

. . . And one day the young priest said to us, 'Well, do any of you want
to get together some day and study the Bible? I've been told by some of
you that you used to meet with the other Father. . . . ' Those that were
there began to shout 'I do!' And when others heard about it, they
wanted to as well. And he began to sit down with us and with the Bible.
He began to read to us from James 5, the criticism against the rich and
all that. . . .

'What's this?' we said to one another without believing it. He said,
'Look, you can clearly understand this if you see that you are all children of God, and that Christ came through his birth to a poor woman,
and. . . . ' He began to explain to us what the Bible had to teach about
the poor.

I remember that day well. It was then that we began to become con-
scientized that criticizing the wealthy was not a sin. But that even God
condemned them there in the Bible. And if God condemned them, how

is it that God nurtured and blessed them with so much money? Yet, in the Bible they are condemned. And a grand contradiction arose in our minds. There was a long argument among ourselves for even taking up these thoughts. We began to throw ideas from one side of the room to the other. We began taking positions.

The time came when the priest told us: 'We ought to form a community of people that would go to all the local villages and preach the gospel, and to teach doctrine. How would we possibly be able to do that? Well, for that we are going to need to locate the Bible, the word of God, within the reality in which we live.' 'Locate?,' we asked ourselves. What did that mean? And he began to explain to us new words. 'Reality,' for instance. And the more we understood, the more we were liking our new world of understanding....

... Slowly and probingly he went. The priest also had his tactics. Fair enough, one does not wake up in one day.[18]

One thing becomes quite obvious in the course of Lito's testimony: there is no such thing as an immediate representation of socio-historical reality, be it from the 'court priest' of the landowners and military colonels or from the 'subversive' priest of the people, nor even from Lito himself. This observation highlights the fact that an explanation of any socio-historical phenomenon will entail a conscious or unconscious theory which makes sense out of a people's experience of objective data. "The reading of reality is still the reading of a code," explains Boff, "and this code is read in alphabets whose seeming immediate spontaneity is merely the product of 'habit'—that is, of the degree of internalization of the culture to which these alphabets belong."[19]

Of course, the reading of that reality will also naturally be a product of where one is socially located within the society. That point was clearly driven home to me on an extended visit I made to Nicaragua several years after the triumph of the revolution. My stay was arranged by a small Baptist church which believed that a North American would surely not be comfortable staying in the home of a low-income family, even though the majority of the church's membership fell into that economic category. One woman in the church, however, was married to a medical doctor, Roberto, who did not share any of his wife's religious convictions yet nonetheless kindly agreed to open his home for hospitality.

Roberto's family was fairly well off by Nicaraguan standards: they owned two modest houses, two cars, and ate meat with their meals at least two times a day. During the time of the Somoza regime, he had worked in a private hospital and had maintained a medical practice for those patrons who had the ability to pay for consultations. Of course, that select group only included perhaps fifteen percent of the Nicaraguan population. Nevertheless, Roberto was free to carry out his career in those ways he determined beneficial.

With the triumph of the revolution, health care was nationalized throughout Nicaragua. Doctors and other health professionals were required to devote a large percentage of their consulting hours to popular clinics, and for their services they were compensated with a fixed salary which was considerably lower than that which they had previously earned. Roberto was livid about these changes, and regularly vented his anger with me: "Can you believe the totalitarian system which we have in this country?! You wouldn't allow this to happen in the United States. You wouldn't let your government tell you where to work and how much you are to be paid for doing it. The Sandinistas have taken our *freedom* from us!"

When I was not listening to Roberto's diatribes in the evenings, during the daytime I was traveling to the city barrios and countryside of Nicaragua in conjunction with the Protestant relief agency CEPAD. Everywhere I went, campesinos and workers were sharing with me the thrill of receiving medical attention for the first time in their lives. No longer did they have to face the inexpressible tragedy of sitting back and watching their children die simply because they did not have the money to buy medicine for them. "We now have the *freedom* to see a doctor," they repeatedly exclaimed to me. "We thank God that the revolution has given us the possibility of life!"

To give yet one more perspective on how we view reality from the place where our feet are planted, it would be of interest to note the response I have commonly received when I retell this story to churches in the United States. In an adult Sunday school class held at a Baptist church in Oakland, I was sharing how we more often than not read both the Bible and our own history through the grid set by our social and economic commitments. To illustrate that point, I recalled the story of Roberto who, consciously or not, held his rights of individual gain over the freedoms of the vast majority of the poor people in his country. At the end of the story, I was mildly shocked to hear one of the class members, the wife of a bank executive, respond: "No, Roberto was right! That government must be acting as a dictatorship; no one has the right to take away what he has worked so hard to earn!"

Once again it is clear that the perception of reality is never self-disclosing. Though neither Roberto nor the Baptist woman from Oakland would likely dispute the objective fact that poor people exist in society, they firmly resist any explanation for that condition which might challenge the privilege which they personally gain from that system which creates poverty. Assuming that their response is illustrative of a whole series of values which legitimates their place in that world, it would be safe to say that the poor should not expect any change in their situation to be initiated from those sectors which hold economic and social power in the society. More realistically, the poor should anticipate a forceful opposition, both 'moral' and rational, to any alternative rendering of that world to which they might arrive grounded in their own experience of history.

In that context, it was shown above that Lito and his community formed and modified their relationship with the world based on their own critical (or acritical) awareness of their social situation and its determining structures. What was required for them to regain a sense of their own identity, and subsequently become the autonomous creators of their own destiny, was an analysis which enabled them to actually see their world as a problem. This transformation involved the process of deciphering those themes — e.g. "we deserve what we have earned" or "my individual freedom is inalienable" — which define and justify the world. The movement from mystification to conscientization then helped them to begin to imagine new themes for reshaping the world.[20]

It is at that point where their 'theologizing' about the world took its departure as well. For "Christians have the right to think . . . out the experience of their own liberation," Gutiérrez reminds us. Theologically speaking, it means that they also "have the right to reclaim their faith — a faith that is continually diverted away from the experience of being poor — in order to turn it into an ideological exposé of the situation of domination that makes and keeps them poor."[21]

Just as there is no immediate appropriation of the absolute significance of those socio-cultural categories which structure our view of 'world,' neither is there a monistic, singular meaning of the Scriptural texts and theological affirmations of the church which may be applied a priori to objective reality. Of course, this thesis itself is predicated upon the assumption that the object of theology is not to be found unto itself, but is the product of a process of reflection upon the 'nontheological.'

If Jesus Christ is to be seen as the logos of the world and of all reality, then the mystery of God's presence may not be excluded from an evaluation of the ultimate meaning of any object or event. However, that divine presence is not revealed to the naked eye (theo-phany), but is comprehended only through later reflection (theo-logy). "Theology, therefore, is not to be conceived as something static, like a deposit, or a sum total of knowledge — but as something dynamic, a practice, a process, a labor, a production. Theological effort transforms the nontheological into the theological."[22]

We who are Christians living in the developed world generally find it difficult to reconceptualize our understanding of theology along these

lines. For that reason, the new theologies which are being written in
Latin America often seem so alien to our notion of religious faith. We are
offended to hear that God may have a predisposed predilection for one
social class over another, or that the gospel could be especially good news
for those who are in conditions of poverty (and may even contain some
bad news for those of us who are wealthy!).

Surely one of the primary factors contributing to our mental block
— besides the obvious threat we perceive to our vested interests — is the
nature of 'truth' which dominates our religious thinking. Be it manifest
in the preoccupation with literalism and the inerrancy of the Bible
within the evangelical and fundamentalist camps, or in the crisis regarding the authority of dogma and the ecclesial office in the Catholic
church, or in a crumbling confidence in technology and the scientific
method which the mainline churches had once taken for granted, it is
clear that our faith is all too reliant upon the certainty of knowledge. A
theological statement is validated in our eyes only if it logically follows
from those propositions which we have previously accepted as reliable.
Once that foundation of knowledge cracks, our whole faith enterprise
subsequently enters into a period of crisis. Since these truth-claims have
little relevancy for daily life, it should come as no surprise that a growing
number of people in our country are developing an ambivalent attitude
towards religious faith.

The question of truth comes up quite regularly in the Bible. For example, the gospels record that when John the Baptist was in prison he
sent a group of his followers to find Jesus and ask him if he were the one
in whom God was to reveal the messianic future, i.e., if he was the *true*
Messiah. Jesus answered: "Go tell John what you are seeing and hearing
— the blind can see, the lame can walk, those who suffer from dreaded
diseases are made clean, the deaf hear, the dead are brought back to life,
and the good news is preached to the poor" (Matt. 11:2–6).

We are not told if Jesus' response sufficiently dispelled all of John's
doubts regarding Jesus' messianic ministry, but we certainly recognize
its inadequacy to answer the complex questions which we bring to the
Christological task. Perhaps if Jesus had addressed himself to the mysterious relationship between the human and divine, or possibly if he had
delivered a definitive collection of beliefs which could be readily identified as revelation, we would be convinced that this human being was chosen to reveal the nature and activity of God in the world. For as it stands,
the only information which John's followers could report back to him is
that Jesus is devoting his time caring for those who suffer and is preaching a message which is particularly good news for those who have been
marginalized to classes of economic poverty. Surely, we say to ourselves,

John would have been disappointed that his disciples could provide him no further clarification to the messianic question than a reaccount of Jesus' activities in the Galilean countryside.

Growing up in an evangelical, Protestant church in the United States, it was always curious to me that every sermon I heard preached on this passage pointed to Jesus' response as a 'proof' of his fulfillment of Old Testament prophecy; in our language, it was 'evidence that demanded a verdict.' It was assumed that if we could only gather enough hard data that would substantiate our beliefs — viz., that he was indeed the one whom the Old Testament prophets had predicted would come — others would also be convinced to believe in Christ as a true reality in their world as well. We determined the truth of his messianic existence, therefore, in relation to our own rational system, while virtually ignoring the very practical implications of Jesus' response for our historical existence.

In Latin America today, however, it is out of these very stories of historical ministry that the popular church has reformulated the approach to Christological inquiry. It has shifted the question of faith from rational truth to that realm which is implicitly found in Jesus' response to John: what kind of action does that faith produce? This manner of doing theology witnesses to the activity of God in the world as a reflection upon its engagement with the poor and suffering. It does so convinced that the character of God is revealed when love is shown to the "least of our sisters and brothers." The theological word in the popular church, then, is subject to a constant reinterpretation in relation to the unfolding of history as it is experienced in praxis. In this context is to be understood Gutiérrez' now famous statement, "Theology follows; is the second step. What Hegel used to say about philosophy can likewise be applied to theology; it rises only after sundown."[23]

Reading the Scripture with New Eyes

A Christological process so conceived implicitly gives hermeneutical priority to the current experiences of the Christian community. In what is surely to be a scandalous claim for textual positivists who trust in infallible deposits of truth ostensibly contained within the Bible, it must be confessed that it is more important to reflect upon what the Spirit is saying in contemporary communities than to apprehend what the Spirit said once upon a time.[24] That statement is in no way meant to imply a denigration of the value of Scripture; rather, it points to its proper function as a light for present reality. The work of Biblical interpretation does not concern itself with the questions which are raised as an outgrowth of its own method, but devotes itself to the questions which are raised by Christian or other Christic activity within the present context. The written text thereby becomes "the channel of meaning through a succession of historical moments. Now word ceases to be simply text to be interpreted, and itself becomes interpretive code. Now word is no longer world to be seen but eyes to see, no longer landscape but gaze, no longer thing but light."[25]

It is in this sense that Scripture may be said to have a pedagogical function within the Christian community. It presents itself as a paradigm of the dialogical interplay existing between past foundational events of history and their word of explication and illumination for present activity (cf. chapter Four). The Biblical text offers the community a narrative of the history of salvation which challenges it to read its own reality as part of that story. The community is invited to discern the movement of the Spirit in its own experiences and struggles. In that way the arena of God's activity does not remain fossilized within any one limited moment in that history (past or present), but is presented as an open process which continues to grow and develop wherever people struggle to be faithful to that vision. Carlos Mesters warns that to read the Scripture in any other way leads to tragic consequences: "... When the group closes itself up in the letter of the Biblical text and does not bring in the life of a community or the reality of the people's struggles, then it has no future and will eventually die."[26]

In truth, the 'memory' of the early Christian community is only activated when it is brought into contact with historical currency; metaphorically speaking, it is allowed to become a catalytic agent. The community may then begin to uncover Christological and soteriological images within its own world which subvert the vision legitimated by the religious and social vision promoted by the dominant sector. When that happens, the memory of Jesus is apt to become a dangerous force within the social system. If Christology were to entail no more than the simple reconstitution of the words of Jesus, on the other hand, it would pose no real threat to anyone. Therefore, Christology "performs its entire task only when it seeks to comprehend the words of the Spirit, who applies Jesus' words at a determinate time."[27]

The operation of this dynamic interplay is exemplified in a remarkable narrative related to me by María, a young campesina woman who lives in eastern El Salvador. She is one of numerous refugees who were forced to flee their villages in the fertile aprons of the San Vicente volcano region. María's family, along with the majority of campesino families in her village, had been involved in the local base community. After several years of critical reflection on their own reality as it interacted with the Biblical message of human redemption, they made the bold move of planting crops on idle land which was part of the private estate of the wealthy landowner—the same one for whom they had worked for years at slave wages. Although the community had offered to pay a reasonable rent for the land, the landowner did not want to see the community organized and self-sufficient (Where else do you get good labor for $1/day?). To make a long story short, the landowner called in the National Guard who forcibly displaced the people from his land and killed the community's leaders.

Subsequent military operations and heavy aerial bombardments eventually made it impossible for María and the other campesinos to live in their village. The community made a mass exodus to a coastal zone where the war was being carried out at a lower intensity. Nonetheless, like the other hundreds of thousands of displaced people throughout the country of El Salvador, they have been unrelentingly harrassed by the military for being alleged members of the *masas* of the guerilla front; since they are native to a zone where the rebels have strong support, then so runs the military's logic, they must be supporters of their cause.[28]

From time to time, though without announcement, the military would surround the community's new relocation village for days at a time, ostensibly to watch for subversive activity. María told me of the morning her brother, Enrique, had traveled to the provincial capital in order to buy some medicine for their family's malnourished and diseased children. While he was gone, the military set up camp around the village and were waiting for him upon his return. At the checkpoint they saw that Enrique was carrying medicine and immediately charged that he was gathering medicine for the rebels. His denials notwithstanding, they tortured him throughout the night to extract collaborative evidence until there was hardly any breath left in his body.

The next day, María related, the soldiers dragged him by his hair from house to house in the village in search of his family (the family is guilty by association in El Salvador, and often suffers the same fate as the accused one).

> Four Guardsman got out dragging the man, pulling him as if he were a sick animal. He was so disfigured, you couldn't even see what he looked like because of all the blood covering his face and drenching his shirt and pants.
>
> 'Bring him over here to see if they know him,' [said Private Martinez].
>
> It wasn't until I got close that I realized it was you, that you had your face covered with blood, and I could see one of your eyes was tattered, one eye that had observed your life around here, because the eye was

showing, it was hanging out. . . . When I see your pants my head is filled with nightmares. I don't know you, I don't know you. From where do I get the idea that I don't know you? Who instructed me to deny knowing you, or was my hope that it really wasn't you? Who could have had that exact pair of pants, a similar shirt, even though with all the blood it was barely distinguishable did you ever have a shirt the color of blood . . . ?

And the voice of the authorities saying, 'Perhaps you know him?' My legs on the point of giving up, of ceasing to flow through my veins. I feel paleness scurrying all over my skin. 'Do you know this man?'

Then I said no. It had to be without any quavering of my voice, without the least bit of hesitation. And at the moment your good eye opened, the one they had left you, which perhaps for that reason you had kept closed so as not to talk, so as not to be recognized. Your coffee-colored eyes, the same ones I had seen with my pair for more than thirty years.[29]

María was visibly shaken simply by the retelling of her tragic story; obviously, it is not the type of experience that would easily fade from one's memory in a lifetime, let alone in a year. After a few moments pause to collect herself, she continued to explain to me how the base community met together to deal with the crisis caused by the death of her brother and the communal denial of acknowledgment:

At first we expressed our guilt—can you imagine the pain of denying your own brother and compañero? We tried to make sense about whether we had done the right thing or if we had merely been cowards. Someone brought up the fact that we were not alone in this question: after Jesus had been picked up by the Roman soldiers and was being tortured on the night before his trial, Peter, when asked, also denied that he ever knew Jesus. Wasn't he too trying to save his own life? Geez, he had to go through the agony of doing it three times!

Then it hit me. Didn't Jesus understand why Peter did what he did? We began looking at how Jesus treated Peter by the lake after his resurrection [John 21:15 – 19]. He understood. He forgave him. Someone else remarked that three times—the same number as Peter's denial—Jesus assured Peter that all he needed to know was that Peter loved him. And how was he to show it? By loving and serving others: 'Feed my sheep.'

Enrique knew that we loved him too, and has already forgiven us. The best thing that we can do to show that love is go on with our struggle for others. Both he and Jesus will walk forward [adelante] with us.

María and her community have worked together to see the word of God as it is hidden within their own struggles, not as it is enclosed within a text. They have shifted the axis of interpretation: "basically they are not trying to interpret the Bible; they are trying to interpret life with the help of the Bible."[30] Their hermeneutical circle runs from the 'pre-textual' critical awareness of their own experience to a 'con-textual' reading of the Scripture with each other, and then on to an active praxis which informs their pretext.

Some rather profound Christological images emerge from María's interpretation of Jesus/Enrique's torture and death and Peter/the community's act of denial. Especially in light of the popular images of the suffering Christ which have reinforced the notion of a predetermined fate of the powerless in Latin America, it might be expected that Enrique's death would have been internalized as yet another instance of defeat, sacrifice, and pain. In other words, death appropriated not as a temporary reversal to be overcome in struggle, but as an inevitable necessity, a condition for the privilege of living. Within that thematic universe, they would surely have then rationalized their denial as the only possible response of an impotent people.

But quite the opposite took place. Certainly, Enrique is identified with Jesus as an innocent victim brought to his death by injustice, but only insofar as he also lives with him to empower the community which must now carry on with its struggle. Even greater emphasis is placed on the salvific role of forgiveness which frees the community from the paralysis of guilt and self-immolation. Theirs is a Christ who understands the twisted conundrums of historical realities which admit no simple solutions, and often lead only to painful failure. And yet this Christ not only forgives, but as *El Salvador* [the Savior] still encourages them to move ahead on a path which will surely land them in more snares and setbacks, i.e. failure. But even after each setback, this Christ is there to tell them that at the end of the road is liberation, not only for themselves but for their larger community as well. Love for this Christ, then, may only authentically be expressed by an active commitment to create the conditions by which others may be "fed," i.e., justice.

It would be misleading, however, to give the impression that the hermeneutical circle which the base communities employ for their interpretation of Biblical passages always relies, or even should rely, on an analogical key — e.g., Jesus and his socio-historical context corresponds to the base community and the current socio-historical context. Regardless of the fact that certain resemblances may be identified between similar historical contexts of oppression, it would be anachronistic to hold that applicability would simply carry across two thousand centuries. Though some form of mediation is required to challenge present-day communal reflections, that mediation cannot simply be an "automatic process of imitation which pays no heed at all to our own concrete situation and bypasses political, anthropological, and socio-economic analysis."[31]

In certain situations, such as in the experience of María and her community, the relationships between context and message will seem compatible. But even in such cases, the level of applicability is not primarily dependent upon the identity of those contexts but the challenge and direction which that message gives to human faith. Does faith, then, signify an encounter with God's word on a distinctly ahistorical plane of reality? No, for quite to the contrary, faith is a radically historical mode of being. It is simply the case that Scripture cannot prescribe the specific ideologies which are required to concretize a faith response within another socio-historical context; it may only manifest those relative ideologies by which faith has been practiced in its own time and place. That is why Scripture is said to have a pedagogical relationship to the contemporary community: the latter is taught how to search for the truth of its own existence based on a creative fidelity to the former.

> We need not, then, look for formulas to 'copy,' or techniques to 'apply,' from Scripture. What Scripture will offer us are rather something like orientations, models, types, directives, principles, inspirations — elements permitting us to acquire . . . a 'hermeneutic competency,' and thus the capacity of judge . . . 'according to the mind of Christ' . . . the new, unpredictable situations with which we are continually confronted.[32]

A U.S. priest working in the highlands of Guatemala, Tom Melville, discovered that even what might be considered the most universal of gospel teachings may not always find its complete application in new contexts. Melville's pastoral ministry was directed primarily to the indigenous tribes which make up a significant portion of Guatemala's highland population, a percentage which is rapidly decreasing because of the genocide — itself the outgrowth of a twisted prejudice which has deep racial and socio-economic roots — which the Guatemalan military has carried out against them for centuries.

On one occasion, Melville presented during mass the parable of the good Samaritan to the gathered faith community as a model of exemplary Christian action toward one's neighbor. The community members patiently listened as he urged them to treat all human beings with the respect and dignity which the Samaritan accorded to the beaten man lying beside the side of the road. After the mass was over, a proud, yet troubled Indian man approached the priest and thanked him for teaching them how to help the neighbor who has been maltreated and left to die on the road; yet, he politely related, in knowing how to do that they had already had plenty of experience. The most difficult and pressing question, suggested the man, had not been addressed by the sermon on the parable: what do you think that we should do to defend the neighbor if we come upon him *while* he is being beaten and exploited? How do we act towards those who are administering the blows? Startled by these unexpected queries, Melville was then forced to return to his own hermeneutical circle.[33]

Without a doubt, the parable of the good Samaritan has some rather profound, direct applications within the context of the Guatemalan situation. In fact, an interpretive model which relies on a correspondence of terms has elicited some rather radical implications for this context in which the attribution of heroic status is clearly defined along racial and class lines. What the Indian campesino had suggested to Melville, however, is that its meaning potential is not exhausted by mere recourse to analogical significations. The historical, cultural, political, and religious elements which constitute any specific event form a complex of irrepeatable conditions which require their own analysis and resolution. Moreover, human relationships are determined within this matrix of conflictual realities in such a way which at times precludes the viability of, say, an ethical appeal to universal love. For instance, in the scenario posed by the Indian campesino, *how* is universal love to become operative and *for whom?* What would it mean to effectively love the victim; or again, the thieves/oppressors?

Tokihiro Kudó discovered in his work with the oppressed in Peru that the translation of the Christian message into general religious statements has often encouraged a form of religious conduct which tends to be ahistorical and apolitical.

> Fundamental elements such as 'unity,' 'peace,' 'order,' 'liberty,' 'love for one's enemies,' 'the will of God,' etc. have, in point of fact, acted among other things, as *intrusive channels and mechanisms* of ideological legitimation that justify the established social order to the extent that they have deprived these messages of their dialectical force of protest and historical transformation.[34]

The Indian campesino, however, insightfully cut through the potential manipulation of the parable as a call to a patient and fraternal nonresistance to evil, the universal application of which might only serve to prolong the domination of the status quo.

Inevitably, this Guatemalan example points to a larger ethical dilemma, namely, that of the practice of 'defensive' violence in the quest for justice.[35] Although the topic is much too complex for a proper consideration here, it must at least be noted in passing that a definitive answer to the debate is not mandated by reference to Jesus as 'a man of nonviolent love' or as 'the man who did not resist evil.' To begin with, the latter case is patently untrue — Jesus was quite energetic in resisting the evil perpetrated by his enemies, as argument after argument with the Pharisees and other Jewish authorities demonstrate. Moreover, while exegetical attempts to portray Jesus as anything other than nonviolent in his earthly practice are bound to fail, so will all attempts which seek to make his relative, historical option of nonviolence into an absolute ethical criteria for discipleship.

It would be equally wrong to conclusively promote an absolute legitimation of violent activity on the basis of God's commandment to the Israelites to violently conquer the people of Canaan in order to take over the land God had promised them. Citing selected Scriptural texts from either side of the issue does not bring the modern faith community any closer to a solution of its own ethical crisis. "To put it another way," Segundo writes, "all the remarks we find in the Bible about violence or nonviolence are ideologies — necessary, of course, since we will always be confronted with the task of filling the void between faith and concrete historical realities."[36]

Of course, the Scriptural witness adds yet another fundamental factor to these considerations which go beyond the mere determination of 'us' and 'them' or 'ally' and 'enemy': forgiveness. The notion of forgiveness is filled with many concrete images in the one who "died for the sins of the many," images which manifest that grace can arrive to even the most outrageous situations of injustice. Although most Christians are able to affirm the possibility of forgiveness, its application within personal and social conflict is all too often quite absent. Perhaps the knowledge of forgiveness, then, comes only through the risk of putting it into practice.

One would think that forgiveness would have been long forgotten in Nicaragua. It was hoped that a people's revolution in 1979 would have put an end to the decades of misery which the country had experienced under the U.S.-backed Somoza dictatorship. But peace was short-lived, for within two years the Central Intelligence Agency was organizing and arming Somoza's deposed National Guard to form a contra-revolutionary force capable of carrying out significant destruction to Nicaragua's socio-economic infrastructure.

The ecclesial base community in the city of Leon has walked a pilgrimage of faith even in the midst of these national crises. During the latter years of the Somoza dynasty, the community linked with other groups to establish a movement which sought to change the conditions which were killing so many of their neighbors. Its activities toward this end inevitably brought tremendous repression down upon it. When the brutal National Guard arrived in Leon ostensibly to restore order, many of its members suffered torture and, in some cases, execution. Then, as

Sandinista victory drew unmistakably nearer, Somoza sent his bomber planes to destroy Leon and many of Nicaragua's other major cities so that the society would be left in shambles for the new government. In many respects, Somoza's strategy worked; when I walked the streets of Leon for the first time in 1984, five years after the aerial bombardments, the city was still half in ruins.

In more recent times, the tears of the community have once again been brought to a tragic flow. The bodies of two of its young boys, sent to the mountains to defend the border of Honduras against incursions by the Contras, were returned in wooden boxes. The bloom of life had been stolen from them. The community was torn with grief as it came together to remember their lives. Deep emotions broke loose in songs which called it back to hope in the love of God from which nothing could separate them. The remembrances recalled and the blessings given, the funeral ended with the community gathered in a circle around the caskets. In the center of the circle, near the lifeless bodies of their close friends and Christian brothers, stood several young men dressed in military green. They joined with the entire community in prayer for those who had died and for their families who had been left behind. Then something remarkable happened. The community asked forgiveness for those who had killed the boys, for those very ex-National Guardsmen who have brought so much suffering to their country. Asking that they too might find the way of the gospel, the community repeated the ancient prayer of forgiveness.

Grace had once again appeared unexpectedly. One would think that hate and bitterness might dominate the lives of the Leon community; yet, to our surprise the doors of reconciliation and conversion are left open for their enemies. It is so difficult for us to forgive those who have abused us, for the violation of trust endures, remaining a block to severed relationships and unimaginable violations. The message from Leon and Calvary, however, is that hate and conflict are not the only realities in the world. Jesus, nailed to a cross, looks on those who have opposed his project of bringing God's reign near and asks God to forgive them. He can acknowledge the humanity even in his enemies. To find those possibilities in our own world certainly requires the reading of Scripture with 'new eyes' that are able to envision not only who we are, but who we can indeed become.

The Theologian and the Community

As was exemplified in the case of Lito's community, the achievement of conscientization within the oppressed community, and thus a regaining of their true selves, most generally requires the intervention of an outside agent who will work *with*, though not *for*, the oppressed to uncover the thematic universe which encloses them.[37] Since those who have been marginalized from the social sector are often unable to critically evaluate their objective situation and its causes, the pedagogical agent, who is not in a co-dependent relationship to the dominant ideology, may pose their own reality to them in ways which provides glimpses of momentary breaks in a seemingly impenetrable system.

In Freire's estimation, it is vital that this "dialogical teacher" present the oppressed community not with a new thematic universe which is alien to its own world, but one which 're-presents' that very universe to the people from whom it was first received. In order to pose that world itself as a problem, then, the educator must first become immersed in an investigation of those themes and symbols which have served to maintain that world in the first place. It was suggested in chapter Two that, in this manner, Jesus used parables as narrative sketches which represented situations familiar to his hearers, but which at the same time opened up their world to unexplored possibilities and themes. In the same way, the dialogical teacher must utilize relevant metaphors which represent situations familiar to a specific community and the thematics which constitute its world so that it may readily recognize its own relationship to those situations of oppression.[38]

Freire warns of the propensity of the 'enlightened' educator, who either does not realize or simply ignores the fact that liberative education must fundamentally begin with thematic investigation, to eschew a dialogical pedagogy in favor of a "moralistic" approach. The moralistic educator may be thought of, at least on a literal level, as one who sermonizes *to* the community and thereby conveys a prescribed body of virtues which are necessary to save the community from its problems. On a much more subtle and potent level, however, the moralistic educator typically seeks to move the community beyond the motifs of the local situation in order to introduce themes which he or she believes are more intellectually salient. Such a pedagogical method, however, is geared more to impart 'true' ideas than it is to prepare the members of the community for the struggle against the obstacles to their own humanization.[39]

Mesters has discovered in his pastoral work with the base communities in Brazil that the theological "expert" who comes to teach biblical interpretation to the 'common' people is always in danger of falling into a paternalistic style of pedagogy:

> The expert may arrive with his or her more learned and sophisticated approach and once again expropriate the gains won by the people. . . . We say it is scientific. When the people get together to interpret the Bi-

ble, they do not proceed by logical reasoning but by the association of ideas. One person says one thing; somebody else says another. We tend to think that approach has little value, but actually it is just as scientific as our approach![40]

It is not that Mesters the Scriptural scholar would want to eliminate scientific, critical analysis from the hermeneutical process of Biblical and theological interpretation. He considers it invaluable, but only when it is put in the service of the questions which the people themselves are raising and which are formulated in a cultural universe which is their own.

It is in the very process of dialogue that the marginalized community has its first opportunity to regain the dignity which has been stolen from it. It is not so much assistance that the marginalized community requires as it does accompaniment. For "when the hungry ask for bread and receive it," observes Tamez, "their dignity is not necessarily taken into consideration." But when they are allowed "to think, to enter into theological dialogue (in their own way), and to make their contribution," the potential for their own human dignity is given fertile ground to grow and flourish.[41]

As insightful and sincere an educator as Ernesto Cardenal is generally found to be in his role as a dialogical teacher within the Solentiname community of Nicaragua, he nevertheless from time to time turned to a moralistic pedagogy by means of which he imposed his own conceptual world onto the concrete thematic universe of the campesino. In one particularly vivid example, Cardenal is leading the community in a discussion of the parable of the wise virgins (Matt. 25:10–13):

'[The five] were awake because they knew neither the day nor the hour in which the Son of Man would come.'

Esperanza: It means that the change could come at any moment . . .

[Cardenal]: It's going to be a surprise, according to this, and when it is least expected. . . .

Oscar: What tremendous happiness! In a fiesta we all get together and we share everything that's there, and we all take part in everybody else's conversations and we're happy to be hearing everyone. For that reason I believe the kingdom is like a fiesta, a joyful time.

[Cardenal]: The gathering has to be for everyone, and that's why the resurrection is needed. All those that have died will also share in that joy, provided they lived with their lamp oil ready.

Laureano: Now only a few people can afford to have big fiestas, with whiskey and fancy things.

Olivia: It won't be a fiesta like those other fiestas, it'll be more like the fiesta there is when in a country in which every single person eats and every single person has medicine and every single person has clothes. If it was like that here, all Solentiname would be a fiesta, and all Nicaragua would be a fiesta, because there would be love, and because there would be everything for everybody. And it's pretty much like that kind of fiesta that the kingdom of heaven will be.

Oscar: Look, when a rich bastard has a fiesta, the poor people can't share. But when the people have a fiesta, it's a joy for everybody, and even the rich can share in it. It seems to me it'll be like that, like the people's fiestas, the one that God offers in the kingdom.

[Cardenal]: I've wondered about one thing: why does the bridegroom of this parable get to the fiesta so late? . . . I think it must have been because the fiesta, for some reason, was delayed. The parable seems to be trying to tell us that the marriage of God and the people has also had a delay in history. We don't know why, but it will take place later than planned. . . . [42]

While the campesinos of the Solentiname community are focussed on the image of the reign of God as a country fiesta to which everyone is invited and within which everyone has their place, Cardenal repeatedly tries without success to bring the discussion around to an explanation for the failure of the Parousia to arrive. It is not that the campesinos ignore the fact that the bridegroom has been delayed in his arrival; several times they allude to the fact that the virgins have been left waiting. All the same, even despite Cardenal's prompting, they hardly concern themselves with the bridegroom, and certainly do not make his belated appearance the hermeneutical key to the parable's interpretation.

Possibly because their lives are so accustomed to waiting—for transport to the capital, for work at the haciendas, for medicine for their families—time does not become the primary consideration. They are more interested in discussing how the ten women, as the waiting ones, respond to their insecure conditions in order to actively prepare for the fiesta, and in so doing, actually shape the character which that coming fiesta will take. Thus, while Cardenal seeks to intellectualize the problem of the parable, the community visualizes it as a concrete injustice which unsettles its world.

The reason for this divergence in focus is a product of the conceptual universes which are relied upon in their respective hermeneutical circles. Cardenal, unquestionably with the best of intentions, has sought to orient the community's reflections within an exegetical framework which is alienated from the campesino's own conceptual universe. He utilizes static categories of time and world: there is one, monistic world which moves in a linear fashion through time to a predetermined end. Since the definitive new world has failed to arrive and put the old world to an end — neither in the life of Jesus (as he so eagerly anticipated) nor in the two thousand years hence — the primary theological problem of the parable revolves around time, that is, the delay of the bridegroom (cf. chapter Two).

But for the campesinos, the categories of time and world are sustained in a fluid relationship. The parameters of world are not fixed by determined points in time but by the social relationships which maintain that world. The present world is one in which rich landowners are the only people who can afford to have lavish fiestas, while the remainder of that world struggles to find food to eat, clothes to wear, and medicine to heal. The limit of that world is marked by a selfish mentality. But within time (and not necessarily at its linear end), that seemingly invincible world will crumble and give way to the new world of country fiestas which are bordered by a communal spirit.[43] The central theological problem here is the creation of a new world, that is, how to prepare its coming.

What this example from Solentiname helps to demonstrate is the difficulty of redoing theology from the underside of history. Orthodox theology has for so long been in the hands of the dominators that without an exegetical suspicion of the theoretical underpinnings which determine any method, theological and Biblical hermeneutics will always risk falling into an ideology of oppression. The theologian, however unwittingly, will then play a "superversive" role as one who bolsters and supports the prevailing domination.[44]

In order for the theologian to be truly subversive, that is, one who makes possible a rereading and remaking of theology from below, requires a respect for the right of the exploited themselves to participate in theological reflection. It is an appropriation of the Bible and faith in solidarity with the struggles of the poor, a rendering of theology which prevents "the private proprietors of this world's goods from being the private proprietors of the word of the Lord as well," and returns to the poor the right to exercise power in history.[45]

Within the life of the Christian community, then, the theologian is presented with an exceptional challenge: to articulate the consciousness and practice of the faith community both in light of the gospel and in regard to the specific historical commitments to which it is engaged. Of course, as has already been indicated, it would be wholly naïve to suppose that the theologian need only approach an oppressed community and spontaneously gather images and concepts which may serve as a

foundation for a people's theology of liberation. It would be equally simplistic, however, to expect that a determined theoretical framework, free
of ambiguity, would reflexively correspond to each and every concrete
praxis. The relationship between theory and praxis is much more dialectical than that which many proponents of historical theology are willing to admit.

Acknowledging that complexity, Clodovis Boff has criticized those
theologies which seek their font of knowledge in that reality which,
though it has been expressed by a number of different terms, actually
denotes the selfsame object: the poor, the exploited, the praxis of liberation, the experience of the base. Although he thinks these notions may
serve a very useful and positive ideological function, he believes that
they "are bereft of any very great theoretical vigor" and inevitably lead
to an "empiricism" which "mires itself in the concrete."

What partly lies behind Boff's critique is a legitimate concern that a
direct path will be swathed from praxis to theology which will bypass the
essential mediation of socio-critical analysis. In a nutshell, such an immediate identification of theory with praxis would ignore the fact that
every concrete praxis, be it oppressive or liberative, is engaged to a particular ideological commitment which boasts its own theoretical elaboration. The dominant ideology, no less than the revolutionary one, seeks
a theoretical explication which makes sense of the construction of reality
which corresponds to its interests. Therefore, when a hermeneutical
methodology situates theory and praxis on the same continuum, with
the latter posited as the criterion of the former, a major problem—at the
same time theoretical and ethical—is overlooked: *which* praxis and *which*
theory are to be advanced?[47] In Boff's system, then, theory and praxis
are presented as "irreducible orders" that are separated by a radical, dis-
continuous breach which may only be crossed by a decisive leap of human creativity.[48]

He does not thereby wish to place praxis and theory in a completely
autonomous relationship. Despite their relative independence, praxis,
by virtue of the fact that it is the "producer of social reality," sets the
agenda and serves as the material source (though not the actual result)
of theological theory. Therefore, he assumes that the theologian's engagement in a given cause and within a defined group or class determines, to a large extent, the objects or themes which one will treat within
one's own theological system.[49] Moreover, he accepts that it is only by
means of praxis that theory may move beyond its own transcendence in
order to enact practical realizations in history.

Nevertheless, he emphasizes that praxis does not thereby become
the criterion for theory; at most it may be said to be an indirect norm

which exerts pressure on theory by way of mediation. To even speak of praxis as a criterion for theological reflection is inappropriate, for theological theory is of another order of "practice" incomparable to that of concrete engagement. In that regard, he assumes that theological theory is not beholden to any practice external to itself, for it operates according its own logic and contains its own empirical verification. In short, "theology is a self-policed practice."[50]

For all of these reasons and more, Boff deems "ambiguous" any theological method which locates theory and praxis within the same realm of meaning. For example, so labeled is this statement crafted by Gutiérrez: "The theology of liberation attempts to reflect on the experience and meaning of faith based on the commitment to abolish injustice and to build a new society; this theology must be verified by the practice of that commitment."[51] Gutiérrez' "error," Boff claims, is to seek an external criterion of truth which springs from an "existential order" of the concrete practice of the community and brings it to bear upon an "epistemological order" which has its own rules of practice by which the theologian must operate. Theoretical quality cannot be judged, he repeatedly insists, on the social positioning of a theological production, nor its political theology, nor even its thematic relevance, but within its own "epistemological perimeter."[52]

Although one may grant Boff that efficacy may never be the sole criterion of faith and its theological rationale (the scandal of the cross is sufficient evidence of that!), his own proposal for the verification of theological theory—an 'in-house' self-validation based on internal criteria—must be seriously questioned as well. It is not as if theory, be it theological or otherwise, simply drops from the sky as a revelation of the interrelationship of dynamic factors which fashion historical realities. It is itself a product of the continual process of reflection which seeks to analyze and explain the cumulative human experience within history. For as his brother, Leonardo, explains:

> To know is to interpret, and there are no exceptions. The hermeneutic structure of all knowledge ... with its models, paradigms, and categories, enters into the composition of the experience of the object via the mediation of language. ... The subject is immersed in history, in a socio-political context, and is moved by personal and collective interests.[53]

It is nonsensical, then, to suppose that theory operates according to its own logic, that is, in reference to a set of predetermined rules which are given within a distinct (transcendent), epistemological order. That does not suggest, however, that theory is simply formulated by means of a direct deduction from empirical research. This latter assumption, viz., that science moves from neutral observation to theory, has been the *modus operandi* of the classical scientific model since the Enlightenment. In its most basic form, its method seeks to accumulate raw data and propose hypothetical theories which might account for that which has been observed.

Thomas Kuhn, in his study entitled *The Structure of Scientific Revolutions*, suggests that these two models of theoretical formulation are not the only possible alternatives.[54] Kuhn proposes that human beings perceive their world through the medium of an established "paradigm," i.e., a specific view of the world which incorporates the concepts, ideas, values, and hopes which undergird its existence.

Explaining Kuhn's theory in my own theological terms, as long as a community's theological paradigm coherently explains the activities and perceptions which shape its world, then the members of the community will continue to accept it as a true representation of its reality. However, when its praxis gives rise to an anomaly which contradicts the perceptual field offered by its paradigm, the community is intuitively thrown into a state of theoretical dissonance, i.e., confusion. The anomaly may very well be such that requires only a slight modification in a community's paradigm. Yet again, it may create such a considerable dissonance within the community that the entire paradigm is scrapped, thereby instigating a 'revolution' in its theoretical formulation and forcing the community to search for new paradigms which might orient its praxis. Such a paradigmatic shift would entail the radical reformulation of a community's theological model, introducing new symbols, more meaningful metaphors, more appropriate categories, and more relevant issues.

When their proper functions are duly respected, then, theory and praxis operate in a dialectical fashion; that is, as two keys which mutually inform one another. Praxis, in that sense, does not unfold in an existential vacuum. It is shaped in reference to those theoretical paradigms to which its basic identity is conformed. The limitations of human energy alone — regardless of the host of other complex factors which limit the vast universe of potential theoretical choice — obviate the feasibility of preparing anew, antecedent to every praxis, a theoretical elaboration specific to it alone. More realistically, human beings tend to trust those paradigms which adequately explain their world and subsequently orient their praxis.

To speak of 'trust,' though, may be misleading because it seems to imply that every community makes the free, intentional choice for that paradigm — theological, social, economic, political — which best responds to its experience of the world. Such a Pollyannaish view of theoretical formation denies a fundamental datum of human experience:

the conflictual character of all historical reality. In this real world of division at the level of praxis and theory, oppository sectors of the social system seek to impose that paradigm which best corresponds to its own interests and which legitimates the social status to which it has arrived.

Thus, theory may serve as part of a larger ideological mechanism which seeks not so much to explain reality as to mask its full meaning from those over whom the dominant sectors seek to maintain hegemony. In the exercise of their authority over the means of information and education within the society, as well as their control of the major institutions (political, economic, religious) which largely determine a social identity, the dominant sectors are able to daily bombard the oppressed sectors with a theoretical view of the world and their practice within it which is alienated from their own experience of that reality. In the relationship between theory and praxis, the dialectic is broken; theory becomes immune to the fruits of praxis and, consciously or not, seeks its ideological manipulation. Often times the oppressed, in a tragically ironic twist, come to trust paradigms which frame their practice in such a way as to reinforce their own subjugation within a closed world.

The opening of that world requires a reclamation of the dialectical relationship which theory and praxis may potentially enjoy. In this process of conscientization, the community may begin to analyze its own reality and become aware of its prior, distorted perceptual field. "This discovery cannot be purely intellectual but must involve action; nor can it be limited to mere activism, but must include serious reflection: only then will it be praxis."[55] What is called for, then, is a critical intervention (theory) which leads to an active transformation (praxis) of the community's objective situation.

Once this break in consciousness is effected, the oppressed inevitably become disillusioned with those paradigms which have misrepresented their reality and are impelled to choose, and even help create, new paradigms. Realistically, that task will often be facilitated by those specialists, such as the theologian, who are best equipped educationally to offer a theoretical systematization of the reflections gained from the engaged community. But in order to authentically fulfill that task, the theoretician is compelled to be in relationship to the transformative process of the community and theorize with it as a co-creator and co-subject of that unfolding reality. If not, the theologian's results will likely be something else than a theology of authentic liberation. So warns Gutiérrez,

> If theology is to be a reflection from within, and upon, praxis, it will be more important to bear in mind that what is being reflected upon is the praxis of liberation of the oppressed of the world. To divorce theologi-

cal method from this perspective would be to lose the nub of the question and fall back into the academic.[56]

In respect to all that has been written thus far, it would appear that all interpretation is irreducibly subjective. For "however academic it may be, theology is intimately bound up with the psychological, social, or political status quo though it may not be consciously aware of the fact."[57] From that perspective, the danger manifest in a theological theory that asserts its own independent verification is that it will, on the basis of its own ideological self-purging, claim to speciously function with complete neutrality and objectivity. Or, on another level, it will always herald itself as the protector of transcendent truth from the onslaught of historical contingencies.

In light of those dangers, Segundo contends that theological method is in many respects more important even than content in securing the liberative character of any theology which seeks to break with the existing system, for it ensures that the horizon of a particular theology will not be co-opted.[58] In order for method to function in that manner, however, it must be infused by a suspicion that "anything and everything involving ideas, including theology, is intimately bound up with the existing social situation in at least an unconscious way." Perhaps then it may prevent theology from being reabsorbed by the deeper mechanisms of oppression, for it invites an ongoing modification within whatever paradigm as is obliged by the continuing changes, both individual and social, that each new reality brings.[59] Segundo believes that this method is mandated by the pedagogical principle discovered in divine revelation: "The fact is that God shows up in a different light when his people find themselves in different historical situations. ... If God continually presents himself in a different light, then the truth about him must be different also."[60]

Therefore, Segundo begins his "hermeneutical circle" with the demand for a committed attitude which is not satisfied to simply reflect on the world, but one which requires a commitment to work for its actual transformation. This manner of experiencing reality as a participant in a process which is changing the world — and that primarily in and through the historical praxis of the struggling poor—engenders within the theologian an ideological suspicion regarding those paradigms which explain and justify the world as it presently is. The theologian might very well discover deeper layers of meaning in that reality which might serve to undermine the ideological assumptions upon which those paradigms rest. These suspicions may then be brought to bear on the society's ideological superstructure in general and to theology in particular.

These steps are deemed necessary since theology indelibly forms a part of any society's moral universe; consequently, it cannot declare itself exempt from the diverse ideological mechanisms which operate to maintain it and shape its character. For that reason, theological theory must always be confronted with a criterion which resides external to its own "epistemological perimeter." Informed by a critical evaluative judgment of its own relationship to the historical process, theological theory is forced to examine whether it will be truly liberative or whether it will reinforce that world maintained by the status quo.

Yet, Segundo's hermeneutical process does not end there; as suggested by its title, it comes back around full 'circle.' And as it returns to interpret reality, theological theory does so with the purpose of making the community's commitment for a transformation of the world more profound and clear. It seeks to illuminate history with the word of God so as to create a vision of that praxis which is consonant with the irreversible movement of divine redemption within the structures of that reality itself. Hence, the concrete praxis of the faith community is the soil into which the hermeneutical circle "stubbornly and permanently sinks its roots and from which it derives its strength."[61]

It is the truth about reality which is discovered in historical praxis which prevents theoretical explication from ever becoming comfortable or fixed within any status quo. That is not the sign of an empirical method, but a critical one which leads from theory to praxis and back again. Therefore, it should not be considered misguided when various theologians of liberation announce that the criteria of their undertaking will be 'the praxis of liberation' or 'the struggle of the poor in history.' They are making a radically distinct statement about the foundation of theological knowledge itself. For within a theology written from the underside of history, the poor serve a dual hermeneutical function: to determine the full significance of liberation in history and to discover within that history the hidden revelation of a liberating God. "These are the challenges," Gutiérrez announces, "that constitute the initial locus and criterion of discernment of all the other questions that arise in the course of its endeavors."[62]

The Community and Its Thematic Universe

Juan Carlos Scannone, a Jesuit priest from Argentina, laments the fact that liberation theology in Latin America has not gone far enough in shifting the hermeneutical center of its reflection toward the thematic universe of its own *pueblo*. He admits that one of the primary reasons for this situation is the inescapable truth that all too many liberation theo-

logians, having received their training and education in "the culture of
the Enlightenment," lose touch with the popular culture and its historical experience. Scannone proposes that if liberation theology is to speak
to and for the *pueblo,* it must be shaped in such a way that coincides with
a distinctively Latin American meaning-world.

> Now if theology does wish to accompany our people in history, discern-
> ing the signs of God in their history, life, and praxis from its own the-
> ological vantage point, then it obviously must confront the various
> socio-cultural mediations . . . through which the faith of the *pueblo* or of
> different groups read the signs of the times [and] the projects and uto-
> pias that articulate hope.[63]

Scannone concludes that this may very well require that the theologian
"undergo a real *cultural conversion,* [yet] without denying the values of
the tradition and critique they got from their training."[64]

This last point should not be overlooked, for it is historically naïve
and methodologically blind to suppose that the solution to the modern
Christological task in Latin America is a return to some earlier phase of
history when human thought was untainted by the ideological biases of
the Enlightenment; as if it and its Christological tradition are singularly
unique in respect of being determined by a horizon of interest! In truth,
the birth of the historical, social and physical sciences which occasioned
the development of modern thought during the last three centuries in
the countries of the North Atlantic have contributed to the formation of
those critical theories of knowledge which are central to liberation theology itself.[65]

Therefore, when it is proposed here that the Christological task in
Latin America is in need of further indigenization, that does not imply
a purging of all that which is not indigenous to its own culture.[66] Nor is
it an idealization of all that which might arise from a privileged fount, in
this case the struggle of the oppressed masses for their own liberation.
More to the point, it is simply underscoring that which other self-critical
liberation theologians have already noted elsewhere: "It is obvious . . .
that the native peoples and cultures of Latin America are not sufficiently
taken into account in our present efforts at theological reflection."[67]

In order for the indigenization of Christology to deepen in Latin
America, it would seem necessary for its theologians to presuppose two
fundamental propositions: (1) the Spirit of Christ is presently active in
the historical struggle of the Latin American *pueblo* for cultural, socio-
economic, and political freedom from colonial and neo-colonial domination and (2) a "veiled Christ" is somehow present in the pre-Columban
religion of the native people.[68]

A Christological commitment so conceived signals the complete reversal of that hermeneutical method employed by the Spanish 'court theologians' of the conquest and their ecclesiastical heirs. As Cook explains, "the failure to recognize even the possibility of Christ incarnating himself by transforming the Indian culture from within led to the massive rejection of everything indigenous and the imposition of a foreign Christ."[69] Ironically, due to the fact that the seed of Christianity in Latin America was sown with such a violent upturning of the native 'soil,' some of the most profound Christological images which arise out of the culture are defined in *opposition* to that religion rather than in *continuity* with it, e.g., the "beaten Christs of the Indies" (Las Casas).

Despite the apparent bankruptcy of the community's own popular religiosity, once the poor reach conscientization of their situation and the causes lying behind their exploitation, these symbols, myths, values and beliefs regularly serve as vital expressions of a dynamic faith. In fact, to theologize out of any other conceptual world always risks a reappropriation of the ideology of the dominant sector. In that regard, the process of a people's own liberation is inextricably linked to their capability to articulate their faith and identity in their own terms. To the extent that the Latin American base communities are able to intervene in their oppressive reality and free themselves from the dominant ideologies which dehumanize them, it will clear away the most deeply rooted obstacles preventing the possibility of their own cultural liberation. For the cultural and religious consciousness of a people is a vital element in the force for social transformation. As artist/theologian Brett Greider confirms:

> Essential to the development of a liberation theology is the conscientization of the people who forge a theology which represents their identity. A relationship with God implies a unique perspective that must be respected. Indigenous literature, narratives, songs, dance, folk arts, and oral traditions inform and uphold the identity of a people. This foundation is the source of community identity, an essential element in the formation of authentic religious expression.[70]

It is inevitable then, and even necessary, that cultural elements enter into the creation of contemporary Christologies. Boff attests that it has been this very practice—the continual assimilation of cultural values to the mystery of Christ—which has "prolonged" the incarnation of Christ throughout history. On the negative side, however, he warns that when Biblical or other traditional titles of Christ are adopted uncritically, i.e., without an awareness of their own "historical relativity," they are likely to degenerate into alien symbols. When that happens, these symbols are manipulated, more times than not, to absolutize a social or religious structure which is foreign to the cross of Jesus Christ. As an example, Boff points to a medieval European history in which popes and kings were thereby able to find an "ideological base" in such titles as "Christ the King" for the support of their feudal societies. Hence, concludes Boff, no title conferred on Christ can be absolutized independent of the culture within which it is confessed.[71]

Ironically, liberation theologians may find that even those Christological titles which have their roots in a modern emancipatory history take on different value significations in another cultural context. For instance, Stephen Judd, a Maryknoll missioner working with the base communities of the Quechua Indians in Peru, has discovered that the title "Jesus Christ Liberator" — a term with European roots which is widely used in liberation theology — has little or no meaning for the Quechuans.[72] Although it clearly has a greater degree of potency within the Spanish *mestizo* population, "liberator" has played virtually no role in the cultural identity of the Indian culture. Judd has discovered that the Quechuans find other Christic symbols which function within their culture to nourish and stimulate resistance to oppression:

> When ... [they] are asked 'Who is Christ for you?' the most frequent response is *Cristo humilde* [humble Christ]. ... *Humilde* is symbolically a highly-charged word. Such a designation is an honor reserved for the most respected people, those who are just, kind, compassionate. It is, moreover, an ironic term; for, like their dances, which 'mask' a deeper meaning, it expresses as well a hidden form of resistance to oppression. Thus, it is an ironic protest of the popular culture against the status quo and it implies a kind of imaginative challenge similar to the scene of Jesus' entry into Jerusalem.[73]

In like manner, Gutiérrez indicates that such subtle, yet nonetheless subversive, images of Christ have been sustained within the native culture despite centuries of domination. These Christological images retain that spirit of protest which has sparked indigenous rebellions against their oppressors over the course of that long history of subjugation.

> From the beginning of the conquest, the indigenous peoples of America revolted against their oppressors. The written history speaks very little of this. However ... the Indians who received the gospel found in it reasons for rejecting the oppression to which they were being submitted. They interpreted the gospel from their own situation and from their own culture.[74]

It would be wrong to assume, then, that all that is Christian in the continent's popular religion is the product of a wholesale appropriation of the colonists' theological world; much was covertly integrated into their own pre-Christian understanding of faith.

The cultural universe of a people is always a reflection of their own historical experience, an amalgamation of elements which has its origin both within the people themselves and the outside forces which affect them.[75] It is not surprising, therefore, that the Indian culture of Latin America has woven a patchwork of traditional Christian symbols mixed with the myths, legends, and utopic visions which were spawned by its own native culture. In one example of this cultural phenomenon from Peru, the campesinos often tell and retell the story of Inkarri, a figure of the religious folklore of the Inca culture. It is presented below as it appears in a catechism written and practiced by a network of Christian base communities located in the Northern Andes.

> Inkarri was the child of the Sun and of a poor woman; he shared the sufferings of Andean farm-workers: his feet were often bleeding from long walks through the mountains, but the blood was merely mingling with Mother Earth [*Pachamama*], his real mother.
>
> At a later time there is a struggle; Inkarri dies, killed by Spanish conquistadors or by his own brother. But his head still exists and his body is still growing. One day Inkarri will come back: 'When the world turns over, Inkarri will return and take power to himself as in former times. Then all people, Christians and non-Christians alike, will be as one.'
>
> The history of Inkarri tells of a harsh reality: that Peru is divided. One part wants 'progress' and economic domination, while the other is faithful to the ancient Peruvian society where everybody felt themselves to be children of the Sun and of Mother Earth.[76]

The agrarian spirituality of the Inca legend is reappropriated by these base communities to express the redemption which the Christ figure Inkarri promises despite his apparent defeat and death by the oppressors of the *pueblo*. The goddess of the earth, the *Pachamama*, shares in the 'bleeding' and suffering of her son and yearns for the day when the ownership of the land is 'turned over' and once again returned to its rightful tillers. In the background of this legend, salvation is tied to the sacredness of the land and its communal ownership by the *pueblo*. The utopic vision of a new society which is once again ruled by the Sun and the Mother Earth stimulates creative action to resist those who have sought to usurp their place. Meanwhile, the faithful are called to nourish the growing body of Inkarri in their midst. Its gospel is captured in the words of an ancient Quechuan song: *Nucanquis purinanchis, nuannyun puscananchis* [the strong person who weeps with the weak person—the one who suffers with us—will live].

The Inkarri legend is an alternative vision of life which incorporates elements of the Inca tradition together with those of the Christian faith to create an indigenous Christology which speaks to the fundamental hopes of the Latin American people. Yet, despite the deep value it has for its own culture—a quality it shares with other equally profound legends and myths which lie as an immense treasure hidden in the veins of Latin America's native culture—its cultural universe is strikingly absent from the vast majority of writings which have been produced by Latin American theologians. The Christological images which they have utilized are all too often the fruits of a North Atlantic church and its history.

Gutiérrez, perhaps more than any other Latin American liberation theologian, has manifested this concern to articulate God's proclamation "in Quechua and Spanish, of joy and pain, of liberation and oppression, of life and death, which is a part of this country."[77] Although it is not evident to the same degree in his Christology, much of Gutiérrez' work has been infused by the popular culture which he has drawn from Peru's native literature, art and traditions.

That interest is perhaps best exemplified in the interchange Gutiérrez enjoyed with one of Peru's most renowned novelists, José María Arguedas. Both authors have sought to make the poor not only the subjects, but also the co-artisans of their creative endeavors. Arguedas, for instance, tried to recapture the profound memory of his country's history and faith in such expressions as "a God who rejoins." Gutiérrez subsequently borrowed this image, enabling him to integrate into his theology a Peruvian vision of a God who makes life whole.

> Unlike the divinity of Spanish Catholicism who is distant and severe, the God who rejoins nourishes and makes whole. Much like Pachamama, or Earth Mother, whom campesinos have reverenced for centuries, Arguedas' God sustains the community of the oppressed with the gifts of nature and a collective belief in life.[78]

The power of Arguedas' imagery as it is reflected here is not due to the cleverness of his thought (alone!); it resounds with meaning because it goes to the depths of Peruvian identity.

In conclusion, if Gutiérrez is to be judged correct when he states that "theology is a reading of faith from the cultural universe that corresponds to [a specific] involvement in history and [its] religious experience,"[79] then it becomes imperative for an indigenous theology of liberation to reflect both the current historical engagement of its people for liberation and the heritage of its rich past which still breathes life into the present culture. A Latin American Christology committed to this task will strive to speak of Christ in a manner which is truly good news ('gospel') within that context. To be true to that task it must critically appropriate the historical experiences, cultural symbols, beliefs and utopic visions of the Latin American *pueblo* as a vital expression of that liberative work which the Spirit is effecting within its own reality. It is a work of creative imagination which affirms that the path of the struggling and resurrected Jesus is still open. *"Caminante, no hay camino. Se hace camino al andar"* [traveler, there is no road; the way is made by walking].[80]

Notes

1. José María Arguedas, "La Novela y el Problema de la Expresión Literaria en el Perú," in *Yawar Fiesta* (Santiago: Editorial Universitaria, 1973), 17, quoted in Cadorette, *Heart of the People*, 31.

2. Segundo, *Liberation of Theology*, 241. Boff remarks in a similar vein, "This kind of urgent reflection is presupposed in the liberation Christology now being elaborated on our continent. It is rarely written down or presented in theoretical detail; instead it is being bruited about in discussion groups and passed along in mimeographed texts," *Liberator,* Epilogue, 278.

3. Gutiérrez, *We Drink From Our Own Wells*, 27.

4. Gutiérrez, "The Irruption of the Poor in Latin America and the Christian Communities of the Common People," in *The Challenge of Basic Christian Communities: Papers from the International Congress of Theology, February/March 1980, São Paulo, Brazil,* eds. Sergio Torres and John Eagleson (Maryknoll: Orbis Books, 1981), 116.

5. Ernesto Cardenal, *El Evangelio en Solentiname,* vol. 1 (Managua: Editorial Nueva Nicaragua, 1983); *The Gospel in Solentiname,* vol. 1, trans. Donald Walsh (Maryknoll: Orbis Books, 1976), 77–79.

6. Míguez Bonino, *Revolutionary Situation,* 173. "Ecclesiogenesis" was brought into nomenclature during a congress celebrated jointly by the base communities and church hierarchy in Brazil. See Boff, *Ecclesiogenesis: The Base Communities Reinvent the Church* (Maryknoll: Orbis Books, 1986).

7. Míguez Bonino, "Who is Jesus in Latin America Today?," 5.

8. Gutiérrez and Richard Schaull, "Freedom and Salvation: A Political Problem," in *Liberation and Change* (Atlanta: John Knox Press, 1977), 92.

9. C. Boff, *Theology and Praxis,* 8.

10. Gutiérrez, "Liberation, Theology, and Proclamation," in *The Mystical and Political Dimension of the Christian Faith, Concilium*, vol. 96, eds. Claude Geffré and Gustavo Gutiérrez (New York: Herder & Herder, 1974), 71.

11. Gutiérrez, *Power of the Poor*, 123–4.
In kind, Tamez writes, "It is said our Latin American peoples are eminently Christian. . . . But the statement is a contradiction, because while the gospel preaches life, justice, and freedom, the masses of our peoples live in abject poverty and are oppressed and repressed," *Bible of the Oppressed*, 75.

12. Galilea, "New Tasks Facing Christians," 173. The Spanish phrase *toma de conciencia* is practically an idiomatic expression. It is admittedly not adequately rendered by the common translation which I give here: "process of conscientization." It is much more profound than an intellectual paradigmatic shift, although it is clearly that as well; it entails concrete engagement.

13. Freire, *Pedagogy*, 100.

14. Ibid., 32, 94.

15. Vidales and Kudó, *Práctica Religiosa y Proyecto Histórico*, 114.

16. Freire, *Pedagogy*, 51.

17. Indeed, the Santa Fe Document which was compiled by Ronald Reagan's 'kitchen cabinet' in 1980 and which served as a guide for U.S. policy towards Latin America over the course of the Reagan administration's eight year term, identified the liberation movement as a formidable enemy which must be fought on religious and ideological lines. It is no wonder, therefore, that the term "liberation theology" in the U.S. has become a pejorative label which is used to disparage those churches and Christian movements which do not support the status quo—the religious equivalent of labeling someone a communist.

18. María López Vigil, *Don Lito de El Salvador: Habla un Campesino* (San Salvador: UCA Editores, 1982), 29–39. Excerpts taken from the chapter of Don Lito's testimony entitled "Despertando" [awakening].

19. C. Boff, *Theology and Praxis*, 21.

20. Herzog, "Quest," 37.

21. Gutiérrez, *Power of the Poor*, 101.

22. C. Boff, *Theology and Praxis*, p. 138. "For the 'bestowal of meaning,' " writes Boff, "is not to be understood as capricious invention, but as a decision and determination of meaning in the space that 'hermeneutic reason' has opened and circumscribed," ibid., 37.

23. Gutiérrez, *Theology of Liberation*, 11.

24. C. Boff, *Theology and Praxis*, 151.

25. Ibid., 137.

26. Mesters, "Use of the Bible," 200.

27. José Comblin, "Autour de la 'Théologie de la Révolution," *La Foi et le Temps*, vol. 5 (1975), 530, quoted in C. Boff, *Theology and Praxis*, 303, n. 85.

28. One of my companions on this visit to María's base community was a Baptist pastor from the United States who instigated a fascinating discussion with the gathered base community with what may only be conceived as a quintessentially U.S. preoccupation:

U.S. Pastor: "Do you people fear communism?"

Miguel (Delegate of the Word): "I don't think we know what communism is exactly. We are more worried about where our next meal will come from, whether our family can get medicine, how we can escape the wrath of the army. . . . I think communism is something only the wealthy in our country worry about. In fact, it may very well be a *fantasma* of the wealthy to keep us from changing our reality!" [After a morning full of frank and honest discussion with the community, Miguel approaches our table as we are finishing lunch. The entire community looks on, listening]

Miguel: "Now that we have built some confidence in one another, maybe you could answer some questions for us" [one campesino gets up and goes outside, circling the church to make sure no one is listening in beneath a window—a process which is repeated every five minutes thereafter]. "What exactly is communism?"

U.S. Pastor: "To tell you the truth, I really don't know either" [Laughter breaks out on all sides].

29. The actual words used here to describe what happened to María's brother are taken from a novel written by Manlio Argueta because it remarkedly matches down to even the most minute detail that of María's own testimony. The remainder of the narrative is told completely in the words of María. See Manlio Argueta, *One Day of Life*, trans. Bill Brow (New York: Aventura, 1980).

Argueta, a personal friend, has told me that his novel, which recounts the story of one woman's struggle in El Salvador, was based on the testimony of the wife of one of the leaders of the Christian campesino cooperative movement (FECCAS) formed in Chalatenango during the mid-1970s. Her husband was killed for his leadership role. The coincidence of Argueta's narrative with that of María's serves to demonstrate that these events are not isolated incidents, but daily realities for thousands of Latin Americans.

30. Mesters, "Use of the Bible," 205.

31. Sobrino, *Christology at the Crossroads*, 12.

32. C. Boff, *Theology and Praxis*, 149.

33. Story as told to me by Margarita Melville. Tom and Margarita (Sister Marian Peter) were both Maryknoll missioners in Guatemala during the late 1950s and 1960s. Due to their close contacts with the urban and rural poor of the country, they eventually accompanied the people in their option for a revolution-

ary change. Because of their specific option, they were ordered out of the country by the Maryknoll superiors (with pressure by Guatemalan Cardinal Casariego). They later left the Maryknoll order and married.

34. Kudó, *Práctica Religiosa y Proyecto Histórico II: Estudio sobre la Religiosidad Popular en Dos Barrios de Lima* (Lima: Centro de Estudios y Publicaciones, 1980), 113.

35. When I call it "defensive," I do so because those in Latin America who have taken up arms for liberation have often done so as a 'third response.' The first level of violence is the effect which the socio-economic structures exact against the people (hunger, disease, etc.) In actuality, this type of violence is the cause of the greatest number of deaths. The second level is the violence enacted by the dominant minority in order to silence any opposition created by the first wave of violence. Third, is the defensive violence of the people against the first two forms of violence. See Dom Helder Camara, *The Spiral of Violence* (London: Sheed & Ward, 1971).

36. Segundo, *Liberation of Theology*, 166.

37. Freire, *Pedagogy*, 33.

38. Ibid., 100–108.

39. Ibid., 112.

40. Carlos Mesters, "The Use of the Bible in Communities of the Common People," in *Challenge of Basic Christian Communities*, 203.

41. Elsa Tamez, "A New Stage in the Development of the Christian Community," in Samuel Amirtham and John S. Pobee, eds., *Theology by the People: Reflections on Doing Theology in Community* (Geneva: World Council of Churches, 1986), 114.

42. Cardenal, *El Evangelio en Solentiname*, vol. 4, 29–30.

43. In his study of popular religious and class consciousness in Nicaragua, anthropologist Roger Lancaster finds material which reinforces the point which I am attempting to make in this example. Lancaster discovers that the popular religion of the Nicaraguan people contains "an assortment of social leveling mechanisms." Most pertinent here is the practice of popular fiestas for patron saints. He notes that the responsibility to host the fiesta falls upon the *mayordomos* [stewards], who typically are better off economically than the majority of campesinos. "Such sponsorship means temporary economic ruin for the 'big men' *[hombres grandes]* compelled, as a result of their good fortune, to fund these fiestas," *Thanks to God and the Revolution: Popular Religion and Class Consciousness in the New Nicaragua* (New York: Columbia University Press, 1988), 52.

Lancaster found the same expectations present in the popular consciousness of the poor barrios of Managua. For example, in the *Purísma,* a week-long celebration of the Virgin Mary's purity, it is incumbent on the more prosperous members of the community to host a fiesta and give a large number of gifts away to one's neighbors. See ibid., 52.

These traditions which exist within the popular religion of the Nicaraguan people are potent themes for the re-establishment of world. As Lancaster notes, "They already constitute a real bulwark against capitalistic accumulation and exploitation, and they provide a moral paradigm that might readily be mobilized within a newly articulated class consciousness. Further, they already suggest a working model for revolutionary redistribution," ibid., 52. It seems evident, then, that the campesinos of Solentiname were seeking to relate those themes to the disappointment of the virgins in the Biblical story who were not able to participate in the fiesta. In their own experience, the large landowners of the Somoza dynasty had broken the basic moral code of human decency, refusing to share with those who were less fortunate and accumulating their wealth for themselves.

44. Gutiérrez, *Power of the Poor*, 21.

45. Ibid., 101.

46. C. Boff, *Theology and Praxis*, 175.

47. Ibid., 231.

48. Ibid., 193.

49. Ibid., 167–8, 207–8. Kudó further enriches this point: "Since, then, concrete people, the rich and the poor, live in social conditions in this society which are not only unequal but distinct, in the final analysis concrete people, viz., the rich and the poor, have a distinct sense of life and different ways of relating with nature, other groups of people and themselves," *Hacia una Cultura Popular* (Lima: Centro de Estudios y Promoción del Desarrollo, 1982), 118.

50. C. Boff, *Theology and Praxis*, 199.

51. Gutiérrez, *Theology of Liberation*, 307, quoted in C. Boff, *Theology and Praxis*, 323, n. 16.

52. C. Boff, *Theology and Praxis*, 15.

53. C. Boff, *Passion of Christ*, 1.

54. Thomas Kuhn, *The Structure of Scientific Revolutions*, 2nd ed. (Chicago: University of Chicago Press, 1970).

55. Freire, *Pedagogy*, 52.

56. Gutiérrez, *Power of the Poor*, 201.

57. Segundo, *Liberation of Theology*, 13.

58. Ibid., 39–40.

59. Ibid., 8.

60. Ibid., 31.

61. Gutiérrez, *Theology of Liberation*, 3.

62. Gutiérrez, *Power of the Poor*, 169.

63. Scannone, "Theology, Popular Culture, and Discernment," 255–6. Gutiérrez voices this same conviction at the conclusion of *Theology of Liberation:* "But in the last instance we will have an authentic theology of liberation only when the oppressed themselves can freely raise their voice and express themselves directly and creatively in society and in the heart of the People of God, when they themselves 'account for the hope' which they bear, when they are the protagonists of their own liberation. For now we must limit ourselves to deepen and support that process, which has barely begun," 307.

64. Ibid., 225.

65. See Gutiérrez, *Power of the Poor*, 173.

66. I use "indigenization" in the sense conveyed by Cook's superb definition: "By indigenization I mean simply a particular people getting in touch with their own uniquely proper roots ('radicalization' in the best possible sense of the word) through a profound recognition (memory) of themselves in their history, their culture, their spirituality, and their communal (ecclesial?) experience." Cook adds that "indigenization" must be "critically appropriated through a specific politico-communal commitment," i.e., conscientization, in order that a particular view of culture and history does not become romanticized, "Christology in Latin America," 277.

67. Gutiérrez, "Liberation Praxis and Christian Faith," in *Frontiers*, 33, n. 13. When does he believe that this will begin to happen?: "We will get a new and distinctive theological perspective only when our starting point is the social praxis of the real population of Latin America, of those whose roots are buried deep in the geographical, historical, and cultural soil of our region, but who now stand mute. It is from that source that we will get a new reading and interpretation of the gospel message as well as a fresh expression of the experiences it has occasioned throughout history and their meaning," ibid., 25.

68. Enrique Jordá Arias, "El Cristo velado del pueblo andino," *Pastoral Andina* 12 (1975) 15–25, cited in Cook, "Christology in Latin America," 279. The main thrust of Jordá Arias' article is directed towards the appropriation of the images of Christ among the Andean people, and does not address the Christological implications of the wider cultural and racial diversity of the Latin American continent.

69. Cook, "Christology in Latin America," 279.

70. Brett Greider, *Crossing Deep Rivers: The Liberation Theology of Gustavo Gutiérrez in Light of the Narrative Poetics of José María Arguedas* (Berkeley: Graduate Theological Union unpublished Ph.D. dissertation, 1988), 282.

Cf. Kudo: " ... The revitalization of popular religiosity in Latin America can be construed ... as an intergral part of the process of rediscovering the *pueblo* as subjects of their own history," *Práctica Religiosa 11*, 33.

71. Boff, *Liberator*, 229–230.

72. Cook, "Christology in Latin America," 284, n. 68. Judd is also director of the Andean Pastoral Institute in Peru. Based on his experiences in Latin America, he is convinced that all peoples infuse the Christian message with their own distinctive character: "That's the challenge of evangelization. We have to allow the culture to speak its own Christianity, to embrace the Gospel with its own symbols and rituals," quoted in John McCoy, "Expressing People's Soul," *Maryknoll* 83, no. 2 (February 1989), 13.

73. Cook, "Christology in Latin America," 284. Cook here credits Judd with his insight on the significance of the word *humilde*. Cook further explains that like *humilde*, the connotation of the word 'meek' ['and the meek shall inherit the earth' (Matt. 5:3)] does not convey the meaning of passivity and conformity which is suggested by their literal English translation. Rather, they imply the active embodiment of justice on behalf of oneself and for others. Cook also notes that after *Cristo humilde*, the second most common Christological image is *justo juez:* "Christ as judge who will bring justice where it is lacking," 283–5.

74. Gutiérrez & Shaull, "Freedom and Salvation," 75. Kudó reminds us, however, that popular religiosity is by no means a unified force for liberative change, and is dialectically both a legitimation of oppression and resistance against it: "Popular consciousness, that is, the social consciousness of the dominated popular classes, is, by definition, partially dominated, alienated, penetrated, and partially specific, autonomous, and resistant in terms of the ideology of the dominant class. In other words, cultural penetration and cultural resistance are two faces of the same historical reality of oppressed peoples. If domination-oppression and resistance-liberation are dialectical terms in permanent tension within a concrete historical process, *it is impossible, in an isolated way, to measure the force of domination on one hand and that of resistance on the other*," *Cultura Nacional Popular*, 22–3.

75. Kudó, *Cultura Nacional Popular*, 24.

76. Pastoral Team of Bambamarca. *Vamos Caminando: A Peruvian Catechism*.

77. Gutiérrez, *Entre las Calandrias* (Lima: Centro de Estudios y Publicaciones del Desarrollo, 1982), 243. Gutiérrez is actually referring here to the literary work of José María Arguedas, but I believe it is a quite appropriate description of his own theological work.

78. Cadorette, *Heart of the People*, 74.

79. Gutiérrez, *Power of the Poor*, 37. Gutiérrez adds that in this respect the greatest work for Latin American theologians and their communities still lies

ahead: "Our record of the interpretation of the faith that rises up from among the poor is generally fragmentary and oral, as manifested in customs, rites, and the like. . . . And yet the memory of history, the memory of faith, is there, awaiting reconstruction. The task will be complex, and it is urgent. It is the task of reconstructing the memory of the poor, a memory that is always subversive of a social order that despoils and marginalizes," 94–5.

80. A poetic expression created by Antonio Machado.

Bibliography

Alves, Rubem A. *A Theology of Human Hope*, Washington, D.C.: Corpus Books, 1969.

Argueta, Manlio. *One Day of Life*. Translated by Bill Brow. New York: Aventura Press, 1980.

Assmann, Hugo, "The Actuation of the Power of Christ in History: Notes on the Discernments of Christological Contradictions." In *Faces of Jesus: Latin American Christologies*, ed. José Míguez Bonino, 125–136. Translated by Robert R. Barr. Maryknoll: Orbis Books, 1984.

———. "The Power of Christ in History: Conflicting Christologies and Discernment." In *Frontiers of Theology in Latin America*, ed. Rosino Gibellini, 133–150. Translated by John Drury. Maryknoll: Orbis Books, 1979.

———. *Theology of a Nomad Church*. Translated by Paul Burns, Maryknoll: Orbis Books, 1975.

Batstone, David. "The Transformation of the Messianic Ideal in Judaism and Christianity in Light of the Holocaust: Reflections on the Writings of Elie Wiesel. *Journal of Ecumenical Studies* 83, no. 4 (Fall 1986): 587–600.

Berger, Peter. *Pyramids of Sacrifice: Political Ethics and Social Change*. New York: Basic Books, 1974.

———. *The Sacred Canopy*. Garden City, New York: Doubleday Press, 1967.

———, and Thomas Luckmann. *The Social Construction of Reality*. Garden City, New York: Doubleday Press, 1966.

Berryman, Phillip. *The Religious Roots of Rebellion: Christians in Central American Revolutions*. Maryknoll: Orbis Books, 1984.

Bloch, Ernst. *Das Prinzip Hoffnung*. 2nd. ed. Frankfort: Suhrkamp, 1969.

Boff, Clodovis. *Theology and Praxis: Epistemological Foundations*. Translated by Robert R. Barr. Maryknoll: Orbis Books, 1987.

Boff, Leonardo. "Christ's Liberation via Oppression: An Attempt at Theological Construction from the Standpoint of Latin America." In *Frontiers of*

Theology in Latin America, ed. Rosino Gibellini, 100 – 132. Translated by John Drury. Maryknoll: Orbis Books, 1979.

————. *Ecclesiogenesis: The Base Communities Reinvent the Church.* Translated by Robert R. Barr. Maryknoll: Orbis Books, 1986.

————. *Jesucristo y La Liberación del Hombre.* Madrid: Ediciones Cristiandad, 1981.

————. *Jesucristo y Nuestro Futuro de Liberación.* Bogotá: Indo-American Press Service, 1978.

————. *Jesus Christ Liberator: A Critical Christology for Our Time.* Translated by Patrick Hughes. Maryknoll: Orbis Books, 1978.

————. *Passion of Christ, Passion of the World: The Facts, Their Interpretations, and Their Meaning Yesterday and Today.* Translated by Robert R. Barr. Maryknoll: Orbis Books, 1987.

————. "Salvation in Jesus Christ and the Process of Liberation." In *The Mystical and Political Dimensions of Christian Faith, Concilium,* vol. 96, eds. Claude Geffré and Gustavo Gutiérrez, 78–91. Translated by J. P. Donnelly. New York: Herder & Herder, 1974.

Bonhoeffer, Dietrich. *The Cost of Discipleship.* Translated by R. H. Fuller. London: SCM Press, 1959.

————. *Christ the Center.* Translated by John Bowden. New York: Harper & Row, 1966.

Borhek, James T. and Richard F. Curtis. *The Sociology of Belief.* New York: Krieger Press, 1983 (1975).

Bornkamm, Günther. *Jesus of Nazareth.* Translated by Irene and Frank McLuskey with James Robinson. New York: Harper & Row, 1960.

Bultmann, Rudolph. *Faith and Understanding.* Translated by J. C. G. Greig. New York: Charles Scribner's Sons, 1932.

————. *Jesus and the Word.* Translated by Louise Pettibone Smith and Erminie Huntress Lantero. New York: Charles Scribner's Sons, 1934.

————. "New Testament and Mythology." In *Kerygma and Myth,* ed. H. W. Bartsch. Translated by Reginald H. Fuller. New York: Harper & Row, 1961.

Bussmann, Claus. *Who Do You Say?: Jesus Christ in Latin American Theology.* Translated by Robert T. Barr. Maryknoll: Orbis Books, 1985.

Cadorette, Curt. *From the Heart of the People: The Theology of Gustavo Gutiérrez.* Oak Park, IL: Meyer-Stone Books, 1988.

Cardenal, Ernesto. *The Gospels in Solentiname.* Translated by Donald Walsh. Maryknoll: Orbis Books, 1976.

Carney, Padre J. Guadelupe. *To Be a Revolutionary.* San Francisco: Harper & Row, 1985.

Casalis, Georges. "Jesus: Neither Abject Lord nor Heavenly Monarch." In *Faces of Jesus: Latin American Christologies,* ed. José Míguez Bonino. Translated by Robert R. Barr. Maryknoll: Orbis Books, 1984.

Chopp, Rebecca. *The Praxis of Suffering: An Interpretation of Liberation and Political Theologies.* Maryknoll: Orbis Books, 1986.

Cook, Michael. "Jesus from the Other Side of History: Christology in Latin America," *Theological Studies,* 44 (June 1983): 258–287.

Croatto, J. Severino. *Exodus: A Hermeneutics of Freedom.* Translated by Salvator Attanasio. Maryknoll: Orbis Books, 1981.

———. "The Political Dimension of Christ the Liberator." In *Faces of Jesus: Latin American Christologies,* ed. José Míguez Bonino, 102–122. Translated by Robert R. Barr. Maryknoll: Orbis Books, 1984.

Dupertuis, Atilio René. *Liberation Theology: A Study in Its Soteriology.* Burrian Springs, MI: Andrews University Press, 1982.

Dussel, Enrique. *América Latina: Dependencía y Liberación.* Buenos Aires: Fernando García Cambeiro, 1973.

———. "Sobre la Historía de la Teología en América Latina." In *Liberación y Cautiverio: Debates en Torno al Método de la Teología en América Latina,* ed. Enrique Ruiz Maldonado, 55–70. Mexico City: Venicia, 1976.

Ellacuría, Ignacio. *Freedom Made Flesh: The Mission of Christ and His Church.* Translated by John Drury. Maryknoll: Orbis Books, 1985.

Fiorenza, Elisabeth Schüssler. "Toward a Feminist Biblical Hermeneutics: Biblical Interpretation and Liberation Theology." In *The Challenge of Liberation Theology: A First World Response,* eds. Brian Mahan and L. Dale Richesin. Maryknoll: Orbis Books, 1981.

Frei, Hans. *The Eclipse of Biblical Narrative: A Study in Eighteenth and Nineteenth Century Hermeneutics.* New Haven: Yale University Press, 1974.

Freire, Paulo. "Education and Cultural Action: An Introduction." In *Conscientization for Liberation,* ed. Louis M. Colonnese, 109–122. Washington, D.C.: U.S. Catholic Conference—Latin American Division.

———. *Pedagogy of the Oppressed.* Translated by Myra Bergman Ramos. New York: Seabury Press, 1970.

Fuchs, Ernst. *Studies of the Historical Jesus.* Translated by A. Scobie. London: SCM Press, 1964.

Galeano, Eduardo. *Memory of Fire.* Three volumes. Translated by Cedric Belfrage. New York: Pantheon Books, 1987.

————. *Open Veins of Latin America: Five Centuries of Pillage of a Continent.* Translated by Cedric Belfrage. New York: Monthly Review Press, 1973.

Galilea, Segundo. *Following Jesus.* Translated by Sister Helen Phillips. Maryknoll: Orbis Books, 1981.

————. "Liberation Theology and New Tasks Facing Christians." In *Frontiers of Theology in Latin America,* ed. Rosino Gibellini, 163 – 183. Translated by John Drury. Maryknoll: Orbis Books, 1979.

————, and Raúl Vidales. *Cristología y Pastoral Popular.* Bogotá: Paulinas, 1974.

Greider, Brett. *Crossing Deep Rivers: The Liberation Theology of Gustavo Gutiérrez in Light of the Narrative Poetics of José María Arguedas.* Berkeley: Graduate Theological Union unpublished Ph.D. dissertation, 1988.

Guerrero, José Ramón. *El Otro Jesús.* Salamanca: Ediciones Sígueme, 1976.

Gutiérrez, Gustavo. "Entre las Calandrias." In *Arguedas: Mito, Historia y Religión,* 239 – 277. Lima: Centro de Estudios y Promoción del Desarrollo, 1982.

————. "The Irruption of the Poor in Latin America and the Christian Communities of the Common People." In *The Challenge of Basic Christian Communities: Papers from the International Ecumenical Congress of Theology, February 20 – March 2, 1980, São Paulo, Brazil,* eds. Sergio Torres and John Eagleson, 107 – 123. Translated by John Drury. Maryknoll: Orbis Books, 1981.

————. "Freedom and Salvation: A Political Problem." In *Liberation and Change,* 3 – 94. Atlanta: John Knox Press, 1977.

————. "Liberation Praxis and Christian Faith." In *Frontiers of Theology in Latin America,* ed. Rosino Gibellini, 1 – 33. Translated by John Drury. Maryknoll: Orbis Books, 1979.

————. "Liberation, Theology, and Proclamation." In *The Mystical and Political Dimension of the Christian Faith, Concilium* 96, eds. Claude Geffré and Gustavo Gutiérrez, 55 – 77. Translated by J. P. Donnelly. New York: Herder and Herder, 1974.

————. *The Power of the Poor in History.* Maryknoll: Orbis Books, 1983.

————. "Praxis, Liberación, Teología y Anuncio." In *Liberación: Dialogos en el CELAM,* 68 – 85. Bogota: CELAM, 1974.

————. *A Theology of Liberation: History, Politics and Salvation.* Translated by Sister Caridad Inda & John Eagleson. Maryknoll: Orbis Books, 1973.

————. *We Drink From Our Own Wells: The Spiritual Journey of a People.* Translated by Matthew J. O'Connell. Maryknoll: Orbis Books, 1984.

Hanson Paul. *The Dawn of Apocalyptic: The Historical and Social Roots of Jewish Apocalyptic Eschatology.* Rev. ed. Philadelphia: Fortress Press, 1979 (1975).

Hegel, G. W. F. *Philosophy of Religion.* Vol. 3. London: Routledge and Keegan Paul, 1968.

Herzog, William II. "Apocalypse Then and Now: Apocalyptic and the Historical Jesus Reconsidered." *Pacific Theological Review* 18, no. 1 (Fall 1984): 17–25.

———. "The Quest for the Historical Jesus and the Discovery of the Apocalyptic Jesus." *Pacific Theological Review* 19, no. 2 (Spring 1985): 25–39.

Hodgson, Peter. *The Formation of Historical Theology: A Study of Ferdinand Christian Baur.* New York: Charles Scribner's Sons, 1966.

Jordá Arias, Enrique. "El Cristo Velado del Pueblo Andino." *Pastoral Andina* 12 (1975): 15–25.

Kasper, Walter. *Jesus the Christ.* Translated by V. Green. New York: Paulist Press, 1976.

Kudó, Tokihiro. *Práctica Religiosa y Proyecto Histórico II: Estudio sobre la Religiosidad Popular en Dos Barrios de Lima.* Lima: Centro de Estudios y Publicaciones, 1980.

———. *Hacia una Cultura Nacional Popular.* Lima: Centro de Estudios y Promoción del Desarrollo, 1982.

Kuhn, Thomas. *The Structure of Scientific Revolutions.* 2nd ed. Chicago: University of Chicago Press, 1970.

Küng, Hans. *On Being a Christian.* Translated by E. Quinn. Garden City, New York: Doubleday, 1976.

Lancaster, Roger N. *Thanks to God and the Revolution: Popular Religion and Class Consciousness in the New Nicaragua.* New York: Columbia University Press, 1988.

López Vigil, María. *Don Lito de El Salvador: Habla un Campesino.* San Salvador: UCA Editores, 1987 (1982).

MacKay, J. *The Other Spanish Christ: A Study of the Spiritual History of Spain and Latin America.* New York: Macmillan Co., 1932.

McCoy, John. "Expressing People's Soul." *Maryknoll* 83, no. 2 (February 1989): 12–18.

McGrath, Alister. *The Making of Modern German Christology: From the Enlightenment to Pannenberg.* Oxford: Basil Blackwell, Inc., 1986.

Mesters, Carlos. "The Use of the Bible in Christian Communities of the Common People." In *The Challenge of Basic Christian Communities: Papers from the International Ecumenical Congress of Theology, February 20 – March 2, 1980, São Paulo, Brazil*, eds. S. Torres and J. Eagleson, 197–211. Translated by John Drury. Maryknoll: Orbis Books, 1981.

Míguez Bonino, José. *Doing Theology in a Revolutionary Situation*. Philadelphia: Fortress Press, 1975.

———. "Historical Praxis and Christian Identity." In *Frontiers of Theology in Latin America*, ed. Rosino Gibellini, 260–283. Translated by John Drury. Maryknoll: Orbis Books, 1979.

———. *Polémica, Diálogo, y Misión: Catolicismo Romano y Protestantismo en América Latina*. Centro de Estudios Cristianos, 1966.

———, ed. "Who is Jesus Christ in Latin America Today?" In *Faces of Jesus: Latin American Christologies*, 1–6. Translated by Robert T. Barr. Maryknoll: Orbis Books, 1984.

Miranda, Jose Porfirio. *Being and the Messiah: The Message of St. John*. Translated by John Eagleson. Maryknoll: Orbis Books, 1977. (Spanish ed., *El ser y el mesias*, Salamanca, Spain, Ediciones Sígueme, 1973.)

Melano Couch, Beatriz. "Statement." In *Theology in the Americas*, eds., Sergio Torres and John Eagleson, 304–308. Maryknoll: Orbis Books, 1976.

Moltmann, Jürgen. *The Crucified God: The Cross of Christ as the Foundation and Criticism of Theology*. Translated by R. A. Bowden and John Bowden. New York: Harper & Row, 1974.

———. *Theology of Hope*. Translated by James Leitch. London: SCM Press, 1967.

———. "Open Letter to José Míguez Bonino." *Christianity & Crisis* 29 (March 1976): 57–63.

Montgomery, Tommy Sue. *Revolution in El Salvador: Origins and Evolution*. Boulder, CO: Westview Press, 1982.

Pannenberg, Wolfhart. *Jesus — God and Man*. Translated by Lewis L. Wilkens and Duane A. Priebe. London: SCM Press, 1968.

Pastoral Team of Bambamarca. *Vamos Caminando: A Peruvian Catechism*. Translated by John Medcalf. London: SCM Press, 1985.

Perrin, Norman. *Jesus and the Language of the Kingdom: Symbol and Metaphor in New Testament Interpretation*. Philadelphia: Fortress Press, 1976.

———. *Rediscovering the Teaching of Jesus*. New York: Harper and Row, 1967.

Richard, Pablo. "Teología de la Liberación en la Situación de América Latina." *Servir* 13 (1977): 27–38.

Reuther, Rosemary Radford. *Sexism and God-Talk: Toward a Feminist Theology*. Boston: Beacon Press, 1983.

Robinson, James M. *A New Quest of the Historical Jesus.* Chatham: W & J MacKay Co., Ltd., 1959.

Scannone, Juan Carlos. "Theology, Popular Culture, and Discernment." In *Frontiers of Theology in Latin America,* ed. Rosino Gibellini, 213 – 239. Translated by John Drury. Maryknoll: Orbis Books, 1979.

Schweitzer, Albert. *The Quest of the Historical Jesus: A Critical Study of Its Progress from Reimarus to Wrede.* New York: The Macmillan Co., 1956 (1901).

Segundo, Juan Luis. "Condicionamientos Actuales de la Reflexión Teologíca en Latinoamerica." In *Liberación y Cautiverio: Debates en Torno al Método de la Teología en América Latina,* ed. Enrique Ruiz Maldonado. Mexico City: Venecia, 1976.

———. *Faith and Ideology.* Vol. 1, *Jesus of Nazareth Yesterday and Today.* Translated by John Drury. Maryknoll: Orbis Books, 1984.

———. *Historía y Actualidad: Las Cristologías en la Espiritualidad.* Vol. 2, no. 2, *El Hombre de Hoy Ante Jesús de Nazaret.* Madrid: Ediciones Cristianidad, 1982.

———. *The Historical Jesus of the Synoptics.* Vol. 2, *Jesus of Nazareth Yesterday and Today.* Translated by John Drury. Maryknoll: Orbis Books, 1985.

———. *The Humanist Christology of Paul.* Vol. 3, *Jesus of Nazareth Yesterday and Today.* Translated by John Drury. Maryknoll: Orbis Books, 1976.

Sobrino, Jon. *Christology at the Crossroads: A Latin American Approach.* Translated by John Drury. Maryknoll: Orbis Books, 1978.

———. "El Conocimiento Teologíco de la Teología en la Teología Europea y Latinamericana." *Estudios Centroamericanos* 30 (1973): 428–445.

———. "El Jesús Histórico, Crisis y Desafío para la Fe." *Christus* (Mexico) 40, no. 481 (1974): 6–18.

———. *Jesus in Latin America.* Translated by John Drury. Maryknoll: Orbis Books, 1986.

———. "Tesis sobre una Cristología Histórica." *Estudios Centroamericanos* 30 (1975): 462–478.

Stout, Jeffrey. *The Flight From Authority: Religion, Morality, and the Quest for Autonomy.* Notre Dame: University of Notre Dame Press, 1981.

Tamez, Elsa. *Against Machismo.* Translated by John Eagleson. Oak Park, IL: Meyer-Stone Books, 1987.

———. *Bible of the Oppressed.* Translated by Matthew J. O'Connell. Maryknoll: Orbis Press, 1982.

———. "A New Stage in the Development of the Christian Community." In *Theology by the People: Reflections on Doing Theology in Community,* eds. Samuel

Armirtham and John S. Pobee, 113 – 115. Geneva: World Council of Churches, 1986.

Trinidad, Saúl. "Christology, *Conquista,* Colonization." In *Faces of Jesus: Latin American Christologies,* ed. José Míguez Bonino, 49 – 65. Translated by Robert R. Barr. Maryknoll: Orbis Books, 1984.

Tyrrell, George. *Christianity at the Crossroads.* London: George Allen & Unwin Ltd., 1963 (1909).

Vidales, Raúl. "How Should We Speak of Jesus Christ in Latin America Today?" In *Faces of Jesus: Latin American Christologies,* ed., José Míguez Bonino, 137– 161. Translated by Robert R. Barr. Maryknoll: Orbis Books, 1984.

————. "Methodological Issues in Liberation Theology." In *Frontiers of Theology in Latin America,* ed. Rosino Gibellini, 34 – 57. Translated by John Drury. Maryknoll: Orbis Books, 1979.

————. "La Práctica Histórica de Jesús: Notas Provisorias." *Christus* (Mexico) 40, no. 481 (1974): 43–55.

————, and Tokihiro Kudó. *Práctica Religiosa y Proyecto Histórico: Hipótesis para un Estudio de la Religiosidad Popular en América Latina.* Lima: Centro de Estudios y Publicaciones, 1975.

Index

MAR 2 5 2019

U.S. History

4th Edition

by Steve Wiegand
Award-winning political journalist
and history writer

U.S. History For Dummies®, 4th Edition

Published by: **John Wiley & Sons, Inc.,** 111 River Street, Hoboken, NJ 07030-5774, www.wiley.com

Copyright © 2019 by John Wiley & Sons, Inc., Hoboken, New Jersey

Published simultaneously in Canada

For general information on our other products and services, please contact our Customer Care Department within the U.S. at 877-762-2974, outside the U.S. at 317-572-3993, or fax 317-572-4002. For technical support, please visit https://hub.wiley.com/community/support/dummies.

Wiley publishes in a variety of print and electronic formats and by print-on-demand. Some material included with standard print versions of this book may not be included in e-books or in print-on-demand. If this book refers to media such as a CD or DVD that is not included in the version you purchased, you may download this material at http://booksupport.wiley.com. For more information about Wiley products, visit www.wiley.com.

Library of Congress Control Number: 2019931104

ISBN 978-1-119-55069-3 (pbk); ISBN 978-1-119-55073-0 (ePDF); ISBN 978-1-119-55074-7 (epub)

Manufactured in the United States of America

C10008347_022119

Contents at a Glance

Table of Contents

Introduction

"Those who cannot remember the past," said American philosopher George Santayana, "are condemned to repeat it."

Generally in the 12th grade.

Lots of people think of learning U.S. history as a punishment. It's just a subject you had to take in school. You memorized a bewildering array of dates, absorbed definitions for terms like *Manifest Destiny,* and wondered whether America really needed two presidents named Harrison. Historical figures were presented as if they were characters in a junior high school costume pageant. Their blemishes were airbrushed out, and their personalities were drained away.

Sure, you were taught George Washington warned the country about foreign entanglements in his "Farewell Address." But it might have been more interesting to also learn he never actually gave that speech. It was printed in the newspapers. Washington didn't like giving speeches, partly because of his false teeth, which were not made of wood but of hippopotamus ivory.

Alas, textbooks often overlook the fascinating moments and details of U.S. history. They present it as something dry and distant — events, facts, trends, movements — and don't focus on what it really is. U.S. history is the story of people: what they thought, did, and tried to do; what they ate and drank; what made them angry; and what made them laugh.

About This Book

This book is not a textbook, nor is it an exhaustive encyclopedia covering everything that ever happened in the United States. Instead, it focuses on people: famous and infamous, well-known and obscure. It gives you a basic foundation of information about U.S. history. You can use it as a handy reference. Haul it off the shelf to settle an argument — or to start one.

Which brings me to a key point. This book is not 100 percent, straight-down-the-middle-you'll-agree-with-everything objective. Although I've tried to stick to the facts — or at least the most widely accepted historical interpretations of the facts — the bottom line is that my own thoughts, biases, and interpretations will inevitably intrude. It happens in every nonfiction book ever written. Sorry. If you think something is factually wrong, please let me know. If you just don't agree with something, object. You're reaffirming one of the best things about America: the right to freely express indignation.

Because U.S. history hasn't always been bright and shining, especially when it comes to topics such as slavery or the treatment of Native Americans, this book doesn't always deal with pleasant or uplifting subjects. Some of what you read may anger you, sadden you, or even make you feel a little ashamed. In that regard, America's history shares something in common with just about every country ever. But the truth is that overall, America's story is a positive one. For a nation in its third century, America still does a whole lot of things right. One of them is recognizing past mistakes and generally — and sometimes gradually — striving to do better.

Enough time on the soapbox. I'm also happy to report you can find things in this book that you won't find in other U.S. history books (which may or may not be a good thing, depending on your sense of humor or taste for trivia). Although they may be of little importance in the overall scheme of things, they're kind of fun to know — and trot out at dinner with your boring in-laws. Some examples: the Civil War general whose name helped to popularize a common term for prostitutes (Joseph Hooker); which canned meat product helped win World War II (Spam); and the major league baseball team that overcame the curse of a man with a goat (Chicago Cubs). And if you're a history purist, I think there's a mention of Manifest Destiny in here somewhere.

Conventions Used in This Book

To help you find your way around in the book, I use the following conventions:

>> *Italics* are used both to emphasize a word to make a sentence clearer and to highlight a new word that's being defined.

>> **Bold** highlights keywords in bulleted lists.

What Not to Read

As you ramble around the book, you'll encounter blocks of text in shaded boxes. They contain quotes; mini-profiles of both famous and semi-obscure people; the origins of things; factoids and numbers; and other historical debris. You don't need to read them to get what's going on. They're just there as little extras that I've thrown in at no additional charge. Feel free to read them as you find them, come back to them later, or save them for recitation at your next poker game.

Foolish Assumptions

I'm assuming you picked up this book because you have some interest in U.S. history (which is why I chose the title). But it doesn't matter if you know a little or a lot about the subject. I think you may enjoy it either way, even if it's just to settle arguments about the Louisiana Purchase (Chapter 7) or what Iceland had to do with the Great Recession (Chapter 22). Enough facts are in here to make this a good (if I do say so myself) basic U.S. history book and enough trivia to irritate party guests who won't go home.

Beyond the Book

You got more than you bargained for when you bought this book. In addition to what you're reading right now, this product also comes with a free access-anywhere Cheat Sheet that puts scads of facts about U.S. history at your fingertips. You'll be able to make substantive points in discussions about politics, impress potential employers as a well-rounded individual, and convince people you actually remember something from 11th grade. To get this Cheat Sheet, simply to go www.dummies.com and search for "U.S. History For Dummies, 4th Edition Cheat Sheet" in the Search box.

This product also comes with an online test bank of practice questions to test your knowledge. To gain access to the online practice:

1. **Find your PIN access code:**

   - *Print-book users:* if you purchased a print copy of this book, turn to the inside front cover of the book to find your access code.

- *E-book users:* If you purchased this book as an e-book, you can get your access code by registering your e-book at www.dummies.com/go/getaccess. Go to this website, find your book, and click on it. Answer the security questions to verify your purchase. You'll receive an email with your access code.

2. **Go to Dummies. com and click on** *Activate Now.*

3. **Find your product and then follow the on-screen prompts to activate your PIN.**

Icons Used in This Book

Throughout the book, you can find icons in the margins or alongside boxed sidebars that alert you to particular aspects or features of history. Here's what they mean:

TECHNICAL STUFF

The names, numbers, and other stats behind the news are the focus of this icon.

REMEMBER

This icon alerts you to a fact or idea that you may want to stash in your memory bank.

Where to Go from Here

Congratulations! By reading this far, you've already learned something about U.S. history: It doesn't bite, induce deep comas, or poke you in the eye with a sharp stick. Read a few more pages, and you may get the itch to keep going even further.

Remember, history is the story of people.

And people are the most interesting story of all.

1
Getting Started with U.S. History

IN THIS PART . . .

The early settlers make their way in a new land.

The colonies establish themselves.

The American Revolution leads to the creation of a new country.

IN THIS CHAPTER

» **Tracing America's roots**

» **Establishing a national identity**

» **Dealing with growing pains**

» **Fighting wars of a different kind**

» **Donning a new look for a new millennium**

Chapter **1**

America: A Short Biography

Long before it was a nation, America was an idea, a dream, a fanciful tale. For most of humankind's history, it didn't exist as anything but a blank slate, waiting to be filled. Eventually it was filled, with people who came for all sorts of reasons and with all sorts of ideas on how to assemble a country. Sometimes the ideas and the people clashed. But out of the clashes and struggles grew a country founded on a system of government that made it unique in the world.

America was lucky to have great leaders in bad times, when it most needed them. It had abundant natural resources, generally peaceable neighbors, and plenty of room to grow. And boy, did it grow. But before all this could happen, someone had to transform it from a fantasy to a very real place. This chapter gives you the lowdown on how that came about and directs you to the places in the book that give you the nitty-gritty in more detail.

They Came, They Saw, They Stayed

The first Americans probably wandered over from Asia about 14,000 years ago, which in geologic terms is an eye blink ago. Over the succeeding four or five millennia, they spread out over the North and South American continents.

There weren't a whole lot of these first Americans, at least not in what became known as the United States of America, but they were wildly diverse in their customs and culture. Many of the differences had to do with the environment in which they settled. Around AD 985, Northern Europeans popularly known as *Vikings* showed up on the North American continent but stuck around only long enough to irritate the Native Americans.

But two things — greed and imagination — prodded other Europeans into taking their place. Looking for a new route to the riches of the East (particularly spices), explorers such as an Italian weaver's son named Christopher Columbus thought they might sail west around the globe until they hit Asia. Of course, the Americas got in the way. Rather than reverse course, Columbus and his counterparts refocused their priorities to exploring and exploiting the New World.

The exploiting part of that plan included enslaving or killing off the native population. Sometimes the killing was deliberate; sometimes it was inadvertent, through the introduction of diseases for which the Native Americans had no defenses, for example. See Chapter 2 for more details on Native Americans and explorers.

Catching up to the Spanish

Spain got a head start in the Americas, mainly because it was the first to get enthusiastic about exploring the Americas. But other European countries eagerly sought to catch up. France split its efforts between colonizing and just carting off resources like fish and furs. But the English took steps to make their presence more permanent.

English settlements were founded for both economic and ecclesiastical reasons. In the South, colonists hoped to make money by growing tobacco, and later, cotton. To make their enterprises more profitable, they imported slaves from Africa. It was a practice that would prove far costlier in terms of human misery than the crops were ever worth.

In the North, settlers who had fled religious persecution established colonies based more on religious principles than making a buck (although they weren't averse to the latter). Like the Spanish, English settlers often found the easiest way to deal with the Native Americans was to shove them aside or kill them. The English colonies grew rapidly. Chapter 3 has the stories of Pilgrims, Puritans, and entrepreneurs.

It's revolutionary!

It was probably of small comfort to the Native Americans, but the French and British also spent an inordinate amount of time killing each other. Throughout much of the 18th century, the two nations squared off in a series of wars that were fought in both Europe and the New World. When the dust settled, Britain had cemented its position as top dog among the European powers in North America. But a new power — whose members increasingly called themselves *Americans* — was beginning to assert itself.

Stung by slights both real and imagined from the mother country, American colonists grew restless under British control. In 1776, after a series of provocations and misunderstandings, the colonies declared themselves independent. Details about the pre-Revolution period are in Chapter 4.

The American Revolution took seven years for the colonists to win. To do so took a brilliant leader in George Washington, a timely ally in France, and healthy helpings of tenacity and luck. Chapter 5 has the details.

Making a country out of the victorious colonies also took tenacity, luck, and genius. Over the summer of 1787, a remarkable group of men gathered in Philadelphia to draw up the rules for the new nation. The United States of America elected Washington as its first president, set up a reasonable financial system, and avoided war with European countries long enough to get itself established. All these events are in Chapter 6.

Putting America on the Map

Thomas Jefferson was a great example of America finding the right man at the right time. He helped the country make a smooth transition from one political party being in charge to another. Plus, he had the imagination to pull off a pretty big land deal — the Louisiana Purchase. That not only doubled the size of the country, it gave Lewis and Clark a good reason for an expedition. Meanwhile, the U.S. Supreme Court asserted itself as a co-equal branch of government. That's all in Chapter 7, along with fighting pirates and getting into another war with Great Britain. (Spoiler alert: It ended in a draw.)

Nationalizing a nation

The end of the War of 1812 also marked the fading of the Revolution generation. People increasingly began to identify themselves as Americans rather than New Yorkers or Virginians. But it wasn't the end of tensions among sections of the country when their interests diverged. Those divergent issues included fights over banking, tariffs — and especially slavery.

With the invention of the cotton gin, growing the fiber became quite profitable in the South, and along with a surge in sugar growing, made the region intensely dependent on slave labor. Many people in Northern states opposed slavery, for a variety of moral, political, and economic reasons. A fight over the question of allowing slavery to spread was avoided, at least temporarily, with a fragile compromise in 1820.

Beyond its borders, the United States was nervously watching European nations who were avariciously watching former Spanish colonies in Latin America gain their independence. In 1823, Pres. James Monroe formally warned Europe to keep its hands off the Americas.

Not all the political squabbling was international. In 1824, a crusty military-man-turned-politician named Andrew Jackson lost a hotly contested and controversial election to John Quincy Adams. In 1828, Jackson avenged the loss after one of the sleaziest campaigns (by both sides) in U.S. history.

As president, Jackson found himself confronted by a theory — most eloquently championed by South Carolina Sen. John C. Calhoun — called *nullification*. It held that states could decide for themselves which federal laws they did and did not have to obey. The theory served to deepen the divide between North and South.

Despite a national recession brought on by speculation and shady financial dealings, Americans were busy coming up with ways to make life better. Improvements in equipment triggered a boom in railroad building. The development of steel plows and rolling harvesters greatly enhanced grain production. And the invention of the telegraph signaled the start of a national communications medium.

Down in Texas, meanwhile, American expatriates led a successful revolt against Mexico and then waited for nine years to become part of the United States. The annexation of Texas, in turn, helped start another war. Chapter 8 has a lot of stuff in it.

Fighting with a neighbor

In 1844, America elected its first *dark horse,* or surprise, presidential candidate. He was James K. Polk. Polk was a hard worker with a yen to expand the country to the Pacific Ocean by acquiring territory from Mexico. Polk saw it as the nation's *Manifest Destiny.*

Mexico saw it as intolerable bullying. After the Mexican government refused to sell, Polk sent U.S. troops to the border. A fight was quickly provoked and just as quickly escalated into war. The Americans' quick and decisive victory resulted in their grabbing of about 500,000 square miles of Mexican territory, comprising much of what became the western United States.

These actions not only fulfilled Polk's vision of Manifest Destiny but also gave California to America. That addition proved to be particularly fortuitous when gold was discovered there in early 1848. By the end of 1849, the California gold rush had sparked a human stampede and given America all the elbowroom it would need for decades.

That was a good thing because immigration was again booming, particularly from Ireland and the European states that would become Germany. But the acquisition of Mexican territory also renewed the struggle to balance the interests of slave states and free states.

In 1850, Congress worked out a five-bill compromise. California was added as a free state. The free-or-slave question was postponed in other areas of the former Mexican lands. And Congress enacted a law that made it easier for slave owners to recover fugitive slaves.

While a movement to give women rights and opportunities equal to men's began to gather steam in the 1850s, the slavery issue overshadowed it. Violence broke out in Kansas and Virginia. An 1857 Supreme Court decision that held that slaves had no more rights than mules infuriated slavery opponents.

And in 1860, the badly divided country gave a plurality of its votes to a 51-year-old Illinois lawyer in a four-way race for the presidency. The election of Abraham Lincoln was the last straw for Southern states, which began leaving the Union. See Chapter 9 for accounts of the war with Mexico, the California gold rush, and America's divorce from itself.

Fighting among ourselves

Talk about timing: America had its best president at the worst time in its history — the Civil War. Underestimating Lincoln was easy, and many did. But he had a knack for getting the best out of most of the people around him and a self-deprecating sense of humor that disarmed others.

Lincoln was no fan of slavery, but even more important to him was preserving the Union. The North seemed well-equipped to accomplish that. It had a larger population, better manufacturing and transportation systems, and an established navy and central government. The South had the home-field advantage and better military leaders, and it only had to fight to a draw.

While the North was largely successful in establishing a naval blockade of Southern ports, the South won most of the early land battles. Its best general, Robert E. Lee, even succeeded in taking the fight to Northern territory for a while. But eventually, the North's superiority in numbers and supplies asserted itself, and the tide turned.

It took four years and 600,000 American lives for Northern forces to prevail, restore the Union, and end slavery. But less than a week after the surrender of the South's main army, Lincoln was assassinated. With him went the nation's best chance of healing its wounds. The details are in Chapter 10.

Making up is hard to do

The postwar South was a mess, and that's putting it mildly. The infrastructure was wrecked, the economy in shambles, and the best and brightest of its leaders gone. Millions of African Americans were free — with no education, no place to work, and nowhere to go.

With Lincoln gone, many of the North's leaders were more in the mood for revenge than for reconstruction. Andrew Johnson, Lincoln's successor, had few friends in Congress and fewer leadership skills. Such a climate resulted in the North imposing draconian laws on the South, which led, in turn, to economic and physically violent reprisals by white Southerners on black Southerners.

Reconstruction efforts suffered further when the great Northern general Ulysses S. Grant turned out to be a not-so-great president. Political corruption infected every level of government. The corruption peaked — or bottomed out — with a sleazy deal that gave the 1876 presidential election to a former Ohio governor named Rutherford B. Hayes. It's all there in Chapter 11.

Struggling with Greatness

With the North-South struggle over, America began stretching west in earnest. Great tracts of land were available to settle, and money could be made in mining, ranching, and farming.

Tragically, that meant pushing out or bumping off the original human residents. Most of America's surviving Native Americans were on the Great Plains. But by 1890, wars, murders, disease, starvation, and forced emigration had largely "solved" the "Indian problem."

Other minorities fared little better. In the South, the failures of Reconstruction led to a series of Jim Crow laws that sanctioned racial segregation. Immigration from China was temporarily banned in 1882, and the ban lasted six decades. Immigrants from other nations poured in, however, many of them populating vast slums in rapidly growing cities.

But Big Business boomed in what Mark Twain dubbed *The Gilded Age.* Railroads, steel, and oil were the objects of monopolistic cartels, and new industries sprang up around new inventions like the telephone and electric lighting.

With its frontier rapidly settled, America cast its eyes beyond its borders. In 1898, it went to war with Spain. The conflict lasted four months and resulted in Guam, Puerto Rico, and the Philippines becoming U.S. territories. See Chapter 12 for details.

Finding a place in the world

As the 20th century began, the nation marched along to the twin drums of *imperialism* — running other people's countries for America's benefit — and *progressivism* — improving the bad habits of Big Business and Big Politics. At the forefront of both was a human dynamo named Theodore Roosevelt.

The country was also undergoing labor pains, with unions striving, often violently and not very successfully, with business leaders. Women were also struggling to gain a place in the polling booth and in the pay line.

Chapter 13 winds up with America trying to stay out of World War I — and failing. America's participation in the war turned out to be a good thing for the rest of the world, as it helped the war get over with sooner.

Roaring through the '20s

After the war, America decided to mind its own business and restricted immigration to keep the rest of the world out. It also gave up drinking — at least legal drinking. Prohibition resulted in a lot of illegal drinking, which seemed in turn to affect the country's mores in other areas.

America also elected a string of rock-ribbed Republicans as president, all of whom did what they could to make the rich richer. Everyone else made do by buying things on installment plans and looking for ways to get rich themselves.

And Americans spent their increasing leisure time going to the movies, listening to the radio, and paying homage to heroes like Babe Ruth and Charles Lindbergh. As Chapter 14 closes, the Roaring Twenties sputter to an end with a stock market crash, which makes for a depressing next chapter.

What's so great about a depression?

A whole fistful of factors helped cause the Great Depression: the stock market crash, a host of bank and farm failures, even terrible weather. It all added up to an economically catastrophic decade. Unemployment and foreclosures soared. Tens of thousands of farm families migrated to the promise of better times in California. Minority groups were even worse off than usual. About the only groups to make progress were labor unions.

Trying to untangle the mess was a patrician New Yorker named Franklin D. Roosevelt. As president, FDR launched an alphabet's worth of federal programs to combat the Depression, with mixed results. For Depression distractions, America had an array of demagogic politicians, dangerous criminals, and long-winded radio personalities. They're all right there in Chapter 15.

The big one

As the 1930s ended, most Americans were too preoccupied with their own problems to worry about problems in the rest of the world. As it turned out, however, the country couldn't get by indefinitely just selling war materials to friendly nations.

By the end of 1941, America was in another world war, and the country was up to the task. Industrial production ramped up. Women went to work, taking the place of men at war. Minority groups gained ground in the struggle for equality by making invaluable contributions to the effort.

American efforts overseas were even more valiant. After helping to secure North Africa, U.S. troops were at the vanguard of the allied invasions of Italy and France. In the Pacific, the military recovered quickly from the devastating attack on Pearl Harbor and began a methodical hopscotch across the Pacific. As Chapter 16 concludes, America ends the war by using nuclear weapons — and begins a very uneasy chapter in world history.

A Cold War and a Brave New World

After years of struggling with totalitarian regimes in other countries, America marked the end of World War II by beginning a decades-long struggle with different totalitarian regimes in other countries. Instead of fascists, these were communists, especially those in the Soviet Union and, eventually, China. After helping get the United Nations off the ground, the United States began diplomatically, and sometimes not so diplomatically, dueling with communists who were trying to overthrow governments in other countries.

In 1950, UN troops, consisting mainly of U.S. troops, began what was termed a *police action*, trying to push back a Chinese-supported North Korean invasion of South Korea. It took until mid-1953, and 33,000 U.S. dead, to end the war in a stalemate. At home, meanwhile, Americans' antipathy toward communism resulted in demagogic persecution of U.S. citizens. Commie hunting became something of a national pastime. It took until mid-1954 for a poison of innuendo and smear tactics spread by a Wisconsin senator named Joe McCarthy to run its course.

Communists aside, Americans were doing pretty well after the war. Returning veterans came home to plenty of jobs and government aid programs, which meant a booming economy. People bought houses and cars in new suburban communities, where they watched a new cultural phenomenon called television and listened to a new kind of music called rock 'n' roll.

But not everyone was having fun. After helping win two world wars, African Americans decided it was past time to be treated as equals. A 1954 U.S. Supreme Court decision and a 1955 boycott of a bus company helped jump-start the civil rights movement. It's all in Chapter 17.

From a Kennedy to a Ford

After eight years of Dwight Eisenhower (a great general but a pretty dull president), America was ready for some charisma in the White House. It got it with the election of John F. Kennedy in 1960. Kennedy proved his leadership skills in 1962 when he pulled the country, and the rest of the world, back from the brink of nuclear war over the presence of Soviet missiles in Cuba. But his assassination the following year ended the promise of his presidency.

In Kennedy's place came Lyndon B. Johnson, a practiced politician. Johnson inherited a messy U.S. involvement in a civil war in Vietnam, which grew increasingly messier in his five years in office. Antiwar sentiment grew almost as fast and kept Johnson from seeking a second full term. At home, the civil rights movement that began in the '50s picked up speed in the '60s, fueled by a confluence of Johnson-pushed federal legislation; nonviolent demonstrations led, most notably, by the Reverend Martin Luther King, Jr.; and the violence of race riots in many U.S. cities.

African Americans weren't the only ones protesting. Latinos, women, and gay and lesbian Americans took their grievances to the streets. Young people embraced freer attitudes toward drugs, sex, and personal appearance. Their parents, meanwhile, elected Richard Nixon president — twice.

Except for Vietnam, Nixon enjoyed reasonable success in foreign policy, warming up relations with China and gingerly seeking middle ground with the Soviet Union. After expanding the U.S. role in Vietnam by bombing targets in neighboring Cambodia, Nixon administration officials decided it was time to exit and announced a peace settlement with North Vietnam in early 1973. At home, Nixon's paranoid fixation on getting even with political foes led to a spying-and-lying scandal that, in turn, led to him becoming the only U.S. president to resign his office. The Watergate dirt is in Chapter 18.

Good intentions, mixed results

After Nixon quit, the country had two very good men who were not very good presidents — Gerald R. Ford and Jimmy Carter. Ford angered many Americans by pardoning Nixon of any crimes connected with the Watergate scandal. Carter, who defeated Ford in the 1976 presidential race, angered many Americans by pardoning Vietnam War draft dodgers. And both men had trouble with a national economy that suffered from runaway inflation and an embargo by oil-producing nations that resulted in long lines and high prices at gas stations. Carter did broker a peace deal between Egypt and Israel, but he also oversaw a mess in America's relations with Iran.

The successor to Ford and Carter was seemingly about as improbable a presidential choice as America ever made: a former B-movie actor who had served two unremarkable terms as governor of California. But Ronald Reagan turned out to have as much impact on the country as any president since FDR. He was charismatic, optimistic, stubborn, decisive, and lucky — all of which were just what the country needed to restore its self-confidence.

An ardent anti-communist, Reagan heated up the Cold War, in part by proposing an ambitious "Star Wars" military program based on laser-shooting satellites. But his tenacity, combined with tough economic and political times in the Soviet Union, pushed the Soviet bloc closer to its demise in the late '80s and early '90s.

Chapter 19 ends with the one-term presidency of George H. W. Bush, a short war with Iraq, the worst riot in a U.S. city in a century, and the election of a president whose hometown was Hope. Really.

Finishing out the century

A native of Hope, Arkansas, Bill Clinton was the nation's first president born after the end of World War II. Although he successfully pushed for a major trade agreement with Canada and Mexico and helped restore some order in the war-torn states of the former Yugoslavia, most of the Democratic president's energies were aimed at domestic issues.

A major effort to reform America's healthcare system failed, but he was more successful in working with a Republican majority in Congress to reform the welfare system. He also shone when it came to economic matters, turning a federal budget deficit into a surplus, and a 1993 tax hike into a 1997 tax cut, after he won reelection in 1996.

But in 1998, Clinton was caught lying about a sexual affair with a White House intern. The GOP-controlled House impeached him, and he became just the second president to be tried by the Senate. (Andrew Johnson was the first, in 1868.) The Senate acquitted the president, mostly on the grounds that getting caught with his zipper down and trying to cover it up wasn't sufficient reason to throw him out of office.

Clinton's budgetary success was tied to the overall success of the U.S. economy in the '90s. That, in turn, was driven by technological advances (home computers, cellphones, the Internet) that helped foster tighter economic ties with the rest of the world.

But the '90s also saw the broadening of America's experience with a problem it heretofore had associated mostly with other countries: terrorism. Bombings of the World Trade Center in New York City, of a federal office complex in Oklahoma City, and at the 1996 Olympic Games in Atlanta brought home the chilling realization that America wasn't immune from horrific acts of sudden mass violence.

The country also battled the less sudden but more widespread problems of illicit drug use and the spread of AIDS. And as Chapter 20 (and the 20th century) ends, America and the rest of the world found themselves on the cusp of technological and economic changes that made a seemingly smaller planet spin at a faster pace.

America in the 21st Century

There's nothing like kicking off a new millennium with a nail-bitingly close presidential election, and that's where Chapter 21 begins. The contest between George W. Bush (the eventual winner) and Al Gore wasn't decided until seven weeks after the polls closed, and only then by a 5–4 U.S. Supreme Court decision. Over the eight years of the Bush presidency, America suffered the worst terrorist attack in modern times, got into two wars, toppled one dictator, and got hit with a couple of nasty hurricanes. All in all, it's one untidy chapter.

Bursting economic bubbles

As the biggest economic calamity to hit the country since the 1930s, the Great Recession seemed to warrant its own chapter, which is what Chapter 22 is all about. People lost their houses and their jobs at dizzying rates. As it had in the Great Depression, the federal government tried to fix things with ambitious and expensive programs. And as America gradually got back on its fiscal feet, it found its economy had reshaped itself into a form that didn't fit all Americans the same.

Politics and healthcare are no tea party

In 2008, the country elected an African American as its president for the first time. Barack Obama faced a deeply divided nation when it came to choosing which political philosophy to be guided by, on issues that ranged from federal government spending to devising an efficient and broad-based healthcare system. Take a look at Chapter 23 to see how it worked out for him.

Stormy times and a new kind of president

The economy was humming along, America was still the world's most dominant country when it came to military might and cultural influence — and yet the nation was perhaps more deeply divided along ideological, political, and financial lines than it had been since the Civil War.

Part of the reason was a new president who was either loved or hated — there seemed to be no middle ground when it came to assessing Donald J. Trump. Elected in one of the biggest upsets in U.S. presidential history, Trump's approach to governing seemed to stir controversy at every turn, and in nearly every part of the world.

At home, meanwhile, Americans struggled with problems that ranged from opioid addiction and gun violence to hurricanes, sexual harassment, and racial divides. It all makes for an unsettling Chapter 24.

Changing technology, changing America

As the new century moved along, Americans found themselves riding a wave of technological innovation that upended old ways of news-gathering, communicating, socializing, shopping, and entertaining. The new technology also crept into the country's political processes in sometimes troubling ways. At the same time, changes in both the demographics — a lot of people got a lot older — and cultural norms were dramatically reshaping who Americans were and how they lived. The new reflection is revealed in Chapter 25.

Chapter **2**

Native Americans and Explorers: 14,000 BC (?)–1607

Because U.S. history is most often written about by the descendants of Europeans (me included), there has been a tendency to overemphasize the experiences of European settlers at the expense of others who dropped by the New World (Native Americans included).

But tracking what the Native Americans did can be difficult because they left no written records of their activities. In this chapter, I make some educated guesses and then get on with all those Europeans.

Coming to America

Once upon a time, about 14,000 years ago, some people from what is now Siberia walked across what was then a land bridge but is now the Bering Strait and into what is now Alaska. They were hunters in search of ground sloths the size of hippopotamuses, armadillos the size of Volkswagens, mammoth-sized mastodons, and other really big game.

They weren't in any kind of hurry. Their descendants kept walking south for 4,000 or 5,000 years — not stopping until they got to Patagonia, at the tip of South America. Along the way, they split up and spread out until people could be found in all parts of the continents and islands of North and South America. <u>Maybe.</u>

REMEMBER

Actually, no one knows when humans first showed up in the New World. For most of the 20th century, the most widely accepted view among scholars was the one told in the preceding paragraphs: People got to the Americas by walking across a land bridge during the Ice Age, when there was more ice and the water level of the world's oceans was lower than it is today.

But recent discoveries have caused many scientists to think Americans, in one form or another, have been around a lot longer. Archaeological sites in Alaska, Oregon, Florida, Chile, and other places have yielded clues, such as tools, animal bones carved and smashed by humans, and even DNA from human remains, that indicate people may have been in the Americas for as long as 20,000 to even 40,000 years. And there is evidence that despite the presence of the land bridge, thousands of square miles of ice on the North American side would have been too difficult to cross.

If that's the case, Americans may very well have come some other way, such as by water. One theory is that the first Americans followed The Kelp Highway, traveling by boat and hugging the shoreline where they would have found food, such as shellfish. (Imagine being the first guy in your tribe to put an oyster or lobster in your mouth.) The boat people were followed, the theory goes, by those crossing the land bridge when the vast ice fields retreated but before water covered the bridge.

Other puzzles have popped up to cause scientists to look hard at the Bering Strait theory. One study of human blood types, for example, found that the predominant blood type in Asia is B, and the blood types of Native Americans are almost exclusively A or O. This finding seems to indicate that at least some of the Native Americans' ancestors came from somewhere other than Siberia.

Exploring Early Civilizations

Although it's unclear who got here first and when, it's known that the forerunners of Native Americans were beginning to settle down by about 1000 BC. They cultivated crops, most notably *maize*, a hearty variety of corn that takes less time to grow than other grains and can also grow in many different climates. Beans and squash made up the other two of the "three sisters" of early American agriculture.

GETTING THE POINT

In the early 1930s, researchers near Clovis, New Mexico, found long spearheads made of chert, obsidian, and other stone materials. The spearheads, which were found with the bones of dead animals, had grooves in their base, where they could be attached to wooden shafts and hurled with great force by using a throwing stick.

These spearheads have since been found in a wide area of North America. Scientists called them *Clovis points* and offered them as proof that man was here during the Ice Age. Many scientists believe the point-chucking hunters were so efficient that they helped hasten the extinction of most of the period's great mammals.

For decades it was believed the Clovis people represented the oldest widespread culture in the Americas. Although that belief became widely disputed in recent years, it's well-accepted that most modern Native American people can trace their ancestry to the Clovis folks.

Growing their own food enabled the groups to stay in one place for long periods of time. Consequently, they could make and acquire things and build settlements, which allowed them to trade with other groups. Trading resulted in groups becoming covetous of other groups' things, which eventually led to wars over these things. Ah, civilization.

The Anasazi

One of the earliest cultures to emerge in what's now the United States was the *Anasazi.* The group's name comes from a Navajo word that has been translated to mean "ancient people" or "ancient enemies." Although they were around the southwestern United States for hundreds of years, they flourished from about AD 1100 to 1300.

At their peak, the Anasazi built adobe-walled towns in nearly inaccessible areas, which made the communities easy to defend. The towns featured apartment houses, community courts, and buildings for religious ceremonies. The Anasazi made artistic pottery and tightly woven baskets. The baskets were so good the culture is sometimes referred to as the *Basket Makers.*

Because of the region's arid conditions, the Anasazi people couldn't support a large population and were never numerous. But just why their culture died out so suddenly around the beginning of the 14th century is a puzzle to archaeologists. One theory is that a prolonged drought simply made life unsustainable in the region.

A more controversial theory is that marauding Indians from Mexico conquered the Anasazi or drove them off. However the Anasazi's demise came about, their culture was developed enough to be reflected in some of the Southwest tribes of today.

The Mound Builders

East of the Anasazi were groups of early Americans who became known as *Mound Builders*, after their habit of erecting large earthworks that served as tombs and foundations for temples and other public buildings. One group, known as the *Woodland Culture*, was centered in Ohio and spread east. Their mounds, which took decades to build, reached more than seven stories in height and were surrounded by earthwork walls as long as 500 yards. The largest of these mounds was near what's now the southern Ohio town of Hopewell.

The largest Mound Builder settlement was on the Illinois side of the Mississippi River, about 8 miles from what's now St. Louis. It was called *Cahokia*. At its zenith, around AD 1100, Cahokia covered 6 square miles and may have been home to as many as 30,000 people. To put that in perspective: Cahokia was about the same size as London was in 1100, and no other city in America grew to that size until Philadelphia did, 700 years later.

The residents of Cahokia had a knack for astronomy, building — and human sacrifice. Their largest mounds, like pyramids of cultures in Mexico, were four-sided, had a flat top, and covered as much ground as the biggest pyramids of Egypt. The Cahokia Mound Builders also had a penchant for constructing stout, wooden stockades around their city. In doing so, however, they cut down most of the trees in the area, which reduced the amount of game in the region and caused silt to build up in nearby waterways. The city also may have suffered from nasty air pollution because of wood fires that were constantly burning.

By 1200, people were leaving Cahokia and its suburbs in large numbers. By 1400, the city was abandoned, an early victim of the ills of urban growth.

Many Tribes, Not Many People

Although what's now the United States didn't have a lot of Native Americans — maybe 1 million to 1.5 million or so at the time of Christopher Columbus's arrival in 1492 — it certainly had a wide variety. Historians estimate that at least 250 different tribal groups lived in America at that time. Some estimates have put the number of distinct societies as high as 1,200. They spoke at least 300 languages, none of them written, and many of the languages were as different from each other as Chinese is from English.

In the Northwest

The Northwest Indians were avid traders. Acquisitions of material goods — including slaves — resulted in higher status, and gift-giving in ceremonies called *potlatches* marked public displays of wealth. Tribes such as the Chinook, the Salishan, and the Makah lived in well-organized, permanent villages of 100 or more. Abundant fish and a mild climate made many of the tribes relatively prosperous, especially because they dried fish to save for the times of year when food was less available. The Northwest cultures carved elaborate and intricate totem poles, which represented their ancestral heritage.

In the Southwest

Arid conditions made life tougher for tribes in the Southwest. Tribes such as the Apache were foragers, scrounging for everything from bison to grasshoppers, while tribes such as the Hopi scratched out an existence as farmers. In what's now California, most of the scores of different tribes were pretty laid-back. They lived in villages, as hunters and gatherers.

On the Great Plains

Game, especially bison, was plentiful on the Plains. But hunting bison was tough on foot, and the Plains Indians didn't have horses until the mid-16th century. Eventually, the tribes domesticated the wild offspring of horses that Spanish explorers brought from the Old World, and tribes like the Cheyenne and Lakota became expert riders. Until then, the Plains tribes made do by stalking, ambushing, and occasionally stampeding a herd of bison over a cliff. The tribes were semi-nomadic: They packed up their teepees and moved on when the local food got scarce.

In the Northeast

Tribes fell into two large language groups in the Northeast: the Iroquoian and the Algonquian. Because history shows that human beings divided into two groups but living in the same area tend to fight, guess what? They fought a lot. Both groups used tools and weapons made of copper or slate, which they traded back and forth when they weren't fighting. The Northeast Indians lived in communal longhouses and invented a light, maneuverable canoe made out of birch bark.

NATIVE AMERICAN GIFTS

Native American contributions to modern culture are plentiful, varied, and often over-looked. They include the names of 27 states and thousands of rivers, lakes, mountains, cities, and towns; foods such as potatoes, sweet potatoes, artichokes, squash, turkey, tomatoes, vanilla, cacao (which is used to make chocolate), and maple sugar; medicines like coca (used to make Novocain), quinine, curare, and ipecac; and other items such as hammocks, toboggans, parkas, ponchos, and snowshoes — oh yeah, and tobacco, too.

A remarkable event involving the Northeast tribes occurred around 1450, when five tribes — the Cayugas, Mohawks, Oneidas, Onondagas, and Senecas — formed the Iroquois League. The purpose of this league was to form an alliance against the Algonquin and settle disputes among themselves. Some scholars believe the uniting of individual tribes for a common cause may have been studied by the country's founding fathers, particularly Benjamin Franklin, when they were putting together the federalist form of government after the American Revolution.

In the Southeast

The dominant tribes in the Southeast included the Cherokees, the Choctaws, the Chickasaws, the Creeks, and the Seminoles. These tribes got by through a mix of hunting, gathering, and farming. Europeans would later refer to them as the *Five Civilized Tribes*, in part because they developed codes of law and judicial systems but also because they readily adopted the European customs of running plantations, slaveholding, and raising cattle. They also often intermarried with Europeans. However, despite European admiration for the Southeast tribes' abilities to adapt, these Native Americans were still exploited, exterminated, or evacuated.

De-stereotyping the Native Americans

Both historians and Hollywood have often stereotyped pre-Colombian Native Americans as either noble people who lived in constant harmony with nature or mindless knuckleheads who sat around in the dirt when they weren't brutally killing one another.

The truth is somewhere in between. Like people everywhere else, Native Americans had both virtues and faults. They showed remarkable ingenuity in areas like astronomy and architecture, yet lacked important cultural advances like the plow, the wheel, and sailing ships. Some tribes had no clue what a war was; others lived and died for little else. Some Native Americans were environmentally conscientious, others were eco-clueless.

Although different tribes and cultures sometimes traded with one another for necessities, they generally kept to themselves — unless they were fighting one another. Groups tended to refer to themselves as "human beings" or "the people" and referred to other groups as simply "others" or something less flattering.

But it wasn't character traits, good or bad, that ultimately hurt Native Americans. Instead, it was a conspiracy of other elements: an unwillingness or inability to unite against the European invader, a relatively small total population, a lack of biological defenses against European diseases, and the unfortunate tendency of many of the newcomers to view Native Americans not as human beings but as just another exotic species in a strange New World.

Visiting by the Vikings

Native Americans got their first look at what trouble was going to look like when Vikings showed up in North America. All Vikings were Norsemen, but not all Norsemen were Vikings. *Viking* meant to go raiding, pirating, or exploring. Although some of the Scandinavians of 1,000 years ago surely did all these things, most of them stayed in Scandinavia and fished or farmed.

For about 300 years, the Vikings conquered or looted much of Western Europe and Russia. In the ninth and tenth centuries, sailing in ships was made speedy and stable by the addition of keels. Consequently, the Vikings journeyed west, not so much for loot as for new lands to settle.

Like many things in human history, the Vikings' first visits to the North American continent were by accident. The first sighting of the New World by a European probably occurred around 987, when a Viking named Bjarni Herjolfsson sailed from Iceland to hook up with his dad and missed Greenland. Herjolfsson wasn't impressed by what he saw from the ship, and he never actually set foot on land before heading back to Greenland.

Herjolfsson was followed about 15 years later by the son of Eric the Red, the Viking who had settled Greenland. Eric's son, Leif Ericsson, was also known as Leif the Lucky. Leif landed in what's now Labrador, a part of Newfoundland, Canada. Mistaking seasonal berries for grapes, Leif called the area Vinland. He spent the winter in the new land and then left.

His brother Thorvald visited Vinland the next year. Thorvald got into a fight with the local inhabitants and thus gained the distinction of being the first European to be killed by the natives in North America. (Vikings called the natives *skraelings,* a contemptuous term meaning "dwarves.") After his death, Thorvald's crew went back to Greenland.

The next Viking visit was meant to be permanent. Led by a brother-in-law of Leif's named Thorfinn Karlsefni, an expedition of three ships, some cattle, and about 160 people — including a few women — created a settlement. The Karlsefni settlement lasted three years. There were chronic troubles with the natives, who had a large numerical advantage, as well as weapons and fighting abilities that were equal to the Vikings. There were also too few Viking women in the settlement to keep things peaceful. So the settlers sailed back to Greenland. By 1020, most scholars agree, the Vikings had given up on North America. Supply lines to the homelands were long, the voyages back and forth were dangerous, and the natives were unfriendly. The Norsemen apparently felt that the new land wasn't worth the trouble.

REMEMBER

The Vikings' forays to the North American continent were relatively brief and had no lasting impact. The main evidence that they were even here is fairly limited: two long sagas written in the Middle Ages and the scattered ruins of three housing clusters and a forge at a place called L'Anse aux Meadows, on the northern tip of Newfoundland. But tales of their voyages were well reported around Europe, and they served to whet the exploration appetites of people in other places. Other nations, however, plagued by troubles like, well, plagues, weren't ready to follow them west for almost 500 years.

Spicing Up Life — and Other Reasons for Exploring

For centuries, people in Europe had no way of preserving food other than salting it, which doesn't make it very palatable. When Europeans were fighting in the Middle East during the Crusades, however, they established overland trading routes that supplied a whole condiment shelf of spices: cinnamon from Ceylon, pepper from India, and cloves and nutmeg from the Moluccan Islands. They also developed a taste for silks from China and Japan, and they already liked the gold and precious metals of the East.

But in 1453, the Turkish Empire conquered Constantinople (now Istanbul), which had been the capital of the Eastern Roman Empire and the crossroads of the overland supply routes. The Turks closed the routes, and Europeans had to begin thinking about finding a sea route to reopen the trade.

Countries were also putting aside the feudal disputes of the Middle Ages and unifying. In Spain, for example, 700 years of war between the Spaniards and the Moors (Arabs from North Africa) were finally over in 1492. The marriage of

Ferdinand of Castile and Isabella of Aragon had united the country's two major realms. And Europe was stepping briskly toward the Renaissance. People were beginning to believe in the power of the individual to change things and were more willing to take chances.

The Portuguese, the best navigators and sailors in the world at that time (except perhaps for the Polynesians), were pushing farther into the Atlantic and down the coast of Africa. In 1488, the Portuguese explorer Bartolomeu Dias reached the tip of Africa, named it the Cape of Good Hope, and verified that a sea route to India did exist.

Meanwhile, other explorers who knew the earth was a sphere were thinking about reaching the Indies and the East by sailing west across the Atlantic. One of them was named Columbus.

Christopher Columbus was obsessive, religious, stubborn, arrogant, charming, and egotistical. He was physically striking, with reddish-blond hair that had turned white by the time he was 30, and he stood 6 feet tall at a time when most adult males were six inches shorter. Born the son of a weaver in Genoa Italy in 1451, Columbus became a first-class sailor. He also ran a successful mapmaking business with his brother Bartholomew. But he became convinced his ticket to fame and fortune was in finding a western route to the Indies.

Starting in the 1480s, Columbus and his brother began making the rounds of European capitals, looking for ships and financial backing for his idea. His demands were exorbitant. In return for his services, Columbus wanted the title Admiral of the Oceans, 10 percent of all the loot he found, and the ability to pass governorship of every country he discovered to his heirs.

The rulers of England and France said no thanks, as did some of the city states that made up Italy. The king of Portugal also told him to scram. So in 1486, Columbus went to Spain. Queen Isabella listened to his pitch, and she also said no, for the time being. But she did appoint a commission to look into the idea and decided to put Columbus on the payroll in the meantime. The meantime stretched out for six years. Finally, convinced she wasn't really risking much because chances were that he wouldn't return, Isabella gave her approval in January 1492. Columbus was on his way.

REMEMBER

Partly because of error and partly because of wishful thinking, Columbus estimated the distance to the Indies at approximately 2,500 miles, which was about 7,500 miles short. But after a voyage of about five weeks, he and his crews, totaling 90 men, did find land at around 2 a.m. on October 12, 1492. It was an island in the Bahamas, which he called San Salvador. The timing of the discovery was good;

it came even as the crews of the *Nina*, *Pinta*, and *Santa Maria* were muttering about a mutiny. Columbus dubbed the locals Indians, believing he was in the Indian Ocean. The name stuck.

Columbus next sailed to Cuba, where he found few spices and little gold. Sailing on to an island he called Hispaniola (today's Dominican Republic and Haiti), the *Santa Maria* hit a reef on Christmas Eve, 1492. Columbus abandoned the ship, set up a trading outpost he called Navidad, left some men to operate it, and sailed back to Spain in his other two ships.

So enthusiastically did people greet the news of his return that on his second voyage to Hispaniola, Columbus had 17 ships and more than 1,200 men. But this time he ran into more than a little disappointment. Natives had wiped out his trading post after his men became too grabby with the local gold and the local women. Worse, most of the men he brought with him had come only for gold and other riches, and they didn't care about setting up a permanent colony. Because of the lack of treasures, they soon wanted to go home. And the natives lost interest in the newcomers after the novelty of the Spanish trinkets wore off.

Consequently, Columbus took harsh measures. He demanded tribute in gold, which the Indians didn't have. He also divided up the land on Hispaniola and enslaved the natives, thousands of whom died. And he hanged some of the "settlers" for rebelling against his authority.

A CIGAR A DAY KEEPS THE DOCTOR AWAY

Of all the fabulous tales Columbus's men brought back to Europe, one of the strangest was about how many Indians had this weird habit of sticking dried leaves in a slingshot-shaped pipe called a *tabaco* and lighting it on fire. They then put the forked end of the pipe in their nostrils and inhaled. Another method was to roll the leaves into a big tube, light one end, put the other end in their mouths, and breathe in.

Columbus's men brought some of the plant's seeds, which they called *tobacco,* back to Spain with them, and they soon spread to other parts of Europe. (In France, a leading distributor was a guy named Jean Nicot — hence the word *nicotine* to describe the key ingredient in tobacco.) Europe marveled at the "miracle" herb, which was believed to help heal sword wounds, ward off plague, and help clear congested lungs.

Not everyone, however, was in love with the stuff. "Smoking tobacco is loathsome to the eye, hateful to the nose, harmful to the brain, dangerous to the lungs," fumed England's King James I in 1604. Forsooth! He knew whereof he spoke!

COULD'VE BEEN WORSE; COULD'VE BEEN "VESPUCCI"

Amerigo Vespucci was an Italian who settled in Spain and helped supply Columbus's voyages. He then took several trips to South America under the command of one of Columbus's captains. In 1504, somewhat exaggerated letters by Vespucci about what he called Mundus Novus — the *New World* — were printed throughout Europe.

A German mapmaker read the letters, was impressed, and decided in 1507 to call the massive new lands on his maps *America,* in Vespucci's honor — which is why we're not called the United States of Christopher.

The third and fourth voyages by Columbus also failed to produce the fabulous riches he had hoped for. When he died in 1506, he was largely considered a failure. But even if Columbus was unaware that he never reached the Orient, he knew he had not failed.

"By the divine will," he said shortly before his death, "I have placed under the sovereignty of the king and queen an 'other world,' whereby Spain, which was considered poor, is to become the richest of all countries."

Dropping Names of Others Who Dropped By

Remember in school when your history teacher would give you a sheet with a list of 15th-century explorers' names on one side and a list of their accomplishments on the other side, and you had to match them? Well, here's that list again. But before I sum up these people in a line or two, it may be a good idea to marvel at what they did. They sailed across unknown stretches of water in cramped, leaky ships no longer than a tennis court, provisioned with food that would gag a starving pig, and commanded crews who were more than willing to cut their throats if things went wrong.

When they reached the Americas, they wandered for months (sometimes years) through strange lands populated by people who, though not always hostile, were certainly unpredictable. And then they had to try to get home again to tell someone about what they'd found. Although their motives were rarely pure, they displayed a lot of courage and determination.

Here are eight of these daring explorers:

» **John Cabot (England):** An Italian, Cabot was commissioned by King Henry VII to explore the New World. Using the old Viking northern route, Cabot sailed to Newfoundland in 1497, saw lots of fish, and claimed the area for England. In 1498, he took a second trip with five ships, but only one ever returned to England. The other ships and their crews, including Cabot, disappeared. Even so, Cabot may have been the first non-Viking European to set foot on what's now the continental United States, and he gave England its first real claim on America.

» **Vasco Nunez de Balboa (Spain):** Balboa is credited with being the first European to see the South Seas from the New World. He named it the Pacific because it appeared to be so calm. He was later beheaded by his successor to the governorship of Panama.

» **Ferdinand Magellan (Spain):** Magellan, a Portuguese explorer who was one of the greatest sailors ever, led a Spanish expedition of five ships in 1519. He was looking for a quick passage to the East from Europe. He sailed around the tip of South America and into the Pacific. Magellan was killed by natives in the Philippines, but one of his five ships made it back to Spain in 1522 — the first to sail around the world.

» **Jacques Cartier (France):** He made two trips to the New World in 1534 and 1535, sailing up the St. Lawrence River. He went back in 1541 with a sizable expedition to look for gold and precious stones but returned to France with what turned out to be just a bunch of quartz. Still, his trips helped France establish a claim for much of what is now Canada.

» **Francisco Coronado (Spain):** This guy led an incredible expedition in 1540 that went looking for the "Seven Cities of Cibola," which were supposedly dripping with riches. Instead, in two years of looking for the elusive cities, Coronado's group explored Arizona, Texas, New Mexico, Kansas, and the Gulf of California and discovered the Grand Canyon. But they never found gold.

» **Hernando de Soto (Spain):** He marched around what are now the Gulf states before discovering the Mississippi River in 1541. He died of a fever on its banks.

» **Samuel de Champlain (France):** A mapmaker, Champlain landed in the New World in 1603 and explored extensively in the northeastern part of the continent. He founded the colony of Quebec in 1608.

» **Henry Hudson (Netherlands):** Hudson sailed up the bay and river that now bear his name in present-day New York in 1609. He was looking for a northwest passage to the Indies. Instead, he found an area rich in fur-bearing mammals and helped the Dutch lay claim to a piece of the continent. He was cast adrift by his crew in a mutiny in 1611 and was never heard from again.

The Sword, the Cross, and the Measles

One of the problems in "discovering" a new land that's already inhabited is deciding how to interact with the people who got there first. When it came to the Native American populations of the New World, the Europeans generally decided on fighting with them or enslaving them.

Native American slavery

It started with Columbus. By his second voyage to Hispaniola, he set up a system, called the *encomienda*, which amounted to slavery. Under it, a colonist who was given a piece of land had the right to the labor of all the natives who lived on that land — whether they were interested in a job or not. Columbus also imposed a gold tax on the Indians and sometimes cut the hands off of those who couldn't or wouldn't pay it. Between slavery, killings, and diseases, the population of Hispaniola's natives plummeted from an estimated 250,000 to 300,000 at the time of Columbus's arrival in 1492 to perhaps 60,000 by 1510, to near zero by 1550.

As the Indians on the main islands died off, the Spanish settlers in the Caribbean simply raided other, smaller islands and kidnapped the residents there. A historian at the time wrote that you could navigate among islands "without compass or chart . . . simply by following the trail of dead Indians who have been thrown from ships."

When even the populations of the little islands waned, the Spanish looked for other cheap labor sources. They found them in Africa. African slaves were first imported to the New World within a few years after Columbus's first trip. By 1513, King Carlos I of Spain had given his royal assent to the African slave trade. He made his decision in part, he said, to improve the lot of the Indians.

Of course, the fact that many Spanish landholders in the New World were beginning to prefer African slaves made his decision easier. They believed the Africans had better immunity to European diseases and were more used to hard agricultural labor because they came from agricultural cultures.

The men in the brown robes

Whatever his other motives, King Carlos I and his successors did have their consciences regularly pricked by some church leaders, as well as missionaries who accompanied the early voyagers. In 1514, Pope Leo X declared that "not only the Christian religion but Nature cries out against the slavery and the slave trade." In 1537, Pope Paul III declared Indians were not to be enslaved.

AND FOR THE SERIOUS SWEET TOOTH . . .

On his second trip to the Americas in 1493, Columbus stopped by the Canary Islands and picked up some sugar cane cuttings. He planted them in Hispaniola, and they thrived. In 1516, the first sugar grown in the New World was presented to King Carlos I of Spain. By 1531, it was as commercially important to the Spanish colonial economy as gold.

Planters soon discovered a byproduct as well. The juice left over after the sugar was pressed out of the cane and crystallized was called *melasas* by the Spanish (and *molasses* by the English). Mixing this juice with water and leaving it out in the sun created a potent and tasty fermented drink. They called it *rum* — perhaps after the Latin word for sugar cane, *saccharum officinarum*. The stuff was great for long sea voyages because it didn't go bad. Sugar and rum became so popular that sugar plantations mushroomed all over the Caribbean.

REMEMBER

With 21st-century hindsight, it's tempting to shrug off the work of the early European missionaries as sort of a PR effort designed to make the nastier things the conquerors did look less nasty. Although the idea that the cross was used to justify bad treatment of the "heathens" has some truth (a 1513 proclamation required natives to convert or be enslaved or executed), most of the people who committed the worst atrocities apparently didn't much care who knew about their violent actions. Thus, they didn't need an excuse.

The horrendous actions of some of their fellow Europeans certainly didn't make the missionaries' jobs easier. One Native American chief, who was being burned at the stake — by government officials, not missionaries — for refusing to convert, reportedly replied that he feared if he did join the religion, he "might go to Heaven and meet only Christians."

Destruction through disease

If they managed to survive slavery, the sword, and the excesses committed in the name of the cross, the New World's natives were then likely candidates to die from the Europeans' most formidable weapon: disease. Because they had never been exposed to them as a culture, the Native Americans' immune systems had no defense when faced with diseases such as measles and smallpox.

The first major epidemic — smallpox — started in 1518 after the disease arrived at Hispaniola via a shipload of colonists. From there, it gradually and sporadically spread through North, Central, and South America by following the Native Americans' trade and travel routes. Sometimes, disease spread so fast that it decimated tribes before they ever saw a European.

A POX ON THE CONQUERORS

New World Native Americans may have gathered a measure of revenge in the disease department by giving Europeans syphilis. Many researchers believe that Columbus's sailors brought the disease back to Spain from the Americas, where it was relatively common among different Native American groups. The theory was bolstered in early 2008, when a study led by Emory University scientist Kristin Harper determined through molecular genetics that the sexually transmitted version of the disease originated in the New World.

In 1495, after Columbus returned from his first voyage, the rulers of Spain and France sent large armies to besiege the Italian city of Naples. After the city was captured, the soldiers returned and helped to spread the new venereal disease. The French called it "the Neapolitan disease," and the Spanish called it "the French disease." They proved that there are some new things for which no nation wants credit.

Some historians believe that disease was spread less by the Europeans and more by the livestock they brought with them, particularly the pigs. The theory is that the pigs passed on microbes to the native wildlife, allowing disease to spread more quickly than it could have by mere human transmission.

What's certain is that over the next 400 years, smallpox, measles, whooping cough, typhus, and scarlet fever killed thousands of times more Native Americans than guns or swords did.

Arriving Late for the Party

Spain's early explorations of the New World gave that country a great head start over its European rivals. Spanish conquerors defeated mighty empires in Mexico and Peru — the Aztecs and Incas. Both empires had huge caches of gold and silver and sophisticated cultures with built-in labor classes. All the Spanish had to do was kill the old bosses and become the new bosses, so they didn't have to import slaves as they had done in the Caribbean. Moreover, the conquests spawned a herd of *adelantadaos* (or "advancers"), who roamed all over the lower half of America in search of the next big empire.

But Spain's position of preeminence was short-lived. In 1588, Spanish plans to invade England with an armada of ships blew up when the fleet was scattered by the English navy and a fierce storm. Within 30 years, both England and France had established colonies in the New World.

Eventually, a growing spirit of independence would strip Spain of its New World empire. Early on, it was pretty clear that war-weary Europe would soon be fighting again over the spoils of the New World. In an effort to head that off — and also find a way to put his mark of authority over matters in the Americas — Pope Alexander VI divided the Americas between Spain and Portugal by drawing a line on the map.

This decision left Portugal with what's now Brazil, Spain with everything else, and the rest of Europe pretty peeved. King Henry VII of England declared that he would ignore the papal edict. King Francis I of France sniffed, "We fail to find this clause in Adam's will." The countries left empty-handed by the Pope's decree got over it in part by picking off Spanish ships laden with treasure on their way home.

France

Throughout much of the 16th century, France's efforts to get its share of the Americas were marred by civil wars and inept leadership. The French forays to the New World were limited to fishermen who came each year to mine the cod-rich banks off Newfoundland and explorations of areas that are now New England and eastern Canada.

Moreover, while the Spanish were in it for the loot and the English for the land, the French weren't quite sure what they wanted. They eventually settled on a little of both. Fur franchises were awarded private companies on the condition that they also start permanent colonies. But the companies didn't try very hard, and as the 1500s ended, the French had little more than a tenuous hold on its New World dominion.

England

Despite early explorations by John Cabot just on the heels of Columbus's voyages, England lagged behind Spain when it came to exploring and exploiting the New World. Part of the problem was that the English were broke, and part of it was that England feared Spain's military might.

By the end of the 16th century, however, the English were encouraged by the success of raids against Spanish-American cities and ships by *privateers* (a cross between patriots and pirates) such as John Hawkins and Francis Drake. The defeat in 1588 of the Spanish Armada, the invasion fleet that met with disaster off the coast of England, encouraged England even more.

In 1587, Walter Raleigh, who had the royal right to colonize in the Americas, sent a group that consisted of 89 men, 7 women, and 11 children to what is now North Carolina. They called their colony Roanoke.

Unfortunately, the looming threat of the Spanish invasion meant the little colony got no support from the homeland. In 1590, when a relief expedition finally arrived, the colonists had vanished. They left behind only rotting and rummaged junk and a single word carved in a tree: *Croatoan*.

The word referred to an island about 100 miles south of Roanoke. No one knows the meaning behind the carved word. And no one knows exactly what happened to the first English colony in the New World.

Chapter **3**

Pilgrims' Progress: The English Colonies, 1607–1700

With the defeat of the Spanish naval armada off the coast of England in 1588, Spain seemed to lose interest in expanding its empire in the New World. England, on the other hand, was eager to make up for lost time.

In this chapter, England establishes its American colonies, slavery establishes itself as an enduring evil, and colonists wrestle with religious differences among themselves and with Native Americans over nearly everything else.

Seeing Potential in the New World

For most of the 16th century, England was too poor and too timid to do much about the opportunities presented by the opening of two new continents. By 1604, however, when England and Spain signed a tenuous peace treaty, the English had good reasons to think about branching out to the new lands of the West. Among them were

>> **Economic incentive:** A middle class of merchants, speculators, and entrepreneurs had formed. By pooling their resources in "joint-stock companies," these capitalists could invest in schemes to make money in the New World by backing colonists who would produce goods England and the rest of Europe wanted. They could also harvest resources, such as timber, for which England had to depend on other Old World countries.

>> **Overpopulation:** Even though the entire population of about 4 million was less than half that of modern-day London, many Englishmen pined for a less-crowded land.

REMEMBER

>> **Religious dissent:** Protestantism, a rival Christian religion to the one led by the Pope in Rome, had developed in the 16th century and become firmly rooted in England. Even though the country's own state church was Protestant, many English Protestants felt it wasn't different enough from the Roman Catholic faith they had left. Religiously restless, they looked to America as a place to plant the seeds of their own version of Christianity.

>> **Wool:** England's woolen industry was booming in the late 1500s and early 1600s. Farms were turned into pastures for more and more sheep, and the tenant farmers on the former farms were forced off, with no particular place to go — except the New World.

Settling in Jamestown

It's pretty safe to say that the first permanent English colony in America was put together about as well as a soup sandwich. Those who set out to establish the colony weren't sure where they were going or what to do when they got there.

A group of investors known as the Virginia Company of London was given a charter by King James I to settle somewhere in the southern part of the New World area known as Virginia. After a voyage on which roughly 27 percent of the original 144 settlers died, three ships arrived at the mouth of a river they ingratiatingly named the James, after the king. On May 14, 1607, they began the settlement of Jamestown.

Early troubles

Some of the settlers were indentured servants who had traded seven years of their labor for passage to America. Most of the others were far more interested in finding gold than creating a colony and lacked skills, such as hunting or farming, that might actually be useful in the wilderness. As one historian put it, "It was a colony of people who wouldn't work, or couldn't."

Worse, the site they had chosen for a settlement was in a malaria-ridden swamp, and the local inhabitants were both suspicious and unfriendly. In fact, the Native Americans launched their first attack against the newcomers within two weeks of their arrival. Within six months, half of the 105 settlers who had survived the trip were dead of disease or starvation.

Making Native American friends

Those who survived did so largely because of a character named John Smith. An experienced and courageous adventurer, Smith was also a shameless self-promoter and a world-class liar, with a knack for getting into trouble. On the voyage over, for example, he was charged with mutiny, although he was eventually acquitted.

But whatever his faults, Smith was both gutsy and diplomatic. He managed to make friends with Powhatan, the chief of the local Native Americans, and the tribe provided the colonists with enough food to hold on. Smith provided much-needed leadership, declaring, "He that will not work neither shall he eat." Without Smith, the colony may not have survived.

As it was, Jamestown came pretty close to disaster. In the winter of 1609, called "the starving time," conditions got so bad colonists resorted to eating anything they could get — including each other. One man was executed after eating the body of his dead wife. In 1610, the survivors were actually on a ship and ready to head home when a military relief expedition showed up and took charge.

Finding a cash crop

One of the biggest problems the colonists faced was coming up with a product that people in England wanted and which could form the basis of a profitable economy. They found one in 1613, when a fellow named John Rolfe developed a variety of tobacco that was a huge hit in the mother country. Within a few years, Jamestown had a thriving cash crop.

REMEMBER

In 1619, three things happened in the Virginia colony that had a large impact on the British in America. One was the arrival of 90 women, who became the brides of settlers who paid for their passage at a cost of 120 pounds of tobacco each.

The second was the meeting of the first legislative body of colonists on the continent. Known as the House of Burgesses, it met for about a week, passed laws against gambling and idleness, and decreed all colonists must attend two church services each Sunday — and bring their weapons with them. Then the legislators adjourned because it was too hot to keep meeting.

The third event — three weeks after the House of Burgesses had become a symbol of representative government in the New World — was the arrival of a Dutch ship. From its cargo, Jamestown settlers bought 20 human beings from Africa to work in the tobacco fields (see Figure 3-1).

FIGURE 3-1: The arrival of slaves in Jamestown: One of the key elements in America's history.

Courtesy of the Library of Congress, Prints & Photographs Division, LC-USZ62-53345

Instituting Slavery

While it was a Dutch ship that brought the first slaves to Virginia, no European nation had a monopoly on the practice. The Portuguese were the first Europeans to raid the African coast for slaves, in the mid-15th century. They were quickly followed by the Spanish, who used Africans to supplant the New World Indians who had either been killed or died of diseases. By the mid-16th century, the English sea dog John Hawkins was operating a thriving slave trade between Africa and the Caribbean.

Most slaves were seized from tribes in the continent's interior and sold from West African ports to the New World. Some were hunted down by European and Arab slave traders. Many were sold by rival tribes after being captured in wars or on raids. And some were sold by their own tribes when they got into debt or ran afoul of tribal leaders.

Although the use of African slaves in the tobacco fields proved successful and more slaves were gradually imported, slavery was by no means a strictly Southern colony phenomenon. While the Northern colonies had less use for slaves as agricultural workers, they put Africans to work as domestic servants or as unpaid laborers in various trades. One reason was that slaves represented more or less permanent labor, while *indentured servants* — people who traded five to seven years of work in return for passage to the New World — would eventually have to be freed.

REMEMBER

Not everyone in the colonies was enamored with slavery. In 1688, a radical Protestant group in Pennsylvania known as the Mennonites became the first American religious group to formally oppose the practice. In 1700, a New England judge named Samuel Sewall published a three-page tract called "The Selling of Joseph," in which he compared slavery to what Joseph's brothers did to him in the biblical story and called for the abolition of slavery in the colonies.

But voices such as Sewall's were few and far between. Although the total population of slaves was relatively low through most of the 1600s, colonial governments took steps to institutionalize slavery. In 1662, Virginia passed a law that automatically made slaves of slaves' children. In 1664, Maryland's assembly declared that all black people in the colony were slaves for life, whether they converted to Christianity or not. And in 1684, New York's legislators recognized slavery as a legitimate practice.

As the 17th century ended, it was clear that African slaves were a much better bargain, in terms of costs, than European servants, and the numbers of slaves began to swell. In 1670, Virginia had a population of about 2,000 slaves. By 1708, the number was 12,000. Slavery had not only taken root; it was sprouting.

Colonizing: Pilgrims and Puritans

While Virginia was being settled by gentlemen farmers, servants, slaves, and some people you wouldn't trust with your car keys, a very different kind of people were putting together England's second colony in America.

These people, who settled New England, came to America for wealth of another type. They were spurred by their deep religious beliefs and their zeal to find a haven for the freedom to practice their faith — although not necessarily for anyone else to practice theirs.

The Mayflower Compact: A Dutch pilgrimage

The Pilgrims (actually, they called themselves "the Saints" and everyone else "the Strangers," and they weren't dubbed *Pilgrims* until much later by one of their leaders) were mostly lower-class farmers and craftsmen who had decided the Church of England was still too Catholic for their tastes. So they separated themselves from the Church, thus resulting in everyone else calling them "Separatists." This didn't please King James I, who suggested rather forcefully that they rejoin or separate themselves from England.

The Separatists did just that, settling in Holland in 1608. But after a decade of watching their children become "Dutchified," the English expatriates longed for someplace they could live as English subjects and still worship the way they wanted. The answer was America.

After going back to England and negotiating a charter to establish a colony, taking out a few loans, and forming a company, a group of 102 men, women, and children left England on September 16, 1620, on a ship called the *Mayflower.* (A second ship, the *Speedwell,* also started out but sprang a leak and had to turn back.) The *Mayflower* was usually used for shipping wine between France and England. Its cargo for this trip was decidedly more varied than usual. Although the Pilgrims didn't really pack any smarter than had the Jamestown colonists, they did show some imagination. Among the things they took to the wilderness of North America were musical instruments, all kinds of furniture, and even books on the history of Turkey (the country, not the bird). One guy even brought 139 pairs of shoes and boots.

Despite a rough crossing that took 65 days, only one passenger and four crewmen died, and one child was born. After some preliminary scouting, they dropped anchor in a broad, shallow bay now known as Plymouth. (No evidence exists to indicate they landed on any kind of rock.)

REMEMBER

Two important things happened on the way over. One was that the Pilgrims missed their turnoff and failed to land within the borders laid out by their charter. That meant they were essentially squatters and didn't fall under the direct governance of anyone in England. Secondly, concerned by mutterings from some members of the group that they should go home, the colony's leaders drew up a *compact*, or set of rules, by which they all agreed to abide. This became known as the Mayflower Compact.

The Mayflower Compact was remarkable in that it was drawn up by people who were essentially equal to one another and were looking for a way to establish laws they could all live under. Although it certainly left out equal rights for women, slaves, Native Americans, and indentured servants, it was still a key early step in the colonists' journey toward self-rule and independence from England.

Despite their planning, the Plymouth colony had a very rough first winter. Just like the Jamestown colonists, half the Plymouth settlers died in the first six months. But unlike many of the Jamestown colonists, the Pilgrims were hard workers. They had an extremely able leader in William Bradford, who was to be governor of the colony for more than 30 years, and an able, although diminutive, military leader in Miles Standish (his nickname was "Captain Shrimpe"). They were also extremely lucky because the local Native Americans proved not only to be great neighbors but also had one among them who spoke English.

The locals showed the newcomers some planting techniques and then traded the colonists' furs for corn, which gave the Pilgrims something to send back to England. By the fall of 1622, the Plymouth colonists had much to be thankful for.

The Plymouth colony never got all that big, and by 1691 it was absorbed by the larger Massachusetts Bay colony. But the impact of its approach to government and its effect on the American psyche far outstripped its size or longevity. Ever since (greatly aided by countless elementary school Thanksgiving pageants), the Pilgrims have dominated most Americans' images of the country's earliest settlers.

SQUANTO

His real name was Tisquantum, and he was a member of the Pawtuxet tribe. In 1605, Squanto was taken to England, possibly as a slave, by a passing explorer named George Weymouth. In 1613, he returned to the New World as a guide for Capt. John Smith and remained there. A short time later, however, Squanto was abducted by yet another English expedition and sold as a slave in Spain. This time he escaped. He made his way to England and eventually onto a 1619 expedition to New England, only to find his tribe had been exterminated by disease, most probably brought by the white newcomers.

So, when the Pilgrims arrived, Squanto spoke fluent English, a little Spanish, and was essentially rootless. He was also apparently extremely tolerant. Until he died a little more than a year after their arrival, Squanto stayed with the Pilgrims, acting as their interpreter and advisor. Talk about a good sport!

THANKS-A-DRUMSTICK

When the first Thanksgiving feast took place is uncertain, but it was probably between September 21 and November 9, 1621. Under a decree by Gov. William Bradford, Chief Massasoit and his Wampanoag tribe were invited to share a few days' worth of wild fowl, venison, leeks, watercress, plums, berries, eels, oysters, corn bread, and "popped" corn. It was such a good idea that only 242 years later, Pres. Abraham Lincoln made it a national holiday.

The Massachusetts Bay colony:
A pure haven

It's easy to confuse the Pilgrims and the Puritans. Both groups moved to journey to America for religious reasons. Both were remarkably intolerant of other people's beliefs. And neither was much fun at parties.

But they had differences. The Puritans were less radical and less interested in leaving the Church of England than in "purifying" it. Their leader was a well-to-do lawyer named John Winthrop. He had some qualities that came to be part of the stereotypical New England Yankee. He was deeply religious but a practical businessman. He advocated — and put into practice — such egalitarian principles as trial by jury, yet regarded democracy as "the meanest and worst" of all forms of government.

Armed with a charter that gave the colonists extraordinary independence in making their own rules, Winthrop led about 500 Puritans to the Massachusetts Bay colony in New England in 1630, establishing the city of Boston later that year. An even larger group of Puritans had settled at Salem, in another part of the colony, the year before, and by 1642, as many as 20,000 Puritans had left England for America.

The Puritans established fur, fishing, and shipbuilding industries. They set up a system of compulsory free education, institutions of higher learning, and a model for what would eventually become a typical two-house state government in America. They developed crafts such as silversmithing and printed their own books.

They were also pretty puritanical. Religious dissidents, especially Quakers, were routinely beaten and banished, and sometimes hanged. "If they beat the gospel black and blue," one Puritan minister said in explaining this treatment, "it is but just to beat them black and blue." Adultery was punishable by death until 1632, when the penalty was reduced to a public whipping and the forced wearing of the letters "AD" sewed onto the clothing.

WHICH IS WITCH?

Witch hunting in America started with kids fooling around. It ended with 20 executions and a wave of hysteria that swept through New England. In early 1692, three young girls in Salem, Massachusetts, threw fits and claimed they had been bewitched by a West Indian slave and two other local women. The accusations begat more accusations as the girls and their friends basked in the attention. When they admitted they had made it up, it was too late. Witchcraft accusations were used to settle all sorts of petty personal and political scores.

By the time Gov. William Phips (whose own wife was accused) had put an end to it, 150 people had been charged with consorting with Satan. Of that number, 28 were convicted: 5 confessed and were released, 2 escaped, 1 was pardoned, and 20 — 14 women and 6 men — were executed. All the women and five of the men were hanged. One man, who refused to speak at his trial, was pressed to death under heavy stones. Despite widespread belief to the contrary, none was burned at the stake, as witches were commonly dealt with in Europe.

REMEMBER

The impact of the Puritan society of New England was huge. In it were the roots of the modern corporate system, the representative form of state and federal government, the American legal system, and the moral conflict between wanting the freedom to think and act as you please and the authority to control how others think and act.

Bringing Religious Freedom: Dissidents, Catholics, and Quakers

The Massachusetts and Jamestown colonies were only the beginning. Throughout the rest of the 17th century, English settlers of all kinds moved to America. Some of those didn't like where they landed — or the place they landed didn't like them. But it was a big country, so they began the American tradition of moving on.

Some of the colonies — Maine, New Hampshire, Connecticut, and North and South Carolina — were either privately founded or were offshoots of the Massachusetts and Virginia colonies (see Figure 3-2). But three of them had very different beginnings.

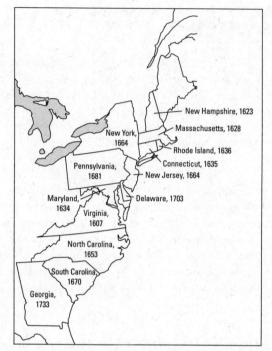

FIGURE 3-2: The original 13 colonies and their dates of establishment.

New Hampshire, 1623
Massachusetts, 1628
New York, 1664
Rhode Island, 1636
Connecticut, 1635
New Jersey, 1664
Pennsylvania, 1681
Maryland, 1634
Delaware, 1703
Virginia, 1607
North Carolina, 1653
South Carolina, 1670
Georgia, 1733

© John Wiley & Sons, Inc.

Sneaking off to Rhode Island

In 1633, a smart and sociable guy named Roger Williams became a minister in Salem, Massachusetts. He also became an expert in Native American languages and was troubled by the way his fellow settlers treated the natives. His fellow settlers, meanwhile, were troubled by Williams's insistence that land shouldn't be stolen from the Native Americans and that there should be a separation between the institutions of church and state. So troubling was this latter idea to Puritan leaders that they decided to ship the troublemaker back to England.

But Williams was tipped off to the plan by John Winthrop, and with the help of friendly Native Americans, Williams and his family slipped off in 1636 to an unsettled area. By 1644, it had become the colony of Rhode Island. Small and disliked by its neighbors, Rhode Island became a haven for those seeking religious freedom — or those who just plain didn't like life in the rest of Puritan New England.

"No person in this country shall be molested or questioned for the matters of his conscience to God, so he be loyal and keep the civil peace," Williams said. "Forced worship stinks in God's nostrils."

Collecting Catholics in Maryland

While the Puritans may have had some religious differences among themselves, they did agree on one thing: They didn't like Roman Catholics. Undaunted, Catholics established a colony north of Virginia in 1634. Called Maryland, it was the result of a grant given by King James I to his former secretary, George Calvert, who had converted to Catholicism.

The colony prospered as a tobacco exporter. But so many Protestants were allowed in that its Catholic founders were threatened with the prospect of being persecuted in their own colony. So they struck a compromise in 1649, which recognized all Christian religions — and decreed the death penalty for Jews and atheists.

Promoting tolerance in Pennsylvania

If Puritans didn't like Catholics, they really didn't like Quakers. Quakers (who referred to themselves as "Friends") were steadfast pacifists who had no paid clergy, refused to use titles or take oaths of allegiance, and were said to "quake" from deep religious emotion.

In 1681, a wealthy Quaker named William Penn got a charter to start a colony in America. He advertised it exhaustively, attracted a diverse group of settlers, and founded Pennsylvania. Penn treated the Native Americans fairly, set up a relatively liberal system of laws, and made it easy for most people to settle in his colony. By 1700, Pennsylvania's leading city, Philadelphia, was, after Boston, the colonies' leading cultural center.

Penn died in poverty and in social and political disrepute. But more than any other colony, Pennsylvania was truly tolerant of differing religions, cultures, and national backgrounds.

Dealings of the Dutch

While the English, French, and Spanish were noisily tromping all over the New World, the Dutch were establishing themselves as the most successful maritime traders in the Old World. Intent on getting their share of the American trade, they formed the Dutch West India Company and in 1626 established a colony in the New World at the mouth of the Hudson River, calling it New Amsterdam. Three other settlements added up to a colony the Dutch called New Netherland.

FAIR TRADE?

The chief purpose of the New Amsterdam colony was trade, and in one of the first such transactions, Dutch leader Peter Minuit gave the local Indians a couple of boxes containing stuff like hatchets and cooking pots and in return took title to the island of Manhattan, which the Indians didn't claim to own in the first place.

The goods have since been estimated to have been worth 60 Dutch guilders, the equivalent of 2,400 English pennies — hence, the idea that Manhattan was sold for $24.

New Amsterdam was different from the New England settlements in that it wasn't founded for religious reasons. So its attitude was more relaxed when it came to activities like drinking and gambling. In addition, land for the colonists wasn't an issue because New Amsterdam was basically a company town, run for the benefit of the Dutch West India stockholders.

After awhile, this began to chafe on the settlers. So in 1664, when English ships and troops showed up to attack the settlement, it surrendered without firing a shot. New Amsterdam became New York, named after its new owner, James, the Duke of York. The duke gave some of his new colony to a couple of friends, who thus began the colony of New Jersey. Despite its new English ownership, New York kept much of its Dutch flavor for decades.

Coping with Native American Troubles

When it came to the Native Americans, English colonists had varying opinions. Some thought they should be treated as pets, others as pests. Some thought the Native Americans should be treated with respect. Others thought they should be exterminated, and still others thought they should be tricked out of their lands and then exterminated.

In the Southern colonies, trouble between the two groups started almost as soon as the English got off the ships. In 1642, Native Americans under Chief Opechen-canough attacked settlers over a large area of the Virginia colony and killed about 350 of them. The settlers counterattacked a few months later and killed hundreds of Native Americans. In New Netherland, the Dutch settlers murdered nearly 100 Native Americans in their sleep, cut off their heads, and kicked them around the streets of New Amsterdam. That launched a nasty war that ended when 150 Dutch soldiers killed about 700 Native Americans at a battle near present-day Stamford, Connecticut.

In New England, thanks in part to the good initial relations between the Pilgrims and local tribes, war was averted until 1634, when a rowdy pirate named John Stone and seven of his crew were murdered by Native Americans the settlers decided were from a tribe called the Pequot. After an uneasy two-year truce, Puritan soldiers and their Native American allies attacked a Pequot fort near Mystic River, Connecticut. In about an hour, they burned the village and slaughtered 600 men, women, and children. In September 1638, the Pequots surrendered. As many as 2,000 of them were sold as slaves in the West Indies or given to rival tribes. The Pequots were all but exterminated, and the Native American wars in New England were over for nearly 40 years.

But in 1675, a Native American chief named Metacom (called King Philip by the settlers because he liked English customs), decided to push the white invaders out once and for all. The result was King Philip's War.

This time, the Native Americans used guns and attacked everywhere. By the time the two-year war was over, half the settlements in New England had been destroyed, and the English were on the edge of being driven into the sea. Finally, however, the colonies united while the Native Americans did not, and the tide began to turn. King Philip was killed in August 1676, and the war finally ended. It would be 40 years before the area recovered enough to begin expanding its boundaries into the frontier again.

Chapter 4

You Say You Want a Revolution: 1700–1775

B y the beginning of the 18th century, European powers had been alternately exploring the New World and sparring over what they found. It was time for the main event: a showdown for control of the American continent. Actually, it was time for a series of main events. As this chapter unfolds, Europe engages in a succession of wars in which America is not only a pawn but also a battleground. Britain comes out on top, but her relationship with the American colonies is dramatically changed.

Britain views the colonies mainly as economic enterprises, whereas the colonists have a growing dislike for being told what to do by a distant government. The differing perspectives clash until, as the chapter ends, Britain gets popped in the snoot.

Looking at America in 1700

The English colonies in America had filled in the gaps between the first two settlements in Virginia and Massachusetts by 1700 and, in fact, had gone beyond them. They now stretched from Maine to South Carolina. But they were a pretty skinny bunch, as colonies go. Few settlers lived more than 75 miles from the Atlantic coast, and vast stretches of land lay unsettled by any nation, although claimed by more than one.

The population had reached 275,000 to 300,000, including 25,000 African slaves. Most people — as many as 90 percent — lived in small communities or farms. The population of New York City was about 5,000; Charles Towne (now Charleston) about 2,000.

Many of the newcomers weren't English but people from other Western European regions, such as Ireland, France, Scotland, and Germany, as well as the Scandinavian countries.

The colonies were maturing as they grew. Boston and Philadelphia were major publishing centers. Small manufacturing firms were turning out goods such as furniture and iron products that lessened the colonies' dependence on goods from England. And increasing secularism was loosening the hold of religious authority on everyday life. In fact, things were going along okay, except for all that fighting in Europe.

Colonizing New France

While New England was filling up with Puritans and the Southern colonies with tobacco growers, the area of North America dominated by the French was progressing more slowly.

By 1663, when what is present-day Canada officially became a French crown colony, Quebec had only about 550 people, and the entire region had fewer than 80,000 Europeans by 1750. French officials did take steps to increase the population. Bachelors were censured, and fathers of unwed 16-year-old girls were fined. But the population remained low, especially compared to the English colonies.

One reason for the lack of settlers was that the colony was strictly Catholic, and Protestants from France were banned. Many French Protestants thus settled in the English colonies. Another reason was a looney-tunes system carried over from the Middle Ages that awarded vast tracts of the best land to just a few people. A third reason was the emphasis on fur trading — conducted by men called *courers de bois* (runners of the woods) — instead of on agriculture, for which people had to settle down.

Although few in number, the French were daring explorers, roaming as far south as present-day New Orleans and as far west as the Rocky Mountains. But the lack of permanent settlements by the French in the vast areas they explored, coupled with their small numbers, spelled trouble for their efforts to hold on to what they had when the wars in Europe spilled over to America.

Fighting the First True World Wars

Eighteenth-century royalty didn't need much of an excuse to start a war — they fought over everything from who should be the next king of Spain to the lopping off of a sea captain's ear. Their willingness to fight was based partly on greed for more territory and the wealth it could bring and partly on their fear that other countries would beat them to it and become more powerful.

REMEMBER

What made these wars different from their predecessors was that they were global in scope, fought all over Europe, India, North and South America, and the Caribbean. The main combatants were the French and English, although the Spanish, Dutch, and Austrians did their share of fighting.

France and England were pretty even matches. England had a better navy, but France had a better army. In North America, England's colonies had a much larger population: 1.5 million compared to the French colonies' 80,000 in 1750. England's colonies had a much more varied economy, the protection of the English navy, and the support of the Iroquois Confederacy, a six-tribe alliance of Native Americans who hated the French. The French colonists, on the other hand, had better military leaders, did less quarreling among themselves than the English colonists, and had Native American allies of their own.

So, here's what happened in the first three true world wars.

King William's War

King William's War was the warm-up bout. After a revolution by Protestants in England, James II, a Catholic, was tossed out. Protestant William III and his wife Mary were brought in from the Netherlands and put on the throne in 1689. This didn't sit well with the French king, Louis XIV, a Catholic. After William III sided with other countries against France in a territorial dispute, a war was on in Europe that lasted until 1697.

In America, the war went back and forth. The French led Native American raiding parties into New York and practiced a kind of warfare that was to become known as *guerilla fighting*: ambushes and hit-and-run attacks. The English outlasted the attacks but botched attempts to conquer Quebec and Montreal. The war pretty much ended in a draw.

Queen Anne's War

After King William's War ended, Europe took all of four years to catch its breath. Then in 1701, Louis XIV of France tried to put his grandson on the throne of Spain. Queen Anne, who had succeeded William in England, objected, and they were back at it again.

This time the English colonists found themselves fighting the Spanish in the South and the French in the North. As with the previous war, there were few big battles and lots of raids and counter-raids, with both sides employing Native American allies.

When the war finally ended in 1713, Louis XIV got to put his grandson on the Spanish throne, but England got Nova Scotia, Newfoundland, and the Hudson River Valley, which put it in good position to take over even more of Canada in future wars.

King George's War

Most wars have more than one cause, but historians with a whimsical side like to start the story of King George's War with an English smuggler named Robert Jenkins. Spanish revenue agents caught Jenkins in 1731, and in the course of being interrogated, he involuntarily had one of his ears removed. "Take this back to the king, your master," a Spanish official was said to have said, "whom, if he were present, I would serve in the same fashion."

THE RIGHT TO COMPARE GOVERNORS TO MONKEYS

John Peter Zenger was a German-born printer who, in 1734, was also the editor of a New York newspaper called the *Weekly Journal*. After articles appeared attacking the policies of Governor William Cosby and comparing Cosby and his supporters to monkeys and dogs, Zenger was charged with seditious libel and jailed.

At his trial, Zenger's attorney, a Philadelphia lawyer named Andrew Hamilton, argued the articles were basically true, and truth was a valid defense against libel. The judge, a friend of Cosby, told the jury to ignore Hamilton's argument. Instead, the jury ignored the judge and set Zenger free.

Although the case didn't immediately win the press the freedom it would enjoy later, it did help establish the foundation that prevents U.S. government officials from stifling printed material. It also reaffirmed the old English tradition of juries ignoring judges when impressed by an eloquent lawyer.

Jenkins did take his ear back to England, but he took his time about it and didn't actually tell his tale to Parliament until 1738. It didn't matter much, and a new war was on anyway. It eventually merged with a larger war that broke out in Europe. In America, the same kind of fighting that had taken place in the earlier wars was taking place again. The British colonists took a key port called Louisbourg, which commanded the Gulf of St. Lawrence, but they had to give it back as part of the 1748 treaty that settled the war.

Awakening to Greater Religious Freedom

Despite the nagging presence of almost-continual war, the American colonies were doing pretty well. And as the colonists did better economically, they began to loosen up in terms of their religious beliefs, too. "Pennsylvania," said a German observer, by way of example, "is heaven for farmers, paradise for artisans, and hell for officials and preachers."

It wasn't so much that Americans were becoming less devout, but more a function of their becoming less rigid and more likely to question the practice of most clergy to dictate exactly what they were to think and believe.

In the 1730s, a reaction to this shifting of religious attitudes resulted in what came to be known as the *Great Awakening.* Its catalyst was a genius named Jonathan Edwards. Tall and delicately built, Edwards entered Yale at the age of 13. By the time he was 21, he was the school's head tutor. He was a brilliant theologian and wrote papers on insects that are still respected in entomological circles.

Edwards was also — excuse the expression — a hell of a public speaker. "The God that holds you over the pit of hell, much as one holds a spider or some loathsome insect over the fire, abhors you and is dreadfully provoked," he thundered in a sermon called "Sinners in the Hands of an Angry God."

But Edwards's message, preached to mass audiences throughout New England in the 1730s and 1740s, was not just fire-and-brimstone yelling. Edwards believed that God was to be loved and not just feared and that internal goodness was the best way to be happy on this earth.

Edwards was eventually surpassed on the revival circuit by a Georgia-based minister named George Whitefield. Called the *Great Itinerant* because of his constant traveling, Whitefield drew crowds in the thousands. On one crusade, he traveled 800 miles in 75 days and gave 175 sermons. Equipped with an amazing voice and a flair for the melodramatic, Whitefield quite literally made members of his crowds wild. He made seven continental tours from 1740 to 1770, and it's safe to say he was America's first superstar.

REMEMBER

Although the Great Awakening had run its course by the time of the American Revolution, its impact was deep and lasting. It sparked widespread discussions about religion that in turn led to the development of new denominations, which in turn helped lead to more religious tolerance among the colonists. Several of the new or revitalized denominations were encouraged to start colleges, including Brown, Princeton, Dartmouth, and Columbia, to ensure a steady stream of trained ministers.

The Great Awakening also helped break down barriers among the colonies and unify them through their common experience with it. And as the first spontaneous mass movement in America, it heightened the individual's sense of power when it was combined with that of others — and emboldened them to question the status quo.

The French and Indian War

Despite being filled with the divine spirit of the Great Awakening — or maybe because of it — American colonists were ready by 1750 to once more fight the French and Native Americans. The first to do so were led by a tall, 22-year-old Virginia militia captain named George Washington.

This time the world war, called the *Seven Years' War* in Europe and dubbed the *French and Indian War* in the New World, started in America. English speculators had secured the rights to 500,000 acres in the Ohio River valley. At about the same time, the French had built a series of forts in the same area as a way to keep lines of communication and supply open between Canada and Louisiana.

In 1754, a year after he had conducted a diplomat/spy mission, Washington was sent to the Ohio Country with 150 men. They ran into a French detachment, the Virginians fired, and the French fled. "I heard the bullets whistle," Washington wrote later, "and, believe me, there is something charming in the sound."

The French set out to "charm" Washington by counterattacking a fort the young Virginian had hastily put up (and aptly named *Fort Necessity*) and by forcing Washington to surrender — on July 4. Then, in a stroke of luck for a nation yet unborn, the French let Washington lead his men home.

Unifying the colonies

While Washington was savoring his first taste of battle, representatives of 8 of the 13 colonies were meeting in Albany, New York, at the request of the British government. The purpose was to see whether the colonies could be more unified.

The British wanted more unity because they figured it would make it easier to fight the French and also to govern the colonies.

But a few far-seeing colonists — most notably a Philadelphia printer, inventor, scientist, and man-about-town named Benjamin Franklin — saw the meeting as an opportunity to increase the colonies' economic and political clout.

Franklin engineered a sound plan for a colonial union, and the gathered representatives approved it. But the assemblies in the individual colonies rejected it, mostly because they felt they would give up too much of their independence.

Defeating British General Braddock

On the battlefield, meanwhile, the British had sent two of their worst regiments to the colonies and given command to a general named Edward Braddock. Though undeniably brave (he had five horses shot from under him in one battle), Braddock was arrogant and a plodding bozo when it came to military strategy. He was also contemptuous of the American militia under his command.

In 1755, Braddock and a force of about 1,400 men, including Washington, marched on French forts in the Ohio Country. A force of French and Native Americans surprised the British force. Braddock was killed, along with almost a thousand of his men.

Braddock's defeat was just one of a bunch of losses the British suffered over the next two years. The war in America merged with a war in Europe that involved all the major European powers. It went badly for the British in both theaters.

Outfighting the French

In 1757, however, things began looking up. An able administrator named William Pitt became head of the London government. Pitt skillfully used the superior British navy and appointed good military leaders.

REMEMBER

Among them were James Wolfe and Jeffrey Amherst. Wolfe and Amherst led a British force against the French fortress-city of Quebec in 1759. In one of the most important battles fought in North America, the British took the city. Montreal fell in the following year, and the French were finished in the New World.

The war was formally settled by the Treaty of Paris in 1763. The British got all of Canada, all of America east of the Mississippi, Florida, and some Caribbean islands.

The American colonists got rid of the decades-old threat from the French. More than in previous wars, men from different colonies fought alongside one another, lowering barriers among the colonies. Future leaders matured. And the animosity and friction that sprang up between British military leaders and the Americans lingered long after the war was over.

To see what land holdings that Britain, France, and Spain maintained in the mid–18th century, take a look at Figure 4-1.

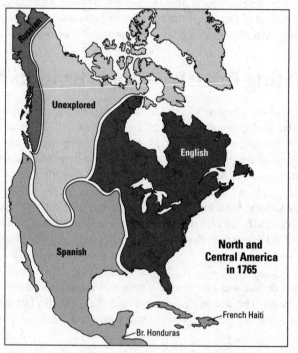

FIGURE 4-1:
Map of North and Central America during the mid-18th century showing what belonged to Britain, France, and Spain.

© John Wiley & Sons, Inc.

Growing like a Weed

If there was one inarguable fact about the American colonies in the mid- to late 18th century, it was that they were growing like crazy. In 1730, the population of the 13 colonies was about 655,000. Boston was the biggest city, with a population of about 13,000, while New York and Philadelphia were home to about 8,500 people each.

By 1760, the population had reached 1.6 million, not including African slaves, and by 1775, the nonslave population stood at 2.5 million. Philadelphia was now the largest city, with a population of about 34,000.

Accounting for the population explosion

The population explosion was caused by two things. One was the natural birthrate of the colonists. Partly because of the time-honored farm family tradition that large families meant more people to work (and maybe because there wasn't much else to do on those long winter nights in the country), the size of many American families was astounding. Benjamin Franklin wrote of a Philadelphia woman who had 14 children, 82 grandchildren, and 110 great-grandchildren by the time she died at the age of 100. The growth rate was even more astounding when you consider the high infant mortality rate. One woman was reported to have lost 20 children at birth or soon thereafter.

But the growth was by no means all from within the colonies. Immigration continued at a brisk pace, not only from England but also from other Western European countries. A 1909 population study estimated that at the time of the American Revolution, about 82 percent of the white population was from England and Wales; 5 percent from Scotland; 6 percent from the German states; and about 7 percent from Holland, Ireland, and other countries.

REMEMBER

Despite a postwar recession after the fighting with the French stopped in 1763, the colonies were on a fairly sound economic foundation. About 90 percent of the colonists were involved in agriculture, with tobacco, corn, rice, indigo, and wheat being the main crops. Fishing and whaling were big in New England. Timber was the top manufacturing product, and because trees were plentiful and cheap, shipbuilding boomed. By the time of the American Revolution, one-third of the British navy had been built in America.

THE INVOLUNTARY ARRIVALS

One of the fastest-growing segments of the 18th-century American population didn't grow voluntarily. In 1725, an estimated 75,000 African slaves resided in the colonies. By 1790, the number was 700,000. The 1790 census reported that all but three states had slaves: Maine, Massachusetts, and Vermont. Forty-three percent of the people living in South Carolina belonged to other people; in Virginia, 39 percent were slaves.

More than a few colonists raised their voices in alarm at the increasing number of slaves. Some protested for humanitarian reasons. Benjamin Franklin argued the slave system didn't make sense from an economic perspective. Even the most ardent pro-slavery apostles had their doubts. Some were afraid of slave uprisings if the numbers continued to grow, while others wanted to stop the importation of slaves so the value of the ones already in America would increase. But the British government refused to allow bans on slave importation by the colonies for fear of damaging the lucrative trade. This refusal became a sore spot between Britain and America.

Living the good life

Although the colonists shared problems common to people all over the world in the 18th century, such as nasty epidemics, they generally ate better, lived longer, and were more prosperous than any of their European counterparts. Land was cheap and had to sustain fewer people because the population was smaller. Because labor was often in short supply, wages were higher, which raised the standard of living.

While enjoying the protections of the formidable British Empire's military, the average American colonist, if he paid any taxes at all, paid far less than his British cousin. The argument against British taxes, put forth by the eloquent Boston lawyer James Otis, that "taxation without representation is tyranny," was a bit hypocritical. After all, more than a few Americans had to pay taxes to American local governments and still couldn't vote or didn't have a representative in the colonial assemblies.

Moreover, for the most part, Britain didn't interfere in the colonies' internal affairs. Mostly, the mother country concerned itself with defense and trade issues, and many of the trade laws were mutually beneficial to both sides of the water (unless you happened to be a big-time smuggler like John Hancock, who later became the first to sign the Declaration of Independence and was Public Enemy Number One as far as the British were concerned).

So, most Americans in the 1760s and early 1770s had no interest in independence from Britain. What they wanted was what they had: protection by the world's mightiest navy, generally cozy trade rules, and freedoms and rights unequalled in the rest of the world.

Britain, however, couldn't, or thought it couldn't, afford to maintain the status quo.

Heading Toward Divorce with Britain

After more than 60 years of almost continuous war, the British national debt had soared. Because a lot of the debt had come about by defending Americans from the French and Native Americans in America, the British government concluded that it was only fair that the Americans pay for part of it.

In addition, the British and the Americans fundamentally disagreed on what role Parliament, the British governing body, should play in the colonists' lives. For Britain, it was simple: Parliament made the rules for Britain and all its colonies. For America, however, the role of Parliament was negligible. The colonists wanted to come up with their own rules in their own mini parliaments and deal directly with the king. In the end, it came down to a fight over who should tell whom what to do.

Starting in 1763, Britain and her American colonies began to irritate each other almost incessantly. Like an impatient parent with a headstrong child, Britain tried different methods to instill discipline. Only America wasn't such a kid anymore, or as Ben Franklin put it in verse: "We have an old mother that peevish is grown / She snubs us like children that scarce walk alone / She forgets we're grown up and have sense of our own."

And as happens in family quarrels, incidents and issues that by themselves could be smoothed over began to pile up. In this case, the irritants helped lead to a revolution.

The Proclamation of 1763

One of the first things Britain wanted to do after finally whipping the French was to calm down the Native Americans, who were understandably upset by the generally pushy, and often genocidal, actions of the colonists. So King George III decided that as of October 7, 1763, no colonist could settle beyond the crest of the Appalachian Mountains. That decision meant America would remain basically a collection of coastal colonies.

The idea was to give everyone a sort of timeout after all the fighting. But even if it was well intentioned, it was impractical. For one thing, a bunch of colonials were already living west of the dividing line and weren't about to move just because some potentate thousands of miles away said so.

Worse, the decree was a slap in the face to those who had fought against the French and Native Americans with the expectation that winning meant they could move west to vast tracts of free land. In the end, it was an unenforceable law that did nothing but anger the colonists and vex British officials when it wasn't obeyed.

The Revenue Acts (1764)

On the other side of the sea, more than a few Brits were peeved that their colonial cousins paid relatively little in taxes, especially because the British were among the highest taxed people in the world. So British Prime Minister George Grenville pushed a bill through Parliament that was explicitly designed to raise money from the colonists to pay for their defense.

The law actually lowered the tax on molasses but raised or imposed taxes on other things like sugar, wine, linen, and silk. Colonists objected, asserting that Parliament had no right to impose taxes on them without their assent. They also organized boycotts of the taxed goods and increased their already booming smuggling enterprises.

The Stamp Act (1765)

Unsatisfied with the revenue from the Revenue Acts, Parliament imposed a new levy on 50 items, including dice, playing cards, newspapers, marriage licenses, college degrees, and just about every other kind of legal document. Some of the taxes doubled the cost of the item. Not only that, the items had to be stamped or have a stamped receipt on them, showing the tax had been paid.

British citizens had been paying similar taxes for years, at even higher rates. But American colonists saw the Stamp Act taxes as only the beginning. Paying anything, they argued, was an invitation to be milked dry later.

In reaction to the tax, nine colonies sent 27 delegates to a meeting in New York City. The group drew up a petition and sent it to England, where it was ignored. But the colonies also began a boycott of British goods, which was not ignored. Groups calling themselves the *Sons of Liberty* encouraged and bullied their fellow colleagues to wear "homespun" clothing instead of British wool. They also tarred and feathered more than a few would-be tax collectors.

SAMUEL ADAMS

He was a flop at business and a crummy public speaker — and perhaps America's first truly great politician. More than any of his contemporaries, Samuel Adams kept the colonies on the road to independence. Born to a prosperous family, Adams graduated from Harvard. After failing at a business of his own, he took over a bustling family brewery and managed to run it into the ground. Then he became a tax collector and narrowly avoided jail for mismanaging funds.

But Adams was a success at backroom maneuvering. He helped organize the Sons of Liberty, the Boston Tea Party, and the minutemen. He wrote tirelessly for colonial newspapers on the urge to stand up to Britain, and his letters urging action were circulated throughout America. When the movement seemed to be sputtering, Adams kept it alive almost single-handedly with his writing and organizing.

He attended both Continental Congresses as a delegate and was a signer of the Declaration of Independence. But once independence was won, there was no need for a rabble-rouser. Although elected governor of Massachusetts for one four-year term in 1794, Adams had dropped from national prominence by the time of his death in 1803, at the age of 81.

The boycott had its desired effect. In 1766, under pressure from British manufacturers, Parliament repealed the taxes. But it also tried to save face by declaring that henceforth it had the right to pass any laws it wanted to govern the colonies. Americans rejoiced at the tax repeal. They praised "Good King George." In New York, they even erected a statue of him in his honor. And they blithely ignored the warning from Parliament.

The Townshend Act (1767)

British Prime Minister William Pitt was a capable leader. But when he had a mental breakdown in 1766, he handed over the government to one of his lieutenants, Charles Townshend, also known as *Champagne Charley* because he was quite eloquent when drunk. A cocky sort, Townshend vowed to squeeze some money out of the obstinate American colonies, and he got Parliament to impose taxes on a number of goods, including glass, paper, paint, and tea. The revenues were to be used to pay the salaries of royal judges and governors in the colonies. To be fair, Townshend also dropped import duties on some American products entering England, thus making their export more profitable for the colonies.

It was too small a gesture as far as many colonists were concerned. For one thing, many of them had grown extremely fond of tea and were not keen on paying any tax on it. For another, they didn't like the idea of the money going to pay judges and governors. Up until that point, the officials' salaries had been controlled by colonial legislatures, which gave them a fair amount of influence over their policies.

Eager to show he meant business, Townshend sent two regiments of red-coated British troops — sneeringly dubbed *lobsterbacks* by the locals — to Boston in 1768. That set up the next confrontation.

The Boston Massacre (1770)

Because the soldiers sent to Boston were poorly paid, some of them tried to find part-time work, a practice that didn't sit well with many Bostonians. So it wasn't unusual for fights to break out between soldiers and groups of colonists.

On the night of March 5, a small mob of lowlifes began throwing rocks and snowballs at a British sentry outside the customs house. Another 20 British soldiers appeared with fixed bayonets, the crowd grew to as many as 300 boys and men, and after about 30 minutes of being taunted and pelted with rocks and sticks, one of the soldiers opened fire. A few minutes later, 11 members of the mob were dead or wounded.

At a subsequent trial, the soldiers were ably defended by a Boston lawyer named John Adams, and all but two were acquitted. The two soldiers found guilty were branded on the hand and then let go. But the radicals among the colonists milked the incident for all it was worth. A highly exaggerated engraving of the "massacre" was made by a silversmith named Paul Revere, and copies of it circulated all over the colonies.

Ironically, on the day of the incident, the Townshend Acts were repealed by Parliament — except for the tax on tea.

The Boston Tea Party (1773)

Despite the widespread publicity surrounding the tragedy in Boston, cooler heads prevailed for the next year or two. Moderates on both sides of the Atlantic argued that compromises could still be reached.

Then the powerful but poorly run British East India Company found it had 17 million pounds of surplus tea on its hands. So the British government gave the company a monopoly on the American tea business. With a monopoly, the company could lower its prices enough to undercut the smuggled tea the colonists drank instead of paying the British tax. But even with lower prices, the colonists still didn't like the arrangement. It was the principle of the tax itself, not the cost of the tea, that bothered them. Shipments of English tea were destroyed or prevented from being unloaded or sold.

On December 16, 1773, colonists poorly disguised as Native Americans boarded three ships in Boston Harbor, smashed in 342 chests of tea, and dumped the whole mess into the harbor, where, according to one eyewitness, "it piled up in the low tide like haystacks." No one was seriously hurt, although one colonist was reportedly roughed up a bit for trying to stuff some of the tea in his coat instead of throwing it overboard.

King George III wasn't amused. "The die is now cast," he wrote to his latest prime minister, Lord North, who had succeeded Townshend upon his sudden death. "The colonies must either submit or triumph."

The "Intolerable" Acts (1774)

In response to the tea party, Parliament passed a series of laws designed to teach the upstarts a thing or two. They were called the *Repressive Acts* in England, but to Americans, they were *Intolerable*. The new laws closed Boston Harbor until the colonists paid back the damage they had wrought, thus cutting the city off from sources of food, medical supplies, and other goods. The laws also installed a

British general as governor of Massachusetts and repealed such liberties as the right to hold town meetings.

At the same time, the Brits passed the Quebec Act, a law that gave more freedom to conquered French subjects in Canada, including the right to continue customs such as nonjury trials in civil cases.

Though a sensible thing to do from a British perspective, the Quebec Act incensed Americans, especially at a time when they felt their own freedoms were being messed with. The act also pushed the borders of the Quebec province well into the Ohio River valley, which infuriated colonials who had fought several wars to keep the French out of that same valley.

The acts galvanized the colonies into a show of unity that had only occasionally been shown before. Food and supplies poured in by land to Boston from all over America. And in Virginia, the colonial legislature decided to try to get representatives from all the colonies together for a meeting.

Congressing for the First Time

On September 5, 1774, leaders from all the colonies but Georgia gathered in Philadelphia to talk things over. There were 56 delegates, all of them men and about half of them lawyers. Some, such as New York's John Jay, were politically conservative. Others, such as Virginia's Patrick Henry, were fire-breathing radicals. Despite their differences, the delegates to what is called the *First Continental Congress* did reach agreement on a number of issues, even though they had no real powers.

Several delegates wrote essays that suggested the colonies stay under the supervision of the king but have nothing to do with Parliament. They petitioned Parliament to rescind the offending laws. The group also proclaimed that colonists should have all the rights other British subjects had, such as electing representatives to make the laws they were governed by, and that all trade with Britain should cease until the "Intolerable" Acts were repealed.

The Congress also resolved that if one of the colonies was attacked, all the rest would defend it. And, probably much to the dismay of some members, the Congress resolved to abstain from tea and wine (but not rum) and to swear off recreational pursuits like horse racing and cock fighting until the troubles with England were resolved.

The meeting served to draw the colonies closer together than ever before. "The distinctions between New Englanders and Virginians are no more," declared Patrick Henry. "I am not a Virginian, but an American."

The Congress adjourned on October 26, pledging to come back in May if things didn't get better by then. Things didn't.

Mr. Revere, Your Horse Is Ready

The Congress's decision to boycott all trade with Britain was embraced with enthusiasm almost everywhere. Lists of suspected traitors who continued to trade were published, and tar and feathers were vigorously applied to those who ignored the boycott.

While businessmen in England fretted, the colonists' actions were met with disdain by a majority of the members of Parliament. Lord North, the prime minister, resolved to isolate the troublemakers in Massachusetts and thus stifle dissent in other areas.

But some British knew better. Gen. Thomas Gage, the British commander in chief in America, reported that things were coming to a head. "If you think ten thousand men are enough," he wrote to North, "send twenty; if a million [pounds] is thought to be enough, give two. You will save both blood and treasure in the end."

In April 1775, Gage decided to make a surprise march from his headquarters in Boston to nearby Concord, where he hoped to seize a storehouse of rebel guns and ammunition and maybe arrest some of the rebels' leaders.

But the colonists knew he was coming, thanks to a network of spies and militia called the *minutemen*, aptly named because they were supposed to be ready to quickly spring into action. One of these was Paul Revere, the son of a French immigrant.

In addition to being a master silversmith, Revere made false teeth and surgical tools, and he was pretty good on a horse, too. So when word came on the night of April 18 that the British were marching on Concord, Revere and two other men, William Dawes and Doctor Samuel Prescott, rode out to warn that the British were coming. After rousing the town of Lexington, Revere and Dawes were captured and briefly detained. But Prescott escaped and made it to Concord. (Revere became the most famous of the three, however, because a poet named Henry Wadsworth Longfellow made him the star of a wildly popular poem in 1863.)

REMEMBER

When the 700 British soldiers marched through Lexington on the morning of April 19 on their way to Concord, they encountered 77 colonials. "Don't fire unless fired upon," said the minutemen's leader, John Parker. "But if they mean to have a war, let it begin here."

Shots were fired, and eight of the minutemen were killed. By the time the British reached Concord, however, resistance had been better organized. At a bridge near one of the entrances to the town, British soldiers were attacked, and the fighting began in earnest.

Now facing hundreds of colonists who prudently stood behind trees and in houses and fired at the redcoats, the British soldiers beat a disorganized retreat to Boston. More than 250 British were dead, missing, or wounded, compared to about 90 Americans killed or wounded.

The war of words was over. The war of blood and death had begun.

Chapter 5

Yankee Doodlin': 1775–1783

After blood was spilled at Lexington and Concord, war between Britain and her American colonies was inevitable, even though there were some efforts on both sides to avoid it. British leaders weren't too worried about quelling the disturbance. One British general suggested it wasn't anything that "a capable sheepherder" couldn't handle.

But there's an old saying that it's good to be good, better to be lucky, and best to be both. In this chapter, the American colonists are good when they need to be — and really lucky much of the rest of the time — and win their independence from Britain. They also lay out their reasons for doing so in a remarkable declaration.

In This Corner, the Brits . . .

The first thing the British had going for them when it came to fighting the Americans was a whole bunch of fighters. The British army consisted of about 50,000 men. They "rented" another 30,000 mercenary German soldiers. In addition, they had the best navy in the world. And the people the Brits were fighting, the colonists, had no regular army, no navy at all, and few real resources to assemble them.

But, as America itself was to find out about two centuries later in Vietnam, having the best army and navy doesn't always mean that much. For one thing, the British people were by no means united in a desire to rein in the colonies. When war broke out, several leading British military leaders refused to take part. Some British leaders also recognized the difficulty of winning a war by fighting on the enemy's turf thousands of miles from Britain, especially when the enemy was fighting for a cause.

"You may spread fire, sword, and desolation, but that will not be government," warned the Duke of Richmond. "No people can ever be made to submit to a form of government they say they will not receive."

Three factors contributed to Britain's ultimate downfall:

>> **The British political leaders who did support the war were generally inept.** Lord North, the prime minister, was a decent bureaucrat but no leader, and he basically did what King George III wanted. And some of the British generals were nincompoops. One of them, leaving for duty in early 1777, boastfully bet a fair sum of money that he would be back in England "victorious from America by Christmas Day, 1777." By Christmas Day, he had surrendered his entire army.

>> **Britain couldn't commit all its military resources to putting down the rebellion.** Because of unrest in Ireland and the potential for trouble with the French, who were still smarting from their defeats by the British in the New World, Britain had to keep many of its forces in Europe.

>> **Because the Brits didn't take their opponents seriously, they had no real plan for winning the war.** That meant they fooled around long enough to give the Americans hope. And that gave the French a reason to believe the colonials just might win, so they provided the Americans with what proved to be indispensable arms, money, ships, and troops.

In This Corner, the Yanks . . .

When you look at the problems the British had and then look at the dilemmas the Americans faced, it's no wonder the war took eight years.

In the early years at least, probably as few as a third of Americans supported the revolution. About 20 percent, called loyalists or Tories after the ruling political party in Britain, were loyal to the crown, and the rest didn't care much one way or another.

Because they weren't professional soldiers, many of those who fought in the American army had peculiar notions of soldiering. They often elected their officers, and when the officers gave orders they didn't like, they just elected new ones. The soldiers signed up for a year or two, and when their time was up, they simply went home, no matter how the war — or even the battle — was going. At one point, the colonial army under George Washington was down to 3,000 soldiers. They also weren't big on sticking around when faced with a British bayonet charge. Many, if not most, battles ended with the Americans running away, so often that Washington once observed in exasperation that "they run from their own shadows."

Regional jealousies surfaced when soldiers from one colony were given orders by officers from another, and at least one mutiny had to be put down by other American units. The American soldiers were ill-fed, ill-housed, and so poorly clothed that in some battles, colonial soldiers fought nearly naked. About 10,000 soldiers spent a bitter winter at Valley Forge, Pennsylvania, literally barefoot in the snow, and about 2,800 of them died. "The long and great sufferings of this army are unexampled in history," wrote Washington.

They were also paid in currency called *continentals,* which became so worthless the phrase "not worth a continental" became a common American saying for decades after the Revolution. Because the money was so worthless, unpatriotic American merchants often sold their goods to the British army instead, even when American troops wore rags and starved. Others cornered the markets on goods such as food and clothing, stockpiling them until the prices rose higher and higher. As a result, desperate army leaders were forced to confiscate goods from private citizens to survive.

About the best thing the Americans had going for them was a cause, because men who are fighting for something often fight better. Indeed, as the war wore on, the American soldier became more competent. By the end of 1777, a British officer wrote home that "though it was once the tone of this [British] army to treat them in a most contemptible light, they are now become a formidable enemy."

The fact that there were 13 colonies was also an advantage because it meant there was no single nerve center for which the British could aim. They conquered New York, they took Philadelphia, and still the colonies fought on. America also had rapid growth in its favor. "Britain, at the expense of 3 million [pounds] has killed 150 Yankees in this campaign, which is 20,000 pounds a head," observed Ben Franklin early during the fighting. "During the same time, 60,000 children have been born in America."

But maybe most important, the Americans were lucky enough to choose an extraordinary leader and smart enough to stick with him.

Mr. Washington Goes to War

George Washington has become so mythic a figure that some people think his importance has been blown out of proportion. That's too bad because Washington was truly one of the most remarkable people in American history.

At the time of the revolution, Washington was 43 years old. He was one of the wealthiest men in the colonies, having inherited land and money and married into more. Although he was a soldier in the wars against the French and Native Americans, Washington had never commanded more than 1,200 men at any one time. Other colonials had more military command experience.

But the Second Continental Congress, which had convened in May 1775 and taken over the running of the Revolution (even though no one had actually asked it to), decided on Washington as the Continental army's commander in chief. Their choice was based more on political reasons than military ones. New England leaders figured that putting a Virginian in charge would increase the enthusiasm of the Southern colonies to fight; the Southern leaders agreed. And it didn't hurt that being quite wealthy, Washington could dig into his own wallet when it got tough to finance the fighting.

For his part, Washington wasn't so sure he was up to the task. "I declare with the utmost sincerity, I do not think myself equal to the command I am honored with," he told Congress and then refused to take any salary for the job.

Finding faults in George

Washington had his flaws. He wasn't a military genius, and he lost a lot more than he won on the battlefield. In fact, his greatest military gifts were in organizing retreats and avoiding devastating losses. He had no discernible sense of humor and was a snob when it came to mixing with what he considered the lower classes.

He also had a terrible temper. Disgusted with the lack of discipline and acts of cowardice in the American army, he unsuccessfully asked Congress to increase the allowable number of lashes for punishing soldiers from 39 to 500. Once he was so angry at a subordinate, he broke his personal rule against swearing. "He swore that day till the leaves shook on the trees," recalled an admiring onlooker. "Charming! Delightful! . . . sir, on that memorable day, he swore like an angel from heaven."

Commanding a country

In spite of his flaws, Washington was a born leader, one of those men who raised spirits and expectations simply by showing up. He was tall and athletic, an expert horseman, and a good dancer. He wasn't particularly handsome — his teeth were bad, and he wasn't proud of his hippopotamus ivory and gold dentures, so he seldom smiled. But he had a commanding presence, and his troops felt they could depend on him. He was also a bit of an actor. Once while reading something to his troops, he donned his spectacles and then apologized, explaining his eyes had grown dim in the service of his country. Some of his audience wept.

His spirit was indomitable. His army was ragged, undisciplined, and undependable, with a staggering average desertion rate of 20 percent. His bosses in Congress were often indecisive, quarrelsome, and indifferent. But Washington refused to give up. Just as important, he refused the temptation to try to become a military dictator, which he may easily have done.

One of the reasons men loved him was that Washington was personally brave, often on the battle's front lines, and always among the last to retreat. He was also very lucky: In one battle, Washington rode unexpectedly into a group of British soldiers, most of whom fired at him at short range. They all missed.

Declaring Independence

Despite the fact that fighting had actually started, many in the Continental Congress and throughout the colonies still weren't all that keen on breaking away completely from Britain. The radicals who were ready for a break needed a spark to light a fire under those who were still reluctant to act. Not only did they get the spark they needed, but they also got it in writing with the Declaration of Independence.

Stirring up colonists' emotions

The first motivator was a political blunder by the British government. The Brits needed more fighters, but British citizens didn't fall all over themselves trying to sign up. Being a British soldier often meant brutal treatment, poor pay and food, and the chance that someone would kill you. So British officials hired the services of soldiers who worked for a half-dozen German princes. Eventually, they rented about 30,000 of these *Hessians*, named after the principality of Hesse-Kassal, from which many of them came.

The Americans were outraged at this. It was one thing for the mother country and her daughters to fight, but it was a real affront for Mom to go out and hire foreigners to do her killing for her. (Eventually, about 12,000 Hessians deserted and remained after the war as citizens of the new country.)

The second spark came from the pen of a 38-year-old, tomato-faced Englishman with a big nose. Thomas Paine arrived in the colonies in November 1774. He had been a seaman, schoolmaster, corset maker, and customs officer, and he wasn't successful at anything. But with the help of Ben Franklin, Paine was hired as editor of a Philadelphia magazine.

On January 10, 1776, Paine anonymously published a little pamphlet in which he set forth his views on the need for American independence from Britain. He called it "Common Sense."

This pamphlet was straightforward, clear, and simple in its prose. Basically, it said the king was a brute, with no reasonable mandate to rule in Britain, let alone America; that Britain was a leech feeding off the back of American enterprise; and that it was time for the colonies to stand up on their own and become a beacon of freedom for the world.

The pamphlet electrified the country. Within a short time, 120,000 copies were sold, and the number eventually rose to a staggering 500,000 copies, or one for every five people in America, including slaves. (Paine never made a dime, having patriotically signed over royalties to Congress.) It was read by soldiers and politicians alike, and it shifted the emphasis of the fight to a struggle for independence and not just for a new relationship with Britain.

Writing history

On June 7, 1776, Congress began to deal with the independence issue in earnest. Virginia delegate Richard Henry Lee prepared a resolution stating the colonies "are, and of a right ought to be, free and independent states." A few days later, delegates appointed a committee of five to draft a formal declaration backing Lee's resolution, just in case Congress decided to adopt it.

The committee consisted of Benjamin Franklin, John Adams, a Connecticut lawyer named Roger Sherman, a New York iron mine owner named Robert Livingston, and a 33-year-old, red-haired lawyer from Virginia named Thomas Jefferson. (The committee got on well, although Sherman had a habit of picking his teeth, which provoked Franklin into warning that if he didn't stop, Franklin would play his harmonica.)

REMEMBER

Jefferson set to work at a portable desk he had designed himself, and a few weeks later he produced a document that has come to be regarded as one of the most eloquent political statements in human history. True, he exaggerated some of the grievances the colonists had against the king. True, he rather hypocritically declared that "all men are created equal," ignoring the fact that he and hundreds of other Americans owned slaves, whom they certainly didn't regard as having been created equal.

Overall, though, it was a magnificent document that set forth all the reasons America wanted to go its own way — and why all people who wanted to do the same thing should be allowed to do so. After a bit of tinkering by Franklin, the document was presented to Congress on June 28. (See Appendix B for the full text.)

At the demand of some Southern representatives, a section blaming the king for American slavery was taken out. Then, on July 2, Congress adopted the resolution submitted by Lee. "The second day of July, 1776, will be the most memorable epoch [instant of time] in the history of America," predicted John Adams. He missed it by two days because America chose to remember July 4 instead — the day Congress formally adopted the Declaration of Independence, or as one member put it, "Mr. Jefferson's explanation of Mr. Lee's resolution."

With independence declared, Congress now had to find a substitute form of government. Starting in August 1776 and continuing into 1777, members finally came up with something they called the Articles of Confederation. Basically, it called for a weak central government with a virtually powerless president and congress. The power to do most key things, such as impose taxes, was left to the states. Even so, it took the states until 1781 to finish ratifying the articles, so reluctant were they to give up any of their power. It was a poor excuse for a new government, but it was a start. In the meantime, the new country was looking for a few foreign friends.

Cozying Up to the French

Still smarting from its defeats by Britain in a series of wars, France was more than a little happy when war broke out between its archenemy and the American colonies and almost immediately started sending the rebels supplies and money. By the end of the war, France had provided nearly $20 million in aid of various kinds, and it's estimated as much as 90 percent of the gunpowder used by the Americans in the first part of the Revolution was supplied or paid for by the French.

In December 1776, Congress sent Benjamin Franklin to Paris to see whether he could entice even more aid from the French. Personally, he was a big hit with most of France, especially the ladies. But King Louis XVI wasn't overly impressed (he is reported to have given one of Franklin's lady friends a chamber pot with Franklin's picture on the bottom), and the king took a wait-and-see attitude before committing the country to a more entangling alliance.

News of a great American victory at the Battle of Saratoga, however, caused Louis and his ministers to think the rebels just might win. On February 6, 1778, France formally recognized America as an independent nation and agreed to a military alliance. Two different fleets and thousands of French soldiers were sent to the war and played key roles in the deciding battles. The French entry also caused Britain to have to worry about being invaded by a French army and about having to fight the French navy in the West Indies — or wherever else they encountered it.

Undergoing Life Changes: The Loyalists and the Slaves

Before I get to who fought whom where and how it all came out, it's worth taking a look at the war's impact on two very different parts of the American population: the Loyalists and the slaves.

Remaining loyal to the crown

Slightly less than one of every three white colonists didn't side with the Revolution and remained loyal to the crown. Many, but by no means all, were from the aristocracy or had jobs they owed to the British government. Some of these Loyalists, or *Tories* as they were also called, kept quiet about their allegiances, but many acted as spies or guides for the British forces. As many as 30,000 actually fought against their rebel neighbors, and some battles were purely American versus American affairs. One of the Tories, Banastre Tarleton, rose to a major command in the British army and was feared and hated for his savagery and reputation for executing prisoners.

In some areas, such as New York City and parts of North and South Carolina, Loyalists were dominant, but in areas where they weren't, they paid a heavy price for their loyalty. Their taxes were sometimes doubled, their property trashed, and their businesses shunned.

When the war ended, things got even worse. A new verse was added to "Yankee Doodle" by victorious rebels: "Now Tories all what can you say / Come — is this not a griper? / That while your hopes are drained away / 'Tis you must pay the piper." Tory property was confiscated, and as many as 80,000 Loyalists eventually left America for Canada, England, and the West Indies.

Confronting slavery issues

One of the thorniest — and most embarrassing — problems Congress was confronted with during the Revolutionary War was what to do about slaves. At first, Congress declared that no Africans, freed or not, could fight in the Continental army. But when Washington pointed out that they might end up fighting for the British, who were offering freedom in exchange for fighting the rebels, Congress relented and allowed freed slaves to enlist.

More than a few American leaders were also red-faced about fighting for freedom while owning slaves — a hypocrisy not lost on their critics. In the end, some slaves fought for the American cause, and some fled to the British side. The issue of slavery, meanwhile, grew as a divisive issue between North and South. In most of the Northern states during the war, the slave trade was outlawed. In the South, the number of slaves actually grew, mostly because of the birthrates among slaves already there. And slavery spread as Southerners moved west, into Kentucky and Tennessee.

Winning a War

Okay, here's pretty much how the actual fighting unfolded: The Americans started off pretty promisingly — winning an early battle in New York and holding their own at a big battle outside Boston — mostly because the British were slow to recognize they had a real war on their hands. But then the Americans launched an invasion of Canada, which proved to be a really bad idea. Shortly after the Canada failure, Washington got his tail kicked in New York and escaped total disaster only through great luck.

But Washington learned a valuable lesson: He couldn't possibly win by fighting the British in a series of open-field, European-style major battles. The trick, the Continental army learned, was to be a moving target. "We fight, get beat, rise, and fight again," noted Gen. Nathanael Greene.

Washington did win a couple of smaller victories, which were great for morale, but he also suffered through a couple of hideous winters at Valley Forge, Pennsylvania, and Morristown, New Jersey, which were bad for morale.

But the British made a series of tactical blunders and lost an entire army in upstate New York. Then they turned their attentions to the South, made more blunders, and lost another entire army in Virginia. Having apparently run out of mistakes, they quit, and America won. Figure 5-1 shows the highlights of ten key battles or campaigns in the American Revolution.

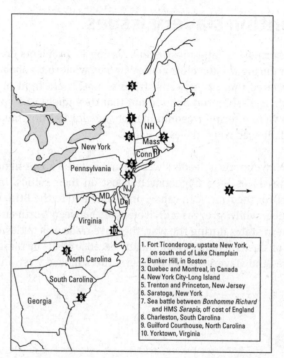

FIGURE 5-1: Ten key battles of the American Revolution.

1. Fort Ticonderoga, upstate New York, on south end of Lake Champlain
2. Bunker Hill, in Boston
3. Quebec and Montreal, in Canada
4. New York City-Long Island
5. Trenton and Princeton, New Jersey
6. Saratoga, New York
7. Sea battle between *Bonhomme Richard* and HMS *Serapis*, off cost of England
8. Charleston, South Carolina
9. Guilford Courthouse, North Carolina
10. Yorktown, Virginia

© *John Wiley & Sons, Inc.*

Felling a British fort

Less than a month after Lexington and Concord, American troops under Vermont frontiersman Ethan Allen surprised and captured a British fort — Fort Ticonderoga — on the shores of Lake Champlain in New York. They captured 60 cannons and mortars, which they eventually used to drive the British out of Boston. The victory was a big confidence booster.

Battling over Bunker, uh, Breed's Hill

This battle, on June 17, 1775, was actually fought on Breed's Hill, which is next to Bunker Hill, just outside Boston. About 1,400 Americans held the hill. About 2,500 British troops attacked them in a frontal assault rather than by surrounding them.

The Brits won after two charges, but they paid a heavy toll. About 1,000, or 40 percent, of their troops were killed or wounded, while the Americans suffered about 400 killed or wounded. The carnage shook British commander William Howe so much he became overly cautious and conservative in future battles.

Losing the campaign in Canada

In late 1775, American leaders Richard Montgomery and Benedict Arnold launched an invasion of Canada. The Yanks thought the Canadians wouldn't put up much of a fight. Bad thought. Americans lost battles at Quebec and Montreal and were forced to retreat. The losses left Canada firmly in British hands and gave the Brits a good base from which to launch attacks on New York and New England.

Nixing plans to take New York

In mid-1776, Washington and his entire army of about 18,000 men moved to the area around New York City, hoping to hem in and defeat a British army of about 25,000. But many of the American troops were raw recruits, who panicked and ran in a series of battles in the area. By the fall, it was Washington who was nearly trapped. Under protection of a heavy fog that materialized at just the right time, the American army slipped away into New Jersey and then to Pennsylvania. It was a major defeat for the American army, but it could've been a lot worse.

Winning at Trenton and Princeton

Smarting from about six months of running away, Washington moved his army across the ice-choked Delaware River on Christmas Eve 1776 and surprised a Hessian brigade in Trenton, New Jersey. The result was that Washington captured more than 900 Hessian troops and 1,200 weapons without losing a single man. Washington then followed up with a victory over the British a few days later at Princeton, New Jersey. The victories were smashing morale boosters for the Yanks.

Making the Brits surrender at Saratoga

In 1777, British General "Gentleman Johnny" Burgoyne proposed to lead a British army into New York and New England from Canada, while the British army already in New York City sailed down to capture Philadelphia. It turned out to be a disaster for the Brits. Burgoyne had no concept of a march through enemy-infested wilderness and took along officers' wives and children. Continually harassed by American troops and running low on food and supplies, Burgoyne's army lost two battles near Saratoga. On October 17, 1777, the British army of nearly 6,000 men surrendered. News of the victory helped convince France to enter the war on the American side.

Sparring at sea

On September 23, 1779, an American navy ship named the *Bonhomme Richard* took on the British warship *Serapis* off the coast of England. The American captain, John Paul Jones, saw two of his major guns explode on the first discharge. Undismayed, he pulled alongside the *Serapis* and the two ships pounded each other for more than two hours. At one point, when asked if he would surrender, Jones replied, "I have not yet begun to fight!"

Finally, faced with the arrival of another American ship, the *Serapis* surrendered. Jones's own ship was so badly damaged it had to be abandoned, and he transferred his flag to the British ship. But the victory was the greatest single naval feat of the war and shook British confidence in its navy.

Losing big in Charleston

This was the worst American defeat of the war. In the spring of 1780, about 8,500 British and Loyalist troops and 14 ships surrounded the city of Charleston, South Carolina, trapping an American army under the command of Gen. Benjamin Lincoln. On May 12, Lincoln surrendered his entire army of 5,500 men, along with huge amounts of weapons.

Minimizing a loss at Guilford Courthouse

Most of the war in the South consisted of British troops beating American troops, chasing them, and then beating them again. In December 1780, Congress finally put a competent general in charge of the American forces in the South while Washington fought in the North. He was 38-year-old Nathanael Greene, who was probably the only American general to consistently outstrategize his opponents.

After victories at the battles of Cowpens and Eutaw Springs, Greene faced British Gen. Charles Cornwallis at Guilford Courthouse in North Carolina. The British won what was one of the bloodiest and most bitter battles of the war, but they suffered almost 30 percent casualties, while Greene's losses were light. Cornwallis was forced to withdraw out of the Carolinas and back to Virginia, taking his troops to Yorktown.

Turning things around at Yorktown

After trying for months to coordinate his own troops with the French troops and ships that were supposedly ready to aid the American cause, Washington finally hooked up with his allies in May 1781. Together with two French fleets, French and American armies converged on Yorktown and hemmed in the British army under Cornwallis. The British, meanwhile, mishandled two fleets of their own and were unable to come to Cornwallis's rescue.

On October 19, 1781, Cornwallis surrendered his entire army of 8,000 men. The British band played a tune called "The World Turned Upside Down," and a band hired by the French played "Yankee Doodle." In London, when Lord North, the British prime minister, heard the news, he cried out "O God! It is all over!"

Actually, it wasn't over for more than a year. The British army still held New York, and there were some small battles until the formal peace treaty was signed on February 3, 1783.

The British were gracious losers, mainly because they wanted to drive a wedge between America and France. They gave up rights to all the land from the Atlantic Coast to the Mississippi River and from Canada to Florida, which was far more than the Americans actually controlled. The Americans promised to treat the Loyalists in their midst fairly and set up fair rules so that British creditors could collect prewar debts. (Neither promise was kept.)

American independence was won. The question now was what to do with it.

Chapter **6**

Blueprints and Birth Pains: 1783–1800

After winning its independence from Britain, America felt a little like a kid who has just moved out of his parents' house and isn't sure what step comes next in growing up. The country had no real government, no sound financing system, and no true foreign friends.

Fortunately, it did have a group of extraordinary individuals — some of whom had helped lead it through the Revolution — who were willing to try to find a form of government that would fit. Putting aside most of their personal differences and aspirations (at least at first), they came up with a system of governing the new country that became a true wonder of the world.

Making the Rules

America limped through the Revolutionary War guided by the Continental Congress, a group of men selected by colonial legislatures. The Congress, in turn, came up with something called the Articles of Confederation.

Drafted in 1777 but not ratified by all the states until 1781, the Articles were based on the idea that the individual states would be friendly with one another and cooperate when it was in their mutual interest. Each state had one vote in Congress, and it took 9 of the 13 states to ratify any decision.

Congress ran matters of war and peace, operated the post office, coined money, and dealt with Native Americans when the states didn't want to. It had no power to tax or to establish a federal judicial system, and it lacked any real power to make the individual states pay attention to its legal authority to make postal, coin, or war-and-peace decisions.

It wasn't an awful system, but it guaranteed a continual stream of squabbles among the states. Making things worse were schemes by agents of Spain, France, and Britain. They tried to get Americans who lived in the western parts of the new country to break away. War hero Ethan Allen, for example, met with British agents to discuss making his beloved Vermont a British province and narrowly escaped being tried for treason.

REMEMBER

Still, at least two good bits of legislation came out of the loose-knit confederation. The first was the Land Ordinance of 1785, which set up the way land owned by the federal government — which basically was territory won from Britain that wasn't claimed by one of the states — would be divided and sold. The ordinance called for the land to be surveyed into square townships, which were six miles on each side. Each township was then surveyed into 36 areas of one square mile each (640 acres). The parcels were then listed for sale at public auction and could, in turn, be subdivided by the owner into smaller parcels for sale. Part of the revenue went to the establishment of public schools.

The second piece of legislation was enacted in 1787. Called the Northwest Ordinance, it stated that as new states were admitted to the country, they would be equal in every way to the original 13. It also banned slavery in the new territories, although this was later changed. Both laws were good starts to stabilizing the new country. But ongoing troubles in trying to regulate commerce among the states and in trying to raise money for the federal government still plagued the nation, especially because every state had its own currency and assigned it its own value.

Going back to Philly

By 1787, it was apparent to many leaders that the Articles of Confederation needed an overhaul, or the union of states would eventually fall apart. So Congress agreed to call a convention of delegates from each state to try to fix things. The first of the delegates (selected by state legislatures) to arrive in Philadelphia in May 1787 was James Madison, a 36-year-old scholar and politician from Virginia who was so frail he couldn't serve in the army during the Revolution. Madison had so many ideas on how to fix things he couldn't wait to get started.

Not everyone else was in such a hurry. Although the convention was supposed to begin May 15, it wasn't until May 25 that enough of the delegates chosen by the state legislatures showed up to have a quorum. Rhode Island never did send anyone.

Eventually, 55 delegates took part. Notable by their absence were some of the leading figures of the recent rebellion against England: Thomas Jefferson was in France, Thomas Paine was in England, Sam Adams and John Hancock weren't selected to go, and Patrick Henry refused.

But those who did show up were hardly second-stringers. George Washington was there and was unanimously selected the convention's president. Benjamin Franklin, at 81 the oldest delegate, was there. But Madison and a handsome 32-year-old, self-made success story from New York named Alexander Hamilton were the true stars of the group.

Half of the group's members were lawyers, and 29 were college-educated. Many were wealthy and thus had a bigger-than-most stake in straightening out the country's financial mess. Their average age was 42.

They met in long and highly secret sessions, with armed guards at the doors. Their reasoning was that their task was so difficult that any leaks about what they were doing would only increase outside pressures. They studied other forms of government; they debated. And after 17 weeks, on September 17, 1787, they voted 39 to 3, with 13 absent, to approve a ten-page document that became the United States Constitution. Then most of them adjourned to a local tavern and hoisted a few.

REMEMBER

The document the delegates created was a masterpiece of compromises. Big states gained more clout when it was decided that representation in the House of Representatives would be based on population, while small states got protection from being bullied when it was decided that each state would have the same number of members (two) in the Senate. The South won the right to count slaves as three-fifths of a person when determining population for representation in the House; the North got a promise that the slave trade would end for good in 1807. Actually, the South didn't mind this compromise all that much because it didn't mean slavery itself would end — just the practice of importing more slaves from overseas. In fact, it ensured that the value of slaves already here would increase, thus making their owners richer.

The Constitution gave Congress the power to regulate commerce among states as well as with foreign nations and to pass laws with a simple majority of its members. It gave the presidency a powerful role. It created a federal judicial system, with the Supreme Court at the top. And it left the individual states with a fair amount of independence to make their own laws on most matters. No one thought it was perfect, but most of the delegates thought it was a pretty good blueprint from which to build.

While the last members of the convention were signing the document, Franklin pointed to a sun painted on the chair in which Washington was sitting. "I have often . . . looked at that behind the president, without being able to tell whether it was rising or setting," he said. "But now, at length, I have the happiness to know that it is a rising, and not a setting sun." But they still had to sell the blueprint to the rest of the country.

Selling the Constitution to the states

The convention submitted its work to the Congress that was still laboring under the old Articles of Confederation, and Congress accepted it after three days of sometimes intense debate. But because of the enormity of the issue, Congress also didn't want to be totally responsible if things went wrong (proving that some things never change).

So Congress sent the proposal to the states for ratification. Each state had to elect delegates who would consider the proposed Constitution, and when nine states had approved it, it would become the law of the land.

It was a gamble because if any of the big states — Virginia, New York, Massachusetts, or Pennsylvania — rejected it and went its own way, the whole deal might fall apart. In addition, a lot of people who hadn't thought much about the need for a central government (which was probably the majority of Americans) weren't sold on the idea at all. But the idea of letting "ordinary" people have a say (actually, only about one-fourth of the population was eligible to vote) led to a great deal of spirited debate on the subject, which allowed pro-Constitution forces a chance to make their case.

They did. In a brilliant series of 85 newspaper essays that became known as the Federalist Papers, Hamilton, Madison, and John Jay argued eloquently for adoption of the Constitution. Much more important was the public support of the two most popular men in America: Franklin and Washington. Anti-Constitution forces also made powerful public arguments, but their efforts were not as well organized and lacked star appeal.

GIVING WEIGHT TO THE BILL OF RIGHTS

The first ten amendments to the Constitution were added mainly because a lot of Americans believed in the saying "get it in writing." The drafters of the original Constitution didn't spell out specific rights mainly because they didn't think it was necessary. The document defined the powers of Congress, and, thus, its creators assumed that everything left over belonged to individuals and the states.

But some states insisted the specific rights be spelled out as soon as possible after the Constitution was ratified. So James Madison, at the urging of Thomas Jefferson, came up with a list of 12 amendments, only 10 of which were ratified by 11 of the states in 1791. The two amendments left out had to do with the number of members of the House of Representatives and prohibiting Congress from setting its own salaries. For some reason, Connecticut and Georgia didn't get around to ratifying the remaining ten until 1941. See Appendix A for the list of the ten amendments that made it.

The first five states to ratify did so by January 1788. The following month, Massachusetts agreed — but only on the condition that a list of specific individual rights be added to the Constitution as soon as possible (see the sidebar "Giving weight to the Bill of Rights"). By July, all but North Carolina and Rhode Island had ratified it, and they fell in line by May 1790.

"Our constitution is in actual operation," Franklin wrote, "and everything appears to promise that it will last. But in this world, nothing can be certain but death and taxes."

Dishing Up Politics, American Style

Now that it had rules, America needed a president, and the choice was a no-brainer. George Washington was unanimously elected in April 1789 by the Electoral College, which had been established by the Constitution and was composed of men elected either by popular vote or by state legislatures. Washington set out from his home in Virginia for the temporary capital at New York (which soon moved to Philadelphia, where it stayed until the federal district that is now Washington, D.C., was completed in 1800). Everywhere he went, Washington was greeted by parades and cheering crowds.

Washington the politician

Washington wasn't a great politician, although he did know enough to buy 47 gallons of beer, 35 gallons of wine, and 3 barrels of rum for potential voters in his first campaign for the Virginia legislature. He wasn't a good public speaker, and he wasn't a great innovator.

But he was perfect for the new country. He was enormously popular with the public, even those who didn't like his policies. Because of that, other political leaders were wise to defer to him. (At least publicly: Behind his back, John Adams referred to Washington as "Old Muttonhead," and Alexander Hamilton called him "the Great Booby.")

Washington was also good at assembling competent people around him and playing to their strengths while ignoring their faults. And he assembled a heck of a group: Adams was his vice president, Hamilton his treasurer, Thomas Jefferson his secretary of state, old Revolutionary War buddy Henry Knox his secretary of war, and sharp-tongued Edmund Randolph of Virginia his attorney general.

Family feuding: Jefferson versus Hamilton

But Washington's cabinet wasn't exactly one big happy family. For example, Hamilton and Adams disliked each other even though they shared many of the same political views — Adams once referred to Hamilton as "the bastard brat of a Scotch peddler."

And Jefferson and Hamilton not only disagreed politically, they were different in a host of other ways. Hamilton was short but impeccable in his dress and manners. Jefferson was tall and often looked like an unmade bed. Hamilton grew up poor in New York and was illegitimate; Jefferson grew up wealthy in a leading family in Virginia. Hamilton had a deeply abiding distrust of the common man and a deep affection for wealth. Jefferson disliked the upper classes and professed that the farmer was nature's greatest creation. And although Jefferson was a relatively pleasant guy to be around, Hamilton could be arrogant and snotty.

Given their differences, it shouldn't be surprising that the two men were at opposite ends of the political spectrum. And given their abilities and stature, it shouldn't be surprising that people who thought the same way began to form political parties around them. At the time, most politicians repudiated the idea of political parties — at least publicly. "If I could not go to heaven but with a [political] party," Jefferson said, "I would not go at all." But people being people, the formation of parties revolving around a certain philosophy of governing was probably inevitable.

REMEMBER

The Hamiltonians were called *Federalists.* In essence, they supported a strong central government, a powerful central bank, government support of business, a loose interpretation of the Constitution, and restrictions on public speech and the press. They opposed the expansion of democratic elections and were generally pro-British when it came to foreign affairs. "Those who own the country," said Federalist John Jay, "ought to govern it."

The Jeffersonians were first called *Democratic Republicans*, then just *Republicans.* They favored more power to individual states and state-chartered banks, no special favors for business, a strict reading of the Constitution, giving more people the vote and relatively free speech and a free press. They were generally pro-French. It's too simplistic to say today's Republicans are yesterday's Federalists and today's Democrats are descended from Jefferson's party. Hamilton, for example, supported big federal government programs, which today would make him more of a Democrat, while Jefferson wanted to minimize government, which sounds like the modern Republican. But the dominance of just two parties, Federalists and Republicans, foreshadowed the two-party system that America has pretty much stuck with throughout its history.

By 1796, Washington had had enough of fathering a country. He declined a third term and went home to his plantation in Mount Vernon, Virginia. Hamilton, who was born in St. Croix and therefore under the Constitution couldn't be president, hoped someone he could control would be elected. He backed Thomas Pinckney of South Carolina, who was Washington's minister to England, but Vice President John Adams — whom Hamilton disdained — won.

Jefferson was the Republican candidate, and because he came in second, he became vice president, per the Constitution. (It soon became clear that this wasn't a great idea. So in 1804, the states amended the Constitution to allow candidates to run for either president or vice president, but not both.)

Raising the Dough

Every successful country needs a sound financial plan, and it fell to Hamilton to devise one for America.

The first thing he had to do was establish the new nation's credit. To do that, he needed to clean up its existing debts, such as the $54 million the federal government owed foreign and domestic creditors. Hamilton proposed the debt be paid off in full, rather than at a discount as creditors had feared. Hamilton argued that if America didn't make good on what it already owed, no one would want to lend it money in the future.

In addition, he proposed that the federal government also pay off about $21 million in debts the individual states had run up. The old debts would be paid off by issuing bonds. But states like Virginia, which had paid off much of its Revolutionary War debts, were peeved at the thought of the federal government picking up other states' tabs and then sticking all U.S. residents with the bill. So they engaged in a little horse-trading. Virginia withdrew its objections to the plan, and in return, Hamilton and the Washington administration agreed to locate the new federal district next door to Virginia on the Potomac. Whatever advantage Virginia thought that would give it has certainly evaporated by now.

Many members of Congress supported Hamilton's plan to pay off the debts dollar for dollar, especially because many of them either held the old bonds or had snapped them up for next to nothing and stood to make enormous profits. Hamilton himself was accused of using his office to make money off the bonds, but if he was guilty, he didn't do a very good job, because he died broke.

To raise money to pay off the bonds, the federal government established taxes, called *tariffs,* on goods imported into America. It also slapped a tax of 7 cents a gallon on whiskey, which was pretty steep considering whiskey in many of the southern and western states sold for only 25 cents a gallon.

Finally, Hamilton proposed a nationally chartered bank that would print paper money backed by the federal government and in which the government would be the minority stockholder and deposit its revenues. To be located in Philadelphia, the bank would be chartered for 21 years. Jefferson howled that the whole idea would cripple state banks and was unconstitutional, but Hamilton, with the backing of Washington, prevailed. The bank's stock sold out within four hours after going on sale.

Hamilton's plan worked, in large part because the American economy kicked into high gear in the 1790s. Another war between France and England helped increase America's share of the world market; trade in the West Indies that had been stunted by the Revolutionary War was revived; and industry, particularly in the North, began to develop. America, the new kid on the block, now had some change in its pockets.

Earning Respect

A government is only as good as the respect it commands from its citizens, and respect for the new U.S. government wasn't universal. Whiskey makers, former soldiers, Native Americans, and people who thought some politicians were jerks — and said so publicly — were among the groups whose respect the new government had to earn.

Shaking things up: Shays's Rebellion

Daniel Shays was a Massachusetts farmer and Revolutionary War veteran who, like many of his fellow vets, found himself broke and in debt after the war. Moreover, the constitution Massachusetts adopted in 1780 was drafted mostly by businessmen who lived along the coast, and the state's inland farmers got the short end of the stick when it came to things like paying taxes.

When taxes couldn't be paid, homes, farms, livestock, and personal possessions were seized, and debtors were sometimes thrown into prison. So in 1786, Shays found himself at the head of an "army" of about 1,000 men who were fed up. They marched on Springfield, forced the state Supreme Court to flee, and paraded around town. In January 1787, Shays's group tried to take a military arsenal at Springfield. But the state militia routed them, and after a few weeks of skirmishing, they dispersed and abandoned the fight. Several of the group's members were hanged. Shays fled to Vermont and was eventually pardoned, but he died the next year.

The whole thing wasn't in vain, however. Some of the reforms they wanted — such as lower court costs, an exemption on workmen's tools from debt seizures, and changes in the tax laws — were adopted. Jefferson noted "a little rebellion now and then is a good thing . . . the tree of liberty must be refreshed from time to time with the blood of patriots and tyrants." Washington, however, despaired that the rebellion illustrated how too much democracy would lead to anarchy.

But the biggest impact of Shays's Rebellion may have been that it helped convince some of the delegates to the Constitutional Convention that the country needed a strong central government to handle such things.

Taxing liquid corn: The Whiskey Rebellion

This is how important whiskey was on the American frontier: Americans often used it in place of cash for commercial transactions. It was also the cheapest way to market some of the surplus corn crop. So it's easy to understand why people got upset when the new federal government announced it was slapping what amounted to a 25 percent tax on the drink.

Distillers in western Pennsylvania organized a revolt in 1794, roughing up tax collectors and threatening distilleries that tried to pay the tax. When the state's governor refused to intervene for fear of losing votes, President Washington himself led a massive force of about 13,000 men — a larger army than he had during most of the Revolutionary War — and the rebels scattered.

The short-lived rebellion didn't amount to much, but it provided an early test of the federal government's willingness to enforce federal laws.

Going "mad" over the Native Americans

Despite their loss in the Revolution and subsequent peace treaty, the British still had a string of forts in the American Northwest, which was then defined as the area northwest of the Ohio River, east of the Mississippi, and south of the Great Lakes. The Brits said they were there to protect their interests in Canada, but many Americans suspected they were there to stir up the Native Americans. In 1791, a U.S. army of about 2,000 troops under Gen. Arthur St. Clair marched into what is now Indiana to counter the British/Native American threat. But St. Clair was surprised and routed by a Native American force, and he suffered nearly 50 percent casualties.

In 1793, another force of 2,000 U.S. troops tried again, this time led by Gen. "Mad Anthony" Wayne. A Revolutionary War hero, Wayne got his nickname not from being nuts but from being daring and a bit reckless in battle (which may be the same thing). Anyway, in August 1794, Wayne's troops attacked a Native American force of about the same size at a site called Fallen Timbers in Indiana. Wayne's army rolled over the Native Americans, burning their villages and destroying their crops. The victory ended the Native American threat and restored much confidence in the U.S. Army.

Attempting to censor the press

American newspapers had been used as a political weapon almost as long as there had been American newspapers. But the rise of the two-party system in the 1790s greatly increased their use and their sting. Pro-Jefferson editors, such as Phillip Freneau and Benjamin Bache, squared off against pro-Hamilton scribes, such as John Fenno and William Cobbett.

These were nasty fellows with a quill in their hands. Bache once wrote that "if ever a nation was debauched by a man, the American nation has been debauched by Washington," and Cobbett opined that America would be truly free only "when Jefferson's head will be rotting cheek-to-jowl with that of some toil-killed Negro slave."

By 1798, the Federalist-controlled Congress had had enough. It narrowly approved the Alien and Sedition Acts. The acts extended the naturalization period from 5 to 14 years, to keep out the foreign riff-raff. And Congress also made it a crime to publish "any false, scandalous and malicious writing" about the president, Congress, or the government in general.

Hundreds were indicted under the Sedition Act, but only ten — all of them Republicans — were convicted. Among them was Congressman Matthew Lyon of Vermont, who had already gained notoriety by spitting in the face of Federalist

Congressman Roger Griswold on the floor of Congress. Lyon was sentenced to four months in jail for writing about President Adams's "unbounded thirst for ridiculous pomp, foolish adulation and selfish avarice." Lyon was reelected to Congress while in jail.

Partly because its application was so one-sided, the Sedition Act's popularity quickly waned and in the end probably hurt the Federalist cause much more than it helped. The act expired on March 3, 1801, a day before Republican Jefferson assumed the presidency. It wasn't renewed, and American politicians in both camps decided it was generally better to develop a thick hide when it came to the press than to try to slap a muzzle on the First Amendment.

Finding Foreign Friction

Most Americans applauded when the French Revolution, which eventually overthrew the French monarchy and did away with a feudalistic system of government ruled by an aristocracy, began in 1789. Americans even continued to support it after the revolution was usurped by radical rebels, who turned it into the Reign of Terror. Thousands of French aristocrats, including King Louis XVI, had their heads lopped off by the guillotine. But many Americans shrugged off the excesses and focused on the French revolutionaries' goals of "liberté, égalité, fraternité" (French for "liberty, equality, brotherhood").

REMEMBER

But when the revolt spread to once again engulf Europe in war, more sober Americans started to worry. The Federalists, led by Hamilton, didn't want to take the French side against the British. For one thing, they detested the excesses of the French "mobocracy," or mob rule. For another, they realized that England was America's best customer, and most of the revenues from tariffs paid on imports came from English ships.

The Jefferson-led Republicans, on the other hand, didn't want to side with the British. They reasoned that the French had backed them in their revolution, so they should do the same.

But America's first two presidents, Washington and Adams, didn't want to side with anyone. Both men saw that the longer America could stay out of the European mess, the stronger the country would become and thus the more able it would be to control its own destiny rather than rely on the fortunes of an alliance.

Staying neutral wasn't easy. British naval ships routinely stopped American merchant ships and forced American sailors into service aboard British ships, a practice called *impressments*. French ships also attacked American merchants with England-bound cargoes.

JOHN JAY

John Jay was not your average revolutionary. Jay was born into a wealthy New York family in 1745. He became a lawyer and developed a lucrative law practice, hobnobbing with New York's very pro-British aristocracy.

But during the Revolution and afterward, Jay became one of the busiest of America's statesmen. Over the course of his career, he served in both Continental Congresses; was chief justice of the New York State Supreme Court; helped negotiate the peace treaty with the British in 1783; brokered the 1794 treaty with Britain that avoided another war; was the first chief justice of the U.S. Supreme Court; served as America's first foreign secretary before cabinet posts were created; was New York governor for two terms; and helped abolish slavery in that state.

But luck and skillful negotiating kept America out of the Anglo–Franco fracas for a generation. In 1794, Washington sent diplomat John Jay to England. Jay eventually negotiated a treaty with the British in which the British agreed to give up their forts in the American Northwest and pay for damages caused by seizures of American ships. But the British didn't agree to stop impressing American sailors, and Jay agreed the United States would repay pre-Revolutionary War debts it still owed. The Jay treaty was greeted with widespread howls of rage in America, but it cooled things down with the British for more than a decade.

Although an ardent Federalist, Jay was highly regarded by leaders of both parties for his intelligence, diplomatic skills, and willingness to take the heat on unpopular decisions. But his most remarkable accomplishment may have been this: He did all these things and still managed to fit in 28 years of retirement before dying in 1829, at the age of 83. The Jay treaty also angered the French, who stepped up their attacks on U.S. ships. In 1797, President Adams sent U.S. envoys to Paris to meet with the French foreign minister, Charles Talleyrand. But upon their arrival, the Americans were met by three go-betweens known publicly only as "X, Y, and Z," who tried to get a $250,000 bribe from the Americans just for the chance to meet with Talleyrand. The U.S. envoys told X, Y, and Z to stick it and returned home.

So for about two years, France and the United States waged an undeclared war on the seas. The newly created U.S. Navy captured about 80 French ships, and the French continued to prey on American vessels. Then Adams did a remarkable thing. Ignoring the fact that war fever was raging and declaring war on France could help him win a second term as president, Adams sent another peace team back to Paris in 1800. This time, the two countries made a deal. Adams kept the United States out of war, but he also lost reelection to the presidency and sealed the doom of the Federalist Party in doing so.

2
Growing Pains

Chapter 7

"Long Tom" and One Weird War: 1800–1815

The turn of the century brought what has been called the *Revolution of 1800.* The term, first used by Thomas Jefferson, refers to the fact that for the first time in the young country's history, America saw one political party give up power to another.

In this chapter, you see how well it worked, look at the development of the U.S. Supreme Court in the grand scheme of things, sit in on a big land sale, and fight some pirates. I wrap it up with a pretty weird war with the British.

Jefferson Gets a Job

President John F. Kennedy once hosted a dinner party at the White House and invited a guest list so impressive that he joked it was the finest group of genius and talent to sit at the table "since Thomas Jefferson dined alone."

Kennedy's quip held as much truth as humor. A tall, loose-limbed man who was said to amble more than walk and was thus nicknamed *Long Tom*, Jefferson was a statesman, a writer, an inventor, a farmer, an architect, a musician, a scientist, and a philosopher.

Thus, it may not be surprising that he was also a bundle of contradictions. Jefferson was

>> An idealist who could bend the rules when he needed to accomplish something

>> A slave owner who hated slavery

>> A man who believed Africans were naturally inferior, yet for years had one of his slaves as his mistress

>> A believer in sticking to the letter of the Constitution who ignored it on at least one major issue during his presidency

>> A guy who preached frugality for the country, yet died $100,000 in debt

But Jefferson's contradictory nature made him flexible, and flexibility in a president can be a very valuable asset. In addition, Jefferson was a true man of the people, much more so than his predecessors George Washington and John Adams. He did away with the imperial trappings that had built up around the office, sometimes greeting visitors to the White House in his robe and slippers. That kind of informality added to the popularity he already enjoyed as author of the Declaration of Independence.

REMEMBER

But public popularity meant diddly-squat in the election of 1800 because of the screwy way the Constitution's drafters had set up the presidential election process. Republican Jefferson received the votes of 73 members of the Electoral College, while Federalist incumbent John Adams snagged 65. But the electors were required by the Constitution to list two names (with the second-highest vote-getter becoming vice president). And as it happened, the 73 electors who voted for Jefferson also listed a New York politician named Aaron Burr, who had helped deliver New York to the Republican side. That meant a tie between Jefferson and Burr, and the winner had to be decided by the House of Representatives, which was still controlled by the Federalists. (The goofy system was done away with by the 12th Amendment to the Constitution, which was added before the next presidential election in 1804.)

The Federalists took their cues mainly from Alexander Hamilton. Hamilton disliked Jefferson, but he detested Burr, with good reason. To call Burr a reptile is a slur to cold-blooded creatures everywhere. Born to a wealthy New Jersey family and well-educated, Burr established the first true political machine in the United States. He was a power-hungry schemer and a dangerous opportunist.

SALLY AND TOM

When Jefferson ran for reelection in 1804, the nastiest bit of campaigning against him was a claim that he had an affair with one of his slaves, a woman named Sally Hemings, beginning while he was U.S. envoy to France. Moreover, the story was that he had fathered children by her. Jefferson ignored the charges and easily won reelection.

The issue seemingly died with Jefferson and was largely ignored by historians until the 1970s, when two books revived the rumor and claimed it was true. Jefferson apologists howled, and their arguments ranged from the lack of concrete evidence to back up the assertion to the contention that Jefferson was impotent.

But in 1998, some pretty concrete evidence did surface, in the form of DNA samples taken from the descendants of Jefferson and Hemings. The conclusion: Jefferson and Hemings had children together. In 2000, a commission formed by the Thomas Jefferson Foundation concluded that the weight of all evidence "indicated a high probability" that Jefferson and Hemmings had been more than friends. It was probably no coincidence, then, that the only slaves Jefferson ever freed during his lifetime were Sally Heming's four surviving children.

But even with Hamilton's grudging support, it took 35 ballots before the House gave the presidency to Jefferson, with Burr becoming vice president. In return, Jefferson privately promised not to oust all the Federalist officeholders in the government — a promise he mostly kept.

As president, Jefferson played to his supporters, who were mainly in the South and West. He pushed bills through Congress that changed the time required to become a citizen from 14 to 5 years and repealed the tax on whiskey. Because he wasn't very good at finances, he left the government's financial fortunes in the hands of his Swiss-born secretary of the treasury, Albert Gallatin, and Gallatin managed to cut the national debt almost in half.

Disorder in the Court

One of the last things the Federalist-controlled Congress did before giving way to the Jeffersonian Republicans in early 1801 was to create 16 new federal circuit court judgeships. Federalist Pres. John Adams then spent until 9 p.m. the last day of his term filling the judgeships — with Federalists.

But when the Republicans took over, they promptly repealed the law creating the judgeships, and the judges were out of a job, along with a few dozen other judicial appointees made by Adams in his last days as president. One of them, a guy named William Marbury, didn't take it gracefully. Marbury sued Jefferson's secretary of state, James Madison, for refusing to give him his judicial commission, and the case went to the U.S. Supreme Court.

In 1803, the court made a historic ruling. The justices said that though Marbury's appointment was legal, another section of the 1789 law that created the federal judiciary in the first place was unconstitutional because it gave powers to the judiciary that weren't spelled out in the Constitution and weren't within the power of Congress to create.

The ruling marked the first time the Supreme Court ruled an action taken by Congress to be unconstitutional. The result was that the Court asserted its place as a co-equal with the legislative (congressional) and executive (presidential) branches.

JOHN MARSHALL

John Marshall quite possibly represented the most important accomplishment of the John Adams administration, becoming the patron saint of the U.S. Supreme Court.

A distant cousin of Thomas Jefferson, Marshall was born in 1835 in a log cabin in Virginia, where his father was active in politics. After serving in the Continental army — including the winter at Valley Forge — Marshall earned his law degree and entered politics. In 1799, he went to Congress; in 1800, he became Adams's secretary of state; and in January 1801, Adams appointed him chief justice of the Supreme Court.

It was a job Marshall held until his death, 34 years later. During his tenure as chief justice, he led a series of landmark decisions that established the court's role as a key player in American government and strengthened the power of the federal government. But he also had a good time.

According to one story, Marshall suggested to his fellow justices that on days they were considering a case, they should only drink hard spirits if it was raining. When the sun continued to shine in Washington, however, Marshall decided that because the court had jurisdiction over the entire nation, justices should drink only when it rained somewhere in America.

But the Republicans weren't done. A Supreme Court justice named Samuel Chase, a signer of the Declaration of Independence, so irritated the Jeffersonians with his harangues from the bench that they took to naming vicious dogs after him. Then in 1804, the Republican-controlled Congress took it a step further by impeaching him.

REMEMBER

Chase was tried by the Senate, but because he really hadn't done anything that would warrant removing him from the court, he was acquitted. It was the last formal attempt by elected officials from one political party to reshape the Court by directly pushing justices appointed by another party off the bench, although there have been numerous efforts to block nominees' Senate confirmations. Free from partisan machinations, justices were thus freer to make decisions based on the law as they saw it.

Growing by Leaps and Bounds

The young United States was a restless rascal. And like most kids, it was growing so fast, you couldn't keep it in shoes. The census of 1800 reported a population of 5.3 million (including about 900,000 slaves), a whopping 35 percent increase over 1790. About eight in ten Americans lived and worked on farms.

The largest states were still Virginia, Pennsylvania, and New York. More significantly, the fastest-growing were Tennessee and Kentucky, which had nearly tripled in population since 1790. Americans were moving west.

One of the reasons for this move was that in some areas, they had literally worn out their welcome. Tobacco can be as tough on soil as it is on lungs, and the crop had depleted a lot of land in the South. In the North, the growing population helped drive up the price of land to $14 to $50 an acre.

But in the West — which in 1800 was what was or would become Michigan, Ohio, Kentucky, Tennessee, Indiana, and Illinois — federal government land could be bought for less than $2 an acre. Of course, Native Americans occupied some of it, but in the first few years of the 19th century, government officials such as Indiana Territory Gov. William Henry Harrison were more willing to buy the land than steal it.

So thousands of Americans began to do something they would do for most of the rest of the century — move west. "Out west" was more an idea than a location, the latter of which changed as the country's borders changed. And the borders changed big time, in large part because of a slave revolt in Haiti.

JOHN JACOB ASTOR

He was the founder of America's first great fortune, and he did it the old-fashioned way: through brains, hard work, and political string-pulling.

Astor was born in Germany in 1763 and came to New York at the age of 20. He parlayed a music store business into real estate, and after 1800, he got into fur trading and importing goods from China. When U.S. companies were barred from foreign trade in 1807, Astor had a clerk pretend to be a Chinese VIP who wanted to go to China for his grandfather's funeral. The trip was approved, and, of course, the ship came back with a fortune in Chinese goods.

During the War of 1812, Astor lost his trading post in Oregon — the first American post on the Pacific coast — to the British. But after helping to finance the U.S. war effort, Astor got Congress to pass a law banning "foreigners" from the U.S. fur trade. That allowed him to buy out his Canadian partners cheaply and establish a lucrative monopoly.

By the time he died in 1848, Astor had amassed a $30 million fortune, some of which went to establish the New York Public Library. *Astor* became synonymous with wealth in America. Oh, the name of that Oregon trading post? *Astoria,* of course.

Capitalizing on Napoleon's going-out-of-business sale

Napoleon Bonaparte, emperor of France, scourge of Europe, and namesake of a good dessert pastry, was in kind of a jam. In 1800, Spain had reluctantly transferred its control of the vast territory of Louisiana, including the key city of New Orleans and the Mississippi River, to France. Napoleon took it with plans to create a vast new French empire on the North American continent.

The following year, Spanish and French officials clamped down on the rights of Americans to use the Mississippi to float their goods and produce to New Orleans for overseas shipment. U.S. farmers and traders howled, and Jefferson considered siding with the British against France. "The day France takes possession of New Orleans," he wrote, "we must marry ourselves to the British fleet and nation."

Instead, he decided to first try to buy a way out. So he sent his friend James Monroe to France in 1803 and instructed Monroe and Robert Livingston, the U.S. ambassador to France, to offer up to $10 million for New Orleans and Florida, or $7.5 million for New Orleans alone.

But by 1803, Napoleon's plans for an American empire had hit a snag on what is now the island of Haiti. Napoleon had sent 35,000 crack French troops to the island to crush a rebellion led by a brilliant former slave named Toussaint L'Ouverture, and it proved to be a very bad idea. More than 24,000 of the French soldiers were wiped out by the Haitians or yellow fever, and the disaster soured the French dictator on the whole subject.

So when the Americans made their pitch, the French flabbergasted them with a counteroffer: Why not buy all of Louisiana? After some dickering, they struck a deal. For 60 million francs (about $15 million), the Louisiana Purchase gave the United States an area that stretched from New Orleans to Canada and from the Mississippi River to what is now Colorado and Idaho (see Figure 7-1). That's 828,000 square miles for about three cents an acre, surely one of the best real-estate bargains in history.

But there was a problem. Under the Constitution, Jefferson had no legal power to make such a deal without congressional approval first. And he knew it, confessing privately that he had "stretched the Constitution till it cracked." Undaunted, he pushed a treaty ratifying the sale through the Senate, and America doubled in size almost overnight. Now it was time to go see what the new half looked like.

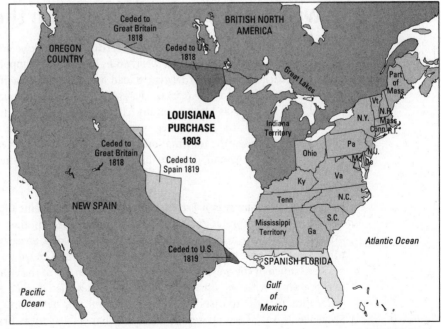

FIGURE 7-1: Territory gained by the Louisiana Purchase.

DUEL TO THE DEATH

Vice President Aaron Burr was a sore loser. So when he lost a bid to become governor of New York in April 1804, he was more than a little angry at his old enemy, Alexander Hamilton, who had helped engineer his defeat. In June, Burr sent a letter to Hamilton demanding an apology for slurs on Burr's character in the newspapers, which had been attributed to Hamilton. When the former treasury secretary refused, Burr challenged him to a duel.

The two met on July 12, on the bluffs above the Hudson River near Weehawken, New Jersey. Hamilton, who detested dueling and who had lost a son in a duel a few years earlier, reportedly fired into the air. But Burr aimed at his rival and shot him. Hamilton died the next day.

Burr continued to be a slime ball. In 1807, he was charged with treason for plotting to overthrow the government, and, failing that, to create a new country in the West. He was acquitted because of a lack of witnesses and then spent the next few years in Europe, trying to find support for an invasion of Mexico. He died in 1836, largely, and deservedly, despised.

Lewis, Clark, and the woman on the coin

Even before the purchase of the Louisiana territory was a done deal, Jefferson had a hankering to send an expedition west. So in late 1803, he appointed a 29-year-old army officer, Meriwether Lewis, to lead a group to the Pacific Ocean. Lewis, who was Jefferson's former private secretary, enlisted a former army colleague named William Clark as his co-captain. Their mission was to find a good route to the Pacific through the mountains, open the area to American fur trading, and gather as much scientific information as they could. Accompanied by 34 soldiers, 10 civilians, and Seaman, Lewis's big Newfoundland dog, the expedition left St. Louis in 1804.

One of the civilians was a French trapper named Toussaint Charbonneau, who served as an interpreter with the Native Americans. Another was Sacagawea, Charbonneau's wife and a member of the Shoshone tribe. Sacagawea was the star of the trip. She gave birth to a son on the expedition and ended up carrying him on her back much of the way. Not only did she know many of the tribes' customs, but her presence with an otherwise all-male group also helped convince Native Americans that the tourists' goals were peaceful. For her efforts, 196 years later, Sacajawea's image was chosen for the U.S. dollar coin that was first issued in early 2000.

The expedition trekked up the Missouri River through what are now the Dakotas and then took a left turn through Montana, Idaho, and Oregon. Traveling by boat, foot, and horseback, the group reached the Pacific near the mouth of the Columbia River in late 1805. After wintering there, they returned to St. Louis in the fall of 1806, having traveled a distance of nearly 7,000 miles in a bit less than three years.

The trip cost $2,500, and it was a smashing success. Only one man died, of a burst appendix. Trouble with the Native Americans was kept to a minimum, and a vast storehouse of knowledge was gained, from information on plants and animals to whether there was land suitable for farming (there was) to whether it was possible to get there and back. Much of the country was thrilled by the stories of a strange new land just waiting to be Americanized.

Fighting Pirates, and a "Dambargo"

Things were going so well for the country in 1804 that Jefferson was reelected in a landslide. But while everyone was excited about what was going on in the West, there was trouble over the eastern horizon.

"To the shores of Tripoli . . ."

For several years, America — as well as other countries — had been paying a yearly tribute to the Barbary States of Algiers, Morocco, Tunis, and Tripoli in North Africa as protection insurance against pirates. But in 1800, the dey (or leader) of Algiers humiliated the U.S. ship that brought the tribute by forcing it to fly the flag of the Ottoman Empire while in Algiers Harbor. The action angered American officials and hastened the building of naval ships that the penny-pinching Jefferson administration had only reluctantly supported.

The following year, the pasha (or leader) of Tripoli declared war on the United States because it wouldn't increase its tribute. Over the next four years, the fledgling American navy dueled with the pasha and his pirates with mixed success. Then in 1805, William Eaton, the former U.S. counsel to Tunis, led a motley force of about 200 Greek and Arab mercenaries — and 9 U.S. Marines (which is where the "to the shores of Tripoli" line in the "Marines' Hymn" comes from) — on a 600-mile desert march. Eaton's force captured the city of Derna. Coupled with the presence of American warships off its harbors, Tripoli was forced to sign a peace treaty, free the American prisoners it was holding, and stop exacting tribute.

Although fighting with other pirates continued off and on for another six or seven years, the victory was a huge shot in the arm for American morale. But the real foreign threat about to surface was from a more familiar source.

AMERICA GETS BOOKISH

On April 24, 1800, Congress passed a resolution creating the Library of Congress, even though it didn't have any books or papers to put in it yet or any building in which to put them. But there were books out there. According to the 1800 census, the country had 50 public libraries, with a total collection of 80,000 books. In 1803, the first tax-supported library opened in Salisbury, Connecticut.

The Library of Congress eventually got settled in Washington and began building a collection under John James Beckley, who was appointed its first chief librarian by Jefferson. Ironically, Jefferson had probably the largest private library in America — some 15,000 volumes. They ended up in the Library of Congress because Jefferson was forced to sell them to the government in later years to pay his private debts.

No one likes a bloodless war

Britain and France were at war again, and the United States was trying to stay out of it — again. One reason for staying out of it was that it was hard to figure out which side to like less. Both countries decided to blockade the other, and that meant French naval ships stopped American ships bound for Britain and seized their cargoes, and the British navy did the same to U.S. ships bound for France or its allies.

But the British also had the maddening habit of *impressments* — pressing Americans into British naval service. Britain relied on its navy for its very survival. But it treated its sailors so poorly that they deserted by the hundreds and sometimes took refuge in the American merchant fleet, where treatment and pay were better. So British warships often stopped American ships and inspected their crews for deserters. And just as often, they helped themselves to American citizens when they couldn't find deserters.

In one particularly galling case in June 1807, the British frigate *Leopard* fired on the U.S. frigate *Chesapeake*, forced the *Chesapeake* to lower its flag, took four "deserters" — including a Native American and an African American — and hanged one of them. The incident infuriated much of the country, and the louder members of Congress called for war.

Jefferson wanted to avoid a fight. Instead, he decided to put pressure on Britain economically. In late 1807, he prodded Congress into passing the Embargo Act, which essentially ended all American commerce with foreign countries. The idea was to hurt Britain — and France, too — in the wallet and force them to ease off American shipping.

Bad idea. While smuggling made up some of the loss, American commerce plunged. U.S. harbors were awash in empty ships, and farmers watched crops once bound for overseas markets rot. Jefferson received hundreds of letters from Americans denouncing the *dambargo,* including one purportedly sent on behalf of 4,000 unemployed seamen. Meanwhile, France and Britain continued to slug it out.

Finally, in early 1809, just before leaving office, Jefferson relented, and Congress passed a milder version of an embargo. But the damage had been done, and the bloodless war was on its way to being replaced with a real one.

"Little Jemmy" Takes the Helm

If James Madison were alive today, he might well be a computer nerd. He was extremely intelligent, conscientious, and focused on the task at hand. A neat dresser who was slight of build (5 feet 4 inches, but he had a big head) and shy in public settings, Madison was referred to by both friend and foe as *Little Jemmy.* He could also be very stubborn.

Madison was easily elected president in 1808. As "the father of the Constitution," he was generally well-regarded. Jefferson, who believed two terms was enough for anyone, had hand-picked Madison to be his successor as the Republican nominee. And the opposing Federalist Party was in such bad shape, it would have had a hard time organizing a one-car funeral.

Madison inherited a messy foreign situation. France and Britain were still at war, and both countries had continued to raid American ships. Jefferson's efforts to stop this practice by cutting off all U.S. trade with foreign countries had nearly sunk a previously buoyant U.S. economy.

So Madison and Congress tried a different approach. In 1809, Congress passed a law that allowed U.S. ships to go wherever they wanted but banned French and British ships from U.S. ports. The following year, Congress lifted all restrictions but gave the president the power to cut off trade with any country that failed to recognize America's neutrality.

The French dictator Napoleon then announced the French would stop their raids if the British agreed to end their blockades of European ports. The British, quite correctly, didn't trust Napoleon and refused. But Madison decided the French despot was sincere and re-imposed the U.S. trade ban on Britain. American merchants, especially in New England, moaned, and the British seethed, but Madison refused to change his mind.

DOLLEY MADISON: PROOF THAT OPPOSITES ATTRACT

If James Madison was kind of a nerd, his wife was anything but. Born in 1768 to a poor Quaker family in Philadelphia, Dolley Payne Todd's marriage to Madison was her second. After her first husband died in 1793, Aaron Burr introduced her to Madison. Within a few months, she was married to "the great little Madison," as she called him.

She took to being First Lady like a duck to water. After all, she had practiced for the job for eight years as the White House's unofficial hostess while Thomas Jefferson, a widower, was president. When Madison took over, Dolley assumed the task of decorating the great house. Her charm also made her a great political asset to her husband. "She is a fine, portly, buxom woman who has a smile and a pleasant welcome for everybody," observed the writer Washington Irving.

Dolley also showed her pluck when the British army invaded Washington and burned the White House. With British soldiers less than a rifle shot away, Dolley stubbornly refused to flee until a portrait of George Washington by the famous artist Gilbert Stuart could be saved. Dolley died in 1849 at the age of 81, 13 years after her husband's death.

New kids on the block

Madison's decision was cheered by a new group of congressmen who took office in 1811. They were led by the new speaker of the House of Representatives, a 34-year-old Kentuckian named Henry Clay, and a 29-year-old lawyer from South Carolina named John C. Calhoun. This new Washington brat pack had missed a chance to participate in the American Revolution, and because so many of them wanted their own chance to fight the British, they became known as the *War Hawks.*

But there was more to the War Hawks' desire for war than just a chance to kick some British butt. Canada belonged to the British Empire, and more than a few land-hungry Americans thought it should belong to the United States. A war with Britain would provide the perfect reason to conquer the neighboring northern nation.

Fighting the Native Americans — again

There was also the perennial vexing issue of what to do about the Native Americans. For the first decade of the century, the American policy had been to buy, coerce, bully, and swindle Native Americans out of their land in the Northwest rather than go to war.

"Sell our country? Why not sell the air, the clouds, and the great sea? Did not the Great Spirit make them all for the use of his children?" —Chief Tecumseh, speaking to Gen. William Henry Harrison, 1810

By 1811, an inspirational Shawnee chief named Tecumseh had had enough. Aided by his religious fanatic brother Tenskwatawa, who was also known as the *Prophet* and who urged a holy war against the whites, Tecumseh rallied tribe after tribe to join his confederacy and stop the white men's invasion. He urged the Native Americans to give up everything white — their clothes, their tools, and especially their alcohol.

By late 1811, Tecumseh had put together a force of several thousand Native Americans. An army of about 1,000 U.S. soldiers, led by Gen. William Henry Harrison, marched to the edge of the territory claimed by Tecumseh at Tippecanoe Creek, Indiana. While Tecumseh was away, his brother led an attack against Harrison. The result of the battle was a draw, but Tecumseh's confederacy began to fall apart.

Why Not Invade Canada This Year?

In Britain, the long war with Napoleon and the trade fights with America had caused hard times, and a lot of British wanted to drop the squabbling with the former colonies and focus on the French. On June 16, 1812, the British government decided to stop raiding American ships. But there was no quick way to get the news to America, which was too bad, because two days later, Congress declared war on England under the rallying cry of "Free Trade and Sailors' Rights."

War was a bold — and foolhardy — move for a country with such a shabby military. The U.S. Army had about 7,000 men and few competent officers. Many of the top officers were antiques from the Revolutionary War 30 years before. One army official, Maj. Gen. Henry Dearborn, was so fat he had to travel in a specially designed cart. The U.S. Navy consisted of 16 ships and a bunch of little gunboats that had been a pet project of Jefferson's and proved to be completely useless. And a sizeable segment of the population was against the war, particularly in New England.

It took about a month to demonstrate just how unready America was. A U.S. command of about 1,500 troops marched to Detroit as a staging ground for an invasion of Canada. When a Canadian army showed up to contest the idea, the American general, William Hull, surrendered without firing a shot.

It was the first of several failed U.S. efforts to conquer Canada, which had looked so easy on paper. After all, the U.S. population was more than 7 million by 1810, while there were fewer than 500,000 white Canadians, many of whom were former Americans. The British army had about 5,000 soldiers in Canada, but there wasn't much chance of them being reinforced because the English were busy fighting Napoleon.

Still, the U.S. efforts managed to fail. After Hull's defeat at Detroit, another U.S. force tried to invade from Fort Niagara. It flopped when many of the New York militia declined to fight outside their own state and refused to cross the river into Canada. A third army set out from Plattsburgh, New York, bound for Montreal and marched 20 miles to the border, only to quit and march back to Plattsburgh.

In September 1813, a U.S. Navy flotilla built and commanded by Capt. Oliver Hazard Perry destroyed a British fleet on Lake Erie. Perry's victory was notable not only for the famous saying that came from it — "We have met the enemy and they are ours" — but also because it forced the British out of Detroit and gave Gen. William Henry Harrison a chance to beat them at the Battle of the Thames River. Tecumseh, the Native American leader who was now a brigadier general in the British army, was killed and, thus, the Native American–Britain alliance was squelched.

The victories kept the British from invading the United States through Canada, but the American efforts to conquer Canada were over.

EVERYONE'S RELATIVE

Sam Wilson was a nice guy. He was born in Arlington, Massachusetts, in 1766; served as a drummer boy and then a soldier in the American Revolution; and in 1789 moved to Troy, New York, to start a meatpacking company. Everyone liked him for his good humor and fair business practices.

In 1812, Wilson's solid reputation landed him a contract to supply meat to the American army. He began the practice of stamping "U.S." on the crates destined for the troops. Because the term "United States" still wasn't often used, federal meat inspectors asked one of Wilson's employees what it stood for. The guy didn't know, so he joked "Uncle Sam," referring to Wilson.

Soon troops began referring to rations as coming from "Uncle Sam," and by 1820, illustrations of Uncle Sam as a national symbol were appearing in newspapers. Wilson died in 1854 at the age of 88. In 1961, Congress recognized his claim to be the original Uncle Sam.

Things were a little better at sea. With most of Britain's navy tied up in Europe, U.S. warships like the *Constitution, United States,* and *President* won several one-on-one battles with British ships and so cheered Congress that it decided to build more ships. But none of the naval engagements were very important from a military standpoint, and after the rest of the formidable British fleet showed up and bottled most of the U.S. Navy up in American ports, the victories at sea ceased.

Three Strikes and the Brits Are Out

By mid-1814, the British had finally defeated Napoleon and sent him into exile. Now they could turn their full attention to the war in America — and America wouldn't be getting any help from France this time.

Britain's first big effort came in August 1814, when a force of about 4,000 veteran British troops landed in the Chesapeake Bay area east of Washington, D.C. At the village of Bladensburg, the Brits encountered a hastily organized force of 6,000 American militiamen who quickly showed they had no stomach for a fight. Almost as soon as the shooting started, the militia ran like scalded dogs, and the British army easily strolled into America's capital.

The government officials fled, and the British burned every public building in the city (see Figure 7-2). The burnings were partially to avenge the American torching of the Canadian city of York and partially to take the heart out of the Yanks. Instead, they enflamed U.S. anger and delayed the British advance on Baltimore, which was the real military target.

REMEMBER

By the time the British forces got to Baltimore, the city's Fort McHenry had been fortified. An all-night bombardment of the fort accomplished nothing, except to inspire a Washington lawyer who watched it from the deck of a British ship, where he was temporarily a prisoner. Francis Scott Key jotted down his impressions in the form of a poem, on the back of a letter. After the battle, he revised it a bit and showed it to his brother-in-law, who set it to the tune of an old English drinking song called "To Anacreon in Heaven." It was published in a Baltimore newspaper as "Defense of Fort McHenry" but was later renamed "The Star-Spangled Banner." Soon soldiers were singing it all over the country. Meanwhile, the British efforts to invade Baltimore ended.

A second, even larger British force attempted an invasion of the United States via a land-water route through New York. In September 1814, a British fleet sailed against an American fleet on Lake Champlain, near Plattsburgh. The U.S. fleet, under the command of Lieutenant Thomas Macdonough, was anchored, and

Macdonough rigged his ships so they could be turned around to use the guns on both sides. After a savage battle, the American fleet prevailed thanks to Macdonough's trick, and the shaken British force retired to Canada.

FIGURE 7-2:
The British army burns the White House.

The third and last major British effort took place at New Orleans. A 20-ship British fleet and 10,000 soldiers squared off against an army of about 5,000 American soldiers, backwoods riflemen, and local pirates who disliked the British more than they disliked the Americans.

The American force was under the command of a tall, gaunt Tennessee general named Andrew Jackson. Jackson had already made a name for himself as a great military leader by defeating the Creek Indians earlier in the war. After a few fights to feel each other out, the two sides tangled in earnest on January 8, 1815.

Actually, it was more of a slaughter than a fight. The British charged directly at Jackson's well-built fortifications, and U.S. cannon and rifles mowed them down. In less than an hour, more than 2,000 British were killed, wounded, or missing, compared to American losses of 71. The British retreated. It was a smashing victory for the United States. Unfortunately for those killed and wounded, it came two weeks after the war had formally ended.

Calling It Even

Almost as soon as the war started, Czar Alexander I of Russia offered to mediate between Britain and America, mostly because he wanted to see Britain concentrate its military efforts against Napoleon. But nothing came of the offer.

Working on a settlement

Early in 1814, both sides agreed to seek a settlement. A few months later, America sent a team of negotiators to Ghent, Belgium, led by its minister to Russia, John Quincy Adams, and House Speaker Henry Clay.

At first, the British negotiators dragged things out while waiting to see how their country's offensive efforts worked out on the battlefield. England then demanded America turn over loads of land in the Northwest Territory and refused to promise to stop kidnapping American sailors off U.S. ships. But when news of the defeats at Plattsburgh and Baltimore reached Ghent, the British tune changed.

They dropped their demands for territory, agreed to set up four commissions to settle boundary disputes, and agreed to stop the habit of impressing American seamen. On December 24, 1814, both sides signed a treaty that basically just declared the war over.

"I hope," said John Quincy Adams in toasting the treaty, "it will be the last treaty of peace between Great Britain and the United States." It was — the countries have never gone to war against each other since.

Squawking about things in New England

In New England, meanwhile, Federalist Party officials had been chafing for a while about the dominance of the Democratic-Republican Party and the waning influence of the region as the country moved west. In late 1814, representatives from five New England states sent delegates to Hartford, Connecticut.

They met for about three weeks and came up with some proposed amendments to the Constitution, including requiring approval by two-thirds of the states before any future embargoes could be set, before war could be declared, or before any new states could be admitted.

There was even some talk about states leaving the Union. (Although it didn't amount to much, it was a chilling harbinger of things to come.) Eventually, three of the delegates were sent to Washington with the demands. They got there just in time to hear about the victory at New Orleans and the treaty at Ghent. They left town quietly.

Thus did a goofy war end. Fewer than 2,000 U.S. soldiers and sailors were killed. No great changes came immediately from it. But the War of 1812 did serve to establish America firmly in the world's eye as a country not to be taken lightly. It may not always choose its fights wisely or fight with a great deal of intelligence. But it would fight.

Chapter 8

Pulling Together to Keep from Falling Apart: 1815–1844

Fresh from a "victory" over England in the War of 1812 (it was really a draw), America was feeling pretty full of itself in 1815. The country made big strides in pulling together. But like any adolescent, America was subject to wild mood swings. As this chapter unfolds, the country suffers an attack of the economic blahs, encounters some pretty sick politicking, and sees one of the most tragic aspects of its national character, slavery, take firm hold.

There's also the election of Andrew Jackson; a speech from Daniel Webster that helps get the North ready to fight the Civil War; the coming of the railroad; and more shameful treatment of Native Americans. Oh, and don't forget the Alamo.

Embracing Nationalism . . . Sort Of

By 1815, the generation that had brought on — and fought through — the American Revolution was fading away. James Monroe, who was elected president in 1816, was the last chief executive to have actually fought in the Revolutionary War. And as the revolutionary crowd faded, so did many of the memories of what it had been like to be individual colonies before uniting to become a single country.

More people began to think of themselves as Americans first and Virginians or Vermonters second. The rising tide of nationalism showed itself in the beginnings of a truly American literature and art. The District of Columbia, rebuilt on the ashes of the capital the British had burned in 1814, became a source of national pride.

But these nationalist feelings were sorely tested by several issues that different sections of the country viewed with different perspectives. These included the banking system, tariffs, public land sales, and Supreme Court decisions on the powers of the central government versus individual states.

Taking it to the bank

The first Bank of the United States, which had helped the nation get a grip on its finances, had been created at the urging of Alexander Hamilton in 1791. But it had been allowed to expire in 1811, and a horde of state-chartered banks swarmed to take its place. In 1811, there were 88 state banks; by 1813, the number was 208, and by 1819, 392. Most of them extended credit and printed currency far in excess of their reserves; when the war with Britain came, most of them couldn't redeem their paper for a tenth of its worth.

In 1816, Congress chartered a second Bank of the United States, with capital of $35 million. The idea was to provide stability to the economy by having a large bank that would serve as the federal government's financial agent. But the new bank's managers were corrupt, stupid, or both, and they lent money like mad to land-crazed Americans flocking to the West.

In 1819, land prices dropped, manufacturing and crop prices collapsed, and scores of overextended banks failed. The yahoos who were first put in charge of the second Bank of the United States finally got the boot; new management stepped in, clamped down hard on credit, and foreclosed on its debtors.

But the Panic of 1819, the nation's first widespread financial crisis, triggered strong resentment toward the Bank, which was nicknamed "the Monster." The Bank was particularly hated in the credit-dependent West, which saw it as a creature of Eastern financiers and speculators. The West's antipathy toward the bank drove a wedge between the regions.

A tariff-ic idea

The largest source of income for the federal government came from *tariffs*, the taxes collected on goods imported into the United States. During the War of 1812, the average tariff doubled, to about 25 percent. In 1816, Congress voted to keep tariffs at those levels.

The idea was that higher tariffs would not only generate money for the government but also drive up prices on foreign goods and thus encourage Americans to buy U.S.-made products. Most sections of the country liked the idea at first, especially the North, where manufacturing of goods from furniture to textiles had developed during the war.

But as time passed, the South and much of the West came to hate tariffs because those regions had little manufacturing to protect, and the taxes just drove up the cost of goods they had to get from somewhere else.

This land is my land, but for how much?

As a new country, America was attracting a crowd. In 1810, the census counted 7.2 million Americans. By 1820, that number shot up to 9.6 million. Much of that was the result of an astonishing birthrate, but an upswing in the number of European immigrants crossing the Atlantic helped as well. The crossing was relatively cheap (maybe $25 from London). No customs, no immigration, no passport. You got off the ship, and you looked for a job. By 1820, an estimated 30,000 people a year were doing just that. Although some immigrant-bashing surfaced when economic times got tough, most newcomers were greeted with a big yawn.

"The American Republic invites nobody to come," wrote Secretary of State John Quincy Adams. "We will keep out nobody. Arrivals will suffer no disadvantages as aliens. But they can expect no advantages either . . . what happens to them depends entirely on their individual ability and exertions, and on good fortune."

One of the reasons for this attitude was that the country had plenty of room. Between 1815 and 1821, six new states joined the Union, bringing the total number to 24. And federal land was cheap and plentiful: $2 an acre for a minimum of 160 acres, with only $80 down and the rest paid over four years.

But when hard times hit in 1819, even those lenient terms were too much. Many folks lost their land to banks when they couldn't pay the mortgage. The banks themselves weren't immune, either: Many failed, taking the settlers' savings with them.

In 1820, Congress lowered the minimum amount of land that could be bought to 80 acres, at $1.25 an acre. The West supported the move, but the North and East, which saw public land as a cash cow to be milked for every dollar that could be squeezed out, were less enthusiastic. Public land thus became another sore point between regions.

Orders from the court

One place where nationalism was secure was in the U.S. Supreme Court. Under Chief Justice John Marshall, the court consistently ruled in favor of a strong central government over the rights of individual states.

In an 1819 case, for example, the court ruled that Maryland had no legal right to try to run the Bank of the United States out of the state by heavily taxing it. "The power to tax is the power to destroy," Marshall wrote, and states had no power to destroy federal institutions. In an 1821 case involving Virginia and an illegal lottery, the court asserted its right to review the decisions of state supreme courts in cases involving powers of the federal government. And the court ruled in 1824 that New York had the power to regulate steamboat commerce only within itself, not between states.

Increasing industry

America was basically a country of farmers for much of the 19th century, but the War of 1812 had cut off the supply of many manufactured goods from Europe and encouraged the growth of domestic industry.

The rise of factories

In 1790, the first factory devoted to spinning cotton into thread opened in New England, and by 1815, there were 213 such factories.

Most goods were still produced and sold by individuals or small companies. But strides in manufacturing interchangeable parts to make assembling objects easier, the use of water- and steam-powered machinery, and increases in demands for American-made goods all helped foster growth in the nonagricultural segment of the economy.

Transportation gets rolling (well, floating)

As the market for goods grew, so did the need for a sound transportation system. Congressional leaders like Henry Clay and John C. Calhoun were eager for the federal government to lead the development of roads and waterways. The idea of federal transportation subsidies was part of what Clay termed *"The American System,"* which also called for U.S. industry-protecting tariffs and a strong national bank system. But Presidents Madison and Monroe balked, claiming that the

Constitution limited the federal government's public works efforts only to projects that crossed state boundaries. Because most states didn't have the money for big road-building projects, traveling or shipping by road remained a real pain in the back pocket.

On the water, however, things were a little different. One of the advantages of moving goods by water is that you can move a lot more with less effort — if you can get the water to go where you want to go and move in the direction you want. The development of the steamboat opened two-way traffic on rivers, particularly the Mississippi, because cargo could go upstream against the current. And construction began in New York in 1817 on a remarkable engineering feat: the 363-mile-long Erie Canal, linking Lake Erie at Buffalo with the Hudson River and Atlantic Ocean. Completed in 1825, the $7 million canal soon repaid its costs through tolls and brought prosperity to the entire region. It also sparked a nationwide canal-building boom as areas raced to link up major natural waterways with man-made ditches.

The Slavery Cancer Grows

In the South, no one was digging canals or building factories. Tobacco, once the major crop, had worn out the soil in many areas, and many Southern planters were looking for a substitute. Cotton was a possibility because of the big demand for it, especially in England. But the variety of cotton that grew well in most of the South was difficult to de-seed.

Cotton and sugar mean more slaves

In 1793, a teacher and inventor from Massachusetts named Eli Whitney visited a plantation in Georgia. Fascinated with the cottonseed problem, Whitney fiddled around and came up with a simple machine that rotated thin wire teeth through the slots of a metal grill. The teeth picked up the cotton fibers and pulled them through the slots, leaving the seeds behind. Whitney's *cotton gin* (short for "engine") could do the work of 50 men. The result was a cotton boom. In 1793, the South produced about 10,000 bales of cotton. By 1820, that amount rose to more than 400,000.

In 1794, a Frenchman in New Orleans named Jean Etienne Bore came up with a method of boiling off sugar cane until it turned into crystals, and the cultivation of sugar spread over the Southeast.

But growing cotton and sugar were labor-intensive activities, and that labor was supplied almost exclusively by slaves. Until the cultivation of cotton and sugar took off, slavery had appeared to be on the decline. A federal constitutional provision had outlawed the importation of any more slaves in 1808, but all the individual states had already banned the practice five years earlier. And the prices of slaves had been steadily dropping, a sign that the economics of the system were too unfavorable to continue it.

Noneconomic reasons also factored in. A religious revival that swept the country in the late 18th and early 19th centuries did much to raise the level of opposition to slavery. In addition, many whites were fearful that an increase in the number of slaves could lead to a massive rebellion such as the one that had happened in Haiti in the 1790s. But the rise of the cotton and sugar crops and the spread of tobacco to new areas increased the dependence of the South on slave labor. Ten to 20 slaves worked every 100 acres of cotton, and they became valuable "commodities." In 1800, the average cost of a slave was about $50; by 1850, it was more than $1,000.

As the need for slaves increased, owners were anxious to increase their holdings through births. But as their value rose, slaves were sold from state to state as the market dictated, often breaking up families. In 1800, the number of slaves in America was put at about 900,000; by 1860, on the eve of the Civil War, the number was 4 million.

In summary, slave owners had a labor force they could force to work at no wages and keep, sell, rape, or kill as they saw fit. To defend the system, the owners often fell back on the rationale that slavery was good for the slave and frequently mentioned in the Bible as a normal human condition.

Opposing slavery

Many Northerners felt compelled to attack the system. Some of the opposition was on moral grounds, but some of it was based on politics. The Constitution allowed slaves to be counted as ³⁄₅ of a person when deciding how many members each state could have in the House of Representatives, and nonslave states resented slave states for gaining more political clout through their nonvoting slaves. In the West, much of the anti-slave sentiment stemmed from free laborers not wanting to have to compete with slave labor.

The truth was that African Americans were discriminated against in the North, too. In most situations, they couldn't vote, testify at trials, marry outside their race, join labor unions, live in "white" areas, or go to school. Free African Americans in the North, especially children, were also at risk of being kidnapped and taken to the South to be sold.

With even well-intentioned antislavery advocates convinced that the two races may not be able to live together, many people supported sending former slaves to

Africa. President Monroe, a Virginia slave owner, pushed in 1819 for the establishment of a colony in Africa where freed American slaves could go. In 1824, the colony of Liberia was established, with its capital of Monrovia named after Monroe. But many American-born freed slaves had no interest in going to a strange country. They preferred to take their chances on staking a claim to their birthrights as American citizens.

Compromising over Missouri

In February 1819, the territory of Missouri petitioned Congress to be admitted as a state. At the time, America consisted of 11 slave and 11 free states, so the question was whether Missouri, with 10,000 slaves, should be admitted as a slave state or be forced to free its slaves before it was allowed into the fold. Debate on the issue raged across the country. Finally, Henry Clay crafted a compromise in March 1820. Under the aptly named *Missouri Compromise*, Missouri was admitted as a slave state, and the territory of Maine came in as a free state, keeping a balance of 12 slave and 12 free. Figure 8-1 shows a breakdown of the slave/free arrangement created by the compromise. Congress also deemed that slavery would be excluded from any new states or territories above latitude 36 degrees, 30 minutes.

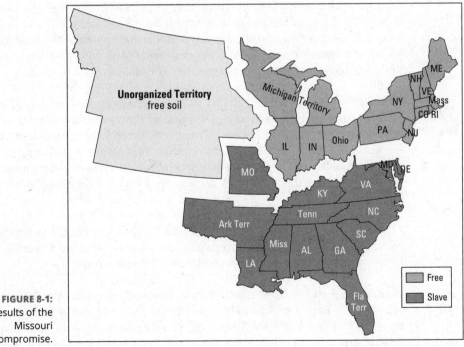

FIGURE 8-1:
Results of the Missouri Compromise.

© *John Wiley & Sons, Inc.*

Proslavery forces grumbled that Congress had no constitutional right to say where slavery could and couldn't occur; antislavery forces complained that the compromise was an admission that slavery was acceptable. But the compromise held for the next three decades, giving the country a little more time to seek a better solution it would not find.

"[T]his momentous question [the spread of slavery], like a fire bell in the night, awakened and filled me with terror. I considered it at once as the knell of the Union," noted slaveholder Thomas Jefferson. "(W)e have the wolf by the ears, and we can neither hold him, nor safely let him go."

Mind your own hemisphere: The Monroe Doctrine

While the issue of slavery was growing at home, big events were happening elsewhere in the Americas. Spain's Latin American colonies were struggling for their independence, and U.S. citizens generally supported the struggles as being like their own with the British.

In 1819, after Spain had sold Florida to America for $5 million and a promise that the United States would keep its hands off Texas, President Monroe urged Congress to formally recognize the newly independent Latin American countries, including Mexico. In Europe, meanwhile, a group of monarchs known as the Holy Alliance was scheming to pick off Spain's former colonies. And on the Pacific Coast, the Russians claimed an area from present-day Washington State to Alaska.

REMEMBER

Declining an offer from the English to go in as partners against the Holy Alliance's plans, Monroe and his secretary of state, John Quincy Adams, decided to issue what became known as the *Monroe Doctrine*, which amounted to a hands-off warning in the Western Hemisphere. In December 1823, Monroe told Congress that America wouldn't tolerate further attempts by European powers to colonize in the New World. What they had, they could keep, he said. Everything else was off limits.

"The American continents, by the free and independent condition which they have assumed and maintained, are henceforth not to be considered as subjects for future colonization by any European powers," Monroe wrote.

Although it probably had little to do with Monroe's warning, the Russians did agree in 1824 to pull back to what is now the southern border of Alaska and stay there. In fact, Monroe's statements didn't really have much to back them up, because American military might was slight. But the Monroe Doctrine was subsequently employed by various presidents as the basis for interfering in, or staying out of, the affairs of neighboring countries.

Mud-Wrestling to the White House

In 1816, presidential politics were pretty dignified. In 1824, they were pretty disgusting. Democratic-Republican James Monroe was elected in 1816, easily beating Rufus King, the last candidate the Federalist Party would ever nominate. Monroe wasn't brilliant. But he had common sense and was so honest Thomas Jefferson said, "[T]urn his soul wrong side outwards, and there is not a speck on it."

Monroe was so immensely popular he won reelection in 1820 with all but one electoral vote. But in 1824 he followed the tradition started by Washington and didn't seek a third term. With no need to unite behind one candidate because the Federalist Party was extinct, plenty of Republicans decided to run. They included Monroe's secretary of state, John Quincy Adams; House Speaker Henry Clay; Treasury Secretary William Crawford; Secretary of War John C. Calhoun; and war hero General Andrew Jackson.

Adams wins, but Jackson isn't done

By the 1824 election, Calhoun had dropped out in favor of running (successfully) for vice president, and Crawford had suffered a stroke that left him unable to serve. Despite a bitter, nasty campaign and the crowded field, voter turnout was only 27 percent.

When the electoral votes were counted, Jackson had 99, Adams 84, Crawford 41, and Clay 37. Because no one had a majority, the Constitution required that the House of Representatives pick the winner. Clay had no love for Adams but even less for Jackson, so he threw his support to Adams.

The son of former president John Adams, Adams was an intelligent and disciplined visionary — and a lousy politician. He refused to use his appointment powers to win support and then appointed Clay as his secretary of state despite their well-known personal differences. Clay's appointment set off howls of protest — many viewed it as a political payoff for Clay's support in the House showdown for the presidency — and it became known as "the Corrupt Bargain." It marred Adams's time in office almost from the start.

Jackson, meanwhile, never stopped running in what turned out to be one of the longest and sleaziest presidential campaigns in American history. His supporters attacked Adams as an aristocrat who had lived his entire life at the public trough. When Adams bought a billiard table and chess set with his own funds, they accused him of turning the White House into "a den of gambling." And Adams was charged with supplying a young American girl for the pleasure of the Russian tsar while he was U.S. minister to Russia.

The Adams camp counterattacked. Jackson, they said, was a murderer, a slave-trader, and a bigamist. A pro-Adams newspaper claimed Jackson's mother was a prostitute brought to America by British soldiers. Posters were distributed listing 18 people Jackson had supposedly killed.

The mudslinging may have been sleazy, but it sure brought out the vote. The turnout in 1828 was 58 percent, more than twice that of 1824. It was also the first truly democratic presidential election because in 22 of the 24 states, the popular vote determined how many electoral votes went to each candidate. When the votes were tallied, Jackson had 178 electoral votes to Adams's 83. Adams returned to Massachusetts, was elected to Congress (the first president ever to do so after his presidency), and served until his death in 1848. Jackson went to Washington and ushered in a new American era.

Old Hickory: The Jackson presidency

Andrew Jackson wasn't in a good mood when he arrived in Washington in early 1829 to become president. His beloved wife, Rachel, had died two months before, shortly after discovering that she had been the target of vicious personal attacks during the 1828 election. Jackson was sure the discovery contributed to her death, and he was bitterly angry.

But if Jackson was angry, the thousands of his supporters who came to see him take the oath of office were jubilant. Jackson was the first Westerner to win the office and the first to come from humble beginnings. Though some came just to cheer their hero, many came hoping for a cushy government job.

More than 20,000 people surrounded the Capitol for the inauguration. Jackson gave a speech that hardly anyone heard and then fought his way through the crowd and went off to a reception at the White House. So did almost everyone else. Hordes of people crowded into the place, drinking, eating, and stealing souvenirs. Jackson escaped through a back window and spent the first night of his presidency in a nearby hotel.

Jackson's supporters were referred to as "the mob" by Washington onlookers used to more refinement and less tobacco-spitting, but the mob also reflected a growing sense of democracy in America. More people had the vote and were using it. Cheap newspapers and magazines were flourishing, giving the common man access to ideas and information. The average guy was finding his voice, and in Jackson, a focus for his admiration.

Jackson was the first president since Washington who hadn't been to college. He was tall and thin (6 feet 1 inch, 145 pounds) with a full mane of silver-gray hair and hawklike features. He was born into a desperately poor Irish immigrant family in the Carolina colonies in 1767.

As a boy, Jackson received a sword cut on his head from a British officer who thought the boy hadn't been humble enough, and Jackson learned never to let a slight or insult go unanswered. He had a violent temper, although he often pretended to be angry just to get his way. Like many military men, he was often inflexible when he made up his mind. His friends called him "Old Hickory" or "Gineral;" his foes called him "King Andrew."

As a Western lawyer and politician, Jackson had seen firsthand how the West was often at the mercy of Eastern financial interests, and he had a Westerner's distrust of banks. But as a wealthy man by the time he became president, he didn't champion the idea that all men are equal. Instead, he believed that every man should have an equal chance to succeed, and that no one's rights were more important than another's — unless you were a woman, a Native American, or an African American.

REMEMBER

Jackson was also a believer in an adage offered by a New York politician at the time: "To the victors belong the spoils of the enemy." That meant replacing federal officeholders who had been appointed by previous administrations with his own appointees in what became known as the *spoils system.* Jackson's theory was that most government jobs weren't very tough and that personnel should be changed up to bring in new ideas.

KILL OR CURE

By 1810, America had five formal medical schools in operation. Still, most "doctors" received their training by spending an apprenticeship with someone who had been trained the same way.

Many doctors followed the teachings of Benjamin Rush, a Philadelphia physician and medical professor. Rush advocated bleeding, purging, blistering, sweating, and puking as ways of relieving disease symptoms. He also believed Africans had dark skin from a form of leprosy. Rush's ideas were popular through the middle of the 19th century. But he wasn't all bad: He did advocate the humane treatment of the mentally ill.

Medicine was so riddled with quacks and so unregulated that distrust of physicians was rampant, and many Americans turned to home remedies, like these described in an 1828 book of household hints: "A good quantity of old cheese is the best thing to eat when distressed by eating too much fruit, or oppressed with any kind of food . . . honey and milk is very good for worms; so is strong salt water . . . for a sudden attack of quincy or croup, bathe the neck with bear's grease, and pour it down the throat."

Jackson didn't invent this idea; all the presidents since Washington had done it to some degree. In fact, in his eight years in office, Jackson only turned out about 20 percent of the 1,100-member federal bureaucracy. And many of them needed turning out because they were inept or corrupt.

But the spoils system changed qualifications to hold a federal post from being able or experienced to being a campaign worker or contributor. It gave rise to political machines by giving them something to reward supporters with, and it reduced the efficiency of government. Jackson's efforts to democratize the government created problems that took decades to fix.

Nullify This

John C. Calhoun had waited a long time to be president. Intelligent but humorless, the South Carolinian had served as vice president under John Quincy Adams and was now vice president under Jackson. Then, as now, the best part about being vice president was that it made becoming president easier, and Calhoun figured to follow Jackson into the White House. But two relatively trivial things happened to throw him off-course and, in a way, helped push the country toward civil war. The first involved the wife of Jackson's old friend and secretary of war, John Eaton. Peggy Eaton had a reputation of being something of a slut, which she may or may not have deserved. But Washington society's leading females — led by Calhoun's wife — snubbed her.

Jackson, whose own wife had been the target of scandalous gossip, was enraged at the snubs. At one point he called an evening Cabinet meeting to defend Mrs. Eaton. The issue, dubbed "Eaton Malaria" by Washington wags, dominated the first months of Jackson's presidency and drove a wedge between Jackson and Calhoun. The second incident involved a letter Jackson received from Calhoun's enemies suggesting that Calhoun had called for Jackson to be court-martialed for invading Florida when it was still owned by Spain. When confronted, Calhoun could provide only vague explanations. The rift between the two men grew, and Jackson turned his favor to his secretary of state, Martin Van Buren, to succeed him as president.

REMEMBER

Calhoun eventually resigned as vice president and was immediately elected a senator from South Carolina. When it was clear he wouldn't become president, Calhoun abandoned his support of a strong central government and became a champion of the rights of states to pick and choose what federal laws they would obey, a theory of government called *nullification*.

The nullification debate hits the Senate

Calhoun's embrace of states' rights and nullification further pushed him from Jackson. Even though he was a Westerner and a slave owner, Jackson was an ardent nationalist. At a White House dinner, when nullification proponents tested his loyalties by offering a series of toasts about states' rights, Jackson responded, "Our Federal Union: It must be preserved!" (To which Calhoun replied, "The Union — next to our liberty, the most dear!")

Despite Jackson's support, nationalism was having a tough time. In the Senate, a January 1830, debate on whether to stop selling public land in the West turned into a debate on nullification. Senator Robert Hayne of South Carolina gave an impassioned and eloquent speech in favor of the idea, pointing out that it was the only way a state could safeguard its interests.

Then Daniel Webster of Massachusetts took the floor. Webster was one of the greatest orators in U.S. history. Dark and imposing, with eyes that glowed like coals and a deep but pleasing voice, Webster spoke for hours. The people, not the states, had ratified the Constitution, he said, and if the states were allowed to decide which sections they would or wouldn't subscribe to, the country would be held together by nothing but "a rope of sand."

Webster's speech had a spectacular effect. Within three months, 40,000 copies had been published, and within a few years, parts of it were standard reading in textbooks throughout the North and West. Hundreds of thousands of young Northerners and Westerners were exposed to its sentiments — including a 21-year-old man on his way to Illinois named Abraham Lincoln. For many of them, the speech became words worth fighting for.

A tarrible idea

In 1828, Congress had passed a bill that set high tariffs on a bunch of imported goods. The tariffs were favored in the North because they drove up prices of imported goods and, thus, made goods from Northern factories more attractive. The West was okay with the bill because tariff revenues were supposed to pay for public works projects the region needed. But the South, without factories and with less need for roads and canals, hated them.

In 1832, Congress passed a new tariff schedule lower than the 1828 rates. But it wasn't enough for South Carolina legislators. They convened a special convention, which decided that not only was the tariff null and void in South Carolina, but the state would also militarily defend its right to nullify the law.

NAT TURNER'S REBELLION

Despite all the rhetoric about how well they treated their slaves and how happy the slaves were, Southern slave owners' deepest fear was that the humans they so degraded would someday rise up to seek freedom — and revenge. Slave rebellions, in fact, had occurred in both Northern and Southern states and had been responded to with harsh brutality.

In 1822, for example, just the rumor of a possible uprising resulted in the execution of 37 slaves in South Carolina. In August 1831, however, a preacher/slave named Nat Turner led 70 followers on a murderous rampage around Southampton, Virginia. Before the uprising was over, Turner's group had murdered 57 white men, women, and children. The rebellion was broken up quickly, and after two months in hiding, Turner was captured and hanged, along with 19 others.

But the rebellion sent shock waves through the South. In retaliation, about 100 slaves were slain at random. New laws were passed to make it harder for owners to free slaves, to restrict the ability of slaves to travel without supervision, and to censor anti-slavery material. Any serious talk of the South voluntarily freeing its slaves ceased.

The move infuriated Jackson, and he sent some army and navy units to the state while he prepared a larger force "to crush the rebellion." Fortunately, cooler heads prevailed. Henry Clay, the great negotiator, came up with a compromise tariff that reduced the rates over a decade. The South decided it could live with that without losing face. Both sides claimed victory, and a bloody civil clash was once again delayed.

Bringing down the Bank

With South Carolina back in the fold, Jackson was easily reelected in 1832, despite his ill health and his earlier statements that he would serve only one term. Part of the reason he sought a second term was to thrash his old foe, Henry Clay, who was the first nominee of the new National Republican Party (which would soon take the name of the opposition party to the English king and become the Whigs). Another factor was that Jackson had some unfinished business with a bank.

The charter of the country's only nationwide bank, the Bank of the United States, was set to expire in 1836, and Clay pushed a bill through Congress in 1832 to extend it. But Jackson vetoed the bill, contending the Bank was a corrupt private monopoly that fed off little banks and benefited only a handful of rich American and foreign investors.

The Bank's stock was in fact controlled by a relatively few men, and the charge of corruption also had its truth. Bank president Nicholas Biddle was a brilliant but arrogant aristocrat who often loaned money at no or low interest to the "right people" — including dozens of members of Congress — while clamping down hard on banks in the West. But since 1819, the Bank had provided stability to the economy by requiring local banks to keep adequate gold and silver reserves to back up the currency they issued and to be careful about making loans.

After his veto, Jackson decided to kill the Bank off rather than wait until 1836. So in 1832, he ordered that all federal funds be withdrawn from it and deposited in smaller banks. When his treasury secretary balked, he got a new one, and when that one also balked, he got a third who agreed to go along.

At first, the plan worked pretty well, mostly because the economy was sailing along. The federal government's budget deficit dropped to zero for the first time in history; the budget even had a surplus, which was shared with the states for projects like road building and education. But then the boom busted.

In 1836, Jackson ordered that all public land could be sold only for silver or gold, not paper currency. Land sales sagged from 22 million acres to 6 million in one year. Local banks held mortgages that weren't being paid, and they couldn't foreclose because the land was worth little and no one could buy it anyway. In 1837, after a bank panic, the country sank into a four-year recession. But by that time, Jackson was out of office, and it was someone else's problem.

Inventing a Better Life

While politicians were debating lofty issues like nullification and national banks, other people were creating better ways to get around, get something to eat, and get their points across.

Riding the train

On September 18, 1830, a nine-mile race on the outskirts of Baltimore pitted a horse pulling a carriage against a noisy contraption on wooden wheels called a steam locomotive engine. The horse won after the engine broke down, but it was a relatively short-lived victory for Old Paint, because the railroad had arrived in America.

Although trains had been operating in England for some years, the Baltimore & Ohio (B&O) line's *Tom Thumb* was the first in the United States. By the end of 1830, the B&O had carried 80,000 passengers along a 13-mile track. In South Carolina, a 136-mile line between Charleston and Hamburg opened in 1833. By 1840,

409 railroads had laid 3,300 miles of track, and by 1860, America had close to 30,000 miles of rail.

Early trains had their flaws. Sparks caused fires along the tracks and in the rail cars, and the rails themselves had a nasty habit of coming up through the bottoms of the cars. Trains were also subject to the occasional explosion, which hardly ever happened with horses.

But trains had an enormous impact. The demands for labor to build tracks encouraged immigration, and the demand for capital to finance the lines attracted foreign investment. The ability to transport large amounts of goods and agricultural products opened new markets and linked old ones. Communications improved vastly, and going from here to there got a whole lot easier. Even philosopher Henry David Thoreau conceded, "When I hear the iron horse make the hills echo with his snort, like thunder, shaking the earth with his feet and breathing fire and smoke . . . it seems the earth had got a race now worthy to inhabit it."

Reaping what you sow

As the nation grew, so did its appetite. Steel plows, most notably the kind developed by Illinois blacksmith John Deere, had made it easier to plant crops. But harvesting, especially grain, was still a laborious process that involved men swinging heavy scythes all day long and then going back and picking up the threshed grain.

In 1831, a Pennsylvanian named Cyrus McCormick came up with a rolling machine that both cut down the grain and threw it onto a platform. McCormick's machine could do the work of 15 men, and more quickly. By 1860, he was making 4,000 harvesters a year and selling them on an "installment" plan so farmers could afford them by paying off a little at a time. America's breadbasket got much bigger because of it.

ON TONIGHT'S MENU . . .

Nineteenth-century Americans didn't waste much when it came to chow. Some samples from an 1836 book called *The Frugal Housewife*: "A bullock's heart is very profitable to use as a steak, broiled just like beef. There are usually five pounds in a heart, and it can be bought for 25 cents . . . . Calf's head should be cleansed with very great care . . . . The brains, after being thoroughly washed, should be put in a little bag, with one pounded cracker, or as much crumbled bread, seasoned with sifted sage and tied up and boiled one hour. After the brains are boiled, they should be well broken up with a knife, and peppered, salted and buttered."

Communicating across America

In New York, a painter named Samuel F.B. Morse was tinkering with a device he called the telegraph, which could send messages using electricity. After he patented it, in 1841, Morse got Congress to put up $30,000 so he could string electric wire between Washington and Baltimore. On March 24, 1844, the first message — "What hath God wrought?" — was sent. In 1856, the Western Union Company was formed, and by 1866, a transatlantic telegraph cable had been laid between America and Europe.

The telegraph was the first true mass communication medium. By 1900, there were few places in the world that couldn't send and receive messages. Not everyone, however, was impressed. When someone remarked that, with the telegraph, Maine could now talk to Florida, writer Ralph Waldo Emerson reportedly observed, "Yes, but has Maine anything to *say* to Florida?"

Staking Out New Land

When not busy inventing things, Americans were on the move, mostly in a westerly direction. That movement was unfortunate for the Native Americans already there. It also proved unfortunate for the Mexican government, which was determined to hold onto an area known as "Tejas" in Spanish. Americans called it Texas.

Pushing out the Native Americans

A Native American name for Andrew Jackson was "Long Knife," and not because they considered him a swell guy. For his part, Jackson contended he didn't hate the Native Americans despite the fact that as a soldier he had killed them and burned their villages. He just didn't want them where they would be in the way.

Therefore, Jackson wholeheartedly supported a policy (actually started by Pres. James Monroe) to systematically move all the Native Americans east of the Mississippi River to west of the Mississippi, or off the fertile acreage of the river valley and onto the dusty prairies of what is now Oklahoma.

In 1830, Congress passed the Indian Removal Act and set aside $500,000 for the task. By the time the odious job was done in the 1840s, more than 100,000 natives had been moved off more than 200 million acres. Proponents contended the forced exodus was humane, because the only practical alternative was to kill them. This conveniently ignored the fact that thousands of Native Americans did die — of disease, hunger, and exposure — on the forced marches, giving rise to the term *Trail of Tears.* Of all the nation's leaders, only Henry Clay spoke out against the policy.

SEQUOYAH

If the Cherokee, or any other Native Americans for that matter, wanted to jot down their thoughts, they had to do it in English because none of the tribes had a written language. Sequoyah, a Tennessee-born Cherokee trader, hunter, diplomat, and genius, changed that.

In 1809, Sequoyah began work on an 86-letter alphabet for the Cherokee language, using symbols from an English grammar book and then adding to them as needed to reproduce the sounds of Cherokee. By 1821, the language could be read and written, and the Cherokee could now preserve their ancient traditions and culture on paper. *Sequoyah,* by the way, means "hog's foot" in Cherokee.

Later in his life, Sequoyah acted as a mediator with federal officials when the Cherokee were forced off their lands in the Southeast and moved to the Indian Territory in present-day Oklahoma. He died in 1843 but left a version of his name behind in the giant sequoia trees of California and Sequoia National Park.

Two tribes, in particular, didn't go easily. The Sauk and Fox tribe, led by Chief Black Hawk, originally crossed the Mississippi and then came back. Met by a large U.S. military force that included an Illinois militia volunteer named Abe Lincoln, the tribe surrendered after bloody fights in which women and children were slaughtered along with the native warriors. In Florida, the Seminoles under Chief Osceola used the swamps and Everglades to fight for a decade before ultimately surrendering. The war with the Seminoles cost the U.S. military $20 million and 1,500 lives.

In the Southeast, the so-called civilized tribes of the Cherokee, Creek, Choctaw, and Chickasaw had actually been pretty adaptable to the encroaching white man's ways. They built roads and houses, raised cattle, and farmed. Some even owned slaves. When the state of Georgia tried to force the Cherokee off their land, they appealed to the U.S. Supreme Court, which ruled in their favor. But the ruling didn't help; what the state couldn't do, the federal government could. By the end of the 1840s, most of the Native Americans in the eastern United States were gone.

Claiming independence for Texas

Everyone wanted Texas. Pres. John Quincy Adams offered $1 million for it; Andrew Jackson upped the offer to $5 million. The newly independent country of Mexico wasn't interested in selling the area, even though it was sparsely settled and Mexico had no firm plans for it. But Mexico did allow Americans to settle there.

Growing the American base

In late 1825, the Virginia-born Stephen Austin had settled 300 American families in an area near San Antonio. By 1834, Austin's colony had 20,000 white colonists and 2,000 slaves. That was four times the number of Mexicans in Texas. Slavery was abolished in Mexico in 1831, but Austin ignored the law, as well as the one requiring the settlers to convert to Roman Catholicism. The settlers began thinking of themselves less as Mexican subjects and more as a cross between Mexicans and Texans — or *Texians,* as they called themselves.

The area began to attract restless and sometimes lawless Americans who weren't as peaceful as the Austin bunch. These folks included Sam Houston, a soldier and good friend of Andrew Jackson's; the Bowie brothers, Louisiana slave smugglers who had designed an impressive long knife that bore their name; and David Crockett, a Tennessee ex-congressman and daredevil backwoodsman with a flair for self-promotion.

Remembering the Alamo

In 1835, Mexican Pres. Antonio López de Santa Anna proclaimed a new constitution that eliminated any special privileges for Texas, and the Texians declared their independence. They kicked the Mexican soldiers out of the garrison at San Antonio, and a motley force of 187 Texians and American volunteers set up a fort in an old mission called the Alamo.

On March 6, 1836, after a 13-day siege and a brief predawn battle, Santa Anna's army of about 5,000 overran the Alamo, despite heavy Mexican losses, and killed all its defenders. The victory accomplished little for Santa Anna, but "Remember the Alamo" became a rallying cry for Texians. Six weeks after the Alamo fell, an army led by Sam Houston surprised, defeated, and captured Santa Anna at the San Jacinto River.

Becoming a state

Texas ratified a constitution that included slavery and waited to be annexed to the United States. But Jackson was in no hurry. He didn't want a war with Mexico that could ruin the election chances of his handpicked successor, Martin Van Buren. And the fact that Texas was proslavery would upset the delicate balance between free and slave states.

Jackson did formally recognize Texas on his last day in office in March 1841, after Van Buren had been elected. But it wasn't until December 1845 that the Lone Star Republic became the Lone Star State.

Changing it up at president

In the 16 years between 1820 and 1836, America had three presidents. In the eight years between 1836 and 1844, it also had three.

"The Little Magician"

The first was Martin Van Buren, who was the first president born under the U.S. flag. Van Buren was a New York lawyer and governor whose political machine had helped elect Jackson. Dubbed "the Little Magician" for his political skills, Van Buren snuggled up to Jackson, serving as secretary of state and vice president and winning Jackson's considerable support in beating Whig candidate William Henry Harrison.

Unfortunately for him, Van Buren took office just as the Panic of 1837 and its subsequent economic recession hit the country. The recession lasted most of his term, and he was blamed for it. But he did manage to strike a blow for labor, agreeing to lower the working day for federal employees to ten hours.

"Old Tippecanoe"

Despite his vast political skills, Van Buren was outfoxed by the Whigs when he ran for reelection. It began when a Democratic newspaper sneered at Harrison, who was again Van Buren's opponent: "Give him [Harrison] a barrel of hard cider and settle a pension of two thousand a year on him, and . . . he will sit the remainder of his days in a log cabin."

That image didn't sound like a bad idea to a lot of voters. Harrison, an old Native-American fighter who had defeated Tecumseh at the Battle of Tippecanoe Creek in 1811, was actually a moderately wealthy Virginia farmer. But the Whigs seized on the chance to present him as a tough frontiersman. Rallies were held featuring log cabins and plenty of hard cider, and "Old Tippecanoe" squashed Van Buren in the election.

At his inauguration on March 4, 1841, a hatless 68-year-old Harrison gave a long and pointless speech in a pouring rainstorm. He fell ill with pneumonia and died a month later, making him the first president to die in office.

And Tyler, too

His successor was the newly elected vice president: John Tyler, a stubborn slave owner from Virginia who had only become a Whig because he had a falling out with the Democrats and Jackson over the nullification issue.

Tyler earned the distinction of being the only sitting president thrown out of his own political party when he refused to go along with Whig policies in Congress and vetoed many Whig bills. In 1844, Tyler started his own party, the Democratic-Republicans, so he could run again, but he gave up after Jackson asked him to step aside.

In 1844, the Whigs put up Henry Clay, who had been running in vain for president for 20 years. Democrats, after a heated convention, nominated a *dark horse*, or surprise candidate, in James K. Polk of Tennessee. Polk was such an ardent follower of Jackson that he was called "Young Hickory."

It was a very close election, but Polk squeaked through. He made few promises during his campaign, among them: to acquire California from Mexico, to settle a dispute with England over the Oregon border, to lower the tariff, and not to seek a second term. When he took over the presidency in March 1845, he kept all of them.

Chapter 9

War, Gold, and a Gathering Storm: 1845–1860

I n the 1840s, it seemed America had an unscratchable itch for elbowroom. It annexed Texas, quarreled with England over Oregon, and took half a million square miles of real estate from Mexico. A good part of the nation — and the world, for that matter — came down with gold fever, too.

In the 1850s, however, much of the country's attention was on trying to cure the seemingly incurable disease of slavery without amputating part of the Union.

Wrenching Land from Mexico

Pres. James K. Polk was a hard worker with a thick hide, which are good traits in a president. He worked 18-hour days, didn't miss many days at the office, and was goal-oriented. One of his goals was to buy California. That would give America a base on two oceans and fulfill its *Manifest Destiny*, a term coined by a New York journalist in 1845. The term referred to the idea it was God's will that America spread across the continent.

But Mexican leaders weren't in a selling mood. They were furious that Texas, which had been independent from Mexico for a decade, was admitted as an American state in 1845. So when Polk sent diplomat James Slidell to Mexico City with an offer to buy California for around $25 million, Mexican leaders refused to even meet with Slidell.

Provoking a war

Polk then decided to take California by force, pushing America into its first war whose primary purpose was simply to gain territory. A young Army lieutenant named Ulysses S. Grant called it "one of the most unjust [wars] ever waged by a stronger against a weaker nation."

It took a little prompting to get it started without firing the first shot. Polk sent an "army of observation," under the command of Gen. Zachary Taylor, to the banks of the Rio Grande River, an area that Mexico considered its territory. The army was gradually built up until there were about 4,000 U.S. troops there in April 1846. Taylor's soldiers managed to provoke a small attack by Mexican troops, and the war was on.

As wars go, it wasn't much. The United States lost 13,000 men, 11,000 of them to disease, and won every major battle. The Mexican army was badly led, badly equipped, and badly trained. The American army, while sometimes short on supplies because Polk was a penny pincher, was very well led, chiefly by Taylor and Gen. Winfield Scott.

Taylor, whose men called him "Old Rough and Ready" because he was tough (and something of a slob), was a career soldier. So was Scott, whose nickname was "Old Fuss and Feathers" because he had a taste for pomp and showy uniforms. Scott and Taylor were ably supported by West Point-trained officers such as Grant and Capt. Robert E. Lee, as well as others to whom the Mexican War would prove a training ground for the Civil War 15 years later.

The first major battle, at Palo Alto, gave a taste of what was to come. Taylor led 2,300 soldiers against a Mexican army of 4,500 and routed them. In a follow-up fight, a U.S. force of 1,700 scattered a Mexican force of 7,500. American losses totaled less than 50 men for the two fights; the Mexicans lost more than 1,000.

In fact, the biggest American worry was that it might have to fight Britain at the same time over a dispute in the Northwest. American officials insisted that a boundary line between America and Canada be drawn at latitude 54 degrees, 40 minutes (which would have given the United States Vancouver, British Columbia). A slogan from Polk's campaign, "54-40 or fight," became popular with some of the more pugnacious members of Congress. But in July 1846, the two sides agreed to compromise at 49 degrees.

Capturing California and the Southwest

The United States then turned its full attention to acquiring California, which was easily captured. Many Mexicans in California considered themselves "Californios" first and weren't too concerned about a U.S. takeover.

In Mexico, meanwhile, U.S. forces kept their undefeated streak going. Mexican forces were now commanded by Gen. Antonio López de Santa Anna of Alamo infamy. Santa Anna, who had been in exile in Cuba, talked U.S. officials into helping him sneak back into Mexico, where he promised he would sell his country out. Once there, he promptly took over command of the army and vowed to crush the hated Yankees.

In September 1846, Taylor's troops took the city of Monterrey, Mexico. In March 1847, Scott captured the fortified seaport of Vera Cruz after a three-week siege. And in September 1847, his forces captured Mexico City, all but ending the war.

The formalities were contained in the Treaty of Guadalupe Hidalgo. It gave America more than 500,000 square miles of Mexican territory (see Figure 9-1), including California, Nevada, Utah, Arizona, and parts of New Mexico, Wyoming, and Colorado. Mexico dropped claims to Texas. Perhaps to soothe a guilty conscience, Polk agreed to pay Mexico $18.25 million, about 80 percent of what he offered before the war.

REMEMBER

Not everyone was thrilled. In Congress, a gangly representative from Illinois named Abe Lincoln attacked the war as unjust aggression. In Massachusetts, the iconoclastic writer Henry David Thoreau refused to pay his poll tax because the money might be used to support the war. His aunt paid it for him after he spent only one night in jail, but the essay that came out of it, "Civil Disobedience," became a handbook for nonviolent protestors and passive resistance demonstrators around the world well into the next century.

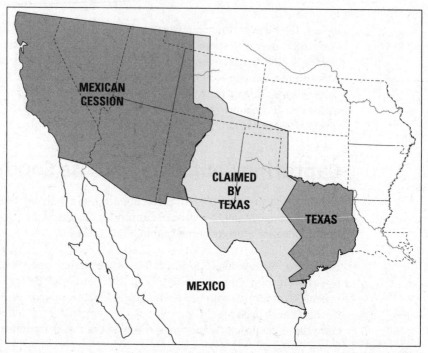

FIGURE 9-1:
Territory won
from Mexico.

Much of the dissent stemmed not just from being uncomfortable about picking on Mexico, but also from fears the war was designed to acquire more territory for the spread of slavery. "They just want Californy / So's to lug new slave states in / To abuse ye and to scorn ye / And to plunder ye like sin," wrote poet James Russell Lowell in 1848. But even as Lowell wrote, a richer reason was lying on the bottom of a California river.

Rushing for Gold

On the chilly morning of January 24, 1848, a man looked down into a sawmill ditch off the American River, about 40 miles east of Sacramento, California (or 120 miles east of Yerba Buena, which soon became known as San Francisco). The man, a dour carpenter from New Jersey named James Marshall, saw a pea-shaped dollop of yellow metal glinting in the gravel.

"Boys," Marshall told the group of laborers who were helping build the sawmill, "by God, I believe I have found a gold mine."

What he had really found was the ignition switch for one of the most massive migrations in human history: the California gold rush. It was quite literally a rush, as soon as the news got out. That took awhile. Although rumors of the find surfaced in the East not long after Marshall's discovery, no one paid much attention. Then President Polk announced in December 1848 that there looked to be enough gold in California to pay for the costs of the Mexican War many times over. That made people sit up and take notice.

Risking life and limb to strike gold

More than 90,000 people made their way to California in the two years following the first discovery and more than 300,000 by 1854 — or 1 of about every 90 people then living in the United States. The stampede ripped families apart and stripped towns of a large percentage of their young men. Not all the prospectors were American. An 1850 census found that 25 percent of those counted were from countries as far away as Australia and China.

REMEMBER

It wasn't easy getting there. From the East Coast, one could take a 15,000-mile, five-month voyage around the tip of South America. More than 500 ships made the voyage in 1849 alone. You could also cut across the Isthmus of Panama and take two months off the trip, if you were willing to risk cholera and malaria. By land, the 2,200-mile journey from trailheads in Missouri or Iowa might take three or four months — with a lot of luck.

History recalls them as the 49ers, because the first big year of the gold rush was 1849. They called themselves Argonauts, after the mythical Greek heroes who sailed in the Argo with Jason to search for the Golden Fleece. Most of them found nothing but disappointment, and many found death.

With few women to add a touch of civilization and balance, and no government, it was a pretty rough place. In just one July week in 1850 in a town called Sonora, two Massachusetts men had their throats slit, a Chilean was shot to death in a gun-fight, and a Frenchman stabbed a Mexican to death. The town of Marysville had 17 murders in one week, and at the height of the gold rush, San Francisco averaged 2 murders a day.

A miner making $8 a day (about $240 in 2018 dollars) was doing eight times better than his coal-mining counterpart in the East. But prices were outrageous, too. A loaf of bread that cost 4 cents in New York cost 75 cents in the goldfields. All in all, most gold seekers weren't any better off than laborers in the rest of the country. But there was gold, and plenty of it. During the Civil War alone, California produced more than $170 million worth of bullion, which helped prop up wartime Union currency.

REMEMBER

The gold rush had other impacts as well. Although many of the 49ers came and left after a relatively short stay, many of them stuck around. From a non–Native American population of about 18,000 in January 1848, California grew to a resident population of 165,000 within three years. San Francisco became a booming U.S. port and doorway to the Pacific. The growth and importance of the state also helped spur long-delayed congressional approval of the proposal for a transcontinental railroad.

Eventually California became a magnet for different kinds of gold rushes. Movies, computers, the aerospace industry, and biotechnology all had California roots. But before all that could happen, it had to become a state.

Compromising on the slavery issue

Zachary Taylor was probably the least political of all American presidents. He served 40 years in the U.S. Army but never held any other office before being elected president. In fact, he had never even voted in a presidential election. But the popularity of "Old Rough and Ready" carried him to the White House in the 1848 election after Polk lived up to his promise not to seek a second term.

Taylor had expressed no opinions during the campaign about the hottest issue of the time, slavery, and had no plans for what to do about all that land he had just helped take from Mexico. At the time, the country was equally, if uneasily, divided into 15 free and 15 slave states. So when California asked to be admitted as a state, the debate raged on which side it should fall. Its own constitution banned slavery, mostly on the practical grounds that gold miners didn't want to compete with slaves digging for their masters. Those aging giants of Congress, Henry Clay of Kentucky and Daniel Webster of Massachusetts, urged yet another compromise approach, which eventually became the Compromise of 1850. But Taylor was adamant that California be admitted without delay as a free state. Southerners, led by their own aging giant, John C. Calhoun of South Carolina, were just as adamantly opposed. Representatives from nine southern states met in Nashville in June 1850 to consider leaving the Union if California was made a free state.

Fortunately for everyone but himself, Taylor helped solve the impasse by suddenly dying. His vice president and successor, a pliable fellow from New York named Millard Fillmore, was more agreeable to compromise. Pushed by the last great speeches by Clay and Webster, and with the help of a U.S. Senate newcomer from Illinois named Stephen Douglas, a deal was reached.

REMEMBER

The Compromise of 1850 consisted of a series of five bills. California was admitted as a free state; New Mexico and Utah were admitted as territories, with the slavery question to be settled later; Texas received $10 million for land it gave the new territory of New Mexico; the slave trade was abolished in Washington, D.C.; and a fugitive slave law was approved that made it much easier for slave owners to recapture escaped slaves by getting federal help.

The Fugitive Slave Law put all African Americans at risk, because all a slave owner had to do was sign a paper saying the person was an escaped slave, show it to a federal magistrate, and slap the chains on. Although only a few hundred African Americans were victims of the law, it outraged many Northerners, and anti-slavery resentment grew. But talk of dissolving the Union died down. For the last time, a compromise worked. Clay, Calhoun, and Webster would all be dead before it fell apart.

Coming Over and Spreading Out

By the middle of the 19th century, there were a lot more Americans than there were when the century started. The country's population in 1860 was 31.4 million, four times more than it had been in 1810. Of the world's predominantly white nations, only France, Russia, and Austria had larger populations.

Many of the new Americans were born elsewhere. The number of immigrants to America in 1830 was about 25,000. In 1855, the number was closer to 450,000. They came from as close as Mexico and Canada and as far away as China and Japan. When they got here, they tended to stay with their fellow expatriates, where the language, food, and culture were more familiar, creating mini-nations.

They also increasingly stayed in cities, even if they had come from a farm background. In 1840, there were 10 Americans living on farms to every 1 who lived in a town. By 1850, that ratio was 5 to 1, and many of the new city dwellers were from foreign shores.

The Germans, the Irish, and the Know-Nothings who opposed them

The parts of the cities they dwelled in were generally dark, smelly, filthy, and violent. Many of the immigrants were so appalled that reality didn't match their glittering visions of America that they went back home.

Because of the glut of people wanting any kind of a job when they got here, wages in the largest cities were pitifully low. In 1851, New York editor Horace Greeley estimated it took a minimum of $10.37 a week to support a family of five, and that didn't include money for medical needs or recreation. The average factory worker, laboring six days a week for 10 or 11 hours a day, might make $5 a week, which meant everyone in the family had to do something to make ends meet.

Because they were newcomers and because most native-born Americans still lived in smaller towns or on farms, there was little appetite for cleaning up the cities. That wouldn't come until the number of immigrants got even larger, and middle-class Americans became more affected by it.

And still they came, from 600,000 immigrants in the 1830s to 1.7 million in the 1840s to 2.6 million in the 1850s. More than 70 percent of the immigrants between 1840 and 1860 were from just two areas in Europe: Ireland and the German states.

For the Irish, it was come or starve. A fungus all but wiped out Ireland's potato crop in 1845, and there was a widespread famine. So more than 1.5 million Irish scraped up the $10 or $12 one-way fare and piled into America-bound ships for an often-hellish two-week trip in a cargo hold. Many of the ships had brought Southern cotton to Britain, and in a way, they were bringing back the North's cash crop — cheap labor to work in factories and build railroads. Many of the Irish settled in New York City or Boston. Politically savvy, they served first as soldiers for the big-city political machines and then as bosses. Even so, they were harshly discriminated against in many places, and "N.I.N.A." signs hung in many employers' windows. It stood for "No Irish Need Apply."

Almost as many Germans as Irish came during this period, although they were more likely to spread out. The Germans also came because of food shortages or other tough economic conditions. But many decided to come after efforts failed to throw off despotic rule in the various German states in the late 1840s. Generally better off financially and better educated than other immigrant groups (they brought the idea of "kindergarten," or "children's garden," with them), many Germans pushed away from the Eastern cities to the Midwest, especially Wisconsin.

The rise in immigration also increased anti-immigrant feeling, especially in areas where the newcomers were competing with people born in America for jobs. In 1849, an organization surfaced called the *Nativists.* They were better known as the *Know-Nothing Party,* because members supposedly replied, "I know nothing" when asked by outsiders what was going on at their meetings. The Know-Nothings demanded an end to immigration, a prohibition on non-natives voting or holding office, and restrictions on Roman Catholics.

The Know-Nothings made a lot of noise for awhile. Renamed the American Party, they attracted more than 1 million members by 1855 and managed to elect several governors and scores of congressmen. Their 1856 presidential candidate, Millard Fillmore, who as a Whig had been vice president under Taylor and served as president from 1850 to 1853 after Taylor died in office, even managed to carry one state, Maryland. But the Know-Nothings faded away as the Civil War approached, torn apart by differences between the party's Northern and Southern members over the slavery issue.

Making waves: The Mormons

Although one of the Know-Nothings' chief targets had been Roman Catholics, Americans in the mid-19th century were generally a pretty tolerant bunch when it came to religion. About three-fourths of them were regular churchgoers, and there were so many denominations that no one church dominated. By 1860, almost every state had repealed laws against Jews or Catholics holding public office, and the question "What can you do?" was more prevalent than "How do you worship?"

Of course, try telling that to a Mormon in 1846. The Church of Jesus Christ of Latter Day Saints began in 1830 with the publication of the Book of Mormon by a New York man named Joseph Smith. To escape persecutions, Smith moved his headquarters to Ohio, and then Missouri, and then to Nauvoo, Illinois, on the banks of the Mississippi. Nauvoo became one of the most thriving cities in the state.

But the Mormons' habits of working hard, sticking to themselves, and having more than one wife at a time seemed to irk outsiders, and the persecutions began again. This time Smith and his brother were killed by a mob, and Mormon leaders decided they needed some distance between themselves and the rest of America.

Led by a capable, if dictatorial, lieutenant of Smith's, Brigham Young, the Mormons moved west, many of them pushing two-wheeled carts for hundreds of miles. Finally, they settled in the Great Salt Lake Basin, a forbidding region in Utah that most people thought of as uninhabitable. Establishing a rigidly run society and economic system, the Mormons thrived. By 1848, there were 5,000 living in the area, many of them Europeans who had been converted by Mormon missionaries.

Many of the Mormons fought in the Mexican War as a way of "earning" what had been Mexican territory. In 1850, Utah became a territory. But its statehood was delayed for almost 50 years, in part because of the Mormons' refusal until then to drop their practice of multiple wives, or *polygamy*.

Wagons ho!

It's often attributed to Horace Greeley, but it was actually Indiana journalist John B. Soule who advised in 1850, "Go west, young man, go west!"

He was a little late. Even before the gold rush, Americans in large numbers were heading that direction. Despite the awesome dangers and hardships, settlers piled their belongings into fortified farm wagons and started out, mostly from St. Joseph or Independence in Missouri.

GIVE HER A CHANCE

"I have heard much about the sexes being equal; I can carry as much as any man, and can eat as much too, if I can get it. I am as strong as any man I know . . . . I can't read, but I can hear. I have heard the Bible and have learned that Eve caused man to sin. Well if woman upset the world, do give her a chance to set it right side up again." – Sojourner Truth, a freed slave who became one of America's most outstanding orators, at a women's rights conference, 1851

Some of them stopped on the Great Plains of Kansas and Nebraska, while others pushed on to the West Coast. By 1846, 5,000 Americans had settled in the Willamette Valley in the Oregon Territory, and by 1859, the territory had become a state. America's Manifest Destiny was being achieved.

Becoming aware of women's rights (or the lack thereof)

As more and more women got involved in the fight over slavery, many of them came to resent how, in many ways, they were also second-class Americans. Like slaves, women couldn't vote, couldn't retain their property when they got married, and could legally be beaten by their husbands.

Leaders, such as Lucretia Mott, Elizabeth Cady Stanton, and Susan B. Anthony, began to publicly demand more rights. In 1848, feminists met at Seneca Falls, New York, at a women's rights convention. Stanton read a *declaration of sentiments* that paraphrased the declaration Thomas Jefferson had written 72 years before: "All men *and women* are created equal."

Although some states began allowing women to keep their own property after marriage and some colleges began admitting women in the 1840s, the feminist crusade was overshadowed by the fight over slavery. For many of their rights, women would have to wait.

The Beginning of the End

The issue of slavery not only overshadowed the women's movement, it overshadowed virtually every part of American life. The Methodist and Baptist churches split into North–South factions because of it. Families with branches in the North and South stopped speaking to each other. It even strained business relations in a country where hardly anything got in the way of making a dollar.

And it was showing no signs of going away by itself. Despite a federal ban on importing slaves, the slave population grew from 3.2 million in 1850 to almost 4 million in 1860, almost all of it through childbirths. Adult slaves who could put in a full day's work had become so expensive that some Southerners began calling for ending the ban on new slaves from Africa.

Factoring a slave's life

REMEMBER

Actually, about 75 percent of Southern families didn't even own any slaves, although it many cases it was because they couldn't afford them rather than because they opposed slavery. But even nonslave owners defended slavery. Slaves, they said, received the benefits of being exposed to the Christian religion, of having cradle-to-grave shelter and food, and of being a contributing part of Southern society. That was more, they said, than many Northern factory workers could say. (Of course, that ignored the fact that even the most miserable factory worker could still make his own choices as to where he worked, didn't have to submit to beatings from his employer, and wasn't likely to see his wife and children taken from him and sold off to some other state.)

Proslavery forces also pointed out that slaves were actually well treated if they behaved. "Negroes are too high [priced] in proportion to the price of cotton," explained a slave owner in 1849, "and it behooves those who own them to make them last as long as possible." And, slavery's defenders said, what would the nation do with them if all the slaves were freed?

That was a question that stumped many Northerners who opposed slavery but did not agree with abolitionists' demand for an immediate end to it. In 1854, Abraham Lincoln, who was then in private practice as a lawyer, admitted, "If all earthly power were given me, I should not know what to do as to the existing situation." But Lincoln and others balked at the idea of slavery being allowed to spread, and that's what the fighting was about.

Battling in Kansas

The South wanted a railroad, Kansas and Nebraska wanted to be states, and the combination of wants caused even more troubles. Spurred by the California gold rush and westward expansion, Congress was getting ready to decide on a route for a transcontinental railroad.

The route that made the most sense, and the route the South wanted, started in New Orleans and moved across Texas before ending up in San Diego. It was the shortest route and went most of the way through already organized states or territories. But Sen. Stephen A. Douglas of Illinois was pressing hard for a central route, starting in Chicago. Douglas owned a lot of real estate in the area and stood to make a sizeable chunk of cash if the trains ran through his property. Trouble was his route went through land that had been given to the Native Americans. (See Chapter 12 for more on the railroads.)

So Douglas pushed a bill through Congress that organized the area into the Kansas and Nebraska territories. To win Southern support, his bill also repealed the Missouri Compromise of 1820, which prevented slavery in the new territories. Instead, it said people in Kansas and Nebraska should decide for themselves, a process he called *popular sovereignty.* Douglas argued that allowing the region's inhabitants to decide the issue was the purest form of democracy. But to many, the idea smacked of just passing the buck. And rather than calm things down, it stirred things up.

The North seethed with anger. Douglas was burned in effigy all around the North and ripped in the press. Pro-slavery interests in the South were disappointed Douglas wasn't stronger in support of slavery's spread. As a practical matter, Nebraska proved to be too far north for crops that would attract much proslavery interest. But what became known as "Bleeding Kansas" became a warmup for the Civil War. Pro- and anti-slavery factions poured into the area, destroying any notion that the question could be decided locally. Both sides resorted to bloody acts of terrorism and guerilla warfare.

THE LITTLE LADY AND THE BIG BOOK

Harriet Beecher Stowe was a diminutive Connecticut woman who dabbled in writing from time to time to bring in a little extra money. But when the Fugitive Slave Law was passed, it ticked her off enough to write a novel about slavery. She called it *Uncle Tom's Cabin.*

The book was published in Boston in 1852 — and it was a sensation. It sold 10,000 copies in one week, 300,000 copies in its first year, and more than 1.5 million copies worldwide. Its chief effect was to put human (if painfully stereotypical) faces on an issue that many Northerners had thought about only in political terms. It outraged Southerners, who felt it was grossly unfair.

Stowe was hailed as a saint; she was also mailed the ear of a "disobedient slave." Stung by accusations that her book exaggerated the plight of slaves, Stowe wrote a second book called *A Key to Uncle Tom's Cabin,* in which she documented all the abuses in the first book. *Uncle Tom's Cabin* became one of the most powerful propaganda pieces ever written. In 1862, Stowe was introduced to Abraham Lincoln. "So," Lincoln reportedly said to her, "you're the little woman that wrote the book that made this great war."

One of the effects of Douglas's bill was to kill the Whig Party, whose leaders were wishy-washy on the subject. In its place came the Republican Party, which was strongly against the spread of slavery. In 1856, the Republicans ran John C. Fremont, a famous explorer and soldier, against the Democrats' James Buchanan, a former Pennsylvania congressman and secretary of state, who had Southern sympathies. Buchanan, a heavy man with tiny feet and almost no backbone, won. He proved to be a worthless president.

Making a "dredful" decision

Dred Scott was a slave who was temporarily taken by his master to Illinois, which was a free state. When they returned to Missouri, Scott sued for his freedom, claiming that his time in Illinois, on free soil, made him an ex-slave.

REMEMBER

But the seven Southern members of the U.S. Supreme Court, led by Chief Justice Roger Taney, found against Scott in 1857. The court decided that as an African American, Scott wasn't a U.S. citizen and, thus, had no right to sue; that as a Missouri resident, Illinois laws didn't apply to him; and that as a slave, he was property, just like a mule, and the government had no right to deprive his master of property without a good reason. The decision absolutely infuriated people in the North. The court's contention that Scott had no more rights than a mule caused many moderate Northerners to take a harder look at the true injustice of slavery.

CANES AND CONGRESSMEN

This is how emotional the issue of slavery was: In the spring of 1856, Massachusetts Senator Charles Sumner, an acid-tongued abolitionist, launched a long and personal attack on South Carolina Senator Andrew P. Butler, an elderly man who had the unfortunate habit of drooling. So nasty was Sumner's attack on Butler, who was not there at the time, that Sen. Stephen Douglas warned "That damn fool will get himself killed by some other damn fool."

The "other damn fool" turned out to be Butler's nephew, a congressman named Preston Brooks. Two days after Sumner's speech, Brooks approached him as he sat at his desk on the Senate floor and began beating Sumner with a cane until he fell bloody and unconscious to the floor. "I gave him about 30 first-rate stripes," Brooks later bragged. Sumner was so badly shaken he could not return to Congress for three years. Brooks resigned his House seat and then was reelected. The North got a martyr out of the deal, the South a hero.

The decision, along with the Fugitive Slave Law of 1850, also added greatly to business on the *Underground Railroad*, the name given to a network of abolitionists in the North and South who worked together to get escaped slaves to freedom, often in Canada. It's estimated that the system, which involved "conductors" and "stations," or hiding places, helped from 50,000 to 100,000 people with their escape.

Squaring Off for a Showdown: The Lincoln–Douglas Debate

In 1858, Lincoln challenged Douglas to a series of seven debates as part of their race for a U.S. Senate seat in Illinois. It was a classic confrontation. Douglas, the incumbent, was barely 5 feet tall, with a big head made larger by his pompadour hairstyle. He was resplendent in finely tailored suits and arrived for the debates in a private railroad car. Lincoln was 6 feet 4 inches, with a homely face topped by a shock of unruly hair. He wore ill-fitting suits that stopped well short of his wrists and ankles and arrived for the debates on whatever passenger train was available.

Their debate strategies were simple. Douglas tried to make Lincoln look like an abolitionist, which he wasn't, and Lincoln tried to make Douglas look like he was proslavery, which he wasn't. But they did have a fundamental disagreement on what the eventual outcome of slavery would be.

Douglas won the election, but Lincoln won a national reputation. In the meantime, the country edged closer to a final showdown, needing only a spark to set off the firestorm. It got two.

Spark number 1: John Brown

John Brown was an Ohio abolitionist who was crazier than an outhouse rat. He believed he had been commanded by God to free the slaves, and he went about it by killing people in the Kansas fighting. On October 16, 1859, Brown led a group of 18 white and black men on a raid on the federal arsenal at Harpers Ferry, Virginia. After killing the mayor and taking some hostages, Brown's gang was surrounded by militia and U.S. troops under the command of Capt. Robert E. Lee. Brown and five others were captured, and the rest killed. After a trial, Brown was hanged. Many Southerners were convinced Brown had done what a lot of Northerners wanted to do; many Northerners considered him a martyr to a noble cause.

Spark number 2: Lincoln's election

Lincoln, now a national figure, was nominated by the young Republican Party as its 1860 presidential candidate, mostly because they thought he would appeal to the North and the West. But the Democrats were split by the slavery issue. Douglas was the official nominee, but a splinter group supported Buchanan's vice president, John Breckenridge of Tennessee. And a fourth group of moderates, called the Union Party, supported John Bell of Kentucky.

When the votes were in, Lincoln had won less than a majority of the popular vote, but easily won the electoral vote and was the new president. Before he could take office, however, seven Southern states had already pulled out of the Union. Buchanan did nothing to try to stop them, and once the fighting started, they were followed by four more.

As the sun rose on April 12, 1861, secessionist guns fired on Fort Sumter, in Charleston Harbor, South Carolina. America's Civil War had begun.

Chapter **10**

A Most Uncivil War: 1861–1865

It pitted brother against brother and killed more American soldiers than any other war in U.S. history. But from this terrible struggle emerged a country that had fought its toughest enemy — itself — and won.

This chapter is a guide to key aspects of the Civil War, from the man who strove to reunite the nation to the beginning of the end of slavery to who won which battle where. (For a closer look at the Civil War, check out *The Civil War For Dummies*, written by Keith D. Dickson and published by Wiley.)

Introducing Abraham Lincoln

Abraham Lincoln began his presidency by sneaking into Washington, D.C. Because of a suspected assassination plot in Baltimore, Lincoln's railroad car was rerouted to arrive at a different time than was publicly announced.

It was an inauspicious beginning to a very tough job. Within a few months of Lincoln taking office, 11 states — Alabama, Arkansas, Florida, Georgia, Louisiana, Mississippi, North Carolina, South Carolina, Tennessee, Texas, and Virginia — had left the Union, and 4 more — Delaware, Kentucky, Maryland, and Missouri — were thinking about leaving. The man in charge of sorting out the whole mess had received only about 40 percent of the popular vote. Although he's now considered one of the most extraordinary men in American — and world — history, Lincoln was more of a puzzle than a leader to most Americans at the time.

Presenting the 16th president

Lincoln was an enormously complex person. He had a great sense of humor but also an air of deep sorrow and melancholy about him (exacerbated by the death of his beloved mother when he was only 9, the deaths of two of his four sons before him and his wife suffering from mental illness). He was ambitious and purposeful, but he was also modest and cheerfully ready to poke fun at himself. Lincoln didn't drink, was skeptical when it came to organized religion (although he professed a belief in God), and delighted in telling racy stories.

He was also at ease with his ungainly appearance (6 feet, 4 inches tall and weighing 180 pounds, with large hands and feet) and usually just smiled when his enemies referred to him as "an ape." He often dressed all in black and wore a stovepipe hat in which he sometimes stored his correspondence. Lincoln spoke with a high squeak, which may have been why he kept his speeches short. One popular and perhaps apocryphal story about Lincoln is that when a young girl suggested he grow a beard to improve his appearance, he whimsically did so between the election and his inauguration.

REMEMBER

Lincoln's greatest gift may have been his ability to use people, in the best sense of the term. He could overlook people's faults — and even their dislike of him — if he thought they had something to offer, and he did so with humor and grace. Case in point: When a troublemaker reported to him that his secretary of war, Edwin Stanton, had called the president a "damned fool," Lincoln replied, "Then I must be one, for Stanton is generally right, and he always says what he means."

He had plenty of need and opportunity to use his gift of getting the most out of people. Throughout his presidency, Lincoln had few close friends or advisors. His cabinet (notably William Seward, secretary of state; Salmon P. Chase, secretary of the treasury; and Stanton, secretary of war) represented a wide range of political philosophies. The biggest thing the men had in common was their low opinion of their boss, at least at the start of the war.

JEFFERSON DAVIS

As president of the Confederate States of America, Jefferson Davis may have been Lincoln's counterpart, but he was in no way his equal. Davis was stiff, unyielding, narrow-minded, and humorless. Born in 1808, Davis was a West Point graduate who was wounded and decorated for bravery in the Mexican War. He was also a U.S. senator and served as secretary of war under Pres. Franklin Pierce. With his brother, Davis owned a Mississippi plantation and believed in good treatment of slaves. But he also firmly believed in the institution of slavery.

After Lincoln's election, Davis resigned his Senate seat. Although he first opposed secession, he accepted the presidency of the Confederate states as a compromise candidate. His presidency was plagued by mediocre cabinet members, quarreling among the rebel states, and his own inability to think other people could possibly be right if they didn't agree with him.

When the South's major armies surrendered, Davis fled with what was left of the government's treasury and vowed to fight on. He was soon captured, however, and thrown in a prison cell for almost two years without a trial. Upon his release, he went to Canada before returning to Mississippi. Davis spent his remaining years writing about how the war's outcome was everyone else's fault. He died in 1889. More than 250,000 people attended his funeral, many of them nostalgic for the "Old South" he represented.

Fortunately, Lincoln had a talent for making his point without being confrontational. Exasperated at the reluctance of General George B. McClellan to fight, for example, Lincoln drolly observed that "if General McClellan does not want to use the army, I would like to borrow it."

Ultimately, Lincoln was able to use his many gifts and unique personality to rally people in the North to keep fighting, first for the cause of preserving the Union and later for the cause of ending slavery.

Understanding Lincoln's views on slavery and the Union

Born in Kentucky in 1809, Lincoln lost his mother when he was 9 and moved with his father (a farmer) to Indiana and then to Illinois. Lincoln had almost no formal schooling. After leaving home, he took a flatboat trip down the Mississippi, worked in a store, became a lawyer, and at 25 was elected to the state legislature. In 1846, he was elected to Congress, but by 1850, he had given up on politics. As the slavery debate grew hotter, however, Lincoln decided to reenter the political arena in 1854 and fight against its spread.

REMEMBER

That Lincoln opposed slavery is clear. "If slavery is not wrong, then nothing is wrong," he once wrote. "I cannot remember when I did not so think and feel." But like most white Americans, he thought black Americans were inferior, and he wasn't in favor of immediate freedom for slaves. He also didn't think blacks and whites could live together: "My first impulse would be to free all the slaves and send them to Liberia, to their own native land," he once said. "But a moment's reflection would convince me, that whatever high hope (as I think there is) there may be in this, in the long run, its sudden execution would be impossible."

As president of the United States, Lincoln put a higher value on preserving the Union than on ending slavery: "If I could save the Union without freeing any slaves," he wrote, "I would do it; and if I could save it by freeing all the slaves, I would do it; and if I could save it by freeing some and leaving others alone, I would also do that."

He was also adamant that no states would be allowed to leave the Union without a fight: "A husband and wife may be divorced," he said, "but the different parts of our country cannot . . . . Intercourse, either amicable or hostile, must continue between them."

Bending the Constitution to preserve the Union — and win reelection

Not everyone in the North felt the same way. As the war progressed, opposition to it formed around *Peace Democrats,* who called for negotiating a way to let the "wayward sisters go in peace." The more radical of these Peace Democrats, who actually called for disloyalty to the federal government, were dubbed *Copperheads* after the poisonous snake that strikes without warning.

The generally patient Lincoln had no patience with the Copperheads. In some areas, he suspended their rights to have a speedy trial and be charged with a specific crime when arrested. More than 13,000 people were arrested and held without trial during the Civil War. By taking these actions, Lincoln disregarded the Constitution in his drive to preserve the Union. (In fact, several of Lincoln's actions were declared unconstitutional by the Supreme Court — but only after the war ended.)

In 1864, Lincoln was up for reelection. He feared he might lose to someone not as devoted to preserving the Union. So he again bent some rules, suspending voting rights in some anti-Union areas of the border states and arranging for Union soldiers to get leave so they could go home and vote, presumably for him.

UH, THANKS FOR COMING ABE

One of the most famous speeches in American history is Lincoln's Gettysburg Address. But the speech wasn't exactly a big hit when he delivered it on November 19, 1863. The occasion was the dedication of the national cemetery at the site of the Battle of Gettysburg in Pennsylvania. The cemetery had been ordered because many of the 8,000 bodies that fell there had been so hastily buried after the battle that they'd become exposed again.

Lincoln wasn't even the featured speaker. That honor fell to Edward Everett, a famous orator who'd been a U.S. senator and president of Harvard University. Everett spoke for nearly two hours and delivered some 1,500 long and windy sentences before he finally sat down.

Lincoln, who, contrary to myth, didn't write his 268-word speech on the back of an envelope during the train trip to Gettysburg, spoke for about three minutes. He was interrupted several times by applause. When he was done, a Philadelphia newspaper reporter on the stage leaned over and whispered to Lincoln, "Is that all?" Lincoln replied, "Yes, for the present."

In addition, the Republican Party formed a temporary alliance with Democrats who favored the war, thereby creating the Union Party. The Democrats against the war put up George McClellan, a general whom Lincoln had twice removed from command. Despite his fears about not being reelected, Lincoln won 55 percent of the popular vote and held a comfortable 212–21 margin in the Electoral College.

Fortunately for the country, the war remained Lincoln's responsibility to the end. "With malice to none, with charity to all, with firmness in the right, as God gives us to see the right, let us strive on to finish the work we are in to bind up the nation's wounds," he said in his second inaugural address.

North versus South: Comparing Advantages and Action Plans

If London bookies had been taking bets on the outcome of the American Civil War, they may have set the odds a little in favor of the South based on the Confederacy's advantages. Sure, the North had some big pluses, including the following:

>> A population of about 22 million, compared to about 9 million in the South (of which 3.5 million were slaves); in addition, immigration during the war added thousands of new recruits for the Union Army

>> Seven times as much manufacturing, which meant the Union Army was always better supplied

>> A far better railroad system (75 percent of all the track in America), which greatly aided the transport of troops and supplies

>> Control of the U.S. Navy and the merchant fleet

>> A central government already in place, and a more diverse economy

>> Lincoln

The South, however, had a number of its own advantages:

>> **The benefit of history:** The Southern secessionists were in good company. Secession by determined regions had previously succeeded in Latin America, the Netherlands, Greece, and the 13 American colonies, just to name a few places.

>> **A defensive stance:** The Confederacy didn't have to conquer the North or even win a lot of big battles; it only had to fight long enough for the North to give up its quest to bring the Southern states back into the Union. A defensive war is much cheaper to fight than an offensive one in terms of both men and materials. Although the South's population was smaller overall, it still had about 200,000 men available to fight within a short time of the war's start.

>> **Home-field advantage:** Much of the fighting was on the South's territory because the North had to conquer the South to get it back into the Union. Southerners not only knew the terrain but also had the incentive of defending their homes and farms. (Of course, as the war progressed, they found that fighting on the home field wasn't all it was cracked up to be.)

>> **Strong military leadership:** The South had more able military leaders right from the start, particularly a courtly and brilliant Virginian named Robert E. Lee and his right-hand man, a former military school instructor who liked to suck on lemons, named Thomas "Stonewall" Jackson.

To win, reasoned Gen. Winfield Scott (the top Northern general, who was 75 and so fat he couldn't get on a horse), the first step was to suffocate the South by blockading its coast. Next, cut it in half by seizing the Mississippi River. Then chop it up by cutting across Georgia and then up through the Carolinas. Finally, capture the Confederate capital of Richmond, Virginia.

HELL NO, WE WON'T GO

Although most men who fought in the Civil War were volunteers, both sides resorted to drafting troops as well. The Confederacy was first, in 1862. A year later, the North followed — but not without serious opposition. One sore point was the fact that draftees who put up $300 or hired someone to go in their place could get out of serving. Men who took advantage of the exemption included tycoons, or soon-to-be tycoons, such as J. P. Morgan and Andrew Carnegie, and future president Grover Cleveland. Another issue was the dislike of many Irish immigrants for African Americans, whom they feared would compete with them for jobs.

The worst anti-draft troubles occurred in New York City. In July 1863, mostly Irish anti-draft mobs, chanting "to hell with the draft and the war," terrorized the city for four days. More than 400 people were killed, and $5 million worth of damage was done. The riots weren't stopped until federal troops arrived. The draft was subsequently suspended in the city for the rest of the war.

Many Northern newspapers sneered at Scott's strategy as too timid. They suggested abandoning his *anaconda plan* (so-called because it envisioned encircling the South and squeezing the life out of it like a giant snake) in favor of marching directly on Richmond and getting the whole thing over with. But Lincoln recognized the worth of Scott's approach.

Confederate Pres. Jefferson Davis, meanwhile, favored a simpler plan for the South: Make the Northern armies press the fight, whip them, and push them back North, thereby breaking the morale of the Northern people. General Lee concurred at first but then realized that the South's limited resources might be better used in a quick and decisive strike to take the heart out of the North. Twice he tried to take the fight to the Union; twice his limited resources forced him to go home.

Freeing the Slaves

One of Lincoln's most pressing problems was what to do about slaves. As soon as Northern troops moved into Southern territory, escaped slaves poured into Union Army camps. One general declared them "seized" property and put them to work in labor battalions so they could earn their keep. But other generals who favored abolition immediately declared them freed.

Lincoln was forced to rescind the latter orders because, as president, he felt that freeing slaves was solely his responsibility and because he had to be careful not to antagonize the slave-holding states that had stayed loyal to the Union: Delaware, Kentucky, Maryland, and Missouri, and later, West Virginia, which broke away from Virginia during the war. Lincoln hoped each state would abolish slavery on its own and compensate slave owners so federal funds could be used to send freed slaves to Africa. When that didn't happen, Lincoln chose a different course.

Proclaiming emancipation

In June 1862, members of Congress who were impatient with Lincoln's caution mustered enough votes to abolish slavery in the District of Columbia and the U.S. territories. Congress also authorized Lincoln to allow the Union Army to enlist African Americans who wanted to fight. Prodded by these congressional actions, Lincoln then told his cabinet in July that he intended to proclaim freedom for slaves as of January 1, 1863. But he wanted to wait until the Union Army had won a big battle before making the announcement.

On September 22, five days after the Union gained what was more of a tie than a win at Antietam Creek, Maryland, Lincoln made his *Emancipation Proclamation* public. As of January 1, he announced, all slaves in any state still in rebellion "shall be, then, thenceforth and forever free."

Surveying the consequences of emancipation

REMEMBER

In reality, Lincoln's proclamation didn't free a single slave. It didn't apply to slaves in the border states, where Union forces could have enforced it, and slave owners in the Confederacy certainly didn't obey it. But it did have effects Lincoln hadn't intended.

>> In the South, the Emancipation Proclamation reinforced the will to fight on because it was clear that if the South lost, slavery would end.

>> In the North, it angered some who were comfortable fighting to preserve the Union but not to free people who might then come north and compete with them for jobs.

>> Abolitionists thought the Emancipation Proclamation didn't go far enough, while other people thought the government had no right to take away the Southern slave owner's "property."

But many Northerners gradually came to embrace the idea of abolishing slavery as a moral cause, and Lincoln's move added another reason for the North to continue to fight. Just as important, working people in England and France cheered the emancipation of slaves. At one point, a letter of support was sent to Lincoln that supposedly came from 20,000 laborers in England. Such support helped ensure that European leaders wouldn't risk the wrath of public opinion by aiding the South.

Reviewing the Troops, the Generals, and the Major Battles

The Civil War was mostly a young man's fight. Most of the enlisted men were under the age of 21, and more than a few were in their early teens. The Civil War was also truly "a brothers' war," with families and friends divided by their allegiances. Mary Lincoln, the president's wife, lost three brothers in the war — they all fought for the South. The Confederacy's leading general, Robert E. Lee, had a nephew who was an officer in the Union Navy.

Because of the fraternal flavor of the two armies, it wasn't unusual for them to engage in friendly banter between battles, sometimes even getting together for a game of baseball or to trade tobacco for coffee during truces.

REMEMBER

The friendliness didn't stop the carnage: More than 600,000 American soldiers died during the Civil War. That's more than the number who died in World War I, World War II, and the Korean War combined. About two-thirds of that number died from diseases rather than battle wounds, and it's estimated the average soldier ended up in the hospital at least once or twice a year. If the soldier ever left the hospital, he was lucky. Sanitary conditions were awful, and 75 percent of the operations consisted of amputations, many of them needless.

Northern forces almost always outnumbered their Southern opponents. At the end of the war, the Union Army had about 960,000 men in uniform compared to the Confederates' 445,000. In addition to having a larger population to draw from, the North's forces also included thousands of European immigrants who took up a rifle almost as soon as they got off the boat.

Additionally, thousands of African Americans fought for the North after being allowed to join the army in 1863. They were paid $7 a month (about a third of what white soldiers got), and they fought well under white officers, earning the grudging respect of those they fought against and alongside.

The men at the top

What each side did have, at least by the close of the war, was a great general at the head of its army. In the South, that man was Robert E. Lee, the son of a Revolutionary War general. A West Point graduate, Lee was asked by Lincoln to lead the Union Army before the war began. But Lee's loyalties were to his native state of Virginia. He was honorable, courteous, skillful, and not afraid to take a chance.

Lee's Northern counterpart was Ulysses S. Grant, the shy and disheveled son of a storekeeper. Grant was also a West Point grad, but he resigned his commission to avoid a court-martial for drunkenness. He rejoined the army and rose through the ranks to command mainly because, unlike some of his contemporaries, he wasn't afraid to get into a fight. Grant was highly intelligent, determined, compassionate — and a cold-eyed killer, if that's what it took to win.

The war at sea

The North's first objective was to blockade the Southern coast and cut off the South's ability to trade its cotton in Europe for arms and supplies. The Union Navy already had ships and guns, but the South somehow managed to scrounge up a navy of its own from refitted private ships or ships built for the South in England, as well as scores of captured Union merchant ships.

REMEMBER

One of the Confederacy's ships was a Union vessel called the *Merrimac*, which had been sunk. Southern ship fitters raised it, covered it with iron plates, and renamed it the *Virginia*. For a few days, it terrorized the Union fleet off Hampton Roads, Virginia, sinking two Union ships and threatening to decimate the entire group. But the North's own hastily constructed ironclad ship, the *Monitor*, showed up in the nick of time. On March 9, 1862, the two met in a four-hour battle that basically ended in a tie. The *Virginia* was eventually burned and the *Monitor* sunk, but their battle was significant in that it was the first battle between two ironclad ships — ultimately spelling the doom of wooden warships. After a slow start, however, the North's sea blockade was ultimately highly effective.

HAIRSTYLES AND HOOKERS

Like most major conflicts, the Civil War gave birth to a number of new terms that are still part of the American language. One of them came from the hairstyle of a Union general who wore his whiskers down the front of his ears along his jaw line, but not as a full beard. His name was Ambrose Burnside, and his whiskers became known as *sideburns*. Another Union general, Joseph "Fighting Joe" Hooker, became known for the large numbers of prostitutes that hung around his army while it was in the Washington area. They were jokingly called "Hooker's Division." Although *hookers* was already a term for ladies of the night, the general helped nationalize it and ensure its lasting place in the language.

The war on land

When it came to the ground war, the North's strategy included capturing the city of New Orleans and gaining control of the mouth of the Mississippi River. Starting in 1862, largely under Grant's command, the Union Army began taking Tennessee and slowly moving up and down the Mississippi River, cutting the South in half just as Gen. Winfield Scott had suggested.

On the Confederate side, Lee twice took the war to the North, but both times he was forced to return to Southern territory when he was outnumbered and faced uncertain supply lines. In late 1863, the North began grinding down Lee's army in Virginia while another Union Army under Gen. William T. Sherman marched diagonally across Georgia and then up into the Carolinas, destroying everything in its path. "We have devoured the land," Sherman wrote to his wife. "All the people retreat before us, and desolation is behind."

Here are ten of the key battles or campaigns of the war (check out Figure 10-1 to get a visual of the various locations):

>> **Fort Sumter:** After the first Southern states seceded, they began seizing federal forts and shipyards inside their borders. Maj. Robert Anderson, commander of the fort in Charleston Harbor, South Carolina, agreed to surrender as soon as the food ran out. But Southern forces wouldn't wait, and at dawn on April 12, 1861, they fired the first shots of the Civil War. Anderson surrendered when he ran out of ammunition, and the only casualties were two Union soldiers killed when a cannon exploded. But the fact that the South fired first helped recruiting efforts in the North.

>> **Bull Run:** The first large fight of the war took place near Manassas Junction, Virginia, on July 21, 1861. Despite the fact that it was a brutally hot day, hundreds of residents from nearby Washington, D.C., came out to picnic and watch the fight, thinking it might be the highlight of what many expected to be a 90-day war. Neither army was trained or prepared, and for most of the day, utter confusion reigned. Then Confederate forces got the upper hand, and Union forces panicked and ran. The rebel army was too tired to chase them.

>> **Shiloh:** Grant's army was caught napping on April 6, 1862, near this Tennessee church, and was on the brink of being routed when Grant launched a counterattack the next day that pushed the Confederate Army back. The battle solidified the Union Army's dominance in the West.

>> **Antietam:** Lee's first push into Northern territory took place near Antietam Creek in Maryland on September 17, 1862. The battle was fought in a narrow field between the creek and the Potomac River. It was one of the bloodiest battles of the war, with 22,000 killed or wounded. Lee was forced to return across the Potomac, providing Lincoln the "victory" he'd been waiting for to announce his Emancipation Proclamation.

>> **Chancellorsville:** The Union Army, under Gen. Joseph Hooker, tried to surround Lee's forces in Virginia from May 1–3, 1863. But Lee took a brilliant gamble, divided his smaller army, and attacked first. It was a complete Confederate victory, but a costly one. Lee's top general, Thomas Jackson, who was nicknamed *Stonewall* for his courage and tenacity, was mistakenly shot by his own troops. He died a week later, creating a leadership hole the South was never quite able to fill.

>> **Gettysburg:** Lee again pushed into Northern territory in early June 1863, this time into Pennsylvania. In a massive battle (a total of more than 50,000 casualties) from July 1 to July 3, Lee's army hurled itself at Union forces led by Gen. George Meade. But the South's effort failed, and Lee was once again forced to withdraw. Considered one of the most important battles in world history, Gettysburg is also regarded by many as the most pivotal fight in the Civil War.

>> **Vicksburg:** This Mississippi town was a major Confederate stronghold on the Mississippi River. Coordinating with Union naval forces moving up from New Orleans, Grant masterfully moved his outnumbered army around the city and laid siege to it. Vicksburg surrendered on July 4, 1863, giving the North control of the Mississippi River. Coming within a day or two of the defeat at Gettysburg, the loss of Vicksburg was a devastating blow to the South.

>> **Chickamauga and Chattanooga:** These confrontations, which ran from August to November 1863, led to Sherman's march across Georgia. At Chickamauga, Union Gen. George H. Thomas withstood a furious attack and saved the Union Army from a rout. After the Union Army was surrounded at Chattanooga, Grant led a rescue effort and drove off the Confederate forces.

>> **The Wilderness:** This was a series of battles in Virginia starting in May 1864 in which Grant used his superior numbers to wear down Lee's army. The carnage was terrible, and Grant's critics accused him of being a butcher. But the strategy worked. Lee's army couldn't break off to try to stop Sherman's march through the heart of the South.

>> **Appomattox Courthouse:** This wasn't a battle, but it was the site in Virginia where on April 12, 1865, Lee formally surrendered to Grant. The Southern Army was exhausted, outnumbered, and half-starved. Grant generously fed the defeated Southerners and allowed them to go home, taking their horses and mules with them. Although some units fought on for a few more weeks, the Civil War, for all intents and purposes, was finally over.

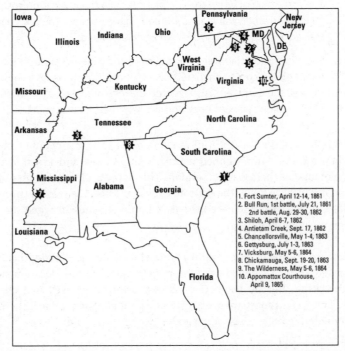

1. Fort Sumter, April 12-14, 1861
2. Bull Run, 1st battle, July 21, 1861
   2nd battle, Aug. 29-30, 1862
3. Shiloh, April 6-7, 1862
4. Antietam Creek, Sept. 17, 1862
5. Chancellorsville, May 1-4, 1863
6. Gettysburg, July 1-3, 1863
7. Vicksburg, May 5-6, 1864
8. Chickamauga, Sept. 19-20, 1863
9. The Wilderness, May 5-6, 1864
10. Appomattox Courthouse,
    April 9, 1865

FIGURE 10-1: Key Civil War battles and campaigns.

© John Wiley & Sons, Inc.

Two More Reasons Why the North Won

Winning a war without money or friends is rather difficult, and the South had neither. Its economy, pardon the expression, went south, and it failed to convince any major European powers to join the fight on its side.

The Southern economy was based solely on agriculture. When the Civil War started, there was only one iron foundry in the entire South. Still, the Confederacy's leaders put their confidence in cotton: "You dare not make war upon our cotton," a Southern politician boasted before the war. "No power on Earth dares make war on it. Cotton is King."

True, European nations had depended on Southern cotton to fuel their textile industries. In fact, some 80 percent of Britain's cotton came from America before the war. The South thought if the Union's blockade cut off Southern cotton, Britain would intervene on the South's behalf.

But this idea had some holes in it:

>> The first was that when the war started, Britain had a cotton surplus. It had stocked up when war clouds loomed on the horizon. The Brits had also started getting more cotton from Egypt and India.

>> Secondly, British laborers hated slavery and wouldn't support the South even if that meant costing them jobs, which it did. British leaders, even those who favored the South and also favored the idea of two smaller Americas over one big one, didn't want to buck popular sentiment that supported the North.

Actually, Britain and the Union came close to war a couple times, most closely when a Union ship stopped a British ship at sea and arrested two Confederate diplomats on their way to London. This act was clearly against international law and might have given the Brits an excuse to enter the war on the side of the South. But Lincoln wisely released the two diplomats and shrugged the whole thing off as a misunderstanding.

With no European allies and the Union blockade succeeding, the South's economy tanked. In 1861, about $1 million in gold-backed Confederate paper currency was circulating. But by 1863, Confederate printing presses had churned out $900 million in currency, with scarcely any gold supplies to back them. Thus, an 1863 Confederate dollar was worth about two cents in gold.

The North's economy was also buffeted by the war. But because it was stronger going in, it handled the conflict better. Advances in agriculture and manufacturing and supplies of gold and silver from California and Nevada helped fuel the economy despite the war's manpower drain.

Losing a Leader

The worst manpower drain of all came on April 14, 1865, just five days after Lee surrendered to Grant at Appomattox. It was Good Friday, and President Lincoln had decided to go to Ford's Theatre in Washington to see the comedy *Our American Cousin*.

REMEMBER

At about 10:30 p.m., during the second act, an actor and Southern sympathizer named John Wilkes Booth snuck into the presidential box and shot Lincoln in the back of the head. Lincoln was taken to a lodging house across the street from the theater, where he lingered until the next morning and then died, surrounded by several members of his cabinet. "Now he belongs to the ages," said Secretary of War Edwin Stanton.

Born in Maryland, Booth was from a family of prominent actors. He was a white supremacist who had plotted to kidnap Lincoln and use him as a bargaining chip to end the war on better terms for the South. But Lee's surrender changed his plot to assassination.

Booth made his escape from the theater after stabbing a Union officer who was in Lincoln's box and jumping to the stage, breaking his leg in the attempt. He was cornered in a Virginia barn a week later and was shot to death or killed himself. Four of Booth's fellow conspirators were hanged. Four others were convicted of helping the conspirators after the fact and were sentenced to prison.

America's Civil War lasted four awful years. Healing from its wounds would take far longer.

Chapter **11**

Putting the Country Back Together: 1865–1876

The bullet that killed Abraham Lincoln at the end of the Civil War may also have killed any chance of coming up with a practical solution toward putting the country back together — and figuring out what to do with nearly four million former slaves who had won their freedom but not much else.

In this chapter, a defiant South, a wrathful and power-mad Congress, and a stubborn and nasty-tempered president combine to make a mess of what's known as the Reconstruction period. Additionally, you also see how a very good military leader became a very bad political leader and how one political party managed to steal a presidential election.

A Southern-Fried Mess: Life in the South after the Civil War

The 11 Southern states that had decided to leave the Union in 1860 and 1861 were basket cases by 1865. Only Texas, where there hadn't been that much fighting, was in relatively decent shape. Southern cities such as Atlanta, Charleston, and Richmond were in ruins.

WHIPPED

"A city of ruins, of desolation, of vacant houses, of widowed women, of rotting wharves, of deserted warehouses, of weed-wild gardens, of miles of grass-grown streets, of acres of pitiful and voiceful barrenness — that is Charleston, wherein rebellion loftily reared its head five years ago. . . . I fell into some talk with [a local resident] . . . when I asked him what should be done, he said 'you Northern people are making a great mistake in your treatment of the South. We are thoroughly whipped; we give up slavery forever; and now we want you to quit reproaching us. Let us back into the Union, and then come down here and help us build up the country.'"

— Massachusetts journalist Sidney Andrews, 1865

Few businesses of any kind were still operating, little capital was available to start new businesses, and few outsiders were willing to risk investing in the area. For example, 7,000 miles of railroad track were laid in the South between 1865 and 1879. In the rest of the country, 45,000 miles were laid.

Before the war, the South's economy had been based almost strictly on agriculture, mainly cotton, tobacco, and sugar, and all these industries suffered, especially cotton. Southern cotton production in 1870 was half what it was in 1860. The education system in the South had virtually disappeared, along with the old plantation system. More than 250,000 of the South's young men were gone, too. "Pretty much the whole of life has been merely not dying," wrote the Southern poet Sidney Lanier about the Reconstruction period.

Two postwar changes dominated Southern life. One was the bewildering new world faced by the freed slaves. The other was a farming practice known as *sharecropping*, which became widespread throughout the South and would ultimately make life more difficult for both ex-slaves and poor whites.

Starting a new life

For an estimated 3.9 million African Americans who had been slaves at the start of the Civil War, the whole of life post–Civil War had become pretty darn confusing. They had their freedom but didn't know what they should do with it. Few former slaves had any education or training. Some thought freedom meant freedom from work; others were fearful that to continue working for white people would put them in danger of being enslaved again. And many believed a widespread rumor that the federal government would be giving each slave "40 acres and a mule" to start their own farms.

Such a plan never existed, but in 1865, the federal government did organize the *Freedman's Bureau*, an agency designed to help freed slaves during their transition from slavery to freedom by providing food, education, and other support. From 1865 to 1868, the bureau helped as many as 200,000 former slaves learn to read. About 10,000 black families were settled by the bureau on land that had been confiscated by Union troops, although most of them were eventually forced off the land by whites who swindled them out of it or used dubious legal means.

Becoming sharecroppers

REMEMBER

Most blacks and many whites couldn't afford to buy land of their own, so a new form of farming became the basis for the Southern agricultural economy: share-cropping. Under *sharecropping*, the farmer farmed land owned by someone else, and the two shared the profits.

That was the ideal, but in most cases, the sharecropper had to borrow money to make ends meet until the next crop was harvested. This borrowing left him with so little when the crop was harvested that he had to borrow on the next crop. Thus, many sharecroppers, both black and white, became virtual slaves to debt. Many former plantation owners, meanwhile, actually did better with sharecropping than slavery, since they didn't have to feed or clothe the "free" sharecroppers.

BLANCHE KELSO BRUCE

Next time you have a $2 bill that was printed in, say, 1880, take a look at the signatures on it. One of them belongs to a Virginia native who started life as a slave and became a prosperous landowner and United States senator.

Blanche Kelso Bruce was born in 1841 and worked as a field hand. When the Civil War began, Bruce escaped. He eventually settled in Missouri, where he organized the state's first school for African Americans. In 1869, Bruce moved to Mississippi, where he held a series of political offices. In 1874, he became the first African American to be elected to a full term in the U.S. Senate. As a senator, Bruce investigated banking scandals, advocated economic aid for freed slaves, and helped obtain levee system and railroad projects for Mississippi.

In 1880, Bruce was appointed registrar of the U.S. Treasury, where his duties required a facsimile of his signature on U.S. currency. He was also a lecturer, a writer, and an educator. Bruce died in 1898, having left his name in American history — and on a lot of money!

The sharecropping system dominated many parts of the South, replacing the plantation system. In 1868, perhaps one-third of the area's farms were tended by renters. By 1900, that percentage grew to about 70 percent. The system, coupled with low cotton prices and the ravages of an insect pest called the boll weevil, virtually guaranteed that few farmers could become successful, no matter how hard they worked.

Piecing the Union Back Together

One of the topics American historians like to speculate on is what might have happened if Lincoln hadn't been assassinated. Would he have been able to come up with a widely accepted plan to reunite the states and give the former slaves their rightful place in society? Would that have led to better race relations sooner in America?

Probably not. Lincoln, like most mid-19th century white Americans, felt it was impossible to just free the slaves and make them socially equal. "There is an unwillingness on the part of our [white] people, harsh as it may be, for you free colored people to remain with us," he told a group of African Americans during the war. Lincoln's hope was to resettle the freed slaves somewhere else, either in Africa or the Caribbean. But most black Americans had no firsthand experience with any country except the United States — the country in which they were born — and they had no desire to leave.

Lincoln did insist, however, that the former slaves be treated as equals when it came to the law. In 1864 and early 1865, he prodded Congress into passing the 13th Amendment to the Constitution, which barred slavery. He also set out a general plan for reuniting the country when the fighting was done (assuming the North won). Under this plan, most Southerners could become U.S. citizens again simply by taking a loyalty oath. Those who couldn't, mostly high-ranking Confederate officials, could apply for the reinstatement of their citizenship on a case-by-case basis. After Lincoln was killed, his vice president, Andrew Johnson, adopted practically the same plan.

Demanding loyalty, legislating equality

When 10 percent of a state's population had taken an oath of loyalty to the Union, the state could set up a new government and apply for readmission to the Union, as long as it agreed to give up slavery and provide an education system for blacks.

By the time Congress convened in December 1865, all the Southern states had organized new governments, ratified the 13th Amendment, and elected new representatives and senators for Congress.

But Congress, dominated by *Radical Republicans* — those who sought harsh reprisals against the South for the war and immediate equal rights for freed slaves — didn't like the deal. For one thing, many of the men elected to represent the Southern states in Washington, D.C., were the same people who'd run the Confederacy — including Alexander Stephens, the ex-Confederate vice president who was in federal prison awaiting trial on treason charges. That kind of in-your-face attitude irritated the Radical Republicans, who felt Southerners weren't sorry enough for causing the war.

REMEMBER

Even more infuriating were the *Black Codes.* These codes were established by Southern state legislatures to keep the former slaves "under control." They varied from state to state and did give blacks some rights they hadn't had, such as the power to sue in court, own certain kinds of property, and legally marry. But the Black Codes also prohibited blacks from bearing arms, working in most occupations other than farming or manual labor, and leaving their jobs without permission. They restricted African Americans' right to travel and fined them if they broke any of the codes. To the Radical Republicans, and even many moderate Northerners, the Black Codes were simply a substitute form of slavery.

To combat the Black Codes, Congress passed a series of bills designed to strengthen the rights of blacks — and President Johnson vetoed them either as unconstitutional interference in states' rights or as infringing on the powers of the presidency. One thing he couldn't veto, though, was the 14th Amendment, because the Constitution required that proposed amendments go directly to the states for approval. The amendment, ratified in 1868, entitled all people born or naturalized in the United States — including slaves — to U.S. citizenship and equal protection under the law.

SORRY — NOT!

"Oh I'm a good old rebel / Now that's just what I am; / For the 'fair land of freedom,' / I do not care a damn. / I'm glad I fought agin it / I only wish we'd won / And I don't want a pardon / For anything I've done."

— from a popular Southern song, 1865–1866

Using violence to keep blacks down

Many whites in the South were outraged by the 14th Amendment, particularly poorer whites who already felt they were competing with ex-slaves for jobs. Groups such as the Ku Klux Klan (KKK), Knights of the White Camellia, and Pale Faces sprang up. They used weird costumes and goofy rituals to intimidate blacks from exercising their rights. When intimidation failed, they and other white mobs and paramilitary groups resorted to violence. Hundreds of African Americans were beaten, driven from their homes, or brutally murdered as a result of these groups' actions.

The terrorist activities of the white supremacist groups were very effective in "keeping blacks in their place." And the groups had de facto, if unwitting, allies in President Andrew Johnson who seemed more intent on squabbling with Congress than solving the woes of ex-slaves, and many Northerners who were losing interest in reforming the South.

TECHNICAL STUFF

Blacks weren't the only targets of the KKK and similar groups; carpetbaggers and scalawags were also terrorized. *Carpetbaggers* were Northerners who came to the South to participate in its reconstruction — and in some cases, make a lot of money in the process. *Scalawags* were Southerners who worked in concert with the carpetbaggers. Although it's true some of these people were basically just vultures feeding off the defeated Southern corpse, many of both groups actually did a lot of good, reviving the school system, helping rebuild the railroads, and so on.

A LAMP, A COW, AND A HOT, HOT TOWN

The year 1871 was a long and dry one in Chicago, Illinois. A drought had made the bustling city tinder-dry and certainly not a place to be careless with fire. But on the morning of October 8, 1871, someone was. Legend has it that someone was a Mrs. O'Leary, on DeKoven Street. Supposedly, she went to her barn to milk the cow, the cow kicked over the kerosene lamp, and one of the most disastrous fires in U.S. history began. (Mrs. O'Leary later denied the story.)

However the fire started, by the time it was out more than 24 hours later, it had killed 250 people, left nearly 100,000 homeless, destroyed more than 17,000 buildings, and done close to $200 million worth of damage.

Contributions poured in from around the world, as did government help. Fortunately, the fire missed the city's vital railroad yards and stockyards, and within a few years, Chicago was able to rise from the ashes.

The Tailor-Made President: Andrew Johnson

Andrew Johnson may have been the poorest president ever, at least in terms of his humble beginnings. He was born in North Carolina to impoverished parents, and his father died when Johnson was just 3 years old. He never went to school and instead became a tailor's apprentice at the age of 14.

Johnson taught himself to read and became involved in politics at the age of 17. When the Civil War broke out, he became military governor of Tennessee. In 1864, the Republican Lincoln picked the Democrat Johnson to be his vice-presidential running mate. The thought was that a pro-Union Democrat would balance the ticket and attract more votes.

But when Lincoln was killed, the country was left with a stubborn and ill-tempered president who had none of Lincoln's gift of leadership. Johnson didn't like blacks, didn't like rich Southerners, and didn't like the Republican-controlled Congress. In 1866, Johnson took what was called a "Swing around the Circle," traveling around the Northern states to campaign *for* Democrats running for Congress and *against* the 14th Amendment, which would give blacks full citizenship.

REMEMBER

Johnson's "Swing around the Circle" was a disaster. The president was booed and jeered by Northern crowds who viewed him as a pro-South bozo. The Republicans dominated the election and had such overwhelming majorities in Congress that they easily passed any bill they wanted — and then just as easily overrode Johnson's vetoes.

Pushed by Radical Republicans, such as Thaddeus Stevens of Pennsylvania and Charles Sumner of Massachusetts, Congress passed a series of Reconstruction acts designed to force the South into line. One Reconstruction act, passed in 1867, divided the South into five military districts, each governed by a general and policed by the army. To be allowed to reenter the Union and get rid of military rule, Southern states had to agree to ratify the 14th Amendment. They also had to modify their state constitutions to give African Americans the right to vote. This stipulation was particularly galling to Southerners, because many Northern states at the time didn't allow blacks to vote.

Adding salt to the wound, Congress also approved and sent to the states the 15th Amendment, which guaranteed all adult males everywhere the right to vote. This amendment was passed to ensure the Southern states didn't go back on their promise to give blacks the ballot (and also because the Radical Republicans were embarrassed to be from Northern states that didn't let African Americans vote).

Enough Southern state legislatures were dominated by carpetbaggers, former slaves, and other people whose loyalties were to the Radical Republicans to ensure the amendment's ratification. However, Southern states gradually got around the law anyway by requiring blacks to pass difficult "literacy" and "citizenship" tests before they could vote.

The 15th Amendment also greatly angered many American women, who found that they were now second-class citizens to black males as well as white ones when it came to voting.

One result of giving newly freed slaves the right to vote was that they elected some of their own to state legislatures. The resulting black-white governments in some states created sound, fair tax and education systems; built roads and levees; and gave property rights to women. In other states, the government was dominated by leeches and thieves of both races, although white politicians were by far the worst offenders. One carpetbagger governor managed to "save" more than $4 million on an annual salary of $8,000 a year.

THADDEUS STEVENS

He had a clubfoot, a razor tongue, and was one of the sincerest white men in America when it came to rights for African Americans. Thaddeus Stevens was born in 1792 in New England. He moved to Pennsylvania, where he practiced law, got into politics, and was first elected to the House of Representatives and later the U.S. Senate.

Stevens was that rarity of rarities — an honest politician. He was unmoved by either flattery or criticism. But he was also fanatical in his hatred for the South, a hatred fueled in part by the destruction of his Pennsylvania factory by Southern troops on their way to Gettysburg. Stevens never married, but for years he had a black housekeeper who was rumored to be his lover. (Stevens never confirmed or denied this gossip.)

As the most radical of the Radical Republicans, Stevens virtually led the country for more than a year because of his power in Congress. He advocated taking the land from the South's wealthiest plantation owners and dividing it among former slaves. But that was too radical even for his colleagues. He did, however, successfully push for other laws designed to protect the basic rights of African Americans.

When Stevens died in 1868, he was buried in a black cemetery. "I have chosen this," read his epitaph, "that I might illustrate in my death the principles which I advocated through a long life: Equality of Man before His Creator."

Radical Republicans weren't satisfied with being able to overturn Johnson's vetoes. They wanted him out of the White House, which, according to the Constitution, would then fall to the leader of the Senate, Ohio's Benjamin Wade.

To get what they wanted, the Radicals laid a trap. Congress passed a bill that required the president to have Senate approval before he could fire any of his appointees. Johnson, who believed the act was unconstitutional, promptly took the bait and fired his secretary of war, Edwin Stanton, whom he considered a Radical Republican stooge.

REMEMBER

Following Stanton's dismissal, Congress impeached Johnson in late February 1868 for violating the law, and the Senate put him on trial. The country regarded the whole situation as a great melodrama: Tickets to the Senate gallery were the toughest buy in town. On May 16, 1868, the first of three votes was taken to remove Johnson from office. All three were 35 to 19 — one short of the two-thirds needed. Seven Republican senators voted against removing Johnson from office.

All these men sacrificed their political careers by voting against Johnson's removal, but they may very well have preserved the U.S. government. Removing Johnson solely on political grounds could have created the basis for a congressional dictatorship, whereby Congress could dominate the presidency by threatening to dump any president who didn't go along with its wishes.

"SEWARD'S FOLLY"

By 1867, Russia was ready to dump Alaska. After all, there didn't seem to be as many fur-bearing animals as there used to be, and the British might take the land anyway. It just so happened that U.S. Secretary of State William Seward was in a buying mood. Seward had heard from Americans in Russia that Alaska had loads of fish, fur, and other natural resources. Plus, buying the area would get the Russians completely out of North America — and keep other European powers from grabbing the region. So in 1867, he offered $7.2 million — about 2 cents an acre — and the Russians said "da."

Most Americans thought buying what they believed amounted to a distant, giant icebox was dumb. The press sneered at the purchase, labeling it "Seward's Folly," "Walrussia," and "Seward's Polar Bear Garden." But Congress went along with the deal, in large part because Russia had been the only European country to support the North during the Civil War. Alaska became the first U.S. possession that wasn't geographically connected to the rest of the country. It also turned out to be a pretty good deal when gold was discovered there in 1897. Then "Seward's Folly" paid off thousands of times over.

The trial may also have marked the beginning of the end of Northern interest in Reconstruction. Many Northerners were as prejudiced against blacks as many Southerners. They were sick of the issue and wanted to put the war, and its aftermath, behind them. "The whole public are tired out with these autumnal outbreaks in the South," wrote a federal official to a Southern governor, in refusing to provide military aid when the KKK interfered in local elections. "Preserve the peace by the forces of your own state."

Growing Corruption in Politics

When Americans elected Ulysses S. Grant president in 1868, they expected him to be the same kind of chief executive as he was a general — brave, tenacious, and inspiring. But Grant had no political experience and little political philosophy. Neither did many of the people he appointed to be his cabinet advisors and top aides. His one asset was his personal honesty, and, unfortunately, it was an asset not shared by the people around him.

Almost from the time Grant took office, his administration was awash in corruption. Scandal after scandal broke over the White House like waves: Cornering the gold market, attempting to annex the Caribbean island of Santo Domingo, speculating on railroads, ripping off the Native Americans, and stealing liquor tax revenues were all grist for the corruption mill. Grant's administration became known as the "Great Barbecue" because everyone helped himself.

Political corruption was by no means limited to the federal government or Grant's administration. State and local governments were tainted by scandal as well, and the country was soon caught up in what writer Mark Twain labeled "The Gilded Age." It seemed everyone (including Mark Twain) was in a fever to make money, and the most money-hungry individuals became known, not always with disdain, as *robber barons*.

In California, Colis P. Huntington and others bribed legislators and congressmen to get concessions for their railroad. In Pennsylvania, John D. Rockefeller bought and bullied lawmakers to aid his Standard Oil Company. The worst situation of all may very well have been in New York City, where a political boss named William M. Tweed created a web of elected officeholders, bureaucrats, and contractors and looted more than $100 million from the city treasury.

Despite the stench of scandal from his first term, Grant was reelected in 1872, easily defeating Democratic candidate Horace Greeley, the longtime editor of the *New York Tribune.* But by 1874, the scandals and the mess of Reconstruction — which ruined Republicans' chances of winning anything in the South — combined to let the Democrats take control of the House of Representatives. The shift added an ingredient of bitter partisan divisiveness to the stinky stew of corruption, but it didn't make it any more palatable. And then an economic panic made things worse.

Riding the railroads to economic ruin

America's post–Civil War economy was driven by a boom in railroad construction. Between 1866 and 1873, 35,000 miles of new track were laid, and railroads trailed only agriculture in their importance to the economic well-being of the country.

For many Americans with a little money to invest, railroads seemed like a can't-miss proposition. Their enthusiasm drove up stock prices far beyond what the stocks were really worth. One such deal involved a major New York-based bank called Jay Cooke & Company.

Cooke, who had become wealthy marketing Union bonds during the war and was known as "the nation's financier," was trying to build a second transcontinental railroad and was seeking investors to pay for it. Sadly for Cooke (and more sadly for his bank's customers), his efforts coincided with a confluence of unfortunate events. One was that banks in Great Britain raised interest rates, which meant fewer Brits were borrowing to invest in U.S. railroad schemes. At the same time, Congress decided to henceforth back U.S. currency with gold only. The U.S. Treasury quit buying silver; silver coins and paper "greenbacks" were devalued; the money supply shrank, and interest rates in America rose.

The economy's tailspin meant Cooke's bank couldn't attract enough cash to keep its vast railroad scheme going. On September 18, 1873, the bank went under. (The bank's collapse was so stunning that a newsboy in Philadelphia was arrested by a disbelieving cop for shouting out the news on a street corner.) The failure triggered a flood of panicked selling on the New York Stock Exchange, which actually closed down for ten days.

The stock market collapse, in turn, touched off a deep economic recession that lasted into 1879. Scores of other banks failed, about a quarter of all U.S. railroads went belly up, thousands of auxiliary businesses closed, and unemployment rose to 14 percent by 1876. The country desperately needed strong, honest, and calm political leadership. What it got was the most tainted presidential race in its history.

BOUNCE THIS IDEA OFF THE WALL

Dr. Benjamin Franklin Goodrich was a Civil War surgeon who became an Ohio business-man after the war. His business was finding things to do with rubber, which a fellow named Charles Goodyear had figured out could be treated with high heat and sulfur — a process called *vulcanization* — so it would stay flexible under hot or cold conditions.

Goodyear died in debt in 1860 before he could find a practical use for the substance. But Goodrich, who had watched a friend's house burn down after a leather fire hose burst, knew exactly what he wanted to produce. In 1870, his company began making the world's first rubber hoses (and one of the first rubber products of any kind).

By the following year, rubber gaskets, bottle stoppers, clothes-wringer rollers, and other items were being produced. Watering can manufacturers may have cursed them, but to gardeners and firefighters, Goodrich's hoses were a godsend.

Fixing a presidency (and not in a good way)

With all the corruption — and the public's growing disgust — it wasn't surprising that in 1876 both political parties nominated presidential candidates known for their integrity. The Republicans put up Rutherford B. Hayes, a former Union general who had been governor of Ohio for three terms. The Democrats countered with New York Governor Samuel B. Tilden, who had gained admiration for helping bring down the Boss Tweed Ring in New York City.

REMEMBER

When the returns came in, Tilden had beaten Hayes by more than 250,000 votes and appeared to have captured 203 of the 369 electoral votes. But Republican Party leaders, who controlled the people who oversaw the elections, arranged to invalidate thousands of Democratic votes in Florida, South Carolina, Oregon, and Louisiana, which changed the electoral vote count to 184–165, with 20 votes in dispute.

Naturally, the Democrats challenged the new results, and a special commission was created to look into the matter. The commission consisted of ten members of Congress, five from each party, as well as five members of the Supreme Court (three Republicans and two Democrats). The commission voted 8–7, not surprisingly along party lines, to give all 20 disputed votes, and the election, to Hayes.

Northern Democrats were outraged, but Southern Democrats saw an opportunity and offered a deal: They agreed to drop any challenge to the commission's vote if Hayes promised to remove the last of the federal troops from Southern states and let the states run their own affairs. The Republicans eventually agreed, and Hayes became president. As a result, the Reconstruction period came to an ignominious end. African Americans were largely abandoned by the federal government, and white Americans outside the South turned their attentions elsewhere, mostly to the West.

INDIGESTION ON WHEELS

One day in 1872, a man from Providence, Rhode Island, one Walter Scott, loaded a wagon with sandwiches, boiled eggs, and other food and parked it outside a downtown newspaper office in the evening. Because all the restaurants in town closed at 8 p.m., Scott had plenty of customers. Soon other "lunch wagons" began rolling down streets all over American cities. In 1884, a guy in Worcester, Massachusetts, named Sam Jones got the idea to put stools in his lunch wagon so customers could sit down.

The wagons drew complaints from residents and competing restaurant owners and were banned or restricted in many towns. So the wagon owners simply rolled their wagons onto vacant lots, took off the wheels, and called themselves restaurants. By the 1920s, people were eating as many breakfasts and dinners at the wagons as lunches, and rather than lunch wagons, people started calling them *diners*.

3 Coming of Age

Chapter **12**

Growing Up: 1876–1898

A mericans have always been restless, and in 1876 they were hungry, too — for success. There seemed to be many ways and places to be successful, and success seemed very important to a whole lot of people.

In this chapter, the country starts its final push toward filling in the gaps between the coasts — and its final pushing aside of the original Americans. Railroads help do both, as well as usher in the birth of truly huge businesses. A string of mediocre presidents don't do much of anything, and a war with Spain launches America on the road to becoming an empire.

Heading West in a Quest for Wealth

When settlers in America first started moving west (about ten minutes after they got here), they generally did so because of the lure of free land and the chance to put down roots. After the Civil War, however, Americans moved west as much to make a buck as to settle into a new life. The West was seen as a bottomless treasure chest of resources to exploit.

Making money from minerals

Some of those resources were mineral. Starting with the California Gold Rush of 1849, the West saw a steady stream of gold, silver, and copper discoveries touch off other "rushes," as hordes of miners careened like pinballs from strike to strike. In 1859, thousands descended on Pike's Peak in Colorado, looking for gold. Later that year, it was the Comstock silver lode in Nevada. In 1861, it was Idaho; in 1863, Montana; in 1874, the Black Hills of Dakota; and in 1876, it was back to Colorado.

Towns with 5,000 inhabitants or more sprang up virtually overnight, composed of miners-who-would-be millionaires, and the gamblers, thieves, swindlers, prostitutes, and liquor sellers who accompanied them. They formed violent societies. Justice was often in the form of vigilance committees or *vigilantes,* who set themselves up as the law and sometimes didn't bother with a trial before stretching a defendant's neck.

Where most of the mining money went reflected what was happening in the rest of the country. Big corporations, financed by stockholders from the East as well as Europe, had the capital to buy the equipment needed to mine on a large scale, and they reaped most of the profits. Most miners made little, and many of them ended up going to work as laborers for the large companies.

REMEMBER

But mining had some positive impact on the West besides the wealth it created. The miners were the first to open much of the West, and they helped encourage the railroads to come. Some of those who came for the booms stayed on after the inevitable busts that followed. Because miners had to set up governments in a hurry to deal with the instant towns, political organization took root. Coupled with the mineral wealth, these organizations gave the mining areas clout in Congress. This helped speed the admission of new states, such as Nevada.

By the dawn of the new century, the big, fever-producing mineral strikes were over in the West. But they were replaced by the rush to extract oil — "Black Gold" — beneath western lands, particularly in Texas and Oklahoma.

Making money from animals

After the Civil War, Texas soldiers returned to find as many as five million cattle roaming around the state. The cattle were descendants of animals brought to the area hundreds of years before by Spanish explorers. There was plenty of grazing land and enough water, and the cattle were a hardy breed.

Now, Texans were as fond of beef as the next state's inhabitants, but they really wanted to find a way to share their wealth on the hoof with the rest of the nation. Cattle worth $3 to $4 a head in Texas could be sold for ten times that much in

Eastern states, if you could get them there. Cattle drives to the East and even California had been tried before. But many of the cattle died before the drives were over, and the survivors were worn thin by the effort.

After the war, however, someone got the idea to shorten the distances by driving cattle to the railroads that were moving west and then shipping them east by rail. Rail met cow at "trailheads" in Abilene and Dodge City in Kansas, Ogallala in Nebraska, and Cheyenne in Wyoming. By 1871, 750,000 head of cattle were moving through Abilene alone. By 1875, the advent of the refrigerated car allowed cattle to be slaughtered and butchered in Midwest cities like Kansas City and Chicago before being shipped east.

The rise of the cattle industry also gave rise to an American icon: the cowboy. Hollywood turned the cowboy into a romantic figure who was quick on the draw with a six-shooter and spent most of his time drinking whiskey and playing poker in town, with a dance-hall girl hovering at his shoulder.

In truth, the cowboy was more likely an ex-Confederate soldier or former slave who spent most of his life on the back of a short-legged cow pony, hundreds of miles from the nearest bar or woman. He was brave and tough, but he was far less likely to use his pistol on his fellow man than he was on rattlesnakes or as a noise-maker. He was likely in his late teens or early 20s, and about one in five was African American. He worked for $25 a month and ate beans, bacon, and black coffee day after day.

By the early 1890s, the day of the cowboy and the cattle drive was coming to an end. Like other aspects of American life, inventions (such as barbed wire) and investments (by Easterners and Europeans) turned ranching into big business, and cowboys became caretakers on large fenced ranches rather than riders of the range. A far less glamorous, but much more numerous, type of Westerner was now dominant: the sodbuster.

Making money from vegetables

In the wake of the miner and the cowboy came the farmer. The railroads were eager to colonize the areas they controlled with potential customers and offered land near their tracks through giant advertising efforts in the East and Europe. The federal government tried various ways to sell public lands, most of them badly managed.

Regardless, the settlers rushed in. The populations of Minnesota, Kansas, and Nebraska doubled or tripled. The Dakotas went from 14,000 residents after the Civil War to 500,000 in 20 years. In 1889, the "Cherokee Strip" in northern Oklahoma was purchased from Native Americans and thrown open to settlement, and by 1900, the Oklahoma Territory had a population of about 800,000.

HAPPY 100TH, AMERICA

In 1871, Congress decided to put on a big to-do to celebrate America's 100th birthday. It took awhile to raise the dough, but on May 10, 1876, 13 giant bells chimed, 100 cannons fired a salute, and an 800-voice choir sang the "Hallelujah Chorus" to open the U.S. Centennial Exhibition in Philadelphia.

The fair, spread over a 248-acre park, featured exhibits from all over the world, but the highlights were the proud displays of Yankee know-how. Crowds, which included Pres. Ulysses Grant and Emperor Don Pedro II of Brazil, gasped and gaped at the largest steam engine ever built up to that time; an ice box that used ammonia as its refrigerant; and a printing process that printed, cut, and sorted pages for up to an hour at a time.

The first prize for new inventions went to Alexander Graham Bell for a device he called the telephone. The Brazilian emperor put the thing to his ear and quickly dropped it, exclaiming, "My God, it talks!" But Bell's invention drew smaller crowds than an exotic exhibit from Central America. It featured a strange fruit, called the banana.

Most of the farmers faced a blizzard of hardships: drought, grasshopper invasions, prairie fires, and, well, blizzards. There was even foreign competition. In the 1870s, crop failures in Europe helped drive up prices and open markets for American farmers. But in the 1880s, crop prices fell as new producers in Australia and India came on the scene.

More and more farmers in the West found themselves in the same plight as those in the Civil War–torn South. The number of farms that were either mortgaged or farmed by tenant farmers steadily increased as the last 20 years of the century passed.

Still, between 1870 and 1900, the number of American acres under cultivation more than doubled, from 407 million to 841 million acres. The frontier had been mined, ranched, and farmed into submission.

Ousting "Undesirables"

Gen. Philip Sheridan never said, "The only good Indian is a dead Indian." What he did say, however, was just as bad: "The only good Indians I ever saw were dead."

There were plenty of dead Native Americans by 1876. When Columbus arrived, there were probably 1 million to 1.5 million Native Americans living in what is now the United States. By the time of the Civil War, that number had dropped to about 300,000, with two-thirds of them living on the Great Plains.

The Plains Indians generally tolerated the white man crossing their territory on the way to California and Oregon. But when the newcomers began to settle in, tensions grew, and both sides resorted to violence.

In 1862, several bands of Dakota went on the offensive in Minnesota against encroaching settlers, killing more than 700 before the militia defeated them and hanged 38 of the tribe's leaders. In 1864, John Chivington, a Colorado militia colonel, attacked a band of Cheyenne at Sand Creek, Colorado, and killed 133 people, most of them women and children. Many white Americans were appalled at Chivington's brutality.

After the Civil War was over, a debate began in earnest on what to do about "the Indian Problem." Ideas ranged from extermination to reservations to ending tribal customs and forcing Native Americans to adopt white culture, a process known as *acculturation*. All the ideas were tried to varying degrees. Between 1859 and 1876, soldiers and Native Americans fought at least 200 pitched battles and signed 370 treaties.

"They made us promises more than I can remember," noted one Sioux leader, "but they never kept but one. They promised to take our land, and they did."

They also all but wiped out the American bison — more popularly, if scientifically inaccurately, known as "buffalo" — which to the Plains Indian was a walking department store. The tribes not only ate bison but also wore clothes and blankets from it and used its bones for tools and its dried dung for fire fuel. In 1840, an estimated 40 million of the animals roamed the Plains.

But bison were dumber than rocks when it came to being hunted, placidly grazing while hunters with long-range rifles picked them off one by one for their hides, their meat, or just for the heck of it. By 1875, only a million were left; by 1893, less than 1,000. The Plains Indians were starved into submission far more than they were outfought.

In 1868, after a series of indecisive battles, both sides agreed to a grand scheme in which two large reservations would be created, one in Oklahoma and one that took in all of western South Dakota. That included the Black Hills, which were sacred to the Sioux, a group of Native American tribes that included the Lakota, Dakota, and Nakota.

Putting up a fight

Six years later, an expedition led by Colonel George Armstrong Custer discovered gold in the Black Hills. White prospectors poured into the area. The federal government, powerless to stop them, offered to buy the land from the Native Americans but was refused. The last great war against the Native Americans began, and for the first time, the Plains tribes united into a formidable fighting force.

On June 25, 1876, the U.S. 7th Cavalry regiment, led by Custer, rashly attacked a Native American encampment at the Little Bighorn River in Montana. It proved to be populated by 2,500 warriors. Custer and nearly 40 percent of his men were killed.

"Custer's Last Stand" horrified people in the East as well as the West, and greatly diminished sympathy for the Native Americans' situation. The battle proved to be the beginning of the end for the Plains Indians. Over the next decade, tribe after tribe was gradually worn down by hunger and continual pursuit by the army. What happened to the Plains tribes was repeated throughout the West — the Apache in Arizona, the Crow and Blackfoot in Montana, the Ute in Colorado, the Nez Percé in Idaho — all were decimated by hunger, disease, and harassment by the whites.

In 1887, Congress passed a law, called the Dawes Act, that divided land into individual allotments for Native Americans, as part of an effort to turn them into small farmers. It also provided for an education system and eventual U.S. citizenship. However well intentioned the law was, it didn't work. Most Native Americans didn't want to be farmers or U.S. citizens, and the education system never amounted to much. Many Native Americans eventually signed away their land for a few cents an acre to speculators, who promptly resold it to settlers for a few dollars an acre.

REMEMBER

In 1890, a misunderstanding led to a cavalry attack on a group of Miniconjou and Hunkpapa Lakota who were under military escort, near a creek called Wounded Knee in South Dakota. The soldiers killed more than 200 men, women, and children and then left their bodies in the snow for three days before burying them in a mass grave. It was the last major violence between the Native Americans and whites, and a tragic and horrifyingly typical response to America's "Indian Problem."

I QUIT

"I am tired of fighting. The old men are all dead . . . it is cold and we have no blankets. The little children are freezing to death. . . . Hear me my chiefs. I am tired; my heart is sick and sad. From where the sun now stands, I will fight no more forever."
— Nez Percé Chief Joseph, before surrendering to U.S. Army troops, 1877

CRAZY HORSE

Crazy Horse was named after his father, after proving himself in battle, which was probably a good thing, because in his early years he was called "Curly." Born around 1842 near the Belle Fourche River in South Dakota, the Lakota (Sioux) warrior began his fight against the white invaders in 1865. He became known as a daring fighter who used tricks and guerilla tactics well. In 1866, he helped lure 80 soldiers into an ambush in which all of them were killed.

Eleven months after leading the combined tribes against Custer at the Little Big Horn, Crazy Horse surrendered to troops that had been relentlessly harassing his band. He was taken to Fort Robinson, Wyoming, where he was held for several months.

"They say we massacred him [Custer]," he said during his captivity, "but he would have done the same thing to us had we not defended ourselves and fought to the last. Our first impulse was to escape . . . but we were so hemmed in that we had to fight."

In September 1877, while still in custody, he was stabbed to death by a soldier under questionable circumstances. Crazy Horse became a mythic figure among Native Americans of all tribes.

Legalizing discrimination

While white America was pushing the Native Americans to adopt white ways and become part of white culture, it was pushing to keep African Americans out. Reconstruction had failed to give blacks equal rights, and a conservative U.S. Supreme Court ensured the failure would last another 50 or 60 years.

REMEMBER

In 1883, the Court ruled the federal government had no right to interfere with discrimination by private enterprises or individuals. In 1896, in a case called *Plessy v. Ferguson*, it decided states had the right to legally segregate public facilities, from schools to trains, as long as the separate facilities were equal in quality — which rarely, if ever, occurred. And in 1899, the Court went a step further by ruling that states could erect new schools for white kids only, even if schools for black kids weren't available.

Encouraged by the decisions, Southern states passed what were called *Jim Crow laws* (named after a popular song that depicted African Americans as shiftless children), which not only tried to completely separate the races, but also take away most of the rights they had been accorded by the 13th, 14th, and 15th Amendments. Blacks couldn't serve on juries, represent themselves in court, or drink from the same public drinking fountains as whites. If they quit a job, they could be arrested for vagrancy. They also established elaborate tests that black would-be voters had to take to get a ballot. Black voting levels dropped like a boulder off a bridge.

In addition to the Jim Crow laws, the South also averaged 130 lynchings a year in the 1890s. They were so commonplace they were sometimes advertised in advance in newspapers. The North generally shrugged at the Jim Crow laws and ignored the lynchings. "The Negro's day is over," observed Yale Professor William Graham Sumner. "He is out of fashion."

Even the best-known African American leader of the day was not ready to challenge the injustices. Born into slavery, Booker T. Washington had become a schoolteacher, the founder of a major vocational school in Alabama called the Tuskegee Institute, and an eloquent advocate of African Americans improving themselves economically.

To improve their economic situations, Washington urged blacks to "accommodate" whites when it came to demands for segregation, in return for white help in obtaining black schools and economic opportunity. "The wisest among my race understand that the agitation of questions of social equality is the extremest of folly," he argued.

White America didn't care much for Chinese immigrants, either. Known as *"The Yellow Peril,"* many Chinese were brought to America to work on the railroads at half the wages paid to white workers. As a result, they were viewed as a competitive labor threat to American-born workers. Anti-Chinese riots broke out in San Francisco in 1877. In 1882, Congress passed a law prohibiting all Chinese immigration for ten years. The ban, called the Chinese Exclusion Act, was later extended to last indefinitely and wasn't repealed until 1943.

Cramming into Cities

The law that excluded immigration by Chinese also banned criminals, the mentally ill or disabled, and those likely to end up as public charity cases. But otherwise, America's front door was wide open, and people poured in. Between 1866 and 1915, 25 million immigrants came to the United States. Most of them came from Italy and Southeastern Europe, but they also came from Scandinavia, Russia, Poland, Germany, Ireland, England, and France. By 1910, 15 percent of the country's total population was foreign-born. Most came to escape hard economic times at home, despotic governments, or both. Often their expectations were unrealistically high. "America is all puddings and pies!" enthused one young man as he stepped off the ship in New York.

Despite the warning of a popular immigrant guidebook to "forget your past, your customs, and your ideals," many of the new Americans clung to their own languages, customs, and cuisines and gravitated to communities populated by others from their country. The presence of so many immigrants in so short a time caused alarm in some "natives," who feared the newcomers would weaken their chances in the job market and pollute American culture. But it wasn't until 1921, after World War I had created millions of refugees in Europe, that Congress tightened immigration policies concerning Europeans.

In the meantime, as much as 80 percent of the immigrant wave settled in Northern cities. By the turn of the century, more than a third of Chicago's populace was foreign-born, and there were more Irish in New York City than there were in Ireland. The immigrants weren't the only newcomers in town, because there were plenty of American-born country folks moving to urban areas, as well. By 1900, 30 million Americans lived in cities, about a third of all U.S. residents. The number of cities larger than 100,000 increased from 9 to 50 between 1860 and 1910.

But many parts of the big cities were festering sores. In those areas, fire protection, street cleaning, sewage systems, garbage collection, and water treatment barely existed. The Chicago River was an open sewer. Baltimore's sewers emptied into the tidal basin and in the summer heat, journalist H. L. Mencken wrote, it "smelled like a billion polecats."

Housing was often designed to cram the most people into the least space. It wasn't uncommon for 24 four-room apartments to be built on a 2,500-square-foot lot. Tenement slums took on fitting names, such as "Hell's Kitchen," "Bone Alley," or "Poverty Gap."

SLUM LIFE

"All the fresh air that enters these stairs comes from the hall-door that is forever slamming. . .. The sinks are in the hallway, that all tenants may have access — and all be poisoned alike by the summer stenches. . .. Here is a door. Listen! That slow, hacking cough, that tiny helpless wail — what do they mean? The child is dying of measles. With half a chance, it might have lived; but it had none."
— Reporter Jacob Riis, in "How the Other Half Lives," 1890

Gradually, things improved in the major urban areas. No one, rich or poor, wanted to live in filth, and after the link between disease and poor sanitation was firmly established, city leaders began to develop adequate sewage and water systems. Public transit systems, based on streetcars or trolleys, were put in place. But none of it happened overnight, and more than a few farmers-turned-city-dwellers must have yearned more than once to be home on the range.

Inventing Big Business

As America reached young adulthood in the last part of the 19th century, it began to shake off its rural roots and become an industrial city slicker. From 1859 to 1899, the value of the country's manufactured products rose 622 percent, from $1.8 billion to $13 billion, and America became the world's leading manufacturer. It rode its way to the top on the train.

Building the railroads

The railroad system was America's first truly big business and its growth and impact were enormous. In the 41 years from 1830 to 1870, about 40,000 miles of track were laid in the country. But in the 20 years from 1871 to 1890, more than 110,000 miles were laid. In 1869, the first transcontinental line linking the East and West coasts was opened, and by 1900, there were four more.

REMEMBER

By 1890, annual railroad freight revenues totaled $1 billion — which was more than twice what the federal government took in. The railroads not only transported goods and people, they dictated where towns would grow and businesses would locate. They employed more than one million people by 1900. They pushed Congress to create four standard time zones across the country so train schedules could be worked out.

The railroads created or greatly expanded other industries with their demands for materials like steel for rails and passenger and freight cars. And they helped speed development of America's telegraph system, because where the rails went, the wires went. With telegraph stations at most train stations, the Western Union Company was sending 40 million messages a year by 1883, over 400,000 miles of wire.

Despite all those grand and glorious numbers, the railroad boom wasn't exactly a shining example of American free enterprise at its best. The rails were laid mostly on public land given to the railroads by the federal government — more than 240,000 square miles, or an area the size of Germany — along with more than $60 million in taxpayer-financed grants or loans.

AND DRIBBLE BEFORE YOU SHOOT . . .

James Naismith had an unruly class on his hands. The Canadian-born YMCA teacher was training would-be YMCA instructors in Springfield, Massachusetts, in the winter of 1891. His boss had ordered him to come up with a new indoor game that would get the class re-enthused about exercise in the winter.

Naismith tried variations of soccer and lacrosse. They proved too rough. After two weeks, he was still stumped. Then a solution began to fall into place. The first notion was to use a big, round ball that didn't require a stick to hit it. Second, running with the ball was eliminated, so no tackling was required. Third, goals were set up through which to chuck the ball.

"I met Mr. Stebbins, the superintendent of buildings," Naismith later recalled, "and I asked him if he had two boxes about 18 inches square. Stebbins thought a minute and then said: 'No, but I have two old peach baskets down in the store room.'" By noon, Naismith had nailed up the peach baskets, and two nine-man teams were playing "basket ball" — as opposed to what presumably would have been "box ball."

Because the federal government didn't want to get directly in the railroad-building business, the land was thought of as an incentive to attract private investment. The idea was the railroad companies would sell most of the land near their tracks, and that's where they would make their money, because rail operations alone weren't expected to turn a profit for years.

The system was ripe for corruption, and scandals were plenty. The Union Pacific line, for example, was built by the Credit Mobilier Construction Company, which was owned by the same people who owned the railroad. They took fat federal grants and awarded themselves exorbitant contracts — and bought off inquisitive congressmen with bribes of heavily discounted railroad stock.

The business attracted titans of industry (or robber barons, depending on how you viewed them). There was Cornelius Vanderbilt in the East, Thomas A. Scott in the Midwest, James J. Hill in the Northwest, and Jay Gould in the Southwest. Each had his railroad fiefdoms and battled with the others for government favors. But not all the country's big wheels concentrated on trains — there were fortunes to be made in other fields, too.

Manufacturing steel more efficiently

Before the Civil War, steel was a rare and expensive building material, mainly because the process to make it from iron ore was a lengthy one. But a method that became widely used in the early 1870s greatly shortened the process while greatly increasing the amount that could be made at one time.

In America, steel-making became synonymous with one man: Andrew Carnegie. Born in Scotland, Carnegie came to America at the age of 13 and got a job working in a Pennsylvania factory for $1.50 a week. He moved on to jobs with Western Union and the Pennsylvania Railroad, made smart investments, and, by the time he was 28, was making $50,000 a year.

Carnegie eventually focused on steel. He hired chemists to perfect the production process, developed markets for steel, reinvested his profits, and expanded. He bought up or leased vast holdings of iron ore and coal in order to corner the supply of raw materials. By 1890, America was producing 4 million tons of steel per year, mostly for the railroads, and 70 percent of it was made by Carnegie's steel plants near Pittsburgh.

In 1901, Carnegie sold out to financier J. P. Morgan for the staggering sum of $447 million. In his later years, he gave away more than $300 million of his fortune through philanthropies that included building 2,811 public libraries and donating 8,000 organs to churches.

Refining (and controlling) oil

In the 1850s, whale oil — the primary fuel for providing light — had become very expensive, and people began to look for an alternative. Gradually, drilling for oil became practical enough that kerosene made from refined petroleum began replacing whale oil.

The most famous — or infamous — of the oil men was John D. Rockefeller, a Cleveland businessman who had made some money during the Civil War selling meat and grain. In 1870, Rockefeller combined five companies he owned into the Standard Oil Company. A ruthless and brilliant businessman, Rockefeller either bought up the competition or drove it out of business by undercutting prices. Political bribery was also a standard tool of Standard Oil: One critic noted that Rockefeller "had done everything to the Pennsylvania legislature except refine it." By 1879, Standard Oil controlled 90 percent of the nation's refining capacity, a huge network of pipelines, and large oil reserves, and by 1892, Rockefeller had amassed a fortune of $800 million.

THE REAL THING

John Pemberton was an Atlanta pharmacist, but he was also a man with a vision: He wanted to make the perfect drink. So he came up with a syrup that combined the coca leaf and the kola nut. Mixing it in a big kettle, he lugged it down to a local drugstore, where he sold it for five cents a glass — and averaged nine sales a day.

Pemberton died in 1888, and the formula for "Coca-Cola" (a name created by Pemberton's bookkeeper from the two main ingredients) was sold to a clever marketing man named Asa B. Candler. Candler realized that advertising was the key to making the product a national brand and devoted an unheard-of $50,000 a year to marketing the drink. Other executives who followed him perfected distribution and bottling techniques, and today billions of bottles and cans of "Coke" are sold in more than 200 countries.

P.S.: Among other things, Pemberton claimed his drink could cure headaches and dyspepsia. He made no rash claims about diet dyspepsia.

Getting wired for sound and light

New industries were also springing up around new inventions. In 1876, a teacher of the deaf, Alexander Graham Bell, invented the telephone. By 1880, 85 cities and towns had phone networks, and by 1900, more than 800,000 telephones were in place throughout the country.

In 1879, inventor Thomas A. Edison came up with a practical electric light bulb. Over the next 20 years, America began to wire up. At first, direct current (DC) was used, but DC didn't work over distances of more than a few miles. Then a man named George Westinghouse began using alternating current (AC), which allowed high voltage to be sent long distances through transformers and then reduced to safer levels as it entered buildings. Switching from steam engines to electricity made factories safer and more efficient, too.

Forming trusts and striking against them

In 1882, Standard Oil organized the first of the nation's trusts. A *trust* oversaw virtually all of an industry's operations, from production to price-setting to distribution and sales. It was supposedly run not by a single company, but by trustees. A trust issued certificates to stockholders in the industry's companies and paid dividends. Virtual monopolies like Standard Oil could then argue that they didn't control an industry; the trust did.

Monopolies weren't all bad. Because of the economies of doing business on a large scale, costs could be kept down and prices lowered. The price of kerosene, for example, dropped a fair amount after Standard Oil dominated the market. Of course, with no competition, prices were at the mercy of the monopolies and could — and often did — swing up again. In addition, the sheer size and power of the monopolies were worrisome to some Americans.

Carnegie and other giants of capitalism immodestly preached the "Gospel of Wealth," arguing that it was natural for a few people to have most of the wealth, a sort of economic "survival of the fittest." As long as they used their fortunes to benefit society, they contended there was nothing wrong with it.

REMEMBER

But opening libraries and donating church organs didn't put bread on the table of the average working guy. Labor unions began to try to do that after the Civil War by organizing on a large scale. Most notable were groups called the Knights of Labor and the American Federation of Labor (AFL). In 1877, America faced its first national labor strike when railroad workers walked off the job after wages were cut. State and federal troops were called in, hundreds of strikers were killed or wounded, and service was restored at the point of a gun.

In May 1886, an AFL strike for an eight-hour day for workers led to a clash at Chicago's Haymarket Square between police and strikers. A bomb killed 7 cops and injured 67 others. The police, who had killed four strikers the day before, fired into the crowd and killed four more. Seven strike leaders were eventually convicted, and four were hanged. The incident was condemned by anti-union forces as an example of how the labor movement was controlled by "anarchists" and "radicals."

In 1894, a strike against the Pullman railroad car company spread over 27 states and paralyzed the country's railroads. Federal troops were called out, and a court order ended the strike. The Haymarket Square riot and Pullman strike dealt severe blows to the chances of things getting better for the average working stiff through labor unions. America was progressing, but not all of its citizens were.

CAVEAT EMPTOR, CHUMP

"Let the buyer beware; that covers the whole business. You cannot wet-nurse men from the time they are born until the time they die. They have to wade, and get stuck, and that is the way men are educated."

— Sugar baron Henry O. Havemeyer, to a congressional committee investigating the sugar industry, 1895

Electing a String of Forgettable Presidents

It's doubtful America ever had as many mediocre presidents in a row as it did between 1876 and 1900. It wasn't a case of boring elections. Party splits and the fact that winners got to milk the government for jobs made for intense and nasty campaigns. There were plenty of big issues, too, from tariffs to bank panics to civil service reform. But the men elected to deal with them were largely a forgettable bunch. Here they are, before I forget them:

>> **Rutherford B. Hayes** (Republican, 1877–1881): Hayes was a Civil War hero who hated making tough decisions, so he avoided them. The Democrats controlled Congress most of the time he was president, so he accomplished little. He chose not to run for a second term and may not have been nominated anyway.

>> **James A. Garfield** (Republican, 1881): Garfield was assassinated by a disgruntled office seeker four months after taking office. He was also the last president to be born in a log cabin.

>> **Chester A. Arthur** (Republican, 1881–1885): Arthur was a lifelong politician who never won an election, except as Garfield's running mate. He was a fairly dignified and businesslike president, but he accomplished little.

>> **Grover Cleveland** (Democrat, 1885–1889 and 1893–1897): Cleveland was the only president to serve two nonconsecutive terms and the only one to have personally hanged a man. He accomplished the latter feat as sheriff in Buffalo, New York. He managed the former by losing his reelection bid in 1888 to Benjamin Harrison and then defeating Harrison in 1892. His second term was marked by an economic depression. He didn't win nomination for a chance at a third term.

>> **Benjamin Harrison** (Republican, 1889–1893): Harrison was the grandson of Pres. William Henry Harrison. Six new states — Washington, Idaho, Montana, Wyoming, North Dakota, and South Dakota — were admitted during his administration. That was pretty much it.

>> **William McKinley** (Republican, 1897–1901): By most accounts, McKinley was a nice guy. He was an Ohio congressman and governor and very devoted to his invalid wife. He also had friends in high places, especially political boss Mark Hanna. Hanna and others helped elect McKinley president. He defeated Democrat-Populist William Jennings Bryan in 1896, and again in 1900. He was assassinated by a crazy anarchist named Leon Czolgosz in 1901. As he lay wounded, McKinley urged that his killer not be harmed. But Czolgosz was executed in the electric chair anyway.

The Rise of Populism

Times were tough on the farm in the 1890s. Crop prices fell as production rose. Credit was hard to get and interest rates were high. Many of the rural areas' best and brightest had taken off to seek their fortunes in the cities.

REMEMBER

These hard times triggered a political movement called *Populism.* Populists sought higher crop prices and lower interest rates. They wanted a system where farmers could deposit crops in storage facilities and use them as collateral for low-interest government loans.

They also wanted more money put into circulation and more silver coins made. The idea was that more money in circulation would raise crop prices, while their mortgage payments would stay the same. But it was also risky. Money based on the amount of gold reserves the country had was more stable than money based on silver, because the amount of silver reserves was increasing and therefore could "cheapen" the value of money as the price of silver dropped.

Republicans generally opposed the Populist ideas, while Democrats generally lined up with the Populists. The Democrats nominated 36-year-old Nebraska Congressman William Jennings Bryan as their 1896 presidential candidate. Bryan, an outstanding orator, gave a rousing speech at the Democratic convention in favor of "free silver," by exclaiming "you shall not crucify mankind upon a cross of gold." But Bryan lost to Republican William McKinley anyway, in large part because McKinley's supporters raised and spent a then-staggering $3 million on his campaign.

"A Splendid Little War"

When Cuba revolted against Spain in 1868, most Americans weren't very interested. But in 1898, when the Caribbean island rebelled again, America took notice. The difference was that by 1898, the United States was Cuba's best customer for its sugar and tobacco crops, and its biggest investor. So when the fighting destroyed American property in Cuba, the country's interest was aroused.

Some Americans wanted to free Cuba from Spanish oppression. Some wanted to protect U.S. economic interests, and others just saw it as a chance to pick off some of Spain's colonies for America.

HOW ABOUT HAWAII?

The islands of Hawaii have always been a great place to visit for Americans. Yankee traders visited there in the 1790s. In the 1840s, the islands were home to American whaling ships. And by 1860, many U.S. citizens owned land there.

In 1875, America dropped a ban on Hawaiian sugar that had been urged by U.S. sugar growers and became the islands' best customer; and in 1887, Hawaii granted America exclusive rights to use Pearl Harbor as a coaling station and repair base for U.S. ships.

But making Hawaii a U.S. territory took some doing. In 1893, white businessmen, looking for a way to exempt Hawaiian sugar from steep U.S. tariffs, led a successful rebellion against Queen Liliuokalani. The rebels promptly petitioned to be annexed to the United States. But Pres. Grover Cleveland rejected the offer. The new Hawaiian government asked again in 1897, but this time the Senate rejected it. Finally, in 1898, Hawaii became a U.S. territory. In 1959, it became the 50th state.

The anti-Spain flames were fanned by New York newspapers that tried to outdo each other in reporting about Spain's "atrocities." "You furnish the pictures," New York publisher William Randolph Hearst told an illustrator for his *New York Journal*, "and I'll furnish the war."

In January 1898, the U.S. battleship *Maine* was sent to Havana when it was reported that American lives were in danger. On February 15, the *Maine* mysteriously exploded, killing 260 U.S. sailors and officers. Possible — and still unexplained — causes ranged from a Spanish mine to an internal coal fire. It didn't matter. By April, America and Spain were at war.

It was, in the words of one American official, "a splendid little war." In the Philippines, a U.S. fleet commanded by Commodore George Dewey blasted a Spanish fleet and U.S. soldiers easily took the islands. Cuba took a little longer to conquer, but the Spanish forces there also fell. The four-month war cost 5,642 American lives, all but 379 to disease. And a grown-up America now had the makings of an empire on its hands.

Chapter **13**

Growing into the 20th Century: 1899–1918

As the 1800s turned into the 1900s, America had just won a short and sloppily fought, but easily won, war with Spain. As a result, the country found itself, for the first time in its history, with an overseas empire formed by the colonies it won from Spain.

This chapter covers how America reacted to its new role as a force to be reckoned with in the world, and how Americans handled changes in how they worked, how they got around, and how they governed themselves.

Here Today, Guam Tomorrow: Colonizing Spain's Lands

At the end of the 19th century, the U.S. government suddenly had a lot more territory on its hands. There was Hawaii, which was formally annexed in 1898, and also Guam, Puerto Rico, and the Philippines, which were all won from Spain. Cuba was technically free, but because of restrictive treaties, it was in reality an American fiefdom.

On February 6, 1899, the U.S. Senate ratified the treaty with Spain that gave the U.S. Guam and Puerto Rico. The Spanish threw in the Philippines, too, after American negotiators offered $20 million for the islands. The Senate vote on the treaty was 57 to 27 — only two more than the two-thirds needed. The close vote mirrored a sharp division of opinion about whether it was a good idea for America to have colonies.

Arguing about American imperialism

Imperialism is a political idea that sounds something like this: "We can run your country better than you can because we have a better system of government." In practical terms, imperialists also often view occupied territory as a sort of automatic teller machine for withdrawals of natural resources or as a great place for strategically located military bases.

In June 1898, opponents to the idea of American colonies formed the Anti-Imperialist League, a group of strange bedfellows that included author Mark Twain, steel tycoon Andrew Carnegie, and labor leader Samuel Gompers. The folks who opposed imperialism all had different reasons for their opposition. Some believed it was un-American to impose American culture or government on other people. Others were afraid of "mingling" with "inferior" races. Laborers feared competition from poorly paid workers in other countries, and conservative business leaders feared foreign entanglements would divert capital.

Proponents, led by Theodore Roosevelt, who was then the governor of New York, argued that annexation would open the Orient for U.S. business. He said it would also prevent other nations from seizing the former Spanish colonies and better position the United States as a world military power. Pres. William McKinley opined it was America's duty to "educate the Filipinos and uplift and civilize and Christianize them," conveniently ignoring the fact that most Filipinos were already Roman Catholic. Such attitudes sparked a war with the newly liberated Filipinos. The war took several years and thousands of casualties on both sides before the United States prevailed.

FIGHTING WITH THE FILIPINOS

After suffering under Spanish rule for 350 years, Filipinos weren't keen on a continuance of domination by a foreign country. But America wanted to hold on to the islands for their strategic value as a base for U.S. naval operations and to protect U.S. business interests there. The result was what is perhaps America's least-known war.

In 1899, led by Emilio Aguinaldo, Filipino *insurrectos* who had fought alongside U.S. troops against the Spanish now took up arms against their former allies. Aguinaldo commanded an army of about 80,000. Many of the insurrectos lacked weapons other than spears or machetes, so the Filipinos resorted to guerilla warfare and terrorism. American soldiers responded with a vengeance, torturing and executing prisoners and burning entire villages.

After four years of fighting, 4,230 Americans and more than 25,000 Filipinos had been killed. After Aguinaldo was captured and took an oath of allegiance to the United States, the fighting ended. A U.S. judge named William Howard Taft (who would later become the 27th president of the United States) took over as civilian governor of the islands. Taft gave the Filipinos wide latitude in governing themselves. But formal U.S. control didn't end until July 4, 1946.

Keeping a high profile in international affairs

To a large extent, the nasty fight in the Philippines soured the American appetite for imperialism. But protecting U.S. business interests overseas remained a priority, and a strong feeling still existed that the country needed to maintain a high profile in international affairs. No one felt that way more strongly than McKinley's new vice president, Theodore Roosevelt. McKinley's original vice president, Garret Hobart, had died in late 1899, and Republican Party leaders added the headstrong Roosevelt to McKinley's ticket in 1900 mainly as a way to shut him up in the obscurity of the vice presidency.

But on September 6, 1901, while visiting the Pan-American Exposition in Buffalo, New York, McKinley was shot by a self-proclaimed anarchist. The president died a week later, and Roosevelt moved into the spotlight.

"Now look!" cried GOP political boss Mark Hanna of McKinley's death and Roosevelt's succession to the presidency. "That damned cowboy is President of the United States!"

Making a Lot of Noise and Carrying a
Big Stick: Roosevelt Takes Office

Depending on whether you liked him or not, Theodore Roosevelt was either the energetic embodiment of the nation he led or a macho blowhard who really should have taken more cold showers.

A puny, asthmatic child, Roosevelt literally built himself into a human dynamo with strenuous exercise and a nonstop personal regimen. His walrus mustache, thick round spectacles, and outsized teeth made him a political cartoonist's dream (see Figure 13-1). However, his relative youth — at 42, he was the youngest president the country had ever had — his energy, and his unpredictability made him the bane of GOP political bosses.

FIGURE 13-1:
Political cartoonists had fun with Theodore Roosevelt's appearance and personality.

THE MAN WHO CAN MAKE THE DIRT FLY.

© Bettmann/CORBIS

Roosevelt was fond of repeating an old African proverb that suggested "Speak softly, and carry a big stick; you will go far." In practice, however, he was much fonder of the stick than of speaking softly. A leading imperialist under McKinley, Roosevelt relished America's role as policeman to the world — and he took great advantage of his position as the top cop. In 1903, for example, Roosevelt encouraged Panama to revolt against Colombia so the United States could secure rights from the Panamanians to build the Panama Canal. In 1905, he brokered the treaty that settled a war between Russia and Japan, for which he won a Nobel Peace Prize. (In 2001, Roosevelt was posthumously awarded the Congressional Medal of Honor for his service in the war with Spain — the only man to win the top prize for peace and war.)

REMEMBER

Roosevelt set the tone for presidents who followed him. Both William Howard Taft and Woodrow Wilson had their own versions of *gunboat diplomacy* (using force, or threat of force, to help negotiations along), particularly in Latin America.

THE PANAMA CANAL

TECHNICAL STUFF

Roosevelt considered the construction of the Panama Canal his greatest accomplishment as president. And so did a lot of sea-goers. After all, it cut 7,800 miles off the voyage from New York to San Francisco by eliminating the necessity to sail around the tip of South America. The canal took about 10 years to build and cost $380 million. That cost broke down to about $7.5 million for each of its 50.72 miles. At the height of construction in 1913, more than 43,400 people were working on the canal; approximately 75 percent of these laborers were from the British West Indies. Hundreds of workers died from disease or accidents. About 240 million cubic yards of earth were moved during construction.

THE WORLD SERIES

For 25 years, the National Baseball League had squashed all challenges to it as *the* only major organization when it came to the national pastime. In 1901, however, a tough and savvy longtime minor-league executive named Byron Bancroft "Ban" Johnson started an eight-team league of his own, with franchises in major cities. Johnson's new American League lured many of the National League's top stars away with higher salaries. Forced to match salaries to keep its best players, the National League sued for peace and signed a National Baseball Agreement in January 1903, recognizing the American League as an equal.

As part of the deal, the leagues agreed to stage a postseason "world" championship between the pennant winners in each league. The first of these, a best-of-nine-games affair, was played in October 1903 between the National League's Pittsburgh Pirates and the American League's Boston Red Sox. To the shock of most baseball fans, the upstart league's Red Sox won, 5 games to 3.

For example, in 1912, Taft sent U.S. Marines to Nicaragua after a revolution there threatened American financial interests. In 1915, when Wilson was commander in chief, U.S. troops went to Haiti when revolution began to bubble; the troops stayed until 1934. In 1916, Wilson sent U.S. Army troops into Mexico under Gen. John J. "Black Jack" Pershing. The troops were to chase Mexican revolutionary Francisco "Pancho" Villa, who had raided American territory. The "punitive expedition" (as it was referred to by the War Department) almost triggered a war with Mexico and added to a widely held notion in the rest of the hemisphere that Uncle Sam was something of a bully. The expedition was also an example of a U.S. tendency to get involved in other countries' affairs. The tendency, which sprang sometimes from idealism and sometimes from pure self-interest, would last the rest of the 20th century.

Progressing toward Political and Social Reform

While America was busy reforming other countries, a burgeoning movement for reforms was in full swing at home, in virtually every business and social institution. At the core of the effort was a loose and diverse coalition of journalists, politicians, and single-cause crusaders who, because they sought progress, were called *Progressives*. These Progressives helped turn the first two decades of the century into what's known as the *Progressive Era*.

The "muckrakers" expose evil and initiate change

The first step in many of the causes undertaken by the Progressives was exposing particular evils. This was often done by reporters and writers who looked into everything from machine politics to child labor to the preparation of food. Roosevelt dubbed them "muckrakers," after a character in the 17th century allegorical novel *Pilgrim's Progress*, who constantly labored to clean up the moral filth around him.

While journalists had written exposés for years, the muckrakers' impact was magnified by the fact that they were often published in a fairly new medium: the popular (and cheap) magazine. The magazines included *McClure's, The Saturday Evening Post,* and the *Ladies' Home Journal.* The muckrakers included Ida Tarbell, who exposed the inner workings of the Standard Oil monopoly; Lincoln Steffens, who wrote about the corruption of many big-city governments; and Upton Sinclair, whose novel on meatpacking practices in Chicago, called *The Jungle,* made the entire country queasy.

The muckrakers were joined in their quest for reforms by political figures at the local, state, and national levels, such as California Governor and then-U.S. Senator Hiram Johnson, Mayor Tom Johnson of Cleveland, and Governor Robert LaFollette of Wisconsin.

When the Progressives couldn't prevail over entrenched corrupt political machines, they sought to change the rules, pushing for reforms such as

>> **Direct primary elections:** Voters — not bosses — picked party nominees

>> **The initiative:** Allowed voters to circumvent balky legislatures and propose laws directly

>> **The recall:** A means of removing officials before their terms expired

>> **The referendum:** Voters could repeal unpopular laws

Improving working conditions — and other people's drinking habits

Other groups, meanwhile, fought to improve working conditions for women and children, secure welfare assistance for widows, and get insurance for workers who were hurt in industrial accidents. Spurred mainly by fundamentalist religious groups in the South and Midwest and women's temperance groups, a decade-long effort to abolish the production and sale of alcoholic beverages gained momentum, culminating in the 18th Amendment — also referred to as "Prohibition" — which went into effect on January 16, 1920. The amendment was repealed in 1933. (See Chapter 14 to find out why.)

One of the Progressives' ideas was that people who made more money could afford to pay more taxes. A federal income tax had been tried before — once during the Civil War and once during the hard economic times of 1894 — but neither attempt was successful. In fact, the U.S. Supreme Court, on a 5 to 4 vote, struck down the 1894 effort as unconstitutional. The 16th Amendment, which was pushed by Progressives, was proposed in 1909 and ratified in 1913. This amendment gave Congress the power to slap a federal tax on income, which it promptly did. Congress required a 1 percent tax on annual income above $4,000, and a 2 percent tax on income above $20,000. Of course, the rates have gone up since.

REMEMBER

The result of all this progress was impressive and included

>> **The Meat Inspection Act and Pure Food and Drug Act in 1906:** This act created new rules and regulations for the preparation and handling of food and medicine.

ANYONE FOR VEGETABLES?

"There would be meat that had tumbled out on the floor, in the dirt and sawdust where workers had tramped and spit uncounted billions of consumption germs. There would be meat stored in great piles in rooms; and the water from leaky roofs would drip over it, and thousands of rats would race about on it . . . a man could run his hand over these piles of meat and sweep off handfuls of the dried dung of rats. These rats were nuisances, and the packers would put out poisoned bread for them, they would die, and then rats, bread and meat would go into the hoppers together."

— Upton Sinclair, writing in *The Jungle* about meatpacking practices in Chicago

» **The breakup of monopolies:** The bank and beef monopolies ended in 1907, and the Standard Oil trust came to a halt in 1911.

» **The Federal Reserve Act of 1913:** This act divided the country into 12 districts, each with its own bank and board of directors. This division helped to better oversee banking practices and policies and prevent panics and bank failures.

» **The 17th Amendment in 1913:** This amendment provided for the direct election of U.S. Senators instead of having them selected by state legislatures.

Contracting Labor Pains

While the nation generally prospered in the early 20th century, it was by no means a uniform prosperity. For every oil millionaire or steel tycoon in 1900, hundreds of thousands of people were making the average annual wage of $400 to $500 — about $100 less than was needed to maintain what was deemed a "decent" standard of living. To make matters worse, the working conditions for these people were often miserable.

Struggling in a changing workforce

REMEMBER

A change was occurring in the U.S. workforce. As manufacturing expanded, jobs moved from the farm to the factory. In 1900, for example, there were about 10 million farm-related jobs as opposed to about 18 million nonfarm jobs. By 1920, there were still about 10 million farm-related jobs, but there were more than 30 million jobs not related to agriculture. Women held 20 percent of all manufacturing jobs, and 1.7 million children under the age of 16 had full-time jobs.

"Full-time" meant just that. In the Pittsburgh steel mills, for example, 10-year-old boys were paid 14 cents an hour to work 12 hours a day, six days a week. Factory conditions were often horrendous. Between July 1906 and June 1907, 195 people died in the steel mills of Pittsburgh — about one person every other day. In 1911, 146 workers, most of them women, were killed when a fire roared through the Triangle Shirtwaist Factory in New York. Casualties were high because fire exits had been locked to keep workers from sneaking out for breaks.

Initiating improvements to working conditions

Eager to improve conditions, American workers increasingly tried to follow the example of the industrialists and combine into large groups — labor unions — to have strength through numbers. In 1904, the American Federation of Labor, which focused mainly on skilled workers, had 1.7 million members. The number grew to more than 4 million by 1920. But the unions often faced brutal reprisals from companies and law enforcement. In Ludlow, Colorado, a 1914 strike against the Colorado Fuel & Iron Company resulted in state militia and private police firing on strikers. Fourteen people were killed, 11 of which were children.

Sometimes the federal government intervened. In 1902, a strike of more than 800,000 coal miners dragged on for months when mine operators refused to negotiate. Fed up, President Roosevelt summoned both sides to Washington and threatened to send troops into the mines and appropriate the coal for the national good. Finally, a presidential commission granted the miners a raise and a shorter workday.

A more typical work stoppage was the 1912 textile mill strike in Lawrence, Massachusetts. After a state law required mill owners to limit the weekly hours of women and children to 54, the owners responded by speeding up production paces and cutting wages by 32 cents a week — the price of eight loaves of bread. The International Workers of the World organized a strike of more than 10,000 men and women. After 63 days that included beatings by police, the killing of a woman, the sending of strikers' children to other cities because strikers couldn't feed them, and a failed attempt to bomb one of the mills and frame the strike leaders, the owners gave in and granted the strikers all their demands. Within a year, however, most of the concessions had been rescinded, and the pre-strike conditions returned. It would be at least another generation before unions became a national force.

"THE WOBBLIES"

Formed in 1905 by socialists and militant unionists, the Industrial Workers of the World (IWW) was a radical labor force that favored action rather than negotiations, and it often resorted to violence. For reasons somewhat unclear, the IWW was disparaged as "The Wobblies." Foes of the union also said IWW stood for "I Won't Work."

The group favored one all-encompassing union rather than many unions divided by craft or industry, and it targeted unskilled laborers, minorities, and women. Although it probably never had more than 150,000 members in any one year, the IWW had great influence on labor relations because of its zeal and the threat it posed to business owners. By the end of World War I, however, the union had become hugely unpopular because of its association with socialism, and it was all but defunct by 1920.

Transporting America

Unions weren't alone in their aspirations for improving the lives of working-class Americans. In Detroit, a generally unlikable, self-taught engineer named Henry Ford decided that everyone should have an automobile, and thus the right to go where he wanted, when he wanted. So Ford's company began making one model in 1908 — the Model T. Contrary to popular belief that it came painted only in black, it actually came in a choice of several colors.

REMEMBER

Because of his innovative and highly efficient assembly-line approach to putting them together, Ford could afford to sell his cars at relatively affordable prices. The cost of a Model T dropped from $850 in 1908 to $290 by 1924. As prices dropped, sales went up: from 10,000 in 1909 to just under a million in 1921. Within two decades, Ford and other carmakers had indelibly changed American life. The average family could now literally get away from it all, which created a new sense of independence and self-esteem. Because of the availability of the automobile, new industries and businesses — from tire production to roadside cafes and "motor courts" — sprang up. By the end of the 1920s, it could be persuasively argued that the automobile had become the single most dominant element in the U.S. economy.

When it came to getting from here to there, others were looking up to the skies. In December 1903, two brothers who owned a bicycle shop in Dayton, Ohio, went to Kitty Hawk, North Carolina. There they pulled off the world's first powered, sustained, and controlled flights with a machine they had built. Fearful of losing their patent rights, Orville and Wilbur Wright didn't go public with their airplane until 1908, by which time other inventors and innovators were also making planes. Unlike the automobile, however, the airplane's popularity didn't really take off until after its usefulness was proven in World War I.

Suffering for Suffrage

By the time the 20th century arrived, American feminists had been seeking the right to vote for more than 50 years. Their desire was fanned even hotter in 1869, when African American males were given the right to vote through the 15th Amendment, while women of all races were still excluded.

One place where women were increasingly included was in the workplace. As the country shifted away from a rural, agrarian society to an industrial, urban one, more and more women had jobs — eight million by 1910. Moreover, they were getting better jobs. In 1870, 60 percent of working women were in domestic service. By 1920, it was only 20 percent, and women made up 13 percent of the professional ranks. Women were getting out of the house for more than just jobs, too. In 1892, membership in women's clubs was about 100,000. By 1917, it was more than one million. And women's increasing independence was reflected in the fact that the divorce rate rose from 1 in every 21 marriages in 1880 to 1 in 9 by 1916.

Because women had always had nontraditional roles in the West, it wasn't surprising that Western states and territories were the first to give females the right to vote: Wyoming in 1869, Utah in 1870, Washington in 1883, Colorado in 1893, and Idaho in 1896. By 1914, all the Western states except New Mexico had extended the voting franchise to women.

By 1917, the suffrage movement was building momentum (see Figure 13-2). In July of that year, a score of suffragists who were picketing the White House were arrested and taken to the county workhouse. President Woodrow Wilson pardoned some of the picketers, but the protests continued despite women picketers sometimes being beaten by gangs of men. The next year, a constitutional amendment — the 19th — was submitted to the states. When ratified in 1920, it gave women the right to vote in every state.

FIGURE 13-2:
Women marching for the right to vote.

Despite the significance of the 19th Amendment, many leaders of the women's movement recognized that the vote alone wouldn't give women equal standing with men when it came to educational, economic, or legal rights.

"Men are saying, perhaps, 'thank God this everlasting women's fight is over,'" said feminist leader Crystal Eastman after the 19th Amendment was ratified. "But women, if I know them, are saying, 'now at last we can begin.'"

JEANNETTE PICKERING RANKIN

Jeanette Pickering Rankin was the first woman to serve in Congress and the only member who voted against both world wars. Born on a ranch near Missoula, Montana, in 1880, Rankin graduated from the University of Montana in 1902 and was a social worker before becoming a field secretary for the National American Woman Suffrage Association. After Montana approved the vote for women in 1914, Rankin decided in 1916 to run for one of the state's two seats in the House of Representatives as a Republican and won. As a congresswoman, she was one of 56 members of Congress who voted against President Wilson's call for a war resolution in 1917.

As a result, she lost the race for a U.S. Senate seat in 1918, moved to Georgia, and devoted her energies to pacifist organizations. In 1940, Rankin returned to Montana, where she ran again for Congress and won — in time to be the lone member of either house to vote against war with Japan in 1941. She didn't run for reelection and died in California in 1973 at the age of 92.

Of Rankin's vote against two world wars, John F. Kennedy said: "Few members of Congress have ever stood more alone while being true to a higher honor and loyalty."

Leaving the South: African Americans Migrate to Northern Cities

Women weren't the only Americans on the move. Between 1914 and 1918, more than 500,000 African Americans left the farms of the South for jobs in Northern cities. The movement was part of the "Great Migration," which stretched from the 1890s to the 1960s, and eventually resulted in more than 6 million black people leaving the South.

This migration was spurred first by the Jim Crow laws, the lynchings, and the poverty of the post–Civil War South. Then, as the war in Europe simultaneously sparked U.S. industrial expansion and cut off the flow of immigrant workers, Northern jobs opened up by the thousands. Henry Ford, for example, offered to pay the astronomical sum of $5 a day in his plants, and despite his racist views, he hired blacks. The black populations of Northern cities swelled. In Chicago, for example, the African American community grew from 44,000 in 1910 to 110,000 by 1920.

But moving North didn't mean that African Americans left racism behind. Many Northern whites resented their new neighbors. The resentment was fueled in 1915 when the wildly popular new movie, *The Birth of a Nation*, portrayed blacks as deranged and dangerous creatures who lorded their emancipation over white Southerners. Nor was there much interest in black issues among Progressive leaders. When a delegation of black leaders met with Pres. Woodrow Wilson in 1914 to protest segregation in federal offices, he all but pushed them out the door.

Racial unrest led to race riots. In 1917 in East St. Louis, Illinois, white rioters went on a rampage in the black community. When it was over, 39 blacks and 9 whites were dead. In the summer of 1919, more than 25 race riots broke out in cities across the country. The worst was in Chicago, where an incident at a segregated swimming beach sparked a six-day riot that resulted in 38 people dead and more than a thousand left homeless by riot-sparked fires. The beachfront riots didn't stop until federal troops were called in.

W. E. B. DUBOIS

William Edward Burghart DuBois was decidedly not what most white Americans thought of when they thought about black Americans. He was born in 1868 to a poor but respected family in a Massachusetts town with a population that was less than 1 percent black; he had degrees from Harvard and the University of Berlin; he became one of the country's leading sociologists; and he was an eloquent orator and stylish writer.

DuBois was best known for his forceful disagreements with another African-American leader, Booker T. Washington. These disagreements were most famously expressed in DuBois's 1903 book, *The Souls of Black Folk*. Washington stressed self-help and material gain over seeking equal legal and social rights with whites, but DuBois believed Washington's approach would only continue black oppression. In 1905, DuBois took a leading role in the Niagara Movement, the forerunner of the National Association for the Advancement of Colored People (NAACP), which he helped found in 1909. Disillusioned with the direction of the NAACP, he resigned in 1934. From 1934 to 1944, he was head of the Department of Sociology at Atlanta University and has been called the Father of American Sociology. He died in Ghana in 1963, at the age of 95.

REMEMBER

Still, when President Wilson called on Americans to "help make the world safe for democracy" in 1917, more than 375,000 African Americans entered the military. "If this is our country," explained black leader W.E.B. DuBois, "then this is our war." (For more information, check out *African American History For Dummies* by Ronda Racha Penrice, published by Wiley.)

The War to End All Chapters

Theodore Roosevelt had been president nearly eight years by the time of the 1908 election, having filled most of the assassinated McKinley's second term and winning his own term in 1904. Even though there were no term limits to stop him, Roosevelt decided not to run in 1908. Instead, he gave his blessing to William Howard Taft, a fellow Republican. But in 1912, Roosevelt became restless and decided to run against Taft, as the candidate of the Progressive, or "Bull Moose," Party. Americans ended up choosing the Democrat in the race, a scholarly former president of Princeton University and son of the South named Thomas Woodrow Wilson.

Progressive in his domestic policies, Wilson was something of a cautious imperialist abroad. He subscribed to the idea that America had a leading role to play in world affairs; he just didn't want to fight about it. The country did get embroiled in a few Latin American skirmishes, and Wilson did send troops into Mexico in 1916 after Mexican revolutionaries led by Pancho Villa raided onto American soil. But as the European powers squared off in 1914 in what was to be four-plus years of mind-numbingly horrific war, America managed, at least initially, to somewhat nervously mind its own business. Wilson, in fact, won reelection in 1916 using the phrase "he kept us out of war."

REMEMBER

As time passed, however, the country began to side more often with Britain, France, and other countries that were fighting Germany. The sinking of the British passenger ship, *Lusitania*, by a German submarine in 1915, which resulted in the deaths of 128 Americans, inflamed U.S. passions against "the Huns," despite German protests the ship was a legitimate target because it was carrying tons of munitions to England. Propagandistic portrayals of German atrocities in the relatively new medium of motion pictures added to the heat. And finally, when it was revealed that German diplomats had approached Mexico about an alliance against the United States, Wilson felt compelled to ask Congress for a resolution of war against Germany. He got it on April 6, 1917.

The U.S. military was ill-prepared for war on a massive scale. Only about 370,000 men were in the Army and National Guard combined. Through a draft and enlistments, however, that number swelled to 4.8 million in all the military branches by the end of World War I.

At home, about half of the war's eventual $33 billion price tag was met through taxes; the rest was funded through the issuance of war bonds. Organized labor, in return for concessions such as the right to collective bargaining, agreed to reduce the number of strikes. Labor shortages drove wages up, which in turn drove prices up. But demand for goods and services because of the war soared, and the economy hummed along, despite government efforts to "organize" it.

In Europe, however, no one was humming. American troops, like their European counterparts before them, found that modern warfare was anything but inspiring. The first U.S. troops were fed into the lines as much to shore up the morale of the Allies as anything else. But by the time the Germans launched their last desperate offensive, in the spring of 1918, more than 300,000 American troops had landed in France. By the war's end in November, the number of Yanks had swelled to 1.4 million.

Led by Maj. Gen. John "Black Jack" Pershing, a celebrated veteran of the Spanish-American and Philippines wars, the U.S. forces, known as the American Expeditionary Force (AEF), fought off efforts by Allied commanders to push the AEF into a subordinate role as replacement troops.

THE GREAT "SPANISH" FLU OF 1918

Despite conflict and war, civilians and soldiers around the world had at least one thing in common in 1918 — a killer flu. Erroneously dubbed "Spanish influenza" because it was believed to have started in Spain, it quite possibly started in America at U.S. Army camps in Kansas and was quickly spread by the concentration of troops in military camps and hospitals in various countries.

Wherever it started, it was devastating. Unlike normal influenza outbreaks, whose victims are generally the elderly and children, the Spanish flu often targeted healthy young adults. By early summer, the disease had spread around the world. In New York City alone, 20,000 people died. Western Samoa lost 22 percent of its population, and entire Inuit villages in Alaska were wiped out. More than 500,000 Americans died, which was a greater total than all the Americans killed in all the wars of the 20th century. By the time it had run its course in 1921, the flu had killed more than 50 million people around the world, rivaling the deadly efficiency of the most horrific epidemics in history.

Starting with the battles of Cantigny, Chateau-Thierry, and Belleau Wood in France, the AEF proved itself an able force. In September 1918, the Americans launched an attack on a German bulge in the lines near Verdun, France. U.S. and French troops captured more than 25,000 prisoners, and the German military's back was all but broken. At the 11th hour of the 11th day of the 11th month of 1918, Germany called it quits, and the fighting stopped.

American losses — 48,000 killed in battle, 56,000 lost to disease — seemed trifling compared to the staggering costs paid by other countries. Germany lost 1.8 million people; Russia, 1.7 million; France, 1.4 million; Austria-Hungary, 1.2 million; and Britain, 950,000. "The War to End All Wars," as it was called, turned out to be just another test of humans' aptitude for killing other humans in large quantities.

Chapter **14**

Gin, Jazz, and Lucky Lindy: 1919–1929

With World War I over, America turned its attention back toward itself — and it was kind of uneasy about what it saw. Things seemed to be happening at too fast a pace. Young people were challenging old ways. An attempt to make the country more moral with a prohibition on liquor had the opposite effect, and the economy was making some Americans rich (and causing a lot more to spend like they were rich).

In this chapter, I visit the heroes and villains of the 1920s, along with the rise of mass media and its impact on the country. It was only a decade-long trip, but it was a helluva ride.

Wilson Goes Out of His League for Peace

Nearly a year before World War I was over, President Woodrow Wilson had already come up with a plan of *14 Points,* in which he outlined his version of a peace treaty. Leaders of America's allies viewed it as both simplistic and overly optimistic. The French prime minister even sneered that because humankind couldn't keep God's 10 Commandments, it was unlikely that folks could keep Wilson's 14 Points.

But so eager was Wilson to play a major role in the making of peace that he did something only one U.S. president (Teddy Roosevelt) had done before: He left the country while in office. In December 1918, a month after the fighting ended, Wilson went to Paris to meet with the leaders of France, England, and Italy. The Big Four (which soon became the Big Three after the minister from Italy left in a snit) soon drafted a peace treaty that included *almost* nothing that Wilson wanted.

Instead, the Treaty of Versailles required Germany to accept the blame for the war, pay $15 billion to the winning countries, give up most of its colonies, and limit the future size of its military forces. But the treaty did include at least one thing Wilson *really* wanted: the formation of a League of Nations, whose members would promise to respect one another's rights and settle their differences through the league.

Wilson brought the treaty and the idea of the league back to America and presented them to the U.S. Senate for its constitutionally required approval. But the Democratic president was facing a Senate dominated by Republicans and led by Massachusetts Sen. Henry Cabot Lodge, chairman of the Foreign Relations Committee.

REMEMBER

Lodge, California Sen. Hiram Johnson, and some other "isolationist" senators were adamantly against the idea of "foreign entanglements" like the league. Lodge used his position to both stall consideration of the treaty and offer amendments to it that would have watered it down somewhat.

PEACE PLAN NOW OR WAR LATER

"I can predict with absolute certainty that within another generation there will be another world war if the nations of the world do not concert the method by which to prevent it."

— Woodrow Wilson,
during his tour to drum up support for the League of Nations,
September 1917

If Wilson had agreed to go along with a few changes, he may have gained the two-thirds approval he needed. But Wilson stubbornly refused to negotiate. Each side dug in and launched thunderous attacks on the other. Wilson made more than 40 speeches in three weeks on an 8,000-mile journey around the country.

In the end, Wilson's valiant effort proved politically futile and personally tragic. In early October, he had a stroke. The next month, the Senate resoundingly rejected the league and the peace treaty. The Senate rejected it again in March 1920 when Democratic senators brought it back for reconsideration. America would go it alone for another generation, or until the next world war.

Restricting Immigration and Challenging the Natives

One of the reasons many Americans opposed joining a League of Nations was because they connected foreigners with growing domestic economic problems, even though the problems had more to do with the war's end than anything else. Labor shortages during the fighting had driven up wages and strengthened workers' bargaining — union membership rose more than 40 percent between 1915 and 1918.

But with the war over, more than $3 billion in federal war-related contracts were canceled almost overnight. Hundreds of thousands of returning soldiers and sailors crowded into the labor market, crowding out women and African Americans. An oversupply of food and other products caused prices — and wages — to drop, and unemployment to rise. Human nature being what it is, Americans bewildered by the sudden downturn from good times looked for someone to blame.

They found plenty of targets. One group was the communists. The Russian Revolution scared many Americans by demonstrating how an uprising by a small group of radicals could overthrow the government of a mighty nation. Actually, relatively few communists were in America, and they wielded relatively little clout. But nearly every labor strike was denounced as communist-inspired. A series of bombs mailed to leading American capitalists like J. P. Morgan and John Rockefeller, as well as some elected officials and judges, also alarmed the country, even though few of the explosives reached their targets. It all added to what became known as the *Red Scare*.

The chief Red-hunter was U.S. Attorney General A. Mitchell Palmer, who had hopes of becoming president. In August 1919, Palmer created the General Intelligence Division within the Justice Department and put an ardent young anti-communist named J. Edgar Hoover in charge of it. On January 2, 1920, Palmer's agents arrested about 6,000 people — many of whom were U.S. citizens — in 33 cities. Some were held for weeks without bail. Many were beaten, and some were forced to sign confessions. But only 556 were eventually deported. When a gigantic communist uprising predicted by Palmer failed to materialize, the Red Scare, and his presidential hopes, deflated.

Closing the gate

The bad taste left by World War I also showed itself in anti-immigration feelings. Immigration increased from 110,000 in 1919 to 430,000 in 1920 and 805,000 in 1921. Fear that war-torn Europe would flood America led to the Emergency Quota Act of 1921. The act limited immigration from any one country to 3 percent of the number from that country already in the United States.

Later, in 1924, the quotas were cut to 2 percent, and all Japanese immigration was banned, an action that deeply humiliated and angered Japan. In 1929, Congress limited total immigration to no more than 150,000 per year. The fire under America's melting pot had cooled off considerably.

Return of the Klan

Xenophobia — the fear or hatred of strangers or foreigners — also showed itself in the resurgence of the Ku Klux Klan in the early 1920s. The Klan had all but died out by 1880, but it was revived in 1915 in Georgia and spread around the country. The Klan's spread was aided by its support of Prohibition, which gave it a moral "in" with many people and allowed it to more easily spread its racist bile. By 1924, it probably had 4.5 million members, many of them in the Midwest. Approximately 40,000 Klansmen marched in Washington, D.C., in August 1925. Both major political parties felt the organization's influence in local, state, and even national elections.

The new Klan targeted not only African Americans but also Latinos, Jews, Roman Catholics, socialists, and anyone else who didn't embrace the Klan's views of what was moral and patriotic.

AND WE LOOK STUPID, TOO

"We are a movement of plain people, very weak in the matter of culture, intellectual support, and trained leadership. . .. It lays us open to the charge of being 'hicks' and 'rubes' and 'drivers of secondhand Fords.' We admit it."

— Hiram Evans, Imperial Wizard of the Ku Klux Klan, 1926

But in 1925, an Indiana Klan leader was convicted of abducting and assaulting a young girl, who subsequently killed herself. The widely publicized scandal, coupled with exposés about how some Klan leaders had siphoned off funds from the group, led to a demise in its popularity. The klowns of the KKK never again approached their earlier influence.

Darwin versus God

The Klan's greatest influence developed in smaller cities and in rural areas. The repressive attitudes it catered to were also quick to embrace *fundamentalism*, or the idea that everything in the Bible was literally true. In 1925, fundamentalists pushed a law through the Tennessee legislature prohibiting the teaching of Darwin's evolution theory in public schools.

When a young high school teacher named John Scopes decided to challenge the law, America had the show trial of the decade (and the basis for the play *Inherit the Wind*). Scopes was defended by Clarence Darrow, a famous trial lawyer and a leader of the American Civil Liberties Union. William Jennings Bryan, the aging, thrice-defeated Democratic presidential candidate and celebrated orator, joined the prosecution.

Bryan repeatedly ridiculed the idea that humans could be descended from apes. But he made a big mistake when he took the stand himself to defend the Bible. Under shrewd questioning by Darrow, Bryan admitted that parts of the Bible couldn't logically be interpreted literally. Scopes was found guilty anyway and fined $100, but the conviction was later overturned on a technicality. The trial took the wind out of the fundamentalist sails for a while, but debate over evolution and education has never fully left the American scene.

AIMEE SEMPLE MCPHERSON

Aimee Semple McPherson preached glory and salvation instead of fire and brimstone; thought heaven would look like a cross between Washington, D.C., and Pasadena, California; and was adored by millions as *Sister*.

McPherson was born in 1890 in Canada. With her first husband, she became a missionary and toured the world, but when her husband died in China, she returned to America and married an accountant. That marriage fell apart, however, when McPherson refused to give up her evangelical career.

In 1921, she showed up in Los Angeles and started the Foursquare Gospel Mission. She opened the Angelus Temple in Los Angeles's Echo Park in 1923 and used brass bands, massive choirs, and fancy sets to draw nightly crowds in the thousands. She became a national figure, and people came from all over the country to hear her preach and to be "healed" by her touch.

While swimming at a local beach in 1926, McPherson disappeared. Thirty-seven days later, she reappeared with a story about being kidnapped and held in the Arizona desert before escaping. The story was a sensation, at first for its own sake and then when skeptical reporters suggested she had really been on a month-long tryst with a married man.

McPherson's popularity waned in the 1930s, but she continued to preach until 1944, when she died at the age of 53 from a possible accidental overdose of sleeping pills. The church she founded still uses Angelus Temple as its headquarters and claims a worldwide membership of nearly 8 million.

Warren, Cal, and Herbert: Republicans in the White House

Three Republicans succeeded Wilson as president in the 1920s — Warren G. Harding, Calvin Coolidge, and Herbert Hoover — and all three were firmly in favor of the status quo, or at least what the status quo was before the war.

Harding was a handsome, affable newspaper publisher and politician from Ohio. His record as a state legislator and U.S. senator was almost entirely without distinction, but he was a popular guy anyway — especially with newly enfranchised women voters — and was easily elected in 1920.

Harding's administration was ripe with scandal, much of it involving buddies he appointed to various offices. The worst scandal was called *Teapot Dome* and involved the secret leasing of public oil reserves to private companies by Harding's Secretary of Interior Albert B. Fall, in return for $400,000 in interest-free "loans."

Harding himself was never implicated in any of the scandals, but he suffered nevertheless. "I have no trouble with my enemies," he told a reporter, "but my damned friends . . . they're the ones that keep me walking the floor nights."

Harding died suddenly while visiting San Francisco in August 1923, probably of a stroke. (His wife inexplicably refused to allow an autopsy, so the exact cause was never established.) He was succeeded by Coolidge, his vice president.

Silent Cal, as he was called, was from Vermont and was quite possibly less interested in being president than any man who ever held the office. (But he did enjoy playing practical jokes on the White House staff and having his photo taken while wearing silly headgear.) After finishing out Harding's term, Coolidge was easily elected to his own term in 1924. His winning platform was that government should do what it could to promote private enterprise and then get out of the way.

"The man who builds a factory builds a temple," Coolidge pronounced. "The man who works there worships there." Coolidge fit the times perfectly. His philosophy was that not doing anything was the best course nine times out of ten. Most of the voting public didn't want or need anything from the federal government other than a military in time of war and someone to deliver the mail. Even though he wasn't exactly overworked in the job, Coolidge decided he had had enough in 1928 and chose not to run again.

In 1928, the country elected Hoover as president. He was an Iowa farm boy turned civil engineer who had won international kudos for organizing massive food programs for Europe after World War I. Hoover easily defeated New York Gov. Al Smith, extending Republican control of the White House. Like Harding and Coolidge, Hoover was a firm believer that America was on the right track economically.

"We in America are nearer to the final triumph over poverty than ever before in the history of the land," Hoover said. "We shall with the help of God be in sight of the day when poverty will be banished from the nation." As it turned out, he was wrong.

MARCUS GARVEY

Marcus Garvey was born in Jamaica, lived in New York and England, and wanted to go to Africa and take all of black America with him. The youngest of 11 children, Garvey moved to New York in 1916, started a newspaper, and organized a back-to-Africa movement he had begun in Jamaica, called the *Universal Negro Improvement Association*.

Garvey believed African Americans would never get a fair chance in America and should therefore go to Africa — a philosophy that, ironically, was enthusiastically supported by the Ku Klux Klan. He was openly contemptuous of whites, opposed interracial marriages, and denounced efforts by some African Americans to "look white" by using skin lighteners and hair straighteners.

Some black leaders thought Garvey — who liked to wear outlandish military-style uniforms in public — was a demagogue, but his appeal to black pride earned his efforts a large following. By the early 1920s, Garvey had more than 2 million followers. He used their financial support to start more than 30 black-owned businesses, including a steamship company that he hoped would help take African Americans to Liberia. But those plans fell apart when Liberia's government, fearful of a possible Garvey-led revolution, refused to deal with him.

In 1925, Garvey was convicted on what quite possibly were trumped up federal mail fraud charges. He served two years of his prison sentence, and then he was deported to Jamaica on orders of President Coolidge. When Garvey died in 1940 in England, he was largely forgotten. But his efforts helped form the roots of black pride and black nationalism that flourished later in the 20th century.

Good Times (or Were They?)

One of the overriding themes sung by Harding and chorused by Coolidge and Hoover was "a return to normalcy," and nothing was more normal, as far as they were concerned, than the pursuit of financial wealth. So their administrations established policies that were designed to help that pursuit.

Helping the rich

Harding, Coolidge, and Hoover all reduced the national debt by cutting spending on government programs. They increased tariffs to protect U.S. manufacturing from foreign competition. They also cut taxes for the wealthy, arguing it would help create incentives for the rich to invest more, which would create more jobs, more products, and more wealth for everyone. And the Federal Reserve Board kept interest rates low so that those who weren't wealthy could borrow money to invest.

"You can't lick this prosperity thing. Even the fellow that hasn't got any is all excited over the idea."

— Will Rogers, American humorist, 1928

REMEMBER

These tactics seemed to work. Businesses became more productive by using new techniques that made workers and machinery more efficient. Chemical processes, for example, tripled the amount of gasoline that could be extracted from crude oil. Advances in electricity transmission sped development of larger manufacturing plants. U.S. manufacturing output rose 60 percent in the 1920s. And greater efficiency and productivity naturally translated to more profit for business owners.

Increasing American spending habits

The 1920s saw the rise of two elements that are still both banes and blessings to the American consumer: advertising and installment buying. Advertising was spurred by the development of national media, such as radio and popular magazines, which made it possible to reach audiences from coast to coast. It became a $1.25 billion-a-year industry by 1925.

In addition, the idea of buying *on time* — paying a little each week or month, plus interest — became more and more popular. Between 1920 and 1929, installment buying increased 500 percent. By 1929, more than 60 percent of American cars, large appliances, and pianos were being purchased on time.

The drive to sell government bonds during World War I made the average American more confident in buying securities like stocks and more willing to invest money rather than save it. The increased availability of capital enabled industries and retailers to expand, which in some cases meant lower prices. The Piggly Wiggly grocery store chain grew from 515 stores in 1920 to 2,500 in 1929; A&P grew from 4,621 stores to more than 15,000.

Making it difficult on the poor

Below the veneer of prosperity, there were indications of trouble. More and more wealth was being concentrated in fewer and fewer hands, and government did far more for the rich than the poor. It was estimated, for example, that federal tax cuts saved the hugely wealthy financier Andrew Mellon (who also happened to be Hoover's treasury secretary) almost as much money as was saved by all the taxpayers in the entire state of Nebraska.

BRUCE BARTON

Bruce Barton invented Betty Crocker, wrote one of the bestselling books of the 1920s, and proclaimed that "advertising is the very essence of democracy," even though he privately had doubts about its worth.

Born in Tennessee in 1886, Barton graduated from Amherst College in 1907 and had trouble finding a job. After a mediocre career as a writer and editor, Barton started a New York City advertising firm that eventually became Batten, Barton, Durstine & Osborn, one of the largest such companies in the world. It was a perfect 1920s fit: Barton had a genius for catchy phrases, and America had a big thirst for buying stuff. In addition to creating the ultimate housewife character in Betty Crocker, Barton ran campaigns for U.S. Steel, General Electric, and Lever Brothers, among others.

A deeply religious man, Barton also wrote books designed to renew the public's enthusiasm for religion. In 1925, he published *The Man Nobody Knows,* which portrayed Jesus Christ as a super salesman and a role model for businessmen. The book sold a hefty 700,000 copies in two years.

Even though he spent most of his life in advertising, Barton privately expressed misgivings as to whether much of it was wasteful and dishonest. Perhaps fittingly for a consummate pitchman, he spent two terms as a congressman from New York City. Barton died in 1967 at the age of 80.

Supreme Court decisions struck down minimum wage laws for women and children and made it easier for big businesses to swallow up smaller ones and become de facto monopolies. And union membership declined as organized labor was unable to compete with the aura of good times.

REMEMBER

Probably worst off were American farmers. They had expanded production during World War I to feed the troops, and when demand and prices faded after the war, they were hit hard. Farm income dropped by 50 percent during the 1920s, and more than 3 million farmers left their farms for towns and cities.

For farmers in ten states along the Mississippi River and its tributaries, things were made tragically worse in 1927, when rains of biblical proportions triggered the most devastating river flood in U.S. history. More than 27,000 square miles of mostly agricultural land were inundated. At least 250 people were killed, and hundreds of millions of dollars in damage was done before the waters finally receded.

Most of those hit the hardest were poor farmers, and unfortunately for them, the affection the Harding, Coolidge, and Hoover administrations felt for business didn't extend to agriculture. Flood relief was scant and sporadic, and much of it was siphoned off to benefit white landowners in the region at the expense of African-American tenant farmers.

Coolidge also twice vetoed bills that would have created government-guaranteed minimum prices for some farm goods, an idea called *parity.* "Farmers have never made money," he explained. "I don't believe we can do much about it."

Ain't We Got Fun?

A lot of people think the Roaring Twenties was a decade in which everyone spent a huge amount of time dancing the Charleston and drinking. That, of course, isn't true. People also went to the movies, listened to the radio, read, and played games. The decade, in fact, was marked by an explosion of popular culture, pushed by the development of mass media, which was pushed by postwar advances in technology.

Going to the movies

By the mid-1920s, moviemaking was one of the top five industries in the country in terms of capital investment. A former farm community in California called Hollywood recently had become the film capital of the world. In 1928, America had 20,000 movie theaters, and movie houses that looked like ornate palaces and seated thousands of patrons were built in every major city. Millions of Americans flocked each week to see stars like Charlie Chaplin and Rudolph Valentino on the silent screen.

CLARA BOW

One producer said Clara Bow "danced even while she was standing still," and the writer F. Scott Fitzgerald called her "someone to stir every pulse in the nation." She was the movies' first true female sex symbol.

Bow was born in 1905 in Brooklyn to an alcoholic father and a mother so unbalanced she tried to cut Bow's throat when she learned her daughter was going into movies. By the time she was 25, Bow had already starred in almost 50 films and was making as much as $7,500 a week. Moreover, she was the ultimate 1920s flapper: the "It Girl" ("it" referring to sex appeal) who did what she wanted when she wanted with whom she wanted.

Personal scandals and the coming of sound to movies (she had a thick Brooklyn accent) marked the end of Bow's career by 1933. She married a cowboy star named Rex Bell (who later became lieutenant governor of Nevada) and was in and out of mental institutions until her death in 1965. Like many of her successors, it's questionable how much Bow really liked the role of femme fatale. "The more I see of men," she once observed, "the more I like dogs."

In 1927, with the release of *The Jazz Singer*, the screen was no longer silent, and "talkies" made the movies even more popular. Perhaps fittingly, the first words spoken in the first talkie were "Wait a minute! Wait a minute! You ain't heard nothin' yet!"

Movies and their stars had a huge impact on the culture of the '20s. They influenced fashion, hairstyles, speech patterns, and sexual mores — and reinforced cultural and racial stereotypes and prejudices.

Listening to the radio

At the beginning of the 1920s, radio was entirely for amateurs. "Ham" operators listened mostly to messages from ships at sea over homemade sets. But in 1920, the Westinghouse Company in Pittsburgh established the first commercial radio station, KDKA. Almost overnight, stations sprang up all over the country. By 1924, there were more than 500 stations, and by 1927 the Radio Corporation of America (RCA) had organized a 19-station National Broadcasting Company (NBC).

REMEMBER

Radio brought major sporting events and election returns "live" into American homes. It also encouraged the makers of soap, the sellers of life insurance, and the purveyors of cornflakes to reach out to consumers over the airwaves. U.S. business had its first true national medium for advertising, and Americans accepted that the price of "free" radio was commercials. By 1929, more than 12 million American families had radio sets.

Listening to music and writing literature

Radio, along with the increasing popularity of the phonograph, made popular music even more popular. The hottest sound was called *jazz*, which stressed improvisation and rhythm as well as melody. This sound had its roots deep in the musical traditions of African Americans. Its stars included Bessie Smith, Ferdinand "Jelly Roll" Morton, and Louis Armstrong, and it was a key part of what became known as the *Harlem Renaissance*, a confluence of African-American genius in the arts that flourished in the 1920s in New York City. Jazz became wildly popular in other parts of the world as well and was recognized as the first truly unique form of American music.

Literature, on the other hand, was most heavily influenced by writers who were disillusioned with postwar America or who chose to satirize Americans' seeming penchant for conformity. These writers included novelists F. Scott Fitzgerald (*The Great Gatsby*, 1925), Sinclair Lewis (*Babbitt*, 1922), and Ernest Hemingway (*A Farewell to Arms*, 1929); playwright Eugene O'Neill (*Strange Interlude*, 1928); and poets E. E. Cummings, Carl Sandburg, and Langston Hughes.

Playing games

When it wasn't being entertained, America was seemingly entertaining itself in the 1920s, so much so that one contemporary observer called it "the age of play." Shorter workdays and weeks and more disposable income (or at least what seemed like more disposable income) gave Americans more time and money to enjoy themselves. Sports like golf and tennis boomed. Public playgrounds for kids became popular. Crossword puzzles and a game called Mah Jong were all the rage.

TILED OUT

Parlor games have come and gone in American culture, but the Mah Jong craze of the 1920s may have been the only one to require costumes. An ancient Chinese game played with a set of 144 colored tiles, Mah Jong hit the West Coast in 1922 and soon became immensely fashionable across the nation. Many women refused to play, however, unless they were suitably attired in elaborate Oriental robes.

So many Mah Jong sets were being produced at the height of the craze that Chinese manufacturers ran out of the traditional calf shins they made the tiles from. As a result, they were forced to ask Chicago slaughterhouses for cow bones. The fad faded after about five years of wild popularity. One possible reason was ennui created by confusion: By mid-decade, more than 20 different sets of rules for the game had been published.

Drying Out America: Prohibition Begins

Even before the country's formal inception, Americans had been a hard-drinking bunch, and the social and private costs they paid for it had been high. But on January 16, 1920, the nation undertook a "noble experiment" to rid itself of the effects of "demon rum." It was called *Prohibition*, and it was a spectacular failure.

There is some statistical evidence that Americans drank less after Prohibition started than they did before it began. But overall, the ban on booze was a bad idea. For one thing, it encouraged otherwise law-abiding citizens to visit *speakeasies* where alcohol was sold illegally. The number of "speaks" in New York City at the end of the decade, for example, was probably double the number of legal saloons at the beginning.

Gangsters like "Scarface" Al Capone and George "Bugs" Moran made fortunes selling bootleg booze, and they became celebrities doing it, despite the violence that was their normal business tool. Capone's Chicago mob took in $60 million a year at its peak — and murdered more than 300 people while doing it. But bullets weren't the gangsters' only tools. They also bought off or bullied scores of federal, state, and local officials to look the other way, which only added to public disrespect for law and government.

REMEMBER

Part of the disrespect for government was well deserved. Even though Congress and a string of presidents paid lip service to the idea of Prohibition to make the anti-liquor lobby happy, many of the politicians were regular customers for the bootleggers. Congress provided only 1,550 federal agents to enforce the ban throughout the entire country, and criminal penalties for bootlegging were relatively light. Over one two-year period in New York, 7,000 Prohibition-related arrests were made with only 17 convictions. Some states, in fact, passed laws restricting state and local police from actively enforcing the ban.

GEORGE REMUS

He was known as *King of the Bootleggers,* an attorney whose most famous client turned out to be himself. Remus was born in Germany in 1876 and came to America when he was 5 years old. He trained as a pharmacist but became a lawyer in 1900 and specialized in criminal defense. When Prohibition began, his clients were often bootleggers, and Remus observed that the occupation paid a lot more than practicing law.

Moving to Cincinnati, which was near most of the major distilleries that could still legally make alcohol for medicinal purposes, Remus used his pharmacist's license to buy huge amounts of legal alcohol. Then he had an army of employees "steal" it on the way to his warehouses and turn it into illegal hooch. Despite five arrests, Remus lived a lavish life, complete with a $125,000 swimming pool at his mansion. He once threw a party where each of the 200 guests received diamond jewelry or cars.

During one of his jail stints, Remus's wife took up with a federal Prohibition agent. On his release from prison, Remus promptly shot and killed his errant spouse. Acting as his own attorney, he pleaded temporary insanity and was acquitted after the jury deliberated all of 19 minutes. Remus eventually retired from bootlegging when the business got too violent for him. He died in 1952 at the age of 75. One more thing: The King of the Bootleggers never touched the stuff himself.

Changing Morals

At the time, many observers saw Americans' unenthusiasm for Prohibition as an example of the country's slipping morals. So, they observed, was the behavior of young people. Perhaps more than any generation before them, the youth of the 1920s embraced their own music, fashion, and speech. The automobile gave them a way to get away from home, at least temporarily, and also a place to be sexually intimate.

Other things contributed to the shifting moral patterns of the times: the sexy images from Hollywood, the growing availability of birth control devices, the use of sex by advertisers to sell everything from cars to toothpaste, and the growing emancipation of women.

REMEMBER

There was no question, however, that the inequities between the sexes continued. Women made less than men in the same jobs and were still subject to a double standard that their place was in the home with the kids. But women now had the right to vote, and more and more of them were entering the workplace — from 8.4 million in 1920 to 10.6 million in 1930.

GIRLS JUST WANNA HAVE MORE . . .

"The outstanding characteristic of the flapper is not her uniform, but her independence and will to be prosperous . . . they will no longer marry men who merely support them . . . they have awakened to the fact that the 'Superior Sex' stuff is all bunk."

— journalist Samuel Crowther, 1926

Short-haired, short-skirted young women — referred to as *flappers*— flaunted their freedom to smoke and drink and go out with men alone without the certainty of being morally condemned as "loose." And perhaps most important, fewer of them cared if they were.

An Age of Heroes

If there was one thing the 1920s had a lot of, it was heroes. The advent of radio and the increasing popularity of national magazines and tabloid newspapers provided an arena for stars to shine. And armies of public relations agents pushed and shoved their clients into the spotlight.

There were movie stars. Clara Bow reportedly got 45,000 fan letters a week. When screen heartthrob Rudolph Valentino died of a perforated ulcer in 1926, several women reportedly committed suicide. More than 30,000 mourners filed past his $10,000 casket, which had a glass plate above his face so they could have one last look. There were also vaudeville stars like magician Harry Houdini and humorist Will Rogers.

Every sport had its own gods or goddesses: In swimming, there were Gertrude Ederle and Johnny Weissmuller; in football, Red Grange and Knute Rockne; in boxing, Jack Dempsey and Gene Tunney; in golf, Bobby Jones; and in tennis, Bill Tilden.

And in baseball, there was the moon-faced son of a Baltimore saloonkeeper. His name was George Herman Ruth, but everyone called him *Babe*. For most of the decade, Ruth was perhaps the most photographed man in the world. A fine pitcher, he became the greatest slugger in history and almost single-handedly restored baseball as the national pastime after a fixed World Series in 1919 had threatened to ruin it. Ruth was so popular that when his team, the Yankees, moved into a new stadium in New York, it was dubbed "the house that Ruth built."

REMEMBER

But as big as Babe Ruth was, he was only second to a tall, thin, and modest airmail pilot from Michigan named Charles A. Lindbergh. On May 20, 1927, Lindbergh lifted off alone from a New York airfield in a $6,000 plane laden with gasoline and sandwiches. When reporters asked him if sandwiches were all he was taking to eat, Lindy replied, "If I get to Paris, I won't need any more, and if I don't, I won't need any more either." Lindbergh headed over the Atlantic, and 33½ hours later, he landed in Paris. He was proclaimed the first man to fly nonstop between the two continents.

The world went nuts. Lindbergh was mobbed everywhere he went. In New York City alone, an estimated 4 million people turned out for a parade and celebration in his honor. In later years, Lindbergh's luster was badly tarnished by his pre–World War II enthusiasm for Hitler's Germany.

But his flight proved a giant shot in the arm for aviation (even though Lindbergh somewhat prudently returned from France by ship.) Suddenly, flying wasn't so scary. By the end of the decade, more than 40 U.S. airline companies were carrying close to 200,000 passengers per year.

Lindbergh's *Spirit of St. Louis* wasn't the only thing in the air as the 1920s came to a close. The economy continued to hum along at a frenetic pace as well. "Stock prices have reached what looks like a permanently high plateau," said Yale economics professor Irving Fisher on October 16, 1929. Eight days later, the plateau collapsed. An overinflated stock market crashed, costing investors $15 billion in a week. America was plunged into an economic mess the likes of which it had never seen.

» Fashioning a New Deal

» Failing minorities

» Dealing with naysayers, crusaders, nuts, and desperadoes

Chapter **15**

Uncle Sam's Depressed: 1930–1940

During one of his last speeches as president, in December 1928, Calvin Coolidge noted that America could "regard the present with satisfaction and anticipate the future with optimism." Much of the country did both. But as the 1930s dawned, it became painfully apparent that Americans had been prematurely satisfied and overly optimistic.

This chapter takes a look at what triggered the Great Depression and what it meant. You also meet Franklin Roosevelt, another of those great men who seem to come along every now and then in American history just when the country needs them. (For a more detailed look at this era, see *Lessons from the Great Depression For Dummies*, written by Steve Wiegand — that's me! — and published by Wiley.)

The Great Depression: Causes and Consequences

America had gone through economic hard times before. There had been bank panics, recessions, and boom-and-bust cycles of varying degrees of severity and length triggered by political battles, the collapse of particular industries, or world events. But never did it suffer an economic illness so deep and so long as the Great Depression of the 1930s. Economists have argued ever since as to just what caused it. But it's safe to say that a bunch of intertwined factors contributed. Among them were

>> **Bank failures:** Many small banks, particularly in rural areas, had overextended credit to farmers who, for the most part, had not shared in the prosperity of the 1920s and often couldn't repay the loans. Big banks, meanwhile, had foolishly made huge loans to foreign countries. Why? So the foreign countries could repay their earlier debts from World War I. When times got tough and U.S. banks stopped lending, European nations simply defaulted on their outstanding loans. As a result, many banks went bankrupt. Others were forced out of business when depositors panicked and withdrew their money. The closings and panics almost completely shut down the country's banking system.

>> **Environmental disasters:** The vast production of crops during World War I and the decade that followed contributed to what already had been decades of over-plowing much of America's farmland. The prairie grasses that held topsoil in place were stripped. Coupled with one of the worst droughts in recorded history, the unprotected soil turned the Great Plains into what would become known as the *Dust Bowl.* Dry winds picked up tons of topsoil and blew it across the prairies, creating huge, suffocating clouds of dirt that turned farms into deserts.

>> **Farm failures:** Even before the Depression and Dust Bowl disasters, farmers were having hard times, mostly because they were producing too much and product prices were too low. The situation was so bad in some areas that farmers burned corn for fuel rather than sell it.

>> **Government inaction:** Rather than try to jump-start the economy through public-works programs or financial system reforms, President Herbert Hoover's first instinct was to handle the financial crisis by largely ignoring it. He insisted the U.S. economic system was fundamentally sound and would get better by itself. By the time the federal government began taking small, tentative actions, it was too little too late.

>> **The stock market crash:** The stock market soared throughout most of the 1920s, and the more it grew, the more people eagerly poured money into it. Many bought *on margin,* which meant they paid only part of a stock's price when they bought it and the rest when they sold it. That worked fine as long as stock prices kept going up. When the market crashed in late October 1929, they were forced to pay up on stocks that were worth far less than what they had paid for them. Many had borrowed to buy stock, and when the stock market went belly up, they couldn't repay their loans. Lenders were left holding the empty bag.

>> **Too many poor people:** That may sound goofy, but it's a real reason. Though the overall economy had soared in the 1920s, most of the wealth was enjoyed by relatively few Americans. In 1929, 40 percent of the families in the country were still living at or below the poverty level. That made them too poor to buy goods and services and too poor to pay their debts. With no markets for their goods, manufacturers laid off tens of thousands of workers, which, of course, just created more poor people.

REMEMBER

Whatever the causes, the consequences of the Great Depression were staggering. In the cities, thousands of jobless men roamed the streets looking for work. It wasn't unusual for 2,000 or 3,000 applicants to show up for one or two job openings. If they weren't looking for work, they were looking for food. Bread lines were established to prevent people from starving (see Figure 15-1). And more than a million families lost their houses and took up residence in shantytowns made up of tents, packing crates, and the hulks of old cars. They were called *Hoovervilles*, a mocking reference to President Hoover, whom many blamed for the mess the country was in.

FIGURE 15-1:
Many wait hours in line for bread.

© Bettmann/CORBIS

Americans weren't sure what to do. In the summer of 1932, about 20,000 desperate World War I veterans marched on Washington, D.C., to claim $1,000 bonuses they had been promised they would get, starting in 1946. When Congress refused to move up the payment schedules, several thousand members of the *Bonus Army* built a camp of tents and shacks on the banks of the Potomac River and refused to leave. Under orders of President Hoover, federal troops commanded by Gen. Douglas MacArthur used bayonets and gas bombs to rout the squatters. The camp was burned. No one was killed, but the episode left a bad taste in the mouths of many Americans.

Thousands of farmers left their homes in states like Oklahoma and Arkansas and headed for the promise of better days in the West, especially California. What they found there, however, was often a backbreaking existence as migrant laborers, living in squalid camps and picking fruit for starvation wages.

TECHNICAL STUFF

PLUS TO MINUS

If you doubt that the Great Depression deserves that "Great" adjective, look at these numbers:

- More than 5,000 banks closed between 1930 and 1933, 9 million savings accounts were wiped out, and depositors lost $2.5 billion.

- Unemployment rose from less than 1 million in 1929 to more than 12 million by 1933 — equal to about 25 percent of the total U.S. workforce.

- Capital investment dropped from $10 billion in 1929 to $1 billion in 1932, and the stock market's industrial index dropped from 452 in September 1929 to 58 in July 1932.

- The gross national product went from $104 billion in 1929 to $59 billion in 1932.

- Farm income dropped 60 percent in the three years after 1929. In 1932, per capita income from farming was only $80 a year for farmers.

THE LINDBERGH KIDNAPPING

Almost everybody loved Charles Lindbergh. The lanky aviator had remained a true American hero after his historic solo flight across the Atlantic in 1927. So it made national headlines in March 1932 when someone climbed in a second-story window of Lindbergh's Hopewell, New Jersey, home and snatched his 20-month-old son, Charles, Jr.

The nation held its breath for six weeks, during which time Lindbergh responded to a ransom demand by paying $50,000. But on May 12, the body of the missing baby was found in the woods about 5 miles from the Lindbergh home. An illegal immigrant and escaped convict from Germany named Bruno Richard Hauptmann was arrested for the crime after most of the ransom money was found in his garage. Hauptmann was convicted and executed in the electric chair in 1936, still declaring his innocence.

As a result of the crime, Congress passed what became known as the *Lindbergh Law,* which made kidnapping a federal crime and thus allowed the FBI to enter the hunt for kidnappers.

FDR: Making Alphabet Soup

In 1932, Herbert Hoover was the U.S. president. In 1933, he was toast. Much of the country blamed Hoover for the Depression, although the groundwork for it had been laid long before he was elected in 1928. Hoover's big mistake was that he kept saying things would get better if everyone was just a little patient — and things just got worse.

Electing a reformer

By the time the 1932 presidential election came along, it was pretty clear that the Democrats could nominate a dead dog and still beat Hoover. Fortunately for the country, they passed up deceased canines and chose the governor of New York. His name was Franklin Delano Roosevelt, an appellation reduced in newspaper headlines and the popular parlance to *FDR*.

A distant cousin of Theodore Roosevelt and the only son of a wealthy railroad executive, FDR attended the best private schools and graduated from Harvard. Trained as a lawyer, Roosevelt served in the state legislature, became assistant secretary of the Navy, and had a boundless future. Then, in 1921, he was struck by polio and crippled.

ELEANOR ROOSEVELT

She began her marriage to her distant cousin in his shadow — and became his "legs." She also became one of the most beloved — and hated — First Ladies in U.S. history.

Eleanor was born into a wealthy New York family in 1884. After an unhappy childhood marked by the death of her parents, she married Franklin in 1905. Over the next decade, Eleanor had six children, found out her husband was playing around, and seemed destined to be either divorced or in the background as a politician's wife.

But Eleanor rose to the occasion. As First Lady, she broke tradition and held more than 350 press conferences of her own — but for female journalists only. She was a tireless champion for civil rights and women's issues and often represented her husband, whose polio prevented him from traveling easily, around the country. But her activism also earned her vitriolic hatred from people who didn't like her husband, her politics, or the fact that she was an independent woman.

After FDR's death, Eleanor served as a U.S. delegate to the United Nations and as a roving ambassador-at-large. She died in 1962 at the age of 78.

WHO'S AFRAID OF A LITTLE DEPRESSION?

"First of all, let me assert my firm belief that the only thing we have to fear is fear itself — nameless, unreasoning, unjustified terror that paralyzes needed effort to convert retreat into advance."

— Franklin Roosevelt, inaugural address, March 4, 1933

"We ain't gonna die out. People is goin' on — changin' a little, maybe, but goin' right on."

— Ma Joad in John Steinbeck's *The Grapes of Wrath*, 1939

But Roosevelt had an indomitable spirit. He was elected New York's governor in 1928, earning a reputation as a reformer. The Democrats nominated him for the presidency in 1932 after some behind-the-scenes maneuvering by newspaper publisher William Randolph Hearst and business tycoon Joseph Kennedy. He campaigned on a New Deal platform and easily defeated Hoover.

Despite his aristocratic background, Roosevelt was wildly popular with the average guy, many of whom didn't know he could walk only with leg braces and crutches. (News photographers and newsreel cameramen took care not to take shots of him in "awkward" poses.) But many conservatives and business leaders, who considered him a traitor to his class, hated him.

FDR may have been the perfect president for the time. He was friendly and approachable and exuded sympathy and self-confidence. He knew how to compromise, and like Lincoln and Washington, he knew how to get the best out of people. He was lucky — before taking office he narrowly escaped an assassin's bullets while riding in a car with Chicago Mayor Anton Cermak in Miami (Cermak was killed). He wasn't afraid to do something, even if it proved to be wrong: "Take a method," he said, "and try it. If it fails, try another. But above all, do something."

Creating hope through a New Deal

Roosevelt heeded his own advice and did something. Supported by healthy Democratic majorities in Congress, FDR pushed through a dazzling array of programs (many of them best known by their initials) in his first 100 days in office. The products of the first 100 days (and in some cases a bit longer) included the

>> **Agricultural Adjustment Act (AAA):** Basically, it paid farmers not to produce so much food. That bailed farmers out, at least a little, and increased farm prices to more profitable levels.

>> **Civil Works Administration (CWA):** The CWA provided about 4 million jobs in building roads, airports, schools, sewer systems, and other civic projects.

>> **Civilian Conservation Corps (CCC):** This created 1,300 camps around the country to give young men new jobs (at $30 a month, with $22 sent home to their families) in conserving natural resources. By 1941, the CCC employed 2.5 million men who planted more than 17 million trees and made improvements in scores of state and national parks.

>> **Emergency Banking Act:** Three days after he took office, FDR closed all banks. Then, on March 9, he pushed through Congress a bill that reopened the banks under close supervision. The bill, which took all of eight hours to go through, also authorized the Treasury to issue more currency.

>> **Federal Emergency Relief Act (FERA):** The FERA eventually provided a total of $500 million in aid to state and local governments.

>> **Glass-Stegall Banking Act:** This act mandated that banks get out of the investment business and restricted use of bank money on stock speculation. It also created federal guarantees for personal bank accounts.

>> **Homeowners Loan Act:** This provided funds to help keep homeowners from losing their homes to mortgage foreclosures.

>> **National Industrial Recovery Act (NIRA):** This ambitious program was designed to get industries to cooperate in setting maximum hours, minimum wages, and price controls through an organization called the National Recovery Administration (NRA). The NIRA was declared unconstitutional by the Supreme Court in 1935 for giving too much power to the program's nongovernment administrators.

>> **Tennessee Valley Authority Act (TVA):** One of the most innovative of the New Deal programs, the TVA created an independent public agency that oversaw the development of dams and other projects in the Tennessee River Valley. The TVA covered 40,000 square miles in seven states. It built 16 dams, took over 5 more, and provided electric power to 40,000 families who previously had none. The TVA also supplied fertilizer, provided flood control and better river navigation, and reforested vast areas.

>> **Truth in Securities Act:** This act required new stocks and bonds offered for sale to be registered with the new Securities Exchange Commission (SEC) and required brokers to fully disclose all background information.

>> **Work Projects Administration (WPA):** This organization created a host of federal projects that ranged from cleaning slums and providing electricity to rural areas to painting murals on the walls of public buildings and putting on plays for audiences who paid only what they could afford.

HARRY HOPKINS

He was the big dealer in the New Deal, a super social worker who was Franklin Roosevelt's most trusted aide and whose no-b.s. approach to things earned him the nickname *Lord Root of the Matter* from Winston Churchill.

Hopkins was born the son of a harness maker in Iowa in 1890. After graduating from college, he became a social worker and eventually ran relief programs in New York for FDR when Roosevelt was governor. In the White House, Hopkins ran several New Deal programs and agencies and was made secretary of commerce in 1938.

He wasn't shy about spending government money, either: One Hopkins-run program spent $1 billion in less than six months, making even FDR wince. When a New Deal congressional critic suggested there were better ways to deal with the Depression in the long run, Hopkins snapped: "People don't eat in the long run, senator; they eat every day."

When World War II broke out, Hopkins served as FDR's alter ego and go-between with other world leaders. After FDR's death, Hopkins helped plan the United Nations. Never in good health, he died in 1946 at the age of 55.

In 1935 Roosevelt added to his alphabet soup of programs by getting Congress to pass the Social Security Act, which began a sweeping federal system of unemployment insurance and retirement pensions paid for by both employers and employees through payroll taxes. In 1938, he signed the Fair Labor Standards Act, which created a national minimum wage of 25 cents per hour and a maximum workweek of 44 hours.

By the time the 1936 elections rolled around, things were looking up. Unemployment had dropped from 12 million to about 9 million. Average weekly earnings had increased from $17 to $22. So despite Republican predictions that the Democrats were creating a socialist state, FDR was easily reelected.

Packing the Supreme Court

One of the things that stuck in FDR's craw during his first term was the nine-member U.S. Supreme Court. Dominated by conservatives, the court had thwarted some of Roosevelt's plans. So in February 1937, he proposed that he be allowed to appoint a new federal judge for every judge who refused to retire within six months of reaching the age of 70. This "court-packing" tactic would have raised the number of Supreme Court justices to 15.

Roosevelt's ploy worked — sort of. Although Congress ultimately rejected it, the high court began making decisions that were more favorable to the New Deal. Within a few years, six justices retired, enabling Roosevelt to appoint liberals to the court. But the fight also weakened FDR politically because it was widely viewed as a presidential power play.

Assessing the New Deal

How well the New Deal actually worked is still widely debated. Many of the programs had big price tags. The national debt, which was about $22.5 billion when FDR took office, was nearly double that by 1940, and so was the size of the federal bureaucracy. After winning reelection in 1936, FDR began scaling back federal spending to help keep inflation in check. As soon as he did, unemployment began to climb again, and industrial production slowed.

What is undebatable, however, is the fact that the New Deal greatly increased the role of the federal government in people's lives. It laid the foundation for a government "safety net" of services for Americans most in need, it fostered the development of the modern labor movement, and it made the federal government a key player in regulating the U.S. economy.

And whether all that was a good or bad idea, most people felt a lot better in 1940 than they did in 1932. Americans were pleased enough, in fact, with FDR's performance by 1940 to give him what they had given no other president — a third term.

THE BIRTH OF A HERO

You may have read that Superman was born on the planet Krypton, but it was really in Cleveland, Ohio, on a hot summer night in 1934. And his parents were a couple of teenagers looking for careers in Depression-ravaged America.

Jerry Siegel was a 19-year-old would-be writer who dallied in science fiction. His pal, 19-year-old Joe Shuster, was an artist. So when Siegel came up during a sleepless night with an idea for a character with superpowers, the two decided to put together a comic strip. They dressed their hero in a red, blue, and yellow costume and took him around to every comic strip syndicate in America — and were rejected faster than a speeding bullet.

In 1938, however, DC Comics decided to take a chance, and Superman appeared for the first time in Action Comics #1 (a near-mint copy of which sold in 2014 for $3.2 million.) Siegel and Shuster got relatively little for their creation, despite decades of legal battles over who owned the rights to the Kryptonian crusader.

Created as an antidote for Depression blues, the Man of Steel has become an icon perhaps second only to Mickey Mouse as a larger-than-life pen-and-ink character. And who knows? Without him, we might not have Super Bowls, superstars, or super-sized fast-food meals.

Shoving Aside Racial Minorities

The majority of America's minorities had never had it good, so it's not surprising that the Depression made their lot even more miserable.

More than half of African Americans still lived in the South, most as *sharecroppers,* meaning they farmed someone else's land. Almost all of those who worked and weren't farmers held menial jobs that whites hadn't wanted — until the Depression came along. When it did, the African Americans were shoved out of their jobs. As many as 400,000 left the South for cities in the North, which didn't help much. By 1932, it's estimated that half of the black U.S. population was on some form of relief.

Segregation continued in nearly every walk of life. Proposals for federal anti-lynching laws were blocked in Congress, and more than 60 blacks were murdered by lynching and other mob violence during the decade. Even some of FDR's bold federal programs blatantly discriminated against blacks. Wage-setting schedules allowed employers to pay black workers less than whites, farm aid schemes often ignored African-American farmers, and job creation programs provided disproportionately fewer jobs to African Americans.

REMEMBER

Some of the programs, however, helped everyone. Segregation in federal jobs slowly began to crumble, and some labor unions opened their membership to minorities. Such crumbs were enough to make many black voters abandon the Republican Party. Since the Civil War, most African American voters had remained loyal to the GOP, particularly as Democrat-dominated Southern states routinely imposed repressive laws and voting-rights restrictions.

But as the Depression deepened and African Americans increasingly moved to Northern cities, black voters began to shift their allegiance from the party of Lincoln, which they felt had done little for them since Reconstruction, to the party of FDR, which offered at least part of the pie to them. In 1932, only 44 percent of black voters supported Roosevelt. By 1936, it was 74 percent. The black vote became one of the Democrats' most reliable blocs of support for decades to come.

Other minority groups suffered similarly to African Americans during the decade. Mexico had been exempted from the immigration restrictions of the 1920s, and as a result, hundreds of thousands of Mexicans came to America, mostly to the Southwest. Prior to the Depression, they were at least tolerated as a ready source of cheap labor. In the 1930s, however, they were pushed out of jobs by desperate white Americans. Thousands of Latinos were deported, even some who were U.S. citizens, and as many as 500,000 returned to Mexico. Those of Asian descent, mostly on the West Coast, were likewise forced from jobs or relegated to work only within their own communities.

THE SCOTTSBORO BOYS

In March 1931, nine young black males were taken from a freight train near Scottsboro, Alabama, and arrested for vagrancy. Then two white women who were traveling in the same freight car accused the boys of gang-raping them.

Despite mountains of evidence that the women were lying, an all-white jury quickly convicted the youths, and eight of them were sentenced to death. A communist-backed group called the *International Labor Defense* took up their cause, and the U.S. Supreme Court ordered a new trial. Five of them were retried and found guilty again, and again the verdict was thrown out by the Supreme Court as unconstitutional because blacks had been excluded from the jury.

None of the defendants were ever executed. One escaped, and the other four were paroled after serving years in prison for the crime of being black in the wrong place at the wrong time. In November 2013, the state of Alabama posthumously pardoned the three men who had not yet been formally exonerated. "The Scottsboro boys have finally received justice," said Alabama Gov. Robert J. Bentley.

Native Americans had been largely ignored by the federal government for decades. The idea had been to have them gradually disappear into the American mainstream. In 1924, Congress made U.S. citizens of all Native Americans, whether they wanted to be or not.

But preliminary studies done in the 1920s found that assimilation had failed. In 1934, Congress changed direction and passed laws that allowed Native Americans to retain their cultural identity. That did little for their economic well-being, and they remained perhaps the worst off of America's minority groups.

Keeping Women at Home — or Work

With jobs scarce, a strong feeling prevailed that women should stay home and let men have the jobs. There was even a federal rule that two people in the same family couldn't both be on the government payroll. But two things occurred that actually slightly increased the number of women in the workforce during the decade. The first was that women would work for lower pay — a fact that was not only allowed by federal law but followed by some federal government agencies. The second was that more women had no man to rely on as a breadwinner: U.S. marriage rates dropped for the first time since the early 1800s.

Charles B. Darrow had known better times. Broke and unemployed in 1933, the Germantown, Pennsylvania, heating engineer combined memories of a past family vacation to Atlantic City, New Jersey, with an existing board game called "The Landlord's Game." Darrow's version used Atlantic City addresses like Marvin Gardens and Park Place. He called his get-rich-quick, real-estate board game "Monopoly." Darrow took his idea to the folks at the Parker Brothers game company in 1934. They promptly kicked him out the door, calling the game too long, too dull, and burdened with at least 52 "fundamental play errors." Undaunted, Darrow produced the game on his own and sold 5,000 sets to a Philadelphia department store. The sale changed the mind of Parker Brothers. It bought the game from Darrow in early 1936; bought the rights to "The Landlord's Game" from its inventor, Elizabeth Magie; and soon was churning out 20,000 sets of Monopoly a week. People forgot their hard times for a few hours while rolling dice, buying railroads, and going directly to jail without passing "Go."

Monopoly is now sold in more than 100 countries and has been produced in 37 languages and in more than 100 variations — including a game made entirely of chocolate and one with 18-carat gold pieces and real U.S. currency. Darrow retired at 46 on his royalties. He lived to 76, the first American millionaire to make his fortune by designing a game — and in the midst of the Great Depression yet!

Developing Organized Labor

If the sun peeked through the Depression's clouds on anyone, it may have been organized labor. The 1930s saw captains of industry and business lose much of their political clout to unions, and new laws made organizing easier.

The decade also saw a telling split in labor. The traditionalists who ran the American Federation of Labor (AFL) wanted to concentrate on organizing workers according to their specific skills or craft. But that left out thousands of workers who had no specific skills and also sometimes pitted workers for the same company against one another.

In 1936, John L. Lewis, the bombastic leader of the United Mine Workers, led a split from the AFL and formed the Congress of Industrial Organizations (CIO). The CIO was more receptive to not only unskilled workers but also women and minorities. By 1938, it had 4 million members.

The United Auto Workers (UAW) also flexed its muscles in the decade. The UAW used sit-down strikes, where workers would simply stop and sit down at their posts, making it much more difficult to use strikebreakers. In 1937, General Motors, the third-largest company in the country, recognized the UAW after a 44-day strike.

That same year, steelworkers won recognition of their union by U.S. Steel, the giant of the industry. Other steel companies, however, refused to go along, and confrontations were often violent. On Memorial Day, 1937, police opened fire on marching strikers and their families in South Chicago, killing 10 and wounding 90. The tragedy became known as the *Memorial Day Massacre* and served as a rallying cry for labor.

All told, there were more than 4,500 strikes in 1937, and labor won more than three-quarters of them. By 1940, more than 8 million Americans were members of organized labor.

Critics, Crooks, and Crime Fighters

Not everyone was in love with FDR. Many Republicans refused to even say his name, referring to him as "that man in the White House." The 1930s also spawned a gaggle of colorful critics and crusaders who made themselves heard above the hard times.

Huey Long

He was a traveling salesman, a lawyer, and a world-class demagogue. Huey Long was elected governor of Louisiana in 1928 on a populist platform, and he actually did some good things for the state, such as making school textbooks free and improving roads and highways. But he also ran a corrupt administration that was not above roughing up, blackmailing, or slandering those who opposed him. By 1930, the "Kingfish" was as close to an absolute dictator as there was in the country. He controlled the legislature and, after winning a U.S. Senate seat, refused to promptly vacate the governor's office, thus holding both jobs for a while.

A "DEMOCRATIC" KINGMAKER

"I'm for the poor man — all poor men. Black and white, they all gotta have a chance. 'Every man a king,' that's my motto."

— Huey Long to a journalist, 1932

Originally an FDR supporter, Long broke with the White House mostly for egotistical reasons. He proposed a "Share Our Wealth" program that called for confiscating family fortunes of more than $5 million and annual incomes over $1 million and guaranteeing every family $2,500 a year, a homestead, and a car. Long had a national following and announced he would run against FDR at the head of a third party in 1936. Private polls showed he might garner 4 million votes, enough to tip the election to the Republicans. But he never got the chance. In September 1935, Long was shot to death on the steps of the Louisiana capitol by a man whose family he had ruined.

Francis E. Townsend

Francis Townsend was an elderly California doctor who was selling real estate in Long Beach in 1935 when he had an idea that he just couldn't help sharing: providing $200 a month for life to everyone 60 or older. It would be financed by sales taxes, and every pensioner would have to spend his entire pension every month, which Townsend said would stimulate the economy. Actually, more experienced economists pointed out the scheme would take half the national income to provide for 8 percent of the population.

Despite the crackpot smell of the idea, "Townsend Clubs" sprang up all over the country, with as many as 5 million members. The idea gradually died out after Roosevelt proposed the Social Security system.

Charles E. Coughlin

A Roman Catholic priest, Charles Coughlin was, after Roosevelt himself, the best radio orator in America. Broadcasting from the Shrine of the Little Flower in Royal Oak, Michigan, Coughlin was a super-patriot who ripped into Wall Street, big business, and oppressive bosses. Originally, he supported FDR, but soon he became an ardent foe, advocating the nationalization of banks and ripping into Roosevelt as a communist tool of Jewish bankers.

Coughlin created the National Union for Social Justice, which drew more than 5 million members in less than two months. But his increasingly shrill attacks on Jews and Roosevelt created a backlash, and by mid-1940, the bombastic cleric had quieted down considerably.

Despite the fact that their schemes were pretty looney-tunes, FDR's more vocal and visible critics did put some pressure on him to continue to press for reform, especially during his first term. "I am fighting communism, Huey Longism, Coughlinism, Townsendism," FDR said with some exasperation. "I want to save our system, the capitalist system [but] I want to equalize the distribution of wealth."

Meanwhile, a guy named Hoover was fighting "outlawism."

Bad guys and G-men

While some were coming up with political proposals to redistribute wealth, others had a more pragmatic approach: They stole it. The 1930s saw the rise of the modern outlaw. Instead of six-guns and horses, they used Tommy guns and Fords. Some of them became folk heroes, robbing banks that many people felt had robbed their customers.

There was Charles "Pretty Boy" Floyd, who reportedly robbed more than 30 banks and killed ten men before he was gunned down in 1934. There was Arizona "Ma" Barker, whose gang consisted mainly of her four sons and who died in a shootout with the law. There were Bonnie Parker and Clyde Barrow, a pair of Texas lovers-robbers-murderers who became folk heroes despite the fact that many of their fellow desperadoes regarded them as trigger-happy bunglers. And there was John Dillinger.

SHIRLEY TEMPLE

She was less than 4 feet tall, and she was the biggest thing in Hollywood: dancing, singing, and mugging her way into the hearts of a country that really needed someone to hug.

Born in 1928 in Santa Monica, California, Shirley Temple made her first movie at the age of 3. She went on to make 24 more during the 1930s and was the No. 1 box-office attraction every year from 1935 to 1938. Movies like *Little Miss Marker* and *Captain January* earned the curly-headed charmer $300,000 a year. And thousands more were added by royalties from the sales of Shirley dolls, dresses, dishes, soap, and books. Little girls all over the country wanted to look like, sound like, and be adored as much as Shirley.

Temple retired from films in the late 1940s and had a brief career on TV. She married oil executive Charles A. Black in 1950 and gradually became active in politics. She served as a U.S. representative to the United Nations, ambassador to Ghana, and chief of protocol for the State Department in the 1970s. She died in February 2014 at the age of 85.

An Indiana native, Dillinger robbed a grocery store in 1924 and was caught. He did nine years in prison, and when he got out, he started a 14-month crime spree that made him one of the most famous, or infamous, men in America. Dillinger killed ten men, engineered three daring jailbreaks, escaped from two gun battles with the law, and stole as much as $265,000.

He also became something of a Robin Hood. "Dillinger does not rob poor people," a fan wrote to the newspapers. "He robs those who became rich robbing poor people. I am for Johnnie." In the end, such popularity did Dillinger little good. Federal agents killed him in 1934 as he left a movie theater in Chicago.

Fighting the bad guys were the *G-men*, a nickname given to Federal Bureau of Investigation (FBI) agents by George "Machine Gun" Kelly. The *G* stood for government, and the head G-man was an owlish-looking, fiercely intense man named J. Edgar Hoover. As head of the FBI, Hoover combined a fanatical sense of duty and a flair for public relations to make his agency a beacon of heroism and integrity.

Serving as director from 1924 until his death in 1972, Hoover was one of the most powerful figures in 20th-century America. His almost pathological hatred of communism, his dictatorial manner, and his unethical and, quite probably, illegal use of the bureau against political and personal enemies eventually stained his name. But in the 1930s, millions of American boys wanted to be him.

THE PANIC OF A MARTIAN INVASION

Mercury Theater players had a dull story on their hands and a deadline looming for their live Halloween-eve performance on CBS radio in 1938. But writer Howard Koch did his best with H. G. Wells's novel *The War of the Worlds,* bringing the Martian invasion into the 1930s and relocating it from England to New Jersey. And Mercury leader Orson Welles used all his considerable acting talent to make it as realistic as possible.

In fact, he and the rest of the cast did too good a job. Despite several announcements that it was just a radio show, many in the show's audience of several million thought there was a real Martian invasion going on. Panic spread (although just how much is a subject of debate among historians). People called police to ask what to do. In New Jersey, families hastily packed and took to the roads. There were several reports of attempted suicides.

It took two days to calm things down, and criminal charges were even considered against Welles. In the end, however, the show got a big new sponsor, Campbell Soup, and Welles was invited to the White House.

"You know, Orson," President Roosevelt told him, "You and I are the two best actors in America."

Chapter 16

The World at War: 1941-1945

Very few Americans had any use for the dictators of Europe and Asia, but even fewer had a burning desire to fight them. World War I had left a bad taste in the mouths of many, and the lingering effects of the Depression were still being felt. The United States didn't need a foreign headache.

But as this chapter shows, sometimes a fight just can't be avoided, particularly when it seems half the world is being run by monsters. Faced with the most widespread and horrific war in human history, Americans respond magnificently. They also develop and unleash a weapon that will forever change the future of mankind.

Trying to Avoid War — Again

Despite the hangover from World War I and America's refusal to join the League of Nations, the country didn't exactly become a hermit in the 1920s and 1930s. In 1922, U.S. government and private interests helped feed more than 10 million starving Russians. The country also provided more than $100 million in aid to Turkey, Greece, and other Mediterranean countries in the 1920s and forgave or reduced World War I debts.

On the diplomatic front, the United States, Great Britain, Japan, France, and Italy agreed in 1922 to limit their warship building. And in 1928, French foreign minister Aristide Briand and U.S. Secretary of State Frank Kellogg convinced themselves and 15 other countries to formally agree not to go to war with each other. As completely unrealistic as the agreement may have been, so eager for peace was the U.S. Senate that it ratified the Kellogg-Briand Pact on an 85-to-1 vote.

Playing the role of a good neighbor

Closer to home, Presidents Harding and Coolidge weren't shy about interfering in Latin American countries' internal affairs if it suited the interests of U.S. businesses. Starting with President Hoover, however, and continuing under Roosevelt, America began a "good neighbor" policy toward Central and South America. The policy basically pledged that America would maintain pleasant relations and generally mind its own business.

America tried to keep to that policy elsewhere in the world as well. In Asia, Japan was becoming more and more hostile toward its neighbors, and U.S. diplomats made periodic attempts to convince the Japanese to slow down. But Japan had been insulted when America closed its doors to Japanese immigration in 1924 and wasn't in the mood to listen. And Americans weren't interested in a fight, even after Japan invaded China in 1931 or when Japanese planes "accidentally" sank a U.S. gunboat in a Chinese river in 1937.

In Europe, Italy, run by a strutting thug, Benito Mussolini, invaded Ethiopia in 1936 with not much more than a whimper from the United States. When Germany, under an evil madman, Adolf Hitler, took Austria and Czechoslovakia in 1938, President Roosevelt sent letters asking the dictators not to conquer any more countries. They laughed at him.

REMEMBER

Roosevelt was not being timid as much as he was being a practical politician. America was still reeling from the effects of the Great Depression, and most Americans were more interested in figuring out how to pay next month's rent than in who ran Austria. A 1937 survey found that 94 percent thought U.S. policy should be directed at keeping out of foreign wars rather than trying to stop them.

An "isolationist" movement, whose most popular leader was aviator hero Charles Lindbergh, gained strength and held rallies around the country, exhorting Roosevelt and Congress to keep the United States sheltered from the growing storm clouds in Asia and Europe. Congress and FDR agreed, approving laws in 1935 and again in 1937 that prohibited the sale of American weapons to any warring nation.

But much of the rest of the world continued to rush toward conflict. On September 1, 1939, Germany invaded Poland. Great Britain and France had signed a pact pledging to come to Poland's defense and declared war on Germany. World War II had begun.

France was badly prepared for war and collapsed quickly under the German "Blitz-krieg," or "lightning war." By mid-1940, England stood alone against Hitler and his allies, which for the time being included the Soviet Union, led by its own evil madman, Josef Stalin.

Sensing the unavoidable

Roosevelt, like most Americans, was still not eager for war. But unlike the ardent isolationists, he also figured it was inevitable and began to take steps to get ready for it in 1940 and 1941. They included

>> Authorizing the doubling of the size of the U.S. Navy.

>> Pledging to come to the aid of any North, Central, or South American country that was attacked.

>> Pushing Congress to approve the first peacetime military draft in U.S. history. The draft required all men between the ages of 21 and 35 (about 16 million) to register. About 1.2 million were drafted for a year's service, and 800,000 reservists were called to active duty. In October 1941, Congress fortuitously voted to extend the draft. But it was a very close vote: 203 to 202.

>> Trading 50 old U.S. Navy destroyers to England in return for leases on military bases on English possessions in the Caribbean.

THE GREAT STONE FACES

John Robinson had this idea for a sculpture. A *big* sculpture. Robinson was the state historian of South Dakota in the 1920s, and he thought it would be cool to turn a cliff in the state's Black Hills into a tribute to figures from the Old West, such as Buffalo Bill Cody. So he and other supporters of the idea hunted up an Idaho sculptor named John Gutzon de la Mothe Borglum. Borglum liked the concept, but not the subject.

In 1927, with the blessing of South Dakota — and eventually about $1 million from Congress — Borglum began using dynamite to blast away granite from the side of a mountain named after a New York lawyer named Charles Rushmore. Instead of Old West figures, however, Borglum carved the heads of four American presidents: George Washington, Abraham Lincoln, Thomas Jefferson, and Theodore Roosevelt. The job wasn't finished until October 1941, when Mt. Rushmore National Memorial opened to the public. Borglum didn't live to see it. He died in March 1941. But his son (somewhat appropriately named Lincoln) carried on his work, and more than 2.7 million visitors view the mammoth effort every year. Very few ask, "Where's Buffalo Bill?"

NO BLOODSHED, I PROMISE

"And while I am talking to you mothers and fathers, I give you one more assurance. I have said this before, but I shall say it again and again and again: Your boys are not going to be sent into any foreign wars."

— Franklin Roosevelt, a few days before being elected to a third term as president, November 1940

>> Pushing the Lend-Lease Act through Congress, which authorized FDR to sell, trade, lease, or just plain give military hardware to any country he thought would use it to further the security of the United States.

>> Ordering the Navy to attack on sight German submarines that had been preying on ships off the East Coast.

REMEMBER

Despite all the preparations, many Americans still refused to believe war was inevitable. Then, on a sleepy Sunday morning less than three weeks before Christmas, 1941, a Japanese naval and air force launched a surprise attack on the U.S. naval base at Pearl Harbor, Hawaii. More than 2,400 U.S. military men were killed, 150 planes were destroyed, and eight battleships were sunk or badly damaged. December 7, in Roosevelt's words, had become "a day which will live in infamy."

THE ANDREWS SISTERS

They didn't have great voices, and they weren't especially beautiful, but they sure struck a chord with Americans in the 1940s. LaVerne (1911–1967), Maxene (1916–1995), and Patty (1918–2013) Andrews were born in Minneapolis and were performing three-part harmonies in vaudeville by the time they were in their teens.

Their first big hit, a Yiddish tune called "Bei Mir Bist Du Schon," came out in 1937 and sold 350,000 copies in a month. Other hit records included "Beat Me Daddy, Eight to the Bar," "Boogie Woogie Bugle Boy," "Don't Sit Under the Apple Tree," "Rum and Coca Cola," and "Don't Fence Me In." They sold more than 70 million records, sang with virtually every big star of the day — from Glenn Miller to Bing Crosby — and appeared in 17 films where they usually played themselves.

But the sisters (who often quarreled and sometimes didn't speak to each other except on stage) were best known as "America's Wartime Sweethearts" because of their tireless travels to entertain U.S. troops, both in the United States and overseas. "We never got tired of trying to bring a little smile and a little music to the boys," Maxene later recalled. "They didn't have much else to smile about."

Gearing Up for War

Despite all the warnings, the United States wasn't completely prepared when war broke out. The Depression had wiped out many of the country's machine and tool industries, the military was woefully under-supplied, and many soldiers found themselves drilling with toy guns and wooden tanks. In a way, however, the Depression was a good preparation for what was to come: Americans had learned to scrimp and persevere. And having been pushed into a fight, they were eager to oblige.

Getting industry and the economy in shape for World War II

Gearing up the industry needed to wage a global war on two fronts was handicapped by a lack of manpower. More than 15 million Americans eventually served in the military. Training and supplying them was a staggering challenge. It took more than 6,000 people to provide food, equipment, medical services, and transportation to 8,000 soldiers. Many raw materials, such as rubber, manila fiber, and oil, were in short supply. And while Roosevelt was a great leader, he was not a great administrator.

Nevertheless, Americans rose to the occasion. When FDR called for the production of 50,000 planes in a year, it was thought to be ridiculous. By 1944, the country was producing 96,000 a year. Technology blossomed. When metals became scarce, plastics were developed to take their place. Copper was taken out of pennies and replaced with steel; nickel was removed from nickels. War-inspired pragmatism even affected fashions: To save material, men's suits lost their pant cuffs and vests, and women painted their legs to take the place of nylons.

Other sacrifices were made as well. Gasoline and tires were rationed, as were coffee, sugar, canned goods, butter, and shoes. But the war proved to be more of an economic inconvenience than a real trial for most people.

Of course, all that military hardware had a hefty price tag. The federal government spent about $350 billion during World War II — or twice as much as it had spent *in total* for the entire history of the U.S. government up to that point. About 40 percent of that came from taxes; the rest came through government borrowing, much of that through the sale of bonds.

All that money had to go someplace. A lot of it went to the West, especially California, where 10 percent of all the federal war spending took place. But the American economy rose just about everywhere else, too. The civilian workforce grew 20 percent. The *Gross National Product* (the total of goods and services produced) more than doubled between 1939 and 1945. Wages and corporate profits went up, as did prices.

THE STATISTICS OF WAR SUPPLIES

Production boomed during the war, to the tune of the following figures:

- **Aircraft:** 296,429
- **Artillery:** 372,431
- **Bullets:** 41.59 million
- **Naval ships:** 87,620
- **Tanks and self-propelled guns:** 102,351
- **Trucks:** 2.46 million

In October 1942, Congress gave the president the power to freeze agricultural prices, wages, salaries, and rents. The Roosevelt administration created the Office of Price Administration (OPA) to oversee prices and wages. But the OPA proved generally ineffective, and the economy mostly ran itself.

Working with labor unions during war times

The serious labor shortage created by the war was a big boost to union membership. Early on, FDR got labor to agree to a "no strike" pledge and a 15 percent limit on wage increases.

Even so, there were numerous work stoppages as the war wore on. The government actually seized the nation's coal mines in 1943 after a major strike and also seized the railroads in late 1943 to avert a strike. Congress eventually passed a law requiring unions to wait 30 days before striking.

Many perceived the strikes as slightly treasonous, and "there are no strikes in foxholes" became a popular response to labor stoppages. Still, as labor leaders pointed out, things were a lot better for a lot of working Americans: Average weekly wages went from $24 in 1939 to $46 in 1944.

"DA" FOR THE WORKING YANK

"To American production, without which this war would have been lost."

— toast by Soviet dictator Josef Stalin, October 1943

HENRY J. KAISER

Henry Kaiser had never built a ship, so he didn't know he was doing it "wrong." All he knew was that he was doing it fast — and helping to win the war. Kaiser was born in New York in 1882. He left school at the age of 13 to go to work and eventually ended up on the West Coast as an engineer. During the Depression, he helped to build major dams in the West, such as Boulder and Grand Coulee, and when the war started, he was asked to help provide ships.

He did it by using assembly line methods, building sections and then welding them together. Traditional shipbuilders were skeptical that it would work. But Kaiser's method streamlined the process of building a cargo vessel, called a *liberty ship*, from 245 days to 17. By 1943, Kaiser's shipyards were producing an average of two ships a day, helping to keep England fed, providing supplies for overseas troops, lowering enemy morale, and earning Kaiser the nickname "Sir Launch-a-lot."

Kaiser's interests were by no means limited to ships. He also built magnesium and aluminum plants to provide parts for planes and built the first steel-producing plant in the West. After the war, he made Jeeps and got into healthcare. He died in 1967, having proven that you can't stop a Kaiser when he's on a roll.

Employing women for the war effort

Millions of women entered the workforce to take the place of the men who were off to the military. By 1943, 17 million women filled a third of civilian jobs, 5 million of them in war factories. "If you've followed recipes exactly in making cakes, you can learn to load shells," proclaimed billboards recruiting women to the workplace.

Some companies offered childcare or provided meals to take home as incentives to lure women into the workplace. But women were still given the short end of the stick when it came to wages: In 1944, women got an average of $31.21 a week for working in war-related factories, while men doing the same jobs were paid $54.65.

Making strides — African Americans achieve greater equality

Many African Americans had hoped their service in World War I would help bring them equality in postwar America. But they were wrong. So when World War II started, some black leaders were wary. "Our war is not against the Hitler in Europe," editorialized one black newspaper, "but against the Hitlers in America." Some black leaders demanded assurances that loyalty this time around would be rewarded with more decent treatment.

ROSE MONROE

It was a classic case of life imitates art imitates life. Early on in World War II, the government started propaganda campaigns to help get women involved in the war effort. One such campaign was built around a poster of an attractive (and well-muscled), bandana-wearing woman named "Rosie the Riveter." There was even a popular song to go along with it.

But Rosie was a fictional character — until actor Walter Pidgeon visited an aircraft plant in Ypsilanti, Michigan, to make a short film promoting war bonds. There he met a young widow named Rose Monroe, who was riveting planes to support her family. Pidgeon signed her up to be in the film, and she became an inspiration for millions of women entering the workforce for the first time.

Born in 1920 in Kentucky, Monroe went to work after her husband died in a car accident. After the war, Monroe drove a cab, owned a beauty shop, started a construction company, and earned a pilot's license. She died in 1997, still an inspiration to new generations of working women.

In response, Roosevelt established the Fair Employment Practices Commission and charged it with investigating cases where African Americans were discriminated against in war industries. The commission enjoyed some success. But the real economic boost for blacks came from the labor shortage, which fueled the movement of many from the South to industrial cities in the North and West.

REMEMBER

About 700,000 African Americans also served in the military and some strides in equality were made. Blacks were admitted into the Air Force and Marines for the first time. The Air Force enlisted some 600 black pilots and the first African-American general was appointed in the Army. Some military units were even integrated toward the end of the war, although it was more for practical reasons than to further civil rights.

Even so, race relations remained mired in racism and distrust. Several cities had race riots, the worst of which was in Detroit in 1943, when 34 people died. Angry that the racism of Hitler was being fought against while the racism at home was largely ignored, many African Americans began taking a more active role in asserting their legal rights. The ranks of the National Association for the Advancement of Colored People (NAACP) swelled from 50,000 before the war to more than 400,000 at war's end.

THE "BATTLE OF LOS ANGELES"

On February 2, 1942, less than two months after Pearl Harbor was attacked, U.S. Naval intelligence in Southern California issued a warning that a Japanese attack might occur that night.

Sure enough, in the wee hours of February 25, radar picked up unidentified blips about 120 miles off the coast of Los Angeles. Then planes were reported near Long Beach, and then four anti-aircraft batteries began firing at something over Santa Monica. Within minutes, other military guns opened fire. Confusion reigned over the next three hours as contradictory reports poured in.

By the dawn's early light, Los Angeles residents saw the results of the attack: no downed enemy planes, no bomb damage, a few traffic accidents, and one man dead from a heart attack.

Eventually it was decided that it had been a false alarm, and the fuss had probably been caused by weather balloons (or UFOs, as some folks now insist). Whatever the cause, for a few hours the fighting had come uncomfortably close to the home front.

Returning for work after being kicked out — Latinos

In 1942, the U.S. and Mexican governments reached an agreement to allow Mexican workers — *braceros* — to enter the United States to help make up the manpower shortage. Thousands of Mexicans, some of whom had been thrown out of America during the Depression, entered the country, mostly to take agricultural jobs in the West.

The sudden influx sometimes caused friction, particularly in California. In Los Angeles, tensions between outlandishly garbed Latino youths and sailors led to the "zoot suit" riots of 1943. To avoid further trouble, city officials passed a law prohibiting the wearing of zoot suits in public.

Treating the Japanese Americans poorly

By far the most shameful aspect of World War II on the home front was the treatment of Japanese residents. About 125,000 people of Japanese descent lived in the United States, 110,000 of them on the West Coast. Seventy thousand, called *Nisei*, were born here. The rest, called *Issei*, were born in Japan and emigrated.

WINNING CUISINE

If an army travels on its stomach, the United States rode to victory in World War II on Spam. Yes, Spam, the ubiquitous canned meat product made from pork shoulder and ham.

Invented in 1937 by the Hormel Foods Corporation, Spam hit its culinary stride when the war began, as a substitute for rationed beef. Because it didn't need refrigeration, it was ideal for feeding troops — and they ate more than 100 million pounds of it.

Spam was also fodder for G.I. humor: "meatloaf without basic training," "the ham that didn't pass its physical," "the reason war is hell." But Spam was a lifesaver for countries whose food supplies had been pinched by the war. Soviet leader Nikita Khrushchev once stated that without Spam, the Russian army would have starved. And it fries up so much better than caviar.

In the wake of Pearl Harbor, many of both groups' neighbors began to view them with suspicion and even hatred. "A Jap's a Jap," said Lt. Gen. John DeWitt, who was in command of the West's defense. "It makes no difference whether he is an American or not."

REMEMBER

In February 1942, Roosevelt ordered the forced evacuation of all Japanese residents from the West Coast, supposedly to lessen the potential for them to engage in seditious or traitorous acts. They were moved to bleak concentration camps in remote areas. Many lost virtually everything they owned: homes, farms, businesses, and even personal possessions.

Despite their treatment, about 8,000 Nisei volunteered to serve in the military. One group, the "Fightin' 442nd," was one of the most decorated combat units of the war.

It wasn't until the 1980s and 1990s that the Nisei were compensated for some of what they lost. In the meantime, Roosevelt's action was upheld by the U.S. Supreme Court as a justifiable hardship. "Hardships are a part of war," said Justice Hugo Black, "and war is an aggregation of hardships."

Dealing with the War in Europe

Shortly after Pearl Harbor, FDR met with English Prime Minister Winston Churchill to decide what the forces of the Allies should do against the *Axis* powers — Germany, Italy, and Japan. The most pressing threat, they decided, was Hitler's

Germany. The German army seemed to be on the brink of defeating the Soviet army, its one-time ally. If the Russians fell, Germany could turn its full attention to Britain.

Soviet dictator Josef Stalin wanted the Allies to launch an invasion of German-held Europe as soon as possible, because Russia was being mauled by the Germans. But Churchill wanted to nibble at the edges of the German empire while bombing Germany from the air. FDR went along with the Brits.

Roosevelt, Churchill, and Stalin managed to put their sharp differences aside and generally cooperate. That proved to be a key ingredient in the Allies' ultimate success. The trio met several times during the war to plot strategy and negotiate about what the world would be like after the war.

Meeting at Yalta

The most important of the meetings of FDR, Churchill, and Stalin actually came toward the end of the war at Yalta, a former palace on the Black Sea in the Soviet Union.

Roosevelt came to Yalta hoping to establish groundwork for a practical and powerful United Nations, to be formed after the war, and also to convince the Russians to enter the war against Japan and help speed up the end of the conflict.

Stalin eventually agreed, but at a price. In return, the Soviet dictator got the other two to agree to give the Soviets control over broad areas of Europe and a promise that each of the major nations on the UN Security Council would have veto power over council decisions. As it turned out, the price Roosevelt paid was far too high for what he got in return.

Winning one step at a time

One of the most immediate problems was dealing with the menace posed by German submarines, or *U-boats*, in the Atlantic. Traveling in packs, the subs sank three million tons of Allied shipping in the first half of 1942 alone. But the Allies worked out a system of convoys and developed better anti-sub tactics. Most importantly, they built far more cargo ships than the Germans could possibly sink.

In the summer of 1942, Allied planes began bombing targets inside Germany. Eventually, the bombing would take a terrible toll. In 1943, more than 40,000 people were killed in the city of Hamburg, and in 1945, the city of Dresden was all but destroyed.

In February 1943, U.S. forces in North Africa had their first significant confrontation with the German army. It did not go well. The green American troops were driven back from the strategic Kasserine Pass in Tunisia. But under a new commander, Major Gen. George S. Patton, the U.S. forces rallied and counterattacked. Combined with victories by the British and other Allies, the effort drove German forces out of North Africa.

From Africa, the Allies invaded Sicily and then advanced into the Italian mainland. Mussolini was overthrown and eventually executed by his own people. But the German army poured troops into the country, and it took until the end of 1944 for Italy to be completely controlled.

On the Eastern Front, meanwhile, the Russian army gradually had turned the tables on the invading Germans and begun pushing them back, despite enormous civilian and military losses. And in England, the Allies, under the leadership of U.S. General Dwight D. Eisenhower, were preparing the greatest invasion force the world had ever seen.

Making the final push

On June 6, 1944 — *D-Day* — the Allied forces swept ashore on the beaches of Normandy in France. It was an astonishing logistical feat. Some 175,000 men were landed on the first day, a number that swelled to 325,000 in the first week and eventually to 2.5 million. They were delivered by 5,300 ships and supported by 50,000 vehicles and 11,000 planes.

By August, the U.S. 3rd Army, under the brash and aggressive Patton, pushed deep into France and to the edge of Germany itself. A little more than a week before Christmas, 1944, however, the Germans launched a desperate counterattack. Known as the Battle of the Bulge, the surprise attack succeeded at first, costing the United States 77,000 casualties. But the Germans were low on men and supplies and could not sustain the attack. By late January 1945, the Allies were again on the offensive.

Discovering the war's greatest crime

REMEMBER

As Allied troops moved deeper into the heart of German-held territory, they began to make stomach-churning, heart-wrenching discoveries: concentration camps holding what was left of millions of Jews and other "undesirables" that German leaders had ordered to be murdered as a "final solution" to "cleansing" Germany of all but the "Aryan Race."

Hitler's "final solution" became known to the civilized world as the *Holocaust* and resulted in the murders of 6 million Jews and 4 million non-Jews, including gays, Gypsies, and the mentally and physically handicapped. The Holocaust was not a complete secret to the Allies. Scores of Jewish organizations and refugee groups sought to bring attention to the horror going on within Nazi-occupied Europe, but finding a way to stop it was not viewed as big a priority as winning the war. And the enormity of the crimes was not fully understood — or believed — until the camps were discovered, and their stories told by survivors.

Late in the war, the Roosevelt administration established the War Refugee Board, which helped organize the rescue of some European Jews. And the United States was the first country to formally recognize the Jewish state of Israel in 1948. But stopping the Holocaust as it was happening was simply not at the forefront of the war effort.

Ending the war in Europe, and the end of FDR

In April, the U.S. and Russian armies joined up at the Elbe River and advanced on Berlin. Hitler committed suicide, and on May 7 — *V-E* or *Victory in Europe* Day — Germany surrendered.

NAZI NITWITS

Adolf Hitler had an itch to bring the war to America. So in mid-June, 1942, German subs landed four men on Long Island, New York, and four more on a Florida beach. They also landed cases of explosives. All the men had lived in America and spoke fluent English. Their mission was to sabotage U.S. factories, incite terror, and disrupt the economy.

But they turned out to be an octet of oafs. Several of them went on shopping sprees. Several blabbed about their mission to relatives — and two of them blabbed to federal agents.

Within two weeks of their arrival, all of them had been arrested by the FBI. After a military trial, all eight were convicted of espionage. Six of the Germans were executed, while the two who confessed were imprisoned for the rest of the war and then deported.

Hitler's itch was never scratched. Not a single case of enemy-directed sabotage was ever verified during the war.

REMEMBER

Roosevelt did not live to see the victory. The president had won a fourth term in 1944, despite rumors about his failing health. But on April 12, 1945, while vacationing at Warm Springs, Georgia, FDR died suddenly of a cerebral hemorrhage. The nation was staggered at the loss of the man who had led them through the Depression and the war. One New York housewife was asked if she heard the radio bulletins of FDR's death and replied "For what do I need a radio? It's on everybody's face."

The new president, a former hat salesman from Missouri named Harry S. Truman, was as stunned as anyone. "Being president is like riding a tiger," Truman later wrote. "I never felt that I could let go for a single moment."

Dealing with the War in the Pacific

Less than 12 hours after the bombing of Pearl Harbor, the Japanese attacked U.S. air bases in the Philippines, destroying scores of U.S. planes. Within a few months, they conquered Guam, Wake Island, Hong Kong, Singapore, the Dutch East Indies, Burma, and the Philippines. Drunk with victories, Japanese forces continued to expand their dominance in the Pacific during the first few months of the war.

About the only good news for the Allies came on April 18, 1942, when a squadron of B-25 bombers launched from an aircraft carrier and led by Col. James Doolittle managed to bomb Tokyo. The planes did little damage, and none of the planes made it back, with most of the crews having to ditch them in China. Still, Doolittle's raid was a huge shot in the arm for sagging American morale.

Fighting back

U.S. strategists decided to strike back on two fronts. The first, under Gen. Douglas MacArthur, would move north from Australia, through New Guinea, and then back to the Philippines. The second, under Adm. Chester Nimitz, would move west from Hawaii and then hopscotch from island to island toward Japan itself.

But first the Japanese offense had to be stopped. The initial halt came in early May 1942, at the Battle of the Coral Sea, northeast of Australia. It was the first naval fight in history where the fighting ships never actually saw each other: All the combat was done by planes from each side's aircraft carriers. The battle was pretty much a draw, but the Japanese fleet carrying invasion troops to New Guinea had to turn back, marking the first time the Japanese had not won outright.

Turning the tide

REMEMBER

The real turning point, however, came between June 3 and June 6, in a fierce naval battle near the U.S.-held Midway Island. Tipped to Japanese plans by intercepting their messages and breaking their codes, U.S. forces managed to sink four Japanese aircraft carriers, losing only one. The victory stopped the Japanese advance in the central Pacific.

A few months after the Battle of Midway, the United States took the offensive in the Solomon Islands, winning battles at Gavutu, Tulagi, and Guadalcanal. It took six grueling months to take Guadalcanal, but by mid-1943, the Japanese forces were either retreating or on defense nearly everywhere.

Now it was America's turn. In February 1944, forces under Nimitz won victories in the Marshall Islands, and in the fall, Allied forces reopened supply lines in Southeast Asia into China. In mid-1944, a U.S. armada struck the Marianas Islands of Tinian, Guam, and Saipan, and on October 20, 1944, MacArthur made good on an earlier promise and returned to the Philippines.

As the Germans did at the Battle of the Bulge, the Japanese threw everything they had into a counteroffensive. And, like the Germans, they lost. The Battle of Leyte Gulf cost Japan four more carriers and all but ended its ability to mount an offensive. Next came the battle for the island of Okinawa, just 370 miles south of Japan itself. The Japanese sent suicide planes called *kamikazes* ("divine wind") on one-way trips into U.S. ships, and while they were horrifyingly effective, they weren't enough. After 50,000 Allied and 100,000 Japanese were killed or wounded, Okinawa fell in late June 1945.

U.S. submarines were taking a huge toll on Japanese supply lines, sinking more than half of all the enemy's cargo ships by the end of the war. American planes, meanwhile, had been softening up the Japanese mainland. In May 1945, they dropped napalm on Tokyo, killing 80,000 people. The bombings were designed to make the eventual invasion of Japan easier. Even so, U.S. strategists figured it would take more than a year of fighting and more than 1 million American soldiers would be killed or wounded before the Japanese homeland would fall.

What the strategists did not count on was a terrible new weapon that had been conceived in New York and Tennessee and spawned on a New Mexico desert.

AUDIE MURPHY

He was a pint-sized Texas orphan who joined the Army as a buck private at the age of 16. When he came home, he weighed a lot more — mostly because of the medals on his chest.

Murphy was born in 1926 to poor sharecropper parents. After joining the Army, Murphy saw action in nine major campaigns in North Africa, Italy, and France, single-handedly killing more than 200 enemy soldiers while rising to the rank of second lieutenant. On Jan. 26, 1945, in France, Murphy took on an attack by six German tanks and supporting infantry. Despite being wounded, he fought until he ran out of ammunition, which was long enough to direct artillery fire and beat back the German attack.

His heroism won Murphy more than 30 citations, including the Congressional Medal of Honor and the French Croix de Guerre. After the war, America's most decorated soldier became a movie actor, making 44 films. One of them, *To Hell and Back,* was based on his own bestselling autobiography. Murphy died in a plane crash in 1971, at the age of 45.

Dropping the Bomb

Even before the war began, scientists fleeing from Nazi Germany had warned U.S. officials the Germans were working on developing a huge new bomb that would be triggered through an atomic reaction. An alarmed U.S. government began pouring what would amount to more than $2 billion into the "Manhattan Project," so called because it started in New York.

Work continued at top-secret bases in Oak Ridge, Tennessee, and Los Alamos, New Mexico, under the direction of physicist J. Robert Oppenheimer. The project was so hush-hush that Vice President Harry Truman wasn't told of it until he assumed the presidency after FDR's death.

On July 16, 1945, the world's first atomic bomb was detonated at a testing ground in New Mexico. "It works," muttered an awestruck Oppenheimer, who later said it made him recall a line from Hindu scripture: "I am become Death; the Shatterer of Worlds."

On July 26, 1945, Allied leaders delivered a surrender ultimatum to Japan, but it was rejected by Japanese military leaders. On August 6, 1945, a single B-29 bomber nicknamed *Enola Gay* dropped an atomic bomb on the city of Hiroshima. The bomb killed 75,000 people and injured another 100,000 in the city of 340,000. Thousands more eventually died from the radiation.

REMEMBER

Debate has raged ever since as to whether Japan would have surrendered if the bomb had not been dropped. But at the time, there was little hesitation about its use on the part of the man who made the decision. President Truman was convinced that bomb's use was an acceptable alternative to the horrific carnage of a U.S. invasion of Japan. "I regarded the bomb as a military weapon," he said later, "and never had any doubt that it should be used."

Japan was stunned by the destruction of the Hiroshima bomb, but its leaders hesitated in surrendering. Three days later, another A-bomb was dropped on Nagasaki. The next day, Japan surrendered. The final ceremony took place on September 2, aboard the USS *Missouri* in Tokyo Bay. World War II, the bloodiest and most devastating war in human history, was over.

About 30 million civilians and military personnel around the world had been killed. American losses, compared to the other major combatant countries, had been light: About 300,000 were killed and another 750,000 were injured or wounded.

But while the war was over, a new age that included the threat of even more horrible wars was just beginning.

4

America in Adulthood

IN THIS PART . . .

See how America emerges as a world power after World War II and engages in a Cold War with the USSR.

Learn about one president's assassination and another's resignation.

Understand how America loses a war and moves slowly toward righting.

Blush at a U.S. president's sex scandal and impeachment, and watch the country move with cautious confidence toward a new millennium.

Chapter 17

TV, Elvis, and Reds under the Bed: 1946–1960

f you had asked most Americans in 1945 how they felt about the Union of Soviet Socialist Republics (USSR), they probably would've responded with warm and fuzzy statements about their brave ally against Hitler. Had you asked them in 1950, however, you would have received a very different answer.

In this chapter, Americans combat communism at home and abroad, real and imagined. They move to the suburbs, eat in their cars, and discover a new medium/religion called television. They also embrace a form of music with its roots in African-American culture — but are much less willing to embrace African Americans themselves.

A Cold War and a Hot "Police Action"

The foundations of the Cold War were broader than just the ideological struggle between capitalism and communism. The Soviet Union had suffered terribly during World War II and was hungry to recover. Soviet leaders feared and distrusted the United States, which was the only country with the atomic bomb — and which had used it. They were also determined to surround the Soviet Union with countries that would not be a threat to it in future wars.

America saw its former ally as a nation led by men who were as duplicitous and dangerous as those the Allies had just defeated. The Soviets' desire to forcibly impose itself on other counties was unacceptable.

Joining the United Nations

After World War I, the U.S. Senate voted against joining the League of Nations. The second time around, however, it jumped at the chance to join the League's successor. On July 28, 1945, senators voted 89 to 2 in favor of joining the United Nations (UN), which had its first meeting in 1946 in London and then moved to its permanent home in New York City.

REMEMBER

The UN's two main bodies were the General Assembly, where every member nation had a seat, and the Security Council, which had five permanent members — the United States, the Soviet Union, Great Britain, France, and China — and six seats that rotated among other countries. Each of the permanent members could veto council actions, which meant it was impossible for the UN to do anything that any one of the top powers didn't like.

While the United Nations did have some success in international cooperation when it came to subjects like health and education, it could do little to slow down the nuclear arms race or prevent the Super Powers from interfering in other countries.

The world as a chessboard

The first big test of wills between the United States and the Soviet Union came in the Mediterranean. Communist-backed rebels in Greece and Turkey were trying to overthrow the governments in those two countries. Britain had been assisting the Greek and Turkish governments, but was in deep economic trouble at home and couldn't continue.

So Harry Truman went to Congress. Truman was a former U.S. senator from Missouri who had been made vice president in 1944 and succeeded Franklin Roosevelt as president when Roosevelt died in 1945. Truman was blunt, honest, and outspoken. He often complained about what a tough job it was to be president. But most of the time, he wasn't shy about doing it — and to hell with anyone who didn't like the way he did it.

REMEMBER

In March 1947, Truman asked Congress for $400 million to help the Greek and Turkish governments. He also asked to send U.S. military advisors to both countries, at their request. In what became known as the "Truman Doctrine," Truman drew a sharp distinction between the communist way of life and the Free World. Congress went along, sending more than $600 million to the two countries by 1950.

Truman's doctrine was part of an overall strategy to "contain" communism. The idea was to make other countries prosperous enough that they wouldn't be tempted to go red. Other elements of the containment strategy included

>> **The Marshall Plan:** Named after General George C. Marshall, who became Truman's secretary of state, the plan provided about $12 billion in U.S. aid to 16 countries in Western Europe to help them recover from the ravages of the war. The plan was a rousing success, and by 1952, much of Western Europe was well on its way to economic recovery.

>> **NATO:** In 1949, the United States and 11 Western nations formed the North Atlantic Treaty Organization (NATO). The countries agreed to come to the aid of any member nation that was attacked and to develop an international security force that would help discourage aggression by non-NATO countries.

>> **The Four Point Program:** This was sort of a junior Marshall Plan. Proposed by Truman in 1949, it provided about $400 million to underdeveloped countries in Asia, Latin America, and Africa for developing industry, communications, and technological systems.

The Berlin airlift

The Soviet Union didn't watch all this U.S. activity while lazing in a hammock. After the war, temporary governance of Germany had been divided among France, Britain, the United States, and the Soviet Union. The city of Berlin was deep in the Soviet sector but run by all four nations. So when the Soviets became irritated at all the containment in 1948, they blockaded Berlin, hoping to force the Western countries out of the city completely.

REMEMBER

Instead, the Western countries mounted a huge airlift, shipping food and other supplies over the blockade and into the city. In May 1949, the Soviets lifted the blockade. But the tensions made both sides realize that there would be no easy solution to reestablishing a new Germany. So the Western powers agreed to create one country out of their half and the Soviets created another country out of the other half. East Germany and West Germany would not be united again for more than 40 years.

BIG RED IN THE CORN

One reason behind the distrust between the United States and the Soviet Union was that the countries didn't really know each other very well. So it was big news in 1959 when leaders of the two countries exchanged visits.

In July, Vice President Richard Nixon went to Moscow to attend an exhibit of American products, including a six-room, ranch-style model home. Nixon and Soviet Chairman Nikita Khrushchev got into a heated — and televised — quarrel over the relative merits of each country's economic system.

In September, Khrushchev came to America. Among his stops were Hollywood, San Francisco, Franklin Roosevelt's grave — and Coon Rapids, Iowa. It seems the chairman had been invited to visit the farm of a fellow named Roswell Garst, who had been selling corn seed to the Soviet Union since 1955, and fancied himself a bit of a diplomat as well as a farmer.

After a tour of Garst's farm, Khrushchev offered what could have been a summary of his whole trip. Garst, the chairman said, was a "class enemy," but was generously willing "to trade secrets with others — even us."

The "miracle of '48"

Despite some success overseas, Truman was considered a political dead duck as the 1948 elections drew near. The Republicans had gained seats in Congress in 1946. Truman's former secretary of commerce, Henry Wallace, had decided to run as a liberal third-party candidate, sure to take votes from Truman. Segregationist Strom Thurmond, governor of South Carolina, also decided to run as an independent candidate. The Republicans were running Governor Thomas Dewey of New York, a man who was considered solid, if a bit dull (someone suggested he looked like the little plastic guy on wedding cakes).

But true to form, Truman decided to "give 'em hell." He stumped around the country, ragging on the Republican-controlled Congress as a bunch of do-nothings and pledging to change things at home and abroad if given another term. When the votes were counted, Truman had pulled off the biggest upset in presidential political history, and the Democrats had taken back Congress. Their reward was another war.

The Korean War

The Cold War was at its hottest in Korea. After World War II ended, the Russians controlled the northern part of the country and the United States the south.

In 1949, the Soviets left a communist government in charge in the north, and the United States left a pro-Western government in the south. China, meanwhile, finished its civil war and was now firmly in the control of communists.

On June 24, 1950, the North Koreans invaded South Korea. A few days later, Truman ordered U.S. troops to the aid of South Korea and convinced the UN to send military aid as well, in what was referred to in diplomatic circles as a "police action."

The UN troops, which were mostly American, were under the command of U.S. General Douglas MacArthur. Because the North Korean attack was such a surprise, the U.S. and South Korean forces were pushed into the far southern corner of the Korean peninsula by September. But MacArthur pulled off a risky but brilliant amphibious landing behind the North Koreans. By November, he had driven the enemy deep into North Korea and was poised to push them into China.

Then the Chinese army poured troops into the fight and forced the UN troops back into South Korea. The UN forces reorganized and counterattacked, forcing the Chinese back behind the 38th parallel of latitude, where the war had started in the first place.

For the next 18 months, an uneasy truce, sporadically interrupted by skirmishing, was in place. Finally, in July 1953, an agreement to call the whole mess a draw was reached.

The Korean War cost more than $50 billion and 33,000 U.S. lives. Another 110,000 or so were wounded. It also cost Truman politically. When MacArthur publicly disagreed with Truman over Truman's decision not to invade China, the general was fired. MacArthur returned to a hero's welcome in America, and Truman was unfairly pilloried as being soft on communism.

REMEMBER

Truman didn't run for reelection in 1952. Instead, the country turned to its most popular military figure in decades, Dwight David Eisenhower. "Ike" was so apolitical he didn't even decide which political party to join until shortly before accepting the Republican nomination.

As Supreme Allied Commander in Europe, Eisenhower had been a bold and decisive military leader during World War II. But as president, his approach, at least on domestic issues, was to move cautiously, if at all. He does deserve credit for investing in and jump-starting America's interstate highway system, but only reluctantly involved the federal government in the struggle for civil rights.

Uncle Sam's big stick

One thing Eisenhower's administration wasn't shy about was injecting itself into other countries' internal affairs. In 1953, Central Intelligence Agency (CIA) operatives helped topple a communist-influenced government in Iran and reinstate the dictatorial Shah. The following year, the CIA aided a coup in Guatemala, ousting a communist-backed but constitutionally elected leader and replacing him with a U.S.-friendly president.

REMEMBER

It wasn't only ideology that motivated America. In Iran, the United States made sure Iranian oil was kept flowing toward America and not the Soviet Union. In Guatemala, the interests of American fruit companies were being protected.

In Asia, the United States was busy providing aid to France to help it fight a communist rebellion in its colony of Vietnam. By 1954, the French had lost the northern half of the country, and by 1956, the United States was steadily increasing the amount of aid it was sending to South Vietnam.

Finding Commies under the Bed

Not all the world's communists were in other countries. Since the 1920s, there had been a communist party in the United States that had taken orders from party leaders in the Soviet Union. But the average American didn't pay much attention. After World War II, however, "communist" became a much dirtier word. U.S. government officials helped fuel the fire by talking almost daily about spies and the dangers of communists and communist sympathizers.

REMEMBER

Part of the reason for the anti-communist fears was that communists ran America's biggest post-war rivals, the Soviet Union and China. Part was bewilderment over the success the communists were having in Asia and Eastern Europe. And part was there really were some spies, and the U.S. government failed to keep the atomic bomb the exclusive property of America.

Whatever the reason, commie hunting became a national pastime. In 1947, the House Un-American Activities Committee (HUAC) — dominated by Republicans who included a freshman member from California named Richard M. Nixon — began searching for communists within and without government. One place they looked was Hollywood. Actors, directors, and writers were called before the committee, and ten who refused to testify were jailed. Others were "blacklisted" and couldn't get jobs in the industry for years afterward. But no great plot to undermine America through the movies was ever uncovered.

Casting suspicion on Hiss

The committee caught a bigger fish in 1948. Whittaker Chambers, a *Time* magazine editor who said he had been a communist until 1937, told the committee that a former member of Roosevelt's State Department, Alger Hiss, had passed information to Soviet spies.

Hiss denied the charges, even after Chambers produced — from a hollowed-out pumpkin — what he said was microfilm passed between the men. Neither could be prosecuted for espionage because too much time had passed. But Hiss was found guilty of perjury and sentenced to five years in prison. The Hiss conviction helped Nixon get elected to the Senate in 1950 and win a place as Eisenhower's running mate in 1952.

HELEN GAHAGAN DOUGLAS

Helen Gahagan Douglas was the "pink lady" of American politics. Douglas was born in New Jersey in 1900. She left college in 1922 to become an opera singer and a leading Broadway actress. With her husband, actor Melvyn Douglas, Helen moved to California and became active in Democratic politics. After working to better the plight of migrant farm workers, she won a seat in Congress in 1944, representing a heavily African-American district in Los Angeles.

In 1950, Helen ran for the U.S. Senate against another member of Congress, Richard Nixon. Nixon had won a national reputation as a communist hunter and wasted little time implying that Helen was, if not an outright commie, "pink right down to her underwear."

Helen's liberalism did not play well with voters, especially after the Korean War broke out, and Nixon easily defeated her. She left politics, became an author, and died in 1980. As part of her legacy, she left behind a nickname she gave Nixon that stuck with him all the way to the White House: "Tricky Dick."

Leaking scientific secrets: The Rosenbergs

Hiss wasn't the only trophy for the commie hunters. In February 1950, it was revealed that a British scientist had given atomic secrets to the Soviets. Among his allies, it was announced, were a New York couple named Julius and Ethel Rosenberg. The Rosenbergs were charged with getting information from Ethel's brother, who worked on the U.S. bomb project in New Mexico. They were convicted of treason and executed in 1953.

Checking the loyalty of federal workers

Despite some reservations that things were getting out of hand, President Truman didn't leave all the ferreting out of communists to Congress. In 1947, Truman ordered a government-wide "loyalty" review. By the time it was done, more than 3 million federal workers had been reviewed. More than 2,000 workers resigned and about 200 were fired.

Not to be outdone, Congress passed bills in 1950 and 1952 — over Truman's vetoes — that made it illegal to do anything "that would substantially contribute to the establishment . . . of a totalitarian dictatorship." The bills also required "communist front organizations" to register with the Justice Department and denied admission to the country to aliens who had been members of "totalitarian" groups, even as children.

A SHOT AT POLIO

Every summer polio showed up: a crippling disease that most often struck children and left them paralyzed or dead. In 1952 alone, more than 21,000 U.S. children were infected.

Jonas Salk wanted to do something about the poliomyelitis virus. Salk, a University of Pittsburgh Medical School researcher, worked for almost eight years to develop a vaccine. Finally, after exhaustive trials, the government licensed the vaccine on April 12, 1955. Salk refused to become rich by patenting the vaccine and hoped the federal government would take over its distribution. The Eisenhower administration greeted the idea icily. Secretary of Health, Education, and Welfare Oveta Culp Hobby called it "socialized medicine by the back door."

But Salk's vaccine, delivered via injections, eventually was distributed free by the government and saved thousands of children from the disease. In 1961, an oral vaccine developed by Dr. Albert Sabin was licensed and administered around the world. Polio is now virtually unknown in the United States. By 2017, there were only 22 cases of polio reported in the entire world.

Telling tall tales: "Tail-Gunner Joe"

He was a liar and a drunk — and for a few years, he was one of the most powerful men in America. In February 1950, Senator Joseph McCarthy of Wisconsin gave a speech in West Virginia. In the speech, McCarthy said he had a list of 205 known communists working in the State Department. It was nonsense, but it made national headlines, and McCarthy repeated it and similar charges over the next four years.

REMEMBER

McCarthy, who claimed to have been a tail gunner who saw lots of action during World War II, actually had never seen any combat. But he was a formidable opponent in the commie-hunting field. He ripped even General George Marshall and President Eisenhower. Every time he made a charge that proved to be untrue, McCarthy simply made a new charge. The tactic became known as "McCarthyism."

By the summer of 1954, however, McCarthy's antics were wearing thin. When he began a series of attacks on the Army for "coddling" communists during congressional hearings, they were televised. Many Americans got their first look at McCarthy in action and were repulsed. In December 1954, the Senate censured him. He died in obscurity three years later of problems related to alcoholism.

Having It All

After World War II, the American economy hummed along. There were plenty of jobs for returning servicemen. There was also the G.I. Bill of Rights, which passed Congress in 1944 and provided veterans more than $13 billion in the decade after the war for college tuition, vocational training programs, or money to start a business. Perhaps most important, the bill offered vets no-money-down, low-interest loans to buy homes.

A booming economy

Thanks to a $6 billion tax cut and all the savings from buying bonds during the war, Americans had plenty to spend. The high consumer demand for goods triggered high inflation — 14 to 15 percent the first two years after the war for goods in general, and a painful 25 percent for food. Such high costs in turn triggered a lot of labor unrest, with 5,000 strikes in 1946 alone, and major troubles in the coal and rail industries. President Truman reinstated wartime price controls to deal with inflation, and the Republican Congress passed a bill called the Taft-Hartley Act in 1947 that restricted labor union power.

By 1949, the economy had adjusted to the ending of the war, and the country entered an almost unprecedented economic boom. From 1945 to 1960, the *Gross National Product* (the value of the amount of goods and services produced) increased from $200 billion to $500 billion per year. Thousands of smaller companies merged or were gobbled up by large corporations. So were many family farms, by large "company" farms.

The economy wasn't the only thing growing. The birthrate boomed as men and women pushed apart by the war made up for lost time. The population grew 20 percent in the 1950s, from 150 million to 180 million, and the generation born between 1946 and 1964 became known as the *baby boomers*. Along with the economy and the population, Americans' appetite for the good life (the number of private cars purchased doubled in the 1950s) and the perceived need to "keep up with the Joneses" also grew.

Moving to the burbs

Having your own car meant you could live farther away from where you worked. The suburbs grew 47 percent in the 1950s as more and more Americans staked out their own little territory. New housing starts, which had dropped to 100,000 a year during the war, climbed to 1.5 million annually. To fill the need, homebuilders turned to assembly-line techniques.

The leading pioneer was a New York developer named William J. Levitt. A former member of the Navy construction battalion known as the Seabees, Levitt knew how to build things in a hurry. He bought 1,500 acres on Long Island and on March 7, 1949, opened a sales office — with more than 1,000 customers already waiting. A basic Levitt four-room house on a 6,000-square-foot lot sold for $6,900, about 2½ years' wages. The cookie-cutter approach in Island Trees (later changed to Levittown) was criticized as stifling individuality. But to the 82,000 people living in 17,000 new houses, it was home. Other builders followed suit all over the country, and 13 million new homes were sold during the decade.

THE GOLDEN AGE OF GREASE

Brothers Richard and Maurice McDonald were bored with the drive-in barbeque joint they had opened in 1940 in San Bernardino, California, and they were tired of all the teens who hung around the place after they ate, as if it were a clubhouse.

So in 1948, the McDonalds fired their carhops, cut their menu to nine items, dropped the price of a hamburger from 30 cents to 15 cents, replaced tableware with paper bags and cups, and pre-assembled much of the food. The "fast food" was perfect for the speeded-up postwar society.

A Chicago milkshake machine salesman named Ray Kroc loved the idea. Kroc convinced the McDonalds brothers to make him their franchising agent and then bought the brothers out in 1961. By the time Kroc died in 1984, there were 7,500 McDonald's outlets. Today, there are nearly 37,000, serving 69 million people a day in 120 countries.

And why did Kroc stick with the brothers' name even after he bought them out? Because, he once explained, no one was going to buy a "Kroc burger." Or a "Big Kroc," for that matter.

"No man who owns his own house and a lot can be a communist," Levitt said. "He has too much to do." Of course, his sentiments didn't extend to African Americans: They were excluded from buying homes at his developments for fear they would scare away white buyers.

Tuning in to the tube

There was less discrimination when it came to selling consumer products, and one of the most popular products in the 1950s was the TV (see Figure 17-1). At the start of the decade, there were about 3 million TV owners; by the end of it, there were 55 million, watching shows from 530 stations. The average price of TV sets dropped from about $500 in 1949 to $200 in 1953.

REMEMBER

Like radio before it, the spread of TV had a huge cultural impact. Beginning with the 1948 campaign, it made itself felt in U.S. politics. One wonderful effect was that it made speeches shorter. Politicians and commentators alike began to think and speak in "sound bites" that fit the medium. By 1960, the televised debates between candidates Richard Nixon and John F. Kennedy were considered a crucial element in Kennedy's narrow victory. TV also helped make professional and college sports big businesses, and sometimes provided excellent comedy and dramatic shows to vast audiences that might not otherwise have had access to them.

FIGURE 17-1:
A family gathers around a TV to watch their favorite program.

© Frank Martin/ Getty Images

But even to its mildest critics, much of what was on the often-aptly nicknamed "boob tube" was mindless junk. It was designed to sell products, it homogenized cultural tastes to the point of blandness, and it created feelings of inadequacy in some, who felt their real lives should compare with the insipidly happy characters they saw on shows like *Leave It to Beaver*.

Federal Communications Commission (FCC) chairman Newton Minnow called it "a vast wasteland." Nonetheless, it was a popular wasteland. Comedian Milton Berle's show was so loved, for example, that movie theaters in some towns closed down Tuesday nights because everyone was home watching "Uncle Miltie." And in 1954, the Toledo, Ohio water commissioner reported that water consumption surged at certain times because so many people were simultaneously using their toilets during commercial breaks on the most popular shows.

Rockin' 'n' rollin'

America had 13 million teenagers by the mid-1950s, and they had a lot of money to spend — an average of about $10 a week. One of the things they spent it on was their own music. It was a mix of blues and country that was as much about youthful rebellion as it was the sound, and it was called *rock 'n' roll*, a term coined in 1952 by a Cleveland radio personality named Alan Freed, who became the new sound's Pied Piper.

Adult backlash was fierce. Ministers decried it as satanic, racists called it "jungle music," and law enforcement officials deemed it riot-inciting. Most troubling to some older Americans was that the music tended to blur racial divides among young people: You couldn't easily segregate the radio dial.

WHAT A DOLL!

Ruth Handler went shopping in Switzerland in the 1950s — and found retail gold. Handler, with her husband Elliot and his business partner, Harold Mattson, had started a toy company in 1945 that they named by combining Mattson's name and Elliot's to form "Mattel." Anyway, Ruth Handler bought a German-made doll named Lilli while on her Swiss shopping spree. Unlike most American dolls, which were modeled after babies, Lilli was modeled after babes — as in buxom, long-legged young women. Handler had seen her own daughter playing with similar-looking paper dolls and figured a U.S. version of Lilli might catch on.

So in 1959, Mattel introduced a very grown-up-looking doll with an impressive wardrobe (which of course was sold separately). It was a hit, and the company sold $500 million worth of dolls and related products in the first decade after its introduction.

The line has added heaps of supporting characters ever since, but the original main-stays have remained "Barbie" and "Ken," named after the Handlers' own son and daughter. Doll collectors the world over are glad the Handlers didn't name their kids "Attila" and "Hortense."

Of course the more adults squawked about it — surprise! — the more their kids wanted it. In 1954, "Shake, Rattle and Roll" by Bill Haley and the Comets sold more than 1 million records. Scores of rock stars came and went almost overnight. Others, such as Jerry Lee Lewis and Little Richard, were stars with more staying power.

An American king

REMEMBER

And then there was Elvis. Born in Mississippi in 1935 and raised in Tennessee by poor, working-class parents, Elvis Presley became perhaps the most recognized personality in the world during the decade. In 1956 alone, he was selling $75,000 worth of records *per day* and had signed a three-picture movie deal. A staggering 54 million people tuned in to see him on the Ed Sullivan TV show. By the time he died in 1977, Presley was the undisputed "King of Rock 'n' Roll," and composer Leonard Bernstein had referred to him as "the greatest cultural force in the 20th century."

One effect of the new music was to open up new audiences for African-American performers. Chuck Berry became the first black rock star to have a hit on the mainstream charts. More than 90 years after the end of slavery, music was one of the few fields open to African Americans.

BUDDY HOLLY

His career lasted only 18 months, but his influence on American music has lasted more than half a century. Charles Hardin Holley was born in Lubbock, Texas, in 1936. After high school, Holley played in a trio, focusing on country music. But his heart was in the new sounds of rock 'n' roll. In May 1957, "Holly" (his name had been spelled wrong on a record label, and he just went along with it) and his group, the Crickets, released their first hit, "That'll Be the Day." By the end of the year, Holly had three million-sellers, and by the end of 1958, he had sold 10 million records.

Unlike other teen stars, Holly not only played guitar and sang, but also wrote, arranged, and produced most of his music and experimented with techniques such as double-tracking. He was also one of the first U.S. rock stars to tour abroad. But on Feb. 3, 1959, his career came to a sudden end. After a concert in Clear Lake, Iowa, the 22-year-old Holly and three others were killed when their small plane crashed. The tragedy was immortalized in the 1972 song "American Pie" as "the day the music died."

Holly's musical influence lived on not only in America, but overseas as well. A fledgling rock group in Liverpool, England, for instance, named itself a variation of Holly's group, the Crickets. They called themselves "The Beatles."

Moving, Slowly, to the Front of the Bus

By the 1950s, after fighting through two world wars and struggling through the Depression, many African Americans were fed up with their glacial-pace progress in achieving equality. The result was a series of events that added up to the beginning of the civil rights movement.

Brown against the board

On May 17, 1954, the U.S. Supreme Court issued one of its most important decisions. In a case called *Brown v. the Board of Education of Topeka, Kansas*, justices unanimously ruled that the segregation of public schools was unconstitutional. *Brown* overturned an 1896 Supreme Court decision that had said schools could be segregated if the facilities that were offered different groups were equal (which, of course, they seldom, if ever, were). "We conclude that in the field of public education, the doctrine of 'separate but equal' has no place," wrote Chief Justice Earl Warren.

The court followed its decision a year later with broad rules for desegregating America's schools, but they included no timetable. Some communities moved quickly. But others, mostly in the South, made it clear they were in no hurry to comply with the court's ruling. By 1957, only about 20 percent of Southern school districts had even begun the process.

REMEMBER

In September 1957, a federal court ordered Central High School in Little Rock, Arkansas, desegregated. A white mob decided to block the admission of nine black students, and Arkansas Governor Orval Faubus refused to do anything about it. So a reluctant President Eisenhower sent in 1,000 federal troops and activated 10,000 members of the National Guard to protect the students and escort them to class.

In the same month, Congress passed a bill that

>> Authorized the attorney general to stop Southern elected officials from interfering with African Americans registering to vote

>> Established a federal Civil Rights Commission

>> Created a civil rights enforcement division within the U.S. Justice Department.

The sad fact, however, was that in many places in the South, the laws went largely unenforced.

FAIR BALL

Branch Rickey needed an African American who was smart, had the ability to play baseball at the major league level — and could keep his mouth shut under trying circumstances.

Rickey, the general manager of the Brooklyn Dodgers, thought he had found him in John Roosevelt Robinson. Known to his friends as "Jackie," Robinson was a 28-year-old UCLA graduate and former Army officer whom Rickey had signed to play for Montreal in the minor leagues in 1945. Robinson was irritated when Rickey kept telling him about all the virulent hatred he would face as the first African-American player in the major leagues.

"Mr. Rickey, do you want a ballplayer who's afraid to fight back?" Robinson asked.

Rickey replied, "I want a player with guts enough *not* to fight back."

On April 15, 1947, Robinson stepped to the plate for the first time in a major league game. By the end of the year, he was the National League's best rookie, and two years later, its most valuable player. Robinson opened the gates for thousands of African Americans in professional sports and inspired millions of Americans of all races with his dignity, courage, and refusal to lose.

Boycotting the bus

Like a rock dropped in a still pond, the Supreme Court decision on school desegregation started ripples of change throughout the country. One of them hit Montgomery, Alabama, on December 1, 1955. A 42-year-old African-American woman named Rosa Parks was tired after a long day working, and she was tired of being treated as a second-class human being. So Parks refused to get up from her seat on the bus when the driver demanded she give it to a white man. That was against the law, and Parks was arrested.

Her arrest sparked a boycott of the bus system by the black community. Facing the highly damaging boycott and a 1956 Supreme Court decision that declared segregation on public transportation unconstitutional, the Montgomery bus company dropped its race-based seating plan in 1957.

More important than getting to ride in the front of the bus was the example the boycott set as to how effective organized demonstrations against segregation could be. Equally important was the emergence on the national scene of the boycott's leader, an eloquent, charismatic son of a well-known Atlanta minister, who admired the nonviolent protest philosophies of India's Mohandas Gandhi. His name was Martin Luther King, Jr., and he was to become one of the most important men in America in the coming decade.

SPUT-WHAT?

Frankly, it didn't look like much: a little blip of a light in the evening sky that appeared to be moving much slower than its 18,000 miles per hour.

But to Americans watching on October 5, 1957, the blip represented a terrible thought: The commies might someday rule the world from outer space. That's because the little blip was a Soviet satellite called *Sputnik* (Russian for "fellow traveler"). It was the first such object, and within a few weeks it was followed by Sputnik II.

Americans were shocked. Fears of super weapons orbiting above the United States competed with the feeling that a new day was dawning for humanity. During the next year, the United States launched four satellites of its own, and within two years, U.S. efforts to catch up with the Soviet Union in space were in full gear. The Space Race had joined the Arms Race in the political Olympics between the Super Powers.

Chapter **18**

Camelot to Watergate: 1961–1974

The decade of the 1960s began with a defeat for Richard Nixon and ended in victory for him. In between, America became mired in a war it never understood and saw its citizens take to the streets in the name of peace, justice, and racial rage.

By the mid-1970s, U.S. streets were clearing, Nixon had suffered the last — and worst — defeat of his career, and America was trying to figure out just what the heck had happened in the preceding 14 years.

Electing an Icon

He was rich, handsome, witty, and married to a beautiful woman, and he looked good on the increasingly important medium of television. His opponent was middle class, jowly, whiny, and married to a less beautiful woman, and on TV he looked like 50 miles of bad road.

Even so, Massachusetts Senator John F. Kennedy won the presidency in 1960 over Vice President Richard Nixon by a very narrow margin — and only, some said, because his father, bootlegger-turned-tycoon Joseph Kennedy, had rigged the results in Illinois and Texas.

CALL FOR VOLUNTEERS

"Let the word go forth from this time and place, to friend and foe alike, that the torch has been passed to a new generation of Americans. . ... Ask not what your country can do for you, but what you can do for your country."

— John F. Kennedy, inaugural address, January 20, 1961

After eight years of the fatherly-but-colorless Dwight Eisenhower, "Jack" and Jacqueline Kennedy excited the interest of the country. Kennedy — known to headline writers as "JFK" — gave off an aura of youth, vigor, and shiny virtue. In truth, however, he was plagued with health problems from excruciatingly painful osteoporosis to venereal disease. He popped pain pills and took amphetamine injections, was an insatiable womanizer, and didn't mind bending the truth from time to time.

After his death, his widow coined the term "Camelot" (after the mythical realm of King Arthur and his knights) to describe JFK's quest to lead America — and the rest of the world — to a brighter future. Kennedy himself called on Americans to push toward a "new frontier" of challenges, such as landing a man on the moon by the end of the decade. But his first big challenge came very soon after he took office, and much closer to home.

The Bay of Pigs

Cuba had been a thorn in the United States' side since 1959, when dictator Fulgencio Batista was overthrown by Fidel Castro, an aspiring baseball player turned communist firebrand. Castro soon became an ardent anti-American, ordering the takeover of U.S.-owned businesses in Cuba and establishing close ties with the Soviet Union.

Kennedy gave his approval to a scheme that centered on anti-Castro Cuban exiles being trained by the Central Intelligence Agency (CIA) for an invasion of the island. The idea was that the Cuban people would rally to the invaders' side and oust Castro. The invasion took place April 17, 1961, at the Bay of Pigs on Cuba's southern coast. It was a disaster. No one rushed to their side, and many of the invaders were captured and held for two years before being ransomed by the U.S. government.

REMEMBER

The resulting embarrassment to America encouraged the Soviet Union to increase pressure in Europe by erecting a wall dividing East and West Berlin and resuming the testing of nuclear weapons. Kennedy, meanwhile, tried to counter the Soviet moves by renewing U.S. weapons testing, increasing foreign aid to Third World nations, and establishing the Peace Corps to export U.S. ideals, as well as technical aid. The Soviets weren't impressed, and tensions between the two super-powers escalated.

Facing the possibility of nuclear war

During the summer of 1962, the Soviets began developing nuclear missile sites in Cuba. That meant they could easily strike targets over much of North and South America. When air reconnaissance photos confirmed the sites' presence on October 14, JFK had to make a tough choice: Destroy the sites and quite possibly trigger World War III, or do nothing, and not only expose the country to nuclear destruction but, in effect, concede first place in the world domination race to the USSR.

Kennedy decided to get tough. On October 22, 1962, he went on national television and announced the U.S. Navy would throw a blockade around Cuba and turn away any ships carrying materials that could be used at the missile sites. He also demanded the sites be dismantled. Then the world waited for the Russian reaction.

On October 26, Soviet leader Nikita Khrushchev sent a message suggesting the missiles would be removed if the United States promised not to invade Cuba and eventually removed some U.S. missiles from Turkey. The crisis — perhaps the closest the world came to nuclear conflict during the Cold War — was over, and the payoffs were ample.

A hotline was installed between the leaders of the United States and the Soviet Union to help defuse future confrontations, and in July 1963, all the major countries except China and France agreed to stop aboveground testing of nuclear weapons.

A dark day in Dallas

Even with his success in the Cuban missile crisis, Kennedy admitted he was generally frustrated by his first thousand days in office. Despite considerable public popularity, many of JFK's social and civil rights programs had made little progress in a Democrat-controlled-but-conservative Congress. Still, Kennedy was looking forward to running for a second term in 1964, and on November 22, 1963, he went to Texas to improve his political standing in that state.

While riding in an open car in a motorcade in Dallas, Kennedy was shot and killed by a sniper. A former Marine and one-time Soviet Union resident named Lee Harvey Oswald was arrested for the crime. Two days later, a national television audience watched in disbelief as Oswald himself was shot and killed by a Dallas nightclub owner named Jack Ruby, while Oswald was being moved to a different jail. Whether Oswald and Ruby acted alone, or were part of conspiracies, has been debated for decades.

ADVOCATING FOR BIRDS: RACHEL CARSON

Because a friend of hers noticed some birds dying, Rachel Carson saved millions more.

Carson was born in Pennsylvania in 1907. She earned a zoology degree from Johns Hopkins University, and after teaching awhile, went to work for the U.S. Bureau of Fisheries. In 1951, her second book, *The Sea Around Us,* became a bestseller, allowing Carson to devote herself to writing full time.

One day, Carson got a letter from a friend in Massachusetts who had a small bird sanctuary. The friend had noticed that a lot of birds had died after the area was sprayed with the insecticide DDT to kill mosquitoes. Carson decided to investigate.

The result, in 1962, was *Silent Spring,* a carefully researched and eloquently written indictment of the pesticide's impact on the reproductive functions of fish and birds. The book started an avalanche of controversy around DDT. Finally, in 1972, the Nixon administration ordered a ban on the substance.

Carson didn't live to see the ban. She died of cancer in 1964, at the age of 57. But her landmark work is considered by many to be the start of the modern environmental movement in America.

America was stunned. The age of Camelot was over. And a veteran politician from Texas named Lyndon B. Johnson was president of the United States.

Sending Troops to Vietnam

If John F. Kennedy represented a fresh new face in the White House, his successor, Lyndon Baines Johnson, was a classic example of the old school of U.S. politics. A Texan, "LBJ" had served in both houses of Congress for more than 20 years before being elected as JFK's vice president in 1960 and was considered one of the most effective Senate leaders in history.

As president, Johnson inherited a host of problems, not the least of which was a growing mess in Southeast Asia, particularly Vietnam. Before World War II, Vietnam had been a French colony, and after the Japanese were defeated and driven out, it reverted to French control. But despite U.S. monetary aid, France was driven out of the country in 1954 by communist forces led by the French-educated Ho Chi Minh. The country was divided in two, with the communists controlling the northern half. Elections were scheduled for 1956 to reunite the two halves.

But they never took place, mostly because South Vietnam dictator Ngo Dinh Diem was afraid he would lose. The U.S. supported Diem (at least until 1963, when he became so unpopular he was assassinated with the U.S. government's unofficial blessing). At first, the support amounted to financial aid. Then U.S. military "advisors," who were not directly engaged in combat, were sent. But the pressure to do more mounted as the fighting dragged on, and by the time of Kennedy's assassination, 16,000 "advisors" had been sent to Vietnam.

Sinking deeper into a confusing war

Shortly after taking office, Johnson ordered 5,000 more troops to Vietnam and planned to send another 5,000. In August 1964, he announced that U.S. Navy ships had been attacked in international waters near the Gulf of Tonkin. Congress reacted by overwhelmingly approving a resolution that gave Johnson the power to "take all necessary measures" to protect U.S. forces. A few months later, LBJ ordered bombings of targets in North Vietnam. By March 1965, more than 100,000 U.S. troops were in the country. Within three years, that number had swelled to more than 500,000.

It was a lot of people to fight a war no one seemed to understand how to win. America had overwhelming military superiority. But it was mostly designed to fight a conventional war, with big battles and conquered territories.

REMEMBER

Vietnam was different. It was essentially a civil war, which meant it was often tough to figure out who was on whose side. The communists in the south were called the Vietcong. They were aided by North Vietnamese Army troops, referred to as the NVA. The dense jungle terrain made it difficult to locate and fight large concentrations of the enemy. There were conflicts between U.S. political leaders who wanted to contain the war and military leaders who wanted to expand it. Finally, the lack of clear objectives and declining public support demoralized many American soldiers.

Taking a look at the Tet Offensive

On January 31, 1968 — the Vietnamese New Year, called *Tet* — communist forces unleashed massive attacks on U.S. positions throughout Vietnam. The Tet Offensive, televised nightly in the United States, shocked many Americans who had the idea that the United States was rather easily handling the enemy. In fact, U.S. forces eventually pushed the North Vietnamese forces back and inflicted huge casualties on them. But the impact the fighting had on U.S. public opinion was equally huge. Opposition to the war grew more heated and contributed mightily to LBJ's decision not to run for reelection in 1968.

MUHAMMAD ALI

He was the most famous sports figure in the world, perhaps the most famous person, period. If you didn't believe it, all you had to do was ask him. "I am," he would reply, "the Greatest."

Ali was born Cassius Clay in Louisville, Kentucky, in 1942. After winning a gold medal at the 1960 Olympics, he turned pro. In 1964, Clay won the heavyweight championship and successfully defended it nine times over the next three years. Witty, charming, and arrogant, he was resented and disliked by many white Americans for not being humble enough.

He became even more controversial when he became a Black Muslim and changed his name. Then in 1967, he was stripped of his title and sentenced to five years in prison for refusing to be drafted into the military, on grounds of his religious beliefs. The Supreme Court eventually reversed the conviction, and Ali won the title back in 1974 from George Foreman, defending it ten more times before losing it in 1978 to Leon Spinks and then winning it for a third time in a rematch with Spinks later that year.

Ali announced his retirement from the ring in 1979 (although he returned for two losing matches in 1980). The onset of Parkinson's disease made it difficult for him to speak in his later years, but he managed an electrifying appearance as a torchbearer at the 1996 Olympics. Ali died in 2016, still "The Greatest" in the minds of many boxing fans.

Increasing Pressure in 'Nam and Escalating Fears at Home

With Johnson out of the 1968 race, Republican Richard Nixon narrowly defeated Johnson's vice president, Hubert Humphrey, and Alabama Gov. George Wallace, an ardent segregationist who ran as an independent.

Nixon and his top foreign affairs advisor, Henry Kissinger, tried several tactics to extricate the United States from the war without just turning over South Vietnam to the communists. One tactic was to coerce the South Vietnamese government into taking more responsibility for the war. To force the issue, the United States began withdrawing some troops in 1969. At the same time, however, Nixon ordered an increase in the bombing of North Vietnam, as well as in the neighboring countries of Laos and Cambodia. In essence, he was trying to put pressure on both sides to stop the fighting.

In 1970, Nixon approved the invasion of Cambodia by U.S. troops who were pursuing North Vietnamese soldiers based there. The decision intensified opposition to the war, and massive anti-war demonstrations spread across the country. At Kent State University in Ohio, National Guard troops shot and killed four student demonstrators.

Anti-war fever grew even stronger in 1971, when *The New York Times* published what became known as the Pentagon Papers. The documents, leaked by a former defense department worker named Daniel Ellsberg, proved the government had lied about the war's conduct. Later that year, an Army lieutenant named William Calley was convicted of supervising the massacre of more than 100 unarmed civilians at a village called My Lai.

REMEMBER

But despite mounting opposition to the war, Nixon easily won reelection in 1972, in part because of a politically inept opponent (U.S. Sen. George McGovern of South Dakota), and in part because Kissinger announced a few weeks before the election that a peace settlement was not too far off.

After the election, however, Nixon ordered heavy bombing of North Vietnam's capital of Hanoi. The bombing failed to break North Vietnamese resolve, and 15 U.S. bombers were shot down. On January 27, 1973, the United States and North Vietnam announced they had reached an agreement to end the fighting and would work to negotiate a settlement.

TECHNICAL
STUFF

VIETNAM BY THE NUMBERS

The following numbers tell a story of their own:

- Number of Americans killed: 58,174

- Number wounded: 304,000

- Cost, 1950–1974: $150 billion

- Peak number of U.S. troops stationed in Vietnam: 535,000

- Average age of U.S. soldier killed: 23

- Age of youngest U.S. soldier killed: 16

- Age of oldest U.S. soldier killed: 62

- Average number of days in combat by U.S. infantry soldier in one year in Vietnam: 240

The peace treaty proved to be a face-saving sham, allowing U.S. troops to be withdrawn before the communists closed in. In April 1975, North Vietnamese troops overran South Vietnam and took over the entire country. America had suffered its first decisive defeat in a war, touching off a reassessment of its role in the world — and on how it would approach involvement in conflicts in the future.

Continuing the Fight for Civil Rights

Although the civil rights movement began in the 1950s, it reached full steam in the 1960s, marked by several new tactics that proved effective in breaking down discrimination.

Enforcing their rights: African Americans

In February 1960, four African-American students sat down at a segregated lunch counter in Greensboro, North Carolina, and refused to leave after they were denied service. The "sit-in" became a strategy used across the country, and by the end of 1961, some 70,000 people had taken part in sit-ins. In May 1961, black and white activists began "freedom rides," traveling in small groups to the South to test local segregation laws (see Figure 18-1).

The inspirational leader of the movement was the Rev. Martin Luther King, Jr., a courageous and eloquent orator who founded the Southern Christian Leadership Conference and won the 1964 Nobel Peace Prize for his civil rights work.

FIGURE 18-1:
Police removing demonstrators from a restaurant.

© Bettmann/CORBIS

But not all African Americans were enamored of King's non-violent-demonstration approach. They also didn't believe equality could be attained through cooperation among the races. Leaders such as the Black Muslims' Elijah Muhammad and Malcolm X warned African Americans to neither expect nor seek help from whites. "If someone puts a hand on you," said Malcolm X, "send him to the cemetery."

Looking for legal remedies to discrimination

Both approaches eventually put pressure on the federal government to act. President Kennedy and his brother Robert (who was also his attorney general) used federal troops and marshals to force the admission of black students to the state universities in Alabama and Mississippi. In June 1963, JFK proposed a bill that would ban racial discrimination in hotels, restaurants, and other public places and give the federal government more authority to clamp down on state and local agencies that dragged their feet in enforcing civil rights laws. Black organizers gathered 200,000 demonstrators for a march in Washington, D.C., to support the Kennedy proposal.

REMEMBER

After Kennedy's assassination, the cause was taken up by Johnson. Despite his Southern roots, LBJ was a committed liberal whose "Great Society" programs mirrored the "New Deal" of Franklin Roosevelt in the 1930s. In addition to providing more federal aid to America's down-and-outs, an effort known as the "War on Poverty," LBJ pushed the 1964 Civil Rights Act through Congress. It featured many of the same elements Kennedy had proposed. Johnson followed it with another bill in 1965 that strengthened federal safeguards for black voters' rights.

But events and emotions moved faster than politics. In early 1965, Malcolm X, who had softened his earlier opposition to interracial cooperation, was murdered by Black Muslim extremists who considered such talk traitorous. A few months later, a march led by Martin Luther King, Jr. from Selma to Montgomery in Alabama was viciously attacked by state and local police, while a horrified national television audience watched.

Tired of waiting for an equal chance at the U.S. economic pie, many African Americans began demanding affirmative action programs in which employers would actively recruit minorities for jobs. "Black Power" became a rallying cry for thousands of young African Americans.

Taking it to the streets

The anger manifested itself in a rash of race riots in the mid- and late 1960s. The first was in August 1965, in the Los Angeles community of Watts. Before it was over, six days of rioting had led to 34 deaths, 850 injuries, 3,000 arrests, and more than $200 million in damages. Riots followed in the next two years in dozens of cities, including New York, Chicago, Newark, and Detroit, where 43 people were killed in July 1967.

BIG DREAMS

"I have a dream that one day this nation will rise up, live out the true meaning of its creed. . . . I have a dream that my four little children will one day live in a nation where they will not be judged by the color of their skin but by the content of their character."
— Martin Luther King, Jr., August 28, 1963 before the Lincoln Memorial, Washington, D.C.

Then things got worse. On April 4, 1968, Martin Luther King, Jr. was assassinated in Memphis, Tennessee. A white man named James Earl Ray was eventually arrested and convicted of the crime. More riots followed across the country, most notably in Washington, D.C.

The riots, in turn, triggered a backlash by many whites. George Wallace, a racist and ardent segregationist, got 13.5 percent of the vote in the 1968 presidential election, and much of the steam of the civil rights movement had dissipated by the time Richard Nixon moved into the White House.

Challenging the system: Latin Americans

African Americans weren't the only minority group on the move in the 1960s. Americans of Latin American descent had been treated as second-class citizens since the 1840s. While their numbers increased during and after World War II, mainly because thousands of Mexicans came to the country as a source of cheap labor, Latinos were largely ghettoized in inner-city *barrios* and rural areas of the Southwest. They were generally invisible in terms of the political process.

Between 1960 and 1970, however, the number of Latinos in the United States tripled, from three million to nine million, with perhaps another five million living in the country illegally. Cubans came to Florida, Puerto Ricans to New York, and Mexicans to California. With the increase in numbers came an increased interest in better political, social, and economic treatment for *La Raza* (the race). Leaders, particularly among Mexican Americans or *Chicanos*, sprang up: Reies Lopez Tijerina in New Mexico, Rodolfo "Corky" Gonzales in Colorado, and Cesar Chavez in California.

Latinos began to pursue organized efforts to gain access to the educational and economic systems and fight racial stereotypes. Latin Americans were elected to municipal and state offices and gradually began to organize themselves into a formidable political force in some parts of the country.

Maintaining their culture: Native Americans

No minority group had been treated worse than Native Americans, nor had any group been less able to do anything about it. They had lower average incomes, higher rates of alcoholism, and shorter life expectancies than any other ethnic group. And because their numbers were few, the federal government since the turn of the century had largely ignored them.

In the 1950s, federal policies tried to push Native Americans to abandon their traditional ways. In the 1960s, some Native Americans began to push back. In 1961, the National Indian Youth Council was established, followed by the American Indian Movement in 1968. The efforts of these and other groups helped lead to the Indian Civil Rights Act in 1968, which granted U.S. rights to Native Americans living on reservations while allowing them to set their own laws according to tribal customs.

CESAR CHAVEZ

His opponents accused him of "sour grapes," but to Cesar Chavez, it was merely a question of tactics. Chavez was born in 1927 on a small family farm near Yuma, Arizona. During the Depression, his family lost the farm and was forced to move, becoming laborers on other people's farms in California and the Southwest. After serving in the Navy during World War II, Chavez settled in San Jose, California, and became an official in a Latino community service organization.

In 1962, using his life savings, he founded the United Farm Workers (UFW), a union for a group that no other union was interested in. Chavez was an advocate of nonviolence, and he believed the union's interests should extend beyond labor contracts to other areas of social justice for farm workers.

By the mid-1960s, Chavez and the UFW had begun to organize farm workers in earnest. When strikes failed to work, he began boycotting products, particularly grapes. The aim of the boycotts was to get consumers not to buy the product until a fair labor agreement was in place. By the end of the 1970s, the UFW's membership was more than 70,000, the state of California had created a state board to mediate disputes between growers and workers, and for the first time, the nation's most downtrodden workers had union contracts.

Chavez died in 1993. The following year, his work not only as a union leader but also as a civil rights leader and humanitarian was recognized when he was posthumously awarded the Presidential Medal of Freedom, the nation's highest civilian honor.

It would be nice to say that all the racial wrongs in America were made right by the tumultuous events of the 1960s. It would also be absurd. But it isn't absurd to say the period was an overall success in terms of civil rights. It established key new laws, instilled a sense of self-pride in minority groups, and served notice that the issue would not be swept under the rug.

"Lord, we ain't what we ought to be," observed Martin Luther King, Jr. "We ain't what we wanna be. We ain't what we gonna be. But, thank God, we ain't what we were."

Entering a Generation in Revolt

Not all the groups fighting the status quo were tied to each other by race or national origin. The war in Vietnam and the blooming civil rights movement triggered political activism among many young Americans, particularly on college campuses. Groups like Students for a Democratic Society appeared, and activities like draft card burnings became as common as pep rallies.

Draft dodging, drugs, and demonstrations

Because of opposition to the war, thousands of draft-age males fled to Canada and other countries rather than serve in the military. Their actions baffled many of their parents, whose generations had served in World War II and Korea, and widened the gap of misunderstanding between the age groups.

The gap was also evident in the younger generation's freer attitudes toward sex, public profanity, and hairstyles. More troubling, and longer lasting in terms of its impact, was the use of drugs by the counterculture. The use of marijuana and hallucinogenics like LSD became commonplace. Most of it could be attributed to the excesses of youth. But it was also a disturbing preview of the plagues of drug use that would sweep over the country during the rest of the century.

Perhaps nowhere was the generation gap more visible than at the 1968 Democratic National Convention in Chicago. While mostly middle-aged and middle-class delegates debated an anti-war plank for the party platform, hundreds of mostly young and poor demonstrators battled with club-swinging police in the streets outside the convention center. "The whole world is watching!" the demonstrators taunted. Ironically, many of those watching were so troubled by the sight of young people defying authority that they voted for Richard Nixon in 1968, and again in 1972. Nixon appealed to these voters, whom he called the "silent majority," because he spoke out strongly against the demonstrations.

The rise of feminism

Draft cards weren't the only things being burned during the period. Women who resented their secondary roles in the workplace, the home, and the halls of government periodically protested by burning their bras. Women faced barriers in getting jobs in the first place, and when they did find work, they were paid far less than men doing the same tasks: In 1970, women earned 60 cents for every dollar paid a man. Married women were denied credit in their own names, even when they had jobs of their own.

REMEMBER

The women's liberation movement gave birth to the National Organization of Women (NOW) in 1966, and by 1970 NOW was organizing women's rights demonstrations and winning court battles over equal pay for equal work. In 1972, Congress approved a constitutional provision called the Equal Rights Amendment and sent it to the states for ratification. But a coalition of conservative and religious groups combined to fight the ERA, and in 1982 it was dead, 3 states short of the 38 needed for ratification.

As it turned out, the amendment hardly mattered, because many of the rights it would have provided were awarded in court decisions. One key decision came in 1973, when in *Roe v. Wade*, the Supreme Court essentially legalized abortion in the first three months of pregnancy. The ruling meant women now had a wider range of legal choices when faced with pregnancy. It also meant the beginning of an intense political, legal, social, and religious battle over abortion that continues today.

Coming out of the closet

The subject of homosexuality was so unspoken in America for most of its history that many Americans at the beginning of the 20th century had never heard of it or didn't believe it was real. Even into the 1960s, many psychiatrists believed homosexuality was a mental illness, and same-gender sex between consenting adults was still a crime in many states.

That began to change in the late 1960s, however, as gay men and women began to assert themselves. In June 1969, New York City police busted a gay nightclub called the Stonewall and began arresting patrons. The bust sparked a riot in the predominantly gay and lesbian community of Greenwich Village. Gay activist organizations like the Gay Liberation Front were started. But changing anti-gay laws and homophobic attitudes was still a work in progress in the first two decades of the 21st century.

HARVEY MILK

When the first openly gay elected official of any big U.S. city stepped in it, he *really* stepped in it. As a San Francisco supervisor, Harvey Milk once pushed for a city ordinance to force dog owners to clean up after their pets in public places. Accompanied by reporters, he staged a stroll through a city park that ended with his foot in a pile of dog droppings, for the benefit of the cameras. The measure was approved.

Milk was born in 1930 in New York. He served in the Navy during the Korean War as a deep-sea diver, but was dishonorably discharged after his homosexuality was revealed. After a career as a Wall Street stockbroker, Milk moved to San Francisco's predominantly gay Castro Street district, opened a camera store, and began running for office as an openly gay candidate. He was finally elected, on his fourth try, in 1977.

In 1978, Milk and San Francisco Mayor George Moscone were shot to death at City Hall by a disgruntled former city official named Dan White. White received only a five-year sentence for the killings, triggering gay riots. But Milk's death also inspired many gay professionals to "come out of the closet" and encouraged other gays to run for office. "If a bullet should enter my brain," Milk had said in a tape-recorded will, "let that bullet destroy every closet door."

Weirdness in the White House

Vietnam and a whole bunch of unhappy people in the streets of America weren't the only problems Richard Nixon faced when he took over as president in early 1969. Inflation was running wild. Much of the problem was a result of President Johnson's economic policy of "guns *and* butter": paying for the war and expanding social programs at the same time.

Making strides: The Nixon administration

Nixon responded to the situation by cutting government spending and balancing the federal budget for 1969. He also rather reluctantly imposed wage and price freezes on the country. But he wasn't reluctant at all about dropping federal efforts to enforce school integration laws: He had been elected with Southern support and was mindful that polls showed most Americans opposed forcing kids to take buses to schools in other neighborhoods to achieve racial balance.

Outside of Vietnam, Nixon enjoyed success in foreign policy. He went to China in early 1972, ending 20 years of diplomatic silence between the two countries, and he pursued a policy of *détente* (a French term for relaxing of tensions) with the Soviet Union.

These accomplishments, coupled with vague hints of looming peace in Vietnam and a backlash among voters Nixon called the "silent majority" against all the protesting, helped Nixon easily win reelection in 1972. In early 1973, the peace settlement with North Vietnam was announced. And despite Democratic majorities in Congress, Nixon was able to veto bills that challenged his authority in a number of areas. He took advantage of it to greatly expand the White House's power and cloak its actions from public scrutiny. And then an ex–FBI agent named James McCord wrote a letter to a judge, and the wheels of the Nixon White House began to come off.

Watching it all fall apart: Watergate

In a nutshell, here's what happened in the greatest presidential scandal in U.S. history (or second–greatest — see Chapter 20):

>> On June 17, 1972, McCord and four other men working for the Committee to Re-Elect the President, or CREEP (really), broke into the Democratic Party's headquarters in the Watergate, a hotel-office building in Washington, D.C. They got caught going through files and trying to plant listening devices. Five days later, Nixon denied any knowledge of it or that his administration played any role in it.

>> The burglars went to trial in 1973 and either pleaded guilty or were convicted. Before sentencing, McCord wrote a letter to Judge John Sirica, contending that high Republican and White House officials knew about the break-in and had paid the defendants to keep quiet or lie during the trial.

>> Investigation of McCord's charges spread to a special Senate committee. John Dean, a White House lawyer, told the committee McCord was telling the truth and that Nixon had known of the effort to cover up White House involvement.

>> Eventually, all sorts of damaging stuff began to surface, including evidence that key documents linking Nixon to the coverup of the break-in had been destroyed, that the Nixon reelection committee had run a "dirty tricks" campaign against the Democrats, and that the administration had illegally wiretapped the phones of "enemies," such as journalists who had been critical of Nixon.

>> In March 1974, former Atty. Gen. John Mitchell and six top Nixon aides were indicted by a federal grand jury for trying to block the investigation. They were eventually convicted.

>> While Nixon continued to deny any involvement, it was revealed he routinely made secret tapes of conversations in his office. Nixon refused to turn over the tapes at first, and when he did agree (after firing a special prosecutor he had appointed to look into the mess and seeing his new attorney general

resign in protest), it turned out some of them were missing or had been destroyed. (They were also full of profanity, which greatly surprised people who had a much different perception of Nixon.)

» In the summer of 1974, the House Judiciary Committee approved articles of impeachment against the president for obstructing justice.

The tapes clearly showed Nixon had been part of the coverup. On August 8, 1974, he submitted a one-sentence letter of resignation and then went on television and said, "I have always tried to do what is best for the nation." He was the first U.S. president to quit the job.

The Watergate scandal rocked the nation, which was already reeling from the Vietnam disaster, economic troubles, assassinations, and all the social unrest of the preceding 15 years. It fell to Nixon's successor, Vice President Gerald R. Ford, to try to bring back a sense of order and stability to the nation. And no one had voted for him to do it.

SMALL STEPS AND GREAT LEAPS

It started with a challenge from John F. Kennedy and ended with perhaps the greatest technological feat in human history: Man on the moon.

On May 25, 1961, Kennedy asked Congress for money to put a U.S. astronaut on the moon before the end of the decade. Congress agreed, and more than $1 billion was spent to get to the afternoon of July 20, 1969. At 1:17 p.m. (PDT), a craft carrying two men landed on the lunar surface. A few hours later, astronaut Neil A. Armstrong stepped out. "That's one small step for man," he said, "one giant leap for mankind."

Armstrong was joined on the surface by Buzz Aldrin, while a third astronaut, Michael Collins, circled above in the mother ship, *Columbia*. A worldwide television audience estimated at 1 billion people watched from a quarter-million miles away.

Some lunar visit facts: Armstrong and Aldrin spent 21 hours on the surface, but only 2 hours, 15 minutes actually walking around and never ventured farther than 275 yards from their craft. They collected 46 pounds of rocks. And they left behind a plaque attached to the base of the landing craft (they got back to the *Columbia* in the top half of the two-stage lander).

The plaque reads: "Here men from the planet Earth first set foot upon the moon, July 1969 A.D. We came in peace for all mankind."

Chapter **19**

Hold the Malaise, or, Ayatollah So: 1975–1992

Nothing puts a damper on a country's attitude like an unscrupulous president followed by a couple of well-meaning but relatively inept ones, and that's just what occurred in the 1970s. Throw in an oil crisis, a very unsettled economy, and a hostage situation in Iran, and we're not exactly talking about the Golden Age of America here.

In this era, a charismatic figure from, of all places, Hollywood, rides to the rescue, smiles a lot, and generally makes America feel better about itself by the end of the 1980s.

Wearing Nixon's Shoes

No one voted for Vice President Gerald R. Ford when he became president of the United States on August 8, 1974. Come to think of it, no one had voted for him when he became vice president, either.

Ford had been elected to Congress from Michigan in 1948 and reelected every two years through 1972. In December 1973, President Nixon appointed Ford vice president after the incumbent vice president, Spiro T. Agnew, resigned. Agnew was a blustering eccentric who proved to be a crook. Finding himself under investigation for extorting bribes from contractors while he was governor of Maryland, Agnew pleaded no contest to a charge of tax fraud, quit the vice presidency, and faded into richly deserved obscurity.

A month after becoming president when Nixon resigned in the wake of the Watergate scandal, Ford decided the country needed to put Watergate behind it. The best way to do that, Ford determined, was to pardon Nixon for any crimes he may have committed while in office. He also vehemently denied making any deal with Nixon before Nixon resigned. About 40 of Nixon's assistants weren't as lucky as their former boss and were indicted for various offenses. Some of them — including Nixon's attorney general, John Mitchell, and Nixon's top aides, John Ehrlichman and Bob Haldeman — went to prison.

Doing the best he could

As an honest, hardworking, and amiable man, Ford did his best as president. Unfortunately, his best wasn't great. Although he had been a college football star and a leader in Congress, he was stuck by the media with an undeserved image as a not-too-coordinated, not-too-bright guy. Falling down a flight of airplane stairs, hitting a spectator with a ball during a golf tournament, and occasionally misspeaking didn't help. Lyndon Johnson joked that Ford had "played one too many games without his helmet."

Ford's pardon of Nixon angered many Americans who felt the former president shouldn't have escaped facing the justice system. But even without the Watergate hangover, 1975 wasn't a great time to be president, for Ford or anyone.

In late April 1975, the communists completed their takeover in Vietnam. American diplomats scrambled onto escape helicopters from the roofs of buildings near the U.S. embassy in Saigon, with the whole world watching from living room TVs. Most of the rest of Indochina had already fallen under communist control or fell soon after.

NOT ON MY SHIFT

"I did not take the sacred oath of office to preside over the decline and fall of the United States of America."

— Gerald R. Ford, after assuming the presidency, August 1974

Whipping inflation

Even worse for Ford than the humiliation of the fall of Saigon, the U.S. economy was a mess. Inflation was soaring, and the unemployment rate reached 9 percent, the highest level since 1941. Ford's response included asking Americans to wear buttons that bore the acronym *WIN*, for *whip inflation now.* The buttons didn't have much of an impact, however.

Despite the buttons' ineffectiveness, Ford refused to take stronger measures. He neglected to address such issues as wage and price controls and did little to lessen the country's growing dependence on foreign oil. So when oil-producing nations, mainly in the Middle East, dramatically jacked up oil prices — 400 percent in 1974 alone — the United States suffered a price increase on just about every other product as well.

The Nixon pardon, the humiliating end to Vietnam, and the staggering economy proved to be three strikes against Ford. After barely winning the Republican nomination over former California Gov. Ronald Reagan, Ford lost the 1976 presidential election to Jimmy Carter, the former governor of Georgia. The way things turned out, Ford may have been the lucky one.

Good Intentions, Bad Results

America turned 200 in 1976, and for its bicentennial birthday, it gave itself a new president. His name was James Earl Carter, but everyone called him Jimmy. He was a Naval Academy graduate, a nuclear engineer, a peanut farmer, and the former governor of Georgia. He ran for the presidency as a Washington outsider. Because U.S. voters were pretty sick of Washington insiders, they elected him in a close race over the incumbent, Jerry Ford. Carter was the first candidate since 1932 to defeat an incumbent president. He was also the first president from the Deep South since the Civil War.

Ford had started his administration with the controversial pardoning of Richard Nixon, and Carter started his with the controversial pardoning of Vietnam War draft evaders. The two men had other similarities. Both seemed to have a tough time being consistent in their policy- and decision-making. And both had real troubles with the economy because of runaway inflation and oil shortages.

Measuring misery

During the 1976 campaign, Carter added up the nation's unemployment rate and inflation level, called it a "misery index," and used it as an effective rhetorical weapon against Ford. Unfortunately for Carter, by the time he left office, the level of misery was higher than when he took over. The annual *inflation rate* — the change in the price of various consumer goods — went from 5 percent in 1970 to 14.5 percent in 1980. The price of gasoline went from about 40 cents a gallon to more than 70 cents. Part of the reason for both higher inflation and high oil prices was America's increasing dependence on foreign oil. Simply put, the country was using far more oil — for everything from running cars to making textiles — than it was producing.

REMEMBER

In the early 1970s, Arab oil-producing countries cut off supplies to the United States and other Western nations as a way of pressuring Israel to give back Arab territory it had taken during a 1967 war. When the embargo was lifted in 1974, the Western countries' oil reserves had dried up, and the oil-producing countries could charge pretty much whatever they wanted for their product.

Higher oil prices helped fuel inflation, and inflation helped trigger higher interest rates. Companies couldn't afford to borrow money to expand, so unemployment rose. Carter tried various ways to combat the problems, including voluntary wage and price controls, but they didn't help much. Things got so bad that Carter went on national TV to acknowledge that a "crisis of confidence" had struck the nation. The address became known as "the malaise speech," and to many people, it made Carter appear to be a self-pitying crybaby.

A NUCLEAR "OOPS"

One of the great hopes of weaning America from its dependence on foreign oil was nuclear power from plants like the one on the banks of the Susquehanna River in a bucolic area of Pennsylvania called Three Mile Island.

On March 28, 1979, one of the plant's thousands of valves went on the fritz. The malfunction caused temperatures in the plant's reactor chamber to climb to 5,000 degrees, melting the lining of the reactor chamber before being stopped by the thick concrete floor.

Pregnant women and children were evacuated, and as many as 60,000 other people voluntarily fled the area. As it turned out, only relatively low levels of radiation escaped, and no claims of personal or property damage were ever proven.

But the accident effectively exploded the hopes of expanding nuclear power as an energy source in America. Although 60 nuclear plants were still operating 98 reactors in the United States in 2018, supplying 20 percent of the country's energy, more than 100 orders for new nuclear plants were canceled after the Three Mile Island accident, and only two new nuclear plants were under construction as of 2017.

Befriending the enemy

On the foreign front, Carter had mixed results. He negotiated treaties to gradually transfer the Panama Canal territory to Panama. He reached an agreement with the Soviet Union to restrict the development of nuclear arms, and he furthered the restoration of relations with Communist China that Richard Nixon had started.

Carter's biggest triumph was in engineering a historic peace agreement between Israel and Egypt, which had been at each other's throats since Israel's birth in 1948. At Camp David, the presidential retreat in Maryland, Carter brokered a deal in 1978 with Israeli Prime Minister Menachem Begin and Egyptian President Anwar Sadat. Sadat and Begin got the Nobel Peace Prize for their efforts; Carter got nothing but trouble in the form of multiple disasters involving Iran.

JESSE JACKSON

He could've been a professional athlete but became a preacher instead — and as a result became known as "the president of black America."

Jesse Jackson was born in October 1941, the illegitimate son of a South Carolina cotton buyer who ignored Jackson for much of his early life. After a career as an all-state football player in high school, Jackson passed up a pro baseball contract and went to college instead. He also became active in the civil rights movement and was with Martin Luther King, Jr. when King was assassinated in Memphis in 1968. In that same year, Jackson was ordained a Baptist minister.

Basing his work in Chicago, Jackson founded a program in 1971 called Operation PUSH (People United to Save Humanity). The program was designed to address problems facing inner-city youth. In 1984, he formed the National Rainbow Coalition, the aim of which was to bring together members of all races to address common goals. Jackson also ran for president in 1984 and 1988, generating enough support to become a major player in national Democratic Party politics. He has also been something of a diplomat-without-a-portfolio, negotiating the release of hostages in Syria, Cuba, and Iraq.

In 2001, it was revealed that Jackson had had an affair with a staff member and fathered a daughter with her in 1999. The revelation resulted in Jackson temporarily withdrawing from public life, and in late 2017, he announced he had Parkinson's disease. But he continued in his role as an inspirational — if sometimes divisive — advocate for human rights.

The United States had backed the shah of Iran since 1953, when the Central Intelligence Agency (CIA) helped him regain power in that country. When the shah was thrown out again in 1979 and replaced with a Muslim religious leader named the Ayatollah Ruhollah Khomeini, the United States allowed the shah to receive medical treatment in America.

That angered Iranian mobs, which invaded the U.S. embassy in the Iranian capital of Teheran on November 4, 1979. The mobs held the occupants of the embassy hostage. Some hostages were allowed to leave, but 52 were kept as prisoners. In April 1980, Carter ordered a team of Marine commandos to Iran on a rescue mission. Because of a series of screw-ups and accidents involving the rescue aircraft, eight commandos were killed before the actual rescue even began, and the mission was called off.

Finally, after the shah died in July, negotiations for the hostages' release began. They ended with the hostages being freed on January 20, 1981, after 444 days in captivity. The day the hostages were freed was, coincidently, the last day of Carter's presidency.

There's a First Time for Everything

If you told someone in 1951 that Ronald Reagan would someday be president of the United States, he would've suggested you check into a rest home for the politically delusional. After all, the veteran actor had just starred in *Bedtime for Bonzo,* in which his costar was a chimpanzee. That qualified him for Congress, certainly, but hardly the White House.

In addition to being the first president to have starred in a movie with an ape, Reagan was also the first president to have been divorced and, at the age of 69, the oldest president when he took office. Reagan was born in Illinois in 1911 and after college became a sportscaster in Iowa. In 1937, a screen test led to Hollywood, and Reagan became a second-tier star, first in movies and then on TV.

His taste for politics grew from serving two terms as president of the Screen Actors Guild, and as his politics became increasingly conservative, he found himself a favorite of the Republican Party's right wing. He ran for governor of California in 1966, defeating incumbent Pat Brown, and served two terms. As governor, Reagan demonstrated two strengths that served him well: a pragmatic streak that allowed him to compromise, and the willingness to consider the advice of others.

In 1976, he came in a strong second for the GOP presidential nomination, and then in 1980, he swept both the nomination and the presidency over the unpopular

Carter. His two greatest campaign assets turned out to be a single question — "Ask yourself, are you better off than you were four years ago?" — and on not being Jimmy Carter.

As president, Reagan was essentially a cheerleader for a vision of America that counted on everyone trying not to be too different from one another and not relying on the federal government to do much. He seemed to have an inexhaustible supply of both good and bad luck. He bounced back from being shot and seriously wounded after giving a speech at a Washington hotel in 1981, and in 1985, he won a bout with cancer. Despite his health problems, he managed an easy reelection victory in 1984 over Democrat Walter Mondale, who had been vice president under Jimmy Carter.

Reagan greeted political setbacks with boundless good cheer and a joke or two. And no matter what else happened, Reagan's personal popularity stayed high — so much so that he became known as the "Teflon president": Like the nonstick coating used on pots and pans, nothing seemed to stick to him. But his nice-guy persona didn't mean he was wishy-washy. When the country's air traffic controllers ignored federal law and went on strike in 1981, Reagan promptly fired all 11,400 of them and refused to rehire them after the strike ended.

GERALDINE FERRARO

She was a self-made woman who made a pioneering mark in America's democratic process, even though she came from a New York borough with a most undemocratic name — Queens.

Ferraro was born in 1935, the daughter of an Italian immigrant. After graduating college, Ferraro became an elementary school teacher while going to law school at night. After graduating law school, she married and for the next 13 years was a mother and housewife. In 1974, she joined the Queens district attorney's office and in 1978 was elected to Congress. As a congresswoman, Ferraro became an advocate for women's issues, particularly in providing greater job training opportunities and in ending gender discrimination in pension plans. In 1984, she was picked by Democratic presidential candidate Walter Mondale to be his running mate, making her the first woman to be part of the ticket for either of the two major U.S. political parties, as well as the first Italian American.

Mondale and Ferraro were clobbered in the election. It didn't help that a stink arose over allegations Ferraro's husband had done business with organized crime figures. Ferraro subsequently ran unsuccessfully for the U.S. Senate, hosted a TV political talk, show, wrote three books, and became a business consultant. She died in 2011. "We've come a long way since '84," she said in a 1999 interview. "That election really paved the way for women, and not just in politics."

Buying into the "Reagan Revolution"

One of the fastest-growing portions of America's population during the 1980s didn't have a clue what Reagan was talking about when he laid out his vision of the country and probably wouldn't have liked it had they understood. They were immigrants from countries like Mexico, Cuba, Haiti, and Vietnam who came to the United States by the tens of thousands during the 1980s. Many of them were counting on some form of government assistance to get started in their new lives in a new land.

But the people who had voted for Reagan knew exactly what he was talking about. Many of them were part of the *Sunbelt,* the fast-growing states of the Southeast, Southwest, and West. As the region's population grew, so did its representation in Congress — and its political clout. (The area became so powerful that every president elected between 1964 and 2008 was from a Southern or Western state.) In the West, in particular, Reagan's call for less government was in perfect harmony with the *Sagebrush Rebellion.* The rebellion, which was mostly rhetorical, was a reaction to land use and environmental regulations made in faraway Washington that were considered a threat to development of urban areas and resource-based industries, such as timber and mining. Reagan was the beneficiary of the growth in the Sunbelt's clout.

REMEMBER

Reagan also benefited from a revival in Christian evangelicalism that married itself to conservative politics in the late 1970s and 1980s. Conservative evangelicals — those who said they had been "born again" through a direct personal experience with Jesus Christ and who were often referred to in a political sense as the *Christian right* — were alarmed at what they saw as the country's moral laxity in the 1960s and early 1970s. America's real problems, they argued, could be traced to feminism, abortion, rising divorce rates, and homosexuality.

Groups like the Moral Majority, led by a Virginia-based TV evangelist named Jerry Falwell, became powerful political forces in terms of raising money and mobilizing mass support — or opposition — for legislation and political candidates. Another "religious right" leader, Marion G. "Pat" Robertson, founded the Christian Coalition and twice ran for president himself.

Finally, Reagan was supported by followers of a more secular cause — tax-cutting. The high inflation of the 1970s caused many people's income and property values to rise — and also pushed them into higher tax brackets that ate up much of the increases. That naturally fueled taxpayers' anger. In California, a cranky political gadfly named Howard Jarvis successfully pushed through an initiative that dramatically cut property tax rates and required state and local governments to drastically shift their way of financing government operations. The success of Proposition 13 led to similar efforts in other states. It also helped Reagan push through his own brand of tax-cutting.

JIM BAKKER

He once spent $100 on cinnamon rolls so his hotel room would smell nice, which was okay because he was doing God's work — and had plenty of cash to spare.

Jim Bakker was born in 1940 and grew up in a small town in Michigan. After high school, he attended a Bible college and became a minister. In the early 1970s, Bakker began a Christian puppet show on a local TV station in Virginia. He developed a TV ministry that became known as the PTL Club, which to followers stood for "praise the Lord" and to critics stood for "pass the loot."

There was plenty of that. With contributions from hundreds of thousands of his followers, Bakker and his wife Tammy Faye (who wore what seemed to be pounds of makeup and wept at the drop of a psalm) built Heritage USA, a 2,300-acre Christian-themed resort, water park, and entertainment complex in South Carolina. In 1988, however, it was revealed that PTL had paid $265,000 to a former secretary named Jessica Hahn to keep her quiet about a sexual encounter she had had with Bakker eight years before.

The revelation was only one of many that followed over the next year. In 1989, Bakker was convicted of bilking more than 100,000 people of $158 million. He served five years in federal prison, and the scandal helped put the brakes on the momentum of the Christian right. After prison, Bakker resumed his television preaching career, contending that the end of the world was near, and advertising buckets of freeze-dried food for those who survived.

Paying for "Reaganomics"

Reagan figured that if you cut taxes on companies and the very wealthy and reduced regulations on business, they would invest more, the economy would expand, and everyone would benefit. This approach, based heavily on the views of the Nobel Prize–winning economist Milton Friedman, a Reagan advisor, required cutting government services because there would be less tax revenue to pay for them. That would most affect Americans on the bottom of the economic ladder. But the benefits would eventually "trickle down" from those on the top of the ladder to those on the bottom. At least, in theory. So, early in his administration, Reagan pushed through a package of massive tax cuts, and the economy got better. Unemployment dropped from 11 percent in 1982 to about 8 percent in 1983. Inflation dropped below 5 percent, and the gross national product rose.

REMEMBER

While Reaganistas were quick to point to the president's policies as a great deal, critics pointed in a different direction. Although Reagan had cut taxes, he and Congress had failed to cut government spending. In fact, they greatly increased spending, particularly on military programs. Because the government was spending far more than it was taking in, the national debt rose from about $900 billion in 1980 to a staggering $3 *trillion* in 1990. Moreover, most of the benefits of Reagan's trickle-down approach failed to trickle, priming the pump for another economic downturn after he left office.

Dealing with foreign affairs

As a true conservative, Reagan didn't much care for the Soviet Union or communists in general. He heated up the Cold War by, among other things, referring to the Soviets as amoral and irreligious. (Toward the end of his second term, however, Reagan's anti-Soviet feelings began to soften, particularly after a moderate named Mikhail Gorbachev became Soviet leader.)

Reagan also irritated the Soviets by proposing a giant military program called the Strategic Defense Initiative (SDI, more popularly known as "Star Wars" after the popular science-fiction film). Reagan's plan included missile-destroying lasers based on satellites in space. His vision never went anywhere, however, because Congress refused to go along with the program's enormous costs.

THE CHALLENGER TRAGEDY

It was cold and windy at Cape Canaveral the morning of January 28, 1986, but U.S. space program officials were determined to go ahead with the launch of the space shuttle *Challenger*. After all, the *Challenger* had already made 9 successful trips into space, and the National Aeronautics and Space Administration (NASA) had run 24 space shuttle missions without a major problem.

At 11:38 a.m. (EDT), NASA launched its 25th mission. At 11:40, as thousands of spectators watched in horror at the launch site and millions more watched on TV, the shuttle exploded shortly after lifting off. All seven of the crew members were killed, including a Concord, New Hampshire, schoolteacher named Christa McAuliffe, who was along for the ride as a way of increasing children's interest in the space program.

The cause of the explosion was later traced to a flaw in the rocket's booster system and led to a complete reevaluation of the shuttle and an examination of more than 1,000 of its parts. More than 2 years passed before the shuttle program was allowed to resume — and 17 years passed before the next space shuttle disaster: The *Columbia* fell apart over Texas on its reentry on February 1, 2003, killing all seven crew members. The space shuttle program ended in 2011.

Reagan also supported virtually any government that was anti-communist, including repressive regimes in Latin America, and he was quick to respond to provocations by terrorist acts supported by Libya. But he did withdraw American peacekeeping troops from war-torn Lebanon after a 1983 terrorist attack killed 241 U.S. marines stationed there. One of the anti-communist groups Reagan's administration supported was called the *contras* in Nicaragua, and it resulted in the biggest embarrassment of Reagan's presidency. In 1986, it was revealed that the White House had approved the sale of weapons to Iran as part of a mostly unsuccessful effort to win the release of some U.S. hostages in the Middle East.

It turned out that some of the money from the arms deal had been illegally siphoned off to the contras. Most of the blame for the scandal was pinned on an obscure Marine lieutenant colonel named Oliver North. But like other calamities, the Iran-contra mess did little to harm Reagan's popularity or inflict any lasting damage on his administration. In fact, it didn't even hurt the election of his successor in the White House, a one-time Reagan political foe who had become Reagan's dutiful vice president. His name was George H.W. Bush.

Warming Up after the Cold War

For more than four decades, the ideological conflict between the free world and the communist world had influenced just about every aspect of U.S. life. The federal budget was built around the idea of defending the country against communism. Advances in science and medicine were often driven by the fervor to stay ahead of the communists. Schoolchildren were indoctrinated as to the evils of the communist menace and chided to do better than commie kids. Even international sporting events became intense political struggles.

But the boogeyman began to deflate in 1979, when the Soviet Union intervened in a civil war in Afghanistan. Over the following decade, the Soviets poured thousands of troops and millions of rubles into what became the equivalent of America's Vietnam. The difference was that the U.S. economy was strong enough and flexible enough to survive Vietnam, whereas the ponderous Soviet economy all but creaked to a halt.

In 1985, Mikhail Gorbachev became the Soviet leader. Gorbachev realized that the old Soviet system couldn't continue to dominate Eastern Europe. In fact, the Soviet Union couldn't even continue to function as a country without some dramatic changes. He initiated two major concepts: *perestroika*, or changes in the Soviet economic structure, and *glasnost*, or opening the system to create more individual freedoms.

OIL ALL OVER THE PLACE

On March 24, 1989, Alaska's Prince William Sound was one of the most scenic and beautiful inlets in the world, teeming with birds, fish, and marine mammals. On March 25, 1989, it was a heartbreaking, stomach-turning mess: the site of the biggest oil spill in U.S. history.

It began when a giant tanker, the *Exxon Valdez,* hit a well-marked reef after picking up a load of crude oil in the town of Valdez. More than 11 million gallons of oil oozed into the sound and spread over hundreds of square miles. More than 250,000 birds were killed, along with thousands of other animals.

It was quickly determined that the 984-foot ship's captain, Joseph Hazelwood, had been drinking before the accident. He was convicted the following year of negligence and sentenced to 1,000 hours of community service. He began the service in 1999, after nine years of appeals. Exxon spent $2.2 billion on cleanup efforts and paid another $900 million in a settlement to the state and federal government. As of 2018, there was still oil to be found on the shores of Prince William Sound.

On November 9, 1989, the wall that divided East and West Berlin was opened. By the end of the year, Soviet-dominated regimes in a half-dozen European countries, including East Germany, had collapsed and been replaced by more democratic governments. By the end of 1991, the Soviet Union itself had dissolved into a set of mostly autonomous republics. The Cold War was over.

The collapse of the Soviet Union left the United States as the world's only true superpower. But it took no time at all for one of the planet's seemingly inexhaustible supply of thugs and bullies to test the United States' will to live up to its role as the world's leader.

Engaging in the Gulf War

If impressive resumes translated into leadership, they'd be carving George Herbert Walker Bush's bust on Mt. Rushmore right now. After all, he was a Yale graduate, a World War II hero, an ambassador to China, a CIA director, and vice president under Reagan.

Bush was easily elected president in 1988 after waging a rather sleazy campaign against Democratic nominee Michael Dukakis. Voters were so turned off by the campaign and politics in general that the turnout was the lowest for a presidential election since 1924. As president, several things hampered Bush. Democrats controlled both houses of Congress. Reagan's personal popularity was a hard act to follow. And Bush was simply not much of a leader, especially when it came to solving domestic problems.

Bush's leadership was put to a stern test in 1990. On August 2, the Iraq army invaded the small neighboring country of Kuwait and quickly took over. Iraq was led by a brutal bozo named Saddam Hussein, who proclaimed he was annexing Kuwait to Iraq, and anyone who didn't like it could stuff it.

Bush chose not to stuff it. To Bush supporters, his decision to intervene was based on his desire to defend the defenseless. To his critics, it was to protect U.S. interests in Kuwait's oil production. Whatever the reason, in the weeks following the Iraqi invasion, Bush convinced other world leaders to establish a trade embargo on Iraq. Almost simultaneously, the United States, Britain, France, Egypt, Saudi Arabia, and other countries began assembling a massive armed force in case the economic pressure didn't work.

REMEMBER

When that proved to be the case, the United States and its allies launched a gigantic aerial assault on Iraq on January 16, 1991. After six weeks of massive bombardment, the Allied forces sent in ground troops. The vaunted Iraqi military turned out to be made of papier-mâché. U.S. casualties were light, and about 100 hours after the ground war started, Iraq quit.

BYTING OFF THE APPLE

Steve Jobs was a college dropout with marketing talents, and Steve Wozniak was an electronics nerd with an inventive mind. When the two got together, interesting things occurred.

First it was a device that allowed them to make free, if illegal, long-distance calls. Then it was an early video game called "Breakout." But the two Steves yearned to do something really radical: create an affordable computer that the average American could use at home.

So Jobs sold his Volkswagen van and Wozniak his favorite calculator. With the $1,300 they raised, they began work on their "personal" computer, laboring in a garage, an attic, and a spare room in the home of Jobs' parents in Palo Alto, California. They called it "Apple," partly in tribute to The Beatles' recording company of the same name and partly because Jobs just liked apples.

In 1976, the duo sold their first 50 computers for $500 each, but they sold only 125 more through the rest of the year. In 1977, however, they developed Apple II. It was the first true PC, with color graphics, a keyboard, a power supply, memory, a carrying case, and a floppy disk drive. It sold for $1,195 (around $5,150 in 2018 dollars). By 1981, the company's sales had reached $335 million — and by 2018, $229 *billion* worldwide. That's a lot of Apples, no matter how you slice them.

The victory, however, wasn't all that victorious. Kuwait was free, but the Iraqi dictator Hussein remained in power. Nine years after the Gulf War ended in March 1991, the United States was still spending $2 billion a year to enforce a no-fly zone over Northern Iraq, kept an armada of Navy ships in the area, and maintained a force of 25,000 troops in the region.

Back on the home front

While the Gulf War was short if not particularly sweet in terms of its lingering after-effect, things at home weren't much sweeter. For one thing, the economy was in the dumpster. Like the federal government, many individuals and corporations had borrowed heavily in the 1980s, causing the number of bankruptcies in the country to soar. That, in turn, triggered a mess in the savings and loan (S&L) industry.

The Reagan administration, in its quest to lessen the role of government in people's lives, had pushed to loosen up regulations on savings and loan companies. The result was that many S&Ls overextended credit and made stupid investments. Many of them collapsed. Tens of thousands of investors lost their savings, and the federal government had to spend billions of dollars to bail many of the S&Ls out.

Not all the disharmony was economic. On March 3, 1992, a 25-year-old black man named Rodney King was pulled over for reckless driving by Los Angeles police. A witness happened to videotape several of the police officers beating King. Despite the videotaped evidence, an all-white jury acquitted the police. Los Angeles erupted in the worst U.S. domestic violence in more than a century. Before it was over, 53 people died, 4,000 were injured, 500 fires had been set, and more than $1 billion was lost in property damage (see Figure 19-1).

FIGURE 19-1:
Aftermath of the Los Angeles riots.

© Peter Turnley/CORBIS

"People, I just want to say, you know, can we all get along? Can we just get along?"
— Rodney King, to reporters during the Los Angeles riots, May 2, 1992

All this didn't bode well for the incumbent president. Not only were Americans generally dissatisfied with the way things were, but an eccentric Texan named Ross Perot also compounded Bush's troubles. Perot was a billionaire who decided to run for president as a third-party candidate. Despite his immense wealth (he financed his own campaign), Perot ran as a populist, railing against the influence of special interests in the political process.

When the votes were counted, Perot had gathered an impressive 19 percent, the best showing by a third-party candidate since Theodore Roosevelt in 1912. Bush finished second. The winner was a 46-year-old Democrat who had been elected governor of Arkansas five times.

His name was William Jefferson Clinton, and the name of his hometown said a lot about the feelings of the country as it headed down the homestretch of the 20th century. The name of the town was Hope.

Chapter **20**

No Sex, Please, I'm the President: 1993-1999

I n the last decade of the 20th century, America was on top of the world. Communism had crumbled. The economy, after a slow start, spent much of the decade in overdrive, sparked by revolutions in how people communicated and did business with one another and the rest of the world.

But the 1990s weren't all fun and games. Terrorism and violent confrontations between the government and domestic fringe groups came home to this country after having been regarded as events that were confined to foreign shores. Oh, and the president of the United States got caught with his zipper down.

Bill, Newt, and Monica

Fewer than half the people who voted for a presidential candidate in 1992 voted for Bill Clinton, which shows there was a pretty fair number of people who either disliked him or didn't trust him. At 46, he was the youngest president since John F. Kennedy. Like JFK, Clinton could be charming and affable, was a convincing public speaker, and had a weakness for women. A Democrat, Clinton was the first of the baby-boomer generation — those born between 1946 and 1964 — to be president. He had avoided the draft during Vietnam and admitted that he smoked marijuana at least once.

Treading lightly abroad

REMEMBER

On the foreign front, Clinton was cautious. He did push through the North American Free Trade Agreement (NAFTA), which was designed to greatly reduce economic barriers among the United States, Canada, and Mexico. But his biggest challenge came in what was the former country of Yugoslavia. It had split into smaller states after the collapse of Soviet dominance in Europe in the late 1980s. In Bosnia, which was one of those states, Serbian, Croatian, and Bosnian groups were fighting a civil war that threatened to spread. When diplomatic efforts failed, the United States and other nations sent in peacekeeping troops to enforce a fragile truce. Later in the decade, U.S. military forces and other countries also intervened (and eventually restored order) when the former Yugoslavian state of Serbia invaded and terrorized neighboring Kosovo.

Clinton was much less successful — and apparently less interested — in solving problems in Africa. He inherited a mess in Somalia, where U.S. troops had been sent in as part of a United Nations peacekeeping force. They failed to quiet things down. In October 1993, Americans were repulsed by video of the bodies of U.S. soldiers being dragged through the streets of Somalia's capital. U.S. troops were removed in 1994. Clinton also failed to intercede in the genocidal conflict in Rwanda, where millions were killed or forced to become refugees. A decade later, and presumably wiser, Clinton apologized for his "personal failure" to do more.

In 1998, a radical Islamic terrorist group called Al-Qaeda bombed U.S. embassies in Kenya and Tanzania. Clinton ordered retaliatory missile attacks against suspected Al-Qaeda havens in Sudan and Afghanistan, to little effect. Frustrated with Iraqi dictator Saddam Hussein's refusal to cooperate with UN weapons inspections, the United States and Great Britain launched air strikes against Iraq in late 1998, also to little effect. Both the terrorist group and the dictator would prove to be even bigger headaches for Clinton's successor.

Pushing harder on the home front

Clinton was much more interested and engaged when it came to domestic policies. His first big battle as president was over his ambitious plan to reform the country's healthcare system. As the beginning of the 21st century loomed, America was virtually the only major developed nation without a government system of providing health care to all its citizens —generally referred to as *universal health care*. Instead, the U.S. system was plagued by soaring costs, confusing programs, and increasing unavailability to the unemployed and the uninsured. As the baby boomers aged and needed more medical care, the strain on the system would only get worse.

Clinton put his wife, Hillary, in charge of getting his reforms through Congress. But her efforts were hampered when she became embroiled in a probe into the financial dealings of an Arkansas company called the Whitewater Development

Corporation. The Whitewater probe led to Hillary Clinton becoming the first First Lady to be subpoenaed in a criminal investigation.

While neither of the Clintons were charged, 15 others —including the governor of Arkansas — were convicted of various offenses. The scandal, along with Hillary's arrogant stubbornness in refusing to compromise with legislators, and a massive and well-financed campaign by the health and pharmaceutical industries, ultimately sank Clinton's healthcare reforms.

In turn, the failure of Clinton's healthcare reforms, a series of mini-scandals at the White House, and the clever political strategy of a Georgia congressman named Newt Gingrich gave the Republicans control of both houses of Congress in 1995 for the first time since 1946. Gingrich was elected House speaker.

Pushing the "Contract with America"

During the 1994 congressional campaign, Republicans had come up with a conservative litany of policies they said they would pursue if they came to power. They called it the *Contract with America*. After the election, they began pushing an array of programs that were aimed at reducing federal spending on social programs, softening environmental rules, cutting taxes, and easing government regulations on business and industry.

Clinton, sensing that the political mood of the country was shifting to the center, went along for the ride. In August 1996, he signed the Welfare Reform Act, which tightened up federal aid to those who wouldn't or couldn't work and shifted more responsibility to the states. By the end of the decade, welfare rolls in much of the country had shrunk considerably. Well before the welfare bill, however, Clinton had shown his willingness to hug the middle. Shortly after taking office in 1993, he tried to end the ban on gays in the military. When a firestorm of opposition arose, he retreated to a "don't ask, don't tell" policy that said gays could serve in the military as long as they didn't tell anyone they were gay.

But most Americans were far more interested in pocketbook issues than gays in the military, and when it came to the economy, Clinton shone. The federal budget deficit of $290 billion in 1993 was transformed to a surplus of about $70 billion by 1997. Clinton had backed a tax increase in 1993 to balance the budget; when it was balanced in 1997, he signed a bill cutting U.S. income taxes for the first time since 1981.

REMEMBER

He was also more stubborn on economic issues than on some other issues. When the president and Congress couldn't agree on a federal budget, the government all but shut down in November 1995 and January 1996. The public largely blamed the Republicans in Congress, in part because Gingrich was viewed as something of a political weasel outside of Washington. By 1998, the "Republican resurgence" was over, although Republicans continued to hold majorities in both houses of

Congress. In November 1998, Democrats picked up a total of 5 congressional seats when they had expected to lose 20. Gingrich stepped down as speaker and soon left Congress altogether.

The public's apathy toward the Republicans' "contract," combined with the fact that the economy was doing well, allowed Clinton to easily win reelection over Kansas Senator Bob Dole in 1996. One of Clinton's most ardent supporters in his reelection effort was a young White House intern named Monica Lewinsky.

Judging a president

Bill Clinton had troubles with women before Miss Lewinsky. During the 1992 presidential campaign, a nightclub singer named Gennifer Flowers claimed she and Clinton had a long affair while he was governor of Arkansas. Clinton first denied it and then acknowledged that during his marriage he had committed adultery. As president, he was also unsuccessfully sued for allegedly sexually harassing a former Arkansas state employee named Paula Jones while he was governor.

Then in January 1998, it was revealed that an independent investigator named Kenneth Starr — appointed by Congress to look into the Whitewater real estate mess around Hillary Clinton — was looking into a possible sexual relationship between Clinton and Lewinsky. Lewinsky had come to the White House in 1995 as a 21-year-old, unpaid intern. She went on the White House payroll a few months later but was transferred to the Pentagon after some Clinton aides thought she was getting too cozy with the president.

At first, Clinton and Lewinsky denied any hanky-panky. Clinton also adamantly denied he ever asked Lewinsky to lie about their relationship. As the months passed, however, the truth began to emerge. In a national TV address in August 1998, Clinton admitted to "a relationship with Miss Lewinsky that was not appropriate."

On October 8, the GOP-controlled House of Representatives brought impeachment charges against Clinton, basically for fooling around with Lewinsky and then lying about it (although the formal charges were obstructing justice and lying under oath). He was impeached a few weeks later, the second president in U.S. history (Andrew Johnson was the first) to be tried in the Senate.

But public polls showed that while most Americans were pretty disgusted with Clinton's morals, they didn't want to see him thrown out of office for them. The Senate agreed, and on February 12, 1999, it voted to acquit him.

BETTOR DAYS

Americans have always been gamblers. Many American ancestors gambled big-time just to get here in the first place. But chances are that very few of them envisioned just how much legal U.S. gambling would eventually grow.

Fueled by relaxed moral views, more leisure time, and governments looking to raise money without raising taxes, legal gambling boomed in the last quarter of the 20th century and into the 21st. By 2013, 44 states ran lotteries, and 42 had casinos of some kind. Only two states — Utah and Hawaii — had no forms of legal wagering.

Some of the biggest beneficiaries of all this betting were Native Americans — although by no means all. Thanks to their status as sovereign nations and a 1988 congressional act, 243 tribes (out of a total of 566) in 29 states had gambling operations in 2018, with revenues of $32 billion.

And don't bet on Americans giving up their betting ways anytime soon. In 2013, Nevada, New Jersey, and Delaware began allowing their residents to legally gamble online within the state. And in 2018, the U.S. Supreme Court struck down a 1992 federal ban on betting on sporting events, opening the door to legalizing even more ways to take a chance.

Homegrown Terrorism

For most of the 20th century, *terrorism* — using violent acts to make a political point — was something most Americans regarded as a foreign problem. But in the 1990s, a series of events brought it closer to home.

Some domestic terrorism stemmed from small-but-fervent groups or individuals who believed the U.S. government was part of various international conspiracies bent on world domination. By 1997, right-wing paramilitary or survivalist groups had developed in every state. Some were led by Vietnam-era vets who felt betrayed by the government, others by religious fanatics, and still others by white supremacists.

Rallying around Ruby Ridge

One such group formed in Idaho, about 40 miles from the Canadian border, at a place called Ruby Ridge. On August 21, 1992, U.S. marshals were watching a white supremacist named Randy Weaver when shots were fired. A marshal and Weaver's 14-year-old son were killed. The next day, an FBI sniper killed Weaver's wife and wounded another man. At a subsequent trial, Weaver and another defendant were acquitted of all but one minor charge, and the government agreed to pay

$3.1 million to the Weaver family for the incident. "Ruby Ridge" became a rallying cry for militia groups of all types.

Taking down a cult: Waco

By his own admission, Vernon Wayne Howell had an unhappy childhood, and by the time he was 22, he was still seeking somewhere to belong. In 1981, he chose the Branch Davidians, a religious sect that in 1935 had settled about 10 miles outside of Waco, Texas. By 1990, Howell had changed his name to David Koresh and was head of the cult. Koresh called himself "the Messiah" and took multiple wives from among his followers.

On February 28, 1993, federal agents looking for illegal weapons and explosives tried a surprise raid on the Branch Davidian compound. But Koresh had apparently been tipped off that they were coming, and a gunfight erupted. Four agents and two cult members were killed, and a 51-day siege of the compound began.

THE PEOPLE VERSUS "THE JUICE"

It may have been unique in U.S. history: a national icon who was an accused double murderer.

Orenthal James Simpson — better known to his fans as "O.J." or "The Juice" — was a Hall of Fame football player who had been a successful movie actor and TV commercial spokesman. On June 12, 1994, Simpson's former wife, Nicole Brown Simpson, and her friend, Ronald Goldman, were brutally knifed to death in front of Nicole's Los Angeles condominium.

Simpson was a suspect and agreed to surrender to police. Instead, he led them on an incredible, slow-motion, nationally televised chase along L.A. freeways before surrendering in the driveway of his mansion. The evidence against Simpson seemed overwhelming. But after a trial that became an international media circus, Simpson was acquitted.

The verdict was characterized as an example of a rich man being able to buy justice by hiring defense attorneys who were smarter than the jury. Simpson lost a 1997 civil suit to the families of Nicole and Goldman and was ordered to pay $33.5 million for being responsible for their deaths. But he vowed never to pay a dime of the award because he insisted he was innocent of the murders.

In December 2008, Simpson was convicted in Las Vegas of robbery, assault with a deadly weapon, and several other charges. He served nine years in a Nevada prison.

On April 19, after negotiations with Koresh to surrender had stalled, federal agents attacked the compound and fired tear gas inside. A fire broke out and spread rapidly. When it was over, at least 82 people were dead, including 17 children. The government contended it had acted responsibly. Critics contended it was at best a reckless mistake, and at worst, murder. One of the critics was a skinny, 29-year-old, former soldier named Timothy McVeigh.

Bombings rock the nation

Not all the mayhem of the 1990s involved the U.S. government. On February 26, 1993, a 1,210-pound bomb that had been packed in a van rocked the World Trade Center building in New York City. The bomb killed six people. Members of a radical Islamic group, some of whom were also accused of plotting to bomb the UN building and two New York City tunnels, were arrested and convicted.

But it was Waco that stuck in the mind of Timothy McVeigh. A Gulf War veteran, McVeigh believed the U.S. government had become part of an international totalitarian conspiracy. With a friend, Terry Nichols, McVeigh decided to do something about it.

On the morning of April 19, 1995, the nine-story Alfred P. Murrah Building, a federal office complex in Oklahoma City, was blasted by a powerful bomb. The blast rained down concrete and glass for blocks around. A total of 168 people were killed, including 19 children who had been at the building's daycare center. At the time, it was America's worst act of terrorism, and it stunned the nation. "This is why we live in Oklahoma," exclaimed a disbelieving woman. "Things like this don't happen here."

McVeigh and Nichols were arrested shortly after the bombing. At their trials, prosecutors charged that the bomb — a mixture of fertilizer and fuel oil in a truck parked outside the building — had been set to mark the second anniversary of the Waco tragedy. McVeigh was sentenced to death in 1997 and executed in 2001. Nichols received a life sentence.

In between the bombing and the sentencings of McVeigh and Nichols, America was shaken by yet another bombing, this one in a park in Atlanta during the 1996 summer Olympics. Two people died, and 111 were injured. An anti-abortion homophobe named Eric Rudolph was arrested in 2003 for the bombing and sentenced in 2005 to life in prison.

Don't open that mail: The Unabomber

Theodore Kaczynski was a university math professor who retreated to life in a tiny plywood shack in Montana. From there he mailed bombs to people he deemed were part of society's "evil" homage to technology. Over 18 years, Kaczynski mailed 16 bombs, killing 3 people, injuring 23, and triggering a massive manhunt. He became known as the "Unabomber" because his initial targets were universities and airlines.

He was caught after he successfully demanded that *The Washington Post* publish a long and rambling "manifesto" he had written. Kaczynski's brother recognized the thoughts as his brother's and contacted federal agents. Kaczynski was arrested. He pleaded guilty in 1997 to avoid the death penalty and was sentenced to life without parole.

The tragedies served notice on America that it was no longer a safe oasis in a dangerous world. Mindful of potential terrorist attacks, Pennsylvania Avenue, the street in front of the White House, was closed to traffic.

Making Ourselves Sick

While the bombs and terrorism of the 1990s were scary, many more Americans were affected by different kinds of horrors: the twin plagues of AIDS and drugs.

Suffering from AIDS

First documented in 1981, AIDS (acquired immune deficiency syndrome) was found to come from the HIV virus, which in turn was spread by the exchange of bodily fluids, such as blood and semen. People could have the virus — be *HIV-positive* — and not have AIDS. After the virus transmuted, however, death was a near certainty. Most of the early cases were among gay men, and "only" 21,517 total cases were reported in 1986.

Still, AIDS was sobering on two levels besides the most important, which was the loss of life. Medical science had conquered many diseases by the end of the 20th century and lessened the impact of many others. AIDS was a chilling reminder that man was still not master of his own medical fate.

REMEMBER

The other impact was political. Gays and lesbians had made important strides in gaining the status of other minority groups. Openly gay candidates had won elective office, and some states and cities had begun banning discrimination on the basis of sexual orientation. But the spread of AIDS was seen by many homophobes as God's revenge against gays, and many people who previously considered themselves open-minded on the issue began to worry about contracting the disease from even casual contact with homosexuals.

As the disease spread from the gay community to intravenous drug users and heterosexuals, the numbers became epidemic. By the early 1990s, as many as 1.5 million Americans were believed to have the HIV virus, and 280,000 had died. But as the number of victims grew, so did public tolerance of the afflicted. Public sympathy was fueled in part by the revelations of public figures with the disease, such as basketball star Magic Johnson and Olympic diver Greg Louganis.

In 1997, the U.S. Supreme Court ruled that federal disability laws covered people with the HIV virus. Though no cure had been found by the end of 2018, drug treatments had some success in blocking the HIV virus from developing into full-blown AIDs. In 2015, the Centers for Disease Control and Prevention reported that the number of new HIV infections, about 38,500 per year, was slowly declining.

Dealing with drugs

A much longer-lived American malady than AIDS was its non-alcohol drug habit. It was a habit that could be traced back to the addictions of Civil War veterans to laudanum and other painkillers used in the war.

But drug use became epidemic in the 1980s and 1990s, especially in the country's inner cities, with the spread of *crack*, a cheap, potent, and smokable form of cocaine. The production and distribution of crack and other drugs became a multibillion-dollar business, and America became the most lucrative market in the world for drug cartels in Asia and Central and South America.

The blossoming drug trade triggered deadly turf wars in U.S. cities, as rival gangs battled for control of the local drug markets. Not since the gang wars of Prohibition had American streets seen so much gunfire — and this time it was with automatic weapons that sprayed bullets all over the place and killed many innocent bystanders.

By 1990, more people were being sent to U.S. jails and prisons for drug-related offenses than for any other crime. The war on drugs ground on through the 1990s, and when the use of crack declined, the use of methamphetamine, or *crank*, grew.

By the end of the decade and into the new century, it became apparent that the weight of the U.S. justice system had made little lasting impact on America's addictions: As the 21st century dawned, a World Health Organization report concluded that America had the highest level of illegal drug use in the world.

TONI MORRISON

She turned to writing because of an unhappy marriage, and her husband's loss turned out to be the literary world's gain.

Chloe Anthony Wofford was born in Ohio in 1931 to an African-American family who had left the South to escape racism. After graduating from college (where she took the name "Toni" because some people had trouble pronouncing her name), she became a university teacher. She married a young architect named Harold Morrison in 1958. But the marriage was an unhappy one, and she joined an amateur writing group to escape.

After getting a divorce, Morrison moved to New York and became a book editor. She also continued to write, and published her first novel, *The Bluest Eye,* in 1970. Her fifth novel, *Beloved,* won the 1988 Pulitzer Prize, and in 1993 she was given the Nobel Prize for Literature, the first African-American woman to win the award.

"Tell us," she challenged black writers in her acceptance speech, "what it is to live at the edge of towns that cannot bear your company."

A World of Change

The last decade of the 20th century saw America — and the rest of the world — undergo some pretty revolutionary changes. One of the biggest was in the development of technology, particularly in computers. The speed of their development was staggering.

As the chips got more complex, their uses grew, and as their uses grew, their prices dropped. In 1994, a computer sophisticated enough to do high-speed, three-dimensional graphics for things like military flight simulators cost $300,000. In 2000, better computers than that were available in kids' video game systems for $400.

Many of the advances were in communications, and sharing information became as big a business as manufacturing a product. The number of cellphones in the country, for example, jumped from fewer than 10 million in 1990 to more than 100 million in 2000. (For where all this tech stuff took America in the 21st century, see Chapter 25.)

You've got mail!

In the early 1960s, some American scientists began kicking around the idea of a computer system, using research computers called *nodes*, which could continue to function even in the event of a nuclear war. That possibility was of keen interest to the Pentagon, which financed much of the work.

The result, in late 1969, was the birth of the Internet, which led to e-mail, which led to a communications revolution. By the late 1990s, virtually every part of the world was linked to every other part. Americans alone sent an estimated 2.2 billion e-mail messages *per day,* or about 7 times the number of pieces of first-class mail. By the start of the new century, it was estimated that e-mail messages had replaced 25 percent of what was now referred to as "snail mail."

REMEMBER

But the Internet, which gave birth to a network of information sources called the World Wide Web, did far more than make it easier to check in on Grandma or chat with Uncle Louie in the old country. It allowed businesses to reduce their costs and be more efficient by instantly knowing how much inventory they needed to keep on hand, how much of a product they needed to make, and who could supply them with the raw materials and needed parts.

Retail customers could comparison-shop in businesses across the country and around the world — and they did. Online shopping for the Christmas holidays in 1999 was estimated at $7.3 billion. In 2000, it had jumped to more than $12 billion. By 2017, it had soared to a staggering $108.2 billion.

A PAWN FOR DEEP BLUE

Garry Kasparov didn't offer to shake hands after winning a chess match in February 1996. It wasn't just Kasparov's well-known arrogance: His opponent had no arms. Kasparov, the world chess champion since 1985, had beaten IBMRS/6000SP, a computer christened *Deep Blue* by its IBM Corporation designers.

The win was called a victory for man over machine, and Kasparov readily agreed to a rematch the following year. It was a bad move for the grandmaster. On May 11, 1997, Kasparov stormed out of a small room in New York City after being soundly thrashed by the computer, which had been considerably tweaked since the first match and could analyze 200 million possible moves in a second.

Kasparov was a sore loser. Much more gracious was Ken Jennings, a champion of the TV quiz show *Jeopardy!,* after Jennings and another human contestant lost a 2011 match to a room-sized IBM computer named Watson.

"I, for one, welcome our new computer overlords," Jennings jokingly wrote on his video screen at the end of the game.

The computer revolution had impacts far beyond shopping and business. It led to amazing advances in medicine and biological research. It led to a very real reduction in the time and space between America and the rest of the world, creating a true global economy.

Trading under a global economy

The *global economy* — an economy that closely tied together the production and consumer patterns of many nations — was created not only by the development of information-sharing technologies but also by many countries dropping trade barriers and opening their markets to the rest of the world.

One of the effects of the global economy was the creation of a wave of mega-mergers among big corporations from different countries: Daimler Benz of Germany with Chrysler in automobiles, British Petroleum of England with Amoco in oil. The bigger companies promised, and often delivered, more efficiencies, better products, and lower prices.

But there were drawbacks. The intertwining of economies meant America was more affected by downturns in other parts of the world than it had been before. International products were often more attractive to American consumers than their U.S.-made counterparts, and the country's trade deficit steadily rose — from $155 billion in 1997 to $299 billion in 1999.

REMEMBER

And many U.S. companies exported jobs as well as products by transferring their manufacturing operations to countries where the cost of labor was much lower. In Thailand, for example, a worker might be paid $2 for a nine-hour day making footwear, or a worker in Haiti might be paid $2.50 a day to make shirts. But though critics complained that such outsourcing was exploiting foreign workers, the companies responded that the wages were fair by third-world standards and helped the countries build their own manufacturing bases.

Most Americans weren't complaining. In 1997, the average U.S. family's annual income passed $40,000 for the first time. The number of people below the poverty level set by the federal government fell to 11.8 percent, the lowest since 1979, and the poverty rates among African Americans and Asian Americans fell to their lowest levels ever. Even Congress couldn't spend fast enough to keep up. The federal budget went from having an annual deficit of $300 billion at the beginning of the decade to a surplus of $123 billion at the end.

And because it was so easy to spend money, Americans did it with enthusiasm. Savings rates dropped to almost nothing by the end of the decade, leaving many Americans in a precarious position if the economy went into a tailspin.

Which, as you can see in Chapter 22, it did.

5

Facing the New Millennium

Chapter **21**

Terror Comes Home; America Goes to War(s)

s the 21st century began, the United States found itself the Big Kahuna on an increasingly shrinking planet. Technological innovations occurred at a geometric pace and jumped national boundary lines. That helped create an even more tightly knit global economy. Environmental and political problems also crossed borders, all of which added up to the fact that the world's troubles were inescapably America's, and vice versa.

This chapter covers one of the closest presidential elections ever, two wars, the most horrific terrorist attack in modern history, and a pretty nasty natural disaster or two. It was a bumpy start for the new century.

Whew! A Squeaker: Bush and Gore, 2000

One was the son of a former president; the other was the son of a former U.S. senator. By the time the 2000 presidential election campaign was over, George W. Bush and Al Gore had staged a race that was a son of a gun.

Gore, the offspring of former Tennessee Sen. Al Gore, Sr. and a former senator himself, had served dutifully, if a bit distantly, for eight years as vice president to

Bill Clinton and was the obvious choice to succeed Clinton as the Democratic Party's standard-bearer.

Bush, the governor of Texas and the son of the 41st president, George H. W. Bush, was a former oil man and major league baseball executive. The younger Bush parlayed his familiar name and financial backing from much of the Republican establishment to win the GOP nomination, after beating back a challenge from Arizona Sen. John McCain.

The campaign was a roller-coaster affair. Gore tried to run on the positive aspects of the Clinton administration while taking pains not to be too closely associated with Clinton himself, who was viewed as damaged political goods because of the Lewinsky scandal and his subsequent impeachment.

Bush dubbed himself a "compassionate conservative" and focused on the need for a "new morality" in the White House. He also criticized the Clinton administration's military intervention in the Balkans and Somalia, contending that the U.S. military shouldn't be used for "nation building" elsewhere. By the time Election Day arrived, polls showed the two were neck and neck.

Hanging chads and butterfly ballots

It all came down to Florida. Outside the Sunshine State, Gore had captured (or would capture) 266 of the 270 electoral votes needed to win the White House. Bush had 246. It appeared at first that Gore had won Florida's 25 electoral votes, giving him the presidency. But as the night of November 7 turned into the morning of November 8, it looked like Bush had won. TV networks that had originally projected Gore as the winner reversed themselves and declared Bush the winner. Around 2 a.m., Gore called Bush to concede. Around 4 a.m., he called back to withdraw his concession.

And the confusion was just getting warmed up. Over the next 35 days, both sides engaged in a titanic legal struggle over whether recounts should occur and, if so, which votes should be recounted. Ballots where voters had failed to completely punch out the little cardboard squares — and therefore left *hanging chads* — were challenged.

So were *butterfly ballots* that had candidates' names on one page and the punch holes on another, leading to voter confusion. A post-election study of ballots in Palm Beach County found that more than 8,000 voters had punched holes for Gore *and* for one of two minor party candidates.

REMEMBER

The whole mess eventually went to the U.S. Supreme Court. On December 12, the court voted 5–4 to reverse a decision by the Florida Supreme Court that would have continued the recounts. The next day, Gore conceded.

Post-election scrutinizing

Gore's concession ended an election filled with ironies and what-ifs. Gore had won the popular vote by about 500,000 votes out of about 100 million cast. It was only the fourth time in U.S. history that the popular vote winner didn't win the White House (1824, 1876, and 1888 were the others). If Gore had only won his home state of Tennessee or Clinton's home state of Arkansas, he would have won. If Green Party candidate Ralph Nader hadn't been on the Florida ballot, most of his 97,000 votes may have gone to Gore.

Post-election studies by several major newspapers found that if the recount had been limited to only the counties in which Gore had sought recounts, Bush still would have won. But if all the disputed ballots throughout the state had been recounted, Gore would have won.

REMEMBER

As something of a consolation prize, Gore won the 2007 Nobel Peace Prize for his work in bringing attention to the role of humans in global warming. A film that he narrated on the same topic also won an Academy Award for best documentary. Bush, meanwhile, got the job his dad had held eight years before — and some of the same headaches.

Bush came into office with slightly more than half of the voters preferring someone else and with polls showing that more than half the country thought the Supreme Court's decision was politically motivated. That's hardly anyone's idea of a good way to start an administration.

But Americans don't hold a grudge for long. By April 2001, polls were showing that though only 50 percent thought Bush had won fair and square, 59 percent said they supported him, and 62 percent approved of the way he was handling the job. (Of course, it didn't hurt that Bush had started his tenure by proposing a $1.6 trillion tax-cut package.) The new president also unveiled an ambitious energy program that called for relaxing environmental protections in favor of aggressively expanding fossil-fuel development.

But less than nine months into his administration, Bush faced a crisis that would put most domestic programs on the back burner, define his presidency, and change the way many Americans thought about their own security.

A Nation Stunned

At 8:46 (EDT) on the morning of September 11, 2001, a hijacked commercial jet crashed into the North Tower of the World Trade Center in New York City. Seventeen minutes later, a second hijacked passenger jet flew into the center's South Tower (see Figure 21-1). Both towers soon collapsed, pulling down or heavily damaging surrounding buildings.

At 9:37, a third jet plowed into the Pentagon in Washington, D.C., followed 26 minutes later by the crash of a fourth flight into a field about 70 miles southeast of Pittsburgh, Pennsylvania. It appeared passengers aboard the fourth plane, having learned of the fate of the other three through cellphone calls, confronted the hijackers before the plane could reach its intended target, which was believed to have been the Capitol in Washington, D.C.

FIGURE 21-1: Devastation at the World Trade Center.

© AFP/Getty Images

The United States had suffered the worst attack on its soil in its history, and the country plunged into a war against terrorism.

Al-Qaeda and Osama bin Laden

The attacks, carried out by 19 members of a fundamentalist Islamist group called *Al-Qaeda* ("the base"), killed a total of about 3,000 people, including 415 New York City police and firefighters who responded to the disaster at the World Trade Center. More than 6,000 people were injured.

Americans — and much of the rest of the world — were shocked. Millions had watched horrified as TV cameras that had been focusing on the North Tower after the first attack captured the second plane hitting the South Tower. The subsequent collapse of the towers was also carried live. National, state, and local officials scrambled to prepare for more attacks. Air travel was shut down. Stock markets in the United States and around the world were badly shaken and posted severe losses.

On September 17, President Bush formally identified Al-Qaeda leader Osama bin Laden as the mastermind behind the attacks. A wealthy member of a prominent Saudi Arabian family, bin Laden had operated out of Afghanistan since the mid-1990s, under the protection of a group called the Taliban. The *Taliban* (which means "student") followed an extreme version of Islamic law and had seized control in Afghanistan in 1998.

Taking on the Taliban

Speaking to a joint session of Congress on September 20, Bush demanded the Taliban hand over bin Laden and other Al-Qaeda leaders and dismantle terrorist training camps within Afghanistan. "They will hand over the terrorists or share their fate," Bush warned.

On October 7, after Taliban leaders had rejected Bush's demands, U.S. and British aircraft unleashed a massive bombing attack on major Afghan cities. By mid-November, the Afghan capital of Kabul had fallen. By mid-December, air attacks coupled with allied nations' ground forces that included about 30,000 troops from the United States and anti-Taliban Afghan militia had toppled the Taliban regime.

While out of power, the Taliban was not out of business. After a year of licking their wounds, Taliban forces began an insurgency. Their efforts were fueled by funds from control of much of Afghanistan's vast production of poppies from which opium was manufactured. It was the nation's largest cash crop, providing most of the world's opium and 400,000 Afghans with work. The enemy also took advantage of safe havens in mountainous areas along the Afghanistan-Pakistan border by scampering into Pakistan, where it was logistically and politically difficult for U.S. troops to follow.

President Barack Obama, Bush's successor, countered in 2009 by gradually building U.S. forces to more than 100,000 while warning that "our troop commitment in Afghanistan cannot be open-ended." By mid-2013, U.S. forces were down to 65,000, and by the end of 2016, 8,400. The number climbed to 14,000 by mid-2018 under President Donald Trump, however, with no indication that a complete withdrawal would happen in the foreseeable future.

Bin Laden was killed by Navy SEALs in his Pakistan hiding place in May 2011, and Taliban leader Mullah Mohammad Omar died two years later, apparently of tuberculosis. But after suffering more than 2,300 military deaths, spending at least $1 *trillion*, and fighting for three times longer than it had in World War II, the prognosis for peace in Afghanistan remained, at best, uncertain.

Fighting terrorism on the home front

The Bush administration never formally declared war on Afghanistan (which allowed it to claim it didn't have to treat those captured as prisoners of war). But it did declare war on terrorism, and Bush proclaimed the war would continue and be fought on every front "until every terrorist group of global reach has been found, stopped, and defeated."

REMEMBER

A month after the 9/11 attacks, as they came to be known, Bush proposed something called the "Uniting and Strengthening America by Providing Appropriate Tools Required to Intercept and Obstruct Terrorism Act" — or the USA Patriot Act.

The far-reaching "temporary" act (most of which was made permanent by Congress in 2006) greatly expanded the authority of the FBI and other law enforcement agencies to conduct searches, look at medical and other personal records (such as what materials an individual took out from public libraries), and spy without court approval on those suspected of potential terrorist acts. It also allowed foreigners to be held for up to seven days without charges or deportation proceedings.

The act was approved 357–66 in the House of Representatives. In the Senate, the vote was 98–1, with only Sen. Russell Feingold, D-WI, opposed.

In July 2002, Bush secretly authorized the National Security Agency (NSA) to listen in on phone calls American citizens made to other countries and to monitor e-mails. (See Chapter 25 for more on the NSA and electronic surveillance.) The order wasn't made public until 2005, and Congress didn't sanction the actions until 2008. In November, Bush signed a bill creating the Department of Homeland Security, consolidating dozens of government agencies, from the Secret Service to the Coast Guard, into one super-agency.

TERROR WITH A STAMP ON IT

If the events of September 11 weren't enough to stamp the word *terrorism* firmly in the minds of Americans, some letters postmarked September 18 from Trenton, New Jersey, finished the job.

The letters, to NBC News and the *New York Post,* contained a note bearing the date "9-11-01" and a short note. They also contained spores of anthrax, a nasty bacterial disease. Similar letters were apparently received at ABC News and CBS News in New York and the *National Enquirer* in Boca Raton, Florida, because people at those organizations were also exposed to anthrax. A few weeks later, anthrax-bearing letters addressed to U.S. senators Tom Daschle of South Dakota and Patrick Leahy of Vermont were found.

By the end of November, 22 people who either worked at the targeted sites or worked for the postal service had contracted the disease. Five of them died. Americans became nervous about something as mundane as opening the mail. Government officials issued dozens of warnings, while emergency personnel practiced responding to any bioterrorism and chemical attacks.

In late July 2008, Bruce E. Ivins, a longtime researcher at the federal biodefense lab at Ft. Detrick, Maryland, committed suicide. Within a week, federal prosecutors announced Ivins was the man behind the attacks and had acted alone. Some of Ivins's colleagues, however, doubted he had done it, and no convincing motive was established. The attacks remain ample fodder for conspiracy theorists everywhere.

Imprisoning "non-POWs" at Guantanamo Bay

Because America had not actually declared war against Afghanistan, it didn't treat captured Al-Qaeda and Taliban fighters as prisoners of war (POWs). Instead, they were taken to a prison erected on the U.S. Naval base at Guantanamo Bay on the island of Cuba. Administration officials contended that because the prison wasn't on U.S. soil, the prisoners had no rights and could be held indefinitely without trial or even formal charges being filed.

REMEMBER

In 2004, international observers reported some of the detainees at Guantanamo had been subjected to what the U.S. Central Intelligence Agency (CIA) referred to as "enhanced interrogation techniques," which the observers characterized as "tantamount to torture." One such technique, called *waterboarding,* consisted of covering a person's face with a towel and then pouring water over it, creating a sensation like drowning. It was also revealed that the CIA had abducted suspected terrorists and held them in secret prisons in Europe.

Defending controversial tactics

Civil libertarians complained that such actions were counter to American ideals and violated basic human rights. But administration officials, notably Vice President Dick Cheney, defended the practices as justifiable and necessary to fight terrorism. They also pointed out that no terrorist attacks had occurred on U.S. soil since September 11, while several terrorist plots had been sniffed out and stopped.

In 2008, Congress approved a bill to ban some of the interrogation methods used, but Bush vetoed it. Of the 780 people held at the detention camp, most were eventually released without charges being filed or repatriated to other countries. When Bush left office, an estimated 242 prisoners were still at Guantanamo.

His successor, Barack Obama, had promised during his campaign to close the base and repeated variations of that pledge in subsequent years. Shortly after taking office in January 2009, he signed an executive order closing down the CIA's secret prisons in other countries. But Congress repeatedly blocked efforts to completely close Guantanamo, and as of late 2018, 40 prisoners still remained there.

That Damn Saddam

With his approval ratings as high as 90 percent in some polls after the 9/11 attacks and U.S. retaliation in Afghanistan, Bush made the war on terror the centerpiece of his administration's efforts. And with the overthrow of the Taliban at least temporarily accomplished, the administration turned its attention to an old nemesis: Iraqi dictator Saddam Hussein.

The United States, under the first President Bush, had decided in 1991 not to prolong the Gulf War by seeking Saddam's ouster. But it did persuade the United Nations to impose economic sanctions against Iraq, as well as to monitor the country's clandestine development of nuclear, biological, and chemical weapons, known collectively as *weapons of mass destruction* (WMD).

In 1998, after Iraqi officials had consistently interfered with UN inspectors, President Clinton ordered the bombing of several Iraqi military installations. Iraq countered by banning the UN inspectors. Moreover, the impact of economic sanctions had waned as some countries quietly resumed trading goods for Iraqi oil.

Toughening the stance against Iraq

In 2002, the second President Bush began demanding that the UN toughen its dealings with Iraq. Bush argued the Iraqis had, or were close to having, weapons of mass destruction. Further, he said, they were harboring members of the Al-Qaeda terrorist group that had engineered the 9/11 attacks. On October 10 and 11, Congress approved a resolution authorizing the use of military force against Iraq. The vote was 297–133 in the House and 77–23 in the Senate.

On February 5, 2003, U.S. Secretary of State Colin Powell went before the UN Security Council to restate American claims about WMDs, displaying aerial photographs of purported chemical weapons sites and mobile nerve gas labs. "Ladies and gentlemen, these are sophisticated facilities," Powell said. "For example, they can produce anthrax and botulinum toxin — in fact, they can produce enough dry biological agent to kill thousands upon thousands of people." Powell was countered by UN inspectors who said they were again making progress with Iraq and had found no evidence of WMDs.

On March 17, 2003 — despite the objections of U.S. allies, such as France and Germany, but with the backing of most of Congress — an undeterred Bush issued an ultimatum that gave Saddam 48 hours to resign and get out of Iraq. When he didn't, U.S. and British forces on March 20 launched air attacks on Iraqi targets, including a bunker in which Saddam was thought to be meeting with aides.

The U.S. invasion

Within days, U.S. forces invaded from neighboring Kuwait. By April 9, the Iraqi capital of Baghdad had fallen. Saddam's sons were killed, and Saddam went into hiding. He was captured in December and turned over to Iraqi authorities. On December 30, 2006, he was executed.

The ongoing war

On May 1, Bush landed on a U.S. aircraft carrier off the coast of San Diego and declared an end to major combat. Standing in front of a large banner proclaiming "Mission Accomplished," Bush told the crew that "because of you, the target has fallen, and Iraq is free. The war on terror is not over, yet it is not endless. We do not know the day of final victory, but we have seen the turning of the tide."

But if the tide had turned, it seemed to have turned the wrong way. The United States lacked a comprehensive postwar plan for rebuilding the country. Looting and riots dismantled much of Iraq's infrastructure and damaged public buildings. U.S. occupation leaders barred members of Saddam's Baath Party from serving in the provisional government and largely disbanded the Iraqi army. That resulted in a dearth of experienced political leaders and military officers to help with the country's reconstruction.

REMEMBER

In the aftermath, guerrilla warfare caused far more casualties than the brief war had, and fighting between militias of the rival Islamic Sunni and Shiite sects threatened to plunge the country into civil war. Worse for Bush, an intensive search failed to turn up any weapons of mass destruction, and it became clear that Saddam had almost no connection with Al-Qaeda.

Losing popularity at home

At home, the war had quickly lost popularity after its initial successes had given way to a protracted fight. In 2004, Bush won reelection over U.S. Sen. John Kerry of Massachusetts by the narrowest margin of any incumbent president since Woodrow Wilson in 1916. In 2006, public dissatisfaction with the progress of the wars in Afghanistan and Iraq helped Democrats wrest control of both houses of Congress for the first time since 1994.

In January 2007, with no light visible at the end of the dark Iraqi tunnel, Bush announced he was sending in 21,500 more U.S. troops, for a total of 170,000, in an effort to quell the almost ceaseless violence in the country. In what was called "the Surge" strategy, he also announced renewed U.S. efforts to rebuild Iraq's infrastructure and economy.

Although U.S. military deaths reached 907 in 2007, the highest of any year, they dropped to 284 in the first 10 months of 2008. While administration officials claimed the decline was proof the Surge was working, critics contended it was due to the Shiite militia having largely defeated the Sunni and to insurgent forces adopting a strategy of waiting until U.S. forces began withdrawing.

In February 2009, new President Barack Obama announced U.S. combat troops would pull out of Iraq by the end of August 2010, which they did. Thousands of American military "advisers," however, remained for another year. On December 15, 2011, Secretary of Defense Leon Panetta officially declared the war over.

The eight-year war had cost the United States about 4,400 military personnel killed, more than 32,000 wounded, and at least $1 trillion. And the "investment" was by no means complete.

By mid-2014, large areas of Iraq were under attack by a radical group calling itself the Islamic State. Also known as ISIS, the group used the guise of religious fundamentalism as an excuse to murder, rape, loot, vandalize, enslave, and terrorize much of the Middle East. At least 5,000 U.S. troops were redeployed to Iraq, and helped Iraqi forces drive most ISIS fighters out of the country by the end of 2017.

Meanwhile, in the Rest of the World . . .

As the wars in Afghanistan and Iraq dragged on, America was waging wars of words with other countries. In 2002, Bush had labeled Iran and North Korea, along with Iraq, as parts of an "Axis of Evil."

The primary beef with North Korea was the country's defiant insistence in developing its nuclear weapons program. After several years of public posturing and private negotiating, North Korea formally agreed in June 2008 to halt its program in return for the easing of economic sanctions against it.

But the agreement didn't last. In April 2009, North Korea launched a rocket that was believed to be part of a test of the country's nuclear missile capabilities. Later that year, and again in 2013, North Korean leaders announced they had conducted successful nuclear tests. The announcements were surrounded by a flurry of bellicose threats of war against the United States and South Korea. At the center of the country's bellicosity was its dictator, 30-year-old Kim Jong-un, who assumed power after his father, Kim Jong-il, died in December 2011.

The younger Kim, a ruthless despot who loved American basketball and routinely had people killed — including a brother and an uncle — when they crossed him, would prove to be every bit as much of a problem for the United States and the rest of the world as his father had.

Iran was another thorny problem. Bush administration officials insisted Iran was aiding the insurgency in neighboring Iraq by arming the insurgents and was developing a nuclear weapons program that further threatened the already unstable region. Although evidence as to the exact status of the Iranian nuclear program was conflicting, the administration viewed Iran as a real threat to the region's stability.

So did much of the rest of the world. In 2015, representatives of the United States, France, Britain, Russia, China, Germany, and the European Union negotiated a deal with Iranian leaders. If Iran would give up its nuclear aspirations, the other countries would ease financial sanctions against Iran that had crippled that nation's economy.

Critics warned Iranian leaders could not be trusted to follow through on their end of the deal, and that "sunset" clauses in the agreement meant certain parts of the deal would expire in future years. That, critics argued, would at best only postpone, not end, Iran's nuclear aspirations.

OPRAH WINFREY

In nearly every field of human endeavor, there are individuals who are so dominant that they're instantly recognized by just their first name. In rock 'n' roll, it's *Elvis*. In soccer, it's *Pelé*. For nearly everything else, it's *Oprah*. Born in 1954 to an unwed teenage mother, Winfrey was raised in poverty by various relatives. Following college, Winfrey became host of a daytime TV talk show in Maryland and then moved to Chicago in 1984. From 1986 to 2011, she hosted a nationally syndicated program that launched her into a highly varied — and highly lucrative — career. Winfrey became an Academy Award-nominated actress, a movie and TV producer, a magazine publisher, an author, and an arbiter of America's popular tastes.

All that made Winfrey a billionaire several times over and one of the world's most generous philanthropists. It's estimated that through 2013, she had given more than $400 million to various educational programs and raised or donated tens of millions more for other causes.

She also became extremely influential. For example, she was once sued by Texas cattlemen for saying on her show that she wouldn't eat another hamburger because of mad cow disease. The cattlemen claimed her remarks drove down the price of beef. (A Texas jury sided with Winfrey.) In 2013, *Forbes* magazine named Winfrey the world's most powerful celebrity, and *Vanity Fair* magazine suggested she had more cultural influence than any politician or religious leader "except perhaps the Pope." Of course, he's known by his first name only, too.

Winds and Losses

While the war on terrorism dominated Bush's presidency, he did attempt to make changes on domestic issues as well. In 2001, Bush proposed an ambitious education reform program called the *No Child Left Behind Act*. Approved by Congress, the plan boosted federal education funding; increased standards expected of schools, including annual reading and math skills testing; and gave parents more flexibility in choosing schools. The program was variously praised for making schools more accountable and criticized for forcing educators to take cookie-cutter approaches to teaching.

After more than a decade of arguing about it, the program was replaced in 2015 by the Every Student Succeeds Act, which gave states more flexibility in setting standards for testing and measuring schools' and students' progress.

In late 2003, Bush pushed a plan through Congress to reform Medicare, the federal health insurance program for the elderly. The plan gave senior citizens more choices when picking a private insurance plan through which they received medical services, as well as in obtaining prescription drugs.

Bush had far less success in trying to reform Social Security and U.S. immigration policies. He proposed replacing the government-run pension program with a system of private savings accounts. But the plan died in the face of criticism that it would put too much of a burden on individuals and be too expensive in the transition.

Bush also supported a bipartisan plan that would allow an estimated 12 million illegal immigrants to remain in the country on a temporary basis and to apply for citizenship after returning to their own countries and paying a fine. The plan was crushed by the weight of opposition from those who thought it was too draconian and those who thought it was too soft.

But all the blustery rhetoric in Washington was like a gentle summer breeze when compared to a natural disaster that blew into the South.

Big blow in the Big Easy

On August 23, 2005, a hurricane formed over the Bahamas and headed toward the southeastern United States. Called *Katrina*, it crossed Florida, picked up strength over the Gulf of Mexico, and made landfall in southeast Louisiana on August 29.

While Katrina's 125-mile-per-hour winds — sending beds flying out of hotel windows — and 10 inches of rain were bad enough, a storm surge of more than 28 feet devastated the Mississippi coastal cities of Gulfport and Biloxi. But the greatest damage was reserved for the region's largest city — New Orleans.

Nicknamed the *Big Easy*, most of New Orleans is below sea level. Under Katrina's onslaught, levees that were supposed to protect the city gave way in more than 50 places, and 80 percent of the city was flooded. While most of New Orleans's 1.2 million residents were evacuated (many to the city of Houston, Texas), thousands either refused to leave or could not (see Figure 21-2).

The disaster claimed more than 1,800 lives and destroyed 200,000 homes. Damage estimates ranged as high as $125 billion, making it the most expensive hurricane in U.S. history. It wasn't until October 11 that the last of the floodwaters were pumped out.

FIGURE 21-2:
The aftermath
of Hurricane
Katrina.

© AFP/Getty Images

REMEMBER

By then, a hurricane of criticism had whipped up over the federal government's response to the disaster. The criticism ranged from condemning the government's slow response in some areas with regard to the evacuation process to providing adequate temporary housing after the storm. There were also charges that the slow response was due in part to the fact that many of New Orleans's residents were poor African Americans. Bush's approval ratings sank to the lowest of his presidency. But they would go even lower.

Ike hits Texas

In September 2008, New Orleans was again evacuated when threatened by Hurricane Gustav. This time, the preparations and responses were better, and the levees held. But on the heels of Gustav came Ike.

The hurricane hit the Gulf Coast of Texas on September 13, dragging up a massive storm surge that drowned much of the city of Galveston. The storm killed 82 in the United States, with as many as 200 people missing, and did an estimated $27 billion worth of property damage.

Once again, the federal government was criticized for its post-storm performance. Texas officials complained that the Federal Emergency Management Agency (FEMA) had been slow to provide housing for those left homeless by the hurricane and to provide funds for cleaning up the mess. "The response from Washington has been pretty underwhelming," Texas Gov. Rick Perry said in mid-November, two months after the storm. "This is really irritating."

But hurricanes, and even irritated governors, paled in the face of another kind of storm, an economic tempest that enveloped the nation and most of the rest of the world.

Chapter **22**

Recessions Can Be Really Depressing

An old economists' joke (told mainly by old economists) says that a *recession* is when your neighbor loses his job, and a *depression* is when you lose yours. Whatever you call it, the country's unsettled financial situation as the new century unfolded permeated nearly every aspect of Americans' lives, from politics to lifestyles to how Americans got along with the rest of the world — and one another.

In this chapter, I look at the web of elements that ensnared the economy; the impacts that technology, global competition, and corporate profits had on employment; the government's efforts to fix things; and the growing gap between the very richest Americans and everyone else.

Ouch! The Economy Stubs Its Toe

Here's what happened to the U.S. economy in the first years of the 21st century: A lot of people got rich (and then poor) creating and/or investing in high-tech companies. Then people in California bought homes they couldn't afford. And then Iceland went broke. And thus America had what has been called the *Great Recession*.

Of course, that interpretation is way too simple; there really isn't a linear, cause-effect explanation. The recession was actually a lot of causes and effects linked together. Think of it as sort of a spider's web of events and results.

Dot-com dreams and investor nightmares

As the 20th century ended and the 21st century began, there was an explosion of technological innovation, much of it centering on the Internet. This innovation was heralded as the gateway to a new economy, based on information-sharing as much as producing goods and services. And it triggered what was labeled the *dot-com boom.* Investors poured millions of dollars into hundreds of companies that were founded on great ideas but that often lacked sound business plans, large potential markets, and in some cases, even a product or service to sell.

This situation was an example of what Alan Greenspan, the chairman of the Federal Reserve Board, had labeled in 1996 as *irrational exuberance:* when investors' enthusiasm to make dollars overwhelms their common sense. By March 2001, the dot-com bubble had burst. Scores of companies went belly up, their stocks became worthless, and America had its first economic recession in a decade. The terrorist attacks on September 11 of that year also dealt a sharp blow to the economy.

The dot-com bubble-bursting recession was fairly mild. But some economists were still troubled. Although the overall economy began improving by the end of 2001, unemployment rates that had risen when the recession began stubbornly refused to go down again to anything near their previous levels.

The houses that went upside down

A much nastier recession — in fact, the worst the country had suffered since the Great Depression of the 1930s — began with another bubble bursting in late 2007. This one was centered on the American dream of owning your own home and came about partly because of something called *credit default swaps.*

Under federal law, banks and other lending institutions have to keep lots of capital in reserve to protect investors if any of the big loans the lenders make go bad. To free up those reserves so they can be used to turn a profit elsewhere, the lending industry came up with a sort of insurance policy in the 1990s, called a *credit default swap*. It involved having a third party — individual investors, insurance companies, hedge funds, and so on — assume the risk of a loan going bad in return for regular payments from the firm that had actually made the loan.

The federal government didn't regulate the deals, so no one had a good handle on how widespread they were or which companies and economic sectors were most at risk. By the middle of the decade, the arrangements had morphed into more than $60 trillion — that's *trillion*, with a *t* — of swaps, and banks and other lenders had trillions of dollars to lend to people who, say, wanted to buy a house.

Buying up houses

In the late 1990s, interest rates were low, and real estate was an attractive investment. Americans began buying homes like crazy. Annual U.S. home sales set records for five straight years, peaking at 7.5 million in 2005. The greater the demand, the higher real estate prices went. Average home prices soared from less than $200,000 in 2000 to more than $300,000 in 2007.

But as prices climbed, fewer people could qualify for mortgage loans, at least under traditional methods of measuring qualifications, such as whether the borrower had enough income to make the payments.

So lenders and mortgage brokers got creative. They pushed loans with no down payments, loans that started out with low interest rates and then ballooned after a few years, and loans on which the borrower paid only interest for the first few years. By 2005, more than 200 kinds of mortgage products were available. And if there came a time when the borrowers couldn't meet the mortgage payments, heck, they could just refinance or sell the house for more than they paid for it and walk away with a profit. The risky mortgages boomed from about $160 billion in 2001 to more than $600 billion four years later.

There was even a bonus for people who could afford their mortgage payments: Their homes became giant piggy banks! They could borrow on the equity in their homes and buy a new car or pay for Junior's college. And *flipping* — buying a house, fixing it up, and reselling it for hefty profits — became a hip way to get rich quick, as long as prices kept rising.

Meanwhile, the new mortgages were pooled and sold by the lenders, as investment bonds, to commercial banks, mutual funds, pension funds, and investors all over the world. And the bonds were "insured" by credit default swaps issued by many of Wall Street's largest financial institutions.

Defaults and foreclosures

The housing market was fine for a while, but then it cooled off — big time. Sales of all homes sagged from a record 7.5 million in 2005 to an estimated 4.9 million in 2008, a 35 percent drop. Sales of brand-new homes dropped even more precipitously, from more than 1.2 million in 2005 to slightly more than 300,000 by 2011.

Millions found their gimmicky mortgages had caught up with them. They couldn't make their payments, and they owed more than they could sell their houses for — hence the term *upside down* mortgages. So they defaulted — big time. Between July and September 2008 alone, foreclosure notices were sent to 766,000 U.S. homes. A quarter of those were in California, where housing prices had climbed the fastest and came down the same way. Median housing prices across the nation dropped about 10 percent in 2008 compared to 2007 — and more than 30 percent in California.

Mortgage-based bonds went in the tank, and big lenders faced making good on hundreds of billions of dollars in credit default swaps. Some couldn't, and they declared bankruptcy or were bought up by other firms.

DEPRESSION? RECESSION? BROKE?

Never mind the old economists' joke at the beginning of this chapter; here's a more technical explanation of the difference between a recession and a depression: An *economic recession* occurs when a country's *gross domestic product* (GDP) — that's the value of all the country's reported goods and services — goes down for two consecutive quarters (six consecutive months) or more. A *depression* happens when the GDP drops by 10 percent or more.

During America's Great Depression, which stretched over a decade, the GDP dropped a whopping 27 percent between 1929 and 1933 and another 18 percent between 1937 and 1938. In contrast, in the new century's worst year, 2008, the GDP decreased "only" 2.8 percent. In fact, the Great Recession officially only lasted from December 2007 to June 2009, according to the National Bureau of Economic Research, which is the private, nonprofit organization of economists that has kept official track of such things since 1920.

Still, the Great Recession of 2007 is considered by most economists to be the worst of the ten recessions America has suffered since World War II because of its duration, worldwide scope, and stubborn refusal to go away and take all its effects and impacts with it.

Credit dries up, spending shrinks, Iceland sinks

As the financial institutions foundered, lending dried up in other parts of the economy, from car loans to credit card limits. People who had relied on equity in their homes to pay for their boats or college tuition suddenly had no equity. So consumer spending shrunk, which caused businesses to cut back, often resulting in massive layoffs. The nation's unemployment rate doubled, from 5 percent in January 2008 to 10 percent by October 2009. At one point an average of 750,000 people per month were losing their jobs.

And because the U.S. market was the dominant force in the world economy, other countries felt the pain. In Iceland, for example, the government was forced to nationalize the country's three major banks. The banks relied heavily on foreign investment. When the world's credit markets became tight, the Icelandic banks ran short on funds to meet their obligations. And it wasn't just Iceland. The recession spread around the world, which in turn meant less foreign investment and business for the United States.

Brother, Can You Spare a Job?

The most vexing effect of the Great Recession was its swollen jobless numbers. Prior to December 2008, America's monthly unemployment rate had not been *above* 7 percent since June 1993. From December 2008 through November 2013, however, it never went *below* 7.3 percent. And that figure didn't include Americans who were *underemployed* and could find only part-time work or who gave up looking altogether. People were out of work longer, new jobs were being created at a frustratingly slow pace, and many companies found they could make do with fewer employees.

Looking for work. And looking . . .

In November 2013, *The New York Times* ran a story about a 53-year-old Massachusetts woman who had been unemployed most of the time since 2008. A college graduate, she had been turned down for dozens of low-paying, low-skill positions for reasons that included "too pretty," "too articulate," and because "we don't hire the unemployed."

She was far from alone in her lengthy quest for work. By November 2013, more than 4 million people, defined as the *long-term unemployed*, had been out of work for longer than 26 weeks. That was triple the number of long-term jobless before the recession began and 50 percent more than the highest figure in any of America's other recessions since World War II.

In July 2008, Congress approved extending unemployment benefits from 26 weeks to as long as 99 weeks and subsequently approved further extensions. But the extensions came with a $250 billion price tag, and there was growing congressional opposition to continuing the program indefinitely. Some economists suggested extending benefits had exacerbated the problem by serving as an incentive for jobless people not to actively seek work and a disincentive for employers to create new jobs.

Where the work went

An estimated 9.1 million jobs had either been lost or not created as expected during the Great Recession and its aftermath. To create enough new jobs to replace them required plugging the holes through which they had leaked.

One of the holes was *outsourcing,* or the transfer of jobs by American companies to other countries with lower costs of doing business. The Department of Commerce reported that from 2000 to 2012, the largest U.S. multinational corporations cut their domestic workforces by 2.9 million while increasing their foreign payrolls by 2.4 million. The outsourcing issue was hotly debated during the 2012 presidential race, with each candidate accusing the other of supporting the practice.

Many of the outsourced jobs were in manufacturing. Between 2000 and 2009, about 6 million U.S. factory jobs were lost, and only 520,000 had been recovered. Technological changes and automation also contributed to the loss.

Costs of providing benefits, such as meeting new federal healthcare mandates, were also a factor in reduced payrolls. (For more on this subject, see Chapter 23.) Employers with more than 49 workers faced fines if they didn't provide healthcare to full-time employees. Some companies responded by cutting workers to part-time status — or just cutting workers.

Another key factor was cutbacks by state and local governments. In previous recessions, public agencies had been quicker than the private sector to restore jobs. But by the end of 2013, state and local governments and schools still employed about 600,000 fewer people than they had four years earlier.

And as the recession waned, many companies found they could make more money by sharing less of it with employees. As workers scrambled to hold on to their jobs — forget about asking for a raise — productivity increased, which enabled employers to get by with fewer employees. A 2010 Northeastern University study found that while pretax corporate profits increased 57 percent from the end of 2008 to the beginning of 2010, wages decreased 2 percent. By the end of 2012, U.S. corporations had amassed a record $1.45 trillion in cash reserves, more than half of it stashed overseas to avoid U.S. taxes.

As the recession slowly eased, some of the jobs came back — and some didn't. An estimated 1.5 million U.S. manufacturing jobs that existed in 2007, for example, no longer existed in 2017. Moreover, some of the people who couldn't find work just gave up looking altogether. The country's labor participation level — the number of people working or actively seeking jobs — dropped from 67 percent in 2007 to 63 percent in 2018.

On the other hand, America's public sector workforce returned to its pre-recession level. And an average of 208,000 new jobs were created per month during the first nine months of 2018. But many of the new jobs were in industries that provided services — retail stores, restaurants, hotels. Those jobs generally paid less and provided fewer benefits than manufacturing jobs.

"We're from the Government; We're Here to Help . . . "

Perhaps because of lessons learned from the Great Depression of the 1930s, the federal government reacted quickly, if somewhat reluctantly, to the financial calamity. The U.S. Treasury Department seized the government-backed mortgage finance firms known as *Freddie Mac* and *Fannie Mae.* The government also bailed out American International Group (AIG), the nation's largest insurance company, but allowed Lehman Brothers, one of the country's largest savings and loan firms, to crash into bankruptcy.

On September 24, 2008, with his approval ratings wallowing below 30 percent, President Bush warned a national television audience that "the entire economy is in danger." The speech was part of an effort to sell Congress on a plan to bail out the teetering financial industry.

Known as the *Troubled Asset Relief Program* (TARP), the plan was to use $700 billion in taxpayer money to buy up the mortgage-backed securities of floundering financial institutions. "Without immediate action by Congress, America could slip into a financial panic," Bush said, "and a distressing scenario could unfold."

The scenario did unfold five days later, when a defiant House of Representatives rejected the Bush proposal. The U.S. stock market reacted with the biggest one-day point drop in its history. Two days later, the House reversed itself and approved a version of the bailout plan that the Senate had revised. The plan gave Treasury Secretary Henry Paulson wide latitude to use the money to shore up financial and mortgage institutions.

But to work, it would take time, and the bad economic news just kept coming. Toward the end of November, the stock market had sunk to its lowest level in more than a decade, dragging down pension plans and individual retirement accounts with it.

The crash dashed the dreams of millions of baby boomers (those born from 1946–1964), many of whom had counted on cashing in on healthy stock prices and soaring home values to finance an early retirement. Now they were desperately hoping to hold on to their jobs.

Brand new president, same old problems

In January 2009, President Bush handed off the crisis to his successor, Barack Obama. (For the lowdown on Obama and the 2008 presidential campaign, see Chapter 23.) Less than a month later, the new Democratic president and a Democrat-controlled Congress agreed to a sweeping — and expensive — plan to revive the economy and get as much of the country back to work as possible.

REMEMBER

The plan, known formally as the *American Recovery and Reinvestment Act of 2009* and informally as the *stimulus package,* called for spending $787 billion (which eventually climbed to $831 billion) on a combination of tax incentives; direct aid to states and local governments; public works projects; extensions of unemployment benefits and funding for job training; and infusions of cash for education, healthcare, housing, energy, and other programs.

The immediate goals of the act were to save jobs and create new ones; help prop up state and local government programs and services, such as those for public safety and education; and inject capital directly into the economy for public works projects that would encourage private investment.

The act's economic philosophy was rooted in the theories of John Maynard Keynes, a British economist who had been greatly influential in guiding the New Deal policies of President Franklin D. Roosevelt during the Great Depression. Keynes had argued that when recessions cause private spending to shrink, governments should spend more to make up the difference, combat unemployment, and prevent the economy from further decline.

"Today does not mark the end of our economic troubles," Obama said while signing the act in Denver on February 17, 2009. "Nor does it constitute all of what we must do to turn our economy around. But it does mark the beginning of the end."

As it turned out, the stimulus package wasn't a bad financial investment. Of the $631.4 billion in the package that consisted of loans or investments, the federal government got back $728.5 billion in refunds, dividends, and interest, for a profit of $97.1 billion. But by itself, it wasn't enough to right the economic ship.

Buying time by buying bonds

While the president and Congress were busy with bailouts and job-saving, another branch of the federal government was also looking for ways to keep U.S. finances afloat. First, some explanation.

Congress created the Federal Reserve System in 1913 in essence to function as the federal government's bank and oversee U.S. monetary policy. Among other things, "the Fed" sets the *federal funds rate,* which is the interest rate banks charge one another for short-term loans and which influences the rates of almost all other kinds of loans. That comes in handy during recessions because lower interest rates help keep the economy moving.

The Fed can also influence the nation's money supply by buying or selling securities, such as government bonds. If it wants to increase the amount of available money in recessionary times, for example, it buys bonds by crediting the reserves various banks must have on hand. That lets the banks lower their reserves and use the money to make money through loans and investments.

When the Great Recession hit, the Fed wielded its financial tools with frequency. Starting in late 2007, it cut the federal funds rate nine times in 15 months, dropping the rate from 4.75 percent to near zero, the lowest in its history. Moreover, it went on a bond-buying spree, averaging $85 billion a month by late 2013. Overall, the Fed's balance sheet rose from about $900 billion in mid-2008 to more than $3.7 trillion by the beginning of 2014.

"These purchases have made a meaningful contribution to economic growth and improving the outlook," Federal Reserve Board Vice Chair Janet Yellen told a congressional committee in November 2013. "A strong recovery will ultimately enable the Fed to reduce its monetary accommodation and reliance on unconventional policy tools such as asset purchases. I believe that supporting the recovery today is the surest path to returning to a more normal approach to monetary policy."

Did government intervention work?

The answer to the question "Did government intervention work?" is clear: It depends on whom you ask.

Even before much of the Bush/Obama plans were put in place or the Federal Reserve System's actions had taken hold, there was deeply divided debate on what kind of lifeline could rescue America's economy. A few weeks before the stimulus plan was approved, for example, a group of about 200 economists took out ads in national newspapers opposing it. A week after that, a similar-sized group of economists sent a letter to Congress endorsing the plan. (All of which brings to mind the famous quote by President Harry Truman: "Give me a one-handed economist! All my economists say 'on the one hand, on the other.'")

Some studies have suggested that the efforts saved or created more than 3 million jobs while keeping inflation in check. Other studies concluded they were only temporary fixes that would do more harm than good in the long run or had little effect. Some liberal economists contended that the efforts didn't go far enough and even more government spending was needed. Conservatives argued that the recession would have waned without the stimulus plan, and the biggest result of the plan was to increase the size of the federal budget debt. Moreover, they warned, the "free money" policies of the Fed had pumped up stock prices to unsustainable levels and would trigger high inflation down the road.

As it turned out, at least through the end of 2018, the lasting impacts of both the Great Recession — and the efforts to defeat it — were decidedly, indisputably and unreservedly mixed:

>> The stock market enjoyed a nine-year positive run that was unprecedented in modern times for its longevity. Yet it took a decade for the median household income — the amount at which half of U.S. households make more and half make less — to return to its 2007 level.

>> Home foreclosure actions dropped from a peak of more than 200,000 in 2009 to less than 31,000 in 2017, but the percentage of Americans who owned homes also dropped.

>> The nation's unemployment rate dropped from 10 percent in October 2009 to around 4 percent by October 2018. And yet total household debt had climbed $500 billion higher than its peak in 2008.

>> The annual inflation rate dropped from 3.8 percent in 2008 to 2.2. percent in 2018, while the percentage of Americans living below the poverty level — a number set annually by the federal government to determine eligibility for various "safety net" programs — rose slightly.

So, 10 years after the start of the worst economic collapse since the 1930s, many Americans were back to making the same amount of money, more of them were working, fewer of them owned homes but were less likely to lose them if they did, and while prices were going up more slowly, more poor people couldn't afford to buy much anyway.

Unspreading the Wealth

The first two decades of the 21st century weren't painful for all Americans. Those with a substantial part of their money in assets other than real estate — and a substantial enough pile of dough to ride out the rough times — were for the most part sitting pretty by the end of 2013.

The stock market, for example, emerged relatively unscathed from the Great Recession. In October 2007, the Dow Jones Industrial Average (an index of 30 large-company stocks) reached a high of 14,198. By March 2009, it had plunged 55 percent. But by mid-2018, it had passed the 25,000 mark. Trouble was, most Americans had no stocks. In fact, it was estimated nearly 40 percent of all equities in the stock market were owned by just 1 percent of Americans. Quickly recovering from the recession's ills was a boon enjoyed mostly by those at the very top of the wealth scale.

The rich get richer

On March 2, 2009, the giant insurance company AIG announced it had lost a staggering $62 billion during the last quarter of 2008. The government responded by hastily funneling $30 billion to the firm. Federal officials deemed the company "too big to fail," meaning its collapse would do irreparable harm to the nation's economy. Two weeks later, AIG announced it was paying $450 million in bonuses to the firm's top executives, in part so they wouldn't quit.

The outrage was quick — and loud. "The first thing that would make me feel a little bit better towards them [is] if they would follow the Japanese example," said Sen. Chuck Grassley of Iowa, "and come before the American people and take that deep bow and say I'm sorry and then either do one of two things: resign or go commit suicide."

As it turned out, taxpayers "invested" a total of $182 billion in AIG. The firm eventually restructured, and by 2012, the federal government had recouped the bailout and made a $22.7 billion profit. But the flap became a symbol of a deepening divide between America's haves and have-nots.

The divide was intensified by the fact that whatever wealth most middle-class families had was in the value of their homes or in retirement savings. When the housing market flopped and the stock market plunged, so did their nest eggs. Median household wealth plunged a whopping 39 percent between 2007 and 2011. "Overall it is estimated that the bottom 80 percent of households lost two decades' worth of wealth," a congressional research report concluded in 2012.

Worse, the average American couldn't buy more stuff with the money he or she did have. A 2018 study by the Pew Research Center found that despite the low unemployment rate and the steady addition of jobs to the economy from 2010 to 2018, the purchasing power of the average American's wages, adjusted for inflation, hadn't budged since 1978.

The wealthy also took big hits when the stock market dropped. But they had the resources to hold on to their holdings and even buy more stocks when prices were low. That meant they more than made up for their losses when the market recovered. By 2017, it was estimated that just 1 percent of U.S. households controlled 40 percent of the country's wealth — the highest level in almost 60 years.

But the defenders of the *1 percenters* (in 2018, that meant those who earned at least $481,000 a year) were quick to point out that the very wealthy also paid 39 percent of all federal income taxes, contributed more than 30 percent of all charitable giving, and were three times as likely to work more than 50 hours a week as anyone else.

"If those people could camp out in the park all day," a wealthy businessman told *The New York Times* in 2012, referring to anti-rich protesters, "why aren't they out looking for a job? Why are they blaming others?"

The blame game

On September 17, 2011, a group of about 1,000 people showed up in New York City's financial district and set up camp in a park. The *Occupy Wall Street* movement, conceived and organized through the Internet and social media, was designed mainly to protest the social and economic inequities that had grown during the Great Recession. "We are the 99 percent" became the movement's rallying slogan, and allied demonstrations were held in more than 70 other cities around the country.

The occupiers' camp was cleared out by police in mid-November, and the movement rather quickly faded from the public eye. But if nothing else, Occupy Wall Street cemented the terms *1 percenters* and *the other 99 percent* in America's political lexicon and fostered debate about economic inequality.

"We can either settle for a country where a shrinking number of people do really well while a growing number of Americans barely get by," President Obama said in his January 2012 State of the Union address, "or we can restore an economy where everyone gets a fair shot, and everyone does their fair share, and everyone plays by the same set of rules."

Deciding who drew up the rules, however, became the country's biggest — and most bitter — bone of contention in the years ahead.

DETROIT

It began as a small fur-trading post and rose to become the nation's fourth-largest city and center of the automobile universe — and eventually the poster child for urban blight. Founded in 1701, Detroit exploded in size and prominence at the beginning of the 20th century, when Henry Ford and other car manufacturers located there. The city attracted tens of thousands of unskilled workers, many of them immigrants or African Americans from the South, who were seeking stable jobs with decent wages and benefits.

By 1950, the population reached 1.9 million, and Detroit was synonymous with auto-making. But increasing competition from foreign car companies, overreliance on a single industry, and years of incompetent and sometimes corrupt leadership took their toll. By 2010, the city had shrunk to 714,000. Entire blocks consisted of abandoned buildings. City services had deteriorated to the point that police response to emergency calls could take 45 minutes.

And no U.S. city was hit harder by the Great Recession. Billions of dollars in debt, Detroit sought bankruptcy protection in federal court in July 2013, the largest American city ever to do so. Five years later, the city's core was being revitalized with new investment; its $19-billion debt had been restructured, and deserted neighborhoods were being re-inhabited. But it still had a long way to go.

Chapter 23

Reforming Healthcare Is No Tea Party

Although the Founding Fathers warned against them, political parties have been a prominent feature of American politics since the 1790s. Generally, two major parties have been all Americans can stomach at any one time. But every once in a while, a third party or political movement has risen temporarily to prominence, if not lasting influence.

In this chapter, I look at the rise of one such movement. I also detail an ambitious — and ultra-controversial — effort to improve America's health (or at least its healthcare) and chronicle the brief shutdown of the federal government. Oh, and I throw in a couple of presidential elections, no extra charge.

The Great Presidential Race of 2008

A U.S. presidential race with no incumbent chief executive or vice president running hadn't occurred since 1928, so when a wide-open field presented itself in the 2008 contest, it attracted a veritable herd of candidates.

In an effort to enhance their voters' clout in selecting the parties' nominees, a host of states raced to move their primaries to the front of the pack. As a result, six states held caucuses or primary elections before the end of January, and

30 more by mid-February. The earlier primaries meant an earlier start to serious campaigning. By the spring of 2008, Democratic presidential wannabes had participated in 26 debates or forums; Republicans in 21.

In early March, U.S. Sen. John McCain of Arizona sewed up the GOP nomination. It capped a startling comeback for McCain, whose campaign had been broken and almost done just a few months before.

In the Democratic race, Senators Barack Obama of Illinois and Hillary Clinton of New York (the former First Lady) ran away from the rest of the field by mid-February. That guaranteed the 2008 general election would be the first of its kind, with either the first woman presidential nominee by a major U.S. political party or the first African American. But if they outdistanced the rest of the field, they couldn't outdistance each other, trading primary victories in key states throughout the spring. Finally, Obama clinched the nomination in early June.

Obama selected Sen. Joe Biden of Delaware, a well-known political veteran, as his vice presidential running mate. But McCain surprised everyone by picking Sarah Palin, the obscure first-term governor of Alaska. At various times, Palin both energized the McCain campaign and acted as a distraction.

Obama versus McCain

The two top-of-the-ticket candidates offered Americans one of the most disparate choices in U.S. history. At 47, Obama would be the fourth-youngest president ever. At 72, McCain would be the oldest. McCain was a naval veteran of 22 years (5½ as a prisoner during the Vietnam War) and a fourth-term senator. Obama hadn't served in the military and was a first-term senator. Obama was the son of a white American woman and a black Kenyan man. McCain had an ancestor who had served on the staff of George Washington. Obama liked to deliver electrifying speeches before huge crowds. McCain preferred chatting with small groups in informal settings.

The two also had widely differing views on nearly every issue: the war in Iraq, healthcare, taxes, energy, and the environment. Obama fought charges that he was a socialist in progressive's clothing. McCain fought charges that he represented four more years of policies identical to those of the highly unpopular Bush.

Obama's historic victory

Obama held a narrow lead through most of the summer. As Election Day grew closer, the country's staggering economy came to dominate the campaign, and voters decided Obama was better equipped to deal with it.

It was a convincing victory. Obama carried states no Democratic candidate had carried in 30 years. He also galvanized young voters and minorities to vote in record numbers. Obama's campaign leaned heavily on new technology and techniques, such as sending Election Day voting reminders to cellphones and using websites to raise money and organize grassroots efforts.

"If there is anyone out there who still doubts that America is a place where all things are possible, who still wonders if the dream of our founders is alive in our time, who still questions the power of our democracy, tonight is your answer," Obama said during an election night celebration in Chicago.

In 1858, buying and selling human beings was legal in America. In 1958, discrimination based on race was widespread. In 2008, an African American was elected 44th president of the United States. The country had come a long way. But as Obama would find out, it also had a long way to go.

Calling the president a liar

On September 9, 2009, 232 days after taking office, Obama was addressing a joint session of Congress about his proposed healthcare reform program. When the president said that despite claims to the contrary, the plan would not cover illegal immigrants, Rep. Joe Wilson of South Carolina, a Republican, pointed at Obama and shouted, "You lie!" Twice.

REMEMBER

The incident showed just how nasty the partisan split in the nation's capital had become. But it belied just how busy Congress really was during the first two years of Obama's administration. Congress lifted a ban on homosexuals serving in the military; approved a new arms control treaty with Russia; overhauled regulations for the financial industry; enacted a sweeping healthcare plan; called for pay equity for women; approved more regulation of the tobacco industry; confirmed the nominations to the U.S. Supreme Court of two women, one of them Hispanic; and approved a mammoth economic stimulus program and an even bigger tax-cut package.

It did so through Democratic dominance. Along with electing Obama, American voters in 2008 had increased the Democrats' control of the House of Representatives by 21 seats from 2006 and gave Democrats a 16-seat edge in the Senate. Simply put, the majority party did pretty much what it wanted. But American voters can be a fickle bunch, and not everyone was happy with all that congressional activity.

Going to a Tea Party

One of the things that stuck in the craws of many Americans in the Great Recession was the series of decisions by the Bush and Obama administrations, abetted by Congress, to provide hundreds of billions of taxpayer dollars to huge banks and corporations.

They weren't buying the rationale that temporary aid to the companies would provide economic stability and combat unemployment. The average guy was worried about losing his job, paying his mortgage, and sending his kids to college — and without any government "bailout." Moreover, many were weary of what they regarded as too much federal interference in matters they thought were best left to local or state decisions, such as education or voter registration.

"I worked hard and I went for the American dream and I did okay," actor John Ratzenberger told a crowd of 5,000 on the state capitol steps in Sacramento, California, in April 2009. "But now I'm confused . . . why does the government want to take my money and give it to people who don't work?"

Ratzenberger, who was best known for portraying an obnoxious mailman on the TV show *Cheers*, was taking part in one of about 750 rallies throughout the country. Although partly financed by Republican-affiliated groups and individuals and promoted by conservative media, the rallies' organizers insisted they were part of a nonpartisan, loosely organized, grassroots effort that became known as the *Tea Party movement*.

The movement took its name from the 1773 incident in Boston when American colonists dumped British tea into the harbor (see Chapter 4). It sprang up in February 2009, fueled by protests from Seattle to New York about various issues, and it was given national impetus after a Chicago TV reporter named Rick Santelli launched a tirade about the government bailing out people whose house mortgage deals had soured. Santelli suggested it was time for a "Chicago tea party," and the "tea party" name stuck.

The movement wasn't a formal political party, and members prided themselves that it had no leaders or formal central structure. Its message generally focused on economic issues more than social ones: Tea Partyers wanted to reduce the federal budget deficit, cut taxes, reduce government spending, and require strict faithfulness to the U.S. Constitution.

Through 2009, Tea Party devotees focused mostly on protest rallies and recruiting new members and were generally viewed as a minor ingredient in the country's political stew. By 2010, that view changed considerably.

Taking over the House

In January 2010, a special election was held in Massachusetts to fill the U.S. Senate seat of Ted Kennedy, who had died in 2009. Scott Brown, a relatively obscure Republican state legislator, squared off against the state's Democratic attorney general, Martha Coakley. With the state's Democratic voters outnumbering Republicans by a 3-to-1 margin, Coakley was a big favorite. But Brown pulled off a huge upset, becoming the first GOP senator elected in Massachusetts in 38 years.

REMEMBER

It was a harbinger of things to come. A perfect storm of elements converged on Democrats: Unemployment rates remained high, despite federal bailouts of banks and big businesses; many Americans found the new national healthcare plan confusing, and others just didn't like it; and Obama was the target of persistent (if ridiculous) rumors that he was born in Kenya and thus not constitutionally eligible to be president. In addition, Democrats had won many congressional seats in 2006 and 2008 in districts that contained lots of Republican and independent voters, who were ready for a change.

The hundreds of Tea Party groups that had formed in 2009 also played roles. The groups raised money and organized get-out-the-vote efforts. They also endorsed candidates in Republican primaries, often against "establishment" candidates who had the official blessings of GOP leaders. How much substantive impact the movement had in the general election has since been dissected and debated in various academic studies.

But it certainly galvanized the electorate. A November Gallup poll found that 73 percent of Americans thought the Tea Party energized more people into getting involved in the political process (although 55 percent also thought it deepened partisan divisions). Larger percentages of white, senior citizen, and self-described conservative voters turned out in 2010 than in 2008, and they tended to vote Republican. Worse for Democrats, 63 percent of voters describing themselves as independents voted for GOP candidates in 2010, as opposed to just 49 percent in 2008.

REMEMBER

The result was a Republican landslide. The party gained 63 seats and a majority in the House, the biggest gain by either party in a midterm election since 1938. The GOP also picked up 6 seats in the Senate and captured a record 680 state legislative seats. "Tonight there's a Tea Party tidal wave," said Rand Paul of Kentucky, one of the Tea Party–backed Senate winners, "and we're sending a message."

But the movement became a victim of its own success. Mainstream politicians, particularly Republicans, began portraying themselves as Tea Party leaders even while ignoring key movement principles, such as cutting government spending and trimming the federal deficit. By late 2015, polls showed Americans' support of the Tea Party movement had dropped from 32 percent in 2010 to 17 percent. Even so, the movement's distrust of big government, distaste for traditional candidates, and dislike of party leaders setting the parties' agenda found their way into the roots of the Donald J. Trump presidential campaign that won the White House in 2016.

Cutting taxes by compromising

"Taxes," American jurist Oliver Wendell Holmes, Jr. noted in 1904, "are the price we pay for a civilized society." But in 2010, U.S. politicians were more interested in reviving the economy than in civilizing society. So with a set of 10-year-old "temporary" federal tax cuts ready to expire on January 1, 2011 — and Republicans ready to take control of the House of Representatives two days after that — President Obama was ready to make a deal.

On December 6, the president and Republican lawmakers agreed on an $858 billion plan that gave each side some of what it wanted. In addition to extending tax cuts for two years, the package continued lower tax rates on capital gains and dividends; expanded unemployment insurance coverage; cut Social Security tax deductions from paychecks; and extended tax credits for college tuition and business investment in research and development.

Supporters said the plan would save jobs, give families more spending money, and generally goose the economy. The bill passed the Senate on a bipartisan 81–19 vote. But Democrats in the House balked, characterizing it as "a huge giveaway to the super-rich." They tried to limit the tax cuts to households making less than $250,000 and then to less than $1 million. The Senate rejected both efforts.

Eventually, the House approved the package on a 277–148 vote, with 139 Democrats joining 138 Republicans in the majority. Many of the Democrats who voted for it acknowledged the reality that Republicans would be taking over the House and feared any bill the Republicans proposed then would be unlikely to include jobless benefits or the payroll tax cut.

Obama signed the bill on December 17 at a ceremony attended by Republican, but not Democratic, congressional leaders. "I'm hopeful that we might refresh the American people's faith in the capability of their leaders to govern," he said, with no apparent trace of irony.

A GULF FULL OF OIL

The oil spill seemed minimal — at first. The day after the April 20, 2010, explosion in the Gulf of Mexico of an oil rig owned by British Petroleum (BP), officials were keeping their fingers crossed that most of the leaking oil would burn up and that the 11 missing rig crew members would be found.

No such luck. The 11 men were never found. The well gushed oil — 210 million gallons — for nearly three months. Marine life died, the land and sea were polluted, and the Gulf Coast region's economy was walloped. All in all, it turned out to be the worst marine oil spill in history.

A federal investigation concluded that BP and two contractors, Halliburton and Transocean, had cut construction costs on the rig and also that government officials had been too prone to accept assurances from the oil industry that things were being done safely. BP pleaded guilty to 11 felony counts related to the workers' deaths and paid more than $53 billion in fines and costs for cleaning up the mess and indemnifying individuals and businesses.

Lurching Toward Healthcare

One of Obama's biggest first-term goals was to find a cure for America's health-care system. The president, and many others, contended that soaring healthcare costs were bankrupting individuals, shutting down small businesses, and crippling corporations. Getting well, or trying not to get sick in the first place, was sucking up larger and larger percentages of the nation's economy, which wasn't feeling too good itself.

Revamping the healthcare system had been tried by other presidents as far back as Theodore Roosevelt. The last Democratic president before Obama, Bill Clinton, had tried and failed in 1993. But Obama was buoyed by the relative success of a Massachusetts plan that had been signed into law in 2006 by Governor Mitt Romney, a Republican. The system required everyone to have health insurance and provided aid for those who couldn't afford it.

With his public approval rating above 60 percent and comfortable Democratic majorities in both the House and Senate, Obama prodded and cajoled a sweeping healthcare reform bill through Congress, signing it into law on March 23, 2010. Not a single Republican in either house voted for it.

The 906-page "Patient Protection and Affordable Care Act of 2010" — commonly known as "Obamacare" — was humongous in size and excruciating in detail. Basically (and a bit simplistically), here's some of what it was supposed to do:

>> Allow individuals to keep their current health plan if they chose to do so, and allow parents to add children up to the age of 26 to their plans.

>> Prohibit insurance companies from dropping customers who got sick and from denying them coverage because of preexisting conditions.

>> Require healthcare providers to provide preventive services, such as wellness exams and tests for specific problems, such as prostate and breast cancer.

>> Require everyone to buy some kind of health insurance — known as the "individual mandate" — by March 31, 2014, or face a financial penalty and require employers with more than 49 employees to provide a health insurance plan.

REMEMBER

At the heart of the plan was the idea that if everyone had to buy insurance, a lot of young healthy people wouldn't use the health system and thus would help defray the costs of those who did. States were allowed to set up their own insurance exchanges to match people up with plans. If they chose not to, their residents could use a federally run exchange.

The law also required states to expand their Medicaid programs (which provide healthcare for low-income and disabled people) to help those who needed financial assistance in buying insurance. The feds would pay for all the expanded Medicaid costs for three years, and 90 percent thereafter.

"It represents a major step forward toward giving Americans with insurance and those without a sense of security when it comes to their healthcare," Obama said while signing the act into law.

What it gave opponents was political heartburn. Critics said Obamacare would drive thousands of small companies out of business because they couldn't afford to provide health insurance for their workers. It was too complex, they said, would cost state governments millions of dollars in Medicaid payments, and was un-American in forcing people to buy something whether they wanted it or not. Polls showed that more than half of Americans disliked Obamacare within a week of it becoming law, in large part because it was so confusingly complicated.

"One thing all Republicans agree on is we think Obamacare is the worst piece of legislation in 50 years," said Senate GOP leader Mitch McConnell of Kentucky. "Every Republican thinks it was a huge mistake and would like to get rid of it."

Republicans tried. The GOP-controlled House of Representatives voted more than 60 times to strip the healthcare plan of funding, suspend major portions of it, or repeal it altogether. Each time they were blocked by the Democratic-controlled Senate. In July 2017, after Republicans had narrowly wrested control of the Senate in the 2014 elections, three GOP senators joined all 48 Democrats and independents in a defeating yet another repeal effort.

While Congress was persistently but ineptly trying to settle the program's future, other Obamacare foes had taken a different approach.

Courting the Supreme Court

In January 2011, the state of Florida sued to block the healthcare plan from taking effect, on the grounds the federal government didn't have the constitutional authority to require individuals to buy health insurance. Both a trial court judge and an appellate court sided with Florida (whose cause was eventually joined by 25 other states). Similar suits followed with varying degrees of success before various appeals courts. Finally, in December, the U.S. Supreme Court agreed to decide the issue.

In March 2012, justices listened to three days of argument over the act's constitutionality. The prevailing public opinion, both expert and novice, was that the five conservative justices on the nine-member court would overturn the law. That view was buttressed at one point in the proceedings when Justice Antonin Scalia sarcastically asked if Congress could force people to buy broccoli as well as health insurance.

REMEMBER

But the prevailing opinion was proved wrong on June 26, when Chief Justice John Roberts joined the court's four liberal justices in a decision that gave Obamacare supporters most, but not all, of what they wanted. The majority ruled that mandating individuals to buy health insurance or face a financial penalty was essentially just a form of taxation, which Congress had the power to do.

States whose elected leaders opposed the law, however, did get a consolation prize: They could refuse to accept additional federal funds to expand their Medicaid programs to cover low-income people who weren't eligible for current Medicaid help but couldn't afford to buy health insurance.

A stumbling start

The court had ruled, but the Obamacare battles were far from over. For one thing, different states took far different approaches to implementing the plan, which began on October 1, 2013. Although the plan originally envisioned each state setting up its own exchange where its residents could buy insurance, only 14 did so. That left it up to the federal government to set up a national exchange.

AND THE DECISION IS . . .

The fate of Obamacare wasn't the only big ruling to come from the closely divided Supreme Court during the first years of the 21st century. Among the others:

- *Citizens United v. Federal Elections Commission.* On January 21, 2010, the court ruled on a 5–4 vote that the government couldn't prohibit or limit corporations and labor unions from spending on political campaigns and causes. The ruling overturned not only federal election laws but also two decisions by earlier Supreme Courts. The decision was a huge impetus to the blossoming of "Super PACS," which were huge political action committees that raised hundreds of millions of dollars for candidates but made it difficult, if not impossible, to trace precisely the sources of the contributions.

- *Shelby County (Alabama) v. Holder.* On June 25, 2013, on a 5–4 vote, the court struck down a major part of the 1965 Voting Rights Act. The decision allowed states to make changes in their voting laws, such as requiring photo identification, without federal approval.

- *United States v. Windsor.* The next day, the court ruled that married couples of the same sex were entitled to federal benefits and cleared the way for same-sex marriages in California. Both decisions were on — surprise! — 5–4 votes, but different combinations of justices voted with the majority in each case.

While exchanges in some states, such as California and New York, performed reasonably well, others had technical glitches. And the launch of the federal exchange was little short of a disaster: People spent hours vainly trying to even sign in to the system, let alone navigate the labyrinthine application process. By mid-November, only 106,000 people had signed up, of the 7 million-plus the Obama administration estimated might be covered.

REMEMBER

In addition, 25 states decided not to accept additional federal money for extending their Medicaid programs to cover residents who made too much money to qualify for existing aid, but too little to afford health insurance. The result was that many Americans faced the choice of going without coverage — or moving to another state.

To make matters worse, it turned out an Obama promise that people with existing policies could keep them wasn't so. Thousands of policies were canceled by insurance companies because their benefits didn't comply with Obamacare requirements. That resulted in many people facing higher premiums for new policies they didn't want in the first place.

All this infuriated voters and delighted Obamacare opponents. In the November 2014 elections, Republicans swept to their largest congressional majorities since 1928 and won numerous gubernatorial and state legislative seats. Along with concerns about illegal immigration, dissatisfaction with Obamacare was often cited by voters as a key motivator for voting GOP.

And, as it turned out, the legal battles weren't over after all. In June 2014, the Supreme Court voted 5-4 to strike down an Obamacare provision that required private companies to offer birth control insurance coverage to employees, even if the companies' owners objected to it on religious grounds.

Clinging to its legislative life

Still, Obamacare survived through 2018. The National Center for Health Statistics estimated that about 20 million Americans who had lacked health insurance in 2010 now had some form of coverage, although that still left an estimated 28.6 million with no coverage. After soaring price increases in 2016 and 2017, the rate of cost increases for health coverage seemed to have slowed.

Even so, abolishing Obamacare remained a Republican priority. Obama's Republican successor in the White House, Donald J. Trump, was an ardent and vocal opponent of the program. With his backing, Congress approved ending the requirement that taxpayers who declined to seek insurance be fined an average of $695 per year. Trump's administration also announced it would not try to enforce the act's requirement that health insurance companies provide coverage to consumers with preexisting health conditions. As a result of these and other administrative actions, it was estimated that the number of Americans *without* health insurance increased by about 3 million during Trump's first year in office.

Reelecting Obama in 2012

The economy was still shaky. The war in Afghanistan was entering its second decade. Polls showed fewer than half of Americans liked his healthcare plan — and fewer than half liked the job he was doing.

Still, Barack Obama wanted to extend his lease on the White House. Even without all the problems, he was bucking the odds, if you believed in historical precedent: Only once had three consecutive presidents served two full terms (Jefferson, Madison, and Monroe), and that was nearly two centuries before.

The challenger

Mitt Romney had finished second to John McCain in the 2008 GOP presidential derby and had a yen to do better in 2012. The son of former Michigan Gov. Hugh Romney, who had also run for president, Mitt (that was his middle name; his first name was Willard) held both law and business degrees from Harvard. His career had included being governor of Massachusetts for a term, running the Winter Olympics in Salt Lake City in 2002, and operating Bain Capital, a private equity company that bought businesses, tried to increase their market value, and then sold them again.

Romney, 65, outlasted a small army of other GOP candidates in the primaries. By May, the last two challengers, former House Speaker Newt Gingrich and former Pennsylvania Sen. Rick Santorum, dropped out. Romney chose Paul Ryan, a Wisconsin congressman who was considered a whiz at economics and the federal budget, as his vice presidential running mate.

The race

The campaign centered mainly on domestic issues, such as how best to create jobs, Obama's healthcare plan (which hadn't gone into effect yet), and how to balance the needs of programs such as Social Security and Medicare against the growing national debt. Obama and Romney spent a total of more than $2 billion, the overwhelming majority (as much as 80 percent according to some studies) of it going for ads that ripped into each other's characters and often exaggerated their stands on issues.

Obama led in most polls through the summer, albeit narrowly. But Romney briefly took the lead in early October, after a nationally televised debate in Denver, in which Obama appeared tired, whiny, and a bit bored. In two subsequent debates, however, the president acquitted himself much better.

The results

Obama won fairly easily. He took 332 of the 538 electoral votes and 51.4 percent of the popular vote. The president lost only two states — North Carolina and Indiana — that he had won in 2008. Obama crushed Romney among minority voters, winning 93 percent of African-American votes, 71 percent of Hispanic, and 73 percent of Asian Americans. He also won big among voters under the age of 40 and those making less than $50,000 a year. All those margins reflected a deepening political division among Americans along racial, economic, and generational lines.

"Democracy in a nation of 300 million can be noisy and messy and complicated," Obama said on Election Night. "We have our own opinions . . . and when we go through tough times, when we make big decisions as a country, it necessarily stirs passions, stirs up controversy. That won't change after tonight. And it shouldn't."

And it didn't.

Meanwhile, Back at the Budget . . .

Despite all the warm-and-fuzzy talk about "bipartisan cooperation" after reaching a compromise on tax cuts at the end of 2010, America began a three-year pinball game of careening from one federal fiscal crisis to another.

At their essence, the fights boiled down to some deep ideological differences between Republican and Democratic lawmakers. Republicans generally favored cutting taxes — including those at the highest income levels — and limiting government spending. That approach, they reasoned, would leave more money in the hands of individuals and businesses, which in turn would create more jobs. Democrats argued that extending tax cuts to the wealthy was less important than having enough revenue to ensure aid to those Americans at the bottom of the economic ladder.

Add to that the fact that Republicans controlled the House and Democrats the Senate and White House. Then buckle your seat belt for the Great Budget Battles of 2011–2013.

Hitting the debt ceiling

The *federal debt ceiling* is the highest amount the U.S. Treasury can borrow without congressional approval. Formalized by Congress in 1917, the ceiling has been repeatedly, and routinely, raised by Congress with little or no debate.

That changed, however, in 2011, when Republican lawmakers demanded federal spending cuts in return for raising the debt ceiling. The Treasury Department warned that if the ceiling wasn't raised by August 2, the United States would default on financial debts it had already incurred. (The only time in U.S. history that ever happened was in the War of 1812, when the British burned down the Treasury.) After weeks of arguing, the two parties reached a deal, and Obama signed it into law on August 2.

REMEMBER

The deal raised the debt ceiling by $900 billion. But — and it was a big "but" — if the two sides failed to find a way to cut $1.2 trillion from the national debt, the agreement called for automatic across-the-board cuts to take place on January 1, 2013.

The looming cuts amounted to $1.2 trillion in reduced spending over ten years. That was relatively peanuts compared to the size of the national debt, which in late 2013 was about $17 trillion — about 2½ times what it had been in 2003. But it was a fortune if you depended on the government programs that would be chopped.

Most members of both parties didn't favor across-the-board budget cuts (called *sequestration*) because it would include programs and projects each side supported. The hope was that sequestration would put burrs under both parties' saddles and get them to find some long-range solutions. But Congress turned out to have a pretty thick hide.

The deal did spur the credit rating agency Standard & Poor's to downgrade America's credit rating for the first time ever. S&P officials said they just didn't trust Obama and Congress to come up with a stable long-term plan. The downgrade triggered a hefty, if temporary, plunge in the stock market.

Driving off the fiscal cliff

In February 2012, Ben Bernanke, chairman of the Federal Reserve Board, warned that America faced "a massive fiscal cliff of large spending cuts and tax increases."

His reference was to the fact that the tax cuts Obama and Congress had compromised on in late 2010 were set to expire on January 1, 2013. At the same time, the budget cuts the two sides had agreed to postpone in August 2011 were poised to kick in. That was a surefire recipe for a giant economic stomachache.

So everyone sat down to squabble, er, negotiate. Democrats wanted to eliminate tax cuts for the wealthiest Americans. Republicans wanted to continue the cuts for everyone and pay for it by cutting deeper into social programs. After months of rhetorical battle, they reached a deal in the wee morning hours of January 1, 2013. The tax cuts were extended for Americans making less than $400,000 a year, and the budget cuts were kicked down the road again, until March 2013. But despite further negotiations, Congress failed to head off the budget cuts, which kicked in on schedule.

Shutting down the government

Meanwhile, Treasury officials warned that the country would hit its debt ceiling again in mid-October. And throughout the summer, Congress also failed to agree on a spending plan to keep the federal government running.

So on October 1, 2013, the government shut down. About 800,000 federal employees were told to stay home. National parks and monuments were closed. People relying on the approval of various federal agencies for loans, medical procedures, and other services were out of luck.

After 16 days of rhetorically rattling sabers and studying public opinion polls (Congress's approval rating dropped to an abysmal 9 percent), the two sides agreed to fund the government until January 2014 and suspend the debt ceiling until February. In mid-December, a shockingly subdued Congress approved a federal spending plan designed to last through September 2015. The plan eliminated some of the sequestration budget cuts and helped ensure against another embarrassing government shutdown in 2014, an election year.

The wheels of government began — creakily and crankily — to turn once more.

Chapter **24**

America Disagrees with Itself

With apologies to Charles Dickens, it was neither the best nor worst of times. It was, well, pretty mixed. Crime rates were generally down, yet it seemed not a day went by without a violent act dominating the news. Unemployment was at historic low levels and taxes had been cut, but the median household income was basically unchanged from two decades before. Abroad, America quarreled with longtime friends and canoodled with longtime foes. And at home, Americans seemed divided on every issue except which direction the sun came up in the morning — and even that seemed debatable.

This chapter focuses on the uncertainties and divisions that gripped the country as the 2020s loomed. Oh, and there is also a really different kind of U.S. president in there somewhere.

Trumped

Hilary Clinton was supposed to win the 2016 presidential race. Virtually every pre-election survey said so. After all, she had been a fixture in the national spotlight since serving as First Lady to her husband Bill in the early 1990s. Since then, she had been a U.S. senator from New York, a strong 2008 Democratic presidential candidate, and Secretary of State under President Obama. Her GOP opponent, meanwhile, was a flamboyant New York City real estate billionaire and reality television star whose most notable catchphrase was "you're fired," and who had never held, nor even run for, elected office.

In fact, of the 17 Republican presidential hopefuls who entered the race, Donald J. Trump was considered by one *Washington Post* pundit in mid-2015 to be "slightly more likely to become our next president than he is to be the first person to set foot on the surface of a planet circling Alpha Centauri." A late 2015 poll of Republican voters reported that 76 percent "absolutely" or "probably" would not vote for him.

Guess what? Trump won. Actually, he lost the popular vote by a whopping 2.8 million votes. But he carried 30 states, including all of the South and most of the Midwest, winning 304 electoral votes to Clinton's 227. Trump thus became the fifth U.S. president to lose the popular vote and yet win the White House.

How he won left political scientists scratching their heads. In fiery rallies that often resembled religious revival meetings, Trump promised to "make America great again" by banning Muslims, building a wall along the Mexican border, stopping unfair foreign trade deals, and repealing the 2010 national healthcare law referred to as Obamacare. He belittled opponents' physical appearance and personalities, slammed the news media as liars — and never apologized for anything.

But what resonated most with voters was his promise as a Washington outsider to "drain the swamp" of special-interest influence and politics-as-usual government. He eschewed political correctness and said what he thought as soon as he thought it (and sometimes, foes said, before he thought it).

Clinton, meanwhile, ran a lackluster campaign in which she struck many voters as cold and aloof, and part of a government system they felt had let them down and left them behind. There was also a controversy over whether she illegally used a private e-mail server while Secretary of State, an allegation that triggered an FBI probe that was closed, then reopened, and then closed again days before the election. The episode diverted at least some negative media attention away from Trump.

The truth was that most voters didn't like either of them: Clinton's disapproval rating on Election Day was 54 percent, Trump's 61 percent. But Trump's appeal as someone who would shake things up was enough to give him 7 of the 11 most closely contested states, thus delivering the most shocking upset in modern presidential elections.

Getting to know a new kind of president

Depending on whom you asked, he was the best president since Lincoln or the worst president ever. But there was no denying Donald J. Trump was a very different kind of chief executive. Rather than vigorously contest or beg forgiveness for political hot potatoes that ranged from paying a pornographic film actress to keep quiet about an affair to using adroit legal maneuvers to avoid paying taxes on millions of dollars in income, Trump variously ignored, denied, and/or dismissed the controversies — and then changed the subject.

As with all presidents, he exaggerated, hyperbolized, and outright lied. But few, if any, of his predecessors had major news organizations keeping daily track of what they contended were examples of Trump stretching, or breaking, the truth: The *Washington Post*, for example, reported Trump had averaged five false or misleading statements per day during his first nine months in office.

None of it seemed to faze the president, or his followers. "I could stand in the middle of 5th Avenue and shoot somebody, and I wouldn't lose voters," he said during a campaign rally before the election. He was right, at least about those who voted for him. Polls showed that after 18 months in office, almost 60 percent of American adults disapproved of Trump's administration. But a staggering 90 percent of Republican voters liked what he was doing — and that was enough to ensure that the Republican-controlled Congress paid attention to what the president wanted, at least most of the time.

Cutting taxes and picking judges

What Trump wanted had been laid out during his campaign, and he managed to deliver on at least some promises. His call for a complete rejection of Obamacare was stymied (see Chapter 23 for details); his promised Mexico border wall was sidetracked; and his plan to rebuild America's infrastructure remained dormant during his first two years.

But he was successful in making things tougher on both legal and illegal immigrants (see Chapter 25). His administration rolled back or canceled dozens of federal government regulations and programs concerning business and financial institution oversight, the environment, and social service programs. And he scored in two other areas that were high priorities: tax cuts and conservative control of the U.S. Supreme Court.

In December 2017, congressional Republicans pushed through, and Trump signed into law, a bill that featured hefty reductions in business taxes, lower personal income tax rates, changes in income tax calculations, and even permission for oil drilling in the Arctic National Wildlife Refuge.

Nonpartisan studies concluded that most of the bill's benefits would accrue to corporations and the wealthiest individuals and would more than triple the federal government's debt. But Trump and other supporters contended it would more than pay for itself in the long run by stimulating the economy through job creation and investment in business and industry expansion. It was basically the supply-side economics argument — also known as *trickle-down* — that President Reagan had used during the 1980s.

While economists argued about the tax bill's merits, Trump had more immediately measurable success when the Senate narrowly confirmed his appointments to two seats on the nine-member U.S. Supreme Court. The confirmations of Neil Gorsuch in 2017 and Brett Kavanaugh in 2018 cemented a 5-4 conservative majority on the court in terms of judicial philosophy. That, in turn, promised to have an impact on a host of hot-button issues that included abortion, voting rights, and immigration law, among others.

Changing who's in charge of the House

This is how split America was when it came to the 2018 midterm elections (the ones that fall between presidential elections): Six of nine brothers and sisters of an Arizona Republican congressman named Paul Gosar publicly endorsed his Democratic opponent. The congressman's siblings said they were alarmed at what they said were his extremist views on immigration, health care, and white supremacists. Gosar easily won reelection anyway.

Not all GOP incumbents were as lucky, even if all their relatives liked them. Democrats took control of the House of Representatives for the first time since 2010. Republicans, however, held on to control of the Senate.

A number of firsts among the results reflected America's changing face:

>> For the first time, at least 100 women were elected to the 435-member House of Representatives.

>> The first Muslim and Native American women were elected.

>> The first openly gay man was elected governor of a state.

>> Of the new House members, 35 were under the age of 40, when the average age of the current House members was 57.

>> More than $5 billion was spent on the campaigns, another first.

There was nothing unusual about the reigning party losing seats in a midterm election. In fact, in only two midterm elections since 1910 had the party in power actually increased its majority. But seldom had the differences between partisans of the two major parties been as deep: An August 2018 Pew Research Center survey found that 78 percent of Americans were convinced that Democrats and Republicans couldn't even agree on what was fact, let alone on how to handle the country's problems.

There was also nothing unusual about the midterms being seen as a referendum on the president's policies and performance, although the unorthodoxy of the Trump administration certainly heightened the aspect in 2018. The president stumped at 30 campaign rallies in 20 states after Labor Day in early September, with mixed results. He appeared three times in Missouri to successfully help a Republican Senate candidate unseat a Democratic incumbent, for example, while three visits to Montana failed to accomplish the same thing.

Trump nonetheless declared the election results "very close to a complete victory" at a press conference the day after the election and said he was willing to work with the House Democratic majority. But he also threatened to adopt a "warlike posture" if they began investigations into his business dealings, tax returns, or actions as president.

If there was a positive effect to the deep partisan rift, it was that it galvanized voter participation. The 2018 turnout was estimated at 47 percent of eligible voters, far higher than 2014's 36.4 percent or 2010's 41 percent. In fact, it was the highest turnout since 1966 for a midterm election. But even as they voted, exit polls showed most voters weren't happy about things: 56 percent said they didn't like Trump, 55 percent said they didn't like Democratic House leader Nancy Pelosi, and 56 percent said the country was going in the wrong direction.

With Friends Like These . . .

Just like Americans, much of the rest of the world viewed the new president with applause, alarm, and/or puzzlement. At home, he ignored traditional political decorum; abroad he demonstrated a healthy disdain for diplomacy. He referred to the Canadian prime minister as "very dishonest and weak." Mexico was "the number one most dangerous country in the world." Germany was "totally controlled by Russia." He also reportedly complained about "all these people from shithole countries" immigrating to America instead of "more people from places like Norway." Trump later denied using "those exact words," but not expressing that opinion.

Putting America first

At the root of Trump's foreign policy was his fervent embrace of *nationalism*, which is generally defined as embracing the culture, traditions, needs, and wishes of one country above all others. But the term also has more troubling political overtones since it was often used by racist and xenophobic groups to describe themselves.

"From this moment on, it's going to be America First," Trump said in his inaugural address. "Every decision on trade, on taxes, on immigration, on foreign affairs, will be made to benefit American workers and American families. We must protect our borders from the ravages of other countries making our products, stealing our companies, and destroying our jobs."

He rattled America's 28 partners in the North Atlantic Treaty Organization (NATO) by complaining they weren't paying their fair share of the mutual defense alliance's costs. He withdrew the country from the *Paris Agreement*, an international framework designed to reduce environmental pollution and combat climate change, in part because he felt the agreement impinged on U.S. sovereignty. And he pulled America out of the Trans-Pacific Partnership, a 12-country agreement to lower tariffs between member nations and boost trade.

Trading insults on trade

A recurring Trump campaign theme was what he said was a need to decrease the U.S. trade deficit by balancing things America bought from the rest of the world with the stuff the rest of the world bought from America. Other countries, he said, protected their domestic industries with unfair tariffs on U.S. goods, while U.S. tariffs remained low. "We are being taken advantage of," the president declared, "and I don't like it." So in January 2018, Trump cited "national security" concerns in imposing a 30 percent tariff on solar panels and a 20 percent duty on washing machines, most of them from China.

China soon retaliated with a tariff on U.S. sorghum. Trump followed up with more tariffs on Chinese goods, and tariffs on steel and aluminum imports from a host of other nations as well. Canada, the European Union, and other countries countered with higher tariffs on U.S. products. By the end of 2018, U.S. tariffs were being imposed on products from frog legs to socket wrenches, while other countries were levying higher tariffs on U.S. peanut butter, motorcycles, and just about everything else.

The reaction domestically was — as with almost everything else Trumpian — decidedly mixed. Trade associations, business leaders, and industries adversely affected complained the trade wars would drive up prices and drive some companies out of business. Labor unions and companies poised to take advantage of less competition from overseas products applauded. And while many economists warned the trade wars would damage the U.S economy in the long run, Trump argued the result would be more U.S manufacturing jobs.

Closer to home, America reached a new trade deal in October 2018 with its neighbors, Canada and Mexico. Dubbed the U.S.-Mexico-Canada Agreement (USMCA), the deal replaced the 24-year-old North American Free Trade Agreement (NAFTA). Trump and others — including some Democratic political leaders — had long complained that NAFTA had siphoned U.S. jobs to Mexico and unfairly favored some Canadian industries. While the changes made by the new deal were relatively minor, all three countries called it a "win-win-win," in large part because it took 13 months to hammer out and was in danger of falling apart completely up until the last minute.

Sorting out friend from foe

In addition to picking fights over trade, the new president wasn't shy about throwing rhetorical punches on other issues at other countries — both traditional allies and opponents. He critiqued the British government's handling of that country's exit from the European Union; suggested the German prime minister was "ruining Germany"; called North Korean dictator Kim Jong-un "little rocket man," and referred to Syrian President Bashar al-Assad as "Animal Assad" for the dictator's use of chemical weapons in that country's civil war.

Most interesting — or baffling — was Trump's approach to Russia, a longtime U.S. adversary. He extended Obama administration economic sanctions against Russia and Russian individuals and added some of his own. He ordered U.S. missiles fired at Russia-supported military sites in war-torn Syria. And he expelled 60 Russian diplomats after a former Russian spy and his daughter were poisoned by suspected Russian agents in England.

But he was openly skeptical about charges Russia interfered in America's 2016 elections (see Chapter 25 for more details). And he said several times he had no reason to doubt the sincerity of Russian president Vladimir Putin when Putin denied Russian interference. "Is he my enemy? He is not my enemy," Trump said of Putin in July 2018, before meeting with him at a summit conference in Helsinki, Finland. "Hopefully, someday he will be a friend. He has said some nice things about me."

Another subject of Jekyll-and-Hyde diplomacy was North Korea. Angered by that country's nuclear weapons testing and bellicose threats by North Korean officials, Trump said in August 2017 that the Asian country would "be met with fire and fury like the world has never seen" if it continued threatening the United States. A few months later, he suggested war with North Korea might be inevitable.

But in the spring of 2018, Kim Jong-un suddenly reversed course and said North Korea was willing to end its nuclear weapons program. In June 2018, Trump and Kim met in Singapore and signed a statement pledging to better relations between the two countries. The president subsequently took credit for pulling the nation back from the brink of nuclear war. "I was really being tough, and so was he," Trump joked at a political campaign rally in September. "And we were going back and forth, and then we fell in love, okay? No, really. He wrote me beautiful letters. And they're great letters. We fell in love."

By early November 2018, however, the two nations were back to rhetorically dueling over whether America's economic sanctions against North Korea would have to be lifted before North Korea gave up its weapons program.

More consistent was the approach to Iran. Trump had warned before the election he might withdraw America from a 2015 multi-nation deal in which Iran promised to stop its nuclear weapons development if other countries lifted financial sanctions against it that had crippled Iran's economy. In May 2018, Trump announced U.S. withdrawal from the deal. In November, the day before the U.S. mid-term elections, the sanctions were reimposed.

D'oh!

They live in Springfield — the one with the ever-burning mountain of tires, the monorail to nowhere, and the nuclear power plant continually on the verge of a meltdown. The patriarch was a lazy, stupid, alcoholic yet down-deep good-hearted oaf; the matriarch a nagging optimist constantly teetering on the verge of hysteria, with a Bride-of-Frankenstein tower of blue hair. The son was a sociopathic underachiever whose conscience was seemingly just big enough to keep him from serial killings. The eldest daughter was a neurotic saxophone-playing genius, and the youngest was a baby who was at least 30 years old and still didn't talk. Together, they formed one of America's most beloved families.

They were, as virtually anyone who ever watched television between 1989 and November 2018 can tell you, the Simpsons. Through more than 30 seasons and more than 640 episodes, Homer, Marge, Bart, Lisa, and Maggie starred in an animated series that poked fun at and satirically prodded just about every aspect of American culture and the human condition. Created by Portland, Oregon cartoonist and writer Matt Groening, the show won dozens of awards, was the longest running primetime TV program in history, earned the fictional family a star on Hollywood's Walk of Fame, and spun off a 2007 film that grossed more than half a billion dollars. *Time Magazine* declared it the best television show of the 20th century: "Dazzlingly intelligent and unapologetically vulgar, the Simpsons have surpassed the humor, topicality and, yes, humanity of past TV greats."

Oh, and "D'oh?" That was Homer's favorite expression, which he uttered, shouted, groaned, and exclaimed hundreds of times in almost every conceivable situation. It became so familiar that in 2001, it entered the *Oxford English Dictionary*, where it was defined as "expressing frustration at the realization that things have turned out badly." But the dictionary folks for some reason left out the apostrophe. Probably a mistake. D'oh!

Guns, Drugs, and #MeToo

As the 21st century sped through its second decade, America found itself wrestling with two all-too-familiar problems — gun violence and drug abuse — and an old problem that heretofore had not been much in the public eye (sexual harassment).

Shooting each other at alarming rates

While it ran counter to the perceptions of many Americans, violent crime actually fell sharply through the end of the 20th century and the start of the 21st. Statistics compiled by the FBI found there were 747 violent crimes per 100,000 residents in 1993, compared to 386 in 2016. Sadly, however, the decline did not apply to mass public shootings.

The overall number of *mass public shootings* — defined as incidents where four or more people were killed in a public venue — stayed relatively stable, between four and five per year. But the enormity of the crimes in terms of sheer size grew at a horrific pace. Starting in 1948, it took 60 years for America to suffer 14 mass public shootings with 9 or more victims. Starting in 2009 and running through late 2018, it took just 10 years to suffer 15 more. A 2016 study found that while the United States had about 4.5 percent of the world's population, it owned an estimated 42 percent of the guns and played host to 31 percent of the planet's public mass shootings.

The varying scenes of the crimes fostered an impression that nowhere was safe: 58 killed at an outdoor music concert in Las Vegas; 49 killed at an Orlando, Florida nightclub; 26 at a church in Sutherland Springs, Texas; 17 at a high school in Parkland, Florida; and 12 at a Thousand Oaks, California bar and dancehall. "We simply cannot accept this violence as a normal part of American life," Pennsylvania Gov. Tom Wolf said after an anti-Semitic gunman killed 11 people at a Pittsburgh synagogue in late October 2018. "These senseless acts of violence are not who we are as Pennsylvanians and are not who we are as Americans."

There was certainly no paucity of firearms. Although there was no firm count, it was generally accepted that the number of U.S. guns was about 265 million in 2018, or about 80 weapons for every 100 Americans. That was nearly double the next-highest country, Yemen. Americans were also far more likely to die from a gunshot than in other countries: 98 times more likely than a Japanese, 55 times more likely than a Briton, and 38.5 times more likely than an Indonesian.

In some of the shootings, the gunmen adapted their weapons to be more efficient killers. Using a *bump stock* — a device added to a semi-automatic rifle that allows the shooter to continuously pull the trigger as the gun recoils — allowed a 64-year-old man to fire more than 1,100 rounds in 10 minutes from his Las Vegas hotel room in October 2017, spraying death on a crowd assembled below for a concert.

A Pew Research Center poll in October 2018 found that more than 75 percent of both Democratic and Republican voters supported preventing people with mental illness from buying guns; barring gun sales to those on watch lists of federal law enforcement agencies; and requiring background checks when guns changed hands at gun shows or through private sales.

But while some states passed their own gun control laws and regulations, Congress and the Trump administration remained immobilized. Despite an almost-immediate call for a ban on bump stocks, for example, the devices were still legal in most states a year after the Las Vegas massacre.

Black lives matter — and so do cops'

As divisive an issue as gun control was, what seemed like a continual stream of incidents occurred in which police officers shot and killed young African American males who sometimes turned out to be unarmed and whose deaths were often videotaped by police cameras or those of witnesses. The cases included a 22-year-old Sacramento man shot in his grandmother's backyard when police mistook his cellphone for a gun; a 12-year-old Cleveland boy who was playing with a BB gun; and a 17-year-old Chicago youth who was running away from officers when he was shot multiple times.

While cities sometimes paid large cash settlements to the victims' families and officers were fired, criminal convictions of police were rare. Of 15 high-profile cases between 2014 and 2016, only three resulted in guilty verdicts. Part of the reason was a U.S. Supreme Court ruling that police were justified in using deadly force if they had "reasonable apprehension" their lives or the lives of others were threatened. Police and their defenders also pointed out that more than 80 officers were shot and killed in 2017 and 2018 alone.

But the number of incidents caught on video triggered the formation of a loosely structured movement called Black Lives Matter in 2013. Using social media and more traditional marches and demonstrations, the movement heightened public attention to the issue. It also triggered backlash that included the formation of Blue Lives Matter, a group that called for anyone convicted of killing a police officer to be sentenced under hate-crime statutes that generally called for enhanced punishments.

Dying from drugs

In December 2017, the Centers for Disease Control (CDC) published a series of reports with a sobering conclusion: The overall life expectancy of Americans had dropped, in large part because so many people were dying from drug overdoses. According to the CDC, the annual number of U.S. overdose deaths had risen from about 22,000 in 2002 to more than 70,000 in 2017, a 318 percent increase in 15 years.

The drugs of choice were *opioids* — a group that included heroin, a synthetic drug called fentanyl, and prescription pain reducers, such as oxycodone, hydrocone, and morphine. Deaths from opioids rose from about 10,000 in 2002 to 49,000 in 2017, a nearly 500 percent jump. Part of the reason was a dramatic increase in prescriptions written by doctors for painkillers starting in the 1990s. The number of prescriptions tripled between 1991 and 2009.

Patient advocacy groups were lobbying for pain to be treated as a disease in itself and not just a symptom. And pharmaceutical companies pushed newly developed pain reducers such as OxyContin as safe and effective. At the same time, other drugs such as fentanyl, a pain-reducing drug that can be 50 times stronger than heroin and was primarily used for cancer patients, became a popular street drug because of its potency. It was also cheaper to produce than heroin or cocaine and was sometimes mixed into those drugs to bulk up their volume.

There was some evidence the crisis was leveling off by the end of 2018, possibly from the impacts of public awareness programs, the increased availability of an anti-overdose drug called naloxone, and laws passed in some states that made it tougher for doctors to write prescriptions for pain-reducing drugs. In 2017, President Trump declared the problem a national public health emergency, and about $1 billion in federal funds were made available for states to finance anti-drug programs.

But the collective reaction to the issue made many doctors leery about treating pain with drugs at all, which made life more difficult for thousands of people suffering from chronic pain.

Meanwhile, other studies found that Americans were dying sooner than people in other "developed" countries, such as Japan, Canada, and Australia, in part because of increased consumption of alcohol. The CDC estimated America suffered about 88,000 alcohol-related deaths each year, shortening those lost lives by about 30 years. Oh, and if that's not cheery enough, the CDC also reported in 2018 that suicide rates rose nearly 30 percent between 1999 and 2015. More than half were committed by using a gun.

Confronting sexual harassment

In 1997, Tarana Burke, a New York City community activist, was talking to a 13-year-old girl who had been sexually abused and realized she couldn't think of anything to comfort the girl — not even saying "me, too." Ten years later, Burke did respond by creating a nonprofit organization to help victims of sexual harassment and assault. She called it Me Too.

And 10 years after that, an actress, Alyssa Milano, used the web-based social medium Twitter to suggest all women who had been assaulted or harassed write "me too." A *hashtag* (the # symbol that makes it easier to follow a topic or group on social media) was added, and the movement gained national attention.

Milano's tweet was in reaction to a scandal centered on sexual abuse and harassment allegations by scores of women against Harvey Weinstein, a prominent Hollywood film producer. It also followed the pre-2016 election release of a 2005 audiotape in which Donald Trump bragged about sexually harassing women with impunity, because "when you're a star, they let you do it. You can do anything." Trump was elected president; Weinstein was arrested in May 2018 on rape and other charges. But Weinstein was only the start.

By the end of 2018, *The New York Times* reported, at least 200 men in prominent positions had lost their jobs over sexual harassment allegations. They included U.S. Senator Al Franken of Minnesota; television talk show host Bill O'Reilly; actor Kevin Spacey; and Missouri Governor Eric Greitens.

The movement was hailed as empowering women and exposing a societal cancer that had been ignored for decades. It was also criticized for encouraging false or reckless charges that ruined men's careers, and deeming accused men guilty unless they could prove they hadn't done something they hadn't done.

But the movement had an indisputable impact. *Time Magazine* named #MeToo its "Person of the Year" in 2017 and labeled the movement "one of the highest-velocity shifts in our culture since the 1960s."

Weathering the Weather

Mark Twain was said to have once said "everybody talks about the weather, but nobody does anything about it." But through the first two decades of the 21st century, yet another issue dividing Americans was whether human beings actually *were* doing something about the weather, or at least the world's climate — and not for the good.

Most scientists believed they were. More than 200 worldwide scientific organizations and an estimated 97 percent of climate scientists were convinced that human actions, most particularly the burning of fossil fuels such as coal, oil, and natural gas, were causing global temperatures to rise and affecting climate and weather patterns. A June 2017 report by a group of federal agencies found it was "extremely likely" human actions had caused the world's climate to change.

Whatever the cause of bad weather, it seemed to be getting more frequent. In the 30 years from 1980 to 2010, according to the National Centers for Environmental

Information (NCEI), America suffered 136 weather/climate disasters that, adjusting for inflation, each resulted in more than $1 billion in economic losses. In the less than eight years from 2011 through September 2018, there were 102 such incidents. In fact, three of the four costliest years on record were 2016, 2017, and 2018 (the other was 2011).

There were wildfires: California suffered the largest fire in its history in the summer of 2018, when a single blaze consumed 454 square miles and forced tens of thousands to flee their homes — at the same time, 16 other fires were burning in the state. In November 2018, the state was hit with its deadliest wildfire ever, killing at least 56 people and destroying the entire town of Paradise.

And there were hurricanes. In August 2017, Hurricane Harvey hit the Southeast, particularly Texas. The catastrophic storm flooded Houston, the nation's fourth-largest city, killed 106 people, and did a record $125 billion in damage. A month later, Hurricane Maria hit the U.S. territory of Puerto Rico, killing more than 3,000 people and inflicting $91 billion in damage.

The issue wasn't confined only to individual weather disasters. Because of melting ice caps and higher water temperatures, the National Oceanic and Atmospheric Administration (NOAA) projected in 2018 that ocean levels were rising at record rates. That, NOAA said, could increase the chance of flooding in American coastal communities by as much as 900 percent in coming years.

Americans — or at least 61 percent of them, according to an ABC-Stanford University poll in July 2018 — thought the federal government should be doing "a great deal" about the issue, and 62 percent disapproved of President Trump's decision to withdraw the United States from the 2015 Paris Agreement, in which nearly every other country in the world agreed to try to combat climate change by cutting the use of fossil fuels.

But only half of those polled saw climate change as becoming a more serious problem if nothing was done. And, unsurprisingly, there was a deep partisan divide: While 78 percent of Democrats saw it as a serious problem, just 25 percent of Republicans thought so.

Among that latter number was President Trump. In an October 2018 television interview, Trump backed off his often-stated assertion that climate change was a hoax perpetrated by either the Chinese or scientists with a political agenda. Instead, the president said, that even if climate change was real, it might just reverse direction by itself, and that it wasn't worth risking jobs and damage to the national economy to address it.

Trump's comments followed the fatalistic conclusion of an August 2018 report by the National Highway Traffic Safety Administration (NHTSA), which was looking into the validity of the Trump administration's proposal to roll back federal requirements that motor vehicles be more fuel-efficient. The NHTSA said that while average global temperatures would likely rise a devastating 7 degrees by the end of the century, it was too late to do anything about it, so there was no reason to require vehicles to use less gasoline.

GOATS AND CUBS

When ushers at Chicago's Wrigley Field barred Billy Sianis from bringing his pet goat Murphy into Game 4 of the 1945 World Series between the Chicago Cubs and Detroit Tigers, he demanded to know why. After all, he had a ticket for the goat. "Because," Cubs owner Philip K. Wrigley told him, "the goat stinks." Sianis was so incensed, he told Wrigley the Cubs would not only lose the '45 series, they would never win a World Series again.

Or at least that's the legend. Whatever its veracity, the fact was that the Cubs not only lost the series in 1945, they seemed fated to never even reach baseball's ultimate contest again, let alone win it. A National League franchise since the league's founding in 1876, the Cubs won series titles in 1907, 1908 — and that was it. They lost their next seven attempts, including 1945, and thereafter became a national symbol of futility.

For example, in 2003 — the Year of the Goat on the Chinese calendar — the team came within five outs of getting to the series, when a Cubs fan reached out for a foul ball and kept a Cubs player from making the catch. The Cubs went on to lose the game.

Attempts were made over the years to lift the curse of Billy's goat. Sianis forgave the team before he died in 1970. His nephew returned with a goat, and with the intercession of Ernie Banks, a legendary Cubs superstar, was allowed entrance. The Cubs' dugout was sprinkled with holy water. Goats were donated to impoverished families in developing countries. Five fans ate a 40-lb. goat at a local Mexican restaurant. Nothing worked. Finally, in 2016, the team was forced to rely on good players — seven All-Stars and the league's most valuable player — and a baseball-brilliant manager. The Cubs beat the Cleveland Indians in one of the most thrilling World Series of all time. The curse was over.

This did not make for good news in Cleveland: The Indians, having not won a World Series since 1948, donned the mantle of the franchise with the longest baseball world championship drought. And they couldn't blame it on a goat.

Chapter **25**

This New America

Over the years, America's multicultural, multiethnic, multiracial populace has been described by playwrights, demographers, and other assorted deep thinkers as a "melting pot," a "mixed salad," a "fondue," and even "tomato soup." The common ingredient in all those descriptions is that the country has proved itself pretty adaptable, even when change hasn't come easy.

As the new century unfolded, continually evolving technology revolutionized the ways people got their information, talked to one another, and entertained themselves. At the same time, immigration, changing cultural mores, and just plain living longer were altering how they lived and with whom.

The Techno Revolution

In 1965, a California physicist named Gordon Moore made a prediction. Moore was helping to develop semiconductor microchips made of silicon and three years later cofounded Intel, which became the world's largest microchip maker. He observed that the number of transistors that could be crammed onto a single chip had been doubling every two years. He thought they would probably continue to do so for some years into the future.

He was right — and then some. In 1975, 5,000 transistors per chip was a pretty good ratio. By 2018, it was 19.2 *billion.* The microchip had become the foundation for nearly every aspect of American life, from buying socks to falling in love. But first, the news.

Getting the news — real and fake — from new news sources

Throughout most of U.S. history, Americans got most of their news from three kinds of media: first newspapers, then radio, and then TV. In the first years of the 21st century, however, that began to change.

Newspapers nose-dive

In 2000, 56 percent of Americans surveyed said they had watched TV news the day before, 47 percent had read newspapers, and 43 percent had listened to radio news. In 2017, the answers were 50 percent TV, 18 percent newspapers, 25 percent radio, and 43 percent online, a news source not even tabulated in the 2000 survey.

Hardest hit by the advent of online news was the print media. In 2018, only one major weekly news magazine, *Time,* was still publishing a print product. From 2000 to 2017, daily newspaper circulation dropped 45 percent. More ominous for newspapers, print advertising revenue dropped 75 percent between 2003 and 2017. Many papers tried to recover by launching their own websites as adjuncts to their print products. By 2018, far more people read *The New York Times* online each day than read it in print.

The rise of the web as a news medium also saw the rise of a host of new news competitors. Web-based news aggregators, such as the Huffington Post (launched in 2005), or specialized news-gathering organizations, such as Politico (launched in 2007), gave news seekers a cornucopia of choices. The bad news was that many websites focused as much on spreading rumors, gossip, and propaganda as on journalism. Readers had more choices, but not all of them were good ones.

TV troubles

While the web's immediate impact wasn't as great on TV news as it was on newspapers, the traditional Big Three of TV — NBC, CBS, and ABC — found things getting a lot more crowded on America's airwaves. In 1996, Congress approved the first sweeping reform of U.S. telecommunications law since 1934.

One of the law's effects was to pave the way for hundreds of new TV channels and networks, delivered via satellite and through cable systems. By 2013, Americans seeking a dose of TV news could pick from the traditional three broadcast networks — or CNN, Fox News, MSNBC, CNBC, PBS, Univision, and others. By 2018, cable- and satellite-based news networks were drawing more viewers than their broadcast counterparts. But as with web-based news sources, while the variety was a big plus for consumers, the quality of journalism sometimes wasn't.

"We've discovered many smart new voices out there," veteran TV journalist Bob Schieffer observed in late 2013, "and excuse me for being blunt, a lot of people who have absolutely no idea what they are talking about."

Faking it

As far as President Trump was concerned, the news was not only full of mistakes, but full of falsehoods, what Trump called, often in capital letters, "fake news." Although he was far from the first president to hold the news media in low regard, he was among the loudest ever when it came to complaining publicly about it. Trump continually branded negative reports about his administration or himself personally as deliberate lies meant to undermine his presidency. "The FAKE NEWS . . . is not my enemy, it is the enemy of the American People!" he said in 2017. In the wake of the November 2018 elections, Trump went so far as to ban one TV reporter from the White House after a shouting match with him during a press conference.

Trump's opponents — including many in the news media — responded that in many cases, the president was merely blaming the messenger for bad news — or trying to deflect pervasive, and often persuasive, criticism that he played fast and loose with the facts himself. Several news organizations routinely ran "analyses" of Trump's remarks and speeches that pointed out what they said were his exaggerations, half-truths, and outright lies.

But a lot of people agreed with Trump. A June 2018 Gallup Poll reported 62 percent of Americans thought the news they saw or heard was biased, and 44 percent believed it to be inaccurate. The traditional news media's credibility gap, combined with the vast array of online news outlets and the rise of web-based social media, radically changed how Americans got their news. It led to more *tribalism* — people tended to gather information from sources that reinforced the views they already held — and that in turn deepened political and cultural divisions.

Calling all cells

On a brisk clear day in April 1973, 44-year-old engineer Martin Cooper was crossing Sixth Avenue in New York City when he decided to call an engineer friend at a rival company and razz him about a device Cooper's company had just invented. So Cooper took out his newly invented cellphone. It measured 10 inches long, weighed 2.5 pounds, and, if it had been for sale, would have cost at least $3,500 ($20,750 in 2018 dollars).

REMEMBER

Improvements were made. In fact, cellphones became pretty popular. In 2002, an estimated 62 percent of American adults had a cellphone; by 2018, 95 percent did. As cellphone use proliferated, the use of landline phones waned. A government study found that while 95 percent of American households had traditional phones in 2003, just 48.5 percent had them in 2017.

More than two-thirds of cellphones were *smartphones,* which were basically mini-computers. You could use them to navigate, take photos, check sports scores, read restaurant reviews, send text messages, and listen to music. Americans did all those things and more. By 2018, research showed the average adult American spent more than 4 hours a day on the phone, about 3 hours of it using various features and programs referred to as *apps*, shorthand for "applications." They also came in handy in emergencies: An estimated 70 percent of the 240 million calls to the 911 emergency number in the country in 2017 were from cellphones.

Americans not only were almost constantly in touch with one another and most of the rest of the world but also probably carried access to more information in their pockets than their grandparents had access to in their entire lifetimes. Nearly every aspect of daily life was made easier.

Of course, this development wasn't all good. In 2018, it was estimated that cellphone use was a key factor in 25 percent of U.S. traffic accidents, resulting in more than 420,000 injuries. By 2018, 47 states had laws prohibiting texting while driving, and 15 banned the use of hand-held phones for any purpose while behind the wheel.

Cellphones also made for breaches of etiquette. In one survey, 82 percent of Americans said they had been irritated by "loud and annoying" cellphone users in public places. But only 8 percent admitted being scolded for making loud and annoying calls in public places.

Socializing and shopping on the web

If you got a busy signal on your cellphone, there was always e-mail. Like the cellphone, technology for sending electronic text improved considerably from the first attempt to send a message via the Internet in 1969, by scientists at UCLA and Stanford University. (The system crashed as soon as the sender typed the "g" in "login.")

By 2017, an estimated 269 billion e-mails were being sent worldwide each day (about two-thirds of which were believed to be *spam*, the electronic version of junk mail). The average U.S. office worker received 121 e-mails per day. So ubiquitous was e-mail that 50 percent of Americans acknowledged reading e-mails in bed — and 42 percent while using the toilet.

E-mails and the web begat *blogging*, which emerged in the 1990s. Blogs (short for *web logs*) were essentially a discussion site usually focused on a particular subject or person and overseen by an individual, organization, or company. Most blogs allowed people to contribute commentary and information. They also served as marketing tools. And they fostered a panoply of *social media:*

>> **Facebook:** Founded in 2004 and initially designed for college students, this social networking service let friends, relatives, and sometimes perfect strangers exchange messages; share photos, recipes, and favorite books; and join common-interest groups. By 2017, Facebook had more than 2.2 billion

active monthly users — those on the site at least once a month — worldwide and an annual net income of nearly $16 billion.

» **LinkedIn:** Launched in 2003, this site was designed for business people to find jobs and potential employees and keep track of other people in their industry or profession. It had 146 million active U.S. users in 2017 (and more than 260 million globally). In 2016, the software giant Microsoft bought LinkedIn for $26 billion.

» **Twitter:** Created in 2006, Twitter was envisioned as a "micro-blogging" service that let users send text messages — as long as they kept it to 140 characters or fewer. By 2018, its 335 million active monthly users posted 500 million "tweets" per day, and the company had doubled the number of characters per tweet. President Trump was an inveterate — and to some, an incorrigible — tweeter. Trump averaged seven tweets per day during his first year in office. His tweets ranged from rants to ruminations and often became front-page news.

Doing business on the web

E-mail, and the web in general, were both a boon and bane to U.S. business. Though e-mail made staying in touch with customers, suppliers, information sources, and colleagues a snap, studies found that some workers spent up to 28 percent of their day sending electronic messages, interrupting their focus and reducing productivity.

For American retailers, the web presented both peril and opportunity. Sales of goods via websites, called *e-commerce*, accounted for just 8.9 percent of total U.S. retail sales in 2017. But that was double its share from a decade earlier, and the percentage was expected to double again by 2022. Companies that were quick to set up websites as auxiliaries to their traditional brick-and-mortar stores were in many cases able to compete with companies that consisted mostly of "www." addresses and distribution facilities. Those that were slow to embrace e-commerce or tried to sell a multitude of products rather than specialize, sputtered or went out of business.

Entertaining ourselves, by ourselves

Once upon a time, say around 1995, Americans who had a yen to see a movie could visit their neighborhood video store, plunk down a few bucks, and rent a VHS tape for a day or two. Of course, if they brought it back late, they had to pay another buck or two.

Fast-forward to 2018. For less than $15 a month, Americans could click a button and watch all the movies they wanted without ever leaving the couch (which is the major reason most video stores, including the 9,000-store Blockbuster chain, were out of business by 2013).

The shift was emblematic of Americans moving to the Internet for their entertainment. Streaming video companies, such as Netflix and Hulu, offered films and TV shows (sans commercials) on a monthly subscription basis. If you fancied something a bit less polished, there was the no-cost YouTube, a 2005-launched website on which people could post videos. The subjects ranged from an infant biting his brother's finger (863 million people around the world watched it) to a pudgy South Korean pop singer performing (this one topped 3.2 billion views).

There were also online games to play. Americans played tennis, killed zombies, and stole cars, all from their desks or easy chairs. Opponents, often complete strangers, could come from anywhere in the world.

REMEMBER

Entertainment made up a good part of Americans' time online — and that was plenty of time. A 2016 U.S. Census Bureau study found that the average American adult spent about 6 hours a day online, compared to about 3 hours watching television and 30 minutes reading. In fact, the study reported, the average American spent more time just surfing the web than volunteering, attending social events, or going to church. A study by the National Bureau of Economic Research concluded those extra minutes online weren't just coming out of reading or TV time: Americans were spending less time sleeping, eating, cleaning the house, traveling, and hanging with the family.

Some academic studies suggested that all that Internet use was making many people unhappy and unsociable. On the other hand, other studies found that nearly 20 percent of newly married American couples met each other through Internet dating sites.

But one thing everyone agreed on was that all this Internet activity was being watched — and manipulated.

Using technology to spy, lie, and meddle

For all the information Americans got from the web, tech-savvy companies gathered loads of information in return. Retail businesses routinely monitored individuals' web-surfing habits and tailored ads for products and services to pop up when someone opened a web page.

How pervasive — or invasive — web snooping could be was exemplified in 2018 by a cleaning supplies company that teamed with a technology firm that produced thermometers. The thermometers could take a person's temperature and record and update it on a cellphone app. The collected data allowed the cleaning company to target specific geographic areas experiencing flu outbreaks and then ratchet up its advertising in the area for products like disinfectant wipes.

Spying on ourselves

But retail advertisers weren't the only ones using technology to ratchet up their stores of information. In the wake of the September 11, 2001 terrorist attacks, the federal government had quietly expanded its security and surveillance efforts. In June 2013, Americans began finding out how much.

Almost simultaneously, the London-based *Guardian* newspaper and the *Washington Post* ran stories that revealed the FBI and the National Security Agency were gathering information about the e-mails, photos, phone calls, and documents of U.S. citizens. The information, from cellphone and Internet companies, had been secured under a secret order issued by the U.S. Foreign Intelligence Surveillance Court (FISC), which was created by Congress in 1978 to oversee domestic surveillance by federal intelligence agencies in cases where criminal activity was suspected. The information-gathering program was code-named PRISM. The agencies cited anti-terrorism laws that had been passed in 2008 as their authority for the operation.

The 200,000-plus documents the newspaper stories were based on came from Edward Snowden, a 30-year-old former CIA employee who had also worked for the NSA as a contractor. Snowden said he leaked the information because he was appalled at the damage the spying programs were inflicting on Americans' civil liberties. But federal officials saw his acts as traitorous, and he was indicted for espionage shortly after the stories ran. His prosecution was problematic because he had fled the country. As 2018 ended, Snowden was living under a grant of temporary asylum in Russia.

The revelations outraged civil liberties groups, who filed suit in federal courts. The surveillance also worried U.S. tech industry companies, who feared that foreign governments and businesses wouldn't trust U.S. firms with sensitive data because the U.S. government might be sifting through it.

And the spying programs alarmed members of both parties in Congress, angered both at the spying and the fact that they didn't know about it. But while more than 20 bills were introduced to curb the authority of federal agencies to snoop on Americans, nothing of substance passed into law. The biggest impacts were that news stories based on Snowden's documents occasionally surfaced, and large web-based companies, such as Google and Apple, tightened up — sometimes without success — unauthorized access to private data they collected on their customers and users.

Most of the country was ambivalent about the spying — and about Snowden. Opinion surveys showed that while about half of Americans thought the revelations served the public interest, more than half thought Snowden deserved to be prosecuted anyway. And about half were not too confident in the government's ability to protect online data. Or, as it turned out, to prevent foreign meddling in U.S. elections.

The Russian factor

In early September 2016, Secretary of Defense Ash Carter issued a public warning to the Russian government. "We will not ignore attempts to interfere with our democratic processes," he said. Carter's warning came as evidence piled up that Russian-backed computer manipulators, known as *hackers* and *trolls*, were working to undermine America's election system. The cyberattacks ranged from stealing and then publicizing private e-mails from the Democratic National Committee to creating fake websites and blogs designed to sow discord and division.

The Russians' goals, according to a January 2017 joint report by the CIA, FBI, and NSA, were "to undermine faith in the U.S. democratic process" and to help Donald Trump defeat Hilary Clinton in the presidential race. Russian President Vladimir Putin personally ordered the efforts, the report said, in part because he intensely disliked Clinton.

President-elect Trump wasn't buying it. Over the following 20 months, Trump variously expressed doubt there had been any interference; suggested it was someone other than the Russians; said he had no reason to doubt Putin's denial of involvement; and admitted that it was possible after all. But the new president was consistent — and adamant — on one point: Any cyberattacking that took place did not affect the election outcome, and to suggest otherwise was merely sour grapes from sore-loser Democrats. Trump's no-election-effect assertion was backed up by U.S. intelligence agencies, who found no evidence that votes had been tampered with or results rigged in any state.

But Trump's skepticism turned to rage when allegations surfaced that his campaign had colluded with the Russians. In March, FBI director James Comey disclosed the FBI was investigating possible "coordination" between Trump campaign officials and Russian operatives. Congressional intelligence committees also announced inquiries into the matter.

The allegations and investigations set off a head-spinning chain of events:

» Attorney General Jeff Sessions recused himself from participating in probes of the Trump campaign because he had played an active role in the campaign.

» Trump fired FBI director Comey for "politicizing and grandstanding" the investigation.

» Deputy Attorney General Rod Rosenstein, acting in Sessions's place, appointed Robert Mueller, a well-respected former FBI director, to head the investigation as special counsel to the Justice Department.

>> Mueller launched a sweeping, secretive, and lengthy probe that through October 2018 had resulted in indictments or guilty pleas of 4 former Trump advisers, 26 Russian nationals, 3 Russian companies, one man from California, and a London-based lawyer.

>> The day after the November 2018 election, Trump fired Attorney General Sessions and replaced him with Matthew G, Whitaker, who had been Sessions's chief of staff and was harshly critical of the Mueller investigation. While the probe continued — and broadened to include possible obstruction-of-justice actions by Trump — the president continually referred to it as a politically motivated "WITCH HUNT" and called for it to end quickly and/or for Mueller to be fired — although he stopped short of firing Mueller himself. The American public, meanwhile, was predictably split along partisan lines when it came to the question of whether the investigation was being conducted fairly. A September 2018 Pew Research Center poll reported that while 76 percent of Democrats were at least somewhat confident it was a fair process, only 33 percent of Republicans were as convinced.

Surfing the "Silver Tsunami"

There was no getting around it: Americans were getting older. In 2010, there were three times as many Americans over the age of 65 as there had been in 1910. The first of the 78-million-strong *baby boomer* generation (those born between 1946 and 1964; see Chapter 17) reached the ripe old age of 65 in 2011. And 65 wasn't as ripe as it once was. America's life expectancy rate had grown from about 70 in 1960 to 79 in 2017.

As the baby boomers crested normal retirement age, they picked up the collective nickname *silver tsunami* — and not because they looked good in bathing suits. Instead, the reference was to the impact the giant generation was having, or likely to have, on many aspects of American life.

Dealing with tough times

For one thing, living longer was not necessarily synonymous with living better. Many boomers who had counted on company pensions to pay for their retirement were knocked out of work prematurely in the Great Recession and saw their pensions shrink or disappear. Many were also hit by the housing bust and had a potentially large chunk of their retirement nest eggs melt away with the value of their home.

The tough economic times meant many older Americans were staying on the job longer. U.S. Bureau of Labor Statistics in 2018 showed the number of Americans still working past the age of 65 had climbed 56.6 percent since 2000. That meant fewer open jobs for younger people. From 2000 to 2018, the percentage of jobs held by those younger than 44 shrank 10 percent.

Straining Social Security and Medicare

But even with a lot of older Americans staying at work, the sheer size of the boomer/tsunami generation helped put a severe strain on key federal social service programs, such as Medicare and Social Security. Federal officials estimated the number of Americans over the age of 65 would grow from 49 million in 2018 to more than 79 million in 2035. The number of Americans enrolled in Medicare (the federal program that provided subsidized healthcare to those 65 and over) was 44 million in 2018; it was expected to grow to 79 million by 2030.

Meanwhile, the number of working Americans whose payroll taxes supported the programs was shrinking, from 2.8 workers per Social Security recipient in 2018 to an expected 2.2 by 2035. Officials estimated the primary trust fund that financed Medicare could be exhausted by 2026, and the Social Security fund by 2034. "Neither Medicare nor Social Security can sustain projected long-run programs in full under currently scheduled financing," a 2013 federal report warned, "and legislative changes are necessary to avoid disruptive consequences for beneficiaries and taxpayers."

Among the many proposed fixes were *privatizing* Social Security by allowing workers to invest their payroll taxes individually; increasing payroll taxes for the two funds; increasing the minimum age at which workers could become eligible for coverage; and lowering the annual increases in benefits.

All the possible solutions, however, were controversial and the subject of intense partisan debate in Congress — rarely a good place to be a subject.

Stirring the Melting Pot

The idea of America as a *melting pot* — where new arrivals could, and should, blend into the existing culture — was popularized in 1908 by an otherwise forgettable play called, well, *The Melting Pot*. But the metaphor was challenged in the last part of the 20th century by those who thought a better image was America as a sort of recipe, where the ingredients kept their own identities but still worked together to produce something tasty.

One indisputable fact was there were plenty of ingredients to choose from. In 1980, about 6 percent of the U.S. population had been born in other countries. In 2016, it was 13.5 percent. Federal statistics showed that from 2001 to 2016, nearly 11 million people became "naturalized" U.S. citizens.

Many of the legal immigrants were here because they possessed special skills — in medicine, technology, and other areas — that made them highly desirable to American employers. The percentage of legal immigrants with college degrees was almost exactly what it was for U.S.-born Americans.

But a whole lot of other people — an estimated 12.1 million in 2015 — didn't come to the country legally. That number had actually dropped between 2007 and 2009, during the Great Recession, but appeared to have leveled off after 2012.

Arguments raged continually among economists, demographers, politicians, and others about just what impact illegal immigration had. Heaps of studies were done, and the conclusions ranged from "illegal immigration is a horrid drain on America" to "we couldn't function without it." In between were studies suggesting that while illegal immigrants undeniably soaked up taxpayer-financed education, health and social services, their contributions to the overall economy balanced the scales.

Trying to fix the system

Still, they were here in violation of U.S. immigration laws, and for many Americans, that was enough. Frustrated that the federal government had failed to do anything meaningful on the question since 1986, lawmakers in 43 states passed state laws dealing with the issue. The laws ranged from the punitive, such as an Arizona law that required law enforcement officials to determine the immigration status of anyone they stopped if they suspected the person was in the country illegally, to the accommodating, such as a California law allowing illegal immigrants to obtain driver's licenses.

Polls showed that the overwhelming majority of Americans favored an overhaul of the federal immigration system and that most believed that immigrants already here illegally should be allowed to stay if they met certain requirements, such as learning to speak English.

In June 2013, the U.S. Senate passed a sweeping reform measure that included a 13-year path for illegal immigrants to obtain citizenship — and an extra $40 billion for adding 20,000 Border Patrol agents and 700 miles of fencing along the border with Mexico. But the proposal failed to even get a vote in the House, where majority Republicans were divided between those who favored reform and those adamantly against any bill that included a citizenship path for people who were in the country illegally.

Muslims, Dreamers, and Trump's Wall

Immigration was a key issue in Donald Trump's 2016 presidential campaign. In a speech announcing his candidacy, he promised to build "a great, great wall on our Southern border" and coerce Mexico into paying for it.

As president, Trump's early attempts to get anyone — either Mexico or Congress — to pay for the wall were stymied. But he was more successful with a promised ban on immigration and travel from seven predominantly Muslim nations. His first two versions of the ban, which he insisted were based on security and not religious concerns, were struck down by various courts as unconstitutional. But a third, trimmed-down version was upheld in June 2018 by the U.S. Supreme Court, on a 5-4 vote predictably divided along conservative/liberal lines.

The president was equally successful in reducing the admission of refugees and increasing arrests of illegal immigrants. His administration also ended programs that had allowed refugees from several countries devastated by war and natural disasters to seek temporary shelter in America.

More controversial was Trump's decision to end a program known formally as the Deferred Action for Childhood Arrivals (DACA), and informally as the Dreamers Act. Begun by President Obama in 2012, the program allowed about 700,000 unauthorized immigrants who came to America at an early age to receive renewable two-year deferrals from deportation, attend school, and apply for work permits.

In announcing in September 2017 that he would end the program, Trump agreed to delay its cancellation for six months in order to give Congress time to come up with a replacement plan. As usual, Congress failed. Although the program officially ended in March 2018, legal battles through the end of 2018 left the act's ultimate fate in limbo.

As controversial as the decision to end DACA was a Trump Administration announcement in April 2018 to implement a "zero tolerance" policy that called for criminal prosecution of everyone trying to cross U.S. borders illegally. The policy resulted in mass arrests. But because of a 1997 court agreement, migrant children could not be detained for more than 20 days before being placed in foster homes or other protective programs. As a result, more than 3,000 children were taken from their parents and relatives and placed in temporary camps.

The public backlash — and a federal court order — slowly ended the separation program. It also appeared to have failed as a deterrent to illegal immigrants. As October 2018 ended, a single mass of 7,000 migrants were making their way through Mexico from Central America, on their way to the United States.

The country's changing face

The tug of war over immigration had political implications as well as legal ones. The issue was of high importance to Hispanic voters in particular — and along with other minority groups, Hispanic voters were a growing political force. Minority voters accounted for about 27 percent of the electorate in the 2016 presidential race.

Moreover, immigration and higher birth rates among minority groups suggested the voting patterns of 2008, 2012, and 2016 were likely to continue. A Pew Research Center study in 2012 projected that by 2050, the Hispanic share of the U.S. population would reach 29 percent. Coupled with projected 13 percent black and 9 percent Asian shares, that meant slightly more Americans would be nonwhite than white by the middle of the century.

And a lot of Americans just weren't interested anymore in being racially categorized: In the 2010 census, more than 19 million people chose the catch-all classification "some other race" in describing themselves.

Redefining the American Family

If an observer from outer space had tried to figure out the typical American family by watching TV in the 1950s, he would most probably have deduced that it consisted of an employed father, a stay-at-home mother, and two or three children who were the center of their parents' universe.

Had the same extraterrestrial come back in the 2010s, he would doubtless have been a bit more confused by the array of choices: a gay father raising a single child, an extended family so dysfunctional they sometimes forgot the children's names, and a cartoon family where the imbecile father routinely choked the incorrigible son. Clearly, there had been some changes.

"There no longer is any such thing," said Zhenchao Qian, chair of the Dept. of Sociology at Ohio State University, "as a typical American family."

Changing with the times

A raft of studies by Qian and others revealed seismic shifts and variations in American family life in the last decades of the 20th century and first decades of the 21st. More people got married later in life, or not at all. Fewer people had children. There were more mixed-race marriages, more people getting divorced and then remarrying, and more families composed of nonrelated friends or combinations of friends and relatives. And there were fewer families of any kind. Some numbers help illustrate the shifting patterns:

>> In 1970, only 11 percent of U.S. households consisted of a person living alone. In 2017, it was 35 percent.

>> In 1970, 57 percent of U.S. households with children under the age of 18 included a married couple. In 2017, it was 41 percent.

>> In 1980, about 18 percent of all births in America were to unmarried women. In 2016, it was 40 percent.

Oh, and the U.S. birthrate in 2017 was the lowest it had been in 30 years.

Legalizing gay marriage

Perhaps nothing marked the shifting landscape of family life as much as the issue of same-sex marriage. It came to the forefront in 1993, when the Hawaii Supreme Court ruled that state officials couldn't bar gay marriages unless they could show that doing so was for the public good. Alarmed by the ruling, more than 40 states quickly passed laws expressly prohibiting same-sex marriages.

In 1996, Congress passed and President Clinton signed into law the Defense of Marriage Act, which defined marriage as a union between a man and a woman and asserted that no state could be forced to recognize a same-sex marriage ratified in another state.

The issue simmered for a few years. Then in 2003, the Massachusetts Supreme Court ruled that a gay marriage ban was unconstitutional in that state. The ruling led to another reaction by lawmakers, when conservative members of Congress tried vainly in 2004 and 2006 to amend the U.S. Constitution to ban gay marriages throughout the country.

But in two landmark decisions in June 2013, the U.S. Supreme Court ruled that the federal Defense of Marriage Act unconstitutionally denied same-sex married partners federal benefits to which they were entitled, and refused to overturn a lower court's ruling that effectively allowed gay marriages in California.

Supporters of gay marriage were cheered by the two decisions and by polls that showed Americans were changing their mind about same-sex unions: In 2001, gay marriage was opposed by a 57–35 margin. In mid-2017, it was supported by a 62–32 margin.

And in June 2015, the Supreme Court made the issue moot, at least legally if not politically. In a 5-4 decision, the court ruled that states could not deny homosexuals the same marriage rights afforded to heterosexual couples. "They ask for equal dignity in the eyes of the law," Justice Anthony Kennedy wrote. "The Constitution grants them that right."'

6

The Part of Tens

Chapter 26

Ten Innovations That Made It Easier to Be Lazy

My pop used to say, "If necessity is the mother of invention, laziness is the father." To prove the wisdom of that adage, here are ten contrivances and contraptions that help you move around, eat, shop, and entertain yourself. So lean back in your recliner, take a sip of that beverage, and maybe learn a thing or two. Just don't strain yourself.

The Escalator (1896)

If you hate climbing stairs — and who doesn't? — you owe some thanks to Jesse W. Reno and his college education. A Kansas-born engineer, Reno built the first working set of moving steps, which were installed at the Old Iron Pier at New York's Coney Island.

The escalator consisted of a single cast-iron platform that moved up a conveyor belt. It was a hit: More than 75,000 people crowded onto it in its first week of operation to be carried up a distance of about 15 feet. Reno eventually sold his patent to the Otis Elevator Co.

Reno's inspiration was said to have come from the hilly geography of his alma mater, Lehigh University, where it was 300 stair steps from the highest building on campus to the lowest. And engineering textbooks are really heavy.

Sliced Bread (1928)

It was the greatest thing since the escalator. Okay, nobody said that. But they didn't have to anyway after July 7, 1928. On that date in Chillicothe, Missouri, the Chillicothe Baking Co. began offering the public Kleen-Maid Sliced Bread.

Otto Frederick Rohwedder, an Iowa-born jeweler, invented the bakery's slicing machine. Rohwedder sold his patent rights to an Iowa company in 1930. In the same year, the Continental Baking Co. introduced a sliced version of its Wonder Bread product, and the rest is baking history. As a footnote, the U.S. Government banned commercial sliced bread sales in January 1943, as part of an effort to control bread prices and divert materials, such as waxed paper and steel used in slicing blades, to the war effort. After two months of indignant protests by homemakers, the ban was lifted.

Pizza Delivery (~1945)

With the end of World War II in 1945, GIs returning from Italy brought back a taste for pizza. Pizzerias popped up all over. East Coast shops began offering pies to go; West Coast shops began delivering them to the front door. By the early 1960s, the first big pizza chains — Pizza Hut (1958) and Domino's (1960) — had begun to multiply, and deliver . . . and kept delivering. By 2018, it was estimated more than 1 billion pizzas were delivered to U.S. homes, offices, and other venues on a yearly basis.

In August 1994, Pizza Hut began testing the idea of letting computer geeks in Santa Cruz, California, order home-delivery pizzas using something called the Internet.

In August 2016, Domino's delivered a pizza to a New Zealand couple by drone. They weren't sure how much to tip.

And in 2017, pizza companies began exploring the idea of delivery via driverless cars. That would really take care of the tip question.

Drive-Through Restaurants (1948)

Ever faced with that choice of either going out to eat or leaving your pants off? Probably not, thanks to Sheldon Chaney and/or Harry Snyder. Chaney owned Red's Giant Hamburg on Route 66 in Springfield, Missouri. Snyder ran a joint called In-N-Out in Baldwin Park, California. In 1948, both men put in speaker systems that enabled customers to place an order, drive up to a window, and get their food without budging from behind the wheel.

Perhaps surprisingly, McDonald's didn't open a drive-through until 1975. A franchise in Sierra Vista, Arizona, started one to accommodate soldiers from a nearby U.S. Army base who weren't allowed to walk around town in their fatigues. And you were worried about your pants.

TV Remote Controls (1950)

What's TV without a remote? Right, a trip off the couch. The first remote controls were developed in World War II by the German navy to control motorboats that could ram enemy ships.

After the war, the Zenith Corporation developed a unit called, fittingly for this chapter, "Lazy Bones." It was connected to the TV by a cable. People kept tripping over it.

In 1958, engineers developed a unit using ultrasonic waves, and 20 years after that, one using an infrared beam. Couch reupholsterers gleefully applauded.

Pop-Top Cans (1963)

Ermal Cleon Fraze was an Ohio tool and die maker with a problem. As the story goes, Fraze was at a family picnic when he found he had forgotten his "church key" opener used to open beer cans and was forced to use a car bumper. Fraze eventually came up with a removable tab that thirsty folks could simply pull off. He patented his invention and promptly sold it to the Alcoa Company. By 1965, most of the U.S. beer and soft drink makers were using "pop-top" or "pull-tab" cans. But by 1975, there were numerous reports of children swallowing the tabs. And the tabs were a litter nuisance.

A Reynolds Metals engineer named Daniel Cudzik partially solved both problems by designing a "stay tab," which pushed part of the lid into the can but didn't completely separate it. No one had to look for a church key anymore.

Oh yeah, the original ring tab design has been around long enough that old cans with the tabs are considered archaeological finds under federal guidelines. Think about that before you just kick that can down the road.

Microwave Ovens (1967)

At the end of World War II, self-taught physicist Percy L. Spencer was experimenting with radar microwaves when he noticed a candy bar in his pocket had melted. Intrigued, he tested the microwaves on corn kernels and an egg, both of which got hot in a hurry. Spencer's employer, Raytheon, quickly obtained a patent for a "microwave oven," but it wasn't until 1967 that Raytheon subsidiary Amana came up with a model small enough, reliable enough, and relatively cheap enough ($495) to win widespread popularity.

By 1975, more than a million microwave ovens were being sold in the United States, and by 2015, nearly 97 percent of American homes had at least one microwave. I would have starved to death long ago without one.

Microwave Popcorn (1983)

The aforementioned Percy Spencer (see preceding section) actually won a patent in 1949 for his idea of placing an ear of corn in a sealed bag and then sticking it in his microwave. And in 1981, Pillsbury researchers Lawrence Brandberg and David Andreas got a patent for a microwave popping bag. But it wasn't until 1983 that microwave popcorn was available nationally. In 1984, manufacturers replaced real butter with "butter flavor" so the bags wouldn't have to be refrigerated.

"Microwave popcorn is a fad," a popcorn popper maker sniffed to *The New York Times* in 1987. Then she got in the unemployment line with the bread-knife and beer can opener manufacturers.

U.S. sales of microwave popcorn jumped from $53 million in 1983 to more than $750 million in 2017. Heck, it's even got its own control button on most microwaves. Excuse me, my popcorn's ready.

Global Positioning System (1989)

Global Positioning System (GPS) began as a satellite-based navigation system for military use and turned into a providential tool for the lost and lazy. After President Ronald Reagan ordered the technology declassified, the Magellan Co. began selling its GPS NAV 1000 devices to the public in May 1989. They weighed 1.5 pounds, lasted a few hours on six AA batteries — and cost $3,000.

Still, the system caught on. In 1999, the Benefon company began offering a GPS-enabled cellphone. By 2015, 82 percent of Americans with smartphones had given up maps as their favorite mode of navigation.

And even if that anonymous female voice sometimes directs you into one too many U-turns while using your phone to get around, at least you don't have to try to fold it.

Amazon (1995)

Jeff Bezos didn't want to miss the Internet business boom. So in 1995, the New Mexico-born, Princeton graduate, who had left his Wall Street job and moved to Seattle, opened an online bookstore from the garage of his rented house. Twenty-two years later, he was the richest man in the world.

Amazon revolutionized online shopping. In 1997, it had 1 million customers. By 2018, it had a staggering 100 million subscribers to its Amazon Prime service, representing 64 percent of U.S. households. Amazon offered more than half a billion products and scooped up about half of every online dollar Americans spent. And customers didn't even have to leave the house to spend money.

Chapter **27**

Ten U.S. Presidents Who Were, Well, Average

Sure, you can find lots of lists of the ten best and ten worst presidents, but what about all the rest? Glad you asked. I took the aggregate rankings from 19 Wikipedia-compiled popular and scholarly polls conducted from 1948 to 2018. Then I lopped off the top 17 and the bottom 17, leaving me with the ten "in-betweens." (Yes, there have been 45 presidencies. But Grover Cleveland was the 22nd <u>and</u> the 2th, and he only gets ranked once.)

As a bit of a bonus, I include a quirky factoid or two (or four) about each of the Middling Ten. Here they are in order from least lackluster to most mediocre.

Bill Clinton

You'd think being one of the only two presidents ever impeached might move Bill Clinton lower than the middle ten, but he's actually ranked the best of the ho-hums. Despite a bunch of sex scandals — or maybe even because of them — Clinton left office with the highest end-of-term approval rating of any president since World War II.

He's also one of three presidents to win two Grammy awards. They were for spoken-word albums, not for playing the saxophone. He did once perform on that instrument on a national late-night television show. He played well enough to at least avoid a sax scandal.

William McKinley

As one of four presidents assassinated in office, William McKinley may have made it to the middle of the presidential rankings just from sympathy votes. He was mostly known for championing U.S. imperialism and, well, getting shot while visiting Buffalo. But he was also the last president to serve in the Civil War and the first to ride in an automobile. The latter event happened when he was taken to the hospital in an electric ambulance after being shot. It didn't help.

Grover Cleveland

Despite his unremarkable ranking, Grover Cleveland is not only the sole U.S. president to serve two nonconsecutive terms, but also the only one to have a rubber prothesis fitted in his mouth after undergoing secret surgery for a cancerous tumor. The surgery was performed aboard a yacht in New York Harbor. Cleveland kept it quiet because he was afraid the news would make an already shaky national economy worse. Elisha Jay Edwards, a Philadelphia newspaper reporter, broke the story shortly after the operation, but Cleveland vehemently denied it, and the reporter's career was ruined. The truth finally came out more than 20 years later, and the reporter was then lionized. Sometimes "fake news" isn't fake.

John Quincy Adams

At No. 21 on the aggregate rankings list, John Quincy Adams is six spots below his dad, John Adams. The younger Adams also shares the dubious distinction of being the first man to win the presidency despite losing the popular vote. (Four of his successors also managed to win while losing.)

John Q liked to swim naked in the Potomac River each morning, which may be partially explained by the fact he kept a pet alligator in a White House bathtub for several months. It was a gift from the Marquis de Lafayette, the Frenchman who gallantly served the colonists' cause in the American Revolution. Lafayette had been given the gator during an 1824–25 U.S. tour. Some people are so ungrateful. . . .

George H. W. Bush

The nickname of George H. W. Bush, the 41st president, was Poppy, which is certainly easier to remember than that extra initial that separates him from his son, George W. Bush, the 43rd president. The elder Bush (ranked ten spots higher than his son on the aggregate list) was the first sitting vice president to be promoted to the Oval Office by voters since Martin Van Buren did it in 1836, but he wasn't reelected.

A heroic World War II combat pilot, Bush spent 30 days of the war in a submarine. The sub picked him up after his plane was shot down, and he had bailed out over the Pacific.

He also played baseball at Yale, went sky diving on his 90th birthday, and loved to show up for things in colorful socks.

William Howard Taft

William Howard Taft may not have been the best U.S. president, but he certainly was the biggest. At 332 pounds, Taft was too big for the White House bathtubs and had to have at least one of them replaced to accommodate his girth. He also once got stuck on some stairs while inspecting a Navy vessel.

As president, he was best known for relying heavily (no pun intended) on dollar diplomacy, which consisted of the United States getting its way in Asia and Central America by making loans to various countries.

Taft freely admitted he liked being chief justice of the U.S. Supreme Court — which he became after leaving the White House — far more than he liked being president.

He was also the last president to sport facial hair and the last to keep a cow at the White House to supply the First Family with dairy products.

Martin Van Buren

Martin Van Buren became president mainly because he was an ardent supporter of the immensely popular Andrew Jackson, and Jackson anointed the diminutive New Yorker as his chosen successor. But he lost his bid for reelection because of the severe economic recession that struck the country soon after he was elected.

Still, Van Buren enjoys distinction as the first president born a U.S. citizen. His seven predecessors were all born when Americans were still British subjects.

At 5'6", Van Buren was also the second-shortest president, towering only over James Madison (5'4"). And he once complained about trains that were reaching speeds of 15 miles an hour, stating "the Almighty certainly never intended that people should travel at such breakneck speed."

Rutherford B. Hayes

Rutherford B. Hayes was another of those presidents who got elected while garnering fewer popular votes than his opponent.

Despite winning the White House after some slick and sleazy political maneuvering by members of Congress, Hayes was a pretty decent guy. His best efforts were in starting reforms of the civil service system and in trying to make government colorblind when it came to treatment of various races.

On the other hand, Hayes used federal troops to crush a national railroad strike and thought the best way to deal with Native Americans was to force them into adopting European culture and mores.

But Hayes had bled for his country more than most presidents, having been wounded five times during the Civil War. He was the first president to have a telephone and a typewriter in the White House and the first to visit the West Coast. He also hosted the first Easter egg roll on the White House lawn.

Gerald Ford

Besides being the only president who wasn't elected president *or* vice president, Gerald Ford was also the best football player to serve as president, having been offered contracts with two NFL teams.

Ford issued an unpopular pardon of his predecessor, Richard Nixon, presided over an inflation-ravaged economy, and watched, with the rest of the country, as communists completed their takeover of Vietnam. Then he lost to Jimmy Carter.

On the bright side, Ford did survive two assassination attempts — both in California and both by women — and lived to the ripe old age of 93.

By the way, Ford's birth name was Leslie Lynch King, Jr. He legally changed his name to Gerald Rudolph Ford, Jr. after being adopted by his mother's second husband.

Ford was also the only president to have been an Eagle Scout, the highest rank attainable in the Boy Scouts of America.

Jimmy Carter

Rated the least of the average, Jimmy Carter is often referred to as America's best ex-president. He was elected as a Washington outsider and inherited a terrible economy from Ford. He managed — or mismanaged — to make things worse and then lost his reelection bid to Ronald Reagan. Then he found his groove.

Among Carter's post-presidential accomplishments were founding a center for human rights; acting as a freelance diplomat to mediate disputes between the United States and various dictators and despots; working with Habitat for Humanity International, which provides decent housing around the world; and winning the 2002 Nobel Peace Prize "for his decades of untiring effort to find peaceful solutions to international conflicts, to advance democracy and human rights, and to promote economic and social development."

Not bad for a mediocre president.

7

The Appendixes

Appendix A

The Bill of Rights: Amendments 1–10 of the Constitution

The Conventions of a number of the States having, at the time of adopting the Constitution, expressed a desire, in order to prevent misconstruction or abuse of its powers, that further declaratory and restrictive clauses should be added, and as extending the ground of public confidence in the Government will best insure the beneficent ends of its institution;

Resolved, by the Senate and House of Representatives of the United States of America, in Congress assembled, two-thirds of both Houses concurring, that the following articles be proposed to the Legislatures of the several States, as amendments to the Constitution of the United States; all or any of which articles, when ratified by three-fourths of the said Legislatures, to be valid to all intents and purposes as part of the said Constitution, namely:

Amendment I

Congress shall make no law respecting an establishment of religion, or prohibiting the free exercise thereof; or abridging the freedom of speech, or of the press; or the right of the people peaceably to assemble, and to petition the government for a redress of grievances.

Amendment II

A well-regulated militia, being necessary to the security of a free state, the right of the people to keep and bear arms, shall not be infringed.

Amendment III

No soldier shall, in time of peace be quartered in any house, without the consent of the owner, nor in time of war, but in a manner to be prescribed by law.

Amendment IV

The right of the people to be secure in their persons, houses, papers, and effects, against unreasonable searches and seizures, shall not be violated, and no warrants shall issue, but upon probable cause, supported by oath or affirmation, and particularly describing the place to be searched, and the persons or things to be seized.

Amendment V

No person shall be held to answer for a capital, or otherwise infamous crime, unless on a presentment or indictment of a grand jury, except in cases arising in the land or naval forces, or in the militia, when in actual service in time of war or public danger; nor shall any person be subject for the same offense to be twice put in jeopardy of life or limb; nor shall be compelled in any criminal case to be a witness against himself, nor be deprived of life, liberty, or property, without due process of law; nor shall private property be taken for public use, without just compensation.

Amendment VI

In all criminal prosecutions, the accused shall enjoy the right to a speedy and public trial, by an impartial jury of the state and district wherein the crime shall have been committed, which district shall have been previously ascertained by law, and to be informed of the nature and cause of the accusation; to be confronted with the witnesses against him; to have compulsory process for obtaining witnesses in his favor, and to have the assistance of counsel for his defense.

Amendment VII

In suits at common law, where the value in controversy shall exceed twenty dollars, the right of trial by jury shall be preserved, and no fact tried by a jury, shall be otherwise reexamined in any court of the United States, than according to the rules of the common law.

Amendment VIII

Excessive bail shall not be required, nor excessive fines imposed, nor cruel and unusual punishments inflicted.

Amendment IX

The enumeration in the Constitution, of certain rights, shall not be construed to deny or disparage others retained by the people.

Amendment X

The powers not delegated to the United States by the Constitution, nor prohibited by it to the states, are reserved to the states respectively, or to the people.

Appendix B

The Declaration of Independence

IN CONGRESS, July 4, 1776.

The unanimous Declaration of the thirteen united States of America,

When in the Course of human events, it becomes necessary for one people to dissolve the political bands which have connected them with another, and to assume among the powers of the earth, the separate and equal station to which the Laws of Nature and of Nature's God entitle them, a decent respect to the opinions of mankind requires that they should declare the causes which impel them to the separation.

We hold these truths to be self-evident, that all men are created equal, that they are endowed by their Creator with certain unalienable Rights, that among these are Life, Liberty and the pursuit of Happiness. — That to secure these rights, Governments are instituted among Men, deriving their just powers from the consent of the governed, —That whenever any Form of Government becomes destructive of these ends, it is the Right of the People to alter or to abolish it, and to institute new Government, laying its foundation on such principles and organizing its powers in such form, as to them shall seem most likely to effect their Safety and Happiness. Prudence, indeed, will dictate that Governments long established should not be changed for light and transient causes; and accordingly all experience hath shewn, that mankind are more disposed to suffer, while evils are sufferable, than to right themselves by abolishing the forms to which they are accustomed. But when a long train of abuses and usurpations, pursuing invariably the same Object evinces a design to reduce them under absolute Despotism, it is their right, it is their duty, to throw off such Government, and to provide new Guards for their future security. —Such has been the patient sufferance of these Colonies; and such is now the necessity which constrains them to alter their former Systems of Government. The history of the present King of Great Britain is a history of repeated injuries and usurpations, all having in direct object the establishment of an absolute Tyranny over these States. To prove this, let Facts be submitted to a candid world.

He has refused his Assent to Laws, the most wholesome and necessary for the public good. He has forbidden his Governors to pass Laws of immediate and pressing importance, unless suspended in their operation till his Assent should be obtained; and when so suspended, he has utterly neglected to attend to them. He has refused to pass other Laws for the accommodation of large districts of people, unless those people would relinquish the right of Representation in the Legislature, a right inestimable to them and formidable to tyrants only. He has called together legislative bodies at places unusual, uncomfortable, and distant from the depository of their public Records, for the sole purpose of fatiguing them into compliance with his measures. He has dissolved Representative Houses repeatedly, for opposing with manly firmness his invasions on the rights of the people. He has refused for a long time, after such dissolutions, to cause others to be elected; whereby the Legislative powers, incapable of Annihilation, have returned to the People at large for their exercise; the State remaining in the mean time exposed to all the dangers of invasion from without, and convulsions within.

He has endeavoured to prevent the population of these States; for that purpose obstructing the Laws for Naturalization of Foreigners; refusing to pass others to encourage their migrations hither, and raising the conditions of new Appropriations of Lands. He has obstructed the Administration of Justice, by refusing his Assent to Laws for establishing Judiciary powers. He has made Judges dependent on his Will alone, for the tenure of their offices, and the amount and payment of their salaries.

He has erected a multitude of New Offices, and sent hither swarms of Officers to harrass our people, and eat out their substance. He has kept among us, in times of peace, Standing Armies without the Consent of our legislatures. He has affected to render the Military independent of and superior to the Civil power. He has combined with others to subject us to a jurisdiction foreign to our constitution, and unacknowledged by our laws; giving his Assent to their Acts of pretended Legislation:

For Quartering large bodies of armed troops among us: For protecting them, by a mock Trial, from punishment for any Murders which they should commit on the Inhabitants of these States: For cutting off our Trade with all parts of the world: For imposing Taxes on us without our Consent: For depriving us in many cases, of the benefits of Trial by Jury: For transporting us beyond Seas to be tried for pretended offences: For abolishing the free System of English Laws in a neighbouring Province, establishing therein an Arbitrary government, and enlarging its Boundaries so as to render it at once an example and fit instrument for introducing the same absolute rule into these Colonies: For taking away our Charters, abolishing our most valuable Laws, and altering fundamentally the Forms of our Governments: For suspending our own Legislatures, and declaring themselves invested with power to legislate for us in all cases whatsoever.

He has abdicated Government here, by declaring us out of his Protection and waging War against us. He has plundered our seas, ravaged our Coasts, burnt our towns, and destroyed the lives of our people. He is at this time transporting large Armies of foreign Mercenaries to compleat the works of death, desolation and tyranny, already begun with circumstances of Cruelty & perfidy scarcely paralleled in the most barbarous ages, and totally unworthy the Head of a civilized nation.

He has constrained our fellow Citizens taken Captive on the high Seas to bear Arms against their Country, to become the executioners of their friends and Brethren, or to fall themselves by their Hands. He has excited domestic insurrections amongst us, and has endeavoured to bring on the inhabitants of our frontiers, the merciless Indian Savages, whose known rule of warfare, is an undistinguished destruction of all ages, sexes and conditions.

In every stage of these Oppressions We have Petitioned for Redress in the most humble terms: Our repeated Petitions have been answered only by repeated injury. A Prince whose character is thus marked by every act which may define a Tyrant, is unfit to be the ruler of a free people.

Nor have We been wanting in attentions to our Brittish brethren. We have warned them from time to time of attempts by their legislature to extend an unwarrantable jurisdiction over us. We have reminded them of the circumstances of our emigration and settlement here. We have appealed to their native justice and magnanimity, and we have conjured them by the ties of our common kindred to disavow these usurpations, which, would inevitably interrupt our connections and correspondence. They too have been deaf to the voice of justice and of consanguinity. We must, therefore, acquiesce in the necessity, which denounces our Separation, and hold them, as we hold the rest of mankind, Enemies in War, in Peace Friends.

We, therefore, the Representatives of the united States of America, in General Congress, Assembled, appealing to the Supreme Judge of the world for the rectitude of our intentions, do, in the Name, and by Authority of the good People of these Colonies, solemnly publish and declare, That these United Colonies are, and of Right ought to be Free and Independent States; that they are Absolved from all Allegiance to the British Crown, and that all political connection between them and the State of Great Britain, is and ought to be totally dissolved; and that as Free and Independent States, they have full Power to levy War, conclude Peace, contract Alliances, establish Commerce, and to do all other Acts and Things which Independent States may of right do. And for the support of this Declaration, with a firm reliance on the protection of divine Providence, we mutually pledge to each other our Lives, our Fortunes and our sacred Honor.

(Signed) John Hancock, Button Gwinnett, Lyman Hall, George Walton, William Hooper, Joseph Hewes, John Penn, Edward Rutledge, Thomas Heyward, Jr., Thomas Lynch, Jr., Arthur Middleton, Samuel Chase, William Paca, Thomas Stone, Charles Carroll of Carrollton, George Wythe, Richard Henry Lee, Thomas Jefferson, Benjamin Harrison, Thomas Nelson, Jr., Francis Lightfoot Lee, Carter Braxton, Robert Morris, Benjamin Rush, Benjamin Franklin, John Morton, George Clymer, James Smith, George Taylor, James Wilson, George Ross, Caesar Rodney, George Read, Thomas McKean, William Floyd, Philip Livingston, Francis Lewis, Lewis Morris, Richard Stockton, John Witherspoon, Francis Hopkinson, John Hart, Abraham Clark, Josiah Bartlett, William Whipple, Samuel Adams, John Adams, Robert Treat Paine, Elbridge Gerry, Stephen Hopkins, William Ellery, Roger Sherman, Samuel Huntington, William Williams, Oliver Wolcott, Matthew Thornton

Index

A

AAA (Agricultural Adjustment Act), 244
abortion, 303
acculturation, 191
Adams, John (president), 76–77, 90–91, 95–96, 100–102, 125
Adams, John Quincy (president), 10, 115, 119, 124–126, 128, 134, 416
Adams, Samuel (politician), 64, 87
adelantadaos, 35
advertising, 229
AEF (American Expeditionary Force), 219–220
AFL (American Federation of Labor), 200, 213, 250
African American History For Dummies (Penrice), 218
African Americans. *See also* slaves/slavery
  discrimination against, 193–194
  14th Amendment, 177, 178
  during Great Depression, 248–249
  greater equality for, 261–262
  migration of to northern cities, 217–218
  Rosa Parks, 290
  violence and, 176
African slaves, 61
Agnew, Spiro T. (vice president), 308
Agricultural Adjustment Act (AAA), 244
Aguinaldo, Emilio (leader), 207
AIDS, 18, 330–331
AIG, 361–362
airplanes, 215
Alamo, 135
al-Assad, Bashar (president), 385
Aldrin, Buzz (astronaut), 306
Alexander I, Czar of Russia, 115
Algonquian, 25
Ali, Muhammad (boxer), 296
Alien and Sedition Acts (1798), 94
Allen, Ethan (frontiersman), 80, 86
Al-Qaeda, 324, 341, 345
Amazon, 413
American Birth Control League, 217
American Expeditionary Force (AEF), 219–220

American Federation of Labor (AFL), 200, 213, 250
American Recovery and Reinvestment Act (2009), 358
American Revolution
  about, 9, 53, 72–74
  America in 1700, 53–54
  Boston Massacre (1770), 65–66
  Boston Tea Party (1773), 66
  Congress, 67–68
  French and Indian War, 58–60
  George Washington during, 74–75
  growth of American colonies, 60–62
  "Intolerable" Acts (1774), 66–67
  King George's War, 56–57
  King William's War, 55
  New France, 54–55
  Paul Revere (minuteman), 68–69
  Proclamation of 1763, 63
  Queen Anne's War, 56
  relationship with Britain, 62–67
  religious freedom, 57–58
  Revenue Acts (1764), 63–64
  Samuel Adams (politician), 64
  Stamp Act (1765), 64–65
  Townshend Act (1767), 65
  World Wars, 55–57
"The American System," 120–121
Amherst, Jeffrey (military leader), 59
anaconda plan, 161
Anasazi, 23–24
Anderson, Robert (major), 165
Andrews sisters (singers), 258
animals, as resources for money, 188–189
Anthony, Suan B. (leader), 148
anthrax letters, 343
Antietam, 166
antiwar sentiment, 16
Apache, 25
Apple, 319
Appomattox Courthouse, 167, 169
Argonauts, 143
Armstrong, Neil (astronaut), 306

M

MacArthur, Douglas (general), 241, 268, 279

Macdonough, Thomas (lieutenant), 113–114

Madison, Dolley (First Lady), 110

Madison, James (president), 109–111, 120–121

Madison, James (scholar), 86, 88, 89

Magellan, Ferdinand (explorer), 32

Mah Jong, 234

Maine (battleship), 203

Makah, 25

"the malaise speech," 310

Malcolm X (leader), 299

Manhattan Project, 270

Manifest Destiny, 11, 139–140

The Man Nobody Knows (Barton), 230

Marbury, William (judicial appointee), 102

Marshall, George C. (general), 277

Marshall, James (carpenter), 142–143

Marshall, John (Chief Justice), 102, 120

Marshall Plan, 277

Martian invasion, 254

Maryland, 49

mass public shootings, 387–388

Massachusetts Bay colony, 46–47

Mattel, 287

Mayflower (ship), 44

Mayflower Compact, 44–45

McAuliffe, Christa (teacher), 316

McCain, John (senator), 366, 375

McCarthy, Joseph (senator), 15, 283

McClellan, George B. (general), 157, 159

McConnell, Mitch (Senate GOP leader), 372

McCormick, Cyrus (farmer), 132

McDonald, Richard and Maurice (restaurant owners), 284

McDonalds, 284, 411

McGovern, George (historian), 297

McKinley, William (president), 201, 202, 206, 207, 218, 416

McPherson, Aimee Semple (missionary), 226

McVeigh, Timothy (terrorist), 329

Meade, George (general), 166

Meat Inspection Act (1906), 211

Medicare, 349, 402

medicine, in 1800s, 127

Mellon, Andrew (financier), 229

melting pot, 402–405

Memorial Day Massacre, 251

Mencken, H. L. (journalist), 195

Mennonites, 43

Meriwether, Lewis (explorer), 106–107

Merrimac (ship), 164

Metacom (Native American chief), 51

Mexico, 11, 135, 139–142

microchip, 393

microwave ovens, 412

microwave popcorn, 412

Midway, Battle of, 269

Milano, Alyssa (actress), 389–390

Milk, Harvey (supervisor), 304

minerals, as resources for money, 188

Minnow, Newton (FCC chairman), 286

Minuit, Peter (leader), 50

minutemen, 69

Missouri Compromise, 123–124, 150

Model T Ford, 214–215

Mohawks, 26

Mondale, Walter (politician), 313

Monitor (ship), 164

monopolies, 199–200, 212

Monopoly, 250

Monroe, James (president), 10, 104, 118, 120–121, 123–125, 133

Monroe Doctrine, 124

the Monster, 118

Montgomery, Richard (American leader), 81

moon landing, 306

Moore, Gordon (physicist), 393

morals, changing, 235–236

Moran, George "Bugs" (gangster), 234

Morgan, J. P. (tycoon), 161, 223

Mormons, 147

Morrison, Toni (writer), 332

Morse, Samuel F. B. (painter), 133

Moscone, George (mayor), 304

Mott, Lucretia (leader), 148

Mound Builders, 24

moviemaking, 231–232

Mt. Rushmore National Memorial, 257

muckrakers, 210–211

Mueller, Robert (FBI director), 400–401

Muhammad, Elijah (leader), 299

Murphy, Audie (war hero), 270

P

Pacific, World War II in, 268–269
Paine, Thomas (editor), 76, 87
Pale Faces, 176
Palin, Sarah (governor), 366
Palmer, A. Mitchell (attorney general), 224
Panama Canal, 209
Panetta, Leon (secretary of defense), 346
Panic of 1819, 118
Panic of 1837, 136
Paris, Treaty of (1763), 59
Paris Agreement, 384
parity, 231
Parker, Bonnie (robber), 253
Parker, John (leader), 69
Parks, Rosa (activist), 290
parlor games, 234
Patton, George S. (general), 266
Paul, Rand (Senator), 369
Paul III, Pope, 33
Peace Democrats, 158
Pearl Harbor, 258, 264, 268
Pelosi, Nancy (House leader), 383
Pemberton, John (pharmacist), 199
Penn, William (Quaker), 49
Pennsylvania, 49
Penrice, Ronda Racha (author)
  African American History For Dummies, 218
Pentagon Papers, 297
Pequots, 51
perestroika, 317
Perot, Ross (presidential candidate), 321
Perry, Oliver Hazard (captain), 112
Perry, Rick (governor), 350
Pershing, John J, "Black Jack" (general), 210, 219
Philadelphia, PA, 60–61, 86–88
Philip, King, 51
Philippines, 206–207
Pierce, Franklin (president), 157
Pilgrims, 43–45
Pilgrim's Progress, 210
Pinckney, Thomas (minister to England), 91
pirates, 107
Pitt, William (prime minister), 59, 65, 68
Pittsburgh steel mills, 213
pizza delivery, 410

Plains Indians, 25, 190–191
Plessy v. Ferguson, 193
Plymouth colony, 44–45
police action, 15
polio, 282
political reform, 210–212
politics. *See also specific topics*
  in 1816, 125–128
  about, 89
  Alexander Hamilton, 90–91
  George Washington and, 89–90
  growth in corruption in, 180–183
  Thomas Jefferson, 90–91
Polk, James K. (presidential candidate), 11, 137, 139–141, 143, 144
polygamy, 147
pop-top cans, 411–412
popular sovereignty, 150
Populism, 202
Portugal, 36
Portuguese, 29, 42
potlatches, 25
Powell, Colin (secretary of state), 345
Powhatan (Native American chief), 40
POWs (prisoners of war), 343
Prescott, Samuel (doctor), 69
President (warship), 113
Presidents, U.S.
  Abraham Lincoln, 11–12, 46, 134, 141, 149, 150, 152–153, 155–159, 169, 174
  Andrew Johnson, 12, 17, 176–180
  Barack Obama, 18, 342, 344, 346, 358–360, 362, 366–367, 369–378, 404
  Benjamin Harrison, 201
  Calvin Coolidge, 226–229, 231, 239, 256
  Chester A. Arthur, 201
  Donald J. Trump, 19, 342, 375, 380–386, 391–392, 394–395, 400, 403–404
  Franklin D. Roosevelt, 14, 243–247, 257, 264–265, 267–268, 276, 299, 358
  Franklin Pierce, 157
  George H. W. Bush, 17, 18, 318–319, 417
  George W. Bush, 337–340, 344–346, 348–349, 357
  George Washington, 9, 58–59, 73–75, 79, 81–82, 87–90, 93, 95, 110
  Gerald R. Ford, 16, 306, 307–308, 309, 418–419
  Grover Cleveland, 161, 201, 203, 416

About the Author

Steve Wiegand has been around for 27.7 percent of America's history as a nation — and he's gaining ground.

An award-winning political journalist and history writer for more than four decades, he worked as a reporter and columnist for the *San Diego Evening Tribune*, *San Francisco Chronicle*, and *Sacramento Bee*.

In addition to *U.S. History For Dummies*, Wiegand is the author of *Lessons from the Great Depression For Dummies* (Wiley), *Sacramento Tapestry* (Towery Books), and *Papers of Permanence* (McClatchy). He coauthored *The Mental Floss History of the World* (Harper Collins) and was a contributing author to *Mental Floss Presents: Forbidden Knowledge* (Harper Collins). His newest book, *The Dancer, the Dreamers and the Queen of Romania* (Bancroft Press) will be released in October 2019.

Wiegand is a graduate of Santa Clara University, where he majored in American literature and U.S. history. He also holds a Master of Science degree in Mass Communications from California State University, San Jose.

He lives in Arizona.

Dedication

To Ceil, for all my pasts, and to Erin, for all our futures.

Author's Acknowledgments

Thanks first to my friends and colleagues: John D. Cox for launching me on the path to authorship, and Bill Enfield, for his interest and encouragement.

For this fourth edition, thanks to Project Editor Kelly Ewing, Technical Editor Troy Guthrie, and Executive Editor Lindsay Lefevere. All the good stuff is mostly their doing; any mistakes are mine.

Finally, thanks to my mom for having given me the inspiration to read books, so I could someday write them, and to my dad for giving me the sense of humor not to take it — or myself — too seriously along the way.

Publisher's Acknowledgments

Executive Editor: Lindsay Lefevere

Project Editor: Kelly Ewing

Technical Editor: Troy Guthrie

Editorial Assistant: Matthew Lowe

Sr. Editorial Assistant: Cherie Case

Production Editor: Siddique Shaik

Cover Image: © drnadig/Getty Images